The Definitive Guide to Grails

Second Edition

Graeme Rocher and Jeff Brown

Apress®

The Definitive Guide to Grails, Second Edition

Copyright © 2009 by Graeme Rocher, Jeff Brown

ISBN-13 (pbk): 978-1-59059-995-2

ISBN-10 (pbk): 1-59059-995-0

ISBN-13 (electronic): 978-1-4302-0871-6

Printed and bound in the United States of America 9 8 7 6 5 4 3 2 1

Lead Editors: Steve Anglin, Tom Welsh
Technical Reviewer: Guillaume Laforge
Editorial Board: Clay Andres, Steve Anglin, Mark Beckner, Ewan Buckingham, Tony Campbell, Gary Cornell, Jonathan Gennick, Jonathan Hassell, Michelle Lowman, Matthew Moodie, Duncan Parkes, Jeffrey Pepper, Frank Pohlmann, Ben Renow-Clarke, Dominic Shakeshaft, Matt Wade, Tom Welsh
Project Manager: Kylie Johnston
Copy Editors: Nina Goldschlager, Kim Wimpsett
Associate Production Director: Kari Brooks-Copony
Production Editor: Laura Cheu
Compositor: Pat Christenson
Proofreader: Kim Burton
Indexer: Becky Hornyak
Artist: April Milne
Cover Designer: Kurt Krames
Manufacturing Director: Tom Debolski

Distributed to the book trade worldwide by Springer-Verlag New York, Inc., 233 Spring Street, 6th Floor, New York, NY 10013. Phone 1-800-SPRINGER, fax 201-348-4505, e-mail orders-ny@springer-sbm.com, or visit http://www.springeronline.com.

For information on translations, please contact Apress directly at 2855 Telegraph Avenue, Suite 600, Berkeley, CA 94705. Phone 510-549-5930, fax 510-549-5939, e-mail info@apress.com, or visit http://www.apress.com.

Apress and friends of ED books may be purchased in bulk for academic, corporate, or promotional use. eBook versions and licenses are also available for most titles. For more information, reference our Special Bulk Sales–eBook Licensing web page at http://www.apress.com/info/bulksales.

The source code for this book is available to readers at http://www.apress.com.

To Birjinia, the love and support you have given me in the last few years will stay with me forever. Unquestionably yours. Maite zaitut.
—Graeme Rocher

To Betsy, Jake, and Zack, the best team ever.
—Jeff Brown

Contents at a Glance

Contents

About the Authors

GRAEME KEITH ROCHER is a software engineer and head of Grails development at SpringSource (http://www.springsource.com), the company behind the Spring Framework that underpins Grails. In his current role, Graeme leads the ongoing development of the Grails framework, driving product strategy and innovation for the Grails framework.

Graeme started his career in the e-learning sector as part of a team developing scalable enterprise learning management systems based on Java EE technology. He later branched into the digital TV arena, where he faced increasingly complex requirements that required an agile approach as the ever-changing and young digital TV platforms evolved. This is where Graeme was first exposed to Groovy and where he began combining Groovy with Cocoon to deliver dynamic multichannel content management systems targeted at digital TV platforms.

Seeing an increasing trend for web delivery of services and the complexity it brought, Graeme embarked on another project to simplify it and founded Grails. Grails is a framework with the essence of other dynamic language frameworks but is targeted at tight Java integration. Graeme is the current project lead of Grails and is a member of the Groovy JSR-241 executive committee.

Before SpringSource, Graeme cofounded G2One Inc.—The Groovy/Grails Company— along with Guillaume Laforge (Groovy project lead) and Alex Tkachman (former JetBrains COO). G2One provided consulting, training, and support for the Groovy and Grails technologies. In October 2008, SpringSource acquired G2One, and Graeme, along with his colleagues at G2One, joined the number-one provider of enterprise software in the Java space. SpringSource now provides training, support, consulting, and products for Groovy and Grails, as well as the frameworks that underpin them such as Spring and Hibernate.

JEFF BROWN is a software engineer at SpringSource and a member of the Groovy and Grails development teams. Jeff has been involved with software engineering since the early 1990s and has designed and built systems for industries including financial, biomedical, aerospace, and others.

Jeff began his software engineering career building business systems in C and C++ targeting the Unix, OS/2, and Windows platforms. As soon as the Java language came along, he realized that it was going to be a very important technology moving forward. At this point, Jeff joined Object Computing Inc. (http://www.ociweb.com/) based in St. Louis, Missouri, where he spent the next 11 years building systems for the Java platform, coaching and mentoring developers, developing and delivering training, and evangelizing.

While fully appreciating the power and flexibility offered by the Java platform, Jeff was frustrated with the unnecessary complexity often associated with Java applications. In particular, web application development with Java seemed to have a ridiculous amount of complexity that really had nothing at all to do with the real problems solved by the application. Jeff discovered the Grails framework soon after Graeme founded the project. Here were the beginnings of a solution that made so much more sense in so many ways. After digging in to the source code of the project, Jeff began making contributions and eventually became a member of the Grails development team.

Jeff eventually joined the team at G2One Inc.—The Groovy/Grails Company—where he would help drive the professional services side of the business. In late 2008, Jeff joined SpringSource when G2One and SpringSource came together to leverage synergies between the technologies created and supported by each company.

Through his entire career Jeff has always been a hands-on technologist actively involved in software development, training, and mentoring. He is also an international public speaker, having been featured regularly on the No Fluff Just Stuff Software Symposium tour (`http://www.nofluffjuststuff.com/`) for a number of years.

About the Technical Reviewer

GUILLAUME LAFORGE is the Groovy project manager and the spec lead of JSR-241, the Java specification request standardizing the Groovy dynamic language. He coauthored Manning's best-seller *Groovy in Action*.

Along with Graeme Rocher, he founded G2One Inc., the Groovy/Grails company dedicated to sustaining and leading the development of both Groovy and Grails and providing professional services (expertise, consulting, support, and training) around those technologies. In November 2008, SpringSource acquired G2One, and now Groovy and Grails bring additional weapons to the SpringSource portfolio to fight the war on enterprise Java complexity.

You can meet Guillaume at conferences around the world where he evangelizes the Groovy dynamic language, domain-specific languages in Groovy, and the agile Grails web framework.

Acknowledgments

First and foremost, I'd like to thank my wife, Birjinia, for her beauty, wisdom, and continued love and support. Over the last few years you have given me your total support and made sacrifices to the cause that I will value forever. Te quiero. Also, to my kids, Alex and Lexeia, who provide little pockets of inspiration to me every day, and to all of my and Birjinia's family, thanks for your support and encouragement.

Also, thanks to everyone at Apress that I have worked with from Steve Anglin and Tom Welsh to the people on the production team such as Nina Goldschlager and Kim Wimpsett (my copy editors), Laura Cheu (production editor), and, in particular, Kylie Johnston (project manager) for keeping the whole thing on track.

To Peter Ledbrook whose insight and contributions have been unbelievably valuable to the community and me. To Marc Palmer for providing a voice of reason, intelligent debate, and continued valuable contribution to Grails. To Alex Tkachman for his inspirational leadership at G2One and continued friendship. To the core members of the Groovy team, such as Guillaume Laforge and Jochen "blackdrag" Theodorou, whose continued responsiveness makes Grails' existence possible.

Also, without the support of the Grails community in general, we wouldn't have gotten very far. So, thanks to all the Grails users, in particular to Sven Haiges and Glen Smith for producing the Grails podcast and screencasts and to all the plugin developers who make Grails a thriving hive of activity.

Last, but most certainly not least, thanks to Rod Johnson, Adrian Coyler, Peter Cooper-Ellis, and everyone at SpringSource for seeing the potential of Grails and granting me the privilege of working for a fantastic company.

Graeme Rocher

I have to start by thanking my lovely wife, Betsy, and our unbelievable boys, Zack and Jake. Thank you all for putting up with me being closed behind the door of my home office many evenings as I worked on this book. You are all the absolute best!

Thanks to Graeme for his support as we worked through this project. It has been a lot of hard work and a whole lot of fun.

I owe a great debt to Alex Tkachman, Graeme Rocher, and Guillaume Laforge. G2One was absolutely the most exciting, challenging, and rewarding professional experience I have ever been involved with. It truly is an honor and a pleasure to know and work with you guys.

Thanks to Matt Taylor for all of the great work we have done together starting back at OCI, then G2One, and now SpringSource.

For more than a decade of professional accomplishments, I have to thank all my friends at OCI. I especially want to thank my friend Dr. Ebrahim Moshiri for the great opportunities and years of support. Thank you, sir. Also, I thank Mario Aquino. There are so many folks at OCI who

I enjoyed working with and continue to enjoy a friendship with, none of them more than Mario. Thanks for everything, man. The next one is on me.

Thanks to the whole team at Apress. I appreciate all of your hard work and patience. Thanks to Kylie Johnston (project manager) for helping us navigate through the whole thing.

I also have to thank Rod Johnson and the whole team at SpringSource. We have a lot of really exciting stuff ahead of us, and I truly look forward to it.

Jeff Brown

Introduction

In the late '90s I was working on a project developing large-scale enterprise learning management systems using early J2EE technologies such as EJB 1.0 and the Servlet framework. The Java hype machine was in full swing, and references to "EJB that, and Java this" were on the cover of every major IT publication.

Even though what we were doing—and learning as we did it—felt so horribly wrong, the industry kept telling us we were doing the right thing. EJB was going to solve all our problems, and servlets (even without a view technology at the time) were the right thing to use. My, how times have changed.

Nowadays, Java and J2EE are long-forgotten buzzwords, and the hype machine is throwing other complex acronyms at us such as SOA and ESB. In my experience, developers are on a continued mission to write less code. The monolithic J2EE specifications, like those adopted by the development community in the early days, didn't help. If a framework or a specification is overly complex and requires you to write reams of repetitive code, it should be an immediate big red flag. Why did we have to write so much repetitive boilerplate code? Surely there was a better way.

In the end, developers often influence the direction of technology more than they know. Why do so many developers favor REST over SOAP for web services? Or Hibernate over EJB for persistence? Or Spring over JNDI for Inversion of Control? In the end, simplicity often wins the day.

Certainly, working with Spring and Hibernate feels a lot better than traditional J2EE approaches; in fact, I strove to use them whenever possible, usually in combination with Web-Work, and delivered a number of successful projects with this stack. Nevertheless, I still felt I had to deal with the surrounding infrastructural issues and configuration, rather than the problem at hand. After all, the more efficient I could be as a developer when doing "real" work, the more time I would have to do what should be driving every developer: spending time with loved ones and learning new and exciting technologies.

In 2003, Groovy entered the picture. I had always been fond of looser rules governing dynamic languages in certain contexts, having worked extensively with Perl, Visual Basic, and JavaScript in the past, and after quickly hacking the WebWork source code, I was able to write MVC controllers (or *actions* in WebWork lingo) with Groovy in no time.

Groovy was perfect for controllers whose sole responsibility should be to delegate to business logic implemented by a service and then display an appropriate view. I was starting to have even more time for the good things in life. Then came the storm of dynamic language–based frameworks led by Ruby on Rails.

Unfortunately, it was all a little late. Java, the community, the tools, the frameworks, and the mind share are well-embedded. The size that Java has grown to is quite staggering, and having been in the training business for many years, I see it showing no signs of slowing, contrary to popular belief. Still, Java has its problems, and I wanted to write less code. Grails was born with this goal in mind in the summer of 2005 after I, Steven Devijver, and Guillaume Laforge kicked off a discussion about its conception on the Groovy mailing list.

Fundamentally, there is nothing at all wrong with many of the specifications that form part of J2EE. They are, however, at a rather low level of abstraction. Frameworks such as Struts,

WebWork, and more recently JSF have tried to resolve this issue; however, Java and its static typing don't help. Groovy, on the other hand, allows that higher level of abstraction. Having used it for controllers, it was now time to take it to every layer—from controllers to tag libraries and from persistence to the view technology.

The APIs you can create with Groovy's metaprogramming support are amazingly simple and concise. Grails uses every single dynamic trick, at both runtime and compile time, from custom domain-specific languages to compile-time mixins, with two fundamental goals in mind: write less code and be Java friendly.

Are Groovy and Grails a replacement for Java, like other dynamic language frameworks? No, on the contrary, they're designed to work with Java. To embrace it. To have Java at their very core. Grails is Java through and through, and it allows you to pick and choose which features to implement with dynamic typing and which to entrust to the safer hands of static typing.

Grails was born from the realization that there is never only just one tool for the job. Grails is about providing an entry point for the trivial tasks, while still allowing the power and flexibility to harness the full Java platform when needed. I hope you enjoy the book as much as I have enjoyed writing it and being part of the Grails community.

—Graeme Rocher

Who This Book Is For

Grails forms just one framework that is driving the movement toward dynamic language–based frameworks. In this sense, anyone who is interested in dynamic languages, whether Perl, Ruby, or Python, will gain something from reading this book, if just to acquire insight into what the alternatives are.

If platform is not a choice and Java is the way your project is going, Grails can provide features like no other framework. In this circumstance, Grails may have the answers you are looking for. Primarily, however, this book will be of most benefit to those who know and love the Java platform—those who appreciate the Java language for all its strong points but want something better as a web framework.

Grails is providing the answers to the long search for something better in the Java world by presenting a framework that solves the common problems in an unobtrusive, elegant manner. But this does not mean that the subject matter of this book is trivial. We'll be challenging you with advanced usages of the Groovy language and real-world examples.

Furthermore, you'll be pushing the boundaries of what is possible with a dynamic language like Groovy, extending it into every tier of a typical web application from the view layer with Ajax-enabled technology to the persistence tier with rich domain models. For experienced Java developers, it should be an enlightening experience, because we'll explore features not found in Java such as closures, builders, and metaprogramming.

Through all this, however, although the subject matter and examples are advanced, the solutions are simple, and along the way you may learn a new way to approach web application development.

How This Book Is Structured

This book is divided into 17 chapters and one appendix. Unlike the first edition, coverage of Groovy is saved for the appendix. If you have no experience using Groovy, then it is recommended that you read the appendix first as the chapters themselves dive straight into Grails starting with Chapter 1, which covers the basic philosophy behind Grails.

In Chapter 2 we take you through a kick-start, demonstrating how you can quickly get productive with Grails. Then from Chapter 3 onward we delve into detailed coverage of each concept within Grails from domain classes in Chapter 3 to views in Chapter 5. By this point, you should have a good understanding of the basics.

The book will then dive straight into the nitty-gritty details of Grails in Chapter 6 with coverage of URL mappings, followed by the multilingual experience that is internationalization in Chapter 7. If you haven't had enough excitement by this point, then Chapter 8 should solve that with coverage of Grails' support for adaptive Ajax.

In Chapter 9 the book will begin to cover some of the more advanced features of Grails staring with Web Flow. In Chapter 10 you'll get a much better understanding of how GORM works, while in Chapter 11 you'll learn how to leverage declarative transactions with Grails services.

Chapter 12 goes into a lot of detail on how you can integrate Grails into your existing ecosystem; then in Chapter 13 you will get to become a Grails plugin developer as you explore the features offered by Grails' plugin system. Security is the focal point for Chapter 14, while in Chapter 15 we'll cover publishing web services with Grails.

Finally, Chapter 16 and Chapter 17 are dedicated to the more advanced topics of integrating Grails with the underlying Spring and Hibernate frameworks.

Conventions

This book uses a diverse range of languages, including HTML, XML, JavaScript, Groovy, and Java. Nonetheless, each example is introduced appropriately and appears in a fixed-width Courier font. We have also endeavored to be consistent in the use of naming conventions throughout the book, making the examples as clear as possible.

In many cases, the original source code has been reformatted to fit within the available page space, with additional line breaks and modified code indentation being common. To increase the clarity of the code, some examples omit code where it is seen as unnecessary. In cases where the code is omitted between two blocks of code, an ellipsis (…) is used to indicate where the missing code would have been.

Prerequisites

This book shows you how to install Grails; in the examples, we use the 1.1 release. As of this writing, the 1.1 release was not quite final, but by the time of publication, Grails 1.1 should be final (or nearly so). However, Grails itself is dependent on the existence of an installed Java Virtual Machine. As a minimum, you will need to install JDK 1.5 or newer for the examples in this book to work.

Installing an application server, such as Tomcat, and a database server, such as MySQL, is entirely optional, because Grails comes bundled with an embedded server and database. Nevertheless, to use Grails in production, you may at least want to set up a database server.

Downloading the Code

The code for the examples in this book is available in the Source Code section of the Apress web site at `http://www.apress.com`. Chapter-by-chapter source code is also available in the Codehaus Subversion repository at `http://svn.codehaus.org/grails/trunk/samples/dgg`.

Contacting the Authors

Graeme is an active member of the open source community and welcomes any comments and/or communication. You can reach him via e-mail at `graeme.rocher@gmail.com` or via his blog at `http://graemerocher.blogspot.com`. You can reach Jeff via e-mail at `jeff@jeffandbetsy.net` or via his blog at `http://javajeff.blogspot.com`. Alternatively, you can simply pop a message on the Grails mailing lists, the details for which can be found here: `http://grails.org/Mailing+lists`.

CHAPTER 1

The Essence of Grails

Simplicity is the ultimate sophistication.

—Leonardo da Vinci

To understand Grails, you first need to understand its goal: to dramatically simplify enterprise Java web development. To take web development to the next level of abstraction. To tap into what has been accessible to developers on other platforms for years. To have all this but still retain the flexibility to drop down into the underlying technologies and utilize their richness and maturity. Simply put, we Java developers want to "have our cake and eat it too."

Have you faced the pain of dealing with multiple, crippling XML configuration files and an agonizing build system where testing a single change takes minutes instead of seconds? Grails brings back the fun of development on the Java platform, removing barriers and exposing users to APIs that enable them to focus purely on the business problem at hand. No configuration, zero overhead, immediate turnaround.

You might be wondering how you can achieve this remarkable feat. Grails embraces concepts such as Convention over Configuration (CoC), Don't Repeat Yourself (DRY), and sensible defaults that are enabled through the terse Groovy language and an array of domain-specific languages (DSLs) that make your life easier.

As a budding Grails developer, you might think you're cheating somehow, that you should be experiencing more pain. After all, you can't squash a two-hour gym workout into twenty minutes, can you? There must be payback somewhere, maybe in extra pounds?

As a developer you have the assurance that you are standing on the shoulders of giants with the technologies that underpin Grails: Spring, Hibernate, and, of course, the Java platform. Grails takes the best of dynamic language frameworks like Ruby on Rails, Django, and TurboGears and brings them to a Java Virtual Machine (JVM) near you.

Simplicity and Power

A factor that clearly sets Grails apart from its competitors is evident in the design choices made during its development. By not reinventing the wheel, and by leveraging tried and trusted frameworks such as Spring and Hibernate, Grails can deliver features that make your life easier without sacrificing robustness.

Grails is powered by some of the most popular open source technologies in their respective categories:

- *Hibernate*: The de facto standard for object-relational mapping (ORM) in the Java world

- *Spring*: The hugely popular open source Inversion of Control (IoC) container and wrapper framework for Java

- *SiteMesh*: A robust and stable layout-rendering framework

- *Jetty*: A proven, embeddable servlet container

- *HSQLDB*: A pure Java Relational Database Management System (RDBMS) implementation

The concepts of ORM and IoC might seem a little alien to some readers. ORM simply serves as a way to map objects from the object-oriented world onto tables in a relational database. ORM provides an additional abstraction above SQL, allowing developers to think about their domain model instead of getting wrapped up in reams of SQL.

IoC provides a way of "wiring" together objects so that their dependencies are available at runtime. As an example, an object that performs persistence might require access to a data source. IoC relieves the developer of the responsibility of obtaining a reference to the data source. But don't get too wrapped up in these concepts for the moment, as their usage will become clear later in the book.

You benefit from Grails because it wraps these frameworks by introducing another layer of abstraction via the Groovy language. You, as a developer, will not know that you are building a Spring and Hibernate application. Certainly, you won't need to touch a single line of Hibernate or Spring XML, but it is there at your fingertips if you need it. Figure 1-1 illustrates how Grails relates to these frameworks and the enterprise Java stack.

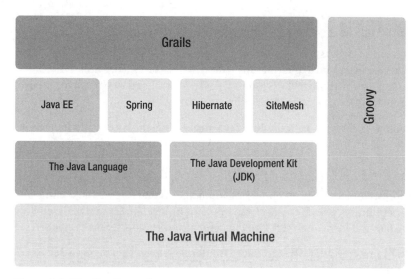

Figure 1-1. *The Grails stack*

Grails, the Platform

When approaching Grails, you might suddenly experience a deep inhalation of breath followed by an outcry of "not another web framework!?" That's understandable, given the dozens of web frameworks that exist for Java. But Grails is different, and in a good way. Grails is a full-stack environment, not just a web framework. It is a *platform* with ambitious aims to handle everything from the view layer down to your persistence concerns.

In addition, through its plugins system (covered in Chapter 13), Grails aims to provide solutions to an extended set of problems that might not be covered out of the box. With Grails you can accomplish searching, job scheduling, enterprise messaging and remoting, and more.

The sheer breadth of Grails' coverage might conjure up unknown horrors and nightmarish thoughts of configuration, configuration, configuration. However, even in its plugins, Grails embraces Convention over Configuration and sensible defaults to minimize the work required to get up and running.

We encourage you to think of Grails as not just another web framework, but the *platform* upon which you plan to build your next web 2.0 phenomenon.

Living in the Java Ecosystem

As well as leveraging Java frameworks that you know and love, Grails gives you a platform that allows you to take full advantage of Java and the JVM—thanks to Groovy. No other dynamic language on the JVM integrates with Java like Groovy. Groovy is designed to work seamlessly with Java at every level. Starting with syntax, the similarities continue:

- The Groovy grammar is derived from the Java 5 grammar, making most valid Java code also valid Groovy code.

- Groovy shares the same underlying APIs as Java, so your trusty javadocs are still valid!

- Groovy objects are Java objects. This has powerful implications that might not be immediately apparent. For example, a Groovy object can implement java.io.Serializable and be sent over Remote Method Invocation (RMI) or clustered using session-replication tools.

- Through Groovy's joint compiler you can have circular references between Groovy and Java without running into compilation issues.

- With Groovy you can easily use the same profiling tools, the same monitoring tools, and all existing and future Java technologies.

Groovy's ability to integrate seamlessly with Java, along with its Java-like syntax, is the number-one reason why so much hype was generated around its conception. Here we had a language with similar capabilities to languages such as Ruby and Smalltalk running directly in the JVM. The potential is obvious, and the ability to intermingle Java code with dynamic Groovy code is huge. In addition, Groovy allows you to mix static types and dynamic types, combining the safety of static typing with the power and flexibility to use dynamic typing where necessary.

This level of Java integration is what drives Groovy's continued popularity, particularly in the world of web applications. Across different programming platforms, varying idioms essentially express the same concept. In the Java world we have servlets, filters, tag libraries, and JavaServer Pages (JSP). Moving to a new platform requires relearning all of these concepts and their equivalent APIs or idioms—easy for some, a challenge for others. Not that learning new things is bad, but a cost is attached to knowledge gain in the real world, which can present a major stumbling block in the adoption of any new technology that deviates from the standards or conventions defined within the Java platform and the enterprise.

In addition, Java has standards for deployment, management, security, naming, and more. The goal of Grails is to create a platform with the essence of frameworks like Rails or Django or CakePHP, but one that embraces the mature environment of Java Enterprise Edition (Java EE) and its associated APIs.

Grails is, however, one of these technologies that speaks for itself: the moment you experience using it, a little light bulb will go on inside your head. So without delay, let's get moving with the example application that will flow throughout the course of this book. Whereas in this book's first edition we featured a social-bookmarking application modeled on the del.icio.us service, in this edition we'll illustrate an entirely new type of application: gTunes.

Our gTunes example will guide you through the development of a music store similar to those provided by Apple, Amazon, and Napster. An application of this nature opens up a wide variety of interesting possibilities from e-commerce to RESTful APIs and RSS or Atom feeds. We hope it will give you a broad understanding of Grails and its feature set.

Getting Started

Grails' installation is almost as simple as its usage, but you must take into account at least one prerequisite. Grails requires a valid installation of the Java SDK 1.5 or above which, of course, you can obtain from Sun Microsystems at `http://java.sun.com`.

After installing the Java SDK, set the `JAVA_HOME` environment variable to the location where you installed it and add the `JAVA_HOME/bin` directory to your PATH variables.

Note If you are working on Mac OS X, you already have Java installed! However, you still need to set `JAVA_HOME` in your ~/.profile file.

To test your installation, open up a command prompt and type **java -version**:

```
$java -version
```

You should see output similar to Listing 1-1.

Listing 1-1. *Running the Java Executable*

```
java version "1.5.0_13"
Java(TM) 2 Runtime Environment, Standard Edition (build 1.5.0_13-b05-237)
Java HotSpot(TM) Client VM (build 1.5.0_13-119, mixed mode, sharing)
```

As is typical with many other Java frameworks such as Apache Tomcat and Apache Ant, the installation process involves following a few simple steps. Download and unzip Grails from `http://grails.org`, create a `GRAILS_HOME` variable that points to the location where you installed Grails, and add the `GRAILS_HOME/bin` directory to your PATH variable.

To validate your installation, open a command window and type the command **grails**:

```
$ grails
```

If you have successfully installed Grails, the command will output the usage help shown in Listing 1-2.

Listing 1-2. *Running the Grails Executable*

```
Welcome to Grails 1.1 - http://grails.org/
Licensed under Apache Standard License 2.0
Grails home is set to: /Developer/grails-1.1

No script name specified. Use 'grails help' for more info or 'grails interactive' to

enter interactive mode
```

As suggested by the output in Listing 1-2, typing **grails help** will display more usage information including a list of available commands. If more information about a particular command is needed, you can append the command name to the help command. For example, if you want to know more about the create-app command, simply type **grails help create-app**:

```
$ grails help create-app
```

Listing 1-3 provides an example of the typical output.

Listing 1-3. *Getting Help on a Command*

```
Usage (optionals marked with *):
grails [environment]* create-app

grails create-app -- Creates a Grails project, including the necessary
directory structure and common files
```

Grails' command-line interface is built on another Groovy-based project called Gant (http://gant.codehaus.org/), which wraps the ever-popular Apache Ant (http://ant.apache.org/) build system. Gant allows seamless mixing of Ant targets and Groovy code.

We'll discuss the Grails command line further in Chapter 12.

Creating Your First Application

In this section you're going to create your first Grails application, which will include a simple controller. Here are the steps you'll take to achieve this:

1. Run the command `grails create-app gTunes` to create the application (with "gTunes" being the application's name).

2. Navigate into the gTunes directory by issuing the command `cd gTunes`.

3. Create a storefront controller with the command `grails create-controller store`.

4. Write some code to display a welcome message to the user.

5. Test your code and run the tests with `grails test-app`.

6. Run the application with `grails run-app`.

Step 1: Creating the Application

Sound easy? It is, and your first port of call is the `create-app` command, which you managed to extract some help on in the previous section. To run the command, simply type **grails create-app** and hit Enter in the command window:

```
$ grails create-app
```

Grails will automatically prompt you for a project name as presented in Listing 1-4. When this happens, type **gTunes** and hit Enter. As an alternative, you could use the command `grails create-app gTunes`, in which cases Grails takes the appropriate action automatically.

Listing 1-4. *Creating an Application with the create-app Command*

```
Running script /Developer/grails-dev/GRAILS_1_1/scripts/CreateApp.groovy
Environment set to development
Application name not specified. Please enter: gTunes
```

Upon completion, the command will have created the gTunes Grails application and the necessary directory structure. The next step is to navigate to the newly created application in the command window using the shell command:

```
cd gTunes
```

At this point you have a clean slate—a newly created Grails application—with the default settings in place. A screenshot of the structure of a Grails application appears in Figure 1-2.

We will delve deeper into the structure of a Grails application and the roles of the various files and directories as we progress through the book. You will notice, however, how Grails contains directories for controllers, domain objects (models), and views.

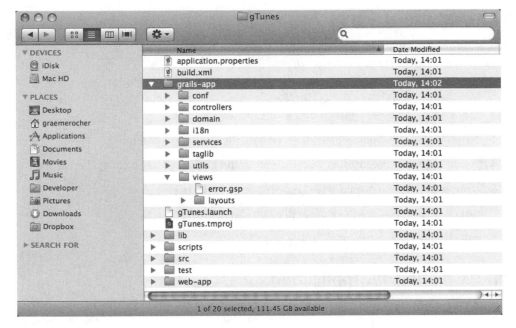

Figure 1-2. *The gTunes application structure*

Step 2: Creating a Controller

Grails is an MVC[1] framework, which means it has models, views, and controllers to separate concerns cleanly. Controllers, which are central to a Grails application, can easily marshal requests, deliver responses, and delegate to views. Because the gTunes application centers around the concept of a music store, we'll show you how to create a "store" controller.

To help you along the way, Grails features an array of helper commands for creating classes that "fit" into the various slots in a Grails application. For example, for controllers you have the `create-controller` command, which will do nicely. But using these commands is not mandatory. As you grow more familiar with the different concepts in Grails, you can just as easily create a controller class using your favorite text editor or integrated development environment (IDE).

Nevertheless, let's get going with the `create-controller` command, which, as with `create-app`, takes an argument where you can specify the name of the controller you wish to create. Simply type **grails create-controller store**:

```
$ grails create-controller store
```

Now sit back while Grails does the rest (see Listing 1-5).

---

1. The Model-View-Controller (MVC) pattern is a common pattern found in many web frameworks designed to separate user interface and business logic. See Wikipedia, "Model-view-controller," http://en.wikipedia.org/wiki/Model-view-controller, 2003.

Listing 1-5. *Creating a Controller with the create-controller Command*

```
[copy] Copying 1 file to /Developer/grails-dev/gTunes/grails-app/controllers
Created Controller for Store
    [mkdir] Created dir: /Developer/grails-dev/gTunes/grails-app/views/store
     [copy] Copying 1 file to /Developer/grails-dev/gTunes/test/unit
Created ControllerTests for Store
```

Once the `create-controller` command has finished running, Grails will have created not one, but two classes for you: a new controller called `StoreController` within the `grails-app/controllers` directory, and an associated test case in the `test/unit` directory. Figure 1-3 shows the newly created controller nesting nicely in the appropriate directory.

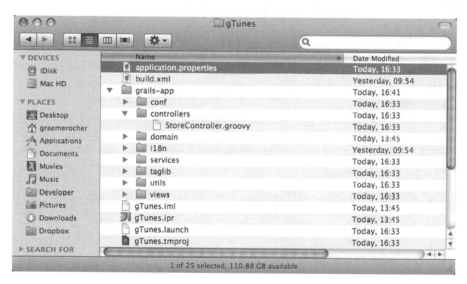

Figure 1-3. *The newly created StoreController*

Due to Groovy's dynamic nature, you should aim for a high level of test coverage[2] in any Grails project (Grails assumes you'll need a test if you're writing a controller). Dynamic languages such as Groovy, Ruby, and Python do not give you nearly as much compile-time assistance as statically typed languages such as Java. Some errors that you might expect to be caught at compile time are actually left to runtime, including method resolution. Sadly, the comfort of the compiler often encourages Java developers to forget about testing altogether.

---

2. Code coverage is a measure used in software testing. It describes the degree to which the source code of a program has been tested.

Needless to say, the compiler is not a substitute for a good suite of unit tests, and what you lose in compile-time assistance you gain in expressivity.

Throughout this book we will be demonstrating automated-testing techniques that make the most of Grails' testing support.

Step 3: Printing a Message

Let's return to the StoreController. By default, Grails will create the controller and give it a single action called index. The index action is, by convention, the default action in the controller. Listing 1-6 shows the StoreController containing the default index action.

Listing 1-6. *The Default index Action*

```
class StoreController {
    def index = {}
}
```

The index action doesn't seem to be doing much, but by convention, its declaration instructs Grails to try to render a view called grails-app/views/store/index.gsp automatically. Views are the subject of Chapter 5, so for the sake of simplicity we're going to try something less ambitious instead.

Grails controllers come with a number of implicit methods, which we'll cover in Chapter 4. One of these is render, a multipurpose method that, among other things, can render a simple textual response. Listing 1-7 shows how to print a simple response: "Welcome to the gTunes store!"

Listing 1-7. *Printing a Message Using the render Method*

```
class StoreController {
    def index = {
        render "Welcome to the gTunes store!"
    }
}
```

Step 4: Testing the Code

The preceding code is simple enough, but even the simplest code shouldn't go untested. Open the StoreControllerTests test suite that was generated earlier inside the test/unit directory. Listing 1-8 shows the contents of the StoreControllerTests suite.

Listing 1-8. *The Generated StoreControllerTests Test Suite*

```
class StoreControllerTests extends grails.test.ControllerUnitTestCase {
    void testSomething() {

    }
}
```

Grails separates tests into "unit" and "integration" tests. Integration tests bootstrap the whole environment including the database and hence tend to run more slowly. In addition, integration tests are typically designed to test the interaction among a number of classes and therefore require a more complete application before you can run them.

Unit tests, on the other hand, are fast-running tests, but they require you to make extensive use of mocks and stubs. Stubs are classes used in testing that mimic the real behavior of methods by returning arbitrary hard-coded values. Mocks essentially do the same thing, but exhibit a bit more intelligence by having "expectations." For example, a mock can specify that it "expects" a given method to be invoked at least once, or even ten times if required. As we progress through the book, the difference between unit tests and integration tests will become clearer.

To test the StoreController in its current state, you can assert the value of the response that was sent to the user. A simple way of doing this appears in Listing 1-9.

Listing 1-9. *Testing the StoreController's index Action*

```
class StoreControllerTests extends grails.test.ControllerUnitTestCase {
    void testRenderHomePage() {
        controller.index()
        assertEquals "Welcome to the gTunes store!",
                              controller.response.contentAsString
    }
}
```

What we're doing here is using Grails' built-in testing capabilities to evaluate the content of the response object. During a test run, Grails magically transforms the regular servlet HttpServletResponse object into a Spring MockHttpServletResponse, which has helper properties such as contentAsString that enable you to evaluate what happened as the result of a call to the render method.

Nevertheless, don't get too hung up about the ins and outs of using this code just yet. The whole book will be littered with examples that will gradually ease you into becoming proficient at testing with Grails.

Step 5: Running the Tests

To run the tests and verify that everything works as expected, you can use the grails test-app command. The test-app command will execute all the tests in the application and output the results to the test/reports directory. In addition, you can run only StoreControllerTests by issuing the command grails test-app StoreController. Listing 1-10 shows some typical output that results when you run the test-app command.

Listing 1-10. *Running Tests with grails test-app*

```
----------------------------------------------------------
Running 1 Unit Test...
Running test StoreControllerTests...
                    testRenderHomePage...SUCCESS
Unit Tests Completed in 233ms
----------------------------------------------------------
...
Tests passed. View reports in /Developer/grails-dev/gTunes/test/reports
```

If you want to review the reports, you'll find XML, HTML, and plain-text reports in the test/reports directory. Figure 1-4 shows what the generated HTML reports look like in a browser—they're definitely easier on the eye than the XML equivalent!

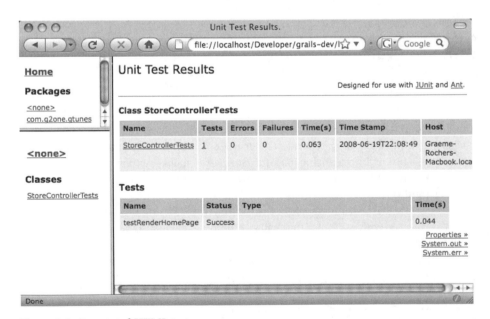

Figure 1-4. *Generated HTML test reports*

Step 6: Running the Application

Now that you've tested your code, your final step is to see it in action. Do this using the `grails run-app` command, which will start up a locally running Grails server on port 8080 by default. Grails uses the popular and robust Jetty container (`http://www.mortbay.org/`) as the default server, but of course you can deploy Grails onto any servlet container that's version 2.4 or above. (You'll find out more about deployment in Chapter 12.)

Get Grails going by typing **grails run-app** into the command prompt:

```
$ grails run-app
```

You'll notice that Grails will start up and inform you of a URL you can use to access the Grails instance (see Listing 1-11).

Listing 1-11. *Running an Application with run-app*

```
...
2008-06-19 23:15:46.523:/gTunes:INFO:  Initializing Spring FrameworkServlet 'grails'
2008-06-19 23:15:47.963::INFO:  Started SelectChannelConnector@0.0.0.0:8080
Server running. Browse to http://localhost:8080/gTunes
```

If you get a bind error such as this one, it probably resulted from a port conflict:

```
Server failed to start: java.net.BindException: Address already in use
```

This error typically occurs if you already have another container running on port 8080, such as Apache Tomcat (`http://tomcat.apache.org`). You can work around this issue by running Grails on a different port by passing the `server.port` argument specifying an alternative value:

```
grails -Dserver.port=8087 run-app
```

In the preceding case, Grails will start up on port 8087 as expected. Barring any port conflicts, you should have Grails up and running and ready to serve requests at this point. Open your favorite browser and navigate to the URL prompted by the Grails `run-app` command shown in Listing 11-1. You'll be presented with the Grails welcome page that looks something like Figure 1-5.

The welcome screen is (by default) rendered by a Groovy Server Pages (GSP) file located at `web-app/index.gsp`, but you can fully customize the location of this file through URL mappings (discussed in Chapter 6).

As you can see in Figure 1-5, the `StoreController` you created earlier is one of those listed as available. Clicking the `StoreController` link results in printing the "Welcome to the gTunes store!" message you implemented earlier (see Figure 1-6).

Welcome to Grails

Congratulations, you have successfully started your first Grails application! At the
moment this is the default page, feel free to modify it to either redirect to a controller or
display whatever content you may choose. Below is a list of controllers that are currently
deployed in this application, click on each to execute its default action:

• **StoreController**

Figure 1-5. *The standard Grails welcome page*

Welcome to the gTunes store!

Figure 1-6. *StoreController prints a message.*

Summary

Success! You have your first Grails application up and running. In this chapter you've taken the first steps needed to learn Grails by setting up and configuring your Grails installation. In addition, you've created your first Grails application, along with a basic controller.

Now it is time to see what else Grails does to kick-start your project development. In the next section, we'll look at some of Grails' Create, Read, Update, Delete (CRUD) generation facilities that allow you to flesh out prototype applications in no time.

CHAPTER 2

Getting Started with Grails

In Chapter 1, you got your first introduction to the Grails framework and a feel for the basic command-line interface while creating the basis for the gTunes application. In this chapter, we're going to build on that foundation by showing how you can use Grails' scaffolding feature to quickly build a prototype application that can generate simple CRUD (Create, Read, Update, Delete) interfaces.

Then we'll start to explain some of the basic concepts within the Grails ecosystem such as environments, data sources, and deployment. Get ready—this is an action-packed chapter with loads of information!

What Is Scaffolding?

Scaffolding is a Grails feature that allows you to quickly generate CRUD interfaces for an existing domain. It offers several benefits, the most significant of which is that it serves as a superb learning tool, allowing you to relate how Grails' controller and view layers interact with the domain model that you created.

You should note, however, that Grails is not just a CRUD framework. And scaffolding, although a useful feature in your repertoire, is not Grails' main benefit. If you're looking for a framework that provides purely CRUD-oriented features, better options are at your disposal.

As with a lot of Grails features, scaffolding is best demonstrated visually, so let's plunge right in and see what you can do.

Creating a Domain

Grails' domain classes serve as the heart of your application and business-model concepts. If you were constructing a bookstore application, for example, you would be thinking about books, authors, and publishers. With gTunes you have other thoughts in mind, such as albums, artists, and songs.

The most significant attribute that differentiates domain classes from other artifacts within a Grails application is that they are persistent and that Grails automatically maps each domain class onto a physical table in the configured database. (You'll learn more about how to change the database setup later in the chapter.)

The act of mapping classes onto a relational database layer is also known as object-relational mapping (ORM). Grails' ORM layer, called GORM, is built on the ever-popular Hibernate library (http://www.hibernate.org).

Domain classes reside snugly in the `grails-app/domain` directory. You create a domain class by using the `grails create-domain-class` helper command, or your favorite IDE or text editor. Type the helper command shown in Listing 2-1 into a command window from the root of the gTunes project.

Listing 2-1. *Creating the Song Domain Class*

```
$ grails create-domain-class com.g2one.gtunes.Song
```

Listing 2-1 shows that you'll be using a package to hold your domain classes. Groovy follows exactly the same packaging rules as Java, and as with Java, it is good practice to use packages. You might not see the benefit of packages in the beginning, but as your application grows and you begin taking advantage of Grails plugins and integrating more Java code, you will appreciate the organization that they provide (for more about plugins, see Chapter 13).

Once the command in Listing 2-1 completes, the result will be a new Song domain class located in the `grails-app/domain/com/g2one/gtunes` directory as dictated by the package prefix specified. Figure 2-1 shows the newly created structure and the `Song.groovy` file containing the domain class definition.

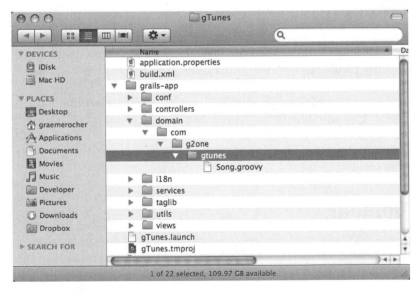

Figure 2-1. *The Song domain class and the Song.groovy file*

Currently, the Song domain isn't doing a great deal; it's simply a blank class definition as shown in Listing 2-2.

Listing 2-2. *The Song Domain Class*

```
package com.g2one.gtunes
class Song {
}
```

At this point, you should think about what aspects make up a "Song". Songs typically have a title, an artist, and a duration, among other things. If you really want to go overboard, you could model your Song domain class on all the fields you can populate in an MP3 file's ID3 tag. But in this case, keep it simple: add only the three previously mentioned properties as shown in Listing 2-3.

Listing 2-3. *Adding Properties to the Song Domain Class*

```
package com.g2one.gtunes
class Song {
    String title
    String artist
    Integer duration
}
```

That was simple enough, and the class doesn't look much different from your typical Groovy bean (see the Appendix for information about Groovy beans). GORM essentially maps the class name onto the table name and each property onto a separate column in the database, with their types relating to SQL types. Don't get too hung up on this now; we'll be digging more deeply into domain classes and GORM in Chapters 3 and 10. For the moment, let's move on to seeing the application in action.

Dynamic Scaffolding

Scaffolding comes in two flavors: dynamic (or runtime), and static (or template-driven). First we'll look at dynamic scaffolding, where a CRUD application's controller logic and views are generated at runtime. Dynamic scaffolding does not involve boilerplate code or templates; it uses advanced techniques such as reflection and Groovy's metaprogramming capabilities to achieve its goals. However, before you can dynamically scaffold your Song class, you need a controller.

You had a brief introduction to creating controllers in Chapter 1, and the controller code necessary to enable scaffolding is minimal. Create the controller for the Song class either manually or via the command line, as shown in Listing 2-4.

Listing 2-4. *Creating the SongController*

```
$ grails create-controller com.g2one.gtunes.Song
```

Again, you should use the package prefix with the grails create-controller command, which will create the SongController within the grails-app/controllers/com/g2one/gtunes directory (see Figure 2-2).

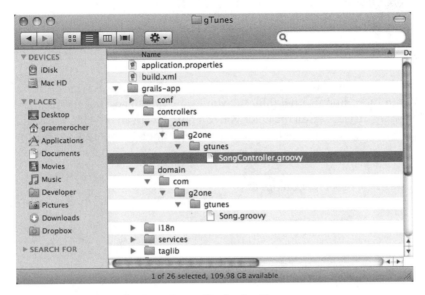

Figure 2-2. *Locating the SongController in the directory*

To enable dynamic scaffolding, within the SongController create a scaffold property with the name of the target class as its value. In this case, it is the Song class, as shown in Listing 2-5.

Listing 2-5. *Enabling Dynamic Scaffolding*

```
package com.g2one.gtunes

class SongController {
    def scaffold = Song
}
```

■**Note** Groovy automatically resolves class names, such as Song in Listing 2-5, to the java.lang.Class instance without requiring the .class suffix. In other words Song == Song.class.

With that done, simply start up Grails with the `grails run-app` command, open a browser, and navigate to the gTunes application at the usual link: `http://localhost:8080/gTunes`.

The Grails welcome page, first demonstrated in Chapter 1, will show the `SongController` instance in the list of available controllers as well as the usual comforting welcome message. Click the `SongController` link to pull up a page listing all the Song objects (perhaps none, as the case may be), as depicted in Figure 2-3.

Figure 2-3. *The Song List page*

Without breaking a sweat, and in a grand total of three lines of code (excluding the package declaration), you have managed to create a useful CRUD interface that lets you create and fully manage the Song instances within the gTunes application.

The Create Operation

The magic doesn't end here. By clicking the "New Song" link at the top of the screen, you can create new songs. While generating the views, Grails does its best to guess what type of field is required to edit a property's value. For example, if Grails finds a `String`, it will create a text field; if it finds a `java.util.Date`, it will render drop-down boxes that allow you to select the date and time. Figure 2-4 shows an example of what the generated song-creation interface looks like.

Grails' built-in validation mechanism, called constraints, can also affect how the interface is rendered, including the order in which fields are displayed and the type of field that is rendered. Try clicking the "Create" button; you'll get a validation error stating that the duration must be specified, as pictured in Figure 2-5. The validation messages hook into Grails' internationalization support (often referred to with the abbreviation i18n). But for now, all you need to know is that Grails is pulling these messages from the properties files within the grails-app/i18n directory. (We'll discuss constraints in Chapter 3 and internationalization in Chapter 7.)

Figure 2-4. *The Create Song page*

Figure 2-5. *How Grails handles validation*

You could customize the message at this point, but for now the defaults will do. Now let's try to create a song with some valid data. Specifically, try to enter these values into the provided fields:

Artist: Kings of Leon

Duration: 176000

Title: The Bucket

Now click the "Create" button and move on to the next section of the chapter.

The Read Operation

Grails has obeyed instructions and duly created a new Song instance with the necessary data in the database. You are then redirected to the "Show Song" screen where you can view and admire a rendered view of the Song instance you just created.

Additionally, as pictured in Figure 2-6, the "Show Song" screen provides two buttons to let you edit or delete the Song instance from the database.

Figure 2-6. *The Show Song screen*

Currently, you're dealing with a trivial domain model with only a single Song domain class to account for. However, another attribute of domain classes is that they typically have relationships such as one-to-many, one-to-one, and so on. If you think about a Song for a moment, it is typically part of a collection of Songs within an album. Let's create an Album domain class to model this using the grails create-domain-class command as shown in Listing 2-6.

Listing 2-6. *Creating the Album Domain Class*

```
$ grails create-domain-class com.g2one.gtunes.Album
```

An `Album` has attributes of its own, such as a title, but it also contains many songs. Listing 2-7 shows how to set up a one-to-many relationship between `Album` and `Song` using the `hasMany` static property of domain classes. The `hasMany` property is assigned a Groovy map where the key is the relationship name and the value is the class, in this case `Song`, to which the association relates.

Listing 2-7. *Defining a One-to-Many Relationship*

```
package com.g2one.gtunes

class Album {
    String title
    static hasMany = [songs:Song]
}
```

The preceding association is unidirectional. In other words, only the `Album` class knows about the association, while the `Song` class remains blissfully unaware of it. To make the association bidirectional, modify the `Song` class to include an `Album` local property as shown in Listing 2-8. Now `Album` and `Song` have a bidirectional, one-to-many association.

Listing 2-8. *Making the Relationship Bidirectional*

```
package com.g2one.gtunes
class Song {
    ...
    Album album
}
```

In Chapter 3, we'll delve into other kinds of relationships and how they map onto the underlying database. For now, create another scaffolded controller that can deal with the creation of `Album` instances. Use the `grails create-controller` command and add the `def scaffold = Album` property to the class definition (see Listing 2-9).

Listing 2-9. *Scaffolding the Album Class*

```
package com.g2one.gtunes

class AlbumController {
    def scaffold = Album
}
```

Now if you return to your browser and refresh the Song list, you'll notice that the Song you entered previously has mysteriously vanished. The reason for this is quite simple: Grails by default is running with an in-memory database, and updating domain classes creates a new instance of it. You might find this useful for testing, but you can configure a different database if you require a less volatile storage mechanism (we'll discuss that later in this chapter).

More significant, however, is the fact that on the welcome page we have an additional AlbumController. Click the AlbumController link, followed by the "New Album" button. Enter a title for the Album such as "Aha Shake Heartbreak" and click the "Create" button to see your newly created Album displayed (see Figure 2-7).

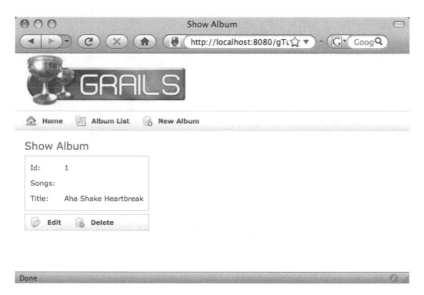

Figure 2-7. *The Show Album screen*

You'll also notice that the Album has a blank Songs field. Let's fix that next.

The Update Operation

You can perform updates by clicking the "Edit" button. In this case, you want to add a Song, so click the "Add Song" link to see the "Create Song" interface. This time, you'll get a useful drop-down box that lets you select which Album the Song should be part of (as shown in Figure 2-8). You'll notice that scaffolding's default behavior is simply to call toString() on each element in the drop-down list. The default toString() that Grails provides uses the class name and instance id, which is not the most pleasant thing to present to a user. You can override this behavior by implementing your own toString() method inside the Album class.

Next, populate the fields as described in the "The Create Operation" section and click the "Create" button. You'll notice that the "Show Song" screen provides a link back to the Album; clicking the link shows the Album with the newly created Song instance appearing in the list of songs (see Figure 2-9). Grails' scaffolding, although not exuding genius, is clever enough to figure out what a one-to-many relationship is and how to manage it accordingly.

Figure 2-8. *The Create Song screen*

Figure 2-9. *Show Album screen with a list of songs*

The Delete Operation

Finally, to complete the CRUD acronym, you can delete a particular Song or Album by clicking the "Delete" button. Grails is kind enough to inquire whether you are completely sure that you'd like to proceed with such a destructive operation.

This completes the tour of Grails' dynamic-scaffolding capabilities; in the next section you'll see how to get access to the underlying controller and view code that makes up these CRUD interfaces.

Static Scaffolding

Dynamic scaffolding can serve a number of purposes, from creating administration interfaces to providing the basis of a real application. However, it often becomes useful to take customization to a new level, particularly in terms of views. Fortunately, Grails provides the ability to take a domain class and generate a controller and associated views from the command line through the following targets:

- `grails generate-views`: Generates views for the specified domain class

- `grails generate-controller`: Generates a controller for the specified domain class

- `grails generate-all`: Generates both a controller and associated views

Called "static" or "template-driven" scaffolding, this approach offers benefits beyond simple code generation. Notably, it provides an excellent learning tool to help you familiarize yourself with the Grails framework and how everything fits together.

You've already created a domain model that relates specifically to the problem you're attempting to solve. Now you can generate code that relates to your domain, increasing your chance of understanding the generated code. Let's start by looking at how to generate a controller.

Generating a Controller

To generate a controller that implements the CRUD functionality you saw in the section about dynamic scaffolding, you can take advantage of the `grails generate-controller` command. Like the other generate commands, generate-controller takes a domain class name as its first argument. For example, Listing 2-10 shows how to use the generate-controller command to output a new controller from the `Album` class.

Listing 2-10. *Outputting a New Controller*

```
$ grails generate-controller com.g2one.gtunes.Album
Generating controller for domain class com.g2one.gtunes.Album ...
File /Developer/grails-dev/apps/gTunes/grails-➥
app/controllers/com/g2one/gtunes/AlbumController.groovy already exists.
Overwrite?y,n,a
y
Finished generation for domain class com.g2one.gtunes.Album
```

Notice that, because the `AlbumController` class already exists, the generate-controller command will ask whether you want to overwrite the existing controller. Entering the value "y" for "yes" followed by hitting Enter will complete the process.

At this point, you should probably examine the contents of this mysterious controller to see how many thousands of code lines have been generated. If you're coming from a traditional Java web-development background, you might expect to implement a few different classes. For example, you would likely need a controller that calls a business interface, which in turn invokes a Data Access Object (DAO) that actually performs the CRUD operations.

Surely the DAO will contain mountains of ORM framework code, and maybe a few lines of Java Database Connectivity (JDBC) mixed in for good measure. Surprisingly (or not, depending on your perspective), the code is extremely concise at well under 100 lines. That's still not quite short enough to list in full here, but we will step through each action in the generated controller to understand what it is doing.

The index action is the default, which is executed if no action is specified in the controller Uniform Resource Identifier (URI). It simply redirects to the list action, passing any parameters along with it (see Listing 2-11).

Listing 2-11. *The index Action*

```
def index = {
    redirect(action:list, params:params)
}
```

The list action provides a list of all albums, as shown in Listing 2-12. It delegates to the static list method of the Album class to obtain a java.util.List of Album instances. It then places the list of Album instances into a Groovy map literal (a java.util.LinkedHashMap under the covers), which is then returned as the "model" from the controller to the view. (You'll begin to understand more about models and how they relate to views in Chapters 4 and 5.)

Listing 2-12. *The list Action*

```
def list = {
    if(!params.max) params.max = 10
    [ albumList: Album.list( params ) ]
}
```

But hold on a second: before we get ahead of ourselves, have you noticed that you haven't actually written a static list method in the Album class? At this point, you will start to see the power of GORM. GORM automatically provides a whole array of methods on every domain class you write through Groovy's metaprogramming capabilities, one of which is the list method. By looking through this scaffolded code, you will get a preview of the capabilities GORM has to offer.

For example, the show action, shown in Listing 2-13, takes the id parameter from the params object and passes it to the get method of the Album class. The get method, automatically provided by GORM, allows the lookup of domain instances using their database identifiers. The result of the get method is placed inside a model ready for display, as shown in Listing 2-13.

Listing 2-13. *The show Action*

```
def show = {
    def album = Album.get( params.id )

    if(!album) {
        flash.message = "Album not found with id ${params.id}"
        redirect(action:list)
    }
    else { return [ album : album ] }
}
```

Notice how, in Listing 2-13, if the Album instance does not exist the code places a message inside the flash object, which is rendered in the view. The flash object is a great temporary storage for messages (or message codes if you're using i18n); we'll discuss it in more detail in Chapter 4.

The action that handles deletion of albums is aptly named the delete action. It retrieves an Album for the specified id parameter and, if it exists, deletes it and redirects it to the list action (Listing 2-14).

Listing 2-14. *The delete Action*

```
def delete = {
    def album = Album.get( params.id )
    if(album) {
        album.delete()
        flash.message = "Album ${params.id} deleted"
        redirect(action:list)
    }
    else {
        flash.message = "Album not found with id ${params.id}"
        redirect(action:list)
    }
}
```

While similar to the show action, which simply displays an Album's property values, the edit action delegates to an edit view, which will render fields to edit the Album's properties (see Listing 2-15).

Listing 2-15. *The edit Action*

```
def edit = {
    def album = Album.get( params.id )
```

```
            if(!album) {
                flash.message = "Album not found with id ${params.id}"
                redirect(action:list)
            }
            else {
                return [ album : album ]
            }
        }
```

You might be wondering at this point how Grails decides which view to display, given that the code for the edit and show actions are almost identical. The answer lies in the power of convention. Grails derives the appropriate view name from the controller and action names. In this case, since you have a controller called `AlbumController` and an action called edit, Grails will look for a view at the location grails-app/views/album/edit.gsp with the album directory inferred from the controller name and the edit.gsp file taken from the action name. Simple, really.

For updating you have the update action, which again makes use of the static get method to obtain a reference to the Album instance. The magical expression `album.properties = params` automatically binds the request's parameters onto the properties of the Album instance. You then save the Album instance by calling the save() method. If the save succeeds, an HTTP redirect is issued back to the user; otherwise, the edit view is rendered again. You can find the full code in Listing 2-16.

Listing 2-16. *The update Action*

```
    def update = {
        def album = Album.get( params.id )
        if(album) {
            album.properties = params
            if(!album.hasErrors() && album.save()) {
                flash.message = "Album ${params.id} updated"
                redirect(action:show,id:album.id)
            }
            else {
                render(view:'edit',model:[album:album])
            }
        }
        else {
            flash.message = "Album not found with id ${params.id}"
            redirect(action:edit,id:params.id)
        }
    }
```

To facilitate the creation of new Albums, the create action delegates to the create view. The create view, like the edit view, displays appropriate editing fields. Note how the create action inserts a new Album into the model to ensure that field values are populated from request parameters (Listing 2-17).

Listing 2-17. *The create Action*

```
def create = {
    [album: new Album(params)]
}
```

Finally, the save action will attempt to create a new Album instance and save it to the database (see Listing 2-18).

Listing 2-18. *The save Action*

```
def save = {
    def album = new Album(params)
    if(!album.hasErrors() && album.save()) {
        flash.message = "Album ${album.id} created"
        redirect(action:show,id:album.id)
    }
    else {
        render(view:'create',model:[album:album])
    }
}
```

In both the save and update actions, you alternate between using the redirect and render methods. We'll cover these further in Chapter 4, but briefly: the redirect method issues an HTTP redirect that creates an entirely new request to a different action, while the render method renders a selected view to the response of the current request.

Clearly, we've given only a brief overview of the various CRUD operations and what they do, without elaborating on a lot of the magic that is going on here. There is, however, method in our madness. The nitty-gritty details of controllers and how they work will surface in Chapter 4. For the moment, however, let's try out the newly generated controller by running the gTunes application once again via the grails run-app target.

Once the server has loaded, navigate your browser to the AlbumController at the address http://localhost:8080/gTunes/album. What happens? Well, not a great deal, actually. The result is a page-not-found (404) error because the generated controller is not using dynamic scaffolding. Dynamic scaffolding renders the views at runtime, but what you have here is just a plain old controller—there's nothing special about it, and there are no views.

■**Note** We can of course set the `scaffold` property to the `Album` class, and the views will be generated with each action overridden.

Generating the Views

It would be nice to have some views for your actions to delegate to. Fortunately, you can generate them with the `grails generate-views` command, which is executed according to the same process described in the section "Generating a Controller" (see Listing 2-19).

Listing 2-19. *Generating Views*

```
$ grails generate-views com.g2one.gtunes.Album
...
Running script /Developer/grails-dev/grails/scripts/GenerateViews.groovy
...
Generating views for domain class com.g2one.gtunes.Album ...
Finished generation for domain class com.g2one.gtunes.Album
```

The resulting output from the command window will resemble Figure 2-10.

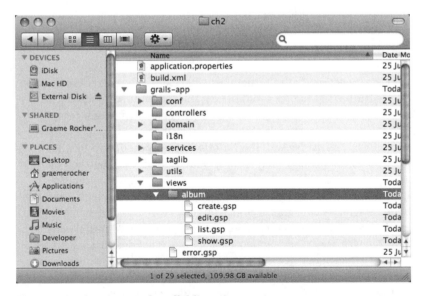

Figure 2-10. *The generated scaffolding views*

All in all, you can generate four views:

- `list.gsp`: Used by the `list` action to display a list of `Album` instances

- `show.gsp`: Used by the `show` action to display an individual `Album` instance

- `edit.gsp`: Used by the `edit` action to edit a `Album` instance's properties

- `create.gsp`: Used by the `create` action to create a new `Album` instance

■**Note** All the views use the main layout found at `grails-app/views/layouts/main.gsp`. This includes the placement of title, logo, and any included style sheets. We'll discuss layouts in detail in Chapter 5.

You now have a controller and views to perform CRUD. So what have you achieved beyond what you saw in dynamic scaffolding? Well, nothing yet. The power of command-line scaffolding is that it gives you a starting point to build your application. Having started with nothing, you now have a controller in which you can place your own custom business logic. You have views, which you can customize to your heart's content. And you accomplished all this while writing minimal code. The developers we know are on a constant mission to write less code, and scaffolding proves a useful tool toward achieving this goal.

With the `AlbumController` and associated views in place, delete the existing `SongController` and repeat the steps in Listings 2-10 and 2-19 to generate a controller and views for the Song domain class. You're going to need the generated code as you build on the basic CRUD functionality in later chapters.

In the meantime, let's move on to understanding more of what's necessary to kick-start your Grails development, beginning with environments.

Being Environmentally Friendly

Typically in any web-application production team, you have a development configuration for the application that might be configured to work with a locally installed database. This configuration sometimes even differs from developer to developer, depending on their specific desktop configurations.

In addition, QA staff who test the work produced by developers have separate machines configured in a similar way to the production environment. So we have two environments so far: the development configuration and the test configuration. The third is the production configuration, which you need when the system goes live.

This scenario is ubiquitous across pretty much every development project, with each development team spinning custom automated-build solutions via Ant or another custom-build system, instead of getting the solution from the framework itself.

Grails supports the concept of *development, test,* and *production* environments by default and will configure itself accordingly when executed. Some of this is done completely transparently to the developer. For example, autoreloading is enabled when Grails is configured in development mode but disabled when it's in production mode (to increase performance and minimize any security risk, however small).

Executing Grails under different environments is remarkably simple. For instance, the following command will run a Grails application with the production settings:

```
$ grails prod run-app
```

If you recall the output of the grails help command, you will remember that the basic usage of the grails command is as follows:

```
Usage (optionals marked with *):
grails [environment]* [target] [arguments]*
```

In other words, the first optional token after the grails executable is the environment, and three built-in options ship with Grails:

- *prod*: The production environment settings. Grails executes in the most efficient manner possible, against all configured production settings.

- *test*: The test environment settings. Grails executes in the most efficient manner possible, against all configured test settings.

- *dev*: The development environment settings. Grails is run in development mode with tools and behavior (such as hot reloading) enabled to optimize developer productivity.

Of course, Grails is not limited to just three environments. You can specify your own custom environment by passing in a system property called grails.env to the grails command. For example:

```
grails -Dgrails.env=myenvironment test-app
```

Here you execute the Grails test cases using an environment called myenvironment. So all this environment switching is handy, but what does it mean in practical terms? For one thing, it allows you to configure different databases for different environments, as you'll see in the next section.

Configuring Data Sources

Armed with your newly acquired knowledge of environments and how to switch between them, you'll see the implications when you start configuring data sources. What initial configuration steps are required to get a Grails application up and running? None. That's right; you don't have to configure a thing.

Even configuring the data source is optional. If you don't configure it, Grails will start up with an in-memory HSQLDB database. This is highly advantageous to begin with, particularly in terms of testing, because you can start an application with a fresh set of data on each load.

However, since it is a pretty common requirement, we will delve into data sources because you'll certainly need to configure them; plus, they'll help you develop your knowledge of environments.

The DataSource.groovy File

When you create a Grails application, Grails automatically provides a `grails-app/conf/DataSource.groovy` file that contains configuration for each environment (see Figure 2-11). You might find this convenient, because it means most of the work is done for you, but you might prefer to use another database such as MySQL rather than the provided HSQLDB database.

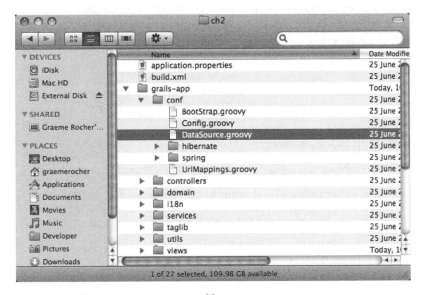

Figure 2-11. *The DataSource.groovy file*

Defining a data source is one area where the strength of the Java platform becomes apparent. Java's database connectivity technology, JDBC, is extremely mature, with drivers available for pretty much every database on the market. In fact, if a database provider does not deliver high-quality, stable JDBC drivers, its product is unlikely to be taken seriously in the marketplace.

A data-source definition is translated into a `javax.sql.DataSource` instance that supplies JDBC `Connection` objects. If you've used JDBC before, the process will be familiar, with the first step ensuring that the driver classes, normally packaged within a JAR archive, are available on the classpath.

The `DataSource.groovy` file contains some common configuration setup at the top of the data-source definition, an example of which is presented in Listing 2-20.

Listing 2-20. *Common Data-Source Configuration*

```
dataSource {
    pooled = true
    driverClassName = "org.hsqldb.jdbcDriver"
    username = "sa"
    password = ""
}
```

The snippet indicates that by default you want a pooled data source using the HSQLDB driver with a username of "sa" and a blank password. You could apply defaults to several other settings. Here's a list of the settings that the `DataSource.groovy` file provides:

- `driverClassName`: This is the class name of the JDBC driver.

- `username`: This is the username used to establish a JDBC connection.

- `password`: This is the password used to establish a JDBC connection.

- `url`: This is the JDBC URL of the database.

- `dbCreate`: This specifies whether to autogenerate the database from the domain model.

- `pooled`: This specifies whether to use a pool of connections (it defaults to true).

- `configClass`: This is the class that you use to configure Hibernate.

- `logSql`: This setting enables SQL logging.

- `dialect`: This is a string or class that represents the Hibernate dialect used to communicate with the database.

Now we get to the interesting bit. Following the global `dataSource` block, you'll see environment-specific settings for each known environment: development, test, and production. Listing 2-21 presents a shortened example of the environment-specific configuration.

Listing 2-21. *Environment-Specific Data-Source Configuration*

```
environments {
    development {
        dataSource {
            dbCreate = "create-drop"
            url = "jdbc:hsqldb:mem:devDB"
        }
    }
```

```
test {
    ...
}
production {
    ...
}
}
```

You'll notice that by default the development environment is configured to use an in-memory HSQLDB, with the URL of the database being `jdbc:hsqldb:mem:devDB`. Also note the `dbCreate` setting, which allows you to configure how the database is autocreated.

■**Note** Hibernate users will be familiar with the possible values because `dbCreate` relates directly to the `hibernate.hbm2ddl.auto` property.

The `dbCreate` setting of the development environment is configured as `create-drop`, which drops the database schema and re-creates it every time the Grails server is restarted. This setting can prove useful for testing because you start off with a clean set of data each time. The available settings for the `dbCreate` property are as follows:

- `create-drop`: Drops and re-creates the database schema on each application load

- `create`: Creates the database on application load

- `update`: Creates and/or attempts an update to existing tables on application load

- `[blank]`: Does nothing

The production and test environments both use `update` for `dbCreate` so that existing tables are not dropped, but created or updated automatically. You might find it necessary in some production environments to create your database schema manually. Or maybe creating your database schema is your DBA's responsibility. If either is the case, simply remove the `dbCreate` property altogether and Grails will do nothing, leaving this task in your or your colleague's hands.

Configuring a MySQL Database

Building on the knowledge you've gained in the previous section about configuring an alternative database, you're now going to learn how to set up MySQL with Grails. You're going to configure Grails to use MySQL within the production environment, and to achieve this you need to tell Grails how to communicate with MySQL. You're using JDBC, so this requires a suitable driver. You can download drivers from the MySQL web site at `http://www.mysql.com`.

In this book's examples, we'll be using version 5.1.6 of MySQL Connector/J. To configure the driver, drop the driver's JAR file into the `lib` directory of the gTunes application, as shown in Figure 2-12.

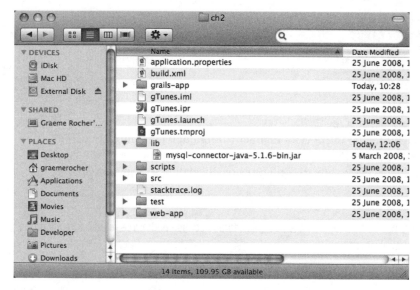

Figure 2-12. *Adding the driver's JAR file to the application's lib directory*

With the driver in place, the next thing to do is configure the Grails DataSource to use the settings defined by the driver's documentation. This is common practice with JDBC (and equivalent technologies on other platforms) and essentially requires the following information:

- The driver class name

- The URL of the database

- The username to log in with

- The password for the username

Currently the production DataSource is configured to use an HSQLDB database that persists to a file. Listing 2-22 shows the production-database configuration.

Listing 2-22. *The Production Data-Source Configuration*

```
production {
    dataSource {
        dbCreate = "update"
        url = "jdbc:hsqldb:file:prodDb;shutdown=true"
    }
}
```

Notice that the remaining settings (username, password, driverClassName, and so on) are inherited from the global configuration, as shown in Listing 2-20. To configure MySQL correctly, you need to override a few of those defaults as well as change the database URL. Listing 2-23 presents an example of a typical MySQL setup.

Listing 2-23. *MySQL Data-Source Configuration*

```
production {
    dataSource {
        dbCreate = "update"
        url = "jdbc:mysql://localhost/gTunes"
        driverClassName = "com.mysql.jdbc.Driver"
        username = "root"
        password = ""
    }
}
```

This setup assumes a MySQL server is running on the local machine, which has been set up with a blank root user password. Of course, a real production environment might have the database on a different machine and almost certainly with a more secure set of permissions. Also note that you must specify the name of the MySQL driver using the `driverClassName` setting.

Configuring a JNDI Data Source

Another common way to set up a production data source in Grails is to use a container-provided Java Naming and Directory Interface (JNDI) data source. This kind of setup is typical in corporate environments where the configuration of a data source is not up to you, but to the deployment team or network administrators.

Configuring a JNDI data source in Grails couldn't be simpler; specifying the JNDI name is the only requirement. Listing 2-24 shows a typical JNDI setup.

Listing 2-24. *JNDI Data-Source Configuration*

```
production {
    dataSource {
        jndiName = "java:comp/env/jdbc/gTunesDB"
    }
}
```

Of course, this assumes that the work has been done to configure the deployment environment to supply the JNDI data source correctly. Configuring JNDI resources is typically container-specific, and we recommend that you review the documentation supplied with your container (such as Apache Tomcat) for instructions.

Supported Databases

Because Grails leverages Hibernate, it supports every database that Hibernate supports. And because Hibernate has become a de facto standard, it has been tried and tested against many different databases and versions.

As it stands, the core Hibernate team performs regular integration tests against the following database products:

- DB2 7.1, 7.2, 8.1

- HSQLDB

- HypersonicSQL 1.61, 1.7.0, 1.7.2, 1.8

- Microsoft SQL Server 2000

- MySQL 3.23, 4.0, 4.1, 5.0

- Oracle 8*i*, 9*i*, 10*g*

- PostgreSQL 7.1.2, 7.2, 7.3, 7.4, 8.0, 8.1

- SAP DB 7.3

- Sybase 12.5 (jConnect 5.5)

- TimesTen 5.1

In addition, although not included in the Hibernate QA team's testing processes, these database products come with community-led support:

- Apache Derby

- HP NonStop SQL/MX 2.0

- Firebird 1.5 with JayBird 1.01

- FrontBase

- Informix

- Ingres

- InterBase 6.0.1

- Mckoi SQL

- PointBase Embedded 4.3

- Progress 9

- Microsoft Access 95, 97, 2000, XP, 2002, and 2003

- Corel Paradox 3.0, 3.5, 4.x, 5.x, and 7.x to 11.x

- A number of generic file formats including flat text, CSV, TSV, and fixed-length and variable-length binary files

- XBase (any dBASE; Visual dBASE; SIx Driver; SoftC; CodeBase; Clipper; FoxBase; FoxPro; Visual Fox Pro 3.0, 5.0, 7.0, 8.0, 9.0, and 10.0; xHarbour; Halcyon; Apollo; GoldMine; or Borland Database Engine (BDE)-compatible database)

- Microsoft Excel 5.0, 95, 97, 98, 2000, 2001, 2002, 2003, and 2004

A few, mostly older, database products that don't support JDBC metadata (which allows a database to expose information about itself) require you to specify the Hibernate dialect explicitly using the `dialect` property of the data-source definition. You can find available dialects in the `org.hibernate.dialect` package. You'll learn more about data-source definitions in future chapters, including Chapter 12. For now, since we have readied our application for the production environment, let's move on to the next step: deployment.

Deploying the Application

When you execute a Grails application using the `run-app` command, Grails configures the application to be reloaded upon changes at runtime, allowing quick iterative development. This configuration does, however, affect your application's performance. The `run-app` command is thus best suited for development only. For deployment onto a production system, you should use a packaged Web Application Archive (WAR) file. Doing this follows Java's mature deployment strategy and the separation of roles between developers and administrators.

As a significant added bonus, Grails' compliance with the WAR format means that IT production teams don't need to learn any new skills. The same application servers, hardware, profiling, and monitoring tools that you use with today's Java applications work with Grails, too.

Deployment with run-war

If you are satisfied with the built-in Jetty container as a deployment environment, you can quickly deploy your application by setting up Grails on your production environment and then checking out your Grails application from the version-control system you have locally. Once you've done this, simply type:

```
grails run-war
```

This command packages up Grails as a WAR file and then runs Jetty using the packaged WAR on port 8080. If you wish to change the port, you can follow the instructions in the "Step 6: Running the Application" section of Chapter 1.

As for the Jetty configuration itself, modifying the `GRAILS_HOME/conf/webdefault.xml` file can customize that.

Deployment with a WAR file

The `run-war` command is convenient, but you might want more control over your deployment environment. Or you might want to deploy onto another container, such as Apache Tomcat or BEA WebLogic, instead of Jetty.

What you need in these cases is a WAR file. The WAR file is the standardized mechanism for deployment in the Java world. Every Java EE–compliant web container supports the format. But some older containers might have quirks, so check out the `http://grails.org/Deployment` page on the wiki for helpful info on container-specific issues.

To create a WAR archive, use Grails' `war` command:

```
$ grails war
```

By default, if no environment is specified, Grails assumes use of the production environment for a WAR file. However, as with other commands, you can change the environment if needed. For example:

```
$ grails test war
```

Once you've run the command, a brand-new WAR file appears in the root of your project directory (see Figure 2-13).

Figure 2-13. *The gTunes WAR file*

If the root directory is not a convenient location for the WAR file, you can always change it by specifying the target WAR location as the last argument to the war command:

```
$ grails test war /path/to/deploy/gTunes.war
```

With the WAR file created, you just need to follow your container's deployment instructions (which might be as simple as dropping the file into a particular directory), and you're done. Notice how the WAR file includes a version number? Grails features built-in support for application versioning. You'll learn more about versioning and deployment in Chapter 12.

Summary

Wow, that was a lot of ground to cover. You generated a simple CRUD interface, configured a different data source, and produced a WAR file ready for deployment. You learned some of the basics about how controllers work in Grails and previewed what is to come with GORM, Grails' object-relational mapping layer.

You also played with Grails' support for running different environments and configured a MySQL database for production. All of this should have given you a solid grounding in the basics of working with Grails. However, so far we've only touched on concepts such as domain classes, controllers, and views without going into much detail. This is about to change as we plunge head first into the gory details of what makes Grails tick.

Starting with Chapter 3, we'll begin the in-depth tour of the concepts in Grails. As we do that, we'll begin to build out the gTunes application and transform it from the prototype it is now into a full-fledged, functional application.

CHAPTER 3

■■■

Understanding Domain Classes

Object-oriented (OO) applications almost always involve a domain model representing the business entities that the application deals with. Our gTunes application will include a number of domain classes including `Artist`, `Album`, and `Song`. Each of these domain classes has properties associated with it, and you must map those properties to a database in order to persist instances of those classes.

Developers of object-oriented applications face some difficult problems in mapping objects to a relational database. This is not because relational databases are especially difficult to work with; the trouble is that you encounter an "impedance mismatch"[1] between the object-oriented domain model and a relational database's table-centric view of data.

Fortunately, Grails does most of the hard work for you. Writing the domain model for a Grails application is significantly simpler than with many other frameworks. In this chapter, we are going to look at the fundamentals of a Grails domain model. In Chapter 10, we will cover more advanced features of the GORM tool.

Persisting Fields to the Database

By default, all the fields in a domain class are persisted to the database. For simple field types such as `Strings` and `Integers`, each field in the class will map to a column in the database. For complex properties, you might require multiple tables to persist all the data. The Song class from Chapter 2 contains two `String` properties and an `Integer` property. The table in the database will contain a separate column for each of those properties.

In MySql, that database table will look something like Listing 3-1.

---

1. Scott W. Ambler, "The Object-Relational Impedance Mismatch," http://www.agiledata.org/essays/ impedanceMismatch.html, 2006.

Listing 3-1. *The Song Table*

```
+----------+--------------+------+-----+---------+----------------+
| Field    | Type         | Null | Key | Default | Extra          |
+----------+--------------+------+-----+---------+----------------+
| id       | bigint(20)   | NO   | PRI | NULL    | auto_increment |
| version  | bigint(20)   | NO   |     | NULL    |                |
| artist   | varchar(255) | NO   |     | NULL    |                |
| duration | int(11)      | NO   |     | NULL    |                |
| title    | varchar(255) | NO   |     | NULL    |                |
+----------+--------------+------+-----+---------+----------------+
```

Notice that the table includes not only a column for each of the properties in the domain class, but also an id column and a version column. The id is a unique identifier for a row and Grails uses the version column to implement optimistic locking[2].

Listing 3-1 shows the default mapping. Grails provides a powerful DSL for expressing how a domain model maps to the database. Details about the mapping DSL appear later in this chapter in the "Customizing Your Database Mapping" section.

Validating Domain Classes

You'll probably encounter business rules that constrain the valid values of a particular property in a domain class. For example, a Person must never have an age that is less than zero. A credit-card number must adhere to an expected pattern. Rules like these should be expressed clearly, and in only one place. Luckily, Grails provides a powerful mechanism for expressing these rules.

A Grails domain class can express domain constraints simply by defining a public static property named constraints that has a closure as a value. Listing 3-2 shows a version of the Song class that has several constraints defined.

Listing 3-2. *The Song Domain Class*

```
class Song {
    String title
    String artist
    Integer duration

    static constraints = {
        title(blank: false)
        artist(blank: false)
        duration(min: 1)
    }
}
```

---

2. Wikipedia, "Optimistic concurrency control," http://en.wikipedia.org/wiki/
   Optimistic_concurrency_control.

The Song class in Listing 3-2 defines constraints for each of its persistent properties. The title and artist properties cannot be blank. The duration property must have a minimum value of 1. When constraints are defined, not every property necessarily needs to be constrained. The constraints closure can include constraints for a subset of properties in the class.

The validators used in Listing 3-2 are blank and min. Grails ships with a lot of standard validators that cover common scenarios (see Table 3-1).

Table 3-1. *Standard Validators in Grails*

Name	Example	Description
blank	login(blank:false)	Set to false if a string value cannot be blank
creditCard	cardNumber(creditCard:true)	Set to true if the value must be a credit-card number
cmail	homcEmail(cmail:truc)	Set to true if the value must be an e-mail address
inList	login(inList:['Joe', 'Fred'])	Value must be contained within the given list
length	login(length:5..15)	Uses a range to restrict the length of a string or array
min	duration(min:1)	Sets the minimum value
minLength	password(minLength:6)	Sets the minimum length of a string or array property
minSize	children(minSize:5)	Sets the minimum size of a collection or number property
matches	login(matches:/[a-zA-Z]/)	Matches the supplied regular expression
max	age(max:99)	Sets the maximum value
maxLength	login(maxLength:5)	Sets the maximum length of a string or array property
maxSize	children(maxSize:25)	Sets the maximum size of a collection or number property
notEqual	login(notEqual:'Bob')	Must not equal the specified value
nullable	age(nullable:false)	Set to false if the property value cannot be null
range	age(range:16..59)	Set to a Groovy range of valid values
scale	salary(scale:2)	Set to the desired scale for floating-point numbers
size	children(size:5..15)	Uses a range to restrict the size of a collection or number
unique	login(unique:true)	Set to true if the property must be unique
url	homePage(url:true)	Set to true if a string value is a URL address

The constraints block in a domain class will help prevent invalid data from being saved to the database. The save() method on a domain object will automatically validate against the constraints before the data is written to the database. Data is not written to the database if validation fails. Listing 3-3 demonstrates how code can react to the return value of the save() method.

Listing 3-3. *Validating a Song Object*

```
// -68 is an invalid duration
def song = new Song(title:'The Rover',
                    artist:'Led Zeppelin',
                    duration:-68)
if(song.save()) {
    println "Song was created!"
} else {
    song.errors.allErrors.each { println it.defaultMessage }
}
```

An interesting aspect of Listing 3-3 is the usage of the errors property on domain classes. This property is an instance of the Spring Framework's org.springframework. validation.Errors interface, which allows advanced querying of validation errors. In Listing 3-3, when validation fails, the code generates a list of all the errors that occurred and prints them to stdout.

Some of the more useful methods in the Spring Errors interface are shown in Listing 3-4.

Listing 3-4. *Methods in the Spring Errors Interface*

```
package org.springframework.validation;
interface Errors {
    List getAllErrors();
    int getErrorCount();
    FieldError getFieldError(String fieldName);
    int getFieldErrorCount();
    List getFieldErrors(String fieldName);
    Object getObjectName();
    boolean hasErrors();
    boolean hasFieldErrors(String fieldName);
    // ...x remaining methods
}
```

Occasionally you'll find it useful to make changes to the domain model before committing to the save() method. In this case, Grails provides a validate() method, which returns a Boolean value to indicate whether validation was successful. The semantics are exactly the same as in the previous example with the save() method, except, of course, that the validate() method doesn't perform persistent calls.

If validation does fail, the application might want to make changes to the state of the domain object and make another attempt at validation. All domain objects have a method called clearErrors(), which will clear any errors left over from a previous validation attempt. Listing 3-5 demonstrates how code might react to the return value of the validate() method.

Listing 3-5. *Validating a Song Object, Revisited*

```
def song = new Song(title:'The Rover',
                    duration:339)
if(!song.validate()) {
    song.clearErrors()
    song.artist = 'Led Zeppelin'
    song.validate()
}
```

Using Custom Validators

Grails provides a wide array of built-in validators to handle many common scenarios. However, it is impossible to foresee every feasible domain model and every specific kind of validation that an application might need. Fortunately, Grails provides a mechanism that allows an application to express arbitrary validation rules (see Listing 3-6).

Listing 3-6. *Constraining the Password Property in the User Domain Class*

```
class User {
    static constraints = {
        password(unique:true, length:5..15, validator:{val, obj ->
            if(val?.equalsIgnoreCase(obj.firstName)) {
                return false
            }
        })
    }
}
```

The validator in Listing 3-6 will fail if the password is equal to the firstName property of the User class. The validator closure should return false if validation fails; otherwise it should return true. The first argument passed to the closure is the value of the property to be validated. The second argument passed to the closure is the object being validated. This second argument is often useful if validation requires the inspection of the object's other properties, as in Listing 3-6.

In addition, when you return false from a custom validator, an error code such as user.password.validator.error is produced. However, you can specify a custom error code by returning a String:

```
if(val?.equalsIgnoreCase(obj.firstName)) {
        return "password.cannot.be.firstname"
}
```

In this example, you can trigger a validation error simply by returning a String with the value password.cannot.be.firstname. You'll be learning more about error codes and how they relate to other parts of the application in later chapters. For now, let's move on to the topic of transient properties.

Understanding Transient Properties

By default, every property in a domain class is persisted to the database. For most properties, this is the right thing to do. However, occasionally a domain class will define properties that do not need to be persisted. Grails provides a simple mechanism for specifying which properties in a domain class should not be persisted. This mechanism is to define a public static property named transients and assign to that property a value that is a list of Strings. Those Strings represent the names of the class's properties, which should be treated as transient and not saved to the database (see Listing 3-7).

Listing 3-7. *A Transient Property in the Company Domain Class*

```
class Company {
    String name
    Integer numberOfEmployees
    BigDecimal salaryPaidYTD

    static transients = ['salaryPaidYTD']
}
```

In Listing 3-7, the salaryPaidYTD property has been flagged as transient and will not be saved to the database. Notice that the default generated schema for this domain class does not contain a column for the salaryPaidYTD property (see Listing 3-8). In other words, the company table does not contain a column for the transient property.

Listing 3-8. *The Company Table*

```
+---------------------+--------------+------+-----+---------+----------------+
| Field               | Type         | Null | Key | Default | Extra          |
+---------------------+--------------+------+-----+---------+----------------+
| id                  | bigint(20)   | NO   | PRI | NULL    | auto_increment |
| version             | bigint(20)   | NO   |     | NULL    |                |
| name                | varchar(255) | NO   |     | NULL    |                |
| number_of_employees | int(11)      | NO   |     | NULL    |                |
+---------------------+--------------+------+-----+---------+----------------+
```

Not all persistent properties necessarily correspond to a field in a domain class. For example, if a domain class has a method called getName() and a method called setName(), then that domain class has a persistent property called name. It doesn't matter that the class doesn't have a field called "name." Grails will handle that situation by creating the appropriate column in the database to store the value of the name property. But you can use the transients property to tell Grails not to do that if the property really should not be persisted, as in Listing 3-9.

Listing 3-9. *A Transient Property in the Company Domain Class*

```
class Company {
    BigDecimal cash
    BigDecimal receivables
    BigDecimal capital

    BigDecimal getNetWorth() {
        cash + receivables + capital
    }

    static transients = ['netWorth']
}
```

Customizing Your Database Mapping

As we have seen already, Grails does a good job of mapping your domain model to a relational database, without requiring any kind of mapping file. Many developer productivity gains that Grails offers arise from its Convention over Configuration (CoC) features. Whenever the conventions preferred by Grails are inconsistent with your requirements, Grails does a great job of providing a simple way for you to work with those scenarios. The Custom Database Mapping DSL in Grails falls in this category.

Grails provides an ORM DSL for expressing your domain mapping to help you deal with scenarios in which the Grails defaults will not work for you. A common use case for taking advantage of the ORM DSL is when a Grails application is being developed on top of an existing schema that is not entirely compatible with Grails' default domain-class mappings.

Consider a simple `Person` class (see Listing 3-10).

Listing 3-10. *The Person Domain Class*

```
class Person {
    String firstName
    String lastName
    Integer age
}
```

The default mapping for that class will correspond to a schema that looks like Listing 3-11.

Listing 3-11. *The Default Person Table*

```
+------------+--------------+------+-----+---------+----------------+
| Field      | Type         | Null | Key | Default | Extra          |
+------------+--------------+------+-----+---------+----------------+
| id         | bigint(20)   | NO   | PRI | NULL    | auto_increment |
| version    | bigint(20)   | NO   |     | NULL    |                |
| age        | int(11)      | NO   |     | NULL    |                |
| first_name | varchar(255) | NO   |     | NULL    |                |
| last_name  | varchar(255) | NO   |     | NULL    |                |
+------------+--------------+------+-----+---------+----------------+
```

That works perfectly if you have a greenfield application that doesn't need to map to an existing schema. If the application does need to map to an existing schema, the schema will probably not match up exactly to the Grails defaults. Imagine that a schema does exist, and that it looks something like Listing 3-12.

Listing 3-12. *A Legacy Table Containing Person Data*

```
+-------------------+--------------+------+-----+---------+----------------+
| Field             | Type         | Null | Key | Default | Extra          |
+-------------------+--------------+------+-----+---------+----------------+
| person_id         | bigint(20)   | NO   | PRI | NULL    | auto_increment |
| person_age        | int(11)      | NO   |     | NULL    |                |
| person_first_name | varchar(255) | NO   |     | NULL    |                |
| person_last_name  | varchar(255) | NO   |     | NULL    |                |
+-------------------+--------------+------+-----+---------+----------------+
```

Notice that the table contains no `version` column and all the column names are prefixed with `person_`. You'll find it straightforward to map to a schema like that using Grails' ORM DSL. But to take advantage of the ORM DSL, your domain class must declare a public property called `mapping` and assign a closure to the property (see Listing 3-13).

Listing 3-13. *Custom Mapping for the Person Domain Class*

```
class Person {
    String firstName
    String lastName
    Integer age

    static mapping = {
        id column:'person_id'
        firstName column:'person_first_name'
        lastName column:'person_last_name'
        age column:'person_age'
        version false
    }
}
```

The example in Listing 3-13 defines column names for each of the properties and turns off the version property, which Grails uses for optimistic locking. These are just a couple of the features that the ORM DSL supports.

The default table name for persisting instances of a Grails domain class is the name of the domain class. Person objects are stored in a person table and Company objects are stored in a company table. If Person objects need to be stored in a people table, the ORM DSL allows for that. Listing 3-14 includes the necessary mapping code to store Person instances in the people table.

Listing 3-14. *A Custom Table Mapping for the Person Domain Class*

```
class Person {
    String firstName
    String lastName
    Integer age

    static mapping = {
        table 'people'
    }
}
```

We'll cover custom database mapping in more detail in Chapter 17.

Building Relationships

Typically an application is not made up of a bunch of disconnected domain classes. More often, domain classes have relationships to one another. Of course, not every domain class has a direct relationship with every other domain class, but it is not common for a domain class to exist in total isolation with no relationship to any other domain class.

Grails provides support for several types of relationships between domain classes. In a one-to-one relationship (the simplest type), each member of the relationship has a reference to the other. The relationship represented in Listing 3-15 is a bidirectional relationship.

Listing 3-15. *A One-to-One Relationship Between a Car and an Engine*

```
class Car {
    Engine engine
}

class Engine {
    Car car
}
```

In this model, clearly a Car has one Engine and an Engine has one Car. The entities are peers in the relationship; there is no real "owner." Depending on your application requirements, this might not be exactly what you want. Often a relationship like this really does have an owning side. Perhaps an Engine belongs to a Car, but a Car does not belong to an Engine. Grails provides a mechanism for expressing a relationship like that, and Listing 3-16 demonstrates how to specify the owning side of it.

Listing 3-16. *An Engine Belongs to a Car*

```
class Car {
    Engine engine
}

class Engine {
    static belongsTo = [car:Car]
}
```

The value of the belongsTo property in the Engine class is a Map. The key in this map is "car" and the value associated with that key is the Car class. This property tells Grails that the Car is the owning side of this relationship and that an Engine "belongs to" its owning Car. The key in the map can be named anything—the name does not need to be the same as the owning-class name. However, naming the key that way almost always makes sense. That key represents the name of a property that will be added to the Engine class, as well as representing the reference back to the owner. The Engine class in Listing 3-16 has a property called car of type Car.

You might encounter situations where a relationship needs an owning side but the owned side of the relationship does not need a reference back to its owner. Grails supports this type of relationship using the same belongsTo property, except that the value is a Class reference instead of a Map. With the approach used in Listing 3-17, the Engine still belongs to its owning Car, but the Engine has no reference back to its Car.

Listing 3-17. *An Engine Belongs to a Car But Has No Reference to Its Owner*

```
class Engine {
    static belongsTo = Car
}
```

One of the implications of having the belongsTo property in place is that Grails will impose cascaded deletes. Grails knows that an Engine "belongs to" its owning Car, so any time a Car is deleted from the database, its Engine will be deleted as well.

One-to-many relationships are equally simple to represent in Grails domain classes. Our gTunes application will require several one-to-many relationships, including the relationship between an Artist and its Albums and between an Album and its Songs. You might say that an Artist has many Albums and an Album has many songs. That "has many" relationship is expressed in a domain class with the hasMany property (see Listing 3-18).

Listing 3-18. *The hasMany Property*

```
class Artist {
    String name

    static hasMany = [albums:Album]
}
```

```
class Album {
    String title

    static hasMany = [songs:Song]
    static belongsTo = [artist:Artist]
}

class Song {
    String title
    Integer duration

    static belongsTo = Album
}
```

In Listing 3-18, an Artist has many Albums and an Album belongs to its owning Artist. An Album also has a reference back to its owning Artist. An Album has many Songs and a Song belongs to its owning Album. However, a Song does not have a reference back to its owning Album.

The value of the hasMany property needs to be a Map. The keys in the map represent the names of collection properties that will be added to the domain class, and the values associated with the keys represent the types of objects that will be stored in the collection property. The Artist class has a domain property called albums that will be a collection of Album objects. The default collection type that Grails will use is a java.util.Set, which is an unordered collection. Where this is the desired behavior, you don't need to declare the property explicitly. Grails will inject the property for you. If you need the collection to be a List or a SortedSet, you must explicitly declare the property with the appropriate type, as shown in Listing 3-19.

Listing 3-19. *The Album Class Has a SortedSet of Song Objects*

```
class Album {
    String title

    static hasMany = [songs:Song]
    static belongsTo = [artist:Artist]

    SortedSet songs
}
```

■**Note** For this to work, the Song class must implement the Comparable interface. This requirement isn't specific to Grails; it's how standard SortedSet collections work in Java.

A domain class might represent the owning side of numerous one-to-many relationships. The `Map` associated with the `hasMany` property might have any number of entries in it, each entry representing another one-to-many-relationship. For example, if an `Artist` has many `Albums` but also has many `Instruments`, you could represent that by adding another entry to the `hasMany` property in the `Artist` class, as shown in Listing 3-20.

Listing 3-20. *Multiple Entries in the hasMany Map*

```
class Artist {
    String name

    static hasMany = [albums:Album, instruments:Instrument]
}
```

Extending Classes with Inheritance

Grails domain classes can extend other Grails domain classes. This inheritance tree might be arbitrarily deep, but a good domain model will seldom involve more than one or two levels of inheritance.

The syntax for declaring that a Grails domain class extends from another domain class is standard Groovy inheritance syntax, as shown in Listing 3-21.

Listing 3-21. *Extending the Person Class*

```
class Person {
    String firstName
    String lastName
    Integer age
}

class Employee extends Person {
    String employeeNumber
    String companyName
}

class Player extends Person {
    String teamName
}
```

How should these classes map to the database? Should there be separate tables for each of these domain classes? Should there be one table for all types of `Person` objects? Grails provides support for both of those solutions. If all `Person` objects—including `Players` and `Employees`—

are to be stored in the same table, this approach is known as a table-per-hierarchy mapping. That is, a table will be created for each inheritance hierarchy (see Listing 3-22). Grails imposes table-per-hierarchy mapping as the default for an inheritance relationship.

Listing 3-22. *The Person Table Representing a Table-Per-Hierarchy Mapping*

```
+-----------------+--------------+------+-----+---------+----------------+
| Field           | Type         | Null | Key | Default | Extra          |
+-----------------+--------------+------+-----+---------+----------------+
| id              | bigint(20)   | NO   | PRI | NULL    | auto_increment |
| version         | bigint(20)   | NO   |     | NULL    |                |
| age             | int(11)      | NO   |     | NULL    |                |
| first_name      | varchar(255) | NO   |     | NULL    |                |
| last_name       | varchar(255) | NO   |     | NULL    |                |
| class           | varchar(255) | NO   |     | NULL    |                |
| company_name    | varchar(255) | YES  |     | NULL    |                |
| employee_number | varchar(255) | YES  |     | NULL    |                |
| team_name       | varchar(255) | YES  |     | NULL    |                |
+-----------------+--------------+------+-----+---------+----------------+
```

Notice that Listing 3-22 includes columns for all the attributes in the Person class along with columns for all the attributes in all the subclasses. In addition, the table includes a discriminator column called class. Because this table will house all kinds of Person objects, the discriminator column is required to represent what specific type of Person is represented in any given row. The application should never need to interrogate this column directly, but the column is critical for Grails to do its work.

The other type of inheritance mapping is known as table-per-subclass (see Listing 3-23).

Listing 3-23. *Table-Per-Subclass Mapping*

```
class Person {
    String firstName
    String lastName
    Integer age

    static mapping = {
        tablePerHierarchy false
    }
}
```

Table-per-subclass mapping results in a separate table for each subclass in an inheritance hierarchy (see Listing 3-24). To take advantage of a table-per-subclass mapping, the parent class must use the ORM DSL to turn off the default table-per-hierarchy mapping.

Listing 3-24. *The Person, Employee, and Player Tables with Table-Per-Subclass Mapping*

```
+------------+--------------+------+-----+---------+----------------+
| Field      | Type         | Null | Key | Default | Extra          |
+------------+--------------+------+-----+---------+----------------+
| id         | bigint(20)   | NO   | PRI | NULL    | auto_increment |
| version    | bigint(20)   | NO   |     | NULL    |                |
| age        | int(11)      | NO   |     | NULL    |                |
| first_name | varchar(255) | NO   |     | NULL    |                |
| last_name  | varchar(255) | NO   |     | NULL    |                |
+------------+--------------+------+-----+---------+----------------+


+-----------------+--------------+------+-----+---------+-------+
| Field           | Type         | Null | Key | Default | Extra |
+-----------------+--------------+------+-----+---------+-------+
| id              | bigint(20)   | NO   | PRI | NULL    |       |
| company_name    | varchar(255) | YES  |     | NULL    |       |
| employee_number | varchar(255) | YES  |     | NULL    |       |
+-----------------+--------------+------+-----+---------+-------+


+-----------+--------------+------+-----+---------+-------+
| Field     | Type         | Null | Key | Default | Extra |
+-----------+--------------+------+-----+---------+-------+
| id        | bigint(20)   | NO   | PRI | NULL    |       |
| team_name | varchar(255) | YES  |     | NULL    |       |
+-----------+--------------+------+-----+---------+-------+
```

Which of these mappings should you use? The answer depends on several factors. One of the consequences of the table-per-hierarchy approach is that none of the subclasses can have nonnullable properties, but because no joins are being executed, queries will perform better. This is because all the subclasses share a table that includes columns for all the properties in all the subclasses. When a Player is saved to the person table, the company_name column would be left null because players don't have a company name. Likewise, when an Employee is saved to the player table, the team_name column would be left null. One of the consequences of using the table-per-subclass approach is that you must pay a performance penalty when retrieving instances of the subclasses because database joins must be executed to pull together all the data necessary to construct an instance.

Grails lets you choose the approach that makes the most sense for your application. Consider your application requirements and typical query use cases. These should help you decide which mapping strategy is right for any particular inheritance relationship. Note that you don't need to apply the same mapping strategy across the entire application. There's nothing wrong with implementing one inheritance relationship using table-per-subclass mapping because you must support nonnullable properties, and implementing some other unrelated inheritance relationship using table-per-hierarchy mapping for performance reasons.

Embedding Objects

Grails supports the notion of composition, which you can think of as a stronger form of relationship. With that kind of relationship, it often makes sense to embed the "child" inline where the "parent" is stored. Consider a simple relationship between a Car and an Engine. If that relationship were implemented with composition, the Engine would really belong to the Car. One consequence of that: If a Car were deleted, its Engine would be deleted with it (see Listing 3-25).

Listing 3-25. *A Composition Relationship Between the Car and Engine Domain Classes*

```
class Car {
    String make
    String model
    Engine engine
}

class Engine {
    String manufacturer
    Integer numberOfCylinders
}
```

Normally Car objects and Engine objects would be stored in separate tables, and you'd use a foreign key to relate the tables to each other (see Listings 3-26 and 3-27).

Listing 3-26. *The Car Table*

```
+-----------+--------------+------+-----+---------+----------------+
| Field     | Type         | Null | Key | Default | Extra          |
+-----------+--------------+------+-----+---------+----------------+
| id        | bigint(20)   | NO   | PRI | NULL    | auto_increment |
| version   | bigint(20)   | NO   |     | NULL    |                |
| engine_id | bigint(20)   | NO   | MUL | NULL    |                |
| make      | varchar(255) | NO   |     | NULL    |                |
| model     | varchar(255) | NO   |     | NULL    |                |
+-----------+--------------+------+-----+---------+----------------+
```

Listing 3-27. *The Engine Table*

```
+---------------------+--------------+------+-----+---------+----------------+
| Field               | Type         | Null | Key | Default | Extra          |
+---------------------+--------------+------+-----+---------+----------------+
| id                  | bigint(20)   | NO   | PRI | NULL    | auto_increment |
| version             | bigint(20)   | NO   |     | NULL    |                |
| manufacturer        | varchar(255) | NO   |     | NULL    |                |
| number_of_cylinders | int(11)      | NO   |     | NULL    |                |
+---------------------+--------------+------+-----+---------+----------------+
```

To treat the relationship between those classes as composition, the Car class must instruct Grails to "embed" the Engine in the Car. You do this by defining a public static property called embedded in the Car class and assign that property a list of strings that contains the names of all the embedded properties (see Listing 3-28).

Listing 3-28. *Embedding the Engine in a Car*

```
class Car {
    String make
    String model
    Engine engine
    static embedded = ['engine']
}
```

With that embedded property in place, Grails knows that the Engine property of a Car object should be embedded in the same table with the Car object. The car table will now look like Listing 3-29.

Listing 3-29. *The Car Table with the Engine Attributes Embedded*

```
+----------------------------+--------------+------+-----+---------+---------------+
| Field                      | Type         | Null | Key | Default | Extra         |
+----------------------------+--------------+------+-----+---------+---------------+
| id                         | bigint(20)   | NO   | PRI | NULL    | auto_increment|
| version                    | bigint(20)   | NO   |     | NULL    |               |
| engine_manufacturer        | varchar(255) | NO   |     | NULL    |               |
| engine_number_of_cylinders | int(11)      | NO   |     | NULL    |               |
| make                       | varchar(255) | NO   |     | NULL    |               |
| model                      | varchar(255) | NO   |     | NULL    |               |
+----------------------------+--------------+------+-----+---------+---------------+
```

Testing Domain Classes

Automated tests can be an important part of building complex applications and confirming that the system behaves as intended. In particular, testing is an important part of building complex systems with a dynamic language like Groovy. With dynamic languages, developers don't get the same kinds of feedback from the compiler that they might get if they were working with a statically typed language like Java.

For example, in Java if you make a typo in a method invocation, the compiler will let you know that you have made the mistake. The compiler cannot flag that same error when you use Groovy because of the language's dynamic nature and its runtime. With a dynamic language like Groovy, many things are not known until runtime. You must execute the code to learn whether it's correct. Executing the code from automated tests is an excellent way to help ensure that the code is doing what it is supposed to do.

Grails offers first-class support for testing many aspects of your application. In this section, we will look at testing domain classes.

Grails directly supports two kinds of tests: unit tests and integration tests. Unit tests reside at the top of the project in the `test/unit/` directory, and integration tests reside in the `test/integration/` directory. You must understand the difference between unit tests and integration tests. Many dynamic things happen when a Grails application starts up. One of the things Grails does at startup is augment domain classes with a lot of dynamic methods such as `validate()` and `save()`. When you run integration tests, all of that dynamic behavior is available, so a test can invoke the `validate()` or `save()` method on a domain object even though these methods do not appear in the domain-class source code.

When you run unit tests, however, that full dynamic environment is not fired up, so methods such as `validate()` and `save()` are not available. Starting up the whole dynamic environment comes at a cost. For this reason, you should run tests that rely on the full Grails runtime environment only as integration tests.

That said, Grails provides advanced mocking capabilities that let you mock the behavior of these methods in a unit test. If you create a domain class using the `create-domain-class` command, Grails will create a unit test automatically. If you execute `grails create-domain-class Artist` (see Listing 3-30), Grails will create `grails-app/domain/Artist.groovy` and `test/unit/ArtistTests.groovy`. Grails is encouraging you to do the right thing—to write tests for your domain classes. If you don't use the `create-domain-class` command to create your domain class, you can create the test on your own. Make sure to put the test in the appropriate directory.

Listing 3-30. *The Unit Test for the Artist Class, Generated Automatically*

```
class ArtistTests extends grails.test.GrailsUnitTestCase {

    void testSomething() {

    }
}
```

As you can see from Listing 3-30, the default unit-test template extends from the parent class `grails.test.GrailsUnitTestCase`. The `GrailsTestUnitCase` class is a test harness that provides a range of utility methods to mock the behavior of a Grails application. To run the test, invoke the `test-app` Grails command from the command line. The `test-app` command will run all the unit tests and integration tests that are part of the project. To run a specific test, invoke the `test-app` target with an argument that represents the name of the test to run. The name of the test to run should be the test-case name without the "Tests" suffix. For example, execute `grails test-app Artist` to run the `ArtistTests` test case.

The `test-app` target will not only run the tests, but also generate a report including the status of all the tests that were run. This report is a standard JUnit test report, which Java developers know very well. An HTML version of the report will be generated under the project root at `test/reports/html/index.html`.

The Song class in the gTunes application has `title` and `duration` properties (see Listing 3-31).

Listing 3-31. *The Song Domain Class*

```
class Song {
    String title
    Integer duration
}
```

The application should consider a nonpositive duration to be an invalid value. The type of the property is `java.lang.Integer`, whose valid values include the full range of values in a 32-bit signed `int`, including zero and a lot of negative numbers. The application should include a unit test like that shown in Listing 3-32, which asserts that the system should not accept non-positive durations.

Listing 3-32. *The Song Unit Test*

```
class SongTests extends grails.test.GrailsUnitTestCase {
    void testMinimumDuration() {

        // mock the behavior of the Song domain class
        mockDomain(Song)

        // create a Song with an invalid duration
        def song = new Song(duration: 0)

        // make sure that validation fails
        assertFalse 'validation should have failed', song.validate()

        // make sure that validation failed for the expected reason
        assertEquals "min", song.errors.duration
    }
}
```

Notice the call to the `mockDomain(Class)` method in Listing 3-32 that provides a mock implementation of the `validate()` method on the Song domain class. Executing `grails test-app Song` will run the test. The test should fail initially because it contains no code specifying that 0 is an invalid value for the `duration` property. Starting with a failing test like this subscribes to the ideas of Test-Driven Development (TDD). The test represents required behavior, and it will "drive" the implementation to satisfy the requirement.

Adding a simple domain constraint to the Song class as shown in Listing 3-33 should satisfy the test.

Listing 3-33. *The Song Domain Class with a Constraint*

```
class Song {
    String title
    Integer duration

    static constraints = {
        duration(min:1)
    }
}
```

With that constraint in place, the unit test should pass. The domain class is written to satisfy the requirements expressed in the test. Specifically, the domain class considers any nonpositive value for duration to be invalid.

Summary

This chapter covered quite a bit of ground by introducing the fundamentals of Grails domain classes. Grails provides slick solutions to common problems like validating domain classes and mapping to a relational database. The GORM technology is responsible for much of that capability. We'll explore GORM in more detail in later chapters, including Chapters 10 and 17.

CHAPTER 4

■ ■ ■

Understanding Controllers

A Grails controller is a class that is responsible for handling requests coming in to the application. The controller receives the request, potentially does some work with the request, and finally decides what should happen next. What happens next might include the following:

- Execute another controller action (possibly, but not necessarily, in the same controller)

- Render a view

- Render information directly to the response

A controller is prototyped, meaning that a new instance is created per request. So developers don't need to be as cautious about maintaining thread-safe code in a singleton controller.

You can think of controllers as the orchestrators of a Grails application. They provide the main entry point for any Grails application by coordinating incoming requests, delegating to services or domain classes for business logic, and rendering views.

Let's look at the basics of how to create a controller before moving on to meatier subjects such as data binding and command objects.

Defining Controllers

A controller is a class defined under the grails-app/controllers directory. The class name must end with "Controller" by convention. Controllers do not need to extend any special base class or implement any special interfaces.

Listing 4-1 shows a typical controller, residing at the location grails-app/controllers/ SampleController.groovy, that defines an action called index. The index action renders a simple textual response.

Listing 4-1. *The SampleController Class*

```
class SampleController {
  def index = {
    render 'You accessed the Sample controller...'
  }
}
```

With this controller in place, a request to /sample/index will result in the String "You accessed the Sample controller . . . " being rendered back to the browser. You can see that actions, like the index action, are defined as fields. Each field is assigned a block of code using a Groovy closure. A controller can define any number of actions, as shown in Listing 4-2.

Listing 4-2. *Defining Multiple Actions*

```
class SampleController {
  def first = { ... }
  def second = { ... }
  def third = { ... }
  def fourth = { ... }
}
```

In Chapter 6, you will learn about the powerful URL-mapping support that Grails provides. By default, URLs are mapped to controller actions by way of a convention. The first part of the URL represents which controller to access, and the second part of the URL represents which action should be executed. For example, /sample/first will execute the first action in the SampleController. Likewise, /sample/second will execute the second action in the SampleController.

Setting the Default Action

You don't necessarily need to specify the action to execute in the URL. If no action is specified, Grails will execute the default action in the specified controller. You can identify the default action using the following rules (see Listing 4-3):

- If the controller defines only one action, it becomes the default action.

- If the controller defines an action called index, it becomes the default action.

- If the controller defines a property called defaultAction, its value is the name of the default action.

Listing 4-3. *The Default Action*

```
// Here the 'list' action is the default as there is only one action defined
class SampleController {
  def list = {}
}

// In this example 'index' is the default by convention
class SampleController {
  def list = {}
  def index = {}
}
```

```
// Here 'list' is explicitly set as the default
class SampleController {
  def defaultAction = 'list'
  def list = {}
  def index = {}
}
```

Logging

Logging, an important aspect of any application, allows the application to report textual information about what is going on inside it. Various logging solutions exist on the Java platform, including third-party logging solutions as well as the standard logging API introduced in Java 1.4. You face a certain amount of complexity in configuring logging for an application.

Often, application developers will avoid this complexity by avoiding logging altogether and opt instead for simply printing messages using System.out.println and System.err.println. For a variety of reasons, this is really not a good idea.

Fortunately, Grails tackles much of the complexity involved with setting up logging. A log property, which is injected into every controller, is an instance of org.apache.commons.logging.Log. You don't need to write any code to initialize the log property because the framework handles that. Listing 4-4 documents the org.apache.commons.logging.Log API.

Listing 4-4. *The org.apache.commons.logging.Log Interface*

```
public interface Log {
  public void debug(Object msg);
  public void debug(Object msg, Throwable t);
  public void error(Object msg);
  public void error(Object msg, Throwable t);
  public void fatal(Object msg);
  public void fatal(Object msg, Throwable t);
  public void info(Object msg);
  public void info(Object msg, Throwable t);
  public void trace(Object msg);
  public void trace(Object msg, Throwable t);
  public void warn(Object msg);
  public void warn(Object msg, Throwable t);
  public boolean isDebugEnabled();
  public boolean isErrorEnabled();
  public boolean isFatalEnabled();
  public boolean isInfoEnabled();
  public boolean isTraceEnabled();
  public boolean isWarnEnabled();
}
```

The log property that is injected into a controller can be used from any controller action or any method within the controller (see Listing 4-5).

Listing 4-5. *Using the log Property*

```
class SampleController {
  def index = {
    log.info('In the index action...')
    // ...
  }
}
```

Logging Exceptions

Groovy translates all exceptions into runtime exceptions, so Groovy code is never forced to catch an exception. This differs from what Java developers are used to. In any case, even though an application is never forced to catch an exception, it makes sense to catch an exception in a lot of scenarios. In Groovy, the details for how to catch an exception are exactly the same as they are in Java. There is no special Groovy syntax for handling exceptions.

When an exception is caught in a controller, you'll almost always want to log details about the exception using the log property (see Listing 4-6).

Listing 4-6. *Logging an Exception*

```
class SampleController {
  def index = {
    try {
      // do something that might throw an exception
    } catch (Exception e) {
      log.error ('some message goes here', e)
    }
  }
}
```

Accessing Request Attributes

Java servlet developers will recognize components such as HttpServletRequest, HttpServletResponse, HttpSession, ServletContext, and others. These are all standard players in the servlet space. The Grails framework differs greatly from your standard servlet-based web frameworks, of course. However, Grails is built on top of those same servlet APIs. Table 4-1 contains a list of standard attributes that are automatically injected into Grails controllers.

Table 4-1. *Standard Request Attributes*

Attribute	Description
actionName	The name of the currently executing action
actionUri	The relative URI of the executing action
controllerName	The name of the currently executing controller
controllerUri	The URI of executing controller
flash	The object for working with flash scope
log	An org.apache.commons.logging.Log instance
params	A map of request parameters
request	The HttpServletRequest object
response	The HttpServletResponse object
session	The HttpSession object
servletContext	The ServletContext object

Many of the previously listed attributes are standard servlet API objects, whose documentation you can find on Sun's Java technology web site at http://java.sun.com/. It is, however, interesting to observe how working with a Grails controller differs from working with these objects.

A common way to interact with the request, for example, is to retrieve or set a request attribute. The session and servlet context also have attributes that you can set or retrieve. Grails unifies these by overriding the dot dereference and subscript operators. Table 4-2 shows the difference between accessing request, session, and servlet context attributes in regular Java servlets compared to accessing them in Grails controllers.

Table 4-2. *Differences Between Request Attributes in Java Servlets and Grails Controllers*

Java Servlet	Grails Controller
request.getAttribute("myAttr");	request.myAttr
request.setAttribute("myAttr", "myValue");	request.myAttr = "myValue"
session.getAttribute("mAttr");	session.myAttr
session.setAttribute("myAttr", "myValue"");	session.myAttr = "myValue"
servletContext.getAttribute("mAttr");	servletContext.myAttr
servletContext.setAttribute("myAttr", "myValue"");	servletContext.myAttr = "myValue"

Of course, if you are accustomed to writing code like that in the left column of the table, you can continue to do so; Grails just makes it a little bit easier.

Using Controller Scopes

You can choose from a number of scopes when developing controllers. The following list defines all the scopes available in order of their longevity:

- request: Objects placed into the request are kept for the duration of the currently executing request.

- flash: Objects placed into flash are kept for the duration of the current request and the next request only.

- session: Objects placed into the session are kept until the user session is invalidated, either manually or through expiration.

- servletContext: Objects placed into the servletContext are shared across the entire application and kept for the lifetime of the application.

As you can see, each scope is unique, and provides very different semantics. In an ideal world, sticking to request scope allows you to maintain a completely stateless application. In terms of scalability, this has significant advantages, as you do not need to consider issues such as replication of session state and session affinity.

However, you can certainly scale stateful applications that use flash and session scope using container-provided replication services or distributed data grids. The advantage of session scope is that it allows you to associate data on the server with individual clients. This typically works using cookies to associate individual users with their sessions.

Finally, the servletContext is a rarely used scope that allows you to share state across the entire application. Although this can prove useful, you should exercise caution when using the servletContext because objects placed within it will not be garbage-collected unless the application explicitly removes them. Also, access to the servletContext object is not synchronized, so you need to do manual synchronization if you plan to read and write objects from the servletContext object, as shown in Listing 4-7.

Listing 4-7. *Synchronized Access to the ServletContext*

```
def index = {
    synchronized(servletContext) {
            def myValue = servletContext.myAttr
            servletContext.myAttr = "changed"
            render myValue
    }
}
```

Of course, writing code like this will result in a serious bottleneck in your application, which leads us to the best-practice usage of the servletContext object: in general, if you really need to use the servletContext, you should prepopulate it with any values you need at startup and then read those values only at runtime. This allows you to access the servletContext in an unsynchronized manner.

Understanding Flash Scope

The flash object is a map accessible in the same way as the params object, the fundamental difference being that key/value pairs stored in the flash object are stored in flash scope. What is flash scope? It's best explained with the problem it solves.

A common usage pattern in web applications is to do some processing and then redirect the request to another controller, servlet, or whatever. This is not an issue in itself, except, What happens when the request is redirected? Redirecting the request essentially creates a brand-new request, wiping out all previous data that might have resided in the request attributes. The target of the redirect often needs this data, but unfortunately, the target action is out of luck. Some have worked around this issue by storing this information in the session instead.

This is all fine and good, but the problem with the session is that developers often forget to clear out this temporarily stored data, which places the burden on the developer to explicitly manage this state. Figure 4-1 illustrates this problem in action.

The first request that comes in sets an attribute on the request called "message." It then redirects the request by sending a redirect response back to the client. This creates a brand-new request instance, which is sent to the controller. Sadly, the message attribute is lost and evaluates to null.

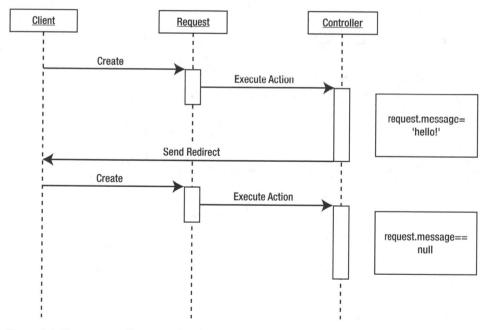

Figure 4-1. *Request attributes and redirects*

To get around this little annoyance, the flash object stores its values for the next request and the next request only, after which they automatically vanish. This feature manages the burden of this kind of use case for you. It's another small but significant feature that allows you to focus on the problem at hand instead of the surrounding issues.

One of the more common use cases for flash scope is to store a message that will display when some form of validation fails. Listing 4-8 demonstrates how to store a hypothetical message in the flash object so it's available for the next request.

Listing 4-8. *Storing a Message in Flash Scope*

```
flash.message = 'I am available next time you request me!'
```

Remember that the flash object implements java.util.Map, so all the regular methods of this class are also available. Figure 4-2 shows how flash scope solves the aforementioned problem. Here, on the first request, you store a message variable to the flash object and then redirect the request. When the new request comes in, you can access this message, no problem. The message variable will then automatically be removed for the next request that comes in.

Note The flash object does still use the HttpSession instance internally to store itself, so if you require any kind of session affinity or clustering, remember that it applies to the flash object, too.

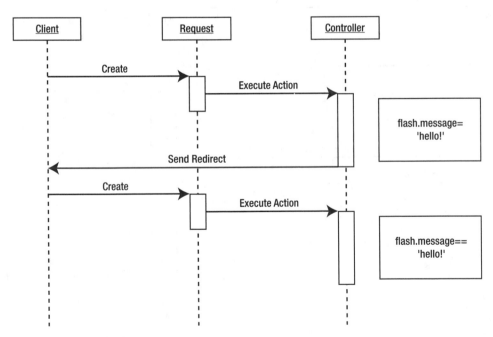

Figure 4-2. *Using flash scope*

Accessing Request Parameters

A controller action is often given input that will affect the behavior of the controller. For example, if a user submits a form that he or she has filled out, all the form's field names and values will be available to the controller in the form of request parameters. The standard servlet API provides an API for accessing request parameters. Listing 4-9 shows how a controller might retrieve the userName request parameter.

Listing 4-9. *Request Parameters via Standard Servlet API*

```
def userName = request.getParameter('userName')
log.info("User Name: ${userName}")
```

One of the dynamic properties injected into a Grails controller is a property called params. This params property is a map of request parameters. Listing 4-10 shows how a controller might retrieve the userName request parameter using the params property.

Listing 4-10. *Request Parameters via params Property*

```
def userName = params.userName
log.info("User Name: ${userName}")
```

Rendering Text

In its most basic form, you can use the render method from a controller to output text to the response. Listing 4-11 demonstrates how to render a simple String to the response.

Listing 4-11. *Rendering a Simple String*

```
render 'this text will be rendered back as part of the response'
```

Optionally, you can specify the contentType:

```
render text:'<album>Revolver</album>', contentType:'text/xml'
```

The most common use of the render method is to render a GSP view or a GSP template. We'll cover GSP in detail in Chapter 5.

Redirecting a Request

Often a controller action will need to redirect control to another controller action. This is a common thing for a controller action to do, so Grails provides a simple technique to manage redirecting to another controller action.

Grails provides all controllers with a redirect method that accepts a map as an argument. The map should contain all the information that Grails needs to carry out the redirect, including the name of the action to redirect to. In addition, the map can contain the name of the controller to redirect to.

Specifying the controller is required only if the request is being redirected to an action defined in a controller other than the current controller. Listing 4-12 shows a standard redirect from the first action to the second action within the sample controller.

Listing 4-12. *A Simple Redirect*

```
class SampleController {
  def first = {
    // redirect to the "second" action...
    redirect(action: "second")
  }
  def second = {
    // ...
  }
}
```

If the redirect is bound for an action in another controller, you must specify the name of the other controller. Listing 4-13 demonstrates how to redirect to an action in another controller.

Listing 4-13. *Redirecting to an Action in Another Controller*

```
class SampleController {
  def first = {
    // redirect to the 'list' action in the 'store' controller...
    redirect(action: "list", controller: "store")
  }
}
```

Although the previous examples are pretty trivial, the redirect method is pretty flexible. Table 4-3 shows the different arguments that the redirect method accepts.

Table 4-3. *Redirect Arguments*

Argument Name	Description
action	The name of or a reference to the action to redirect to
controller	The name of the controller to redirect to
id	The id parameter to pass in the redirect
params	A map of parameters to pass
uri	A relative URI to redirect to
url	An absolute URL to redirect to

As you can see, the redirect method allows you to effectively pass control from one action to the next. However, often you simply want to formulate some data to be rendered by a view. In the next couple of sections, we'll take a look at how to achieve this.

Creating a Model

One of the most fundamental activities carried out in a controller is gathering data that will be rendered in the view. A controller can gather data directly or delegate to Grails services or other components to gather the data. However the controller gathers the data, the data is typically made available to the view in the form of a map that the controller action returns. When a controller action returns a map, that map represents data that the view can reference. Listing 4-14 displays the show action of the SongController.

Listing 4-14. *Returning a Map of Data to be Rendered by the View*

```
class SongController {
  def show = {
    [ song: Song.get(params.id) ]
  }
}
```

Remember that return statements are optional in Groovy. Because the last expression evaluated in the show action is a map, the map is the return value from this action. This map contains data that will be passed in to the view to be rendered. In Listing 4-14, the sole key in the map is song and the value associated with that key is a Song object retrieved from the database based on the id request parameter.

Now the view can reference this song. Whereas this map contains only a single entry, a map returned from a controller action can include as many entries as is appropriate. Every entry represents an object that the view can reference.

A controller action does not have to return a model, so what happens if no model is returned? The simple answer is that it depends on what the action does. If the action writes directly to the response output, there is no model; conversely, if a controller action simply delegates to the view with no model returned, the controller's properties automatically become the model. This allows you to write code like that shown in Listing 4-15 as an alternative to the show action you have already seen.

Listing 4-15. *The Controller as the Model*

```
class SongController {
  Song song
  def show = {
    this.song = Song.get(params.id)
  }
}
```

The technique you choose to use is as much up to personal preference as anything else. You'll often find greater clarity in returning an explicitly defined map. Use whatever makes the most sense in your case, and keep in mind that consistency can be as important as anything else in terms of writing code that is easy to understand and maintain.

Rendering a View

The subject of views in Grails is important, and we'll dedicate an entire chapter to it (see Chapter 5). But for now, you need to understand how Grails goes about view selection from a controller's point of view. First, let's look at the default view-selection strategy.

Finding the Default View

As you saw in Listing 4-15, the SongController has a single action called show. The show action returns a model containing a single key, called song, which references an instance of the Song domain class. However, nowhere in the code can you see any reference to the view that will be used to deal with the rendering part of this action.

That's perfectly understandable because we haven't explicitly told Grails what view to render. To mitigate this problem, Grails makes that decision for you based on the conventions in the application. In the case of the show action, Grails will look for a view at the location grails-app/views/song/show.gsp. The name of the view is taken from the name of the action, while the name of the parent directory is taken from the controller name. Simple, really.

But what if you want to display a completely different view? The ever-flexible render method comes to the rescue again.

Selecting a Custom View

To tell Grails to render a custom view, you can use the render method's view argument as shown in Listing 4-16.

Listing 4-16. *Rendering a Custom View*

```
class SongController {
  def show = {
     render(view:"display",model:[ song: Song.get(params.id) ])
  }
}
```

Notice how you can use the model argument to pass in the model, rather than using the return value of the action. In the example in Listing 4-16, we're asking Grails to render a view called "display." In this case, Grails assumes you mean a view at the location grails-app/views/song/display.gsp. Notice how the view is automatically scoped with the grails-app/views/song directory.

If the view you want to render is in another, possibly shared, directory, you can specify an absolute path to the view:

```
render(view:"/common/song", model:[song: Song.get(params.id) ])
```

By starting with a / character, you can reference any view within the grails-app/views directory. In the previous example, Grails will try to render a view at the location grails-app/views/common/song.gsp.

Rendering Templates

In addition to views, Grails supports the notion of templates—small snippets of view code that other views can include. We'll be covering templates in more detail in Chapter 5, but for now, just know that you can render a template from a controller using the render method:

```
render(template:"/common/song", model:[song: Song.get(params.id) ] )
```

In this case, Grails will try to render a template at the location grails-app/views/common/_song.gsp. Notice how, unlike views, the name of the template starts with an underscore by convention.

Performing Data Binding

Often a controller action will need to create new domain objects and populate the properties of the instance with values received as request parameters. Consider the Album domain class, which has properties such as genre and title. If a request is made to the save action in the AlbumController, the controller action could create a new Album and save it using a technique like that shown in Listing 4-17.

Listing 4-17. *Populating an Album with Request Parameters*

```
class AlbumController {
  def save = {
    def album = new Album()
    album.genre = params.genre
    album.title = params.title
    album.save()
  }
}
```

The approach in Listing 4-17 assigns values to domain properties based on corresponding request parameters. It might work for simple models with a small number of properties, but as your domain model grows in complexity, this code gets longer and more tedious. Fortunately, the Grails framework provides some slick options for binding request parameters to a domain object.

Remember that the params object in your controller is a map of name/value pairs. You can pass maps to a domain class's constructor to initialize all the domain class's properties with the corresponding request parameters. Listing 4-18 shows a better approach to creating and populating an Album object.

Listing 4-18. *Populating an Album by Passing params to the Constructor*

```
class AlbumController {
  def save = {
    def album = new Album(params)
    album.save()
  }
}
```

■**Caution** The features detailed so far can leave your web application open to URL attacks due to the automatic setting of properties from request parameters. This is a common issue among frameworks that perform such conversion (including Ruby on Rails, Spring MVC, WebWork, and so on). If you are developing a web application with heightened security in mind, you should use fine-grained control over data binding through the `bindData` method (described later) and stricter validation.

As you can see, this is a much cleaner approach and scales better as the number of properties in a domain class grows.

Occasionally, setting properties on a domain object that has already been constructed can prove useful. For example, you retrieve a domain object from the database and then need to update it with values passed to the controller as request parameters. In a case like this, passing a map of parameters to the domain-class constructor will not help because the object already exists. Grails provides yet another slick solution here. You can use a domain class's `properties` property in conjunction with request parameters to update an existing object, as shown in Listing 4-19.

Listing 4-19. *Updating an Existing Object with Request Parameters*

```
class AlbumController {
  def update = {
    def album = Album.get(params.id)
    album.properties = params
    album.save()
  }
}
```

Whenever your application accepts user input, there is a chance that said input might not be what your application requires. You've already seen in Chapter 3 how to define custom-validation constraints on domain classes; now you'll begin to understand how you can use data binding in combination with these constraints to validate incoming data.

Validating Incoming Data

The mechanics of Grails' data-binding and data-validation process has two phases. First, let's revisit the following line of code:

```
album.properties = params
```

At this point, Grails will attempt to bind any incoming request parameters onto the properties of the instance. Groovy is a strongly typed language and all parameters arrive as strings, so some type conversion might be necessary.

Underneath the surface, Grails uses Spring's data-binding capabilities to convert request parameters to the target type if necessary. During this process, a type-conversion error can occur if, for example, converting the `String` representation of a number to a `java.lang.Integer` is impossible. If an error occurs, Grails automatically sets the persistent instance to read-only so it cannot be persisted unless you explicitly persist it yourself (refer to Chapter 10 for more information on automatic dirty checking).

If all is well, the second phase of validation commences. At this point, you validate the persistent instance against its defined constraints using either the `validate()` method or the `save()` method as described in Chapter 3:

```
album.validate()
```

Grails will validate each property of the `Album` instance and populate the `Errors` object with any validation errors that might have occurred. This brings us nicely into a discussion of the Errors API.

The Errors API and Controllers

The mechanics of Grails' validation mechanism is built entirely on Spring's `org.springframework.validation` package. As discussed in Chapter 3, whenever you validate a domain instance, a Spring `org.springspringframework.validation.Errors` object is created and associated with the instance.

From a controller's point of view, when you have a domain object in an invalid state—typically due to invalid user input that changes an instance using data binding—you need to use branching logic to handle the validation error.

Listing 4-20 shows an example of how you could use data binding to update an `Album` instance and validate its state.

Listing 4-20. *Dealing with Validation Errors*

```
def save = {
        def album = Album.get(params.id)
        album.properties = params
        if(album.save()) {
            redirect(action: "show", id:album.id)
        }
        else {
            render(view: "edit", model:[album:album])
         }
}
```

Notice how in Listing 4-20 you can call the `save()` method, which triggers validation, and send the user back to the `edit` view if a validation error occurs. When a user enters invalid data, the `errors` property on the `Album` will be an `Errors` object containing one or more validation errors.

You can programmatically decipher these errors by iterating over them:

```
album.errors.allErrors.each { println it.code }
```

If you merely want to check if an instance has any errors, you can call the `hasErrors()` method on the instance:

```
if(album.hasErrors()) println "Something went wrong!"
```

In the view, you can render these using the `<g:renderErrors>` tag:

```
<g:renderErrors bean="${album}" />
```

You'll be learning more about handling errors in the view through the course of the book, but as you can see, it's frequently the controller's job to coordinate errors that occur and ensure the user enters valid data.

Data Binding to Multiple Domain Objects

In the examples of data binding you've seen so far, the assumption has been that you wish to bind parameters to a single domain instance. However, you might encounter a scenario in which you must create several domain instances.

Consider, for example, the creation of `Artist` instances in the gTunes application. The application might require that an `Artist` can exist only if he or she has released at least one `Album`. In this case, it makes sense to create both the `Artist` and the first `Album` simultaneously.

To understand data binding when dealing with multiple domain instances, you first need to understand how parameters are submitted from forms. Consider, for example, the case of updating an `Album` and the line:

```
album.properties = params
```

In this case, the expectation is that parameters are not namespaced in any way. In other words, to update the `title` property of the `Album` instance, you can provide an HTML input such as the following:

```
<input type="text" name="title" />
```

Notice how the name of the `<input>` matches the property name. This clearly would not work in the case of multiple domain classes because you might have two different domain classes that have a property called `title`. You can get around this problem namespacing any parameters passed using a dot:

```
<input type="text" name="album.title" />
<input type="text" name="artist.name" />
...
```

Now create and bind both `Album` and `Artist` instances by referring to them within the `params` object by their respective namespaces:

```
def album = new Album( params["album"] )
def artist = new Artist( params["artist"] )
```

Data Binding with the bindData Method

The data-binding techniques you have seen so far are automatic and handled implicitly by Grails. However, in some circumstances you might need to exercise greater control over the data-binding process or to bind data to objects other than domain classes. To help tackle this issue, Grails provides a `bindData` method that takes the object to bind the data to and a `java.util.Map`.

The map should contain keys that match the property names of the target properties within the passed object. As an example, if you wanted to ensure only the `title` property was bound to an `Album` instance, you could use the code shown in Listing 4-21.

Listing 4-21. *Using the bindData Method*

```
class AlbumController {
    def save = {
            def album = Album.get(params.id)
             bindData(album, params, [include:"title"])
         ...
    }
}
```

Notice how in Listing 4-21 you can pass the `Album` instance as the first argument, and the parameters to bind to the instance as the second argument. The final argument is a map specifying that you wish to include only the `title` property in the data-binding process. You could change the key within the map to `exclude` if you wished to bind all properties *except* the `title` property.

Finally, as you saw in the previous section, you can bind to multiple domain instances using Grails' default data-binding mechanism. You can do this with the `bindData` method too, using the last argument that specifies the prefix to filter by:

```
bindData(album, params, [include:"title"], "album")
```

In this example, the prefix "album" is passed as the last argument, making the `bindData` method bind all parameters that begin with the `album.` prefix.

Data Binding and Associations

The final topic to consider when doing data binding is how it relates to associations. The easiest case to understand is many-to-one and one-to-one associations. For example, consider the `artist` property of the `Album` class, which is a many-to-one association, as shown in Listing 4-22.

Listing 4-22. *The artist Association of the Album Class*

```
class Album {
      Artist artist
      ...
}
```

You need to consider two cases when working with a many-to-one association like this. The first involves creating new instances. Suppose you create a new `Album` instance using this code:

```
def album  = new Album(params)
```

In this case, if any parameters reference the `artist` association, such as `artist.name`, a new `Artist` instance will be automatically instantiated and assigned to the `Album` instance. The names of the properties to set are taken from the value of the right side of the dot in the request-parameter name. With `artist.name`, the property to set is `name`. To further clarify, the following `<input>` tag shows an example of a form field that will populate the `artist` associa-tion of the `Album` class:

```
<input type="text" name="artist.name" />
```

The second scenario occurs when you are assigning an existing instance of an associa-tion (an existing `Artist`, for example) or modifying an association. To do this, you need to pass the association's identifier using a request parameter with the `.id` suffix. For example, you can use the following `<input>` to specify the `Artist` that should be associated with an existing or new `Album`:

```
<input type="text" name="artist.id" value="1" />
```

With single-ended associations out of the way, let's consider associations that contain multiple objects. For example, an `Album` has many `Song` instances in its `songs` associations. What if you wanted to provide a form that enabled you to create an `Album` and its associated songs? To enable this, you can use subscript-style references to populate or update multiple `Song` instances:

```
<input type="text" name="songs[0].title" value="The Bucket" />
<input type="text" name="songs[1].title" value="Milk" />
```

Note that the default collection type for association in Grails is a `java.util.Set`, so unless you change the default to `java.util.List`, the order of entries will not be retained because `Set` types have no concept of order. If you want to create a new `Album` instance and populate the `songs` association with an existing collection of `songs`, then you can just specify their identifiers using the `.id` suffix:

```
<input type="text" name="songs[0].id" value="23" />
<input type="text" name="songs[1].id" value="47" />
```

Working with Command Objects

Sometimes a particular action doesn't require the involvement of a domain class, but still requires the validation of user input. In this case, you might want to consider using a command object. A command object is a class that has all the data-binding and data-validation capabili-ties of a domain class, but is not persistent. In other words, you can define constraints of a command object and validate them just like a domain class.

Defining Command Objects

A command object requires the definition of class, just like any other object. You can define command classes in the `grails-app/controllers` directory or even in the same file as a con-troller. Unlike Java, Groovy supports the notion of multiple class definitions per file, which is quite handy if you plan to use a particular command object only for the controller you're working with.

For example, you could define an `AlbumCreateCommand` that encapsulates the validation and creation of new `Album` instances before they are saved. Listing 4-23 presents such an example.

Listing 4-23. *An Example Command Object Definition*

```
class AlbumCreateCommand {
    String artist
    String title
    List songs = []
    List durations = []

    static constraints = {
        artist blank:false
        title blank:false
        songs minSize:1, validator:{ val, obj ->
            if(val.size() != obj.durations.size())
                    return "songs.durations.not.equal.size"
        }
    }

    Album createAlbum() {
        def artist = Artist.findByName(artist) ?: new Artist(name:artist)
        def album = new Album(title:title)
        songs.eachWithIndex { songTitle, i ->
           album.addToSongs(title:songTitle, duration:durations[i])
        }
         return album
    }
}
```

In Listing 4-23, you can see a command-object definition that is designed to capture everything necessary to subsequently create a valid `Album` instance. Notice how you can define constraints on a command object just like in a domain class. The `createAlbum()` method, which is optional, is interesting because it shows how you can use command objects as factories that take a valid set of data and construct your domain instances. In the next section, you'll see how to take advantage of the command object in Listing 4-23.

Using Command Objects

In order to use a command object, you need to specify the command as the first argument in a controller action. For example, to use `AlbumCreateCommand`, you need to have a save action such as the one shown in Listing 4-24.

Listing 4-24. *Using a Command Object*

```
class AlbumController {
...
    def save = { AlbumCreateCommand cmd ->
            ...
    }
}
```

As you can see from the code highlighted in bold, you need to explicitly define the command object using its type definition as the first argument to the action. Here's what happens next: when a request comes in, Grails will automatically create a new instance, bind the incoming request parameters to the properties of the instance, and pass it to you as the first argument.

Providing the request parameters to a command like this is pretty trivial. Listing 4-25 shows an example form.

Listing 4-25. *Providing a Form to Populate the Data*

```
<g:form url="[controller: 'album', action: 'save'] ">
        Title: <input type="text" name="title" /> <br>
        Artist: <input type="text" name="artist" /> <br>
        Song 1: <input type="text" name="songs[0]" /> <br>
        Song 2: <input type="text" name="songs[1]" /> <br>
        ...
</g:form>
```

You'll probably want to make the input of the songs dynamic using some JavaScript, but nevertheless you can see the concept in Listing 4-25. Once you've given the user the ability to enter data and you're capturing said data using the command object, all you need to do is validate it. Listing 4-26 shows how the save action's logic might look with the command object in use.

Listing 4-26. *Using the Command Object for Validation*

```
def save = { AlbumCreateCommand cmd ->
        if(cmd.validate()) {
                def album = cmd.createAlbum()
                album.save()
                redirect(action:"show", id:album.id)
        }
        else {
                render(view:"create", model:[cmd:cmd])
         }
}
```

As you can see, it's now the command object that is ensuring the validity of the request, and we're using it as a factory to construct a perfectly valid Album instance. As with domain classes, command objects have an Errors object, so you can use the <g:renderErrors> tag to display validation errors to the user:

```
<g:renderErrors bean="{cmd}" />
```

Imposing HTTP Method Restrictions

Often a web application needs to impose restrictions on which HTTP request methods are allowed for a specific controller action. For example, it is generally considered a bad idea for a controller action to carry out any destructive operation in response to an HTTP GET. Such operations should be limited to HTTP POST or DELETE.

Implementing an Imperative Solution

One approach to dealing with this concern is for a controller action to inspect the request method and prevent certain actions from being carried out in response to an inappropriate HTTP request method. Listing 4-27 shows a simple imperative approach to the problem.

Listing 4-27. *Inspecting the HTTP Request Method in a Controller Action*

```
class SongController {
  def delete = {
    if(request.method == "GET") {
      // do not delete in response to a GET request
      // redirect to the list action
      redirect(action: "list")
    } else {
      // carry out the delete here...
    }
  }
}
```

While this approach is fairly straightforward and does get the job done, it's a tedious solution to the problem. In a real-world application, this same logic would appear in many controller actions.

Taking Advantage of a Declarative Syntax

A better solution to limiting actions to certain HTTP request methods is to take advantage of a simple declarative syntax that expresses which HTTP request methods are valid for a particular controller action. Grails supports an approach like this through the optional allowedMethods property in a controller.

The allowedMethods property expresses which HTTP request methods are valid for any particular controller action. By default, all HTTP request methods are considered valid for any particular controller action. If you want an action to be accessible through specific request methods only, then you should include the action in the allowedMethods property.

You should assign the allowedMethods property a value that is a map. The keys in the map should be the names of actions that you want restricted. The value(s) associated with the keys should be a String representing a specific request method or a list of Strings representing all allowed methods for that particular action. Listing 4-28 shows an example.

Listing 4-28. *Restricting Access to Controller Actions Using the allowedMethods Property*

```
class SomeController {
 // action1 may be invoked via a POST
  // action2 has no restrictions
  // action3 may be invoked via a POST or DELETE
  def allowedMethods = [action1:'POST', action3:['POST', 'DELETE']]
  def action1 = { ... }
  def action2 = { ... }
  def action3 = { ... }
}
```

If the rules expressed in the allowedMethods property are violated, the framework will deny the request and return a 405 error code, which the HTTP specification defines as "Method Not Allowed."

Controller IO

As you've learned so far, controllers can control request flow through redirects and rendering views. In addition to this, controllers might need to read and write binary input to and from the client. In this section, we'll look at how to read data, including file uploads, and how to write binary responses to the client.

Handling File Uploads

One of the more common use cases when developing web applications is to allow the user to upload a local file to the server using a multipart request. This is where Grails' solid foundation of Spring MVC starts to shine through.

Spring has excellent support for handling file uploads via an extension to the servlet API's HttpServletRequest interface called org.springframework.web.multipart. MultipartHttpServletRequest, the definition of which is in Listing 4-29.

Listing 4-29. *The org.springframework.web.multipart.MultipartHttpServletRequest Interface*

```
interface MultipartHttpServletRequest extends HttpServletRequest {
        public MultipartFile getFile(String name);
        public Map getFileMap();
        public Iterator getFileNames();
}
```

As you can see, the MultipartHttpServletRequest interface simply extends the default HttpServletRequest interface to provide useful methods to work with files in the request.

Working with Multipart Requests

Essentially, whenever a multipart request is detected, a request object that implements the MultipartHttpServletRequest interface is present in the controller instance. This provides access to the methods seen in Listing 4-30 to access files uploaded in a multipart request. Listing 4-30 also shows how you can define a multipart form using the <g:uploadForm> tag.

Listing 4-30. *An Example Upload Form*

```
<g:uploadForm action="upload">
    <input type="file" name="myFile" />
    <input type="submit" value="Upload! " />
</g:uploadForm>
```

The important bits are highlighted in bold, but an upload form essentially requires two things:

- A <form> tag with the enctype attribute set to the value multipart/form-data. The <g:uploadForm> in Listing 4-30 does this for you automatically.

- An <input> tag whose type attribute is set to the value file.

In the previous case, the name of the file input is myFile; this is crucial because it's the named reference that you work with when using the getFile method of the MultipartHttpServletRequest interface. For example, the code within an upload action will retrieve the uploaded file from the request (see Listing 4-31).

Listing 4-31. *Retrieving the Uploaded File*

```
def upload = {
    def file = request.getFile('myFile')
    // do something with the file
}
```

Note that the getFile method does not return a java.io.File, but instead returns an instance of org.springframework.web.multipart.MultipartFile, the interface detailed in Listing 4-32. If the file is not found in the request, the getFile method will return null.

Listing 4-32. *The org.springframework.web.multipart.MultipartFile Interface*

```
interface MultipartFile {
    public byte[] getBytes();
    public String getContentType();
    public java.io.InputStream getInputStream();
    public String getName();
    public String getOriginalFilename();
    public long getSize();
    public boolean isEmpty();
    public void transferTo(java.io.File dest);
}
```

Many useful methods are defined in the `MultipartFile` interface. Potential use cases include the following:

- Use the `getSize()` method to allow uploads only of certain file sizes.

- Reject empty files using the `isEmpty()` method.

- Read the file as a `java.io.InputStream` using the `getInputStream()` method.

- Allow only certain file types to be uploaded using the `getContentType()` method.

- Transfer the file onto the server using the `transferTo(dest)` method.

As an example, the code in Listing 4-33 will upload a file to the server if it's not empty and if it's fewer than 1,024 bytes in size.

Listing 4-33. *File Uploads in Action*

```
def upload = {
    def file = request.getFile('myFile')
    if(file && !file.empty && file.size < 1024)  {
        file.transferTo( new java.io.File( "/local/server/path/${file.name}" ) )
    }
}
```

Working directly with a `MultipartHttpServletRequest` instance is one way to manage file uploads, but frequently you need to read the contents of a file. In the next section, we'll look at how Grails makes this easier through data binding.

Uploads and Data Binding

In the "Performing Data Binding" section, you saw how Grails handles automatic type conversion from strings to other common Java types. What we didn't discuss is how this capability extends to file uploads. Grails, through Spring MVC, will automatically bind files uploaded to properties of domain-class instances based on the following rules:

- If the target property is a `byte[]`, the file's bytes will be bound.

- If the target property is a `String`, the file's contents as a string will be bound.

Suppose you want to allow users of the gTunes application to upload album art for each album. By adding a new property to the `Album` domain class called art of type `byte[]`, you automatically have the capability to save the image data to the database, as shown in Listing 4-34.

Listing 4-34. *Adding the Picture Property*

```
class Album{
    byte[] art
    ...
}
```

To bind an uploaded file, you simply need to add an art upload field that matches the art property name to a <g:uploadForm> tag:

```
<input type="file" name="art" />
```

The following line automatically handles binding the file to the s:

```
def user = new Album( params )
```

Grails will automatically recognize the request as being multipart, retrieve the file, and bind the bytes that make up the file to the art byte array property of the Album class. This capability also extends to usage in conjunction with the properties property and bindData method discussed previously.

Reading the Request InputStream

The way in which you read the body of an incoming request depends very much on the content type of the request. For example, if the incoming request is an XML request, the parsing is handled automatically for you. We'll cover this subject further in Chapter 15.

However, if you just want to get the text contained within the request body, you can use the inputStream property of the request object as shown in Listing 4-35.

Listing 4-35. *Reading the Request Body*

```
def readText = {
    def text = request.inputStream.text
    render "You sent $text"
}
```

Writing a Binary Response

You can send a binary response to the client using standard servlet API calls such as the example in Listing 4-36, which uses the HttpServletResponse object to output binary data to the response in the form of a ZIP file.

Listing 4-36. *Writing Binary Data to the Response*

```
def createZip = {
  byte[] zip = ... // create the zip from some source
  response.contentType = "application/octet-stream"
  response.outputStream << zip
  response.outputSream.flush()
}
```

The code uses the response object's outputStream property in conjunction with Groovy's overloaded left shift << operator, which is present in a number of objects that output or append to something such as java.io.Writer and java.lang.StringBuffer, to name just a couple.

Using Simple Interceptors

Frequently, it is useful to catch the flow of method execution by intercepting calls to certain methods. This concept is the foundation of Aspect-Oriented Programming (AOP), which allows the definition of "pointcuts" (execution points) to be intercepted. You can then modify the intercepted execution through the use of *before*, *after*, and *around* "advice."

As the names suggest, *before* advice in AOP is code that can be executed before an intercepted method call; *after* advice is code that can be executed after an intercepted method call. *Around* advice is code that can replace the method call entirely. AOP's great strength is providing support for implementing cross-cutting concerns.

The example frequently used for this concept is the logging of method calls. Although Grails' interception mechanism by no means provides the same power and flexibility in terms of what pointcuts can be intercepted, it does fulfill the basic need of intercepting calls to actions on controllers.

Additionally, interceptors are useful if they apply only to a single controller. If your requirement spans multiple controllers, you're better off having a look at Filters (a topic covered in Chapter 14). With interceptors you can either intercept all actions or provide more fine-grained control by specifying which actions should be intercepted. Let's look at a few examples, starting with *before* interceptors.

Before Advice

Luckily, as with the rest of Grails, there is no hefty XML configuration or annotation trickery required, thanks to Convention over Configuration. All it takes to define a *before* interceptor is to create a closure property named beforeInterceptor within the target controller, as shown in Listing 4-37.

Listing 4-37. *A beforeInterceptor*

```
def beforeInterceptor = {
        log.trace("Executing action $actionName with params $params")
}
```

Listing 4-37 uses the log object to output tracing information before any action within the defining controller is executed. This example applies to every action defined in the controller. However, you can apply more fine-grained control using interception conditions.

As an example, say you wanted to trace each time a user views an Album and each user's country of residence. You could define a beforeInterceptor as shown in Listing 4-38.

Listing 4-38. *Using Interception Conditions*

```
class AlbumController {
        private trackCountry = {
                def country = request.locale.country
                def album = Album.get(params.id)
                 new AlbumVisit(country:country, album:album).save()
        }
```

```
        def beforeInterceptor = [action:trackCountry, only: "show"]
        ...
}
```

As you can see from Listing 4-38, you can define a beforeInterceptor using a map literal. The action key defines the code that should execute. In this case, we're using an only condition, which means that the interceptor applies only to the show action. You could change this to an except condition, in which case the interceptor would apply to all actions *except* the show action.

Finally, a beforeInterceptor can also halt execution of an action by returning false. For example, if you want to allow only U.S. visitors to your site, you could send a 403 forbidden HTTP code if the user hails from outside the U.S. (see Listing 4-39).

Listing 4-39. *Halting Execution with a beforeInterceptor*

```
class AlbumController {
        def beforeInterceptor = {
if(request.locale != Locale.US) {

                response.sendError 403
                return false
        }
      }
}
```

After Advice

After advice is defined using the unsurprisingly named afterInterceptor property that again takes a closure. The first argument passed to the closure is the resulting model from the action, as shown in Listing 4-40.

Listing 4-40. *An afterInterceptor Example*

```
def afterInterceptor = { model ->
    log.trace("Executed action $actionName which resulted in model: $model")
}
```

Again, in this rather trivial example, the logging mechanism traces any action that executes.

Testing Controllers

Grails provides a special ControllerUnitTestCase class that you can use to test controllers. Tests that extend from ControllerUnitTestCase are provided with mock implementations of the various Servlet API objects, such as the HttpServletRequest, as well as mock implementations of key methods such as render and redirect.

As an example, the AlbumController class as it stands has no test coverage. To create a test for this controller, you need create a new test class that follows the naming convention for the controller under test. For example, you can create a test for the AlbumController with the create-unit-test command:

```
grails create-unit-test com.g2one.gtunes.AlbumController
```

This will create a new unit test called AlbumControllerTests at the location test/unit/com/g2one/gtunes/AlbumControllerTests.groovy. Now you need to modify the test class to extend from the ControllerUnitTestCase test harness, as shown in Listing 4-41.

Listing 4-41. *Using ControllerUnitTestCase*

```
class AlbumControllerTests extends grails.test.ControllerUnitTestCase {
    ...
}
```

The ControllerUnitTestCase class extends from the parent GrailsUnitTestCase, which contains general mocking capabilities plus utility methods that enable you to mock the behavior of domain classes and controllers. For example, to test the list action of the AlbumController, you can write a trivial test that takes advantage of the mockDomain method (see Listing 4-42).

Listing 4-42. *Mocking a Simple Action That Returns a Model*

```
void testList() {
    mockDomain(Album, [ new Album(title: "Odelay"),
                        new Album(title: "Abbey Road"] )
    def model = controller.list()
    assertEquals 2, model.albumList.size()
}
```

In Listing 4-42, we're testing the returned model, but some controller actions write directly to the response or issue a redirect rather than return a value. To test an action that writes to the response, you can use the response object of the controller, which is an instance of the org.springframework.mock.web.MockHttpServletResponse class.

Several useful methods in the MockHttpServletResponse class allow you to inspect the state of the current response. In particular, the getContentAsString() method provides access to what is currently written into the response as a String. For example, if you have an action that renders some text to the response, you could test it as shown in Listing 4-43.

Listing 4-43. *Testing the Contents of the Response*

```
void testIndex() {
    controller.index()
    assertEquals "Welcome to the gTunes store!",
                    controller.response.contentAsString
}
```

For more complex usages of the render method, such as rendering a view and so on, you can use the renderArgs property of the ControllerUnitTestCase class, which provides a map of the named parameters given to the render method that executed last. For example, say you have a render method that renders a view with a model such as:

```
render(view: "show", model:[album:Album.get(params.id)])
```

You can test this code using the renderArgs property and mock the domain as shown in Listing 4-44.

Listing 4-44. *Testing the render Method*

```
void testShow() {
        mockDomain(Album, new Album(id:1, title: "Aha Shake Heartbreak"))
        mockParams.id = 1
        controller.show()
        assertEquals "show", renderArgs.view
        assertEquals 1, renderArgs.model.album.id
        assertEquals "Aha Shake Heartbreak", renderArgs.model.album.title
}
```

Notice the usage in Listing 4-44 of the ControllerUnitTestCase class's mockParams property. This property provides a mock implementation of the params object that you can populate with values before calling the controller. In addition to a mock implementation of the params object, the ControllerUnitTestCase class provides the following properties that mock various aspects of the controller API:

- mockRequest: An instance of the org.springframework.mock.web.MockHttpServletRequest class that mocks the request object

- mockResponse: An instance of the org.springframework.mock.web.MockHttpServletResponse class that mocks the response object

- mockSession: An instance of the org.springframework.mock.web.MockHttpSession that provides a mock implementation of the session object

- mockParams: A simple map that mocks the behavior of the params object

- mockFlash: A simple map that mocks the behavior of the flash object

Additionally, you can test the redirect method as you test the render method, using the provided redirectArgs property of the ControllerUnitTestCase class. You'll see more examples of testing as we progress through the book, but in the meantime, let's exercise your new knowledge of controllers by implementing the gTunes application's first bit of real functionality.

Controllers in Action

In this section, you'll learn how to build a simple login and registration system using Grails controllers. In Chapter 14, we'll be refactoring this system to use one of Grails' more generic security plugins, but for the moment it will serve as a useful starting point.

One of the first things to consider when developing any site is the point of entry into the site. At the moment, you've just created a bunch of scaffolded pages, but now it's time to think about the real application for the first time, starting with the home page.

Creating the gTunes Home Page

The gTunes application is a music store where users can log in, browse the available music, and purchase music that they can then play. First, you need to establish a home page. You already have a `StoreController`, so you can use that as the controller that deals with the home page. To make sure visitors get routed to this controller, you can modify the `grails-app/conf/UrlMappings.groovy` file to map visitors to the root of the application to this controller (see Listing 4-45).

Listing 4-45. *Routing Users to the Root of the Application to the StoreController*

```
class UrlMappings {
    static mappings = {
                "/"(controller:"store")
    }
}
```

Notice how you can use a forward slash to tell Grails to map any request to the root of the application to the `StoreController`. As you can see from the mapping, it is not mapping onto any particular action in `StoreController`, which will trigger the default action. The default action is the `index` action, which currently writes out a simple-text response. You need to change the `index` action so view delegation kicks in:

```
def index = {}
```

Now instead of returning a textual response, the `index` action delegates to the `grails-app/views/store/index.gsp` view, which you can use to render the home page. We'll start with something simple that just shows a welcome message; we can expand on this later. Listing 4-46 shows the markup code involved.

Listing 4-46. *The gTunes Home Page*

```
<html>
    <head>
        <meta http-equiv="Content-type" content="text/html; charset=utf-8">
        <meta name="layout" content="main">
        <title>gTunes Store</title>
    </head>
    <body id="body">
        <h1>Your online music store and storage service!</h1>
        <p>Manage your own library, browse music and purchase new tracks as they
            become available</p>
    </body>
</html>
```

The next step is to consider how to enable users to register, log in, and log out. Before you can do that, you need to define the notion of a user within the gTunes application. Let's do that in the next section.

Adding the User Domain Class

To model users, you'll need to create a `User` domain class that contains personal information such as first name and last name, as well as the login and password for each user. To do so, you can use the `create-domain-class` command:

```
grails create-domain-class com.g2one.gtunes.User
```

This will create a new domain class at the location `grails-app/domain/com/g2one/gtunes/User.groovy`. With that done, you need to populate the `User` domain class with a few properties, as shown in Listing 4-47.

Listing 4-47. *The User Domain Class*

```
package com.g2one.gtunes
class User {
        String login
        String password
        String firstName
        String lastName
        static hasMany = [purchasedSongs:Song]
}
```

As you can see, the code in Listing 4-47 captures only the basics about users, but you could easily expand this information to include an address, contact number, and so on. One property to note is the `purchasedSongs` association, which will hold references to all the Songs a `User` buys once you have implemented music purchasing.

However, before we get too far ahead of ourselves, let's add a few constraints to ensure domain instances stay in a valid state (see Listing 4-48).

Listing 4-48. *Applying Constraints to the User Class*

```
class User {
    ...
    static constraints = {
        login blank:false, size:5..15,matches:/[\S]+/, unique:true
        password blank:false, size:5..15,matches:/[\S]+/
        firstName blank:false
        lastName blank:false
    }
}
```

With these constraints in place, you can ensure that a user cannot enter blank values or values that don't fall within the necessary size constraints. Also, note the usage of the unique constraint, which ensures that the login property is unique to each User. We'll revisit this in more detail later; for now, let's focus on login and registration.

Adding a Login Form

Because you already have a home page, it might make sense to add the login form there. But further down the line, you'll want to allow users to browse the gTunes music catalog anonymously, so users should be able to log in from anywhere. With this in mind, you need to add a login form to the grails-app/views/layouts/main.gsp layout so that it's available on every page.

Listing 4-49 shows the GSP code to do so. Note how you can check whether a User already exists in the session object and display a welcome box or login form, accordingly.

Listing 4-49. *Adding the Login Form Everywhere*

```
<div id="loginBox" class="loginBox">
    <g:if test="${session?.user}">
        <div style="margin-top:20px">
    <div style="float:right;">
        <a href="#">Profile</a> |
                    <g:link controller="user" action="logout">Logout</g:link><br>
    </div>

    Welcome back
    <span id="userFirstName">${session?.user?.firstName}!</span>
    <br><br>
    You have purchased (${session.user.purchasedSongs?.size() ?: 0}) songs.<br>
        </div>
    </g:if>
    <g:else>
    <g:form
        name="loginForm"
        url="[controller:'user',action:'login']">
        <div>Username:</div>
        <g:textField name="login" ></g:textField>
        <div>Password:</div>
        <g:passwordField name="password" />
                            <input type="submit" value="Login" />
    </g:form>
    <g:renderErrors bean="${loginCmd}"></g:renderErrors>
    </g:else>
</div>
```

In addition to providing a login box, you need to provide a link that allows a User to register. Once logged in, the user will be able to click through the store to browse and click a "My Music" link to view music already purchased. These links won't display when the user isn't logged in, so instead you can use the screen real estate for a prominent link to the registration page. Listing 4-50 shows the registration link added to the main.gsp layout.

Listing 4-50. *Adding a Link to the Registration Page*

```
<div id="navPane">
    <g:if test="${session.user}">
  <ul>
         <li><g:link controller="user" action="music">My Music</g:link></li>
         <li><g:link controller="store" action="shop">The Store</g:link></a></li>
  </ul>
    </g:if>
    <g:else>
  <div id="registerPane">
         Need an account?
         <g:link controller="user" action="register">Signup now</g:link>
         to start your own personal Music collection!
  </div>
    </g:else>
</div>
```

After getting the web designers involved and making a few Cascading Style Sheets (CSS) tweaks, the home page has gone from zero to something a little more respectable (see Figure 4-3).

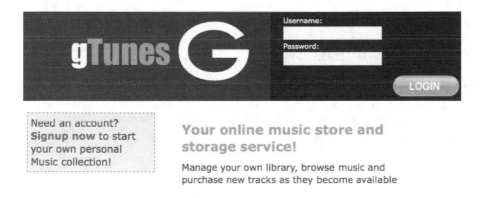

Figure 4-3. *The gTunes home page*

Implementing Registration

Before users can actually log in, they need to register with the site. You'll need to run the create-controller command to create a controller that will handle the site's login and registration logic:

```
grails create-controller com.g2one.gtunes.User
```

Once complete, the command will create a controller at the location grails-app/controllers/com/g2one/gtunes/UserController.groovy. Open up this controller and add a register action, as shown in Listing 4-51.

Listing 4-51. *Adding a register Action*

```
class UserController {
    def register = {}
}
```

As you can see from the example, the register action currently does nothing beyond delegating to a view. Nevertheless, it gives you the opportunity to craft a registration form. Listing 4-52 shows the shortened code from the grails-app/views/user/register.gsp view that will render the form.

Listing 4-52. *The register View*

```
<body id="body">
      <h1>Registration</h1>
    <p>Complete the form below to create an account!</p>
    <g:hasErrors bean="${user}">
                    <div class="errors">
      <g:renderErrors bean="${user}"></g:renderErrors>
                    </div>
    </g:hasErrors>

    <g:form action="register" name="registerForm">
        <div class="formField">
            <label for="login">Login:</label>
            <g:textField name="login" value="${user?.login}" />
        </div>
        <div class="formField">
            <label for="password">Password:</label>
            <g:passwordField name="password"
                             value="${user?.password}"/>
        </div>
        ...
        <g:submitButton class="formButton"
                        name="register"
                        value="Register" />
    </g:form>
</body>
```

The rendered registration form will look like the screenshot in Figure 4-4.

As you can see from Figure 4-4, you can also provide a confirm-password field to prevent users from entering their passwords incorrectly. With that done, let's consider the controller logic. To implement registration, you can take advantage of Grails' data-binding capabilities to bind incoming request parameters to a new User instance. At this point, validation takes over and the rest comes down to a little branching logic. Listing 4-53 shows the completed register action.

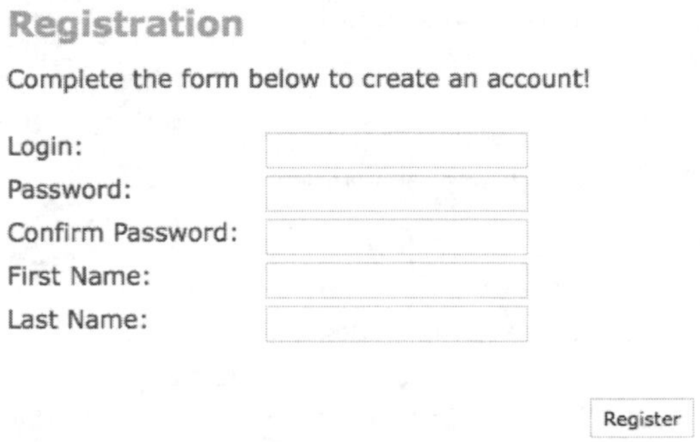

Registration

Complete the form below to create an account!

Login:

Password:

Confirm Password:

First Name:

Last Name:

Register

Figure 4-4. *The Registration screen*

Listing 4-53. *Implementing the register Action*

```
1 def register = {
2    if(request.method == 'POST') {
3        def u = new User(params)
4        if(u.password != params.confirm) {
5            u.errors.rejectValue("password", "user.password.dontmatch")
6            return [user:u]
7        }
8        else if(u.save()) {
9            session.user = u
10            redirect(controller:"store")
11        }
12        else {
13            return [user:u]
14        }
15    }
16 }
```

Many of the key concepts you've learned throughout the course of this chapter have been put to use in Listing 4-53, including a few new ones. Let's step through the code to see what's going on. First, on line 2, the code checks that the incoming request is a POST request because doing all this processing is pointless unless a form is submitted:

```
2    if(request.method == 'POST') {
```

Then on line 3, data binding takes over as it binds the incoming request parameters to the User instance:

```
3        def u = new User(params)
```

On lines 4 though 7, the code confirms whether the user has entered the correct password twice. If not, the password is rejected altogether:

```
4        if(u.password != params.confirm) {
5            u.errors.rejectValue("password", "user.password.dontmatch")
6            return [user:u]
7        }
```

Note how calling the rejectValue method of the org.springframework.validation. Errors interface accomplishes this. The rejectValue method accepts two arguments: the name of the field to reject and an error code to use. The code in Listing 4-53 uses the String user.password.dontmatch as the error code, which will appear when the <g:renderErrors> tag kicks in to display the errors. If you want to provide a better error message, you can open up the grails-app/i18n/messages.properties file and add a message like this:

```
user.password.dontmatch=The passwords specified don't match
```

Here's one final thing to note: directly after the call to rejectValue, a model from the controller action is returned, which triggers the rendering register.gsp so it can display the error.

Moving on to lines 8 through 11, you'll notice that the code attempts to persist the User by calling the save() method. If the attempt is successful, the User is redirected back to the StoreController:

```
8        else if(u.save()) {
9            session.user = u
10            redirect(controller:"store")
11        }
```

Finally, if a validation error does occur as a result of calling save(), then on line 13 a simple model is returned from the register action so that the register view can render the errors:

```
13            return [user:u]
```

Testing the Registration Code

Now let's consider how to test the action using the ControllerUnitTestCase class you learned about earlier. When you ran the create-controller command, a new unit test for the UserController was created for you in the test/unit directory.

You'll notice that the UserControllerTests class extends from a super class called ControllerUnitTestCase:

```
class UserControllerTests extends grails.test.ControllerUnitTestCase {
```

Now write a test for the case in which a user enters passwords that don't match. Listing 4-54 shows the testPasswordsDontMatch case that checks whether a password mismatch triggers a validation error.

Listing 4-54. *The testPasswordsMatch Test Case*

```
void testPasswordsMatch() {
    mockRequest.method = 'POST'
    mockDomain(User)

    mockParams.login = "joebloggs"
    mockParams.password = "password"
    mockParams.confirm = "different"
    mockParams.firstName = "Joe"
    mockParams.lastName = "Blogs"

    def model = controller.register()

    assert model?.user
    def user = model.user
    assert user.hasErrors()
    assertEquals "user.password.dontmatch", user.errors.password
}
```

Notice how the testPasswordsMatch test case populates the mockParams object with two passwords that differ. Then you have a call to the register action, which should reject the new User instance with a user.password.dontmatch error code. The last line of the test asserts that this is the case by inspecting the errors object on the User instance:

```
assertEquals "user.password.dontmatch", user.errors.password
```

The next scenario to consider is when a user enters invalid data into the registration form. You might need multiple tests that check for different kinds of data entered. Remember, you can never write too many tests! As an example of one potential scenario, Listing 4-55 shows a test that checks whether the user enters blank data or no data.

Listing 4-55. *The testRegistrationFailed Test*

```
void testRegistrationFailed() {
    mockRequest.method = 'POST'

    mockDomain(User)

    mockParams.login = ""
    def model = controller.register()
```

```
        assertNull mockSession.user
        assert model
        def user = model.user
        assert user.hasErrors()
        assertEquals "blank", user.errors.login
        assertEquals "nullable", user.errors.password
        assertEquals "nullable",
                        user.errors.firstName
        assertEquals "nullable", user.errors.firstName
}
```

Once again, you can see the use of the errors object to inspect that the appropriate constraints have been violated. Finally, you need to ensure two things to test a successful registration:

- The User instance has been placed in the session object.

- The request has been redirected appropriately.

Listing 4-56 shows an example of a test case that tests a successful user registration.

Listing 4-56. *Testing Successful Registration*

```
void testRegistrationSuccess() {
        mockRequest.method = 'POST'
        mockDomain(User)

        mockParams.login = "joebloggs"
        mockParams.password = "password"
        mockParams.confirm = "password"
        mockParams.firstName = "Joe"
        mockParams.lastName = "Blogs"

        def model = controller.register()
        assertEquals 'store',redirectArgs.controller
        assertNotNull mockSession.user
}
```

With the tests written, let's now consider how to allow users to log in to the gTunes application.

Allowing Users to Log In

Since you've already added the login form, all you need to do is implement the controller logic. A login process is a good candidate for a command object because it involves capturing information—the login and password—without needing to actually persist the data.

In this example you're going to create a LoginCommand that encapsulates the login logic, leaving the controller action to do the simple stuff. Listing 4-57 shows the code for the LoginCommand class, which is defined in the same file as the UserController class.

Listing 4-57. *The LoginCommand*

```
class LoginCommand {
    String login
    String password
    private u
    User getUser() {
        if(!u && login)
            u = User.findByLogin(login, [fetch:[purchasedSongs:'join']])
        return u
    }
    static constraints = {
        login blank:false, validator:{ val, cmd ->
            if(!cmd.user)
                return "user.not.found"
        }
        password blank:false, validator:{ val, cmd ->
            if(cmd.user && cmd.user.password != val)
                return "user.password.invalid"
        }
    }
}
```

The LoginCommand defines two properties that capture request parameters called login and password. The main logic of the code, however, is in the constraints definition. First, the blank constraint ensures that the login and/or password cannot be left blank. Second, a custom validator on the login parameter checks whether the user exists:

```
login blank:false, validator:{ val, cmd ->
    if(!cmd.user)
        return "user.not.found"
}
```

The custom validator constraint takes a closure that receives two arguments: the value and the LoginCommand instance. The code within the closure calls the getUser() method of the LoginCommand to check if the User exists. If the User doesn't exist, the code returns an error code—"user.not.found"—that signifies an error has occurred.

On the password parameter, another custom validator constraint checks whether the User has specified the correct password:

```
password blank:false, validator:{ val, cmd ->
    if(cmd.user && cmd.user.password != val)
        return "user.password.invalid"
}
```

Here the validator again uses the getUser() method of the LoginCommand to compare the password of the actual User instance with the value of the password property held by the LoginCommand. If the password is not correct, an error code is returned, triggering an error. You can add appropriate messages for each of the custom errors returned by the LoginCommand by adding them to the grails-app/i18n/messages.properties file:

```
user.not.found=User not found
user.password.invalid=Incorrect password
```

With that done, it's time to put the LoginCommand to use by implementing the login action in the UserController. Listing 4-58 shows the code for the login action.

Listing 4-58. *The login Action*

```
def login = { LoginCommand cmd ->
    if(request.method == 'POST') {
        if(!cmd.hasErrors()) {
            session.user = cmd.getUser()
            redirect(controller:'store')
        }
        else {
            render(view:'/store/index', model:[loginCmd:cmd])
        }
    }
    else {
        render(view:'/store/index')
    }
}
```

With the command object in place, the controller simply needs to do is what it does best: issue redirects and render views. Again, like the register action, login processing kicks in only when a POST request is received. Then if the command object has no errors, the user is placed into the session and the request is redirected to the StoreController.

Testing the Login Process

Testing the login action differs slightly from testing the register action due to the involvement of the command object. Let's look at a few scenarios that need to be tested. First, you need to test the case when a user is not found (see Listing 4-59).

Listing 4-59. *The* testLoginUserNotFound *Test Case*

```
void testLoginUserNotFound() {
    mockRequest.method = 'POST'
    mockDomain(User)
    MockUtils.prepareForConstraintsTests(LoginCommand)
    def cmd = new LoginCommand(login:"fred", password:"letmein")
    cmd.validate()
    controller.login(cmd)
```

```
        assertTrue cmd.hasErrors()
        assertEquals "user.not.found", cmd.errors.login
        assertEquals "/store/index", renderArgs.view
}
```

As you can see from Listing 4-59, when testing command objects you have to explicitly create the command and call the validate() method on it. Notice also how you can use the prepareForConstraintsTests method of the grails.test.MockUtils class to mock the validation behavior of a command object:

```
MockUtils.prepareForConstraintsTests(LoginCommand)
```

You can then inspect the command for errors as demonstrated by the following two lines from Listing 4-59:

```
assertTrue cmd.hasErrors()
assertEquals "user.not.found", cmd.errors.login
```

The next scenario to test is when a user enters an incorrect password. Listing 4-60 shows the testLoginPasswordInvalid test case that demonstrates how to do this.

Listing 4-60. *The* testLoginPasswordInvalid *Test Case*

```
void testLoginPasswordInvalid() {
        mockRequest.method = 'POST'
        mockDomain(User, [new User(login:"fred", password:"realpassword")])
        MockUtils.prepareForConstraintsTests(LoginCommand)
        def cmd = new LoginCommand(login:"fred", password:"letmein")
        cmd.validate()
        controller.login(cmd)
        assertTrue cmd.hasErrors()
        assertEquals "user.password.invalid", cmd.errors.password
        assertEquals "/store/index", renderArgs.view
}
```

Unlike the example in Listing 4-59, the testLoginPasswordInvalid test case actually provides mock data using the mockDomain method:

```
mockDomain(User, [new User(login:"fred", password:"realpassword")])
```

The second argument of the mockDomain method provides the data that all the query methods should operate on. In this case, the code specifies a mock User instance that has a password with the value of "realpassword." Then you can use the LoginCommand to simulate the entry of an incorrect password:

```
def cmd = new LoginCommand(login:"fred", password:"letmein")
```

The remainder of the test is largely similar to Listing 4-59.

The last test to write is one that tests a successful login. Listing 4-61 shows how to do this.

Listing 4-61. *The* testLoginSuccess *Test Case*

```
void testLoginSuccess() {
    mockRequest.method = 'POST'
    mockDomain(User, [new User(login:"fred", password:"letmein")])
    MockUtils.prepareForConstraintsTests(LoginCommand)
    def cmd = new LoginCommand(login:"fred", password:"letmein")
    cmd.validate()
    controller.login(cmd)
    assertFalse cmd.hasErrors()
    assertNotNull mockSession.user
    assertEquals "store", redirectArgs.controller
}
```

The testLoginSuccess test case again uses the mockDomain method to set up the domain model, and then uses an appropriate LoginCommand to simulate a valid login. As you can see from the last two assertions, you can use the mockSession object to check whether the User instance has been placed in the session and inspect redirectArgs to ensure that an appropriate redirect has occurred.

Summary

And with that, you've implemented the login and registration process for the gTunes application. We'll present throughout the book many more examples of using controllers, but in this chapter you've obtained a strong grounding in the core concepts that apply to controllers.

From data binding and validation to command objects, Grails' controller mechanism offers you a lot of tools. To fully see how everything fits together, you'll need a strong understanding of Grails' view technology—Groovy Server Pages (GSP). In the next chapter, we'll take a much closer look at GSP and what it has to offer, with its dynamic tag libraries and templating mechanisms.

CHAPTER 5

■ ■ ■

Understanding Views

View technologies for web applications in the open source world appear to be a rather popular topic with the seemingly endless number of them available for Java. There always appears to be a newer, better one to learn if you grow tired of the incumbent JSP. JSP, however, remains the most popular view technology; produced by Sun to compete with Microsoft's Active Server Pages (ASP), JSP has become the industry standard, and there is a high level of developer knowledge surrounding JSP.

JSP allows developers to mix traditional markup languages such as HTML with Java code (called *scriptlets*) to produce dynamic output. On the downside, this facility is extremely open to abuse; therefore, there are custom tag libraries that add the ability to abstract logic from a JSP page via tags. JSP has been augmented with two missing ingredients, the JSP Standard Tag Library (JSTL) and an expression language (EL), to bring it up to speed with some of its open source competitors.

So, given JSP's maturity, robustness, and familiarity within the industry, why on Earth would you need yet another view technology for Grails with Groovy Server Pages (GSP)? The answer lies with the Groovy runtime environment:

- To fully take advantage of Grails, the view technology requires knowledge of Groovy's runtime environment and associated dynamic method dispatching.

- Groovy provides a far more powerful expression language, including GPath expressions, Groovy bean notation, and overridable operators.

- Other Groovy features such as regular expression support, GStrings, and an expressive syntax for maps and lists make it perfect for a view technology.

Of course, for any new view technology, it is important not to fall into the same traps that JSP fell into in its early iterations. Mixing scriptlets and markup code is most definitely recognized as a bad thing, and to this end, GSP provides a mechanism for creating custom tags just as JSP does but without sacrificing any agility.

The Basics

You've already been exposed to GSP at various points throughout the book, and we're sure you are verging on the expert level already. Regardless, it will no doubt prove invaluable to discuss the basics of GSP to help you fully grasp all the concepts within it.

It is important to note that GSP is actually remarkably similar to JSP, and you will know from experience that with JSP, by default, a number of objects are simply *available*. These include the request, response, and session objects—the same ones you saw in Chapter 4, which discussed controllers. If you recall, that particular discussion mentioned that a few additional objects are available to controllers, including the flash object. Well, you'll be pleased to know these can also be accessed from GSP views, as can an additional out attribute, which is a java.io.Writer instance representing the response output. Table 5-1 describes the GSP attributes available.

Table 5-1. *GSP Attributes*

Attribute	Description
application	The ServletContext instance
flash	The flash object for working with flash scope, as discussed in Chapter 7
out	The response Writer instance
params	A map of request parameters
request	The HttpServletRequest instance
response	The HttpServletResponse instance
session	The HttpSession instance

You already know how to get to these from controllers, but what about in views? Well, unsurprisingly, GSP supports the same constructs available in JSP as well as a few additional ones. This may start to look a little like a JSP 101 tutorial in the next few examples, but don't be confused; you're definitely dealing with Groovy, not Java.

Understanding the Model

One of the fundamental activities in any MVC pattern, such as that which Grails employs, is to pass information (the model) to the view for rendering. In Chapter 4 you saw this in action, but just to recap, Listing 5-1 shows an example of how you can achieve this in Grails.

Listing 5-1. *Creating the Model*

```
package com.g2one.gtunes

class StoreController {

    def shop = {
        def genreList = Album.withCriteria {
            projections {
                distinct "genre"
            }
        }
        [genres:genreList.sort()]
    }
}
```

In the previous listing (the shop action of the StoreController), the result is a map with one element, the key for which is a string with the value genres. This key (and its value) is then placed in a GSP's model (or *binding* for those more familiar with Groovy lingo), which means it is accessible as a variable in the same way as the page attributes you saw earlier in Table 5-1.

In the following sections, you will see examples of a genres variable being referenced. Just remember that this variable didn't appear by magic. It is passed to the view via the controller in code like in the previous listing.

Page Directives

GSP supports a limited subset of the page directives available in JSP. A *page directive* is an instruction that appears at the top of a GSP that performs an action that the page relies on. As an example, it could set the content type, perform an import, or set a page property, which could even be container-specific.

One of the more useful of these is the contentType directive, which allows you to set the content type of the response. This is useful in that it allows you to use GSP to output formats other than HTML markup, such as XML or plain text. Using the directive is identical to JSP, with the directive appearing at the top of the page and starting with <%@.

Listing 5-2 sets the content type to text/xml, which allows you to output XML; this can be useful when working with technologies such as Ajax.

Listing 5-2. *The contentType Page Directive*

```
<%@ page contentType="text/xml; charset=UTF-8" %>
```

Another page directive available is the import directive, which is analogous to the import statement in a Java or Groovy class. However, because Groovy imports many classes by default and Grails encourages an MVC architecture, where much of the logic should be placed in a controller and not the view, the usage of import is not too common. Nevertheless, Listing 5-3 shows an example of importing the Time class from the java.sql.* package.

Listing 5-3. *The import Page Directive*

```
<%@ page import="java.sql.Time" %>
```

■**Note** Groovy imports the java.lang, java.util, java.io, java.net, groovy.lang, and groovy.util packages by default.

Groovy Scriptlets

GSP tries to stay as true to JSP as possible, and therefore it supports traditional JSP scriptlet blocks using the <%...%> syntax. Essentially, as soon as you type the opening <% declaration, you have entered the world of Groovy and can type whatever Groovy code you so choose up until the closing %> declaration.

What this means is that you can use scriptlets to perform loops and logical if statements merely by combining scriptlet declarations, as shown in Listing 5-4.

Listing 5-4. *Scriptlets in Action*

```
<html>
    <body>
    <% 3.times { %>
        <p>I'm printed three times!</p>
    <% } %>
    </body>
</html>
```

This type of syntax will be familiar to users of Rails, because it bears a striking resemblance to Rails' view technology RHTML (and indeed many other view technologies). However, you should note that scriptlets are available more to align the syntax with JSP and, in practice, are discouraged in favor of GSP tags, which you will see in the section "Built-in Grails Tags."

Although the previous syntax allows arbitrary code to be inserted between the opening and closing declarations, it doesn't actually explicitly output anything when inside the scriptlet block. In other words, as with the previous example, you have to use a closing %> bracket to close the scriptlet expression in order to define what you want repeated three times. You can, however, use the out attribute mentioned earlier to output to the response:

```
<% out << "print me!" %>
```

The previous code will print the text "print me!" to the response using the out attribute. As you can imagine, having all these out << statements all over the place can get a little tedious, so GSP supports another syntax inherited from JSP through the <%=...%> statement (note the equal sign directly after the opening declaration). Essentially, the following example is equivalent to what you saw in the previous code:

```
<%= "print me!" %>
```

Here the = sign after the opening scriptlet bracket ensures that the result of whatever follows is printed to the response. The response in general is a mix of markup and code that results in some text being sent to the browser or client. Now that you've seen GSP's similarities with JSP, let's look at a feature you won't find in JSP: embedded GStrings.

GSP as GStrings

In recent times, since the introduction of JSTL, using scriptlets and declarations such as those shown in the previous section has been looked down on a bit. Instead, there is an expression language in JSP that you can use in combination with the <c:out> standard tag to output values, as shown in Listing 5-5.

Listing 5-5. *JSP c:out Tag*

```
<%-- Output the album title --%>
<p><c:out value="${album.title}" /></p>
```

■**Tip** The previous JSP example uses the syntax `<%--.....--%>` for comments that should not be present in the rendered response. These comments are also supported in GSP using the same syntax.

In addition to the previous rather verbose tag, you would also need to import the tag library, which contains the `<c:out>` tag using a page directive at the top of the JSP. All this amounts to a lot of effort just to use a tag that lets you render values to the response. Luckily, with GSP it is a little bit simpler, because of its support for embedded GString values:

```
<p>${album.title}</p>
```

A GSP, if you think about it, is essentially one big GString, thus allowing the same `${...}` expressions nested within it as found in JSP. The expressions allowed within the GStrings are not, thankfully, limited to simply referencing properties. The full capability Groovy offers in terms of navigating object graphs is at your fingertips, which often becomes useful when iterating, as you will see in the next section.

Built-in Grails Tags

GSP has a number of built-in tags for performing basic operations such as looping, switching, and using logical `if` statements. In general, tags are preferable to embedding scriptlets because they promote a cleaner separation of concerns and allow you to create well-formed markup.

Each GSP tag requires the prefix `g:` before the tag name so that it is recognized as being a GSP tag. Unlike JSP, which requires directives to import tag libraries, no additional page directive is needed.

■**Note** GSP also supports JSP custom tag libraries that can be imported with the standard JSP `taglib` directive.

In the next few sections, you'll see the tags that are built in to Grails. These tags are there by default and require no extra work by the developer.

Setting Variables with Tags

Occasionally, it is useful to set the value of a variable or define a new variable within the scope (commonly referred to as the *page context*) of a GSP. Both use cases can be achieved via the `<g:set>` tag, which will set or define a variable in the page context regardless of whether it already exists. The `<g:set>` tag takes two attributes: the `var` attribute, which defines the name of the variable to set, and a `value` attribute, which is generally an expression:

```
<g:set var="albumTitle" value="${album.title}" />
```

By default, variables set with `<g:set>` are assumed to be within the page scope. Having said that, you can set a variable in the `session` scope simply by using the `scope` attribute:

```
<g:set scope="session" var="user" value="${user}" />
```

In addition to the `session` scope, a number of other scopes are available:

- `application`: Stores variables for the scope of the whole application

- `session`: Stores variables for the scope of the user session

- `flash`: Stores variables for the current request and the next request only

- `request`: Stores variables for the scope of the current request

- `page`: Stores variables for the scope of the rendering page

Another fairly basic requirement, along with setting variables, is the ability to conditionally display information. In the next section, you'll see how you can achieve this.

Logical Tags

As previously mentioned, it is often useful to display information based on a condition. At the most basic level, it is useful to have basic programming constructs in the view such as `if` and `else` to facilitate this. GSP has the aptly named `<g:if>`, `<g:elseif>`, and `<g:else>` tags that, as with any regular programming construct, are used in conjunction with one another to conditionally display output.

The `<g:if>` and `<g:elseif>` tags take an attribute called `test` whose value can be in expression language (that is, statements surrounded by `${..}`), as shown in Listing 5-6.

Listing 5-6. *Usage of Logical Blocks*

```
<g:if test="${album?.year < 1980 && album?.genre == 'Rock'}">
        Classic rock
</g:if>
<g:elseif test="${album?.year >= 1980 && album?.genre == 'Rock'}">
        Modern Rock
</g:elseif>
<g:else>
        Other
</g:else>
```

An interesting aspect of the previous code is the usage of Groovy's safe dereference operator, `?..` The operator really comes into its own when used in views, because it is often useful to navigate an object graph and display information only if all elements navigated through don't evaluate to `null`. If you look at the views generated during scaffolding, you will observe a lot of this in action. Yet another useful feature of the method is that it allows the optional execution of methods. For example, you may for some reason want the title of the album in uppercase, in which case you would use an expression like the following:

```
${album.title.toUpperCase()}
```

Unfortunately, if either the album or title of the album in the previous code is null, a horrid NullPointerException will be thrown. To circumvent this, the safe dereference operator comes to the rescue:

```
${album?.title?.toUpperCase()}
```

Here the toUpperCase method is executed *only* if it can be reached; otherwise, the entire expression evaluates to null. This is useful because null in GSP results in an empty string being printed to the response.

That's it for now on logical tags, although you will see their usage popping up throughout the book.

Iterative Tags

Iterating over collections of objects is one of the more common tasks when working with any view technology, GSP being no exception. Again, scriptlets could be used to achieve iteration, but why would you? You have GSP tags, which allow for a much cleaner transition between code and markup.

The first tag we'll cover is the <g:each> tag, which is essentially the tag equivalent of the Groovy each method and in fact simply delegates to this method internally, as shown in Listing 5-7.

Listing 5-7. *Iterating with <g:each>*

```
<g:each in="${album.songs?}">
    <span class-"tag">${it.title}</span>
</g:each>
```

■**Tip** You can also use the safe dereference operator at the end of expressions as in the previous example, which will not iterate if the songs property is null.

Like its closely related JSTL cousin, the <g:each> tag allows you to optionally specify the name of the object within the current iteration. The name of the object, as with closures, defaults to an argument called it, as shown in Listing 5-7. When using nested tags, however, it is good practice to name the variable being iterated over, which you can do with the var attribute, as shown in Listing 5-8.

Listing 5-8. *Iterating with <g:each> and a Named Variable*

```
<g:each var="song" in="${album.songs?}">
    <span class="song">${song.title}</span>
</g:each>
```

GSP tags are, at their roots, just closures, and in Groovy the variable it refers to the default argument of the *innermost* closure. If you use the <g:each> tag without declaring a var attribute and try to reference the default it variable within a nested GSP tag, this will result in evaluating it to the *current* innermost tag and not the surrounding <g:each> tag. By naming the variable used by `<g:each>` using the var attribute, you circumvent any conflicts such as this. If you remember that GSP tags are closures, you will have no issue at all adapting to the mind-set.

The next iterative tag GSP provides is the `<g:while>` tag that behaves like the traditional while loop by waiting for the expression specified within the test attribute to evaluate to false. As with any while loop, the condition should always end up evaluating to false at some point; otherwise, you will end up in a never-ending loop. Listing 5-9 shows an example that loops while the variable i is greater than zero.

Listing 5-9. *The <g:while> Tag*

```
<g:set var="i" expr="${album.songs?.size()}" />
<g:while test="${i > 0}">
      <g:set var="i" expr="${i-1}" />
</g:while>
```

Here you get the total number of songs from the album and store them in the variable i. You then start a `<g:while>` loop that will decrement the i variable on each iteration. The loop will continue until i reaches zero. The loop is equivalent to the following Groovy code:

```
while(i > 0) i=i-1
```

Using `<g:each>` and `<g:while>` are not the only way to loop over a collection. In the next section, you'll see constructs that provide the powerful combination of filtering and iteration.

Filtering and Iteration

With some of the new methods that accept closures in Groovy that provide the powerful ability to filter and search collections (such as collect, findAll, and grep), it would seem a shame if that power were not extended into GSP tags. Fear not—there are tag equivalents of these three that allow some pretty powerful filtering capabilities.

The collect Tag

The `<g:collect>` tag allows you to iterate over and collect properties of objects within a collection. Say, for example, you want the titles of all albums; you can achieve this simply with `<g:collect>`, as shown in Listing 5-10.

Listing 5-10. *Using <g:collect> to Collect Values*

```
<ol>
    <g:collect in="${albums}" expr="${it.title}">
          <li>${it}</li>
    </g:collect>
</ol>
```

In the previous example, an HTML list of album titles is created by passing a collection of albums to the in attribute via the ${...} syntax. The second attribute, the expr attribute, contains an expression that is used to specify what should be collected (in this case the title property). Again, you use the default it argument within the expression the same way as you would in a closure. In fact, the previous code is equivalent to the scriptlet code in Listing 5-11.

Listing 5-11. *Equivalent Scriptlet Using a Closure*

```
<ol>
    <% albums.collect{ it.title }.each { %>
            <li>${it}</li>
    <%}%>
</ol>
```

As you can see, the expression equates to what is found within the curly braces of the collect closure. Whatever you can place in there can also be placed inside the expr attribute.

Of course, you could also do this with a GPath expression. If you recall what you learned about GPath so far, if you reference the title property and use the dereference operator on a *list* of albums, it will produce a list of titles, as shown in Listing 5-12.

Listing 5-12. *Using GPath to Iterate Over Album Titles*

```
<ol>
    <g:each in="${albums.title}" >
            <li>${it}</li>
    </g:each>
</ol>
```

The <g:collect> tag does, however, give you another option and allows the logic within the expr attribute to be in your control.

The findAll Tag

Collecting properties from a collection via the object graph is handy, but sometimes you want to iterate over only those values that meet a certain criteria. This is often achieved by iterating over all elements and having nested if statements. However, using <g:findAll>, as shown in Listing 5-13, is far more elegant.

Listing 5-13. *Using <g:findAll> to Locate Specific Elements*

```
<g:findAll in="${albums}" expr="${it.songs?.title.contains('Love')}">
    <li>
        ${it.title}
    </li>
</g:findAll>
```

This is an interesting example because it is another demonstration of the power of GPath, Groovy's expression language. The expression in bold references the default argument it, which is the current Album instance being iterated over, and then uses GPath to retrieve a collection of all the names of the songs.

The songs property itself is in fact a collection too (a java.util.Set to be specific) and does not have a title property, but GPath recognizes that the reference to the title property is an attempt to retrieve a collection of name properties from the contained elements within the songs property.

Since the result is a collection, you can invoke the regular JDK contains method to look up all albums that have the world *Love* in their title. The result is far more readable than a bunch of nested if statements and is another case where you can see how a Groovy view technology like GSP just makes a remarkable amount of sense.

You've seen quite a few options to perform different kinds of logical statements and iteration. Controlling the logical flow of a view is not, however, the only task you have when writing the view. One common activity is linking between controllers and actions, which you will look at next; but before that, there is something important to note. This marks the end of the built-in tags. The tags you've seen so far are internally handled and optimized by GSP. The next section shifts focus to Grails dynamic tags and how they differ from the built-in tags.

Grails Dynamic Tags

Dynamic tags in Grails are those provided through classes called *tag libraries*, which can be found within the grails-app/taglib directory of any Grails project. Grails provides a number of tag libraries out of the box that you will see in the next few sections; then you will explore how to create your own tag libraries.

First you need to understand what makes dynamic tags different from other tags besides the fact that they are provided by these libraries. Fundamentally, they can be used the same way as any other tag. For example, you can use the <g:link> tag like the built-in tags you saw previously without requiring any import directive.

More interestingly, dynamic tags can also be invoked as methods from scriptlets and GString expressions. Why is this useful? To maintain a clean syntax and valid XML, it is best to avoid nesting tags within tag attributes. In JSP you often see code like in Listing 5-14 that becomes difficult to read and is not well-formed markup.

Listing 5-14. *Unattractive JSP Example*

```
<a href="<c:out value="${application.contextPath}" />/show.jsp">A dynamic link</a>
```

Clearly, because of GSP's rather JSP-like nature, this problem could have been inherited if it were not for the dynamic nature of Groovy. So, how would you invoke a GSP tag as a method call? Observe the example in Listing 5-15.

Listing 5-15. *An Example of a GSP Tag as a Method Call*

```
<!-- With a regular tag -->
<a href="<g:createLink action="list" />">A dynamic link</a>

<!-- As a method call -->
<a href="${createLink(action:'list')}">A dynamic link</a>
```

The two previous examples produce the same result. They call a tag called createLink, which creates a link to the list action. The second example is notably cleaner and produces well-formed markup. In addition, the body of the tag can be provided as the last argument to the method call.

You can see an example of this in action in the create and edit views generated by scaffolding. As part of form validation, these views highlight the problematic field by surrounding the offender with a red box. You achieve this through the hasErrors tags, which will evaluate if a particular bean field has any validation errors and will set a CSS class, the name of which is the last argument on the surrounding div element if the field does contain errors, as shown in Listing 5-16.

Listing 5-16. *Field Validation Example*

```
<div class="${hasErrors(bean:album,field:'title','errors')}">
    ...
</div>
```

These are just a few examples; as you'll see in a moment, you can create your own tags that can be invoked in the same manner. First, however, let's take a tour through the tags that are already available to you, starting with linking.

Linking Tags

With all these controllers and actions that end up being created, it may become a bit challenging to remember the URL patterns to link to them. Also, the context path of your application could change depending which environment you deploy to. So, how can you make sure you are always linking to the right place in a consistent manner? Well, luckily Grails provides a number of tags to handle linking in an elegant way, the first of which is the aptly named <g:link>.

The Link Tag

The <g:link> tag will essentially create a simple HTML anchor tag based on the supplied attributes, which include the following:

- controller: The controller name to link to

- action: The action name to link to

- id: The identifier to append to the end of the URI

- params: Any parameters to pass as a map

One of either the controller attribute or the action attribute is required. If the controller attribute is specified but no action attribute is specified, the tag will link to the default action of the controller. If, on the other hand, an action attribute is specified but no controller attribute is specified, the *currently executing* controller will be linked to.

Beyond the previous attributes, the <g:link> tag also supports all attributes that the regular HTML anchor tag supports, which can be added as required.

It's time for some examples. Using <g:link> is pretty trivial and intuitive, and of course the values of the attributes could just as well be expressions of the ${...} kind if dynamic linking is required, as shown in Listing 5-17.

Listing 5-17. *Basic Linking with <g:link>*

```
<g:link controller="album" action="list">List Albums</g:link>
<g:link action="show" id="1">Show album with id 1</g:link>
```

Of interest may be the `params` attribute, which takes a map of request parameters to pass via the link. In fact, the current request parameters can even be passed from one action to the other by using this attribute in combination with the `params` object, which if you recall is an instance of `java.util.Map`, as shown in Listing 5-18.

Listing 5-18. *Using Parameters with <g:link>*

```
<g:link controller="album"
        action="list"
        params="[max:10,order:'title']">Show first ten ordered by Title</g:link>

<g:link action="create"
        params="${params}">Pass parameters from this action to next</g:link>
```

The first example uses the `params` attribute in conjunction with a map of parameters and provides your first exposure to another feature of GSP tags: attributes can be specified as maps with the `[key:value]` syntax. This allows for composite attribute values and minimizes the need for messy nested tags.

Finally, the second example demonstrates what was mentioned previously. Instead of specifying a map explicitly, you provide a reference to the `params` object via the `${...}` expression syntax, which then allows passing parameters from the current page to the linked page. Next you'll see how to create links to other resources.

■Note Grails' linking tags automatically rewrite the links based on the URL mappings you have defined. URL mappings will be covered in more detail in Chapter 6.

The createLink and createLinkTo Tags

The `<g:createLink>` tag has already been seen in action and probably needs less of an introduction. Simply put, if it's not clear from the examples, `<g:createLink>` takes the same arguments as the `<g:link>` tag except it produces just the textual link and not an HTML anchor tag. In fact, the `<g:link>` tag actually delegates to `<g:createLink>` when creating its `href` attribute.

So, what is this useful for? You could use it within a regular anchor tag or possibly as a value for a JavaScript variable, as shown in Listing 5-19.

Listing 5-19. *Examples of createLink*

```
<a href="${createLink(action:'list')}">List Albums</a>
<script type="text/javascript">
    var listAlbumsLink = "${createLink(action:'list')}";
</script>
```

Another tag, similar in both name and usage to `<g:createLink>`, is the `<g:createLinkTo>` tag, which allows convenient linking to resources within the web application's context path.

This tag is most commonly used for linking to images and style sheets and again can be seen in action in the views generated by scaffolding:

```
<link rel="stylesheet" href="${createLinkTo(dir:'css',file:'main.css')}"></link>
```

As is apparent from the previous examples and in Listing 5-19, both tags tend to be used via method calls as opposed to markup, because the values produced by them are usually nested within attributes of other tags.

Now that we've covered linking, another common activity is to create forms so that users can enter data to be captured by server-side code. In the following section, you'll see how Grails makes this easier.

Creating Forms and Fields

A form is most commonly a collection of fields that a user populates with data, although occasionally you find forms that consist entirely of hidden fields and no user interaction whatsoever. Nevertheless, how this is achieved depends on the type of field; in other words, the user interacts differently depending on whether it is a text field, a drop-down select, or a radio button.

Clearly, certain fields map nicely onto existing Java (and hence Groovy) types. Check boxes are great for Boolean values, text fields are good for strings, and selects are good when you have strings that can be contained only within a certain list of values (such as enums in Java 5).

To this end, most Java web frameworks provide some mechanism to make form elements (or fields) interoperate smoothly with Java types, Grails being no different. Before you get too deeply involved in looking at the different kinds of fields, let's take care of the basics by looking at how Grails helps in defining forms.

The form Tag

Building on what you have seen in linking, the first tag you are going to look at is the `<g:form>` tag, which is equivalent to the standard HTML `<form>` tag, except it allows the same arguments as those shown with the `<g:link>` tag to allow easy submission to a specific controller and/or action, as shown in Listing 5-20.

Listing 5-20. *An Example Form Tag from grails-app/views/user/register.gsp*

```
<g:form action="register" name="registerForm">
    ...
</g:form>
```

By default, the `<g:form>` tag uses the POST method for form submissions, meaning the previous example is roughly equivalent to the HTML definition (minus the closing tag):

```
<form action="/gTunes/user/register" method="POST" name="registerForm">
    ...
</form>
```

As an alternative to Listing 5-20, you can define the `<g:form>` tag using a single `url` attribute that uses the `key:value` map syntax to define the controller and action combination, as shown in Listing 5-21.

Listing 5-21. *A `<g:form>` Tag with url Attribute*

```
<g:form url="[controller:'user', action:'register']">
    ...
</g:form>
```

Of course, a form is of little use without some fields, the first of which to be discussed is the *text field*. In HTML, most fields are handled by the `<input>` tag, which has a `type` attribute to change its behavior and appearance. The downside of this approach is that it is not clear what its purpose is from simply looking at the tag.

Grails provides a number of wrapper tags that encapsulate the different types of HTML inputs into more meaningful tags.

The textField Tag

First up is the `<g:textField>` tag that, unsurprisingly, handles entry of textual values. The `<g:textField>` tag takes a `name` attribute, representing the name of the parameter to send as part of the form submission, along with the associated `value` attribute, as shown in Listing 5-22.

Listing 5-22. *Example `<g:textField>` Usage*

```
<g:form action="register" name="registerForm">
    ...
    <g:textField name="login" value="${user?.login}"></g:textField>
    ...
</g:form>
```

The previous `<g:textField>` definition will result in HTML input such as the following:

```
<input type="text" name="login" value="A Login Name" />
```

Check Boxes and Radio Buttons

Check boxes are often used as a representation of Boolean values from a domain model. Unfortunately, many frameworks place a lot of burden on the developer both to render check boxes in their correct state and to handle the server-side processing as to whether the check boxes are checked.

Grails, on the other hand, provides a `<g:checkBox>` tag that accepts a Boolean `value` attribute and will render the tag in its correct state. In addition, Grails transparently handles check box processing through its automatic type conversion and data binding facility (discussed in Chapter 7), as shown in Listing 5-23.

Listing 5-23. *Example <g:checkBox> Tag*

```
<g:checkBox name="aBooleanValue" value="${true}" />
```

Closely related to check boxes are radio buttons, which are used in groups, because they represent a one-from-many interaction. For example, two radio buttons must each be given the same name to be placed in the same group, and only one button can be selected at any one time.

Grails has a `<g:radio>` tag that provides a convenient way to define radio buttons and also to calculate that one has been checked.

In Listing 5-24, two radio buttons are defined in the same group. The one that has been checked is calculated using the hypothetical someValue variable.

Listing 5-24. *Example <g:radio> Tags*

```
<p>
    <g:radio name="myGroup" value="1" checked="${someValue == 1}" /> Radio 1
</p>
<p>
    <g:radio name="myGroup" value="2" checked="${someValue == 2}" /> Radio 2
</p>
```

Handling Lists of Values

When dealing with enumerated values (those that can be only a specific set of values), it is often useful to constrain what the user can enter by presenting an HTML select box as opposed to a free text-entry field.

To make creating selects much simpler, Grails provides a `<g:select>` tag that accepts a list or range of values via a from attribute. The currently selected value can be set with the value attribute.

The example in Listing 5-25 creates a select to choose a genre.

Listing 5-25. *Example <g:select> Usage*

```
<g:select name="genre" from="${['Rock', 'Blues', 'Jazz']}"
          value="${album.genre}" />
```

The following is the resulting HTML select, given an album with a genre of Rock:

```
<select name="genre">
    <option value="Rock" selected="selected">Rock</option>
    <option value="Blues">Blues</option>
    <option value="Jazz">Jazz</option>
</select>
```

Clearly, just going by the two examples, using the `<g:select>` tag can save you from writing a few lines of code. Its usefulness extends beyond this thanks to two additional attributes that allow `<g:select>` to be used in combination with object graphs and relationships.

The first is the `optionKey` attribute, which allows customization of the `value` attribute within each option tag of an HTML select. This may seem a little odd that an `optionKey` attribute customizes an attribute called value, but if you think of each `<option>` element as a key/value pair, it begins to make sense. The `optionValue` attribute, on the other hand, allows customization of the value that appears within the body of each option tag.

Using these two in combination can, for example, allow you to create a select from a list of domain object instances, as shown in Listing 5-26.

Listing 5-26. *Using <g:select> on a List of Domain Objects*

```
<g:select name="album.id" from="${Album.list()}"
            optionKey="id" optionValue="title"/>
```

The previous example takes a list of albums and creates an HTML select where the `value` attribute within the option tag is the `id` of the `Album` and the value within the body of each option is the `title` property of each `Album`. The result will resemble something like the following:

```
<select name="album.id">
    <option value="1">Undertow</option>
    ...
</select>
```

In addition to the general-purpose `<g:select>` tag, Grails provides a few others that may come in handy. The `<g:currencySelect>`, `<g:localeSelect>`, and `<g:timeZoneSelect>` tags are convenience tags for working with `java.util.Currency`, `java.util.Locale`, and `java.util.TimeZone` instances, respectively.

Unlike the `<g:select>` tag, each of these takes only two attributes: a `name` attribute for the name of the select and a `value` attribute, which takes an instance of one of the aforementioned classes, as shown in Listing 5-27.

Listing 5-27. *Currency, Locale, and Time Zone Selects*

```
<%-- Sets the currency to the currency of the Locale within the request --%>
<g:currencySelect
            name="myCurrency"
            value="${ Currency.getInstance(request.locale) }" />

<%-- Sets the locale to the locale of the request --%>
<g:localeSelect name="myLocale" value="${ request.locale }" />

<%-- Sets value to default time zone --%>
<g:timeZoneSelect name="myTimeZone" value="${ TimeZone.getDefault() }" />
```

Working with Dates

Dates can be represented in a number of ways, from drop-down selects to advanced JavaScript calendars. One of the more common ways, because of its nonreliance on JavaScript, is to use a combination of HTML select boxes to specify the date or time, with each select representing a unit of time: year, month, day, minute, hour, and second.

Grails provides support for creating such fields (and automatically performing type conversion onto date instances) using the `<g:datePicker>` tag, as shown in Listing 5-28.

Listing 5-28. *A Basic Date Picker*

```
<g:datePicker name="myDate" value="${new Date()}" />
```

At its most basic level, the `<g:datePicker>` tag takes a name attribute and a value attribute as a `java.util.Date` instance. In the previous example, it creates a `<g:datePicker>` for the current time, which consists of selects for the year, month, day, minute, hour, *and* second.

Clearly, it is not always useful to have that level of precision, so the `<g:datePicker>` tag provides the aptly named `precision` attribute for changing how many selects it renders. For example, to render only the year, month, and day selects, the following will suffice:

```
<g:datePicker name="myDate" value="${new Date()}" precision="day" />
```

All in all, Grails provides quite a few tools in your toolbox for simplifying the creation of forms. Given that forms allow users to enter data, often in a free-form fashion, implementing form handling is often one of the most challenging and error-prone activities in web application development.

To ensure data integrity, form validation is necessary and can be achieved on the client side using JavaScript. However, client-side validation should only ever be seen as a usability enhancement and not a replacement for server-side validation. Luckily, Grails provides solid support for performing validation with specialized validation and error-handling tags.

Validation and Error Handling

Having learned how to apply constraints to your domain model in Chapter 3, clearly it becomes useful at some point to display validation errors in the view when they occur. Of course, you could use scriptlets to iterate over the errors of a domain object and output them explicitly, but that's an awful lot of work that Grails can do for you. Just to recap how validation works, take a look at the state diagram shown in Figure 5-1.

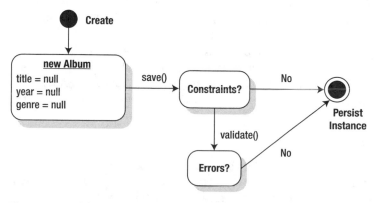

Figure 5-1. *Validation state diagram*

The hasErrors Tag

It is often useful to conditionally display information depending on whether there is an error. To this end, Grails provides a `<g:hasErrors>` tag that supports the following attributes:

- `bean`: A bean instance to inspect for errors

- `field`: The name of the field to check for errors

- `model`: An alternative to specifying a bean; an entire model (map) can be checked

If you recall, you have already seen the `<g:hasErrors>` tag used as a method, but it is also equally applicable as a tag. Interestingly, if no attributes are specified whatsoever, the tag will scan the entire request scope for beans and check each object found for errors. Since the `<g:hasErrors>` tag is often used in conjunction with `<g:eachError>`, we'll cover that next, followed by an example.

The eachError Tag

If a bean instance does have errors, it is useful to iterate over them and display each in turn. This can be done simply with the `<g:eachError>` tag, which takes attributes identical to those expected by the `<g:hasErrors>` tag.

Listing 5-29 demonstrates how to use the `hasErrors` and `eachError` tags to generate a list of error messages for an `Album` instance.

Listing 5-29. *Displaying Errors*

```
<g:hasErrors bean="${album}">
    <ul class="errors">
        <g:eachError bean="${album}">
            <li>${it.defaultMessage}</li>
        </g:eachError>
    </ul>
</g:hasErrors>
```

In this instance, `<g:hasErrors>` checks whether there are any errors in the first place and, if there are, creates an HTML list. These errors are then iterated over via the `<g:eachError>` tag, which creates the list bullets using the *default message*. The default messages for validation errors can be found in the `grails-app/i18n/message.properties` message bundle.

If a list is all that is required, Grails makes it even easier to display errors via the `<g:renderErrors>` tag, which encapsulates everything you've just seen. Essentially, it takes the same arguments as the `<g:eachError>` tag, as well as an optional as attribute, which allows you to specify what to render the errors as. Listing 5-29 shows how to render the errors as a simple HTML list:

```
<g:renderErrors bean="${album}" as="list" />
```

As noted previously, the examples shown so far use the *default message*. Clearly, the default message is not always what is desired, and it is often useful to provide specific messages for each property within a domain class. This is where the `<g:message>` tag comes into play with Grails' support for internationalization (i18n). Internationalization is covered in detail in Chapter 7.

Paginating Views

Rendering lists of data in a web application is a common thing to do. Grails provides an easy-to-use mechanism for retrieving data from the database (GORM) and simple mechanisms for rendering the data (GSPs and GSP tags).

Web applications often serve as a front end to a database that may contain large volumes of data. The application may need to provide mechanisms for the user to manage navigating through those large volumes of data. For example, the gTunes application may contain thousands of artists, albums, and songs. A page that lists all the albums may be overwhelming and difficult for the user to work with, as shown in Figure 5-2.

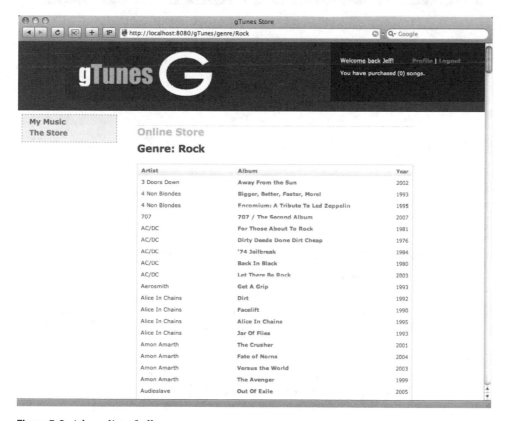

Figure 5-2. *A long list of albums*

Figure 5-2 represents what the user might see if they requested a list of all the albums in the system that belong to the Rock genre. As you can see from the scrollbar on the right, this is a very long page. The page includes several hundred albums. An argument could be made that this is too much data to display on a single page. What if there were thousands of albums? What if there were hundreds of thousands of albums? Clearly, it would not make sense to present all those albums to the user on a single page.

The gTunes application needs to be smart about presenting manageablc lists of data to the user. Instead of displaying hundreds or thousands of albums in a single list, maybe the application should display only five or ten. If the application displays only five or ten albums on the page, then the application also needs to provide a mechanism for the user to navigate around the larger virtual list to view the rest of the albums five or ten at a time.

Figure 5-3 represents a much more manageable interface.

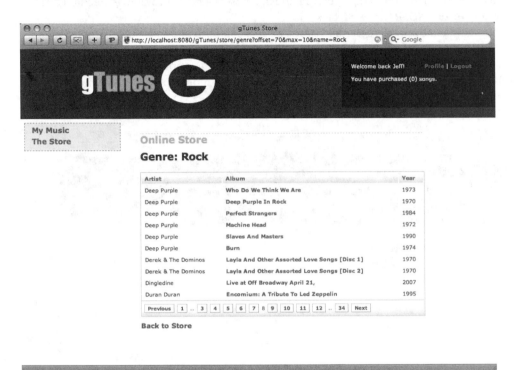

Figure 5-3. *A paginated list of albums*

The list in Figure 5-3 includes only ten albums. The view provides mechanisms for navigating over the larger virtual list, which includes all the albums in this genre. This approach yields a much better user experience, especially for scenarios where the user may be overwhelmed with large sets of data.

Some complexity is involved in generating pagination controls like this. The application needs to retrieve smaller amounts of data from the database for each view. The application needs to provide support for requesting the batch of records that fall immediately before the current batch or immediately after the current batch. The application needs to provide a mechanism for jumping straight to an area of the list, as opposed to navigating through the larger list a single page at a time. The application needs to know the total number of records in the larger list. All of that would normally involve writing a lot of code.

The good news is that Grails provides a really simple mechanism for managing all that. That mechanism is a GSP tag called `paginate`. The `paginate` tag manages a lot of the tedious work that would otherwise be required in order to provide UI elements for navigating over large lists of data.

The GSP responsible for rendering this list is in `grails-app/views/store/genre.gsp`. That page includes the markup shown in Listing 5-30.

Listing 5-30. *The genre.gsp*

```
<h1>Online Store</h1>

<h2>Genre: ${genre.encodeAsHTML()}</h2>
<table border="0" class="albumsTable">
  <tr>
    <th>Artist</th>
    <th>Album</th>
    <th>Year</th>
  </tr>
  <g:each var="album" in="${albums}">
    <tr>
      <td>${album.artist.name}</td>
      <td><g:link action="show"
                  controller="album"
                  id="${album.id}">${album.title}</g:link>
      </td>
      <td>${album.year}</td>
    </tr>
  </g:each>

</table>
<div class="paginateButtons">
  <g:paginate controller-"store"
              action="genre"
              params="[name:genre]"
              total="${totalAlbums}" />
</div>
```

The markup represented there renders an HTML table containing a header row and a row for each of the elements in the `albums` collection. Notice the use of the paginate tag at the bottom of Listing 5-30. That is all the code required in the GSP to render the pagination controls. The paginate tag takes care of all the tedious work involved in generating the "Previous" and "Next" links, all of the links that supporting jumping to a particular page, and all of the appropriate request parameters associated with each of those links. All of that is being handled by this single call to a GSP tag—the whole thing could barely be any simpler!

The paginate tag is generating a number of links. The `controller` and `action` parameters tell the paginate tag where each of those links should submit. In this particular case, all the links submit to the genre action in the StoreController. If all the links reference the same controller action, you might wonder how the application knows the difference between the user clicking one link vs. another. The answer has to do with the fact that the paginate tag is tacking a number of request parameters on the end of each link and those request parameters are used by the controller action. For example, the "7" link points to the URL /store/genre?offset=60&max=10&name=Rock. The "8" link points to the URL /store/genre?offset=70&max=10&name=Rock. Notice that each of those links includes the same value for the max and name parameters, but they include a different value for the offset parameter. That offset parameter is an important part of the request because that is how the controller will know what page of data should be returned when the user clicks one of those links. Let's take a look at the relevant controller action.

Listing 5-31 includes the code that is in the genre action in the StoreController.

Listing 5-31. *The genre action*

```
def genre = {
    def max = Math.min(params.max?.toInteger() ?: 10, 100)
    def offset = params.offset?.toInteger() ?: 0

    def total = Album.countByGenre(params.name)
    def albumList = Album.withCriteria {
      eq 'genre', params.name
      projections {
        artist {
          order 'name'
        }
      }
      maxResults max
      firstResult offset
    }
    return [albums:albumList,
                totalAlbums:total,
                genre:params.name]
}
```

───

■**Note** The previously shown query uses the Hibernate Criteria API. We'll describe the general behavior of the query next. The Criteria API is discussed in detail in the "Criteria Queries" section of Chapter 10.

───

The name request parameter is being used in both of the previous queries. The first query is necessary to count the number of albums in the database that belong to a certain genre. The second query is actually retrieving a list of albums. That second query is not retrieving all the albums that belong to a certain genre but is retrieving a subset of at most ten of those albums.

For example, imagine there is a list of 1,000 albums and each of those albums has an index associated with it starting with 0 and running up through 999. When a request is sent to the /store/genre?offset=60&max=10&name=Rock URL, the call to the `Album.withCriteria(...)` method will return ten of those albums starting with the `Album` at index 60. The max parameter represents the maximum number of albums that should be returned.

Notice that the first line in the genre action is assigning a default value of 10 to max if no max request parameter is found. If a max request parameter is found and the value is greater than 100, the system is falling back to a max of 10. Displaying more than 100 albums per page would defeat the purpose of having the pagination support in place.

The `offset` parameter represents what point in the larger list should this list of ten begin. If no `offset` request parameter is supplied, the system is defaulting the value to 0 or the beginning of the list.

The map of data being returned by the genre action includes not only the list of albums but also includes values for `totalAlbums` and genre, each of which are used in `genre.gsp` as parameters to the `paginate` tag. All of this needs to be kept in sync as part of the interaction between the controller action and the GSP.

The `paginate` tag supports a number of arguments. Table 5-2 lists those arguments.

Table 5-2. *Arguments Supported by the paginate Tag*

Argument	Description
total	Total number of elements in the larger list
controller	Name of the controller to link to
action	Name of the action to invoke
params	Map of request parameters
offset	Offset to be used if `params.offset` is not specified
max	Maximum number of elements per page
prev	Text for the "Previous" link
next	Text for the "Next" link
id	ID to use in links
maxsteps	Number of steps displayed for pagination (the default is 10)

All of the parameters supported by the `paginate` tag are optional except for the `total` parameter.

The default scaffolded list views in a Grails application include support for paginating the list. Define a simple domain class like the `Car` class shown in Listing 5-32.

Listing 5-32. *A Car Domain Class*

```
class Car {
  String make
  String model
}
```

Generate scaffolding for the Car class, and you will see that the default list action in the CarController and the default grails-app/view/car/list.gsp include support for paginating the list of cars. Listing 5-33 shows the relevant part of the GSP.

Listing 5-33. *grails-app/view/car/list.gsp*

```
<div class="list">
  <table>
    <thead>
      <tr>
        <g:sortableColumn property="id" title="Id" />
        <g:sortableColumn property="make" title="Make" />
        <g:sortableColumn property="model" title="Model" />
      </tr>
    </thead>
    <tbody>
      <g:each in="${carInstanceList}" status="i" var="carInstance">
        <tr class="${(i % 2) == 0 ? 'odd' : 'even'}">
          <td>
            <g:link action="show"
                    id="${carInstance.id}">
              ${fieldValue(bean:carInstance, field:'id')}
            </g:link>
          </td>
          <td>${fieldValue(bean:carInstance, field:'make')}</td>
          <td>${fieldValue(bean:carInstance, field:'model')}</td>
        </tr>
      </g:each>
    </tbody>
  </table>
</div>
<div class="paginateButtons">
  <g:paginate total="${Car.count()}" />
</div>
```

The only attribute specified in this call to the paginate tag is the required total attribute. Notice that in this case the value of the total attribute is simply the total number of cars in the database. This is a little bit different from the example shown earlier where the value of the total attribute was not necessarily all the number of albums in the database but was the number of albums in the database that belong to a particular genre.

Listing 5-34 shows the list action in the CarController.

Listing 5-34. *Pagination Support in the CarController*

```
class CarController {

def list = {
    if(!params.max) params.max = 10
    [ carInstanceList: Car.list( params ) ]
  }

  ...
}
```

The default list action in the CarController will assign a value of 10 to the max request parameter if a value is not supplied.

The application may take control over the order of the cars using any number of techniques supported by GORM. The simplest solution for this particular case is to include the order clause in the dynamic method, as shown in Listing 5-35.

Listing 5-35. *Ordering Cars By Model*

```
class CarController {

  def list = {
    if(!params.max) params.max = 10
    [ carInstanceList: Car.listOrderByModel ( params ) ]
  }

  ...
}
```

With all of that in place, if the database includes more than ten cars, then the pagination support in the view will kick in, as shown in Figure 5-4.

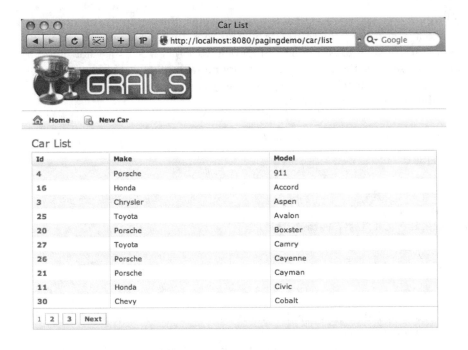

Figure 5-4. *Paginating a list of cars*

Rendering GSP Templates

A GSP template is a special GSP file that contains only a fragment of a page. A GSP template can contain markup that is rendered from various places in an application in which case the template would facilitate reuse. A template can be extracted from a page to simplify the containing page by breaking it down into smaller, more manageable pieces. Whatever the reason for isolating part of a page into a reusable template, Grails provides a really simple mechanism for rendering the template.

A template can contain just about anything that might appear in a normal GSP. One thing that makes a template special is its file name. GSP templates must be defined in a file whose name begins with an underscore. For example, a template that represents a list of albums might be defined in grails-app/views/album/_albumList.gsp.

The render tag can be used in a GSP to render a GSP template. The render tag accepts an attribute called template that represents the name of the template to be rendered. For example, to render the template in the grails-app/views/album/_albumList.gsp file, you would specify /album/albumList as the value of the template attribute when calling the render tag, as shown in Listing 5-36.

Listing 5-36. *Rendering the albumList Template*

```
<div id="artists">
  <g:render template="/artist/artistList"/>
</div>
```

Notice that the template file name contains an underscore, but the name of the template does not.

Rendering a template in a GSP is very much like taking the contents of the GSP template and putting them inline in the containing GSP in place of calling the render tag.

Figure 5-5 shows an updated version of the gTunes application.

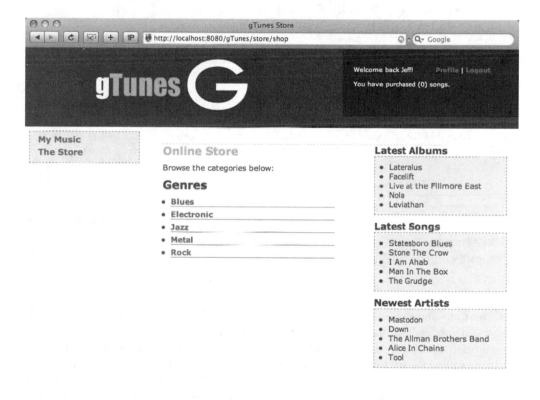

Figure 5-5. *Updated gTunes*

Notice the three boxes on the right of the screen representing the latest albums, latest songs, and newest artists. The markup required to generate each of those boxes would clutter the GSP. Rather than embedding the markup for those boxes in the `views/store/shop.gsp` file, you can pull all of that out into a series of templates and render those templates from `shop.gsp`. Using templates to handle this will yield an easier-to-maintain application compared to an application with monolithic unmodular GSPs.

Listing 5-37 shows what those templates might look like.

Listing 5-37. *GSP Templates for the Top Five Lists*

```
<!-- grails-app/views/artist/_artistList.gsp -->
<ul>
  <g:each in="${artists}" var="artist">
    <li>${artist?.name}</li>
  </g:each>
</ul>

<!-- grails-app/views/album/_albumList.gsp -->
<ul>
  <g:each in="${albums}" var="album">
    <li>${album.title}</li>
  </g:each>
</ul>

<!-- grails-app/views/song/_songList.gsp -->
<ul>
  <g:each in="${songs}" var="song">
    <li>${song.title}</li>
  </g:each>
</ul>
```

■ **Note** For now these are very simple templates that render unordered lists of strings. In Chapter 8 you will evolve these templates to contain some really slick Ajax-driven behavior. At that point, the value of having isolated this markup into templates will be even greater.

Notice that each of those templates is iterating over a different collection (`artists`, `albums`, and `songs`). Those collections are data that must be passed into the template when the template is rendered. The way to pass data into a GSP template is to specify an attribute called `model` when calling the render tag. The value of the `model` attribute should be a map containing all the data that is being passed in to the template. Listing 5-38 shows each of those templates being rendered from the `grails-app/views/store/shop.gsp` and the appropriate data being passed to each of the templates.

Listing 5-38. *Rendering Templates from shop.gsp*

```
<div id="top5Panel" class="top5Panel">
  <h2>Latest Albums</h2>
  <div id="albums" class="top5Item">
    <g:render template="/album/albumList"
              model="[albums: top5Albums]"/>
  </div>
  <h2>Latest Songs</h2>
  <div id="songs" class="top5Item">
```

```
    <g:render template="/song/songList"
              model="[songs: top5Songs]"/>
  </div>
  <h2>Newest Artists</h2>
  <div id="artists" class="top5Item">
    <g:render template="/artist/artistList"
              model="[artists: top5Artists]"/>
  </div>
</div>
```

The templates being rendered here are /album/albumList, /song/songList, and /artist/artistList. Each of those is a fully qualified reference to a template. When a template name is fully qualified like that, the root refers to the grails-app/views/ directory, so /artist/artistList refers to the template defined in the grails-app/views/artist/_artistList.gsp file. Template references may be defined with a relative path as well. Relative template paths are paths that do not begin with a forward slash.

For example, if instead of referring to /artist/artistList the shop.gsp referred to the relative artistList template, then Grails would look for the template in the same directory where shop.gsp lives. Relative references can also include a directory structure. If the artistList template were defined in grails-app/views/store/myTemplates/_artistList.gsp, then the grails-app/views/store/shop.gsp page could refer to the template as myTemplates/artistList since the myTemplates directory is in the same directory as shop.gsp.

Each of the calls to the earlier render tag includes a map of data being passed as the model attribute. For shop.gsp to have that data, the controller action that rendered shop.gsp needs to supply those values. In this case, the controller action is the shop action in StoreController, as shown in Listing 5-39.

Listing 5-39. *The shop Action in StoreController*

```
package com.g2one.gtunes

class StoreController {

  def shop = {
    def genreList = Album.withCriteria {
      projections {
        distinct "genre"
      }
    }

    [top5Albums:  Album.list(max:5, sort:"dateCreated", order:"desc"),
     top5Songs:   Song.list(max:5, sort:"dateCreated", order:"desc"),
     top5Artists: Artist.list(max:5, sort:"dateCreated", order:"desc"),
     genres:  genreList.sort()]
  }

  // ...
}
```

Notice that the controller action is returning values for albums, songs, and artists. The values are lists containing the five most recently created albums, songs, and artists.

These templates have been defined to render these "Top 5" lists in the `shop.gsp`, but they are reusable templates that can be used anywhere that the application needs to render lists of albums, artists, or songs. It is commonplace for web applications to render the same pieces of information on a lot of pages. When you see the same elements showing up in multiple places, consider pulling that markup out of your GSPs and putting it in a reusable template.

Creating Custom Tags

Custom tags in JSP are a wonderfully powerful feature. They provide the ability to cleanly separate concerns between the view and controller logic. In MVC terms, you can think of them as view helpers. Unfortunately, for all their wonderful attributes they are tremendously complicated to develop. The reasons for this are understandable, because JSP tags attempt to account for every possible tag creation scenario including the following:

- Simple tags that have attributes only and no body

- Body tags that have both attributes and a body

- Tags that have parent-child relationships between one another

- Nested tags and a complete API for finding tag ancestors

The implication, however, is that the API for creating JSP custom tags is robust, to say the least. To compound matters, additional information is required about the tag in a tag library descriptor (TLD) file that is loaded on application startup. This makes tags difficult to reload without a server restart, because the application server utilizes this file to configure the tag library. As you can imagine, all this is not very agile and is rather a complete contradiction to the code-by-convention approach.

From a user's perspective, developers rarely go to the effort of creating tags themselves, and typically the ones used tend to be those provided by the frameworks and specifications, such as JSTL. This is rather a shame, because the concept is sound, though the implementation is not.

So, what can Grails and, more specifically, GSP provide to make creating tags simpler? Clearly, supporting every tag type under the sun would result in a complicated API, much like that in JSP. In reality, the most commonly used tags can be broken down into three categories:

- *Simple tags*: Tags that have attributes but no body

- *Logical tags*: Those that have a body that executes conditionally

- *Iterative tags*: Tags that loop and execute the body of the tag one or more times

You will find that the majority of tags you come across fall into one of the previous categories. Since Grails is all about making the common cases simple, creating a simplified API for these tag types seems only logical. The question is, why create a new API at all? This is where Groovy and the power of closures start to shine.

Creating a Tag Library

Having already seen quite a few Grails tags throughout this discussion, it may well be that you've already browsed the source and have become familiar with what a Grails tag is all about. Regardless, it is important to understand how to create a tag library from scratch.

It is generally good practice to place tags inside a library that encapsulate their general function, kind of like a package does in Java.

A *tag library* is quite simply a class that ends with the convention TagLib in the class name and resides snugly in the grails-app/taglib directory. Like the other Grails artifacts you've seen, a convenience target exists for creating tag libraries. To create a new tag library for the gTunes application, you can run the grails create-taglib target and type **gtunes**, as shown in Listing 5-40.

Listing 5-40. *Creating the Gtunes Tag Library*

```
$ grails create-taglib

init-props:

create-taglib:
    [input] Enter tag library name:
Gtunes
    [copy] Copying 1 file to /Developer/grails-apps/gtunes/grails-app/taglib
    [echo] Created taglib: grails-app/taglib/GtunesTagLib.groovy

BUILD SUCCESSFUL
Total time: 8 seconds
```

The result will resemble something like the following:

```
class GtunesTagLib {

}
```

To see how to go about making a tag library, in the next section you'll look at a basic tag and then build some snazzy functionality into the gTunes application for rendering album cover art.

Custom Tag Basics

First let's look at the basics. A tag is essentially a closure property that takes two arguments: the tag attributes as a `java.util.Map` and the body of the tag as a closure, as shown in Listing 5-41.

Listing 5-41. *An Example Tag*

```
class GtunesTagLib {

  def repeat = { attrs, body ->
    attrs.times?.toInteger().times { n ->
      body(n)
    }
  }
}
```

In the example, we've defined a tag called `repeat` that looks for an attribute called `times`, which it attempts to convert to an integer, and then uses Groovy's built-in `times` method to execute the body multiple times.

As mentioned previously, the body is a closure and therefore can be invoked like a method. In addition, you pass the number of the current iteration, as the variable n, to the body as the first argument to the closure call. Why is this useful? It means that the number is available as the default `it` argument in the tag's body. As an example, let's try the new tag in a GSP view as in Listing 5-42. Note that the name of the tag in the markup matches the property name defined in the library shown in Listing 5-41.

Listing 5-42. *Using the repeat Tag*

```
<g:repeat times="3">
        Hello number ${it}
</g:repeat>
```

As you can see, the tag uses the default `it` argument to reference the value passed when the tag calls the body closure. The resulting output will be the following:

```
Hello number 1
Hello number 2
Hello number 3
```

All the tags that are bundled with Grails are defined in the g namespace. By default, all your own custom tags are also put in the g namespace. To avoid naming conflicts with built-in tags and with tags that may be installed into a project as part of a plugin, you should define a namespace for your own tag libraries. Defining a namespace for a tag library is as simple as declaring a static property called `namespace` in the taglib class and assigning that property a `String` value, as shown in Listing 5-43.

Listing 5-43. *Defining a Custom Namespace for a Tag Library*

```
class GtunesTagLib {

  static namespace = 'gt'

  def repeat = { attrs, body ->
    attrs.times?.toInteger().times { n ->
      body(n)
    }
  }
}
```

With that `namespace` property in place, all the tags defined in the `GTunesTagLib` are now in the gt namespace. Instead of referring to `<g:repeat/>`, GSPs should now refer to `<gt:repeat/>`.

Not only are Grails tags amazingly concise when compared to their JSP brethren, but it is important to note that all changes to tags can be reloaded at runtime just like with controllers; there's no need to configure tag library descriptors or restart servers, which makes Grails tags a far more interesting and agile proposition.

Testing a Custom Tag

Like most of your code in a Grails application, the code in custom tag libraries should be tested. Testing tag libraries can be tricky. The test needs a way to invoke a tag, provide parameters, provide a body, and inspect the effect of invoking the tag. Fortunately, Grails provides a really slick mechanism for managing all of that. Unit tests for custom tag libraries should extend from the `grails.test.TagLibUnitTestCase` class. Listing 5-44 contains a unit test for the `GtunesTagLib` class defined earlier.

Listing 5-44. *Testing GtunesTagLib*

```
// test/unit/GtunesTagLibTests.groovy

import grails.test.*

class GtunesTagLibTests extends TagLibUnitTestCase {

  void testRepeat() {
    tagLib.repeat(times: '2') {
      'output<br/>'
    }
    assertEquals 'output<br/>output<br/>', tagLib.out.toString()
  }
}
```

The testRepeat() method here is invoking the repeat tag and supplying a map of parameters and a closure as arguments. In this case, the map contains a single parameter (times), but the map may contain any number of parameters. The closure being passed to the tag method represents the body of the tag. In this case, the closure returns a String. If the tag is behaving correctly, the body of the tag should be rendered twice since the value of the times parameter is 2. The assertion at the bottom of the test method is checking that this did in fact happen.

This test is interacting primarily with the tagLib property. This property is not defined in the test class but is inherited from TagLibUnitTestCase. This property will be an instance of the tag library that is being tested. All the tags defined in this tag library are accessible as method calls on the tagLib property.

A common thing to be asserting when testing a tag is that the tag rendered the expected text. The out property on tagLib contains whatever the tag rendered, so inspecting that property after invoking the tag is the simplest way to make that assertion.

The GtunesTagLibTests class does not define what tag library class is being tested here. How does Grails know where to find the repeat tag? By default, Grails will infer the name of the tag being tested by removing *Tests* from the end of the test class name. Since this class is called GtunesTagLibTests, Grails assumes that this is a test for the GtunesTagLib tag library. If your test does not follow this naming convention, you can be explicit about what tag library is being tested by overriding the default constructor and passing the tag library class as an argument to the superclass constructor. Listing 5-45 shows how to do this.

Listing 5-45. *Being Explicit About Which Tag Library Is Being Tested*

```
// test/unit/MyTagLibTests.groovy

import grails.test.*

class MyTagLibTests extends TagLibUnitTestCase {

  MyTagLibTests() {
    super(GtunesTagLib)
  }

  void testRepeat() {
    tagLib.repeat(times: '2') {
      'output<br/>'
    }
    assertEquals 'output<br/>output<br/>', tagLib.out.toString()
  }
}
```

Summary

You have learned quite a bit in this chapter. You learned about Grails' advanced view technology, GSP, and the array of powerful tags that come packaged with it. You also learned how to build and test your own GSP tags, and you further extended your knowledge of Groovy mocking in the process. We covered a lot of ground, and you should now have a clear idea of how powerful GSP is. Thanks to GPath, an expression language, and dynamic tag libraries, GSP has a lot to offer to increase your productivity and enjoyment.

CHAPTER 6

■■■

Mapping URLs

Grails provides working URL mappings right out of the box. The default URL mapping configuration is yet one more place that the Grails framework leverages the powerful idea of convention over configuration to lessen the burden put on the application developer. Sometimes, though, you will want to deviate from the convention and define your own custom mappings. For example, you may want to create more descriptive and human-readable URLs. Grails gives you the ability to easily define these custom URL mappings.

Defining application-specific URL mappings is something that comes up all the time while building web applications. The technique for configuring URL mappings in Grails is really powerful while remaining very simple to work with. Like a lot of configuration options in a Grails application, configuring custom URL mappings involves writing a little bit of Groovy code, and that's it. In particular, no XML configuration files are involved.

Understanding the Default URL Mapping

The default URL mapping configuration in a Grails app is simple. The first part of the URL corresponds to the name of a controller, and the second, optional part of the URL corresponds to the name of an action defined in that controller. For example, the /store/index URL will map to the index action in the StoreController. Specifying the action name is optional, so if the action name is left out of the URL, then the default action for the specified controller will be executed. Default controller actions are described in detail in the "Setting the Default Action" section of Chapter 4. Finally, the last piece of the URL is another optional element that represents the value of a request parameter named id. For example, the /album/show/42 URL will map to the show action in the AlbumController with a request parameter named id that has a value of 42.

The definition of the default mapping is in grails-app/conf/UrlMappings.groovy. Listing 6-1 shows what UrlMappings.groovy looks like by default.

Listing 6-1. *Default grails-app/conf/UrlMappings.groovy*

```
class UrlMappings {
    static mappings = {
        "/$controller/$action?/$id?"{
            constraints {
                // apply constraints here
            }
```

```
        }
        "500"(view:'/error')
    }
}
```

The key to this mapping is the string `"/$controller/$action?/$id?"`. Notice that the `$action` and `$id` elements are both followed by a question mark. The question mark indicates an optional piece of the URL. The `$controller` element has no question mark, so it is a required piece of the URL. A mapping can define any number of optional elements. If a mapping does contain any optional elements, they must all appear at the end of the pattern.

■**Note** The `constraints` block in the default mapping is empty. The `constraints` block is optional and will be discussed in the "Applying Constraints to URL Mappings" section later in this chapter. The mapping that begins with `"500"` will be discussed later in the "Mapping HTTP Response Codes" section.

Including Static Text in a URL Mapping

In the default mapping, each of the elements in the URL is a variable. Variable elements are prefixed with a $ sign. A URL mapping can contain static elements as well. A static element in a URL mapping is simply text that must be part of the URL in order for a particular mapping to apply. See Listing 6-2 for an example of a mapping that contains static text.

Listing 6-2. *Including Static Text in a Mapping*

```
class UrlMappings {
    static mappings = {
        "/showAlbum/$controller/$action?/$id?" {
            constraints {
                // apply constraints here
            }
        }

        // ...
    }
}
```

This mapping will match URLs such as `/showAlbum/album/show/42` and `/showAlbum/album/list` but will not match URLs such as `/album/show/42` since that one does not begin with `/showAlbum`.

Removing the Controller and Action Names from the URL

The controller and action names do not need to be part of the URL. These special elements can be eliminated from the URL pattern and specified as properties of the mapping. As shown previously, the default mapping supports a URL such as /album/show/42, which will map to the show action in the AlbumController. An application can choose to support a URL such as /showAlbum/42 to access that same controller action. The code in Listing 6-3 includes a mapping to support this.

Listing 6-3. *Specifying the Controller and Action As Properties of the Mapping*

```
class UrlMappings {
    static mappings = {
        "/showAlbum/$id" {
            controller = 'album'
            action = 'show'
        }

        // ...
    }
}
```

The mapping engine in Grails provides support for an alternate syntax to express this same mapping. Which technique you choose is a matter of personal preference. Listing 6-4 shows the alternate syntax.

Listing 6-4. *Specifying the Controller and Action As Parameters to the Mapping*

```
class UrlMappings {
    static mappings = {
        "/showAlbum/$id"(controller:'album', action:'show')

        // ...
    }
}
```

Embedding Parameters in a Mapping

Of course, Grails supports request parameters using the standard HTTP request parameter notation. A URL such as /showArtist?artistName=Rush would work if you had a mapping like the mapping shown in Listing 6-5.

Listing 6-5. *A Mapping for the /showArtist URL*

```
class UrlMappings {
    static mappings = {
        "/showArtist"(controller:'artist', action:'show')

        // ...
    }
}
```

Accessing /showArtist?artistName=Rush would map to the show action in the ArtistController and a request parameter named artistName would be populated with the value Rush. Notice that the artistName parameter is not represented anywhere in the mapping. This is because our mapping applies to the /showArtist URL, and therefore any arbitrary parameters can be passed to that URL without affecting the mapping.

Although this approach works, it has its drawbacks. One drawback is the URL is just ugly, and it would continue to get uglier as more request parameters were introduced.

Grails' URL mapping engine provides a much slicker solution to support custom URLs that have request parameters embedded in the URL. Instead of /showArtist?artistName=Rush, let's support a URL such as /showArtist/Rush. The mapping in Listing 6-6 works perfectly for this.

Listing 6-6. *Embedding a Request Parameter in the URL*

```
class UrlMappings {
    static mappings = {
        "/showArtist/$artistName"(controller:'artist', action:'show')

        // ...
    }
}
```

With this mapping, URLs such as /showArtist/Tool and /showArtist/Cream will be mapped to the show action in the ArtistController with a request parameter named artistName, and the value of that parameter will be whatever is in the last part of the URL; in the previous examples, these were the Tool and Cream values. The action in the AlbumController would have access to the request parameter and could use the parameter however is appropriate. See Listing 6-7.

Listing 6-7. *Accessing a Request Parameter in the Controller Action*

```
class ArtistController {
    def show = {
        def artist = Artist.findByName(params.artistName)
        // do whatever is appropriate with the artist...
    }
}
```

A little snag that must be dealt with here is that the artist names may include characters that are not valid in a URL. One technique you might use is to URL-encode the parameters. A technique like this would support accessing a band named Led Zeppelin with a URL such as /showArtist/Led%20Zeppelin. Notice that the space in the name has been replaced with %20. Yuck! Let's make an application decision here and say that you'll encode artist names by replacing spaces with underscores. This will lead you to a friendlier-looking URL: /showArtist/Led_Zeppelin. The URL mapping doesn't really care about the value of the parameter, so it does not need to be changed to support this. However, the controller action will need to be updated since the underscores in the query parameter must be replaced with spaces. Listing 6-8 represents an updated version of the code in Listing 6-7 to deal with this.

Listing 6-8. *Decoding the Request Parameter to Replace Underscores with Spaces*

```
class ArtistController {
    def show = {
        def artist = Artist.findByName(params.artistName.replaccAll('_', ' '))
        // do whatever is appropriate with the artist...
    }
}
```

Another approach to encoding and decoding an artist name is to write a custom codec. Grails dynamic codecs are covered in the "Using Dynamic Codecs" section of Chapter 14.

■**Note** This encoding/decoding problem exists even if the request parameter is not embedded in the URL. For example, something like /showArtist?artistName=Led%20Zeppelin or /showArtist?artistName=Led_Zeppelin would be necessary to deal with the space in the parameter value.

Specifying Additional Parameters

In addition to embedding parameters in the URL, arbitrary request parameters may be specified as properties of a particular mapping that never show up in the URL. Listing 6-9 includes an example.

Listing 6-9. *Specifying Additional Request Parameters*

```
class UrlMappings {
    static mappings = {
        "/showArtist/$artistName"(controller:'artist', action:'show') {
            format = 'simple'
        }
```

```
        "/showArtistDetail/$artistName"(controller:'artist', action:'show') {
            format = 'detailed'
        }

        // ...
    }
}
```

With this mapping in place, a request to the URL /showArtist/Pink_Floyd would map to the show action in the ArtistController, and the request would include parameters named artistName and format with the values Pink_Floyd and simple, respectively. A request to the URL /showArtistDetail/Pink_Floyd would map to the same action and controller, but the format request parameter would have a value of detailed.

Mapping to a View

Sometimes you might want a certain URL pattern to map directly to a view. This is useful when the view does not require any data to be passed in and no controller action is required. In a case like this, you can define a URL mapping that is associated with a view rather than a controller action. The syntax is the same as mapping to an action except you must specify a value for the view property instead of the action property. Listing 6-10 demonstrates how to do this.

Listing 6-10. *Mapping to a View*

```
class UrlMappings {
    static mappings = {
        "/"(view:'/welcome')

        // ...
    }
}
```

This mapping will handle all requests to the root of the application (/) by rendering the GSP at grails-app/views/welcome.gsp. The mapping engine also allows a mapping to specify a view that belongs to a particular controller. For example, Listing 6-11 demonstrates how to map the /find URL to grails-app/views/search/query.gsp.

Listing 6-11. *Mapping to a View for a Particular Controller*

```
class UrlMappings {
    static mappings = {
        "/find"(view:'query', controller:'search')

        // ...
    }
}
```

Remember that no controller action is being executed for this mapping. The controller is being specified only so the framework can locate the appropriate GSP.

Applying Constraints to URL Mappings

The URL mapping engine provides a really powerful mechanism for applying constraints to variables embedded in a URL mapping. The constraints are similar those applied to domain objects. See the "Validating Domain Classes" section in Chapter 3 for information about domain constraints. Applying constraints to variables in a URL mapping can greatly simplify the job of weeding out certain kinds of invalid data that would otherwise have to be dealt with in an imperative manner in a controller or service.

Consider a blogging application written in Grails. A typical format for a URL in a blogging system might be something like /grailsblogs/2009/01/15/new_grails_release. To support a URL like that, you might define a mapping like the one defined in Listing 6-12.

Listing 6-12. *A Typical Blog-Type URL Mapping*

```
class UrlMappings {
    static mappings = {
        "/grailsblogs/$year/$month/$day/$entry_name?" {
            controller = 'blog'
            action = 'display'
            constraints {
                // apply constraints here
            }
        }

        // ...
    }
}
```

With a mapping like that in place, a URL like /grailsblogs/2009/01/15/new_grails_release would map to the display action in the BlogController with request parameters named year, month, day, and entry_name and the values 2009, 01, 15, and new_grails_release, respectively.

A problem with this mapping is that not only will it match a URL such as /grailsblogs/2009/01/15/new_grails_release, but it will also match a URL such as /grailsblogs/grails/rocks/big/time. In this case, the controller action would receive the value grails for the year, rocks for the month, and so on. Dealing with scenarios like this would complicate the logic in the controller. A better way to manage them is to apply constraints to the mapping that would let the framework know that grails is not a valid match for the year parameter in the mapping, for example. The constraints specified in Listing 6-13 use regular expressions to limit the year, month, and day parameters to match only those values that include the right number of digits and only digits.

Listing 6-13. *Applying Constraints to Mapping Parameters*

```
class UrlMappings {
    static mappings = {
        "/grailsblogs/$year/$month/$day/$entry_name?" {
            controller = 'blog'
            action = 'display'
            constraints {
                year matches: /[0-9]{4}/
                month matches: /[0-9]{2}/
                day matches: /[0-9]{2}/
            }
        }

        // ...
    }
}
```

As is the case with domain class constraints, mapping parameters may have as many constraints applied to them as necessary. All the constraints must pass in order for the mapping to apply.

■**Note**   There is a small syntactical difference between the way constraints are specified in a URL mapping and how they are specified in a domain class. In a domain class, a `constraints` property is defined and assigned a value that is a closure. In a URL mapping, you are calling a method named `constraints` and passing a closure as an argument. This is why no equals sign is needed between `constraints` and the closure in a URL mapping but is needed between `constraints` and the closure in a domain class.

Including Wildcards in a Mapping

You have seen how a mapping may contain static text as well as any number of variable parameters (optional and required), and you've seen how constraints may be applied to variable parameters. One more aid to flexibility that you can use in a mapping definition is a wildcard. Wildcards represent placeholders in a mapping pattern that may be matched by anything but do not represent information that will be passed as request parameters. Wildcards in a mapping definition are represented by an asterisk (*). Listing 6-14 includes a mapping with a wildcard in it.

Listing 6-14. *Wildcards in a Mapping*

```
class UrlMappings {
    static mappings = {
        "/images/*.jpg"(controller:'image')
```

```
        // ...
    }
}
```

This mapping will handle any request for a file under the /images/ directory that ends with the .jpg extension. For example, this mapping will handle /images/header.jpg and /images/footer.jpg, but this mapping will not match requests for .jpg files that may exist in some sub-directory under the /images/ directory. For example, a request for something like /images/photos/president.jpg would not match. A double wildcard can be used to match any number of subdirectories. Listing 6-15 shows a double wildcard mapping.

Listing 6-15. *Double Wildcards in a Mapping*

```
class UrlMappings {
    static mappings = {
        "/images/**.jpg"(controller:'image')

        // ...
    }
}
```

This mapping will match requests for things such as /images/header.jpg and /images/footer.jpg as well as things such as /images/photos/president.jpg.

For some situations, it may be desirable for the value that matched the wildcard to be passed to the controller as a request parameter. This is achieved by prepending a variable to the wildcard in the mapping. See Listing 6-16.

Listing 6-16. *Double Wildcards with a Variable in a Mapping*

```
class UrlMappings {
    static mappings = {
        "/images/$pathToFile**.jpg"(controller:'image')

        // ...
    }
}
```

In this case, the pathToFile request parameter would represent the part of the URL that matched the wildcard. For example, a request for /images/photos/president.jpg would result in the pathToFile request parameter having a value of photos/president.

Mapping to HTTP Request Methods

A URL mapping can be configured to map to different actions based on the HTTP request method.[1] This can be useful when building a system that supports RESTful APIs. For example,

---

1. See http://www.w3.org/Protocols/rfc2616/rfc2616-sec9.html for definitions of all the HTTP request methods.

if a GET request is made to the URL /artist/The_Beatles, then the controller may respond by generating a page that displays details about the Beatles. If a DELETE request is made to that same URL, the controller may respond by attempting to delete the Beatles and all of the band's associated data (albums and so on). An application could deal with all these requests in the same controller action by interrogating the request and reacting differently based on the HTTP request method. Listing 6-17 shows what this might look like in the ArtistController.

Listing 6-17. *Inspecting the HTTP Request Method in a Controller Action*

```
class ArtistController {
  def actionName = {
    if(request.method == "GET") {
      // handle the GET
    } else if(request.method == "PUT") {
      // handle the PUT
    } else if(request.method == "POST") {
      // handle the POST
    } else if(request.method == "DELETE") {
      // handle the DELETE
    }
    // ...
}
```

This is tedious code and would likely be repeated in many places in your application. A better idea is to configure a URL mapping that matches this URL and maps the request to different controller actions based on the HTTP request method. See Listing 6-18 for an example.

Listing 6-18. *Mapping to HTTP Request Methods*

```
class UrlMappings {
    static mappings = {
        "/artist/$artistName" {
            controller = 'artist'
            action = [GET: 'show',
                      PUT: 'update',
                      POST: 'save',
                      DELETE: 'delete']
        }

        // ...
    }
}
```

Note that the value assigned to the `action` property is not the name of an action but is a `Map`. The keys in the map correspond to the names of HTTP request methods, and the values associated with the keys represent the name of the action that should be invoked for that particular request method.

Mapping HTTP Response Codes

URL mappings may be defined for specific HTTP response codes. The default mapping includes a mapping for the 500 response code (Internal Error).[2] This mapping renders the `/error` view for any internal error. This view is located at `grails-app/views/error.gsp`. This GSP renders stack information that may be useful during development and debugging. Listing 6-19 represents the default `error.gsp` page.

Listing 6-19. *The Default grails-app/views/error.gsp Page*

```
<body>
  <h1>Grails Runtime Exception</h1>
  <h2>Error Details</h2>
  <div class="message">
    <strong>Message:</strong> ${exception.message?.encodeAsHTML()} <br />
    <strong>Caused by:</strong> ${exception.cause?.message?.encodeAsHTML()} <br />
    <strong>Class:</strong> ${exception.className} <br />
    <strong>At Line:</strong> [${exception.lineNumber}] <br />
    <strong>Code Snippet:</strong><br />
    <div class="snippet">
      <g:each var="cs" in="${exception.codeSnippet}">
        ${cs?.encodeAsHTML()}<br />
      </g:each>
    </div>
  </div>
  <h2>Stack Trace</h2>
  <div class="stack">
    <pre>
      <g:each in="${exception.stackTraceLines}">
        ${it.encodeAsHTML()}<br/>
      </g:each>
    </pre>
  </div>
</body>
```

---

2. See `http://www.w3.org/Protocols/rfc2616/rfc2616-sec10.html` for definitions of all the HTTP response codes.

You can add your own mappings for specific response codes. For example, if you wanted to map every request for something that cannot be found to the default action in the `StoreController`, you could do so with the mapping shown in Listing 6-20.

Listing 6-20. *Custom Mapping for All 404 Response Codes*

```
class UrlMappings {
    static mappings = {
        "404"(controller:'store')

        // ...
    }
}
```

Taking Advantage of Reverse URL Mapping

You have seen how to support URLs such as `/showArtist/Pink_Floyd` instead of URLs such as `/artist/show/42`. The support you have seen so far relates to handling a request to a URL. The other end of that interaction is equally important. That is, you need a slick mechanism for generating links that takes advantage of custom URL mappings. Fortunately, that mechanism is built into Grails and is as easy to work with as the mapping mechanisms you have already seen.

The `<g:link>` GSP tag that is bundled with Grails is useful for generating links to certain controllers and actions. See Listing 6-21 for a common use of the link tag.

Listing 6-21. *The Link Tag*

```
<td>
  <g:link action='show'
          controller='artist'
          id="${artist.id}">${artist.name}</g:link>
</td>
```

This tag will generate a link like `<a href="/artist/show/42">Pink Floyd</a>`. That link to `/artist/show/42` is ugly. You would definitely prefer `/showArtist/Pink_Floyd`. The good news is that it is easy to get the link tag to generate a link like that. You just tell the link tag what controller and action you want to link to and supply all the necessary parameters that the custom mapping calls for. For example, see the custom mapping in Listing 6-22.

Listing 6-22. *A Mapping for the /showArtist/ URL*

```
class UrlMappings {
    static mappings = {
        "/showArtist/$artistName"(controller:'artist', action:'show')

        // ...
    }
}
```

The link tag will generate a link that takes advantage of this mapping whenever a request is made for a link to the show action in the ArtistController and the artistName parameter is supplied. In a GSP, that would look something like the code in Listing 6-23.

Listing 6-23. *Reverse URL Mapping Using the Link Tag*

```
<td>
  <g:link action='show'
          controller='artist'
          params="[artistName:${artist.name.replaceAll(' ', '_')}]">
    ${artist.name}
  </g:link>
</td>
```

Defining Multiple URL Mappings Classes

When an application defines a lot of custom URL mappings, the UrlMappings class may get long enough to warrant breaking the mappings up into several mappings classes. Having several small, focused mappings classes will be easier to write and maintain than one monolithic class. To introduce new mappings classes, simply define classes under grails-app/conf/ with a name that ends with UrlMappings. The structure of those classes should be exactly the same as the default UrlMappings class. Listing 6-24 shows a custom mappings class that would contain Artist-related mappings.

Listing 6-24. *A URL Mappings Class for Artist Mappings*

```
class ArtistUrlMappings {
  static mappings = {
    "/showArtist/$artistName" (controller:'artist', action:'display')
  }
}
```

Testing URL Mappings

Like most aspects of your application, you are going to want to write automated tests for custom URL mappings to assert that the application does in fact respond to requests in the way you intended. Grails provides a really slick mechanism for writing those tests. The simplest way to test URL mappings is to create an integration test that extends from grails.test. GrailsUrlMappingsTestCase. The GrailsUrlMappingsTestCase class extends GroovyTestCase and provides a number of methods that can be used to test custom mappings.

Listing 6-25 shows a simple mapping to support URLs like /showArtist/Jeff_Beck. A request to a URL like that should map to the display action in the ArtistController.

Listing 6-25. *A Custom URL Mapping*

```
class UrlMappings {

  static mappings = {
    "/showArtist/$artistName" (controller:'artist', action:'display')

    // ...
  }
}
```

The `assertForwardUrlMapping` method in `GrailsUrlMappingsTestCase` can be used to assert that a request to a URL like `/showArtist/Jeff_Beck` is sent to the appropriate controller action. The code in Listing 6-26 demonstrates what this test might look like.

Listing 6-26. *Unit Testing a URL Mapping*

```
class ArtistUrlMappingsTests extends grails.test.GrailsUrlMappingsTestCase {

  void testShowArtist() {
    assertForwardUrlMapping('/showArtist/Jeff_Beck',
                            controller: 'artist', action: 'display')
  }
}
```

The mapping defined in Listing 6-25 includes an embedded variable, `artistName`. The `GrailsUrlMappingsTestCase` class provides a simple mechanism for asserting that mapping variables like this one are being assigned the correct value. The way to do this is to pass a closure as the last argument to the `assertForwardUrlMapping` method and in the closure assign values to properties with names that are consistent with the embedded variable names. See Listing 6-27 for an example. This test will assert not only that the request maps to the `display` action in the `ArtistController` but also that the `artistName` request parameter is being populated with the correct value.

Listing 6-27. *Testing URL Mapping Variables*

```
class ArtistUrlMappingsTests extends grails.test.GrailsUrlMappingsTestCase {

  void testShowArtist() {
    assertForwardUrlMapping('/showArtist/Jeff_Beck',
                            controller: 'artist', action: 'display') {
      artistName = 'Jeff_Beck'
    }
  }
}
```

Listing 6-28 demonstrates a similar approach to testing whether reverse URL mapping is behaving as expected. Note that the assert method is called `assertReverseUrlMapping` this time.

Listing 6-28. *Testing Reverse URL Mapping*

```
class ArtistUrlMappingsTests extends grails.test.GrailsUrlMappingsTestCase {

  void testShowArtist() {
    assertReverseUrlMapping('/showArtist/Jeff_Beck',
                            controller: 'artist', action: 'display') {
      artistName = 'Jeff_Beck'
    }
  }
}
```

Often it is the case that you want to test both forward and reverse URL mapping. One way to do this is to use the `assertForwardUrlMapping` method in addition to using the `assertReverseUrlMapping` method. Although that will work, it is more work than you need to do. If you use the `assertUrlMapping` method, `GrailsUrlMappingsTestCase` will assert that both forward and reverse URL mapping are working, and if either of them fail, the test will fail. See Listing 6-29 for an example.

Listing 6-29. *Testing Both Forward and Reverse URL Mapping*

```
class ArtistUrlMappingsTests extends grails.test.GrailsUrlMappingsTestCase {

  void testShowArtist() {
    assertUrlMapping('/showArtist/Jeff_Beck',
                     controller: 'artist', action: 'display') {
      artistName = 'Jeff_Beck'
    }
  }
}
```

The `GrailsUrlMappingsTestCase` class will load all the mappings defined in an application by default. If you want to take control over which mappings are loaded while the test is running, you can do so by defining a static property in your mapping test called `mappings` and assigning it a value that is either a class reference or a list of class references. If the value of the `mappings` property is a class reference, that class reference should represent the mapping class to be loaded. If the value of the `mappings` property is a list of class references, then all those mapping classes will be loaded. Listing 6-30 demonstrates how to take advantage of the `mappings` property.

Listing 6-30. *Loading Specific URL Mapping Classes in a Unit Test*

```
class ArtistUrlMappingsTests extends grails.test.GrailsUrlMappingsTestCase {

  static mappings = [UrlMappings, ArtistUrlMappings]

  void testShowArtist() {
    assertUrlMapping('/showArtist/Jeff_Beck',
                     [controller: 'artist', action: 'display']) {
      artistName = 'Jeff_Beck'
    }
  }
}
```

Summary

The URL mapping engine provided by Grails is very flexible. Nearly any URL pattern that you might want to map to a particular controller action can easily be configured simply by writing a small amount of Groovy code in `UrlMappings.groovy`. The framework provides a lot of mechanisms that enable you to spend less time configuring the framework and more time solving business problems in your application. The URL mapping engine is one more example of this. Custom URL mappings are simple to write and simple to test.

CHAPTER 7

■ ■ ■

Internationalization

One of the great things about web applications is that they are really easy to distribute to a lot of people. When deploying web applications to a broad audience, often the applications need to adapt and behave differently under certain circumstances. For example, when a request from Spain is made to a web application, the application may want to display messages to the user in Spanish, but the same application will want to render messages in English if the request comes from New York. The adaptations made by the application may involve more complexity than simply displaying different versions of text. An application may need to impose different business rules based on the origin of a particular request.

Grails provides a number of mechanisms for dealing with the internationalization and localization of a web application. In this chapter, we will explore those mechanisms, and you will see that internationalizing a web application does not have to be terribly difficult.

Localizing Messages

When deploying a Grails application to a broad audience, you may want the application to display messages in the user's preferred language. One way of providing this capability is to have a separate version of the application for each language you want to target. That approach has lots of problems. Maintaining all those different versions and trying to keep them all in sync would be an awful lot of work. A much better idea is to have a single version of the application that is flexible enough to display messages in various languages using localized messages.

To support localized messages in your Grails application, you should be defining all user messages in a properties file. So, user messages should not be hard-coded in GSP pages, GSP templates, or anywhere else. Having messages in a properties file means you have a single place to maintain all of them. It also lets you take advantage of the localization capabilities provided by Grails.

Defining User Messages

When a Grails app is created, the project includes a number of localized property files in the `grails-app/i18n/` directory. Figure 7-1 shows the contents of the `grails-app/i18n/` directory.

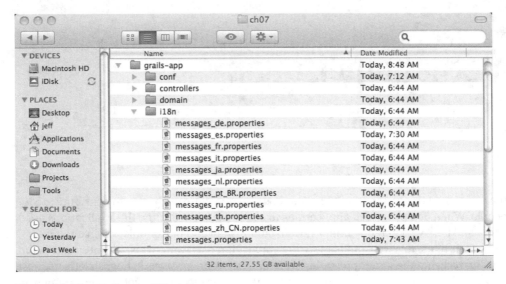

Figure 7-1. *The grails-app/i18n/ directory*

The `messages.properties` file in the `grails-app/i18n/` directory contains default valida-tion messages in English. These messages are used when validation fails in a domain class or command object. You can add your own application messages to this file. In addition to the default `messages.properties` file, this directory has several other properties files that contain the same messages in other languages. For example, "es" is the language code for Spanish, so `messages_es.properties` contains validation messages in Spanish.

■**Note** The naming convention for the messages files follows the standard convention used by the `java.util.ResourceBundle` class. For more information, see the documentation for `java.util.ResourceBundle` and `java.util.Locale` at `http://java.sun.com/j2se/1.5.0/docs/api/`.

Property files are plain-text files, which contain name-value pairs. Listing 7-1 represents a simple properties file.

Listing 7-1. *A Simple Property File*

```
# messages.properties
app.name=gTunes
book.title=The Definitive Guide To Grails
favorite.language=Groovy
favorite.framework=Grails
```

Retrieving Message Values

In a standard Java or Groovy program, you would use the java.util.ResourceBundle class to retrieve values from a properties file. Listing 7-2 demonstrates how you would retrieve and print the value of the app.name property.

Listing 7-2. *Using java.util.ResourceBundle*

```
// JavaMessages.java
import java.util.ResourceBundle;

public class JavaMessages {

    public static void main(String[] args) {
        ResourceBundle bundle = ResourceBundle.getBundle("messages");
        String appName = bundle.getString("app.name");
        System.out.println("application name is " + appName);
    }
}

// GroovyMessages.groovy
def messages = ResourceBundle.getBundle('messages')
def appName = messages.getString('app.name')
println "application name is ${appName}"
```

The java.util.ResourceBundle class takes care of loading the properties file and providing an API to retrieve the values of properties defined in the file. Grails provides a GSP tag called message that will retrieve property values from the messages files in the grails-app/i18n/ directory. For the simplest case, only the code attribute must be specified when calling the message tag. The code attribute tells the message tag which property value should be retrieved. For example, if a property named gtunes.welcome is defined in grails-app/i18n/ messages.properties, the value of that property may be rendered in a GSP using code like that shown in Listing 7-3.

Listing 7-3. *Using the message Tag*

```
<body>
  ...
  <g:message code="gtunes.welcome"/>
  ...
</body>
```

By default, Grails will decide which version of the property file to use based on the locale of the current web request. This means that often you will not need to do anything special in your application code with respect to localization. If you define your message properties in several language-specific versions of the properties files under grails-app/i18n/, then Grails will use the appropriate file based on the client's locale.

Figure 7-2 represents the gTunes home page in English.

Figure 7-2. *gTunes in English*

There are several user messages represented in Figure 7-2. For example, on the left side of the screen is a navigation area, which includes the "My Music" and "The Store" links. The labels for those links will include different text when the application is accessed from different locales. The best way to deal with that is to define those messages as properties and render the messages in the GSP with the message tag. Listing 7-4 shows how those properties might be defined in grails-app/i18n/messages.properties.

Listing 7-4. *User Messages in grails-app/i18n/messages.properties*

```
gtunes.my.music=My Music
gtunes.the.store=The Store
...
```

With those properties defined, a GSP can render those values using the message tag, as shown in Listing 7-5.

Listing 7-5. *Rendering Property Values from a GSP*

```
<div id="navButtons">
  <ul>
    <li><a href="#"><g:message code="gtunes.my.music"/></a></li>
    <li><g:link controller="store" action="shop">
        <g:message code="gtunes.the.store"/>
      </g:link>
    </li>
  </ul>
</div>
```

With that code in place, you may add corresponding properties to as many of the other messages files as you like. To support a Spanish version of the site, add corresponding properties to grails-app/i18n/messages_es.properties, as shown in Listing 7-6.

Listing 7-6. *User Messages in grails-app/i18n/messages_es.properties*

```
gtunes.my.music=Mi Musica
gtunes.the.store=La Tienda
...
```

A simple way to test your Grails application's localization is to include a request parameter named lang and assign it a valid language code, such as "es" for Spanish (`http://localhost:8080/gTunes/?lang=es`). Figure 7-3 shows a Spanish version of the application.

Figure 7-3. *gTunes in Spanish*

Using URL Mappings for Internationalization

As shown previously, a request parameter named lang will tell the framework to use a specific language code while processing this request. One way to specify the request parameter is to include it in the request URL, as in `http://localhost:8080/gTunes/?lang=es`. Another way to specify the request parameter is by defining a custom URL mapping, as shown in Listing 7-7.

Listing 7-7. *A URL Mapping for Localization*

```
class UrlMappings {
  static mappings = {
    "/store/$lang"(controller:'store')

    // ...
  }
}
```

The mapping in Listing 7-7 will map all requests to a URL like `http://localhost:8080/gTunes/en/` or `http://localhost:8080/gTunes/es/` where "en" and "es" could be any valid language code.

Using Parameterized Messages

Often a user message may consist of more than simple static text. The message may need to include some data that is not known until runtime. For example, gTunes displays a message that lets the user know how many songs they have purchased. The message reads something like "You have purchased (97) songs." The "97" part of that message is a piece of information that isn't known until runtime.

Using java.text.MessageFormat

Java includes a class called `java.text.MessageFormat`. One of the things that `java.text.MessageFormat` is useful for is supporting parameterized messages, like the one described earlier, in a language-neutral way. A parameterized message may contain any number of parameters, and the parameters are represented with numbers surrounded by curly braces in the value of the message. Listing 7-8 shows how the "You have purchased (97) songs." message might be represented in `grails-app/i18n/messages.properties`.

Listing 7-8. *Defining a Parameterized Message*

```
# messages.properties
gtunes.purchased.songs=You have purchased ({0}) songs.
...
```

The value of the `gtunes.purchased.songs` message has one parameter in it. As is almost always the case in Java and Groovy, the `java.text.MessageFormat` class uses a zero-based index, so {0} in the message is a placeholder for the value of the first parameter. If the message had multiple parameters, they would be represented in the value of the message with placeholders like {0}, {1}, {2}, and so on.

The code in Listing 7-9 shows how `java.text.MessageFormat` might be used from a Java program.

Listing 7-9. *Using MessageFormat to Populate a Parameterized Message with Java*

```java
// JavaMessages.java
import java.util.ResourceBundle;
import java.text.MessageFormat;

public class JavaMessages {

    public static void main(String[] args) {
        ResourceBundle bundle = ResourceBundle.getBundle("messages");
        String songsPurchased = bundle.getString("gtunes.purchased.songs");
        String message = MessageFormat.format(songsPurchased, 97);
        System.out.println("message: " + message);
    }
}
```

Listing 7-10 shows a Groovy script that does the same thing.

Listing 7-10. *Using MessageFormat to Populate a Parameterized Message with Groovy*

```
import java.text.MessageFormat

def bundle = ResourceBundle.getBundle('messages')
def songsPurchased = bundle.getString('gtunes.purchased.songs')
def message = MessageFormat.format(songsPurchased, 97)

println "message: ${message}"
```

Using the message Tag for Parameterized Messages

Grails allows for parameterized messages to be used without the need for you, the application developer, to deal directly with the java.text.MessageFormat class. The message tag supports an optional parameter named args, and if that parameter is assigned a value, its value will be treated as a list of parameters that need to be applied to the message. Listing 7-11 shows how to pass arguments to the message tag.

Listing 7-11. *Using the message Tag to Populate a Parameterized Message*

```
<div>
  <g:message code="gtunes.purchased.songs" args="[97]"/>
</div>
```

Of course, for a message like this, you will probably not want to hard-code the parameter value in a GSP like that. More likely, you will want that value to be dynamic. The code in Listing 7-12 is passing a parameter to the message to be applied to the gtunes.purchased.songs message. If the currently logged in user has purchased any songs, then the value of the parameter will be the number of songs they have purchased; otherwise, the value of the parameter will be 0.

Listing 7-12. *Using the message Tag to Populate a Parameterized Message Dynamically*

```
<div>
  <g:message code="gtunes.purchased.songs"
             args="[session.user.purchasedSongs?.size() ?: 0]"/>
</div>
```

■**Note** Note the use of the so-called Elvis operator (?:) in the previous code. The Elvis operator is a shorthand version of Java ternary operator where the return value for the true condition is the same as the expression being evaluated. For example, the following expressions accomplish the same thing:

```
size = session.user.purchasedSongs?.size() ? session.user.purchasedSongs?.size() : 0
size = session.user.purchasedSongs?.size() ?: 0
```

Using Parameterized Messages for Validation

You will notice that the default grails-app/i18n/messages.properties file contains a number of messages by default. These messages are there to support the mechanism that is built in to Grails for validating domain classes and command objects. Listing 7-13 shows a domain class that contains some constraints.

Listing 7-13. *A Domain Class with Constraints*

```
class Person {
    String firstName
    String lastName
    Integer age

    static constraints = {
        firstName size: 2..30, blank: false
        lastName size: 2..30, blank: false
        age min: 0
    }
}
```

These constraints are in place to make sure that the firstName and lastName properties are at least 2 characters, no more than 30 characters, and not blank. You might think that specifying a minimum length of two would take care of the blank scenario, but that is not the case. A firstName that is simply three spaces would satisfy the length constraint but not the blank constraint. The age property also is constrained, so it may never have a negative value. If an instance of the Person class is created that does not satisfy all of those constraints, then a call to the validate() method on that instance would return false. Likewise, a call to save() on the instance would fail.

The default scaffolded views for a domain class contain code to display any validation errors. Listing 7-14 shows a piece of the default grails-app/views/person/create.gsp.

Listing 7-14. *create.gsp Containing Code to Render Validation Errors*

```
<h1>Create Person</h1>
<g:if test="${flash.message}">
  <div class="message">${flash.message}</div>
</g:if>
<g:hasErrors bean="${personInstance}">
  <div class="errors">
    <g:renderErrors bean="${personInstance}" as="list" />
  </div>
</g:hasErrors>
```

The hasErrors tag will render its body only if personInstance has errors. If personInstance does have errors, then the renderErrors tag will render a list of all those errors, and that rendering process is using the validation messages defined in grails-app/i18n/messages.properties.

Figure 7-4 shows what the user might see when attempting to create a Person in the user interface with no firstName, no lastName, and a negative age.

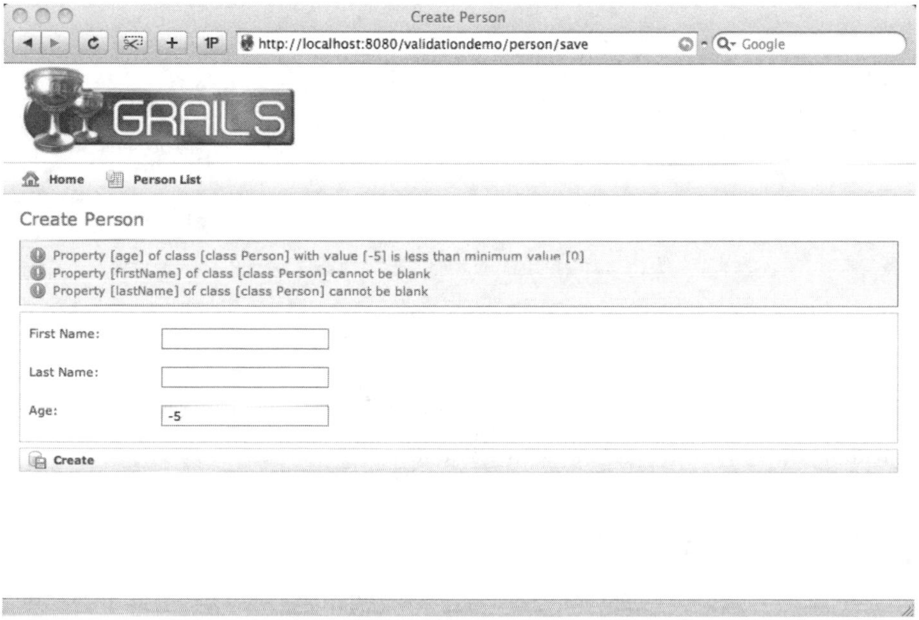

Figure 7-4. *Validation messages in the user interface*

The error messages you see there are all defined in grails-app/i18n/messages.properties as parameterized messages, as shown in Listing 7-15.

Listing 7-15. *Default Validation Messages*

```
default.invalid.min.message=\
  Property [{0}] of class [{1}] with value [{2}] is less than minimum value [{3}]
default.blank.message=Property [{0}] of class [{1}] cannot be blank
...
```

You may modify the values of these messages to suit your application. For example, if the default.blank.message property was given a value of {0} is a required field, then the user would be shown error messages like those in Figure 7-5.

Figure 7-5. *Custom validation messages in the user interface*

Using messageSource

The `message` tag is easy to use and makes sense when a user message needs to be retrieved from `messages.properties` and the message is going to be rendered in a GSP. However, sometimes an application may need to retrieve the value of a user message and do something with it other than render the value in a GSP. For example, the message could be used in an e-mail message. In fact, the message could be used for any number of things, and not all of them involve rendering text in a GSP.

Grails provides a bean named `messageSource` that can be injected into any Grails artefact including controllers, taglibs, other beans, and so on. The `messageSource` bean is an instance of the `org.springframework.context.MessageSource` interface provided by the Spring Framework. This interface defines three overloaded versions of the `getMessage` method for retrieving messages from the source. Listing 7-16 shows the signatures of these methods.[1]

■**Note**   Throughout the source code and documentation of Grails, the word *artefact* is used to refer to a Groovy file that fulfills a certain concept (such as a controller, tag library, or domain class). It is spelled using the British English spelling of *artefact* as opposed to *artifact*, so we will be using that spelling throughout the book to maintain consistency with the APIs.

---

1. See `http://static.springframework.org/spring/docs/2.5.x/api/index.html` for complete documentation of the `MessageSource` interface and related classes.

Listing 7-16. *The MessageSource Interface*

```
String getMessage(String code, Object[] args, Locale locale)
String getMessage(String code, Object[] args, String defaultMessage, Locale locale)
String getMessage(MessageSourceResolvable resolvable, Locale locale)
```

Since the `messageSource` bean participates in Grails' dependency autowiring process, all you need to do to get a reference to the bean is declare a property named `messageSource` in your Grails artefact. The code in Listing 7-17 shows how to use the `messageSource` bean in a controller.

Listing 7-17. *Using messageSource in a Controller*

```
package com.g2one.gtunes

class StoreController {

    def messageSource

    def index = {
        def msg = messageSource.getMessage('gtunes.my.music', null, null)
        // ...
    }
    ...
}
```

Note that the second and third arguments are null. The second argument is an `Object[]`, which would be used to pass parameters to a parameterized message. The third argument is a `java.util.Locale`, which may be specified to retrieve a message for any `Locale` other than the default `Locale` for this request. For example, Listing 7-18 demonstrates retrieving a message in Italian.

Listing 7-18. *Using messageSource and Specifying a Locale*

```
package com.g2one.gtunes

class StoreController {

    def messageSource

    def index = {
        def msg = messageSource.getMessage('gtunes.my.music', null, Locale.ITALIAN)
        // ...
    }
    ...
}
```

Summary

Internationalization is an important aspect of building widely distributed applications. Grails provides a number of mechanisms that make the process much easier than it might otherwise be. All the message property files in a Grails application are located in the same place. This means that, as an application developer, you do not need to tell Grails where to look for these files. It also means that as a Grails developer moves from one Grails project to the next, the developer knows exactly where to look for the property files because they are always in the same place. This is the power of coding by convention at work. Also, retrieving messages from a property file is a snap in a Grails application. The `message` tag is very easy to use from GSP pages and GSP templates. The `messageSource` bean is easily accessible from wherever the application may need it. All of this is built on top of proven and well-understood tools on the Java platform including `java.text.MessageFormat` and `org.springframework.context.MessageSource`.

CHAPTER 8

■ ■ ■

Ajax

Ajax is a technology that has taken the Web by storm and has prompted the Web 2.0 revolution. The technology was originally developed by Microsoft to power a web-based version of its Outlook e-mail software. Microsoft implemented Ajax as an ActiveX control that could be used by its browser, Internet Explorer, and be called from JavaScript to perform asynchronous browser requests.

The advantage of the approach is that the browser doesn't have to refresh the entire page to interact with the server, thus allowing the development of applications that bear a closer resemblance to their desktop counterparts. Since then, browsers other than Internet Explorer have standardized on a native JavaScript object called XMLHttpRequest that has largely the same API as Microsoft's ActiveX control.

The Basics of Ajax

The implications of having different browsers is that you have to write specialized code that detects which browser you are operating in and that loads the XMLHttpRequest object, either as an ActiveX control or as a native object.

Note Microsoft introduced a native JavaScript XMLHttpRequest object in Internet Explorer 7.0, but since Internet Explorer 6.0 is still pretty popular, we recommend you use browser-specific code to obtain the XMLHttpRequest object.

You can see a typical example of obtaining a reference to the XMLHttpRequest object in a cross-browser manner in Listing 8-1.

Listing 8-1. *Example of XMLHttpRequest in JavaScript*

```
var req = null;
if (window.XMLHttpRequest) {
    req = new XMLHttpRequest();
} else if (window.ActiveXObject) {
    req = new ActiveXObject("Microsoft.XMLHTTP");
}
```

```
if(req!=null) {
    // register an event handler
    req.onreadystatechange = processRequest ;
    // open connection
    req.open("GET",
            "http://localhost:8080/a/remote/location",
            true);
    req.send(); // send request
}
function processRequest(obj) {
        alert(obj.responseXML) // Get the result from the response object
}
```

The previous code sends an asynchronous request to the http://localhost:8080/a/ remote/location address and then, using the onreadystatechange callback event, invokes the processRequest function. This function simply displays an alert box with the content of the response. To illustrate the previous code and help you better understand the flow of an Ajax request, take a look at the UML sequence diagram in Figure 8-1. Remember that Ajax calls are asynchronous.

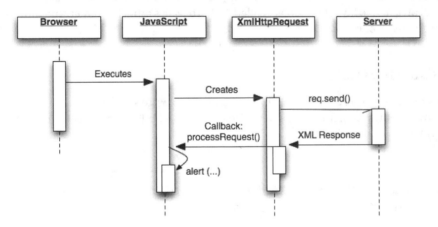

Figure 8-1. *An example Ajax flow*

As Figure 8-1 illustrates, the browser calls some JavaScript, which in turn creates the XMLHttpRequest object that is able to make the remote call. When the remote call has been made, the XMLHttpRequest object then invokes the callback (in this case the processRequest function), which in turn displays the alert.

Writing JavaScript code as shown in Listing 8-1 can become rather repetitive and tedious. Fortunately, there are Ajax frameworks that encapsulate much of this logic, ranging from the simple (such as Prototype) to the comprehensive (such as Dojo). Efforts are underway to standardize on a JavaScript library, but as is always the case with any collaborative effort, this could be a long and painful process that will likely never satisfy everyone.

Knowing this, the developers of Grails have designed an "adaptive" Ajax implementation that allows you to decide which Ajax library is most suitable for your needs. By default, Grails ships with the Prototype library and counterpart Scriptaculous effects library; however, through Grails' plugin system, you can add support for alternative libraries that supply the underlying implementation of Grails' Ajax tags.

Before you delve into the world of Ajax tags, you need to revisit the gTunes application, since you'll be enhancing the gTunes application by adding a range of Ajax-powered features that improve the user experience:

- The ability to log in asynchronously

- A new feature that allows you to search and filter songs within your library and the store using Ajax-powered search fields

- And finally, a slicker way of displaying albums and songs including album art

So, before getting too carried away, let's move on to the guts of the chapter by improving the gTunes application interface, Ajax style.

Ajax in Action

To begin with, let's start with a simple example. At a basic level, Grails provides a set of tags that simplify the creation of Ajax-capable components such as links, forms, and text fields. For example, to create an HTML anchor tag that when clicked executes an Ajax call, you can use the `<g:remoteLink>` tag. Let's try a "Hello World"–style example using `<g:remoteLink>`. First update `StoreController` by adding the action shown in Listing 8-2.

Listing 8-2. *An Action That Renders the Date and Time*

```
def showTime = {
    render "The time is ${new Date()}"
}
```

The `showTime` action in Listing 8-2 uses the `render` method introduced in Chapter 4 to render a plain-text response to the client that contains the current date and time, trivially obtained through Java's `java.util.Date` class. That was simple enough; now open the `index.gsp` file located in the `grails-app/views/store` directory. Before you attempt to use the `<g:remoteLink>` tag, you need to tell Grails which Ajax library to use. You can do this through the `<g:javascript>` tag, which needs to go in the `<head>` section of your `index.gsp` file, as shown in Listing 8-3.

Listing 8-3. *Using the Prototype Library*

```
<g:javascript library="prototype" />
```

In this case, you are telling Grails to use the Prototype library for Ajax. As a side effect, Grails will import all the necessary Prototype dependencies into the page, so you're ready to go. Now, within the body of the `index.gsp` page, add the code shown in Listing 8-4, which uses the `<g:remoteLink>` tag.

Listing 8-4. *Using the Tag*

```
<g:remoteLink action="showTime" update="time">Show the time!</g:remoteLink>
<div id="time">
</div>
```

What this does is add an HTML anchor tag (with the text "Show the time!") to the page, which when clicked will execute an asynchronous request to the showTime action of the StoreController. The update attribute of the <g:remoteLink> tag specifies the ID of the DOM element into which you would like to place the contents of the response. In this case, you've provided an HTML <div> element with an ID of time just below the <g:remoteLink> that will be the target of this Ajax call.

And with that, you have completed a trivial example of Ajax-enabling your application. Try clicking the link to see what happens. You will note that the current date and time gets placed into the <div> each time you click the link! Figure 8-2 shows an example of this behavior.

Figure 8-2. *A Simple Ajax call example*

Changing Your Ajax Provider

So, as it stands, you are using Prototype as the underlying library that powers the <g:remoteLink> tag, but what if you wanted to use a different library? Grails lets you swap to a different implementation via its plugin system. For example, say you wanted to use the Yahoo UI plugin instead; then simply run this:

```
$ grails install-plugin yui
```

Now modify the `<g:javascript>` tag from Listing 8-3, changing the value of the library attribute to yui:

```
<g:javascript library="yui" />
```

Now refresh the page and try the "Show the time!" link again. Like magic, Grails is now using Yahoo UI instead of Prototype. In addition to Yahoo UI, there are plugins for Dojo, Ext-JS, and jQuery. The Grails plugins page at `http://grails.org/Plugins` provides the latest up-to-date information on the available plugins.

Asynchronous Form Submission

Now that you have had a chance to explore a trivial example, let's try something a little more challenging. When building Ajax applications, it is often useful to submit a form and its data to the server asynchronously. Currently, the login process of the gTunes application uses a regular form submission, but wouldn't it be useful to allow users to log in without a refresh?

Right now, the login form contained within the `grails-app/views/layouts/main.gsp` layout submits using a regular form. In other words, the form submission is synchronous and doesn't occur in a background process as an Ajax request would. Luckily, Grails provides the `<g:formRemote>` tag—an enhanced version of the HTML form tag that enables the form to submit as an Ajax request.

However, before you migrate the regular `<g:form>` tag to its infinitely more interesting cousin `<g:formRemote>`, let's move the code that renders the login form into its own GSP template. The importance of doing this will become clear later. For now, create a new file called `grails-app/views/user/_loginForm.gsp`, which will form the basis for the template, and then cut-and-paste the code from the layout so that the template looks like Listing 8-5.

Listing 8-5. *The Login Template*

```
<g:form
        name="loginForm"
        url="[controller:'user',action:'login']">
    ...
</g:form>
<g:renderErrors bean="${loginCmd}"></g:renderErrors>
```

Now within the `main.gsp` layout, use the `<g:render>` tag to render the template, as shown in Listing 8-6.

Listing 8-6. *Using the Tag to Display the Login Form*

```
<div id="loginBox">
    <g:render template="/user/loginForm"></g:render>
</div>
```

With that done, it is time to introduce the usage of `<g:formRemote>`. First simply rename the `<g:form>` tag references to `<g:formRemote>`, and then add the update attribute (mentioned in the previous section about the `<g:remoteLink>` tag) to the `<g:formRemote>` tag. In this case, the update attribute refers to the DOM ID of the loginBox <div>. And that is it; the changes to the code appear in Listing 8-7 in bold.

Listing 8-7. *Altering the Login Form to Use <g:formRemote>*

```
<g:formRemote
            name="loginForm"
            url="[controller:'user',action:'login']"
            update="loginBox">
            ...
</g:formRemote>
```

The remainder of the code stays the same. The <g:formRemote> tag is still submitting to the login action of the UserController, and no change is required to any of the input fields or the submit button. Now if you refresh the page and try to log in, a surprising thing will happen. Astoundingly, you get the contents of the entire page placed within the loginBox <div>! This happens because you updated the client code but paid no attention to the server logic, which is still displaying the entire view. To correct this problem, you need to revisit the server-side code to render only a snippet of HTML instead of the entire page.

Just in case you don't recall the code in question, Listing 8-8 shows what the current code for the login action of the UserController looks like.

Listing 8-8. *The Current login Action Code*

```
def login = { LoginCommand cmd ->
    if(request.method == 'POST') {
        if(!cmd.hasErrors()) {
            session.user = cmd.getUser()
            redirect(controller:'store')
        }
        else {
            render(view:'/store/index', model:[loginCmd:cmd])
        }
    }
    else {
        render(view:'/store/index')
    }
}
```

At the moment, the code in Listing 8-8 renders the entire grails-app/views/store/ index.gsp view, but what you actually want is for only the login form to be displayed again (on login failure) or a welcome message to be displayed if the user successfully logged in. Let's refactor the code to achieve this goal; Listing 8-9 shows the result.

Listing 8-9. *Handing an Ajax Login Request*

```
def login = { LoginCommand cmd ->
    if(request.method == 'POST') {
        if(!cmd.hasErrors()) {
            session.user = cmd.getUser()
            render(template:"welcomeMessage")
        }
        else {
            render(template:'loginForm', model:[loginCmd:cmd])
        }
    }
    else {
        render(template:'loginForm')
    }
}
```

You could, of course, take this further and deal with both Ajax and regular requests, but for the moment that isn't a requirement. As you can see from the code in Listing 8-9, what you're doing is using the template argument of the render method instead of the view argument, which allows you to reuse the _loginForm.gsp template. In addition, you'll need to create a grails-app/views/user/_welcomeMessage.gsp template to deal with a successful login, the contents of which you can see in Listing 8-10.

Listing 8-10. *The _welcomeMessage.gsp Template*

```
<div style="margin-top:20px">
    <div style="float:right;">
        <g:link controller="user"
                    action="profile"
                    id="${session.user.id}">Profile</g:link> |
        <g:link controller="user" action="logout">Logout</g:link><br>
    </div>

    Welcome back <span id="userFirstName">${session?.user?.firstName}!</span>
    <br><br>

    You have purchased (${session.user.purchasedSongs?.size() ?: 0}) songs.<br>
</div>
```

Executing Code Before and After a Call

Each of the Ajax tags supports two attributes called before and after, which allow the insertion of arbitrary JavaScript code to be executed before and after a remote call.

■**Note** The code within the `after` attribute will be executed whether or not the remote call is successful. In this sense, it should not be compared to an `onComplete` event handler.

For example, you could use a before call to programmatically alter the value of the field before it is sent to the server, as shown in Listing 8-11.

Listing 8-11. *Example Before Attribute Usage*

```
<g:javascript>
    function setDefaultValue(form) {
        if(form.elements[0].value == '') {
            form.elements[0].value = 'changed'
        }
    }
</g:javascript>
<g:formRemote action="login"
              before="setDefaultValue(this);"
              update="loginBox"
              name="loginForm">
...
</g:formRemote>
```

Here, you set a default value for the first element of the `<form>` (maybe a hidden or optional field) before it is sent to the server. It is important to understand that the `before` and `after` attributes are not event hooks. This becomes more apparent when using `after`, which will execute directly after an Ajax call and will not wait until it returns. In other words, it has no awareness of whether the Ajax call is successful. Events are a different concept that will be covered in detail in the next section.

Handling Events

An important aspect of Ajax development, and indeed any asynchronous development style, is the ability to receive and act on events. To this end, Grails' Ajax tags allow the registration of a number of different event handlers that you can take advantage of. For example, a common use case in Ajax development is to provide some form of feedback to the user while an Ajax call is happening, be it an activity monitor, a progress bar, or a simple animated icon (such as a spinner or an hourglass).

To accomplish this for a single Ajax call, you could use the `onLoading` and `onComplete` events, as shown in Listing 8-12.

Listing 8-12. *Displaying a Progress Indicator*

```
<g:formRemote
      url="[controller:'user',action:'login']"
      onLoading="showProgress();"
      onComplete="hideProgress();"
      update="loginBox"
      name="loginForm">
   ...
</g:formRemote>
```

> **Note** If you are using the Prototype library, you can take advantage of Prototype's generalized responders mechanism, which allows you to centralize Ajax event logic to provide generic behavior across all Ajax calls (such as displaying a progress indicator). Refer to `http://www.prototypejs.org/api/ajax/responders` for more information.

Listing 8-12 uses two hypothetical JavaScript methods called `showProgress()` and `hideProgress()` to display feedback to the user. These could be as simple as displaying an animated graphic or something more advanced such as polling the server for the current state of a large operation and displaying a progress bar.

Table 8-1 shows the different events. The last event in the table deserves special mention, because it allows you to handle specific error codes. This is often useful to display alert boxes or specific feedback to the user, such as certain codes when the server is down or being maintained. In the next section, we'll cover more advanced ways to perform updates on content.

Table 8-1. *Table of Ajax Events*

Event Name	Description
onSuccess	Called when the remote call is successful
onFailure	Called when the remote call begins to load the response
onLoaded	Called when the remote call has loaded the response, but prior to any
onComplete	Called when the response has been received and any updates are completed
onERROR_CODE	Called for specific error codes such as on404

Fun with Ajax Remote Linking

In your first introduction to the `<g:remoteLink>` tag, you implemented a simple bit of functionality that displayed the time when the anchor tag was clicked. It's not exactly groundbreaking stuff, we know. Let's correct this by looking at a more advanced example.

In Chapter 5, you created a few panels for the right side of the gTunes store that displayed the newest additions to the gTunes library for songs, albums, and artists, respectfully. As a refresher, Listing 8-13 shows the code in question from the `grails-app/views/store/shop.gsp` file.

Listing 8-13. *The Latest Content Panel*

```
<div id="top5Panel" class="top5Panel">
    <h2>Latest Albums</h2>
    <div id="albums" class="top5Item">
        <g:render template="/album/albumList" model="[albums: top5Albums]" />
    </div>
    <h2>Latest Songs</h2>
    <div id="songs" class="top5Item">
        <g:render template="/song/songList" model="[songs: top5Songs]" />
    </div>
    <h2>Newest Artists</h2>
    <div id="artists" class="top5Item">
        <g:render template="/artist/artistList" model="[artists: top5Artists]" />
    </div>
</div>
```

Each of these uses a specific template to render a simple HTML unordered list for each category. It would be nice if the list items, instead of being plain text, consisted of HTML links that used Ajax to display details about the Album, Song, or Artist in question.

Let's start with Album. If you recall from the domain model, an Album has a title, release year, genre, artist, and a list of Songs that apply to that album. To begin with, create a template that can render that information. Listing 8-14 shows the `grails-app/views/album/_album.gsp` template.

Listing 8-14. *Implementing the _album.gsp Template*

```
<div id="album${album.id}" class="album">
    <div class="albumDetails">
        <div class="artistName">${artist.name}</div>
        <div class="albumTitle">${album.title}</div>
        <div class="albumInfo">
            Genre: ${album.genre ?: 'Other'}<br>
            Year: ${album.year}
        </div>
        <div class="albumTracks">
            <ol>
                <g:each in="${album.songs?}" var="song">
                    <li>${song.title}</li>
                </g:each>
            </ol>
        </div>
```

```
        <div class="albumLinks">
    </div>
</div>
```

Now that you have a template, you can alter the grails-app/views/album/_albumList.gsp template to use <g:remoteLink> to call a controller action called display on the AlbumController for each item in the list. Listing 8-15 shows (in bold) the changes made to the _albumList.gsp template.

Listing 8-15. *Updating _albumList.gsp to Use*

```
<ul>
    <g:each in="${albums?}" var="album">
        <li><g:remoteLink update="musicPanel"
                           controller="album"
                           action="display"
                           id="${album.id}">${album.title}</g:remoteLink></li>
    </g:each>
</ul>
```

Notice how you can use the update attribute to specify that you want the contents of the response to be placed into an HTML <div> that has a DOM ID with the value musicPanel. If you refresh the page at this point and try the links, you'll notice that the Ajax part of the picture is working already! The downside is that since there is no display action in the AlbumController at this point, you get a 404 "Page not found" error from the server.

Let's correct that by opening AlbumController and implementing the display action. Listing 8-16 shows the code, which simply obtains the Album instance using the id parameter from the params object and then uses it to render the _album.gsp template developed in Listing 8-14.

Listing 8-16. *The display Action of AlbumController*

```
def display = {
    def album = Album.get(params.id)
    if(album) {
        def artist = album.artist
        render(template:"album", model:[artist:artist, album:album])
    }
    else {
        render "Album not found."
    }
}
```

By adding a bit of CSS magic to enhance the look of the _album.gsp template, all of a sudden you have album details being obtained via Ajax and rendered to the view. Figure 8-3 shows the result of your hard work.

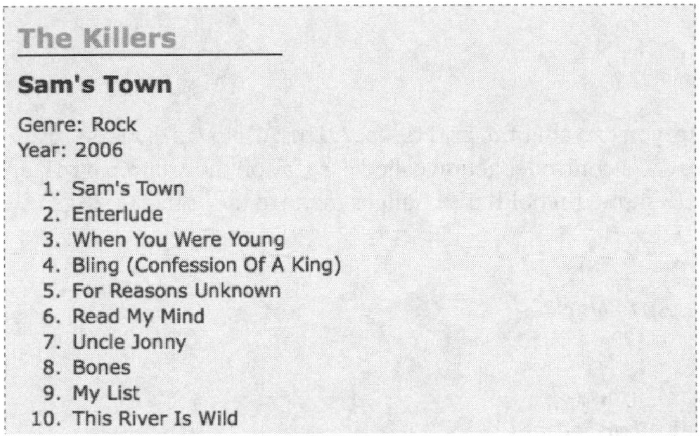

The Killers
_____

Sam's Town

Genre: Rock
Year: 2006

  1. Sam's Town
  2. Enterlude
  3. When You Were Young
  4. Bling (Confession Of A King)
  5. For Reasons Unknown
  6. Read My Mind
  7. Uncle Jonny
  8. Bones
  9. My List
 10. This River Is Wild

Figure 8-3. *Displaying albums using Ajax*

Sadly, even with the CSS enhancements, `Album` details are looking a bit bland with all that text. Wouldn't it be nice to be able to display the album art for each album? Where there is a will, there is a way, and luckily, Amazon has come to the rescue here by providing a web services API that lets developers look up album art from its massive pool of assets.

Even better, it has a Java API, which encapsulates the communication with the web service, perfect for our needs. To complete the initial setup phase, follow these simple steps:

1. Sign up for a free Amazon web services account at `https://aws-portal.amazon.com/gp/aws/developer/account/index.html`, and obtain your Amazon access key (you'll be needing it).

2. Then download the "Java Library for Amazon Associates Web Service" file from the following location: `http://developer.amazonwebservices.com/connect/entry.jspa?externalID=880&ref=featured`.

3. Extract the `.zip` file, and copy the `amazon-a3s-*-java-library.jar` file into your project `lib` directory.

4. Copy the required dependencies `commons-codec-1-3.jar` and `commons-httpclient-3.0.1.jar` from the `third-party/jakarta-commons` directory to your project's `lib` directory.

5. Copy all the JARs contained with the `third-party/jaxb` directory to your project's `lib` directory.

After going through these steps, you should have set up your project's `lib` directory in a similar fashion to Figure 8-4.

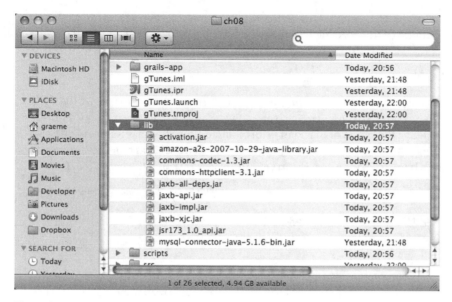

Figure 8-4. *Setting up the appropriate JARs for Amazon Web Services*

With that done, it is time to create your first service. The capabilities of services will be described in more detail in Chapter 11, but as a simple definition, services are useful for centralizing business logic that needs to be shared across layers (such as from a tag library and a controller). You're going to create an `AlbumArtService` that deals with obtaining album art from Amazon. To do this, start by running the grails `create-service` command:

```
$ grails create-service com.g2one.gtunes.AlbumArt
```

The `create-service` command will create a new empty `AlbumArtService` that resembles Listing 8-17.

Listing 8-17. *The AlbumArtService Template*

```
package com.g2one.gtunes

class AlbumArtService {

}
```

One thing to note about services is that they are by default transactional. In other words, each public method is wrapped in a Spring-managed transaction, making all persistence operations atomic. The implications of this are covered in more detail in Chapter 11; for the moment, since this service is not performing any persistence operations, you can disable this behavior by setting the transactional static property to false:

```
static transactional = false
```

With that out of the way, your first job is to provide the `AlbumArtService` with the Amazon access key you obtained earlier. To achieve this, add a `String` property called `accessKeyId` to the `AlbumArtService`, such as the one shown here:

```
String accessKeyId
```

Now you can use a technique called *property override configuration* to specify the value of this property in `grails-app/conf/Config.groovy`. Every service in Grails translates into a singleton Spring bean. The name of the bean is formulated from the class name using bean conventions. Hence, the bean name for `AlbumArtService` will be `albumArtService`. You can set properties on the `albumArtService` bean from `Config.groovy` by using the beans block, as shown in Listing 8-18.

Listing 8-18. *Configuring Beans Using Config.groovy*

```
beans {
    albumArtService {
        // Set to your Amazon Web Services Access key to enable album art
        accessKeyId =  "8DSFLJL34320980DFJ" // Not a real Amazon access key!
    }
}
```

The advantage of this approach is that thanks to the features offered by `Config.groovy`, you can easily specify per-environment access keys rather than hard-coding the key into the `AlbumArtService` class. So, with the `accessKeyId` set, it's time to step through the implementation of the `AlbumArtService`. The first thing you need to do is provide a method called `getAlbumArt` that takes the `Artist` name and `Album` title:

```
String getAlbumArt(String artist, String album) {
    ...
}
```

Now you need to create an instance of the Amazon `ItemSearchRequest` class (remember to import the package!) and populate it with the `Artist` name `Album` title info, the index you want to search, and the response group you're after:

```
import com.amazonaws.a2s.model.*
..
def request = new ItemSearchRequest()
request.searchIndex = 'Music'
request.responseGroup = ['Images']
request.artist = artist
request.title = album
```

After creating an `ItemSearchRequest` instance, you need to pass it to the `AmazonA2SClient` class to obtain a response:

```
import com.amazonaws.a2s.*
..
def client = new AmazonA2SClient(accessKeyId, "")
def response = client.itemSearch(request)
```

With the response in hand, you can extract the information you want by indexing into the response:

```
return response.items[0].item[0].largeImage.URL
```

Great! You have something that works, but it is heavily optimized for the happy path, so what happens when things go wrong? Or if the `accessKeyId` is misconfigured? Or, heaven forbid, if you pass in a `null` artist or album? This is where unit testing best practices come in handy.

So, before you get too far ahead of yourself, let's create some tests to verify this thinking. Create an `AlbumArtServiceTests` test suite within the `test/unit` directory and in the same package as the `AlbumArtService` by running this command:

```
grails create-unit-test com.g2one.gtunes.AlbumArtServiceTests
```

Now let's test what happens if there is no `accessKeyId`:

```
void testNoAccessKey() {
    def albumArtService = new AlbumArtService()
    assertNull albumArtService.getAlbumArt("foo", "bar")
}
```

Run the test by executing the `test-app` command and passing in the name of the test suite. For example:

```
grails test-app com.g2one.gtunes.AlbumArtService
```

The result? An error. Unsurprisingly, the `AmazonA2SClient` was unhappy that you failed to specify a valid `accessKeyId` and threw an exception. You need to deal with the case where there is no `accessKeyId` specified.

The logical thing to do in this case is to return some default image to be rendered since one cannot be obtained from Amazon without an `accessKeyId`. Let's specify a constant that holds the location of this default image:

```
static final DEFAULT_ALBUM_ART_IMAGE =  "/images/no-album-art.gif"
```

Now wrap the code in an `if/else` block to ensure that if no `accessKeyId` is available you return the default value:

```
String getAlbumArt(String artist, String album) {
    if(accessKeyId)
        ...
    }
    else {
        log.warn """No Amazon access key specified.
        Set [beans.albumArtService.accessKeyId] in Config.groovy"""
        return DEFAULT_ALBUM_ART_IMAGE
    }
}
```

Good work, but hang on...the test is still failing? Since the previous assertion was checking for a null return value and not the default image location, you need to change the test:

```
void testNoAccessKey() {
    def albumArtService = new AlbumArtService()
    assertEquals AlbumArtService.DEFAULT_ALBUM_ART_IMAGE,
                           albumArtService.getAlbumArt("foo", "bar")
}
```

Now let's test what happens if an exception emerges from the AmazonA2SClient for any other reason—maybe a network outage or corrupt data. Since this is a unit test, you don't want to actually communicate with Amazon in the test because that would slow the test down. You can use metaprogramming techniques to provide a mock implementation of the AmazonA2SClient's itemSearch method instead via ExpandoMetaClass, as in Listing 8-19.

Listing 8-19. *Mocking Methods with ExpandoMetaClass*

```
void testExceptionFromAmazon() {
    AmazonA2SClient.metaClass.itemSearch = { ItemSearchRequest request ->
            throw new Exception("test exception")
    }
    def albumArtService = new AlbumArtService()
    albumArtService.accessKeyId = "293473894732974"

    assertEquals AlbumArtService.DEFAULT_ALBUM_ART_IMAGE,
                           albumArtService.getAlbumArt("Radiohead", "The Bends")
}
void tearDown() {
    GroovySystem.metaClassRegistry.removeMetaClass(AmazonA2SClient)
}
```

The key line of Listing 8-19 is highlighted in bold as you override the default implementation of the itemSearch method to simply throw an exception. (You can find out more about metaprogramming techniques in Appendix A.) If you run this test now, it will fail with an error. Why? The reason is simple—you are not currently catching any exceptions. This is one area where writing good tests really helps identify potential weaknesses in your code.

To correct the problem, update AlbumArtService to wrap the call to the Amazon client in a try/catch block, as in Listing 8-20.

Listing 8-20. *Gracefully Dealing with Exceptions from Amazon*

```
String getAlbumArt(String artist, String album) {
    ...
    try {
        ...
    }
```

```
    catch(Exception e) {
        log.error "Problem communicating with Amazon: ${e.message}", e
        return DEFAULT_ALBUM_ART_IMAGE
    }
    ...
}
```

Phew. You're nearly done; there is just one more thing to consider. Whenever dealing with any remote resource, you have to consider the performance implications. Currently, you're asking Amazon to look up album art each time you call the getAlbumArt method. However, since there is a high likelihood that you'll be calling the getAlbumArt method repeatedly with the same data, it makes sense to cache the result from Amazon.

To do this, you could just store the results in a local map, but what if the site grows really big? Its memory consumption could become problematic. Really, you need a more mature caching solution where you can configure the eviction policy. You can set up an Ehcache instance to hold the cached data. Ehcache is a mature open source caching library that ships with Grails. To set up Ehcache, open the grails-app/conf/spring/resources.groovy file. This script allows you to configure additional Spring beans that can be injected into any Grails-managed artifact such as a controller, service, or tag library.

We'll be going into a great more detail about Spring and Spring beans in Chapter 16, but for now it's enough to know that each method call within the beans closure translates into a Spring bean. The name of the method is the bean name, while the first argument to the method is the bean class. Properties of the bean can be set in the body of the closure that is specified as the last argument.

■**Note** A Spring bean is, typically, a singleton instance of a Java class that is managed by Spring, which by implication makes it injectable into any Grails instance such as a controller or tag library.

To translate this into practice, Listing 8-21 shows how to use Spring's EhCacheFactoryBean class to set up an Ehcache instance that expires every 5 minutes (or 300 seconds).

Listing 8-21. *Configuring an Ehcache Spring Bean*

```
beans = {
    albumArtCache(org.springframework.cache.ehcache.EhCacheFactoryBean) {
        timeToLive = 300
    }
}
```

With that done, you need to augment the existing AlbumArtService to leverage the albumArtCache bean. The first thing you need to consider is the *cache key*. In other words, what logical variable or set of variables is required to look up the data you are interested in? In this case, the key consists of the artist and album arguments passed to the getAlbumArt method.

To formulate a logical key that models these two arguments, you need to create a new Serializable class called AlbumArtKey and implement equals and hashCode according to the rules defined in the javadocs for these methods. Listing 8-22 shows a possible implementation that assumes that the artist and album are required.

Listing 8-22. *The AlbumArtKey Cache Key Class*

```
class AlbumArtKey implements Serializable {
    String artist
    String album
    boolean equals(other) {    artist.equals(other.artist) &&
                                        album.equals(other.album) }
    int hashCode() { artist.hashCode() + album.hashCode() }
}
```

With the cache key done, it's time to put it to use in the AlbumArtService. Listing 8-23 shows the albumArtCache in action; notice how you can use Groovy's safe-dereference operator so that the code works even if the albumArtCache is not provided.

Listing 8-23. *Enabling Caching in AlbumArtService*

```
import net.sf.ehcache.Element
...
def albumArtCache
...
String getAlbumArt(String artist, String album) {
    ...
    def key = new AlbumArtKey(album:album, artist:artist)
    def url = albumArtCache?.get(key)?.value
    if(!url) {
        // amazon look-up here
        ...
        url = response.items[0].item[0].largeImage.URL
        albumArtCache?.put(new Element(key, url))

    }
    return url
}
```

Excellent—you have now completed the AlbumArtService, and it is ready to be injected into a controller or tag library near you. For reference, Listing 8-24 shows the full code for the AlbumArtService, summarizing all that you have achieved.

Listing 8-24. *The AlbumArtService*

```
package com.g2one.gtunes

import org.codehaus.groovy.grails.commons.*
import com.amazonaws.a2s.*
import com.amazonaws.a2s.model.*
import net.sf.ehcache.Element

class AlbumArtService {
    static transactional = false
    static final DEFAULT_ALBUM_ART_IMAGE =  "/images/no-album-art.gif"

    String accessKeyId
    def albumArtCache

    String getAlbumArt(String artist, String album) {

        if(accessKeyId) {
            if(album && artist) {
                def key = new AlbumArtKey(album:album, artist:artist)
                def url = albumArtCache?.get(key)?.value
                if(!url) {
                    try {
                        def request = new ItemSearchRequest()
                        request.searchIndex = 'Music'
                        request.responseGroup = ['Images']
                        request.artist - artist
                        request.title = album

                        def client = new AmazonA2SClient(accessKeyId, "")

                         def response = client.itemSearch(request)

                        // get the URL to the amazon image (if one was returned).
                        url = response.items[0].item[0].largeImage.URL
                        albumArtCache?.put(new Element(key, url))
                    }
                    catch(Exception e) {
                        log.error "Problem communicating with Amazon: ${e.message}",
                            e
```

```
                    return DEFAULT_ALBUM_ART_IMAGE
                }
            }
            return url
        }
        else {
            log.warn "Album title and Artist name must be specified"
            return DEFAULT_ALBUM_ART_IMAGE
        }
    }
    else {
        log.warn """No Amazon access key specified.
        Set [beans.albumArtService.accessKeyId] in Config.groovy"""
        return DEFAULT_ALBUM_ART_IMAGE
    }


    }
}
class AlbumArtKey implements Serializable {
    String artist
    String album
    boolean equals(other) {    artist.equals(other.artist) &&
                                        album.equals(other.album) }
    int hashCode() { artist.hashCode() + album.hashCode() }
}
```

Now, given that you'll want to display album art in the view, it makes sense to create a custom tag that encapsulates that logic. Enter the `AlbumArtTagLib`. To create the `AlbumArtTagLib`, run the following command:

```
$ grails create-tag-lib com.g2one.gtunes.AlbumArt
```

This will result in a new tag library being created at the location grails-app/taglib/com/g2one/gtunes/AlbumArtTagLib.groovy. As you discovered in Chapter 5, tag libraries can be placed in a namespace. Namespaces provide logical groupings for tags. Let's define a `music` namespace for the `AlbumArtTagLib`; see Listing 8-25.

Listing 8-25. *Defining the music Namespace*

```
package com.g2one.gtunes

class AlbumArtTagLib {
    static namespace = "music"
    ...
}
```

To inject the `AlbumArtService` into the `AlbumArtTagLib`, simply define a property that matches the bean naming conventions for the `AlbumArtService`:

```
def albumArtService
```

Now you need to create a tag within the `AlbumArtTagLib` that is capable of outputting an HTML `<img>` tag with the necessary album art URL populated. The `<music:albumArt>` tag will take three attributes: an `artist`, an `album`, and an optional `width` attribute. The remaining attributes should be added to the attributes of the HTML `<img>` tag that is output. Listing 8-26 shows the implementation of the `<music:albumArt>` tag with usage of the `albumArtService` highlighted in bold.

Listing 8-26. *The <music:albumArt> Tag*

```
def albumArt =  { attrs, body ->
    def artist = attrs.remove('artist')?.toString()
    def album = attrs.remove('album')?.toString()
    def width = attrs.remove('width') ?: 200
    if(artist && album) {
        def albumArt = albumArtService.getAlbumArt(artist, album)
        if(albumArt.startsWith("/"))
                albumArt = "${request.contextPath}${albumArt}"
        out << "<img width=\"$width\" src=\"${albumArt}\" border=\"0\" "
        attrs.each { k,v-> out << "$k=\"${v?.encodeAsHTML()}\" "}
        out << "></img>"
    }
}
```

You can test the `<music:albumArt>` tag using Grails' excellent `GroovyPagesTestCase`, which allows you to test GSP tags directly. The `grails create-tag-lib` command already created an integration test at the location `test/integration/com/g2one/gtunes/AlbumArtTagLibTests`, which serves as a starting point for the test. The functionality being tested is similar to the `AlbumArtServiceTests` suite you developed earlier, so (for the sake of brevity) we won't go through every test. However, Listing 8-27 shows how simple extending `GroovyPagesTestCase` makes testing the `<music:albumArt>` tag, by calling the `assertOutputEquals` method that accepts the expected output and the template to use for rendering.

Listing 8-27. *Testing the <music:albumArt> Tag with GroovyPagesTestCase*

```
package com.g2one.gtunes

import grails.test.*
...
class AlbumArtTagLibTests extend GroovyPagesTestCase {
    ...
```

```
    void testGoodResultFromAmazon() {
        AmazonA2SClient.metaClass.itemSearch = { ItemSearchRequest request ->
            [items:[[item:[[largeImage:[URL:"/mock/url/album.jpg"]]]]]] }

        albumArtService.accessKeyId = "293473894732974"

        def template = '<music:albumArt artist="Radiohead" album="The Bends" />'
        def expected = '<img width="200" src="/mock/url/album.jpg" border="0"></img>'
        assertOutputEquals expected, template
    }
}
```

Finally, to put all the pieces together, you need to change the grails-app/views/
album/_album.gsp template so that it can leverage the newly created <music:albumArt> tag.
Listing 8-28 shows the amendments to _album.gsp in bold.

Listing 8-28. *Adding Album Art to the _album.gsp Template*

```
<div id="album${album.id}" class="album">
    <div class="albumArt">
        <music:albumArt artist="${artist}" album="${album}" />
    </div>
    ...
</div>
```

After further CSS trickery, Figure 8-5 shows what the new album art integration looks like.
Much better!

Figure 8-5. *The _album.gsp template with integration album art*

Adding Effects and Animation

What you've achieved so far is pretty neat, but it would be useful to spice it up with a few effects. As well as Prototype, Grails ships with Scriptaculous (`http://script.aculo.us/`), which is a JavaScript effects and animation library.

To start using Scriptaculous, open the `grails-app/views/layouts/main.gsp` layout, and change the `<g:javascript>` tag that currently refers to prototype to this:

```
<g:javascript library="scriptaculous" />
```

Now say you want albums to fade in when you click the "Latest Album" links; the first thing to do is to make sure albums are hidden to begin with. To do so, open the `grails-app/views/album/_album.gsp` template, and ensure the main HTML `<div>` has its `style` attribute set to `display:none`, as in Listing 8-29.

Listing 8-29. *Hiding the Album*

```
<div id="album${album.id}" class="album" style="display:none;">
    ...
</div>
```

Now you could use Ajax events such as `onComplete`, which were discussed in an earlier section, to execute the effect. However, since that would require ensuring every `<g:remoteLink>` tag contained the `onComplete` attribute, it is probably better to use an embedded script inside the template. Try adding the following to the bottom of the `_album.gsp` template:

```
<g:javascript>
    Effect.Appear($('album${album.id}'))
</g:javascript>
```

This executes the Appear effect of the Scriptaculous library. Now whenever you click one of the "Latest Album" links, the album fades in nicely. Scriptaculous has tons of other effects, so it is worth referring to the documentation at `http://script.aculo.us/` to find out what is available. Also, most notable Ajax libraries—many of which offer Grails plugins—also feature similar capabilities. Make sure you explore what is available in your Ajax library of choice!

Ajax-Enabled Form Fields

Wow, that previous section was quite an adventure. But you're not done with Ajax yet. In this section, you'll learn how you can enable Ajax on form fields such as text inputs.

This is often useful if you're implementing features such as autocomplete or an instant search capability like Spotlight on Mac OS X. In fact, search is exactly what you're going to aim to achieve in this section. Sure, it is useful to be able to click the latest additions to the music library, but it is critical that users of gTunes can search the back catalog of songs and albums.

Luckily, Grails provides an extremely useful tag to help implement the search feature—the `<g:remoteField>` tag. As you might guess from the name, `<g:remoteField>` is a text field that sends its value to the server whenever it changes. This is exactly what you'll need for a Spotlight-like search facility.

As a start, open the `grails-app/views/store/shop.gsp` view, and add the `<g:remoteField>` search box, as shown in Listing 8-30.

Listing 8-30. *Using the <g:remoteField> Tag*

```
<div id="searchBox">
    Instant Search: <g:remoteField
                            name="searchBox"
                            update="musicPanel"
                            paramName="q"
                            url="[controller:'store', action:'search']" />
</div>
```

What you have done here is set up a `<g:remoteField>` that sends a request to the search action of the `StoreController`. Using the `paramName` attribute, you can configure the name of the parameter that will contain the value of the input field when it is sent. If you don't specify the `paramName` attribute, then the `<g:remoteField>` tag defaults to sending a parameter named value. Figure 8-6 shows what the search box looks like.

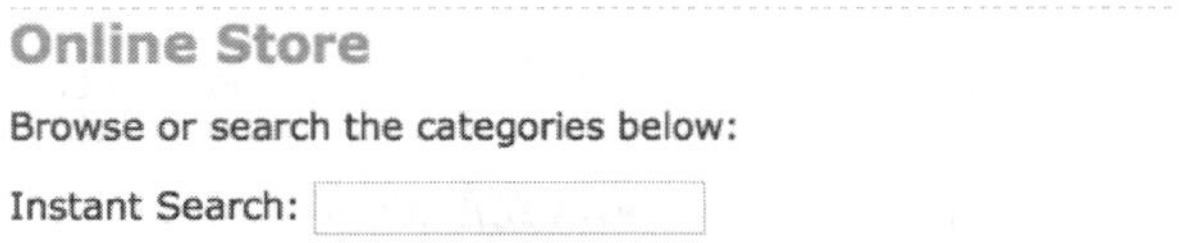

Online Store

Browse or search the categories below:

Instant Search: [   ]

Figure 8-6. *The gTunes instance search box*

If you refresh the page and start typing, you can see that field is already sending remote requests, although you're getting 404 errors in the page rather than anything useful. At this point, it is worth considering how to implement search. You could, of course, use Hibernate queries, but Hibernate is not really designed to be used as a search engine, and designing your own search query language would be a pain.

Needless to say, the Grails plugin system comes to the rescue once again. One of the most popular plugins currently available for Grails is the Searchable plugin, which builds on Compass (`http://www.compass-project.org/`) and Lucene (`http://lucene.apache.org/`).

■**Note** The full documentation for Searchable is available at `http://grails.org/Searchable+Plugin`.

As usual, installing Searchable is trivial. Just run the following command:

```
$ grails install-plugin searchable
```

The Searchable plugin integrates with Grails by providing the ability to expose Grails domain classes as searchable entities. At a simple level, it is possible to add search capabilities by adding the following line to the domain class you want to search:

```
static searchable = true
```

However, it is typically the case that you want to search only a subset of the properties of the domain class. This is, of course, perfectly possible with Searchable, and in fact it defines an entire DSL for mapping between your classes and the search index (a topic beyond the scope of this book).

In this case, you want to be able to search on an album or song's genre and title and on an artist's name. Listing 8-31 shows how to enable the aforementioned behavior using Searchable.

Listing 8-31. *Enabling Search on the gTunes domain*

```
class Song {
    static searchable = [only: ['genre', 'title']]
    ...
}
class Album {
    static searchable = [only: ['genre', 'title']]
    ...
}
class Artist {
    static searchable = [only: ['name']]
    ...
}
```

That was simple enough. Next, it is time to implement the `search` action of the `StoreController`. Like GORM, Searchable provides a bunch of new methods on domain classes that support searching, including the following:

- search: Returns a search result object containing a subset of objects matching the query

- searchTop: Returns the first result object matching the query

- searchEvery: Returns all result objects matching the query

- countHits: Returns the number of hits for a query

- termFreqs: Returns term frequencies for the terms in the index (advanced)

For a full reference on what each method does and how it behaves, refer to the documentation at `http://grails.org/Searchable+Plugin`. For your needs, you're going to use the search method to formulate the search results. Listing 8-32 shows the implementation of the search action of the `StoreController` using Searchable APIs.

Listing 8-32. *Using Searchable to Enable Search*

```
def search = {
    def q = params.q ?: null
    def searchResults
    if(q) {
        searchResults = [
            albumResults: trySearch { Album.search(q, [max:10]) },
```

```
                artistResults: trySearch { Artist.search(q, [max:10]) },
                songResults: trySearch { Song.search(q, [max:10]) },
                q: q.encodeAsHTML()
            ]
        }

        render(template:"searchResults", model: searchResults)
}

def trySearch(Closure callable) {
    try {
        return callable.call()
    }
    catch(Exception e) {
        log.debug "Search Error: ${e.message}", e
        return []
    }
}
```

The code is pretty simple. It obtains the q parameter representing the query and, if it isn't blank, builds a model that contains search results for albums, artists, and songs. One interesting aspect of this code is the trySearch method, which demonstrates a compelling use of Groovy closures to deal with exceptions. Since an exception will likely be because of an error in the search syntax, it is preferable to log that error and return an empty result rather than throwing the error back to the user.

Once the search results have been formulated within a searchResults variable, the code renders a _searchResults.gsp template, passing the searchResults as the model. As Listing 8-33 demonstrates, the grails-app/views/store/_searchResults.gsp template is trivial and simply reuses the existing templates such as _albumList.gsp and _artistList.gsp to display results.

Listing 8-33. *The _searchResults.gsp Template*

```
<div id="searchResults" class="searchResults">

    <g:if test="${albumResults?.results}">
        <div id="albumResults" class="resultsPane">
            <h2>Album Results</h2>
            <g:render template="/album/albumList"
                            model="[albums:albumResults.results]"></g:render>

        </div>
    </g:if>
```

```
<g:if test="${artistResults?.results}">
    <div id="artistResults" class="resultsPane">
        <h2>Artist Results</h2>
        <g:render template="/artist/artistList"
                        model="[artists:artistResults.results]"></g:render>
    </div>
</g:if>

<g:if test="${songResults?.results}">
    <div id="songResults" class="resultsPane">
        <h2>Song Results</h2>
        <g:render template="/song/songList"
                        model="[songs:songResults.results]"></g:render>
    </div>

</g:if>
</div>
```

After calling on your CSS prowess once more, you now have nicely formulated search results appearing, and even better, because they're using the same `<g:remoteLink>` tag as the "Latest Albums" lists on the right of the screen, they're already Ajax-enabled out of the box. Simply by clicking one of the search results, you get an `Album`'s details pulled in via Ajax! Figure 8-7 shows the usage of the search box and demonstrates how wildcard capabilities using the asterisk (*) character are supported thanks to the Searchable plugin.

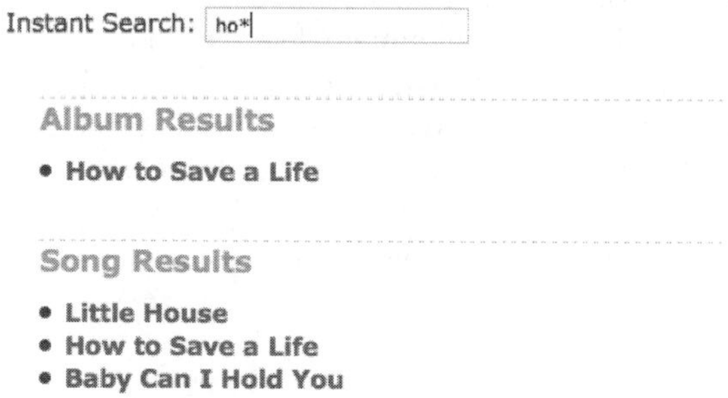

Instant Search: `ho*|`

Album Results

- How to Save a Life

Song Results

- Little House
- How to Save a Life
- Baby Can I Hold You

Figure 8-7. *Instant search results using <g:remoteField> and Searchable*

A Note on Ajax and Performance

It is important to note the impact that using Ajax has on an application's performance. Given the number of small snippets of code that get rendered, it will come as little surprise that badly designed Ajax applications have to deal with a significantly larger number of requests. What you have seen so far in this chapter is a naïve approach to Ajax development. You have waved the Ajax magic wand over your application with little consideration of the performance implications.

Nevertheless, it is not too late to take some of these things into account. You can use several techniques to reduce the number of requests an Ajax application performs before you start throwing more hardware at the problem.

The first thing to remember is that an Ajax call is a remote network call and therefore expensive. If you have developed with EJB, you will recall some of the patterns used to optimize EJB remote method calls. Things such as the Data Transfer Object (DTO) are equally applicable in the Ajax world.

Fundamentally, the DTO pattern serves as a mechanism for batching operations into a single call and passing enough state to the server for several operations to be executed at once. This pattern can be equally effective in Ajax, given that it is better to do one call that transmits a lot of information than a dozen small ones.

Another popular technique is to move more complexity onto the client. Given that Ajax clients, in general, occupy a single physical page, a fair amount of state can be kept on the client via caching. Caching is probably the most important technique in Ajax development and, where possible, should be exploited to optimize communications with the server.

Whichever technique you use, it will pay dividends in the long run, and the server infrastructure guys will love you for it. The users of your application will also appreciate its faster response times and interactivity.

Summary

In this chapter, you learned about the extensive range of adaptive Ajax tags that Grails offers and how to apply them to give your gTunes application a more usable interactive interface. On this particular journey, you also explored advanced Grails development, learning a lot more about how controllers, templates, and the render method function in combination.

In the past few chapters, you've been very much involved with the web layer of Grails in the shape of controllers, GSP, tag libraries, and Ajax. However, everything you have looked at so far has used completely stateless communication. In the next chapter, you'll look at how Grails supports web flows for rich conversations that span multiple pages.

CHAPTER 9

■■■

Creating Web Flows

The majority of modern web frameworks are heavily optimized for dealing with stateless interaction between client and server. In other words, these frameworks assume that you'll be defining simple actions that remember nothing about where the user came from, where the user is going, and what state the user is in. The stateless model offers you advantages, of course, including the ability to scale your application's hardware without the need to consider replication of state.

Nevertheless, you'll occasionally face significant disadvantages to implementing certain use cases with a stateless model. Take, for instance, the good old shopping-cart use case. A shopping cart typically entails a step-by-step process of accepting and displaying information before progressing to the next screen. A shopping-cart user might go through these steps:

- Confirm the basket items and their prices.

- Enter a shipping address.

- Enter a billing address.

- Enter credit-card details.

- Confirm the order.

- Show the invoice.

You don't want one of your users jumping into the middle of this inherently sequential process. Of course, this restriction applies not only to shopping carts, but also to any functionality that is "wizard-like" in nature. To implement a shopping-cart use case with a stateless model, you would need to store the state somewhere—maybe by storing it in the session or using cookies. You would then need code in your actions to ensure users arrive from a point that's appropriate. In other words, you don't want the user going straight from confirming the basket items to showing the invoice. The user needs to have originated from the correct place.

However you look at it, implementing this use case in a stateless model is a pain. One way to alleviate this pain would be to use Asynchronous JavaScript Technology and XML (Ajax) to manage all the state on the client, which we discussed in the previous chapter. You could reasonably push all this state management to the client by eliminating the need to refresh the browser. The individual steps in your flow could be HTML elements that are shown or hidden depending on your current state.

However, Ajax is not an option for everyone just yet, and certainly not the solution to every problem. Occasionally, it makes a great deal of sense to push this job onto the server.

Fortunately, Grails provides built-in support to aid the creation of rich web flows, often referred to as "web conversations." Built on the excellent Spring Web Flow project (http://www.springframework.org/webflow), flows are integrated seamlessly into Grails with a Groovy domain-specific language (DSL) for flow creation.

Getting Started with Flows

Flows in Grails are a mechanism for defining a series of states, beginning with a start state and terminating with an end state. With Grails flows, it is impossible for users to call your server in the "middle" of a flow unless they have gone through the necessary steps (or states) to reach that point.

How does it work? Spring Web Flow is, essentially, an advanced state machine. A flowExecutionKey and event ID is passed between client and server, typically as a request parameter, which allows a user to *transition* from one state to another. Don't get too worked up about the mechanics of this; Grails deals with most of the communication between client and server for you. What you do need to know, however, is how to define a flow.

Defining a Flow

Unlike the Spring Web Flow project itself, Grails doesn't require any XML configuration to get going. To create a flow, simply define an action in your controller whose name ends with the "Flow" suffix (by convention). Listing 9-1 shows how you would define a hypothetical shopping-cart flow.

Listing 9-1. *Defining a Flow*

```
class StoreController {
    def shoppingCartFlow = {
        ...
    }
}
```

Every flow has what is known as a "flow id." The flow id, by convention, is the name of the action minus the "Flow" suffix. In Listing 9-1, you defined an action called shoppingCartFlow; hence the flow id is shoppingCart. The importance of the flow id will become more relevant when we look at linking to flows and creating flow views.

Defining the Start State

Currently, the shoppingCart flow doesn't look all that different from a regular controller action. However, the way you construct a flow differs greatly. First of all, unlike actions, the body of the closure doesn't define the logic; instead, it defines a sequence of flow *states*. States are represented as method calls that take a closure parameter. Listing 9-2 shows how you can define the start state of the shoppingCart flow.

Listing 9-2. *Defining the Start State*

```
def shoppingCartFlow = {
    showCart {
        on("checkout").to "enterPersonalDetails"
        on("continueShopping").to "displayCatalogue"
    }
    ...
}
```

The start state is always the first state in the flow. The start state in Listing 9-2, highlighted in bold, is called showCart. It's a "view" state as well as a start state.

View states pause the flow execution for view rendering, allowing users to interact with the flow. In this case, because the flow id is shoppingCart and the state is called showCart, by convention Grails will look for a GSP at the location grails-app/views/store/shoppingCart/ showCart.gsp. In other words, unlike regular actions, which look for their views relative to the controller directory (grails-app/views/store), flow views exist in a subdirectory that matches the flow id—in this case, grails-app/views/store/shoppingCart.

You'll notice in Listing 9-2 that the showCart state has two event handlers. Invoking the on method and passing the name of the expected event defines an event handler. You can then define what the event handler should do in response to the event by calling the to method of the return value. Here is the example:

```
on("checkout").to "enterPersonalDetails"
```

This line specifies that when the checkout event is triggered, the flow should transition to the enterPersonalDetails state. Simple, really. In programming terminology, DSLs that let you use a method's return value to chain method calls in this way are often referred to as "fluent APIs". You'll learn more about events and triggering events later in the chapter.

Defining End States

A flow's end state is a state that essentially terminates the flow's execution. Users must start at the beginning of the flow once an end state has been triggered. An end state is either a state that takes no arguments, or one that performs an external redirect to another action or flow. Listing 9-3 shows how to define a couple of end states for the shoppingCart flow, called displayInvoice and cancelTransaction.

Listing 9-3. *Defining an End State*

```
def shoppingCartFlow = {
    showCart {
        on("checkout").to "enterPersonalDetails"
        on("continueShopping").to "displayCatalogue"
    }
    ...
```

```
            displayInvoice()
            cancelTransaction {
                redirect(controller:"store")
            }
        }
    }
```

While the `displayInvoice` end state renders a view called `grails-app/views/store/shoppingCart/displayInvoice.gsp`, the `cancelTransaction` end state performs a redirect to another controller.

Action States and View States

Between the start and end states, you'll typically have several other states, which are either the aforementioned view states or *action* states. Just to recap: A view state pauses the flow execution for view rendering; it doesn't define an action or a redirect. As we mentioned, the start state in Listing 9-2 is also a view state.

By default, the name of the view to render comes from the state name. However, you can change the name of the view to render by using the render method, as you do with regular controller actions. Listing 9-4 demonstrates how to render a view at the location `grails-app/views/store/shoppingCart/basket.gsp` simply by specifying the name "basket."

Listing 9-4. *Changing the View to Render in a View State*

```
showCart {
    render(view:"basket")
    ...
}
```

An *action* state differs from a view state in that instead of waiting for user input, it executes a block of code that dictates how the flow should transition. For example, consider the code in Listing 9-5.

Listing 9-5. *An Action State*

```
listAlbums {
    action {
        [ albumList:Album.list(max:10,sort:'dateCreated', order:'desc') ]
    }
    on("success").to "showCatalogue"
    on(Exception).to "handleError"
}
```

The `listAlbums` state defines an action by calling the `action` method and passing in the block of code that defines the action as a closure. In this case, the action obtains a list of the 10 newest albums and places the list items into a Map with the key `albumList`. This map is returned as the *model* for the action and is automatically put into `flow` scope. Don't be too concerned about this statement; `flow` scopes are the subject of the next section.

As well as demonstrating how to supply a model from a flow action, the code in Listing 9-5 introduces a couple of other new concepts. First of all, if no error occurs when the flow action is executed, the success event is automatically triggered. This will result in the flow transitioning to the showCatalogue action.

Finally, the code contains a second event handler that uses a convention we haven't seen yet. By passing in the exception type to the on method, you can specify event handlers for particular types of exception. Listing 9-5 includes a generic exception handler that catches all subclasses of java.lang.Exception, but you could just as easily catch a more specific exception:

```
on(StoreNotAvailableException).to "maintenancePage"
```

In the example in Listing 9-5, the action defines and returns a model. However, action states can also trigger custom events from the action. For example, take a look at Listing 9-6.

Listing 9-6. *Triggering Events from an Action State*

```
isGift {
    action {
        params.isGift ? yes() : no()
    }
    on("yes").to "wrappingOptions"
    on("no").to "enterShippingAddress"
}
```

In the example in Listing 9-6, the code defines an action state that inspects the params object to establish whether the user has requested to have her purchase gift-wrapped. If the user has, the code triggers the yes event simply by calling the method yes(). Note that the return value of the action dictates the event to trigger, so in some cases you might need a return statement as shown in Listing 9-7.

Listing 9-7. *Triggering Events Using the Return Value*

```
isGift {
    action {
        if(params.isGift)
            return yes()
        else
            return no()
    }
    on("yes").to "wrappingOptions"
    on("no").to "enterShippingAddress"
}
```

■**Note** In Groovy 1.6, the notation of returning the last expression in a method or closure was extended to cover if/else blocks. The result is that the return statements in Listing 9-7 are no longer necessary.

Flow Scopes

In addition to scopes found in regular actions such as `request` and `session,` you can use a few other scopes associated with Grails flows: `flash`, `flow`, and `conversation`. Scopes are essentially just containers, like maps. The main difference is how and when the objects contained within these scopes are cleared. The following list summarizes the behavior of each scope:

- `flash`: Stores the object for the current and next request only.

- `flow`: Stores objects for the scope of the flow, removing them when the flow reaches an end state.

- `conversation`: Stores objects for the scope of the conversation, including the root flow and nested subflows.

As demonstrated in the previous section, models returned from action states are automatically placed into `flow` scope. The `flow` scope is typically the most-used scope in flow development because it allows you to store entries for the length of the entire flow, which are then automatically cleaned up when the flow terminates by reaching an end state or expiring.

The `conversation` scope differs in that it stores entries for the scope of the root flow and all nested subflows. Yes, Grails' Web Flow support includes support for subflows, which we will discuss later in the chapter.

Finally, `flash` scope behaves similarly to the regular `flash` scope provided by controller actions. The main difference is that objects placed into `flash` scope within a flow must implement the `java.io.Serializable` interface.

Flows, Serialization, and Flow Storage

The end of the previous section touched on an important issue regarding the use of flows. Whenever placing any object and its associations within one of the flow scopes, you *must* ensure the object in question implements the `java.io.Serializable` interface.

Why? Quite simply, flows differ from regular scopes such as `session` and `request` in that they store their state in a serialized, compressed form on the server. If you prefer a stateless server, you can instead store the state in the client by setting the `grails.webflow.flow.storage` property to `client` in `grails-app/conf/Config.groovy`:

```
grails.webflow.flow.storage="client"
```

In this case, Grails' Web Flow support will store the state in the `flowExecutionKey` that is passed from client to server. Using client storage has two main disadvantages:

- You can use only HTTP `POST` requests—via a form submission, for example—to trigger events, because the `flowExecutionKey` is too large for browsers to include in the URL.

- This method is inherently unsecure unless delivered over HTTPS because you are sending potentially sensitive data, in serialized form, to and from the server.

If security is not a concern for your application, or you are happy running your flow over HTTPS, then using a client flow-storage mechanism might make sense because it allows your server to remain stateless. You should, however, make this decision up front because your storage mechanism affects how you implement the flow. (As we mentioned, choosing client storage means you must use POST requests only.)

Whichever choice you make, the requirement to implement `java.io.Serializable` remains the same. As you will recall from your Java experience, if you have any properties that you don't want serialized in your objects, you must mark them as `transient`. This includes any closures you might have defined (such as GORM events, which we'll discuss in Chapter 10), because Groovy's closures do not implement the `Serializable` interface:

```
transient onLoad = {}
```

Triggering Events from the View

In the previous section on action states and view states, you learned that a view state is a state that pauses flow execution in order to render a view that takes user input. However, how exactly does the view trigger a flow-execution event? Essentially, there are two ways to trigger an event: from a link, or from a form submission.

Let's look at links first. As we discussed in Chapter 4, Grails provides the built-in `<g:link>` tag for producing HTML anchor tags that link to a particular controller and action. Linking to flows is pretty much the same as linking to a regular action. For example, the following usage of the `<g:link>` tag will link to the start state of the `shoppingCart` flow:

```
<g:link controller="store" action="shoppingCart">My Cart</g:link>
```

Note that you use the flow id, discussed earlier, as the value of the `action` attribute. Of course, linking to the start state allows you to trigger a new flow execution, but doesn't answer the original question of how to trigger flow-execution events. Let's revisit the code from the start state of the `shoppingCart` flow:

```
showCart {
    on("checkout").to "enterPersonalDetails"
    on("continueShopping").to "displayCatalogue"
}
```

In the `showCart` state, there are two potential events that could be triggered: `checkout` and `continueShopping`. To trigger one of these events from the `<g:link>` tag, you can use the `event` attribute:

```
<g:link controller="store" action="shoppingCart" event="checkout">Checkout</g:link>
```

Note that the value of the `action` attribute always remains the same when linking to a flow. What differs is the event, and in this case you are telling Grails to trigger the `checkout` event when the link is clicked.

The mechanism to trigger events from forms is slightly different. Essentially, Grails uses the `name` attribute of the submit button that was clicked to figure out which event you want to trigger. Using the view state from Listing 9-7, you can easily trigger each event using the `<g:submitButton>` tag as shown in Listing 9-8.

Listing 9-8. *Triggering Events from Form Submissions*

```
<g:form name="shoppingForm" url="[controller:'store', action:'shoppingCart']">
    ...
    <g:submitButton name="checkout" value="Checkout" />
    <g:submitButton name="continueShopping" value="Continue Shopping" />
</g:form>
```

Transition Actions and Form Validation

In the previous section, we looked at how you can trigger events on form submission. However, we didn't discuss how to validate a form submission. One way is to submit to an action state. In the section on action and view states, we looked at how you can have action states that execute a particular block of code, which is extremely useful for making the state decision dynamic. However, you're better off using a *transition action* to perform validation.

A transition action is essentially an action that executes when a particular event is triggered. Here's the interesting part: if the transition action fails due to an error, the transition is halted and the state is restored back to the originating state. Take, for example, the state in Listing 9-9.

Listing 9-9. *Using Transition Actions for Validation*

```
enterPersonalDetails {
    on("submit") {
          flow.person = new Person(params)
          flow.person.validate() ? success() : error()
    }.to "enterShipping"
    on("return").to "showCart"
}
```

In the example in Listing 9-9, there is a view state called `enterPersonalDetails` that renders a form where users can enter their personal information. When the user submits the form, the `submit` event is triggered. Notice how the on method that defines the `submit` event is passed a closure. This closure is the `submit` transition action. Contained within the body of the transition action is code, which creates a new `Person` domain class and populates the class's properties by passing the `params` object into the constructor of the `Person` class.

Notice how the `submit` transition action then performs validation by calling `validate()` on the `Person` instance within the flow. Using the ternary operator, the transition action will return either a `success` event or an `error` event. If the result is a `success` event, the transition to the `enterShipping` state continues as expected. But if the result is an `error` event, the transition is halted and the user is returned to the `enterPersonalDetails` state, where the view can render the errors contained within the `person` object.

Subflows and Conversation Scope

As we mentioned briefly in the previous section on flow scopes, Grails' Web Flow implementation supports the notion of subflows, or flows within flows. Consider the `chooseGiftWrapFlow` flow in Listing 9-10, which allows users to select their ideal gift-wrap for a given purchase.

Listing 9-10. *The chooseGiftWrapFlow Flow*

```
def chooseGiftWrapFlow = {
    chooseWrapping {
        on("next").to 'chooseRibbon'
        on('cancel').to 'cancelGiftWrap'
    }
    chooseRibbon {
        on("next").to 'confirmSelection'
        on("back").to 'chooseWrapping'
    }
    confirmSelection {
        on('confirm') {
            def giftWrap = new GiftWrap(params)
            if(!giftWrap.validate()) return error()
            else {
                conversation.giftWrap = giftWrap
            }
        }.to 'giftWrapChosen'
        on('cancel').to 'cancelGiftWrap'
    }
    cancelGiftWrap()
    giftWrapChosen()
}
```

The chooseGiftWrap flow basically goes through three view states (chooseWrapping, chooseRibbon, and confirmSelection) to establish the ideal wrapping for the user. Additionally, there are two end states with pretty self-explanatory names: cancelGiftWrap and giftWrapChosen.

To include the chooseGiftWrap flow in the main shoppingCart flow, you can create a new subflow state by calling the subflow method and passing in a reference to the chooseGiftWrap flow. Listing 9-11 shows an example by defining a wrappingOptions subflow state.

Listing 9-11. *Defining a Subflow State*

```
def shoppingCartFlow = {
    ...
    wrappingOptions {
        subflow(chooseGiftWrapFlow)
        on('giftWrapChosen') {
            flow.giftWrap = conversation.giftWrap
        }
        on('cancelGiftWrap'). to 'enterShippingAddress'
    }
}
```

You should note two critical things about the code in Listing 9-11. First, the wrappingOptions subflow state defines two event handlers called giftWrapChosen and cancelGiftWrap. You will note that these event names match the end states of the chooseGiftWrap flow!

The second important thing is that the confirmSelection state from the chooseGiftWrap flow in Listing 9-10 places an instance of a hypothetical GiftWrap domain class in conversation scope. As we mentioned in the section on flow scopes, conversation scope is shared across all flows and subflows, so it's a good way to pass variables between flows. The giftWrapChosen event handler in Listing 9-11 defines a transition action, which takes the giftWrap variable from conversation scope and places it into local flow scope.

Flows in Action

Now that you know the mechanics of Grails flows, you can put this knowledge into action by developing the next use case for the gTunes application. You have the ability to browse the gTunes Music Library, but gTunes won't be a proper store until users can purchase music!

You'll be selling digital music, so you won't have anything to ship to users. So to make it interesting, you're going to offer a unique, possibly misguided, feature in the gTunes music store: the ability to order a hard-copy CD along with a digital purchase—for free!

To spice things up even further, you're going to implement that classic Amazonesque "recommendations" feature, which tries to tempt users into buying other albums before completing a purchase. Figure 9-1 shows the basic decision-making process that the user follows when stepping through the flow.

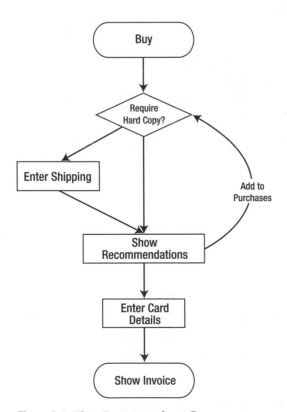

Figure 9-1. *The gTunes purchase flow*

Updating the Domain

The first task is to provide prices for the albums in the music store. To do so, open the `Album` domain class and add a `price` property. Listing 9-12 shows the changes to the `grails-app/domain/Album.groovy` file.

Listing 9-12. *Adding Prices to the Album Class*

```
package com.g2one.gtunes

class Album implements Serializable{
    ..
    Float price
    static constraints = {
        ...
        price scale:2, nullable:false
    }
}
```

The code in Listing 9-12 not only adds a `price` property, but also constrains the `price` property in two ways. First, the `nullable` constraint ensures consistency by not allowing the `price` to be `null`. Second (and more interesting), the `scale` constraint is used to ensure that the `price` is constrained to two decimal places.

With the knowledge that you're developing a flow, you also need to change the `Album` class to implement the `java.io.Serializable` interface as required by flows. In fact, because you're likely to use the rest of the domain in the context of the flow, you will need to update all the other existing domain classes to implement `Serializable`, too.

In addition to these changes to the existing domain, you're going to define three new domain classes to capture various aspects of a transaction. First is a domain class called `Payment`, which holds the invoice number and a reference to the `User` who completed the purchase. Listing 9-13 shows the source for the `Payment` class.

Listing 9-13. *The Payment Domain Class*

```
package com.g2one.gtunes

class Payment  implements Serializable {
    String invoiceNumber
    User user
    static hasMany = [albumPayments:AlbumPayment]

    static constraints = {
        invoiceNumber blank:false, matches:/INV-\d+?-\d+/
    }
}
```

As you can see from the code in Listing 9-13, a `Payment` has many `AlbumPayment` instances. The `AlbumPayment` class is used to track what `Albums` a `User` has purchased, as well as the address to which the CD version of the Album needs to be shipped. The source for the AlbumPayment class is shown in Listing 9-14.

Listing 9-14. *The AlbumPayment Domain Class*

```
package com.g2one.gtunes

class AlbumPayment implements Serializable{
    Album album
    User user
    Address shippingAddress

    static constraints = {
        shippingAddress nullable:true
    }
}
```

Finally, to capture an AlbumPayment instance's shipping address, you'll need an Address class. Listing 9-15 shows the Address class with appropriate constraints applied.

Listing 9-15. *The Address Domain Class*

```
package com.g2one.gtunes

class Address implements Serializable{
    String number
    String street
    String city
    String state
    String postCode
    String country

    static constraints = {
        number blank:false, maxSize:200
        street blank:false, maxSize:250
        city blank:false, maxSize:200
        state nullable:true
        postCode blank:false, maxSize:50
        country blank:false, maxSize:200
    }
}
```

Updating the View

With the updates to the domain done, let's move on to the view. Open the `grails-app/views/album/_album.gsp` template and add the `price` property to the `albumInfo` `<div>`. Now define a new `<div>` that contains a `<g:link>` tag that links to a new action of the `StoreController` called buy. Listing 9-16 shows the changes to the `_album.gsp` template, highlighted in bold.

Listing 9-16. *Updates to the _album.gsp Template*

```
<div id="album${album.id}" class="album" style="display:none;">
    ...
    <div class="albumDetails">
         ...
        <div class="albumInfo">
            Genre: ${album.genre ?: 'Other'}<br>
            Year: ${album.year}<br>
            <strong>Price: $ ${album.price}</strong>
        </div>
        ...
        <div class="albumLinks">
            ...
            <div id="buttons" style="float:right;">
                <g:link controller="store" action="buy" id="${album.id}">
                    <img src="${createLinkTo(dir:'images',file:'buy-button.gif')}"
                                border="0">
                </g:link>
            </div>
        </div>
    </div>
</div>
```

The key addition to the `_album.gsp` template is the link:

```
<g:link controller="store" action="buy" id="${album.id}">
```

The `<g:link>` tag defines a link to the buy action of the `StoreController` that passes the `Album` identifier as part of the request. A few CSS tweaks later, you should have something that resembles the screenshot in Figure 9-2.

Figure 9-2. *Screenshot of the updates _album.gsp template*

Defining the Flow

In the previous section, you created a `<g:link>` tag that referenced an action called buy. As you might have guessed, buy is going to be the name of the flow. Open grails-app/controllers/StoreController and define a new flow called buyFlow, as shown in Listing 9-17.

Listing 9-17. *Defining the buyFlow*

```
def buyFlow {
    ...
}
```

Adding a Start State

Now let's consider the start state. Here's a logical point to start: After a user clicks on the "Buy" button, the application should ask him whether he'd like to receive a CD version of the album. But before you can do that, you should validate whether he is logged in; if he is, you should place him into flow scope.

To achieve this, you can make the first state of the flow an action state. Listing 9-18 shows an action state, called start, that checks if the user exists in the session object and triggers a login() event if not.

Listing 9-18. *Checking Login Details with an Action State*

```
1    start {
2        action {
3            // check login status
4            if(session.user) {
```

```
5              flow.user = User.get(session.user.id)
6              return success()
7            }
8          login()
9        }
10     on('success') {
11         if(!flow.albumPayments) flow.albumPayments = []
12         def album = Album.get(params.id)
13
14         if(!flow.albumPayments.album.find { it?.id == album.id }) {
15             flow.lastAlbum = new AlbumPayment(album:album)
16             flow.albumPayments << flow.lastAlbum
17         }
18     }.to 'requireHardCopy'
19     on('login') {
20         flash.album = Album.get(params.id)
21         flash.message = "user.not.logged.in"
22     }.to 'requiresLogin'
23   }
```

The login event handler contains a transition action that places the Album instance into flash scope along with a message code (you'll understand why shortly). The event then causes a transition to a state called requiresLogin, which is the first example of a redirect state. Listing 9-19 shows the requiresLogin state using the objects that were placed into flash scope to perform a redirect back to the display action of the AlbumController.

Listing 9-19. *Using a Redirect Action to Exit the Flow*

```
requiresLogin {
    redirect(controller:"album",
                    action:"display",
                    id: flash.album.id,
                    params:[message:flash.message])
}
```

Hold on a moment; the display action of the AlbumController doesn't return a full HTML page! In the previous chapter, you designed the code to handle Ajax requests and return only partial responses. Luckily, Grails makes it possible to modify this action to deal with both Ajax and regular requests using the xhr property of the request object, which returns true if the request is an Ajax request. Listing 9-20 shows the changes made to the display action in bold.

Listing 9-20. *Adapting the display Action to Handle Regular Requests*

```
def display = {
    def album = Album.get(params.id)
    if(album) {
        def artist = album.artist
```

```
            if(request.xhr) {
                render(template:"album", model:[artist:artist, album:album])
            }
            else {
                render(view:"show", model:[artist:artist, album:album])
            }
        }
        else {
            response.sendError 404
        }
    }
}
```

The code highlighted in bold changes the action to render a view called grails-app/views/
album/show.gsp if the request is a non-Ajax request. Of course, the shop.gsp view in question
doesn't exist yet, and at this point you can consider refactoring some of the view code developed in the previous section. There is a lot of commonality not only for shop.gsp, but also for
the pages of the buy flow.

Currently the instant-search box and the top-five-songs panel are hard-coded into the
grails-app/views/store/shop.gsp view, so start by extracting those into templates called
_searchbox.gsp and _top5panel.gsp, respectively. Listing 9-21 shows the updated shop.gsp
view with the extracted code replaced by templates highlighted in bold.

Listing 9-21. *Extracting Common GSP Code into Templates*

```
<html>
    ...
    <body id="body">
        <h1>Online Store</h1>
        <p>Browse or search the categories below:</p>
        <g:render template="/store/searchbox" />
        <g:render template="/store/top5panel" model="${pageScope.variables}" />
        <div id="musicPanel">
        </div>
    </body>
</html>
```

Notice how in Listing 9-21 you can pass the current pages' model to the template using
the expression pageScope.variables. With that done, you're going to take advantage of the
knowledge you gained about SiteMesh layouts in Chapter 5. Using the magic of SiteMesh,
you can make the layout currently embedded into shop.gsp truly reusable. Cut and paste the
code within shop.gsp into a new layout called grails-app/views/layouts/storeLayout.gsp,
adding the <g:layoutBody /> tag into the "musicPanel" <div>. Listing 9-22 shows the new
storeLayout.gsp file.

Listing 9-22. *Creating a New storeLayout*

```
<html>
    <head>
        <meta http-equiv="Content-type" content="text/html; charset=utf-8">
        <meta name="layout" content="main">
        <title>gTunes Store</title>
    </head>
    <body id="body">
        <h1>Online Store</h1>
        <p>Browse or search the categories below:</p>
        <g:render template="/store/searchbox" />
        <g:render template="/store/top5panel" model="${pageScope.variables}" />
        <div id="musicPanel">
            <g:layoutBody />
        </div>
    </body>
</html>
```

Notice how you can still supply the HTML `<meta>` tag that ensures the main.gsp layout is applied to pages rendered with this layout. In other words, you can use layouts within layouts!

Now that you've cut and pasted the contents of shop.gsp into the storeLayout.gsp file, shop.gsp has effectively been rendered useless. You can fix that using the `<g:applyLayout>` tag:

```
<g:applyLayout name="storeLayout" />
```

With one line of code, you have restored order; shop.gsp is rendering exactly the same content as before. So what have you gained? Remember that when you started this journey, the aim was to create a grails-app/views/album/show.gsp file that the non-Ajax display action can use to render an Album instance. With a defined layout in storeLayout, creating this view is simple (see Listing 9-23).

Listing 9-23. *Reusing the storeLayout in show.gsp*

```
<g:applyLayout name="storeLayout">
    <g:if test="${params.message}">
        <div class="message">
            <g:message code="${params.message}"></g:message>
        </div>
    </g:if>
    <g:render template="album" model="[album:album]"></g:render>
</g:applyLayout>
```

Using the `<g:applyLayout>` tag again, you can apply the layout to the body of the `<g:applyLayout>` tag. When you do this in conjunction with rendering the _album.gsp template, it takes little code to render a pretty rich view. We'll be using the storeLayout.gsp repeatedly throughout the creation of the rest of the flow, so stay tuned.

Returning to the start state of the flow from Listing 9-18, you'll notice that the `success` event executes a transition action. When the transition action is triggered, it first creates an empty list of `AlbumPayment` instances in `flow` scope if the list doesn't already exist:

```
11 if(!flow.albumPayments) flow.albumPayments = []
```

Then it obtains a reference to the `Album` the user wants to buy using the `id` obtained from the `params` object on line 12:

```
12 def album = Album.get(params.id)
```

With the `album` in hand, the code on line 14 then checks if an `AlbumPayment` already exists in the list by executing a nifty GPath expression in combination with Groovy's `find` method:

```
14 if(!flow.albumPayments.album.find { it?.id == album.id })
```

This one expression really reflects the power of Groovy. If you recall that the variable `flow.albumPayments` is actually a `java.util.List`, how can it possibly have a property called `album`? Through a bit of magic affectionately known as GPath, Groovy will resolve the expression `flow.albumPayments.album` to a new `List` that contains the values of the `album` property of each element in the `albumPayments` `List`.

With this new `List` in hand, the code then executes the `find` method and passes it a closure that will be invoked on each element in the `List` until the closure returns true. The final bit of magic utilized in this expression is the usage of the "Groovy Truth" (`http://docs.codehaus.org/display/GROOVY/Groovy+Truth`). Essentially, unlike Java where only the boolean type can be used to represent true or false, Groovy defines a whole range of other truths. For example, `null` resolves to false in an `if` statement, so if the preceding `find` method doesn't find anything, `null` will be returned and the `if` block will never be entered.

Assuming `find` does resolve to `null`, the expression is then negated and the `if` block is entered on line 15. This brings us to the next snippet of code to consider:

```
15              flow.lastAlbum = new AlbumPayment(album:album)
16              flow.albumPayments << flow.lastAlbum
```

This snippet of code creates a new `AlbumPayment` instance and places it into `flow` scope using the key `lastAlbum`. Line 15 then adds the `AlbumPayment` to the list of `albumPayments` held in `flow` scope using the Groovy left shift operator `<<` — a neat shortcut to append an element to the end of a `List`.

Finally, with the transition action complete, the flow then transitions to a new state called `requireHardCopy` on line 18:

```
18 }.to 'requireHardCopy'
```

Implementing the First View State

So after adding a start state that can deal with users who have not yet logged in, you've finally arrived at this flow's first view state. The `requireHardCopy` view state pauses to ask the user whether she requires a CD of the purchase sent to her or a friend as a gift. Listing 9-24 shows the code for the requireHardCopy view state.

Listing 9-24. *The requireHardCopy View State*

```
requireHardCopy {
    on('yes') {
        if(!flow.shippingAddresses)
            flow.shippingAddress = new Address()
    }.to 'enterShipping'
    on('no') {
        flow.shippingAddress = null
    }.to 'loadRecommendations'
}
```

Notice that the requireHardCopy state specifies two event handlers called yes and no reflecting the potential answers to the question. Let's see how you can define a view that triggers these events. First create a GSP file called grails-app/views/store/buy/requireHardCopy.gsp.

Remember that the requireHardCopy.gsp file name should match the state name, and that the file should reside within a directory that matches the flow id—in this case, grails-app/views/store/buy. You will need to use the <g:link> tag's event attribute to trigger the events in the requireHardCopy state, as discussed previously in the section on triggering events from the view. Listing 9-25 shows the code to implement the requireHardCopy view state.

Listing 9-25. *The requireHardCopy.gsp View*

```
<g:applyLayout name="storeLayout">
    <div id="shoppingCart" class="shoppingCart">
        <h2>Would you like a CD edition of the album
                sent to you or a friend as a gift?</h2>
        <div class="choiceButtons">
            <g:link controller="store" action="buy" event="yes">
                <img src="${createLinkTo(dir:'images',file:'yes-button.gif')}"
                        border="0"/>
            </g:link>
            <g:link controller="store" action="buy" event="no">
                <img src="${createLinkTo(dir:'images',file:'no-button.gif')}"
                        border="0"/>
            </g:link>
        </div>
    </div>
</g:applyLayout>
```

Notice how you can leverage the storeLayout once again to make sure the user interface remains consistent. Each <g:link> tag uses the event attribute to specify the event to trigger. Figure 9-3 shows what the dialog looks like.

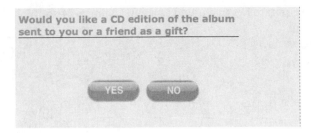

Figure 9-3. *Choosing whether you want a CD hard copy*

As you can see from the `requireHardCopy` state's code in Listing 9-24, if a yes event is triggered, the flow will transition to the `enterShipping` state; otherwise it will head off to the `loadRecommendations` state. Each of these states will help you learn a little more about how flows work. Let's look at the `enterShipping` state, which presents a good example of doing data binding and validation.

Data Binding and Validation in Action

The `enterShipping` state is the first view state that asks the user to do some form of free-text entry. As soon as you start to accept input of this nature from a user, the requirement to validate input increases. Luckily, you've already specified the necessary validation constraints on the `Address` class in Listing 9-13. Now it's just a matter of putting those constraints to work.

Look at the implementation of the `enterShipping` state in Listing 9-26. As you can see, it defines two event handlers called `next` and `back`.

Listing 9-26. *The enterShipping State*

```
1 enterShipping {
2     on('next') {
3         def address = flow.shippingAddress
4         address.properties = params
5         if(address.validate()) {
6             flow.lastAlbum.shippingAddress = address
7             return success()
8         }
9         return error()
10    }.to 'loadRecommendations'
11    on('back') {
12        flow.shippingAddress.properties = params
13    }.to 'requireHardCopy'
14 }
```

We'll revisit the transition actions defined for the `next` and `back` events shortly. For the moment, let's develop the view that will render the `enterShipping` state and trigger each event. Create a GSP at the location `grails-app/views/store/buy/enterShipping.gsp`. Again, you can use the `storeLayout` to ensure the layout remains consistent. Listing 9-27 shows a shortened version of the code because the same <g:textField> tag is used for each property of the Address class.

Listing 9-27. *The enterShipping.gsp View*

```
1  <g:applyLayout name="storeLayout">
2      <div id="shoppingCart" class="shoppingCart">
3          <h2>Enter your shipping details below:</h2>
4          <div id="shippingForm" class="formDialog">
5              <g:hasErrors bean="${shippingAddress}">
6                  <div class="errors">
7                      <g:renderErrors bean="${shippingAddress}"></g:renderErrors>
8                  </div>
9              </g:hasErrors>
10
11              <g:form name="shippingForm"  url="[controller:'store',action:'buy']">
12                  <div class="formFields">
13                      <div>
14                          <label for="number">House Name/Number:</label><br>
15                          <g:textField name="number"
16                                      value="${fieldValue(bean:shippingAddress,
17                                              field:'number')}" />
18                      </div>
19                      <div>
20                          <label for="street">Street:</label><br>
21                          <g:textField name="street"
22                                  value="${fieldValue(bean:shippingAddress,
23                                          field:'street')}" />
24                      </div>
25                  </div>
26                  ....
27                  <div class="formButtons">
28                      <g:submitButton type="image"
29                              src="${createLinkTo(dir:'images',
30                                          file:'back-button.gif')}"
31                              name="back"
32                              value="Back"></g:submitButton>
33                      <g:submitButton type="image"
34                              src="${createLinkTo(dir:'images',
35                                          file:'next-button.gif')}"
36                              name="next"
37                              value="Next"></g:submitButton>
38                  </div>
39
40
41          </g:form>
```

```
42          </div>
43      </div>
44 </g:applyLayout>
```

After creating fields for each property in the `Address` class, you should end up with something that looks like the screenshot in Figure 9-4.

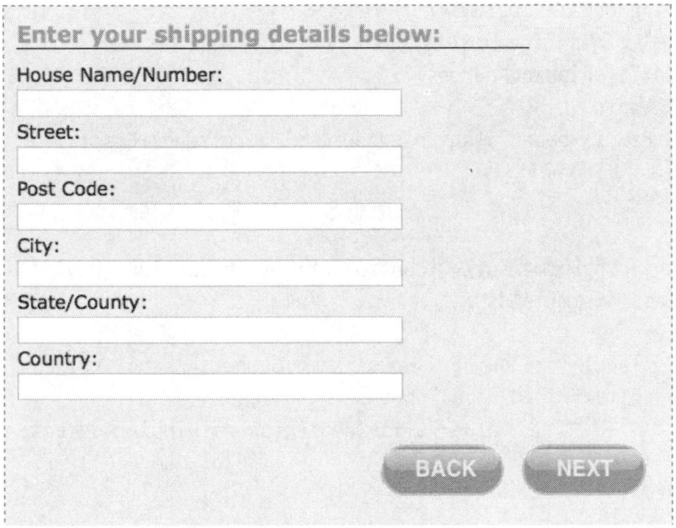

Enter your shipping details below:

House Name/Number:

Street:

Post Code:

City:

State/County:

Country:

BACK   NEXT

Figure 9-4. *Entering shipping details*

As discussed in the previous section on triggering events from the view, the name of the event to trigger is established from the name attribute of each `<g:submitButton>`. For example, the following snippet taken from Listing 9-27 will trigger the next event:

```
33      <g:submitButton type="image"
34              src="${createLinkTo(dir:'images',
35                                  file:'next-button.gif')}"
36              name="next"
37              value="Next"></g:submitButton>
```

Another important part of the code in Listing 9-27 is the usage of `<g:hasErrors>` and `<g:renderErrors>` to deal with errors that occur when validating the `Address`:

```
5           <g:hasErrors bean="${shippingAddress}">
6               <div class="errors">
7                   <g:renderErrors bean="${shippingAddress}"></g:renderErrors>
8               </div>
9           </g:hasErrors>
```

This code works in partnership with the transition action to ensure that the Address is validated before the user continues to the next part of the flow. You can see the transition action's code in the following snippet, taken from Listing 9-26:

```
2    on('next') {
3        def address = flow.shippingAddress
4        address.properties = params
5        if(address.validate()) {
6            flow.lastAlbum.shippingAddress = address
7            return success()
8        }
9        return error()
10   }.to 'loadRecommendations'
```

Let's step through this code line by line to better understand what it's doing. First, on line 3 the shippingAddress is obtained from flow scope:

```
3 def address = flow.shippingAddress
```

If you recall from Listing 9-24, in the requireHardCopy state you created a new instance of the Address class and stored it in a variable called shippingAddress in flow scope when the user specified that she required a CD version of the Album. Here, the code obtains the shippingAddress variable using the expression flow.shippingAddress. Next, the params object is used to bind incoming request parameters to the properties of the Address object on line 4:

```
4 address.properties = params
```

This will ensure the form fields that the user entered are bound to each property in the Address object. With that done, the Address object is validated through a call to its validate() method. If validation passes, the Address instance is applied to the shippingAddress property of the lastAlbum object stored in flow scope. The success event is then triggered by a call to the success() method. Lines 5 through 8 show this in action:

```
5        if(address.validate()) {
6            flow.lastAlbum.shippingAddress = address
7            return success()
8        }
```

Finally, if the Address object does not validate because the user entered data that doesn't adhere to one of the constraints defined in Listing 9-15, the validate() method will return false, causing the code to fall through and return an error event:

```
9 return error()
```

When an error event is triggered, the transition action will halt the transition to the loadRecommendations state, returning the user to the enterShipping state. The view will then render any errors that occurred so the user can correct her mistakes (see Figure 9-5).

Figure 9-5. *Showing validation errors in the enterShipping state*

One final thing to note about the enterShipping state is the back event, which allows the user to go back to the requireHardCopy state and change her decision if she is too daunted by our form:

```
11    on('back') {
12        flow.shippingAddress.properties = params
13    }.to 'requireHardCopy'
```

This code also has a transition action that binds the request parameters to the shippingAddress object, but here you don't perform any validation. Why? If you have a *really* indecisive user who changes her mind *again* and decides she *does* want a hard copy shipped to her, all of the previous data that she entered is restored. This proves to be a useful pattern, because no one likes to fill in the same data over and over again.

And with that, you've completed your first experience with data binding and validation in conjunction with web flows. In the next section, we're going to look at implementing a more interesting action state that interacts with GORM.

Action States in Action

The enterShipping state from the previous section transitioned to a new state called loadRecommendations once a valid Address had been entered. The loadRecommendations state is an action state that interacts with GORM to inspect the user's order and query for other albums she might be interested in purchasing.

Action states are perfect for populating flow data before redirecting flow to another state. In this case, we want to produce two types of recommendations:

- *Genre recommendations*: We show recent additions to the store that share the same genre (rock, pop, alternative, etc.) as the album(s) the user is about to purchase.

- *"Other users purchased" recommendations*: If another user has purchased the same Album the current user is about to purchase, then we show some of the other user's purchases as recommendations.

As you can imagine, both of the aforementioned recommendations will involve some interesting queries that will give you a chance to play with criteria queries—a topic we'll cover in more detail in Chapter 10. However, before we get ahead of ourselves, let's define the loadRecommendations action state as shown in Listing 9-28.

Listing 9-28. *The loadRecommendations Action State*

```
loadRecommendations {
    action {
        ...
    }
    on('success').to 'showRecommendations'
    on('error').to 'enterCardDetails'
    on(Exception).to 'enterCardDetails'
}
```

As you can see, the loadRecommendations action state defines three event handlers. Two of them use the all-too-familiar names success and error, whereas the other is an Exception event handler. The error and Exception handlers simply move the flow to the enterCardDetails state. The idea here is that errors that occur while loading recommendations shouldn't prevent the user from completing the flow.

Now let's implement the first of the recommendation queries, which involves querying for other recent albums of the same genre. To do this, you can use a criteria query, which is an alternative to String-based queries such as SQL or HQL (Hibernate Query Language).

String-based queries are inherently error-prone for two reasons. First, you must conform to the syntax of the query language you are using without any help from an IDE or language parser. Second, String-based queries lose much of the type information about the objects you are querying. Criteria queries offer a type-safe, elegant solution that bypasses these issues by providing a Groovy builder to construct the query at runtime.

To fully understand criteria queries, you should look at an example. Listing 9-29 shows the criteria query to find genre recommendations.

Listing 9-29. *Querying for Genre Recommendations*

```
1  if(!flow.genreRecommendations) {
2      def albums = flow.albumPayments.album
3      def genres = albums.genre
4      flow.genreRecommendations = Album.withCriteria {
5          inList 'genre', genres
6          not {
7              inList 'id', albums.id
8          }
9          maxResults 4
10         order 'dateCreated', 'desc'
11     }
12 }
```

Let's step through the code to understand what it is doing. First, a GPath expression is used to obtain a list of Album instances on Line 2:

```
2 def albums = flow.albumPayments.album
```

Remember that `flow.albumPayments` is a `List`, but through the expressiveness of GPath you can use the expression `flow.albumPayments.album` to get another `List` containing each album property from each `AlbumPayment` instance in the List. GPath is incredibly useful, so much so that it appears again on Line 3:

```
3 def genres = albums.genre
```

This GPath expression asks for all the genre properties for each Album instance. Like magic, GPath obliges. With the necessary query data in hand, you can now construct the criteria query using the `withCriteria` method on Line 4:

```
4 flow.genreRecommendations = Album.withCriteria {
```

The `withCriteria` method returns a `List` of results that match the query. It takes a closure that contains the criteria query's criterion, the first of which is `inList` on line 5:

```
5 inList 'genre', genres
```

What this code is saying here is that the value of the `Album` object's `genre` property should be in the `List` of specified genres, thus enabling queries for albums of the same genre. The next criterion is a negated `inList` criterion that ensures the recommendations you get back aren't any of the albums already in the `List` of `AlbumPayment` instances. Lines 6 through 8 show the use of the `not` method to negate any single criterion or group of criteria:

```
6      not {
7          inList 'id', albums.id
8      }
```

Finally, to ensure that you get only the latest four albums that fulfill the aforementioned criterion, you can use the maxResults and order methods on lines 9 and 10:

```
9       maxResults 4
10      order 'dateCreated', 'desc'
```

And with that, the loadRecommendations action state populates a list of genre-based recommendations into a genreRecommendations variable held in flow scope. Now let's look at the second case, which proves to be an even more interesting query. The query essentially figures out what albums *other* users have purchased that are *not* in the list of albums the current user is about to purchase (see Listing 9-30).

Listing 9-30. *The User Recommendations Query*

```
1 if(!flow.userRecommendations) {
2    def albums = flow.albumPayments.album
3
4    def otherAlbumPayments = AlbumPayment.withCriteria {
5        user {
6            purchasedAlbums {
7                inList 'id', albums.id
8            }
9        }
10       not {
11           eq 'user', flow.user
12           inList 'album', albums
13       }
14       maxResults 4
15    }
16    flow.userRecommendations = otherAlbumPayments.album
17 }
```

Let's analyze the query step-by-step. The first four lines are essentially the same as the previous query, except you'll notice the AlbumPayment class on line 4 instead of a query to the Album class:

```
4 def otherAlbumPayments = AlbumPayment.withCriteria {
```

Lines 5 through 9 get really interesting:

```
5        user {
6            purchasedAlbums {
7                inList 'id', albums.id
8            }
9        }
```

Here, an interesting feature of Grails' criteria support lets you query the *associations* of a domain class. By using the name of an association as a method call within the criteria, the code first queries the user property of the AlbumPayment class. Taking it even further, the code then queries the purchasedAlbums *association* of the user property. In a nutshell, the query is asking, "Find me all the AlbumPayment instances where the User associated with the AlbumPayment has one of the albums I'm about to buy in their list of purchasedAlbums." Simple, really!

In this advanced use of criteria, there is also a set of negated criteria on lines 10 through 13:

```
10      not {
11          eq 'user', flow.user
12          inList 'album', albums
13      }
```

These two criteria guarantee two things. First, line 11 ensures that you don't get back AlbumPayment instances that relate to the current User. The logic here is that you want recommendations only from *other* users—not from the user's own purchases. Second, on line 12, the negated inList criterion ensures you don't get back any AlbumPayment instances that are the same as one of the albums the user is about to buy. No point in recommending that a user buy something she's already about to buy, is there?

With the query out the way, on line 16 a new variable called userRecommendations is created in flow scope. The assignment uses a GPath expression to obtain each album property from the list of AlbumPayment instances held in the otherAlbumPayments variable:

```
16 flow.userRecommendations = otherAlbumPayments.album
```

Now that you have populated the flow.userRecommendations and flow.genreRecommendations lists, you can check whether they contain any results. There is no point in showing users a page with no recommendations. The code in Listing 9-31 checks each variable for results.

Listing 9-31. *Checking for Results in the* loadRecommendations *State*

```
if(!flow.genreRecommendations && !flow.userRecommendations) {
    return error()
}
```

Remember that in Groovy, any empty List resolves to false. If there are no results in either the userRecommendations or the genreRecommendations list, the code in Listing 9-31 triggers the execution of the error event, which results in skipping the recommendations page altogether.

That's it! You're done. The loadRecommendations state is complete. Listing 9-32 shows the full code in action.

Listing 9-32. *The Completed loadRecommendations State*

```
loadRecommendations {
    action {
        if(!flow.genreRecommendations) {
            def albums = flow.albumPayments.album
```

```
                def genres = albums.genre
                flow.genreRecommendations = Album.withCriteria {
                    inList 'genre', genres
                    not {
                        inList 'id', albums.id
                    }
                    maxResults 4
                    order 'dateCreated', 'desc'
                }
            }
            if(!flow.userRecommendations) {
                def albums = flow.albumPayments.album

                def otherAlbumPayments = AlbumPayment.withCriteria {
                    user {
                        purchasedAlbums {
                            inList 'id', albums.id
                        }
                    }
                    not {
                        eq 'user', flow.user
                        inList 'album', albums
                    }
                    maxResults 4
                }
                flow.userRecommendations = otherAlbumPayments.album
            }
            if(!flow.genreRecommendations && !flow.userRecommendations) {
                return error()
            }

        }
        on('success').to 'showRecommendations'
        on('error').to 'enterCardDetails'
        on(Exception).to 'enterCardDetails'
}
```

You've completed the loadRecommendations action state. Now let's see how you can present these recommendations in the showRecommendations state. The following section will also show how you can easily reuse transition and action states using assigned closures.

Reusing Actions with Closures

Once the loadRecommendations action state has executed and successfully accumulated a few useful Album recommendations for the user to peruse, the next stop is the showRecommendations view state (see Listing 9-33).

Listing 9-33. *The showRecommendations View State*

```
1    showRecommendations {
2        on('addAlbum'){
3            if(!flow.albumPayments) flow.albumPayments = []
4            def album = Album.get(params.id)
5
6            if(!flow.albumPayments.album.find { it?.id == album.id }) {
7                flow.lastAlbum = new AlbumPayment(album:album)
8                flow.albumPayments << flow.lastAlbum
9            }
10        }.to 'requireHardCopy'
12        on('next').to 'enterCardDetails'
13        on('back').to{ flow.shippingAddress ? 'enterShipping' : 'requireHardCopy' }
14    }
```

Now, you might have noticed a striking similarity between the transition action for the add-Album event and the transition action for the success event in Listing 9-18. Make no mistake: the code between those two curly brackets from lines 3 to 9 is identical to that shown in Listing 9-18.

In the spirit of DRY (Don't Repeat Yourself), you should never break out the copy machine when it comes to code. Repetition is severely frowned upon. So how can you solve this criminal coding offense? The solution is simple if you consider how Groovy closures operate.

Closures in Groovy are, of course, first-class objects themselves that can be assigned to variables. Therefore you can improve upon the code in Listing 9-31 by extracting the transition action into a private field as shown in Listing 9-34.

Listing 9-34. *Using a Private Field to Hold Action Code*

```
private addAlbumToCartAction = {
    if(!flow.albumPayments) flow.albumPayments = []
    def album = Album.get(params.id)

    if(!flow.albumPayments.album.find { it?.id == album.id }) {
        flow.lastAlbum = new AlbumPayment(album:album)
        flow.albumPayments << flow.lastAlbum
    }
}
```

With this done, you can refactor both the success event from the start state and the addAlbum event from the showRecommendations view state as shown in Listing 9-35, high-lighted in bold.

Listing 9-35. *Reusing Closure Code in Events*

```
def buyFlow = {
    start {
        ...
        on('success', addAlbumToCartAction).to 'requireHardCopy'
    }
    ...
    showRecommendations {
        on('addAlbum', addAlbumToCartAction).to 'requireHardCopy'
        on('next').to 'enterCardDetails'
        on('back').to { flow.shippingAddress ? 'enterShipping' : 'requireHardCopy' }
    }
}
```

With that done, the showRecommendations state is a lot easier on the eye. As you can see, it defines three events: addAlbum, next, and back. The addAlbum event uses a transition action to add the selected Album to the list of albums the user wishes to purchase. It then transitions back to the requireHardCopy state to inquire if the user wants a CD version of the newly added Album.

The next event allows the user to bypass the option of buying any of the recommendations and go directly to entering her credit-card details in the enterCardDetails state. Finally, the back event triggers the first example of a dynamic transition, a topic that we'll cover later in the chapter.

Now all you need to do is provide a view to render the recommendations and trigger the aforementioned states. Do this by creating a file called grails-app/views/store/buy/showRecommendations.gsp that once again uses the storeLayout. Listing 9-36 shows the code for the showRecommendations.gsp file.

Listing 9-36. *The showRecommendations.gsp View*

```
<g:applyLayout name="storeLayout">
    <div id="shoppingCart" class="shoppingCart">
        <h2>Album Recommendations</h2>
        <g:if test="${genreRecommendations}">
            <h3>Other music you might like...</h3>
            <g:render template="/store/recommendations"
                    model="[albums:genreRecommendations]" />
        </g:if>
        <g:if test="${userRecommendations}">
            <h3>Other users who bought ${albumPayments.album} also bought...</h3>
            <g:render template="/store/recommendations"
                    model="[albums:userRecommendations]" />
        </g:if>
```

```
            <div class="formButtons">
                <g:link controller="store" action="buy" event="back">
                    <img src="${createLinkTo(dir:'images',file:'back-button.gif')}"
                            border="0">
                </g:link>
                <g:link controller="store" action="buy" event="next">
                    <img src="${createLinkTo(dir:'images',file:'next-button.gif')}"
                            border="0">
                </g:link>
            </div>
        </div>
</g:applyLayout>
```

The showRecommendations.gsp view contains two <g:link> tags that trigger the next and back events. It then uses an additional template located at grails-app/views/store/_recommendations.gsp to render each list of recommendations. The code for the _recommendations.gsp is shown in Listing 9-37.

Listing 9-37. *The _recommendations.gsp Template*

```
<table class="recommendations">
    <tr>
        <g:each in="${albums?}" var="album" status="i">
            <td>
            <div id="rec${i}" class="recommendation">
                <g:set var="header">${album.artist.name} - ${album.title}</g:set>
                <p>
                  ${header.size() >15 ? header[0..15] + '...' : header }
                </p>
                <music:albumArt width="100"
                                album="${album}"
                                artist="${album.artist}" />
                <p><g:link controller="store"
                        action="buy"
                        id="${album.id}"
                        event="addAlbum">Add to Purchase</g:link></p>
            </div>
            </td>
        </g:each>
    </tr>
</table>
```

The important bit of this template is the "Add to Purchase" <g:link> that triggers the addAlbum event, passing in the Album id. All in all, once users start purchasing albums, they'll start to see recommendations appearing in the flow as presented in Figure 9-6.

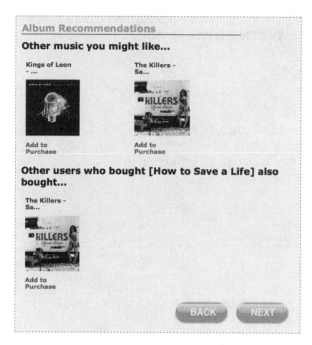

Figure 9-6. *Recommending albums to users*

Using Command Objects with Flows

Once users get through the recommendation system, they arrive at the business end of the transaction where they have to enter their credit-card details.

■ **Tip** If you're security-aware, you will note that it's generally not advisable to take user information, especially credit-card details, over HTTP. To run Grails in development mode over HTTPS, use the `grails run-app-https` command. At deployment time, your container can be configured to deliver parts of your site over HTTPS.

To start off, define a view state called `enterCardDetails` as shown in Listing 9-38.

Listing 9-38. *Defining the enterCardDetails View State*

```
enterCardDetails {
  ...
}
```

Before you can start capturing credit-card details, you need to set up an appropriate form that the user can complete. You can accomplish this by creating a new view at the location grails-app/views/store/buy/enterCardDetails.gsp, which the enterCardDetails view state can render. Listing 9-39 shows the enterCardDetails.gsp view simplified for brevity.

Listing 9-39. *The enterCardDetails.gsp View State*

```
<g:applyLayout name="storeLayout">
<div id="shoppingCart" class="shoppingCart">
    <h2>Enter your credit card details below:</h2>
    <div id="shippingForm" class="formDialog">
        <g:form name="shippingForm"  url="[controller:'store',action:'buy']">
            <div class="formFields">
                <div>
                    <label for="name">Name on Card:</label><br>
                    <g:textField name="name"
                                 value="${fieldValue(bean:creditCard,
                                                 field:'name')}" />
                </div>
                    ...

            </div>
            <div class="formButtons">
                <g:submitButton name="back"
                                value="Back" />
                <g:submitButton name="next"
                                value="Next" />
            </div>
        </g:form>
    </div>
</div>
</g:applyLayout>
```

Figure 9-7 shows what the final view rendering looks like after all the necessary form fields have been added.

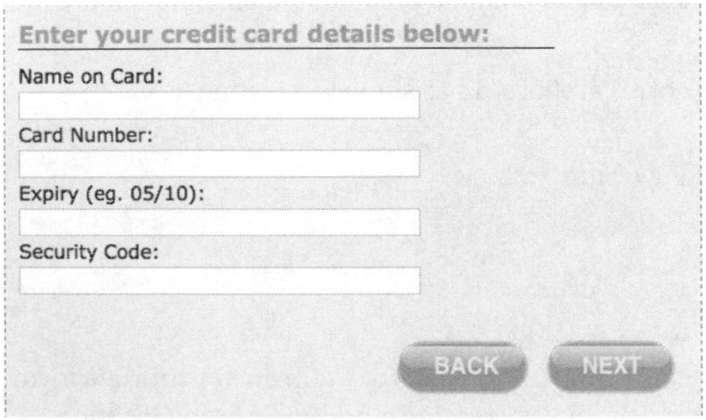

Figure 9-7. *The enterCreditCard.gsp form*

Now let's consider how to capture the credit-card information from the user. A domain class doesn't really make sense because you don't want to persist credit-card information at this point. Luckily, like regular controller actions, flow actions support the concept of command objects first discussed in Chapter 4.

First you need to define a class that represents the command object. Listing 9-40 shows the code for the `CreditCardCommand` class.

Listing 9-40. *A CreditCardCommand Class Used as a Command Object*

```
class CreditCardCommand implements Serializable {
    String name
    String number
    String expiry
    Integer code
    static constraints = {
        name blank:false, minSize:3
        number creditCard:true, blank:false
        expiry matches:/\d{2}\/\d{2}/, blank:false
        code nullable:false,max:999
    }
}
```

Like domain classes, command objects support the concept of constraints. Grails even provides a `creditCard` constraint to validate credit-card numbers. Within the `messages.properties` file contained in the `grails-app/i18n` directory, you can provide messages that should be displayed when the constraints are violated. Listing 9-41 presents a few example messages.

■**Tip** If you're not a native English speaker, you could try providing messages in other languages. You could use `messages_es.properties` for Spanish, for example, as you learned in Chapter 7 on internationalization (i18n).

Listing 9-41. *Specifying Validation Messages for the CreditCardCommand Object*

```
creditCardCommand.name.blank=You must specify the name on the credit card
creditCardCommand.number.blank=The credit card number cannot be blank
creditCardCommand.number.creditCard.invalid=You must specify a valid card number
creditCardCommand.code.nullable=Your must specify the security code
creditCardCommand.expiry.matches.invalid=You must specify the expiry. Example 05/10
creditCardCommand.expiry.blank=You must specify the expiry number
```

Now let's use the `CreditCardCommand` command object to define the next event and associated transition action that will validate the credit-card details entered by the user. Listing 9-42 shows how easy it is.

Listing 9-42. *Using the CreditCardCommand Command Object*

```
enterCardDetails {
    on('next') { CreditCardCommand cmd ->
        flow.creditCard = cmd
        cmd.validate() ? success() : error()
    }.to 'showConfirmation'
}
```

If you simply define the command object as the first parameter to the closure passed as the transition action, Grails will automatically populate the command instance from the parameters in the request. The only thing left for you to do is validate the command object using the validate() method and trigger a success or error event.

You'll notice that in addition to the validation of the command object in Listing 9-42, the command object is placed into flow scope through the variable name creditCard. With that done, you can update the enterCardDetails.gsp view first shown in Listing 9-39 to render any error messages that occur. The changes to enterCardDetails.gsp are shown in bold in Listing 9-43.

Listing 9-43. *Displaying Error Messages from a Command Object*

```
<g:applyLayout name="storeLayout">
    <div id="shoppingCart" class="shoppingCart">
        <h2>Enter your credit card details below:</h2>
        <div id="shippingForm" class="formDialog">
            <g:hasErrors bean="${creditCard}">
                <div class="errors">
                    <g:renderErrors bean="${creditCard}"></g:renderErrors>
                </div>
            </g:hasErrors>
            ...
        </div>
    </div>
</g:applyLayout>
```

Figure 9-8 shows the error messages being rendered to the view. You'll probably need to use one of your own credit cards to get past Grails' credit-card number validator!

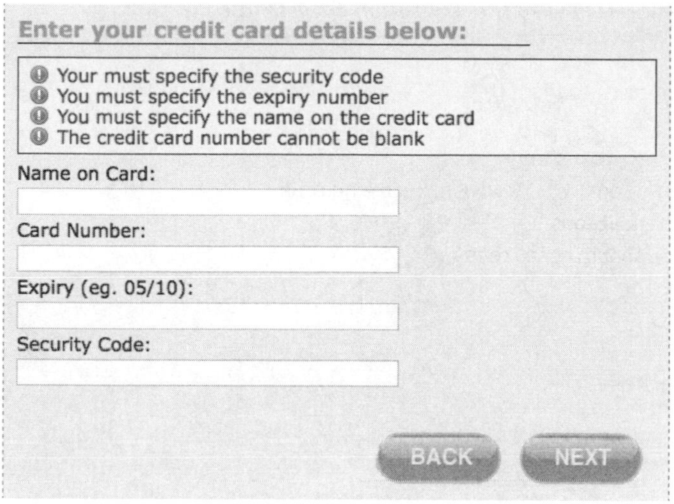

Enter your credit card details below:

⊙ Your must specify the security code
⊙ You must specify the expiry number
⊙ You must specify the name on the credit card
⊙ The credit card number cannot be blank

Name on Card:

Card Number:

Expiry (eg. 05/10):

Security Code:

BACK   NEXT

Figure 9-8. *Validating credit card details*

Dynamic Transitions

Before we move on from the enterCardDetails view state, you need to implement the back event that allows the user to return to the previous screen. Using a static event name to transition back to the showRecommendations event doesn't make sense because there might not have been any recommendations. Also, if the user wanted the Album to be shipped as a CD, then the previous screen was actually the enterShipping view state!

In this scenario, you need a way to dynamically specify the state to transition to, and luckily Grails' Web Flow support allows dynamic transitions by using a closure as an argument to the to method. Listing 9-44 presents an example of a dynamic transition that checks whether there are any recommendations, and transitions back to the showRecommendations state if there are. Alternatively, if there are no recommendations and the lastAlbum purchased has a shipping Address, the dynamic transition goes back to the enterShipping state. Otherwise, it goes back to the requireHardCopy state.

Listing 9-44. *Using Dynamic Transitions to Specify a Transition Target State*

```
enterCardDetails {
    ..
    on('back').to {
        def view
        if(flow.genreRecommendations || flow.userRecomendations)
            view = "showRecommendations"
        else if(flow.lastAlbum.shippingAddress) {
            view = 'enterShipping'
        }
        else {
            view = 'requireHardCopy'
        }
        return view
    }
}
```

Notice how the name of the view to transition to is the return value of the closure passed to the to method. In other words, the following three examples are equivalent, with each transitioning to the enterShipping state:

```
on('back').to 'enterShipping'  // static String name
on('back').to { 'enterShipping' }  // Groovy optional return
on('back').to { return 'enterShipping' } // Groovy explicit return
```

Verifying Flow State with Assertions

Okay, you're on the home stretch. You've reached the showConfirmation view state, which is the final view state that engages the user for input. Listing 9-45 shows the GSP code for the showConfirmation.gsp view.

Listing 9-45. *The showConfirmation.gsp View*

```
<g:applyLayout name="storeLayout">
    <div id="shoppingCart" class="shoppingCart">
        <h2>Your Purchase</h2>
        <p>You have the following items in your cart that you wish to Purchase. </p>

        <ul>
            <g:each in="${albumPayments}" var="albumPayment">
```

```
            <li>${albumPayment.album.artist.name} - ${albumPayment.album.title}
                <br>
                <strong>Cost: </strong> $      ${albumPayment.album.price}
            </li>
        </g:each>

    </ul>
    <g:set var="totalAmount">
            <g:formatNumber
                            number="${albumPayments.album.price.sum()}"
                            format="0.00" /></g:set>
    <p><strong>Total:</strong> $ ${totalAmount}</p>

    <h2>Card Details</h2>
    <p>The following card details will be used to process this transaction:</p>
    <div class="cardDetails">
        <ul>
            <li><strong>Name:</strong> ${creditCard?.name}</li>
            <li><strong>Number:</strong> ${creditCard?.number}</li>
            <li><strong>Expiry:</strong> ${creditCard?.expiry}</li>
            <li><strong>Security Code:</strong> ${creditCard?.code}</li>
        </ul>

    </div>
    <div class="formButtons">
        <g:link controller="store" action="buy" event="back">
            <img src="${createLinkTo(dir:'images',file:'back-button.gif')}"
                border="0">
        </g:link>
        <g:link controller="store" action="buy" event="confirm">
            <img src="${createLinkTo(dir:'images',file:'confirm-button.gif')}"
                border="0">
        </g:link>
    </div>
    </div>
</g:applyLayout>
```

When rendered, the showConfirmation view will display a summary of the transaction the user is about to complete, including all the albums to be purchased, the total price, and the credit-card details. Figure 9-9 shows the showConfirmation view in all its glory.

Figure 9-9. *Confirming the user's purchase*

So the user can trigger one of two events from the showConfirmation view state: confirm or back. The confirm event is where you can implement our transaction processing. To keep the example simple (both in terms of code brevity and later distribution), we're not going to delve into implementing a true e-commerce solution. We'll just happily assume that payments go through without a hitch.

■**Tip** If you want to integrate an e-commerce solution, try the PayPal plugin for Grails at http:// grails.org/Paypal+Plugin.

The confirm state, however, will help you learn how to use assertions inside a flow definition to validate flow state. Remember: by the time the user clicks the "confirm" button, the flow should be in the correct state. If it is not, you probably have an error in your code, which is something assertions exist to solve. Listing 9-46 shows the confirm event and the transition action that deals with taking payments (or not, as the case may be).

Listing 9-46. *Using a Transition Action to Confirm the Purchase*

```
1 showConfirmation {
2    on('confirm') {
3        def user = flow.user
4        def albumPayments = flow.albumPayments
5        def p = new Payment(user:user)
6        flow.payment = p
7        p.invoiceNumber = "INV-${user.id}-${System.currentTimeMillis()}"
8        def creditCard = flow.creditCard
9        assert creditCard.validate()
10        // TODO: Use credit card to take payment
```

```
11        // ...
12
13        // Once payment taken update user profile
14        for(ap in albumPayments) {
15            ap.user = user
16            // validation should never fail at this point
17            assert ap.validate()
18
19            p.addToAlbumPayments(ap)
20            assert p.save()
21
22            ap.album.songs.each { user.addToPurchasedSongs(it) }
23            user.addToPurchasedAlbums(ap.album)
24            assert user.save(flush:true)
25        }
26    }.to 'displayInvoice'
27    ...
28 }
```

On lines 9, 17, 20, and 24 assertions are used via Groovy's built-in assert keyword, to validate the state of the flow. You should not be getting validation errors by the time the flow reaches this transition action; if you are, there is a problem with the code in the flow prior to the showConfirmation view state.

As for the rest of the code in Listing 9-46, on lines 5 through 7 a new Payment instance is created, placed in the flow, and assigned a generated invoice number:

```
5        def p = new Payment(user:user)
6        flow.payment = p
7        p.invoiceNumber = "INV-${user.id}-${System.currentTimeMillis()}"
```

Then on line 10, there is a "to-do" item for when you actually start processing credit-card details. Once the credit card has been processed, on lines 19 and 20 each AlbumPayment is added to the Payment instance, which is then saved through a call to the save() method:

```
19            p.addToAlbumPayments(ap)
20            assert p.save()
```

Finally, on lines 22 through 24 the User is updated. The code adds each of the songs from the Album purchased to her list of purchasedSongs and adds the Album itself to her list of purchasedAlbums:

```
22            ap.album.songs.each { user.addToPurchasedSongs(it) }
23            user.addToPurchasedAlbums(ap.album)
24            assert user.save(flush:true)
```

If all goes well, the confirm event of the showConfirmation view state will transition to the displayInvoice end state. The displayInvoice end state will attempt to render a view located at grails-app/views/store/buy/displayInvoice.gsp. The displayInvoice.gsp view is a simple GSP that displays a summary of the user's just-processed transaction along with her invoice number for future reference. For completeness, we've included the code for displayInvoice.gsp (see Listing 9-47).

Listing 9-47. *The displayInvoice.gsp End State View*

```
<g:applyLayout name="storeLayout">
    <div id="invoice" class="shoppingCart">
        <h2>Your Receipt</h2>
        <p>Congratulations you have completed your purchase.
                Those purchases that included shipping will ship
                within 2-3 working days.
                Your digital purchases have been transferred into your library</p>
        <p>Your invoice number is ${payment.invoiceNumber}</p>
        <h2>Purchased Items</h2>

            <ul>
                <g:each in="${albumPayments}" var="albumPayment">
                    <li>${albumPayment.album.artist.name} -
                            ${albumPayment.album.title}<br>
                            <strong>Cost: </strong> $      ${albumPayment.album.price}
                    </li>
                </g:each>

            </ul>
        <p><strong>Total: </strong> ${albumPayments.album.price.sum()}</p>
    </div>
</g:applyLayout>
```

The user will see the unusually short invoice displayed, as depicted in Figure 9-10 (the legal department hasn't got hold of it yet).

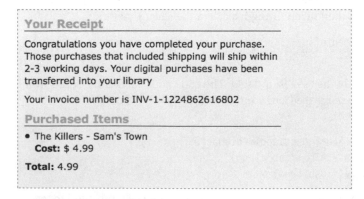

Figure 9-10. *Displaying an invoice*

And with that, you have completed the gTunes checkout flow! Listing 9-48 shows the code for the complete flow you developed over the course of this chapter.

Listing 9-48. *The Finished buyFlow Code*

```
def buyFlow = {
    start {
        action {
            // check login status
            if(session.user) {
                flow.user = User.get(session.user.id)
                return success()
            }
            login()
        }
        on('success', addAlbumToCartAction).to 'requireHardCopy'
        on('login') {
            flash.album = Album.get(params.id)
            flash.message - "user.not.logged.in"
        }.to 'requiresLogin'
    }
    requireHardCopy {
        on('yes') {
            if(!flow.shippingAddresses)
                flow.shippingAddress = new Address()
        }.to 'enterShipping'
        on('no') {
            flow.shippingAddress = null
        }.to 'loadRecommendations'
    }
    enterShipping {
        on('next') {
            def address = flow.shippingAddress
            address.properties = params
            if(address.validate()) {
                flow.lastAlbum.shippingAddress = address
                return success()
            }
            return error()
        }.to 'loadRecommendations'
        on('back') {
            flow.shippingAddress.properties = params
        }.to 'requireHardCopy'
    }
    loadRecommendations {
        action {
            if(!flow.genreRecommendations) {
                def albums = flow.albumPayments.album
                def genres = albums.genre
                flow.genreRecommendations = Album.withCriteria {
                    inList 'genre', genres
```

```
                not {
                    inList 'id', albums.id
                }
                maxResults 4
                order 'dateCreated', 'desc'
            }
        }
        if(!flow.userRecommendations) {
            def albums = flow.albumPayments.album
            def otherAlbumPayments = AlbumPayment.withCriteria {
                user {
                    purchasedAlbums {
                        inList 'id', albums.id
                    }
                }
                not {
                    eq 'user', flow.user
                    inList 'album', albums
                }
                maxResults 4
            }
            flow.userRecommendations = otherAlbumPayments.album
        }
        if(!flow.genreRecommendations && !flow.userRecommendations) {
            return error()
        }
    }
    on('success').to 'showRecommendations'
    on('error').to 'enterCardDetails'
    on(Exception).to 'enterCardDetails'
}
showRecommendations {
    on('addAlbum', addAlbumToCartAction).to 'requireHardCopy'
    on('next').to 'enterCardDetails'
    on('back').to { flow.shippingAddress ? 'enterShipping' : 'requireHardCopy' }
}
enterCardDetails {
    on('next') { CreditCardCommand cmd ->
        flow.creditCard = cmd
        cmd.validate() ? success() : error()
    }.to 'showConfirmation'
    on('back').to {
        def view
        if(flow.genreRecommendations || flow.userRecommendations)
            view = "showRecommendations"
        else if(flow.lastAlbum.shippingAddress) {
            view = 'enterShipping'
```

```
            }
            else {
                view = 'requireHardCopy'
            }
            return view
        }
    }
    showConfirmation {
        on('confirm') {
            def user = flow.user
            def albumPayments = flow.albumPayments
            def p = new Payment(user:user)
            flow.payment = p
            p.invoiceNumber = "INV-${user.id}-${System.currentTimeMillis()}"
            def creditCard = flow.creditCard
            assert creditCard.validate()
            // TODO: Use credit card to take payment
            // ...

            // Once payment taken update user profile
            for(ap in albumPayments) {
                ap.user = user
                // validation should never fail at this point
                assert ap.validate()

                p.addToAlbumPayments(ap)
                assert p.save(flush:true)

                ap.album.songs.each { user.addToPurchasedSongs(it) }
                user.addToPurchasedAlbums(ap.album)
                assert user.save(flush:true)
            }
        }.to 'displayInvoice'
        on('back').to 'enterCardDetails'
        on('error').to 'displayError'
        on(Exception).to 'displayError'
    }
    requiresLogin {
        redirect(controller:"album",
                    action:"show",
                    id: flash.album.id,
                    params:[message:flash.message])
    }
    displayInvoice()
    displayError()
}
```

Testing Flows

As you've seen through the course of this chapter, flows deal with the specific challenge of taking the user through a multistep process. It should come as no surprise that in order to test flows, you must use a specialized test harness called `grails.test.WebFlowTestCase`. Throughout the remainder of this section, we'll show you how to use `WebFlowTestCase` to test flow interactions effectively.

As of this writing, `WebFlowTestCase` cannot be used in a regular unit test. So you need to create an *integration* test by running the `create-integration-test` command:

```
$ grails create-integration-test com.g2one.gtunes.StoreBuyFlow
```

You'll end up with a new test suite in the `test/integration/com/g2one/gtunes` directory called `StoreBuyFlowTests.groovy`. Currently, the `StoreBuyFlowTests` suite extends the vanilla `GroovyTestCase` superclass. You'll need to change it to extend the `WebFlowTestCase` test harness instead, as shown in Listing 9-49.

Listing 9-49. *Extending the WebFlowTestCase Test Harness*

```
package com.g2one.gtunes
import grails.test.*
class StoreBuyFlowTests extends WebFlowTestCase {
    ...
}
```

The next thing to do is provide an implementation of the abstract `getFlow()` method that returns a closure that represents the flow. Listing 9-50 shows how this is done for the `buyFlow` you developed earlier.

Listing 9-50. *Implementing the getFlow() Method*

```
class StoreBuyFlowTests extends WebFlowTestCase {
    ...
    def controller = new StoreController()
    def getFlow() {
        controller.buyFlow
    }
}
```

Now it's time to consider the first test to implement. Recall from Listing 9-18 that if the user is not logged in, the flow ends by sending a redirect in the `requiresLogin` end state. Listing 9-51 shows how to test whether a user is logged in.

Listing 9-51. *Testing if the User is Logged In*

```
1 void testNotLoggedIn() {
2 MockUtils.mockDomain(Album, [new Album(title:"Aha Shake Heartbreak", id:1L)])
3 controller.params.id = 1
```

```
4 startFlow()
5
6 assertFlowExecutionEnded()
7 assertFlowExecutionOutcomeEquals 'requiresLogin'
8 }
```

We've demonstrated a few key concepts in this simple test. First, notice how you can use the mockDomain method of MockUtils to provide some mock data on line 2:

```
2 MockUtils.mockDomain(Album, [new Album(title:"Aha Shake Heartbreak", id:1L)])
```

Then on line 3, you can specify the id of the Album instance that will be looked up in the start action of the buyFlow:

```
3 controller.params.id = 1
```

In this example, we're using an id that matches the id of the mock Album passed to the mockDomain method on line 2. Then to trigger flow execution, you can invoke the startFlow() method on line 4:

```
4 startFlow()
```

With one simple method, the flow execution will begin and proceed to execute the start state of the buyFlow. If you recall, the start state is an action state that checks whether the user is logged in by inspecting whether a User instance exists in the session object. If a user doesn't exist in the session object, the requiresLogin state is triggered, which terminates the flow and redirects to another action. Line 6 checks that the flow has been terminated, by calling the assertFlowExecutionEnded method:

```
6 assertFlowExecutionEnded()
```

On line 7 the assertFlowExecutionOutcomeEquals method is called to ensure that requiresLogin is the end state of the flow:

```
7 assertFlowExecutionOutcomeEquals 'requiresLogin'
```

As you can see, the WebFlowTestCase test harness provides a number of new methods, such as startFlow and assertFlowExecutionEnded, that allow you to manipulate flow execution. The following list summarizes the key extensions to the GroovyTestCase API and what they do:

- assertFlowExecutionActive(): Asserts that the flow hasn't terminated by reaching an end state

- assertFlowExecutionEnded(): Asserts that the flow has been terminated by reaching an end state

- assertFlowExecutionOutcomeEquals(String): Asserts that the outcome (the name of the end state) is equal to the given value

- assertCurrentStateEquals(String): Asserts that the current state in an active flow is equal to the specified value

- startFlow(): Starts a new flow execution

- signalEvent(String): Triggers a flow-execution event for the given name when the flow has paused (for example, at a view state)

- setCurrentState(String): Starts a flow execution and sets the current state to the specified value

Of course, all the regular JUnit assertions are available in addition to those we just mentioned. One key method is the setCurrentState(String) method, which allows you to easily test just parts of a flow. For example, say you wanted to test only the process of entering the shipping address for a purchased album. Listing 9-52 shows how to use the setCurrentState(String) method to move the flow forward to a particular point.

Listing 9-52. *Using setCurrentState(String) to Transition to a Particular State*

```
void testEnterShippingAddress() {
    currentState = "requireHardCopy"
    signalEvent "yes"
    assertCurrentStateEquals "enterShipping"
    signalEvent "back"
    assertCurrentStateEquals "requireHardCopy"
    signalEvent "yes"
    assertCurrentStateEquals "enterShipping"
    signalEvent "next"
    assertCurrentStateEquals "enterShipping"
    ...
}
```

The example in Listing 9-52 sets the currentState to requireHardCopy. The next trick is to use the signalEvent(String) method to transition from one state to the next. Notice how the code in Listing 9-52 uses signalEvent(String) followed by assertCurrentStateEquals(String) to assert that the web flow is transitioning states as expected.

Now note one of the other aspects of the enterShipping state from Listing 9-26: it presents an example of using data binding to populate the Address class. In Listing 9-52, when you try to trigger the next event, the flow transitions back to the enterShipping state because the Address object doesn't validate. Listing 9-53 shows how to build on testEnterShippingAddress to test whether a valid Address object is provided.

Listing 9-53. *Testing Data Binding in Flows*

```
1  void testEnterShippingAddress() {
2  ...
3  signalEvent "next"
4  assertCurrentStateEquals "enterShipping"
5  def model = getFlowScope()
6
7  def errors = model.shippingAddress?.hasErrors()
8  assertNotNull errors
```

```
9   assertTrue errors
10
11  model.lastAlbum = new AlbumPayment(album:new Album(title:"Aha Shake Heartbreak"))
12  model.albumPayments = [model.lastAlbum]
13  controller.params.number = "10"
14  controller.params.street = "John Doe Street"
15  controller.params.city = "London"
16  controller.params.state = "Greater London"
17  controller.params.postCode = "W134G"
18  controller.params.country = "United Kingdom"
19  assertNotNull model.shippingAddress
20  signalEvent "next"
21  assertCurrentStateEquals "enterCardDetails"
22  def shippingAddress = model.shippingAddress
23
24  assertNotNull shippingAddress
25  assertTrue shippingAddress.validate()
26  }
```

The example in Listing 9-53 shows a number of useful techniques. First, it tests failed validation by triggering the next event (without populating parameters for the Address object) and obtaining the model from flow scope using the getFlowScope() method on lines 5 through 9. Then on lines 13 to 18, you can see how to use the controller instance to populate the params object in order for data binding to work effectively. The result is that when the next event is triggered, validation succeeds and state transitions to the enterCardDetails state instead of back to enterShipping.

As you develop the test coverage for your flows, you might need to mock out data-access methods provided by GORM as described in Chapter 10, but overall WebFlowTestCase makes testing flows a lot easier through the provided utility methods.

Summary

Don't be shocked: you have in fact reached the end of the web flow chapter! You've learned a great deal, from the different state types—action, view, redirect—to events and transitions. Along the way, you've completed a pretty comprehensive web flow example by implementing the checkout process for the gTunes application.

We should point out one thing: web flow is not the answer to every problem. For the majority of tasks you face on a day-to-day basis, regular controllers and actions do the job just fine. There's a particular subset of problems that involve taking the user through sequential steps that cannot be compromised, and that's where web flow really shines.

A couple of this chapter's examples in which you used criteria queries touched on the untapped power that is GORM. Never fear; our journey into the world of GORM has only just begun. In the next chapter, we'll jump head first into understanding what else GORM has to offer on the persistence front.

CHAPTER 10

■■■

GORM

As you may have garnered from the table of contents for this book, with no fewer than three chapters dedicated to the subject, the persistence layer of Grails is a critical part of the picture. In Chapter 3, you obtained a surface-level understanding about what domain classes are and how they map onto the underlying database. In this chapter, you're going to plunge headfirst into understanding the inner workings of GORM.

As a starting point, you'll learn about the basic persistence operations involved in reading and writing objects from a database. After going through the basics, you'll then be taken through the semantics of GORM including as many corner cases and surprises as we're able to fit into a single chapter.

Persistence Basics

Fortunately, we won't be spending too long on the foundations, since you've already been exposed to the basic GORM methods as early as Chapter 2, where we took you through the generated scaffolding code. Since then, you've been exposed to various aspects of GORM from dynamic finders to the criteria queries used in Chapter 9.

Nevertheless, as a recap, let's take a look at the basic read operations provided by GORM.

Reading Objects

Each domain class is automatically enhanced, via metaprogramming, with a number of methods that allow you to query for domain instances. The simplest of these is the get method, which takes the identifier of a domain class and returns either an instance or null if no instance was found in the database. Listing 10-1 shows a simple example, highlighted in bold, from the AlbumController you've already developed.

Listing 10-1. *Using the get Method*

```
class AlbumController {
    def show = {
        def album = Album.get(params.id)
```

```
        if(album) {
            ...
        }
        ...
    }
}
```

In addition to the simple get method, there is also a getAll method that can take several identifiers and return a List of instances. You can specify the identifiers as a List or using varargs, for example:

```
def albums = Album.getAll(1,2,3)
```

When using the get method, the object is loaded from the database in a modifiable state. In other words, you can make changes to the object, which then get persisted to the database. If you want to load an object in a read-only state, you can use the read method instead:

```
def album = Album.read(params.id)
```

In this case, the Album instance returned cannot be modified. Any changes you make to the object will not be persisted.

Listing, Sorting, and Counting

A common way to retrieve items from a database is to simply list them. Clearly, it is not always desirable to list every instance, and the order in which they are returned is often important. GORM provides a list() method, which takes a number of named arguments such as max, offset, sort, and order to customize the results, the definitions of which are listed here:

- max: The maximum number of instances to return

- offset: The offset relative to 0 of the first result to return

- sort: The property name to sort by

- order: The order of the results, either asc or desc for ascending and descending order, respectively

In addition to list(), and often used in combination with it, is the count() method, which counts the total number of instances in the database. To demonstrate these, let's look at some examples of their usage, as shown in Listing 10-2.

Listing 10-2. *Using the list() Method*

```
// get all the albums; careful, there might be many!
def allAlbums = Album.list()
// get the ten most recently created albums
def topTen = Album.list(max:10, sort:'dateCreated', order:'desc')
// get the total number of albums
def totalAlbums = Album.count()
```

As you can imagine, it is fairly trivial to use the `list()` method to perform the pagination of results simply by customizing the `offset` argument. In addition, there is a set of `listOrderBy*` methods that are variations on the `list()` method.

The `listOrderBy*` methods provide an example where each method uses the properties on the class itself in the method signatures. They are unique to each domain class, but it is just a matter of understanding the convention to use them. Listing 10-3 presents an example that lists all `Album` instances, ordered by the `dateCreated` property, simply by invoking the `listOrderByDateCreated()`method.

Listing 10-3. *Using listOrderBy*

```
// all albums ordered by creation date
def allByDate = Album.listOrderByDateCreated()
```

Using standard bean conventions, the property name is appended to the end of the method signature starting with a capital letter. You'll see more examples of this later in the chapter when we cover dynamic finders, including a variation of the `count` method.

Saving, Updating, and Deleting

As you've seen already, objects can be persisted by calling the `save()` method. For example, the code in Listing 10-4 demonstrates how to persist an instance of the `Album` class, assuming it validates successfully.

Listing 10-4. *Saving an Instance*

```
def album = new Album(params)
album.save()
```

We'll have more to say about how GORM persists objects to the database in "The Semantics of GORM" later in this chapter. For now, all you need to know is that at some point the underlying Hibernate engine will execute a SQL INSERT to persist the `Album` instance to the database. Updating objects is strikingly similar because doing so involves calling the same `save()` method on an existing persistent instance, as shown in Listing 10-5.

Listing 10-5. *Updating an Instance*

```
def album = Album.get(1)
album.title = "The Changed Title"
album.save()
```

When the `save()` method is called, Hibernate automatically works out whether it should issue a SQL INSERT or a SQL UPDATE. Occasionally, on certain older databases, Hibernate may get this decision wrong and issue an UPDATE when it should be doing an INSERT. You can get around this by passing an explicit `insert` argument to the `save()` method:

```
album.save(insert:true)
```

As for deleting objects, this is done with the `delete()` method:

```
album.delete()
```

So, that's the simple stuff. Next you'll be looking in more detail at associations in GORM and how those work.

Associations

Chapter 3 already provided some detail on associations in GORM in their different incarnations, but there is a lot more to the associations that GORM supports. In a typical one-to-many association such as the `songs` property of the `Album` class, the type is a `java.util.Set`. If you recall the semantics of `Set` as defined by javadoc, they don't allow duplicates and have no order. However, you may want an association to have a particular order.

One option is to use a `SortedSet`, which requires you to implement the `Comparable` interface for any item placed into the `SortedSet`. For example, Listing 10-6 shows how to sort tracks by the `trackNumber` property.

Listing 10-6. *Using SortedSet to Sort Associations*

```
class Album {
    ...
    SortedSet songs
}
class Song implements Comparable {
    ..
    int compareTo(o) {
        if(this.trackNumber > o.trackNumber)
            return 1
        elseif(this.trackNumber < o.trackNumber)
            return -1
        return 0
    }
}
```

Alternatively, you can specify the sort order declaratively using the `mapping` property introduced in Chapter 3. For example, if you wanted to sort `Song` instances by track number for all queries, you can do so with the sort method:

```
class Song {
    ...
    static mapping = {
        sort "trackNumber"
    }
}
```

You may not want to sort by the trackNumber property for every query or association, in which case you can apply sorting to the songs association of the Album class only:

```
static mapping = {
    songs sort: "trackNumber"
}
```

Another way to change the way sorting is done is to use a different collection type such as java.util.List. Unlike a Set, a List allows duplicates and retains the order in which objects are placed into the List. To support List associations, Hibernate uses a special index column that contains the index of each item in the List. Listing 10-7 shows an example of using a List for the songs association.

Listing 10-7. *Using a List Association*

```
class Album {
    ...
    List songs
}
```

Unlike Set associations, which have no concept of order, with a List you can index into a specific entry, for example:

```
println album.songs[0]
```

Finally, GORM also supports Map associations where the key is a String. Simply change the type from List to Map in the example in Listing 10-7 and use a String instead of an Integer to access entries. For both List and Map collection types, Grails creates an index column. In the case of a List, the index column holds a numeric value that signifies its position in the List, while for a Map the index column holds the Map key.

Relationship Management Methods

As well as giving you the ability to map associations to the database, GORM also automatically provides you with methods to manage those associations. The addTo* and removeFrom* dynamic methods allow you to add and remove entries from an association. Additionally, both methods return the instance they are called on, thus allowing you to chain method calls. Listing 10-8 shows an example of using the addToSongs method of the Album class.

Listing 10-8. *Using Relationship Management Methods*

```
new Album(title:"Odelay",
          artist:beck,
          year:1996)
            .addToSongs(title:"Devil's Haircut", artist:beck, duration:342343)
            .addToSongs(title:"Hotwax", artist:beck, duration:490583)
            ...
            .save()
```

As you can see from the example, you can pass just the values of the Song as named parameters to the addToSongs method, and GORM will automatically instantiate a new instance and add it to the songs association. Alternatively, if you already have a Song instance, you can simply pass that into the addToSongs method.

Transitive Persistence

Whenever you save, update, or delete an instance in GORM, the operation can cascade to any associated objects. The default cascade behavior in GORM is dictated by the belongsTo property first discussed in Chapter 3. For example, if the Song class belongsTo the Album class, then whenever an Album instance is deleted, all of the associated Song instances are deleted too. If there is no belongsTo definition in an association, then saves and updates cascade, but deletes don't.

If you need more control over the cascading behavior, you can customize it using the cascade method of the mapping block, as shown in Listing 10-9.

Listing 10-9. *Customizing the Cascading Behavior*

```
class Album {
    ...
    static mapping = {
        songs cascade:'save-udpate'
    }
}
```

A special cascade style called delete-orphan exists for the case where you want a child object to be deleted if it is removed from an association but not deleted explicitly.

■Tip For more information on the different cascade options available, take a look at the related section in the Hibernate documentation at http://www.hibernate.org/hib_docs/reference/en/html_single/ #objectstate-transitive.

Querying

Pretty much every nontrivial application will need to query persistent data. With the underlying storage medium of choice being the database, the typical way to achieve this historically has been with SQL. Relational database systems with their tables and columns are significantly different enough from Java objects that abstracting data access has been a long-term struggle for many an ORM vendor.

Hibernate provides an elegant enough Java API for querying objects stored in a database, but GORM moves up to the next level by completely abstracting the majority of data access logic. Don't expect to see many dependencies on the org.hibernate package in your codebase, because GORM nicely abstracts the details of interaction with Hibernate. In the next few sections, we'll cover the different ways you can query with GORM, from dynamic finders to criteria GORM.

Dynamic Finders

Dynamic finders are among the most powerful concepts of GORM; as with the previously mentioned `listOrderBy*` method, they use the property names of the class to perform queries. However, they are even more flexible than this, because they allow logical queries such as And, Or, and Not to form so-called method expressions. There can be hundreds of combinations for any given class, but, again, they're fairly simple to remember if you know the convention. Let's look at an example `findBy*` method first, shown in Figure 10-1, which locates a unique instance for the specified method expression.

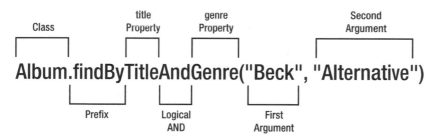

Figure 10-1. *Basic dynamic finder syntax*

The diagram uses the `title` and genre properties to look up an `Album` instance. There is a logical And expression in the middle to ensure both values need to be equal in the query. This could be replaced with a logical Or to look up a `Album` that either has a `title` of Beck or has a genre of `Alternative`.

We have, however, only brushed on what is possible with dynamic finders and method expressions. Dynamic finders support a wide range of expressions that allow `GreaterThan/LessThan`, `Like`, and `Between` queries, to name just a few, simply by appending an additional expression on the end of the property name. Listing 10-10 shows some of these in action.

Listing 10-10. *Dynamic Finders in Action*

```
// retrieve an album where the title contains  'Shake'
def album = Album.findByTitleLike('%Shake%')
// get a album created in last 10 days
def today = new Date()
def last10Days = Album
                    .findByDateCreatedBetween(today-10,today)
// first album that is not 'Rock'
def somethingElse =   Album
                    .findByGenreNotEqual('Rock')
```

Table 10-1 illustrates all the possible expressions that can be appended, the number of arguments they expect, and an example of each in action.

Table 10-1. *Available Dynamic Finder Method Expressions*

Expression	Arguments	Example
Between	2	Album.findByDateCreatedBetween(today-10,today)
Equals	1	Album.findByTitleEquals('Aha Shake Heartbreak')
GreaterThan	1	Album.findByDateCreatedGreaterThan(lastMonth)
GreaterThanOrEqual	1	Album.findByDateCreatedGreaterThanOrEqual(lastMonth)
InList	1	Album.findByTitleInList(['Aha Shake Heartbreak', 'Odelay'])
IsNull	0	Album.findByGenreIsNull()
IsNotNull	0	Album.findByGenreIsNotNull()
LessThan	1	Album.findByDateCreatedLessThan(lastMonth)
LessThanOrEqual	1	Album.findByDateCreatedLessThanOrEqual(lastMonth)
Like	1	Album.findByTitleLike('Shake')
NotEqual	1	Album.findByTitleNotEqual('Odelay")

The findBy* method has two cousins that accept the same method expressions you've already seen. The first is findAllBy*, which retrieves all the instances that match the method expression as a java.util.List. Finally, there is the countBy* method that returns the total number of instances found by the method expression as an integer. It is worth opening up the Grails console, by typing grails console in a command window, and playing with these methods to experiment with the different combinations and discover just how easy they are to use.

You'll find that GORM's dynamic finders pretty much eliminate the need for a Data Access Object (DAO) layer, which you typically need in Java applications. Remember those? No? OK, well, the process is something like this:

1. Define an interface for the data access logic. The signatures will look strikingly like the dynamic finder methods you've seen so far.

2. Implement the interface using a Java class.

3. Using Spring, or your IoC container of choice, to wire in dependencies such as the data source or Hibernate Session.

If you think about it, data access logic is extremely repetitive and heavily violates the DRY principles Grails is founded on. Luckily, with GORM and its dynamic finders, you can forget the DAO.

In the next section, you'll explore how Grails makes criteria more accessible via concise builder syntax.

Criteria Queries

Possibly one of the most powerful mechanisms for querying is with criteria. Criteria use a builder syntax for creating queries using Groovy's builder support. A builder in Groovy is essentially a hierarchy of method calls and closures that is perfect for "building" tree-like structures such as XML documents or a graphical user interface (GUI). Builders are also good candidates for constructing queries, particularly dynamic queries, which are often constructed with the horrifically error-prone StringBuffer.

The Hibernate Criteria API is meant to reduce the risk of errors by providing a programmatic way to construct "criteria" queries. However, Groovy's expressive syntax and powerful metaprogramming support has taken this to a new level of conciseness. Let's start by looking at basic usage patterns of criteria, after which we can move on to some more advanced examples.

Before you can perform a criteria query, you need a criteria instance for the class you want to query. To facilitate this, GORM provides a createCriteria static method on each domain class. Once you have acquired the criteria instance, one of four methods can be invoked, each of which expects a closure argument:

- get: Locates a unique instance for the query

- list: Returns a list of instances for the query

- scroll: Returns a ScrollableResults instance for the query

- count: Returns the total results as an integer for the query

The most common use case is to use the list() method on the criteria instance to perform the query, as shown in Listing 10-11.

Listing 10-11. *A Simple Criteria Query*

```
def c = Album.createCriteria()
def results = c.list {
        eq('genre', 'Alternative')
        between('dateCreated', new Date()-30, new Date())
}
```

The previous example lists all the Album instances with a genre of Alternative created in the past 30 days. The nested method calls within the closure block translate into method calls on Hibernate's org.hibernate.criterion.Restrictions class, the API for which is too long to list here. Nevertheless, the eq and between methods shown here are just two of many for performing all the typical queries found in query languages such as SQL and HQL.

It is worth taking a look at the API on the Hibernate web site (http://www.hibernate.org/ hib_docs/v3/api/org/hibernate/criterion/Restrictions.html) to see what is available and to get a better understanding of the power that is at your fingertips. Of course, you can accomplish queries similar to those in Listing 10-11 with dynamic finder methods. What you haven't really explored is the power of closures and building the query up dynamically.

Consider for the moment that a closure is just a block of code and can be assigned to a variable. Also, consider that a closure can reference variables within its enclosing scope. Put the two together, and you have a pretty powerful mechanism for reusing dynamically constructed queries.

As an example, say you have a map whose keys define the property names to be queried, and the values define the value such as the params object provided by Grails controllers. A query could easily be built up from this map and assigned to a variable. Listing 10-12 provides an example of this concept in action.

Listing 10-12. *Dynamic Querying with Criteria*

```
1 def today = new Date()
2 def queryMap =   [ genre: 'Alternative', dateCreated: [today-10,today]  ]
3 def query = {
4          // go through the query map
5          queryMap.each { key, value ->
6                  // if we have a list assume a between query
7                  if(value instanceof List) {
8                          // use the spread operator to invoke
9                          between(key, *value)
10                 }
11                 else {
12                         like(key,value)
13                 }
14         }
15 }
16
17 // create a criteria instance
18 def criteria = Album.createCriteria()
19
20 // count the results
21 println( criteria.count(query) )
22
23 // reuse again to get a unique result
24 println( criteria.get(query) )
25
26 // reuse again to list all
27 criteria.list(query).each { println it }
28
29 // use scrollable results
30 def scrollable = criteria.scroll(query)
31 def next = scrollable.next()
32 while(next) {
33         println(scrollable.getString('title'))
34         next = scrollable.next()
35 }
```

That's a fairly long example that includes some fairly advanced concepts. To simplify your understanding of it, we've included line numbers, and we'll go through it step-by-step. The first two lines in the following code define a date instance from the current time and a map using Groovy's map syntax that will dictate which properties you're going to query. The map's keys are the property names to query, and the values define the value to query by:

```
1 def today = new Date()
2 def queryMap =   [ genre: 'Alternative', dateCreated: [today-10,today]   ]
```

■Tip In the previous code example, to calculate the date range to be the past ten days, we took a `java.util.Date` instance and subtracted ten from it. This is an example of Groovy's operator overloading feature used to simplify date operations.

On line 3 a closure is assigned to the query variable, which will be used in conjunction with the criteria. The closure's closing bracket is on line 15, but some important stuff is going on in the body of the closure:

```
3  def query = {
      ...
15 }
```

First, a built-in GDK method called each is used to loop over each entry in the Map. Essentially, the method iterates through each element in the map and passes the key and value to the passed closure as arguments.

```
5     queryMap.each { key, value ->
             ...
14   }
```

Next up, the familiar `instanceof` operator is used to check whether the value passed is a List. If the value passed is a List, you can invoke the between method passing the key and the value. The value is split into two arguments using Groovy's * spread operator:

```
7                 if(value instanceof List) {
8                     // use the spread operator to invoke
9                     between(key, *value)
10                }
11                else {
12                    like(key,value)
13                }
```

The * spread operator's job is to split apart a List or an array and pass the separated values to the target. In this case, the between method, which actually takes three arguments, not two, is correctly called, with the first element of the list being the second argument and with the second element being the third argument.

Now let's start to look at how the query, in the form of a closure, works with a criteria instance as a reusable code block. As usual, of course, you have to create the criteria instance, which is accomplished on line 18:

```
18 def criteria = Album.createCriteria()
```

The various methods of the criteria instance are then utilized using the same closure:

```
21 println( criteria.count(query) )
24 println( criteria.get(query) )
27 criteria.list(query).each { println it }
```

The first, on line 21, counts all the results for the query; the next prints out a unique result (if there is one), and finally, the last lists all the results for the query and then iterates through them with the already encountered each method printing each one to standard out.

There is one more usage on line 30, which uses the scroll method on criteria. This returns an instance of the Hibernate class called org.hibernate.ScrollableResults, which has a similar interface to a JDBC java.sql.ResultSet and shares many of the same methods. One major difference, however, is that the columns of results are indexed from 0 and not 1 as in JDBC.

Querying Associations with Criteria

Often it is useful to execute a query that uses the state of an association as its criterion. So far, you have performed queries against only a single class and not its associations. So, how do you go about querying an association?

Grails' criteria builder allows querying associations by using a nested criteria method call whose name matches the property name. The closure argument passed to the method contains nested criteria calls that relate to the association and not the criteria class. For example, say you wanted to find all albums that contain the word *Shake*. The criteria shown in Listing 10-13 would do this.

Listing 10-13. *Querying Associations with Criteria*

```
def criteria = Album.withCriteria {
    songs {
        ilike('title', '%Shake%')
    }
}
```

This is a fairly trivial example, but all the criteria you've seen so far can be nested within the nested songs method call in the code listing. Combine this with how criteria can be built up from logical code blocks, and it results in a pretty powerful mechanism for querying associations.

■**Tip** You can also combine association criteria as shown in Listing 10-13 with regular criteria on the class itself.

Querying with Projections

Projections allow the results of criteria queries to be customized in some way. For example, you may want to count only the number of results as opposed to retrieving each one. In other words, they are equivalent to SQL functions such as count, distinct, and sum.

With criteria queries, you can specify a `projections` method call that takes a closure and provides support for these types of queries. Instead of criteria, however, the method calls within it map to another Hibernate class named `org.hibernate.criterion.Projections`.

Let's adapt the example in Listing 10-14 by adding a projection that results in counting the distinct `Album` titles in the `Alternative` genre.

Listing 10-14. *Querying with Projections*

```
def criteria = Album.createCriteria()
def count = criteria.get {
        projections {
                countDistinct('name')
        }
        songs {
                eq('genre', 'Alternative')
        }
}
```

Query by Example

An alternative to criteria queries is to pass an instance of the class you're looking for to the `find` or `findAll` method. This is an interesting option when used in conjunction with Groovy's additional implicit constructor for JavaBeans, as shown in Listing 10-15.

Listing 10-15. *Query by Example*

```
def album = Album.find( new Album(title:'Odelay') )
```

As you can see from Listing 10-15, the `find` method uses the properties set on the passed `Album` instance to formulate a query. Querying by example is a little limiting, because you don't have access to some of the more advanced expressions such as `Like`, `Between`, and `GreaterThan` when passing in the example. It is, however, another useful addition to your toolbox.

HQL and SQL

Another way to perform queries is via the Hibernate Query Language (HQL), which is a flexible object-oriented alternative to SQL. A full discussion of HQL is beyond the scope of this book; however, the Hibernate documentation does cover it splendidly at `http://www.hibernate.org/hib_docs/reference/en/html/queryhql.html`. We will look at some basic examples of how GORM supports HQL via more built-in methods.

Those who know SQL should not find it hard to adapt to HQL, because the syntactic differences are minimal. GORM provides three methods for working with HQL queries: `find`, `findAll`, and `executeQuery`. Each method, when passed a string, will assume it's an HQL query. The example in Listing 10-16 presents the most basic case combined with `findAll`.

Listing 10-16. *HQL via the findAll Method*

```
// query for all albums
def allAlbums = Album.findAll('from com.g2one.gtunes.Album')
```

In addition, JDBC-style IN parameters (queries with question mark [?] placeholders) are supported by passing a list as the second argument. Thanks to Groovy's concise syntax for expressing lists, the result is very readable, as presented in Listing 10-17.

Listing 10-17. *HQL with Positional Parameters*

```
// query for an Album by title
def album = Album.find(
                    'from Album as a where a.title = ?',
                ['Odelay'])
```

If positional parameters aren't your preferred option, you can also use named parameters using the syntax shown in Listing 10-18.

Listing 10-18. *HQL with Named Parameters*

```
// query for an Album by title
def album = Album.find(
                    'from Album as a where a.title = :theTitle',
                [theTitle:'Odelay'])
```

Notice how you use the colon character directly before the named parameter :theTitle. Then instead of passing a list as the final argument to the find method, you pass a map where the keys in the map match the named parameters in the query.

The methods find and findAll assume the query is a query specific to the Album class and will validate that this is so. It is possible, however, to execute other HQL queries via the executeQuery method, as shown in Listing 10-19.

Listing 10-19. *HQL via executeQuery*

```
// get all the songs
def songs = Album.executeQuery('select elements(b.songs) from Album as a')
```

Clearly, there is a lot to learn about HQL, since it is possible to perform more advanced queries using joins, aggregate functions, and subqueries. Luckily, the documentation on the Hibernate web site is an excellent overview of what is possible and can help you on your way.

Pagination

Whichever way you query, a typically useful thing to be able to do is paginate through a set of results. You've already learned that the list() method supports arguments such as max and offset that allow you to perform pagination. For example, to obtain the first ten results, you can use the following:

```
def results = Album.list(max:10)
```

To obtain the following ten, you can use the offset argument:

```
def results = Album.list(max:10, offset:10)
```

While we're on the topic of querying, you'll be happy to know that the same arguments can be used to paginate queries. For example, when using dynamic finders, you can pass a map as the last argument, which specifies the max and offset arguments:

```
def results = Album.findAllByGenre("Alternative", [max:10, offset:20])
```

In fact, you can use any parameter covered in the previous "Listing, Sorting, and Counting" section, such as sort and order:

```
def results = Album.findAllByGenre("Alternative", [sort:'dateCreated',
                                                    order:'desc'])
```

In the view, you can take advantage of the <g:paginate> tag that renders "Previous" and "Next" links as well as linked numbers to jump to a specific set of results à la Google. In its simplest form, the <g:paginate> tag requires only the total number of records:

```
<g:paginate total="${Album.count()}" />
```

This example assumes you want to paginate the current controller action. If this is not the case, you can customize the controller that is actually performing the pagination using the same attributes accepted by the <g:link> tag such as controller and action:

```
<g:paginate controller="album" action="list" total="${Album.count()}" />
```

You can change the default "Previous" and "Next" links using the prev and next attributes, respectively:

```
<g:paginate prev="Back" next="Forward" total="${Album.count()}" />
```

If internationalization (i18n) is a requirement, you can use the <g:message> tag, called as a *method*, to pull the text to appear from message bundles:

```
<g:paginate prev="${message(code:'back.button.text')}"
            next="${message(code:'next.button.text')}"
            total="${Album.count()}" />
```

■**Tip** If you're interested in the mechanics of i18n support in Grails, take a look at Chapter 7, which covers the details of message bundles and switching locales.

Configuring GORM

GORM has a number of attributes that you may want to configure. Pretty much all the options available in Hibernate are also available in GORM. One of the most fundamental things you're likely to want to achieve is to enable some form of SQL logging so that you can debug performance issues and optimize queries.

SQL Logging

If you're purely interested in monitoring the amount of SQL traffic hitting the database, then a good option to use is the `logSql` setting in the `grails-app/conf/DataSource.groovy` file:

```
dataSource {
    ...
    logSql = true
}
```

With this enabled, every SQL statement issued by Hibernate will be printed to the console. The disadvantage of the `logSql` setting is that you get to see only the prepared statements printed to the console and not the actual values that are being inserted. If you need to see the values, then set up a special `log4j` logger in `grails-app/conf/Config.groovy` as follows:

```
log4j = {
    ...
    logger {
        trace "org.hibernate.SQL",
              "org.hibernate.type"
    }
}
```

Specifying a Custom Dialect

Hibernate has, over the years, been heavily optimized for each individual database that it supports. To support different database types, Hibernate models the concept of a *dialect*. For each database it supports, there is a dialect class that knows how to communicate with that database.

There are even different dialects for different database versions. For example, for Oracle, there are three dialect classes: `Oracle8iDialect`, `Oracle9iDialect`, and `Oracle10gDialect`. Normally, the dialect to use is automatically detected from the database JDBC metadata. However, certain database drivers do not support JDBC metadata, in which case you may have to specify the dialect explicitly. To do so, you can use the `dialect` setting of the `grails-app/conf/DataSource.groovy` file. As an example, if you use the InnoDB storage engine for MySQL, you'll want to use the `MySQL5InnoDBDialect` class, as shown in Listing 10-20.

Listing 10-20. *Customizing the Hibernate Dialect*

```
dataSource {
    ...
    dialect = org.hibernate.dialect.MySQL5InnoDBDialect
}
```

Other Hibernate Properties

The `logSql` and `dialect` settings of the `DataSource.groovy` file demonstrated in the previous two sections are actually just shortcuts for the `hibernate.show_sql` and `hibernate.dialect` properties of the Hibernate `SessionFactory`. If you're more comfortable using Hibernate's configuration model, then you can do so within a `hibernate` block in `DataSource.groovy`. In fact, you'll note that the Hibernate second-level cache (discussed in the "Caching" section later in the chapter) is already preconfigured in this manner, as shown in Listing 10-21.

Listing 10-21. *Regular Hibernate Configuration*

```
hibernate {
    cache.use_second_level_cache=true
    cache.use_query_cache=true
    cache.provider_class='com.opensymphony.oscache.hibernate.OSCacheProvider'
}
```

You can configure all manner of things if you're not satisfied with the defaults set up by Grails. For example, to change your database's default transaction isolation level, you could use the `hibernate.connection.isolation` property:

```
hibernate {
    hibernate.connection.isolation=4
}
```

In this example, we've changed the isolation level to `Connection.TRANSACTION_REPEATABLE_READ`. Refer to the `java.sql.Connection` class for the other isolation levels.

Tip To find out all the other configuration options available, take a look at the Hibernate reference material on the subject at `http://www.hibernate.org/hib_docs/reference/en/html/session-configuration.html`.

The Semantics of GORM

As you have discovered so far, using GORM is pretty easy. It's so easy, in fact, that you may be lulled into a false sense of security thinking that you never have to look at a database again. However, when working with any ORM tool, it is absolutely critical to understand how and what the ORM tool is doing.

Tip Since GORM is built on Hibernate, it may well be worth investing in a book specifically targeting Hibernate; however, we'll do our best to cover the key aspects here.

If you start using an ORM tool without understanding its semantics, you will almost certainly run into issues with the performance and behavior of your application. ORM tools are often referred to as an example of a leaky abstraction (see http://www.joelonsoftware.com/articles/LeakyAbstractions.html) because they attempt to isolate you from the complexities of the underlying database. Unfortunately, to follow the analogy, the abstraction leaks quite frequently if you're not aware of features such as lazy and eager fetching, locking strategies, and caching.

This chapter will provide some clarity on these quirks and ensure that you don't use GORM with the expectation that it will solve world hunger. GORM is often compared, understandably, to ActiveRecord in Rails. Unfortunately, users with Rails experience who adopt Grails are in for a few surprises because the tools are really quite different. One of the primary differences is that GORM has the concept of a persistence context, or *session*.

The Hibernate Session

Hibernate, like the Java Persistence API, models the concept of a persistence session using the org.hibernate.Session class. The Session class is essentially a container that holds references to all known instances of persistent classes—domain classes in Grails. In the Hibernate view of the world, you think in terms of objects and delegate responsibility to Hibernate to ensure that the state of the objects is *synchronized* to the database.

The synchronization process is triggered by calling the flush() method on the Session object. At this point, you may be wondering how all of this relates to Grails, given that you saw no mention of a Session object in Chapter 4. Essentially, GORM manipulates the Session object transparently on your behalf.

It is quite possible to build an entire Grails application without ever interacting directly with the Hibernate Session object. However, for developers who are not used to the session model, there may be a few surprises along the way. As an example, consider the code in Listing 10-22.

Listing 10-22. *Multiple Reads Return the Same Object*

```
def album1 = Album.get(1)
def album2 = Album.get(1)

assertFalse album1.is(album2)
```

The code in Listing 10-1 shows a little gotcha for developers not used to the session model. The first call to the get method retrieves an instance of the Album class by executing a SQL SELECT statement under the covers—no surprises there. However, the second call to the get method doesn't execute any SQL at all, and in fact, the assertion on the last lines fails.

■**Note** In the example in Listing 10-22, the final assertFalse statement uses Groovy's is method because == in Groovy is equivalent to calling the equals(Object) method in Java.

In other words, the Session object appears to act like a cache, and in fact it is one. The Session object is Hibernate's first-level cache. Another area where this is apparent is when saving an object. For example, consider the code in Listing 10-23.

Listing 10-23. *Saving a Domain Class in Grails*

```
def album = new Album(..)
album.save()
```

Now, assuming the Album instance validates, you may think from the code in Listing 10-2 that GORM will execute a SQL INSERT statement when the save() method is called. However, this is not necessarily the case, and in fact it depends greatly on the underlying database. GORM by default uses Hibernate's native identity generation strategy, which attempts to select the most appropriate way to generate the id of an object. For example, in Oracle, Hibernate will opt to use a sequence generator to supply the identifier, while in MySQL the identity strategy will be used. The identity generation strategy relies on the database to supply the identity.

Since an identifier must be assigned by the time the save() method completes, if a sequence is used, no INSERT is needed because Hibernate can simply increment the sequence in memory. The actual INSERT can then occur later when the Session is flushed. However, in the case of the identity strategy, an INSERT *is* needed since the database needs to generate the identifier. Nevertheless, the example serves to demonstrate that it is the Session that is responsible for synchronizing the object's state to the database, not the object itself.

Essentially, Hibernate implements the strategy known as *transactional write-behind*. Any changes you make to persistent objects are not necessarily persisted when you make them or even when you call the save() method. The advantage of this approach is that Hibernate can heavily optimize and batch up the SQL to be executed, hence minimizing network traffic. In addition, the time for which database locks (discussed in more detail in the "Locking Strategies" section) are held is greatly reduced by this model.

Session Management and Flushing

You may be worried at this point that you're losing some kind of control by allowing Hibernate to take responsibility for persisting objects on your behalf. Fortunately, GORM provides you with the ability to control session flushing implicitly by passing in a flush argument to the save() or delete() method, as shown in Listing 10-24.

Listing 10-24. *Manually Flushing the Session*

```
def album = new Album(..)
album.save(flush:true)
```

In contrast to the example in Listing 10-23, the code in Listing 10-24 will persist the object but also call flush() on the underlying Session object. However, it is important to note that since the Session deals with all persistent instances, other changes may be flushed in addition to the object that is saved. Listing 10-25 illustrates an example of this behavior.

Listing 10-25. *The Effects of Flushing*

```
def album1 = Album.get(1)
album1.title = "The Changed Title"
album1.save()
def album2 = new Album(..)
album2.save(flush:true)
```

The example in Listing 10-25 demonstrates the impact of passing the `flush` argument to the second `save()` method. You may expect that a SQL UPDATE would be executed when `save()` is called on `album1`, and then an INSERT would occur when `save()` is called on `album2`. However, the actual behavior is that both the UPDATE and the INSERT occur on the call to `save()` on `album2`, since the `flush:true` argument passed forces the underlying Session object to synchronize changes with the database.

You may be wondering at this point how the code in the listings you've seen so far can possibly use the same Session instance and where this Session came from in the first place. Basically, when a request comes into a Grails application, directly before a controller action executes, Grails will transparently bind a new Hibernate Session to the current thread. The Session is then looked up by GORM's dynamic methods like get in Listing 10-8. When a controller action finishes executing, if no exceptions are thrown, the Session is flushed, which synchronizes the state of the Session with the database by executing any necessary SQL. These changes are then committed to the database.

However, that is not the end of the story. The Session is not closed but instead placed in read-only mode prior to view rendering and remains open until view rendering completes. The reason for this is that if the session were closed, any persistent instances contained within it would become detached. The result is that if there were any noninitialized associations, the infamous org.hibernate.LazyInitializationException would occur. Ouch! Of course, we'll be saying more about LazyInitializationException and ways to avoid the exception, including in-depth coverage of detached objects later in the chapter.

To elaborate, the reason for placing the Session into read-only mode during view rendering is to avoid any unnecessary flushing of the Session during the view-rendering process. Your views really shouldn't be modifying database state after all! So, that is how the standard Session life cycle works in Grails. However, there is an exception. In the previous chapter, you explored Web Flow, which allows you to construct rich conversations that model multistep processes. Unlike regular requests, the Session is not scoped to the request but instead to the entire flow.

When the flow is started, a new Session is opened and bound to flow scope. Then whenever the flow resumes execution, the same session is retrieved. In this case, all the GORM methods work with the session bound into flow scope. Finally, when the flow terminates at an end state, the Session is flushed, and any changes are committed to the database.

Obtaining the Session

Now, as mentioned previously, the Session is basically a cache of persistent instances. Like any cache, the more objects it has within it, the more memory it's going to consume. A common mistake when using GORM is to query for a large number of objects without periodically clearing the Session. If you do so, your Session will get bigger and bigger, and eventually you may either cause your application's performance to suffer or, worse, run out of memory.

In these kinds of scenarios, it is wise to manage the state of your Session manually. Before you can do so, however, you need a reference to the Session object itself. You can achieve this in two ways. The first involves the use of dependency injection to get hold of a reference to the Hibernate SessionFactory object.

The SessionFactory has a method called currentSession() that you can use to obtain the Session bound to the current thread. To use dependency injection, simply declare a local field called sessionFactory in a controller, tag library, or service, as shown in Listing 10-26.

Listing 10-26. *Using Dependency Injection to Obtain the Hibernate Session*

```
def sessionFactory
...
def index = {
    def session = sessionFactory.currentSession()
}
```

As an alternative, you could use the withSession method that is available on any domain class. The withSession method accepts a closure. The first argument to the closure is the Session object; hence, you can code as in Listing 10-27.

Listing 10-27. *Using the withSession Method*

```
def index = {
    Album.withSession { session ->

        ...
    }
}
```

Let's return to the problem at hand. To avoid memory issues when using GORM with a large amount of data (note this applies to raw Hibernate too), you need to call the clear() method on the Session object periodically so that the contents of the Session are cleared. The result is that the instances within the Session become candidates for garbage collection, which frees up memory. Listing 10-28 shows an example that demonstrates the pattern.

Listing 10-28. *Managing the Hibernate Session*

```
1 def index = {
2    Album.withSession { session ->
3       def allAlbums = Album.list()
4       for(album in allAlbums) {
5          def songs = Song.findAllByAlbum(album)
6          // do something with the songs
7          ...
8          session.clear()
9       }
10   }
11 }
```

The example in Listing 10-28 is rather contrived, but it serves to demonstrate effective Session management when dealing with a large number of objects. On line 2, a reference to the Session is obtained using the withSession method:

```
2     Album.withSession { session ->
         ...
10    }
```

Then, on line 3, a query is used to get a list of all the albums in the system, which could be big in itself, and then iterate over each one:

```
3         def allAlbums = Album.list()
4         for(album in allAlbums) {
            ..
9         }
```

Critically, on line 5, a dynamic finder queries for all the Song instances for the current Album:

```
5             def songs = Song.findAllByAlbum(album)
```

Now, each time the findAllByAlbum method is executed, more and more persistent instances are being accumulated in the Session. Memory consumption may at some point become an issue depending on how much data is in the system at the time. To prevent this, the session is cleared on line 8:

```
8             session.clear()
```

Clearing the Session with the clear() method is not the only way to remove objects from Hibernate's grasp. If you have a single object, you can also call the discard() method. You could even use the *. operator to discard entire collections of objects using this technique:

```
songs*.discard()
```

The advantage of this approach is that although the clear() method removes all persistent instances from the Session, using discard() removes only the instances you no longer need. This can help in certain circumstances because you may end up with a LazyInitializationException because removing the objects from the Session results in them being detached (a subject we'll discuss in more detail in the "Detached Objects" section).

Automatic Session Flushing

Another common gotcha is that by default GORM is configured to flush the session automatically when one of the following occurs:

- Whenever a query is run

- Directly after a controller action completes, if no exceptions are thrown

- Directly before a transaction is committed

This has a number of implications that you need to consider. Take, for example, the code in Listing 10-29.

Listing 10-29. *The Implications of Automatic Session Flushing*

```
1    def album = Album.get(1)
2    album.title = "Change It"
3    def otherAlbums = Album.findAllWhereTitleLike("%Change%")
4
5    assert otherAlbums.contains(album)
```

Now, you may think that because you never called save() on the album there is no way it could possibly have been persisted to the database, right? Wrong. As soon as you load the album instance, it immediately becomes a "managed" object as far as Hibernate is concerned. Since Hibernate is by default configured to flush the session when a query runs, the Session is flushed on line 3 when the findAllWhereTitleLike method is called and the Album instance is persisted. The Hibernate Session caches changes and pushes them to the database only at the latest possible moment. In the case of automatic flushing, this is at the end of a transaction or before a query runs that might be affected by the cached changes.

You may consider the behavior of automatic flushing to be a little odd, but if you think about it, it depends very much on your expectations. If the object weren't flushed to the database, then the change made to it on line 2 would not be reflected in the results. That may not be what you're expecting either! Let's consider another example where automatic flushing may present a few surprises. Take a look at the code in Listing 10-30.

Listing 10-30. *Another Implication of Automatic Session Flushing*

```
def album = Album.get(1)
album.title = "Change It"
```

In Listing 10-16, an instance of the Album class is looked up and the title is changed, but the save() method is never called. You may expect that since save() was never called, the Album instance will not be persisted to the database. However, you'd be wrong again. Hibernate does automatic dirty checking and flushes any changes to the persistent instances contained within the Session.

This may be what you were expecting in the first place. However, one thing to consider is that if you simply allow this to happen, then Grails' built-in validation support, discussed in Chapter 3, will not kick in, resulting in a potentially invalid object being saved to the database.

It is our recommendation that you should *always* call the save() method when persisting objects. The save() method will call Grails' validation mechanism and mark the object as read-only, including any associations of the object, if a validation error occurs. If you were never planning to save the object in the first place, then you may want to consider using the read method instead of the get method, which returns the object in a read-only state:

```
def album = Album.read(1)
```

If all of this is too dreadful to contemplate and you prefer to have full control over how and when the Session is flushed, then you may want to consider changing the default FlushMode used by specifying the hibernate.flush.mode setting in DataSource.groovy:

```
hibernate.flush.mode="manual"
```

The possible values of the `hibernate.flush.mode` setting are summarized as follows:

- `manual`: Flush only when you say so! In other words, only flush the session when the `flush:true` argument is passed to `save()` or `delete()`. The downside with a `manual` flush mode is that you may receive stale data from queries, and you must always pass the `flush:true` argument to the `save()` or `delete()` method.

- `commit`: Flush only when the transaction is committed (see the next section).

- `auto`: Flush when the transaction is committed and before a query is run.

Nevertheless, assuming you stick with the default auto setting, the `save()` method might not, excuse the pun, save you in the case of the code from Listing 10-15. Remember in this case the `Session` is automatically flushed before the query is run. This problem brings us nicely onto the topic of transactions in GORM.

Transactions in GORM

First things first—it is important to emphasize that *all* communication between Hibernate and the database runs within the context of a database transaction regardless of whether you are explicit about the transaction demarcation boundaries. The `Session` itself is lazy in that it only ever initiates a database transaction at the last possible moment.

Consider the code in Listing 10-15 again. When the code is run, a `Session` has already been opened and bound to the current thread. However, a transaction is initiated only on first communication with the database, which happens within the call to get on line 1.

At this point, the `Session` is associated with a JDBC `Connection` object. The `autoCommit` property of the `Connection` object is set to `false`, which initiates a transaction. The `Connection` will then be released only once the `Session` is closed. Hence, as you can see, there is never really a circumstance where Grails operates without an active transaction, since the same `Session` is shared across the entire request.

Given that there is a transaction anyway, you would think that if something went wrong, any problems would be rolled back. However, without specific transaction boundaries and if the `Session` is flushed, any changes are permanently committed to the database.

This is a particular problem if the flush is beyond your control (for instance, the result of a query). Then those changes will be permanently persisted to the database. The result may be the rather painful one of having your database left in an inconsistent state. To help you understand, let's look at another illustrative example, as shown in Listing 10-31.

Listing 10-31. *Updates Gone Wrong*

```
def save = {
    def album = Album.get(params.id)
    album.title = "Changed Title"
    album.save(flush:true)
    ...
    // something goes wrong
    throw new Exception("Oh, sugar.")
}
```

The example in Listing 10-15 shows a common problem. In the first three lines of the save action, an instance of the Album class is obtained using the get method, the title is updated, and the save() method is called and passes the flush argument to ensure updates are synchronized with the database. Then later in the code, something goes wrong, and an exception is thrown. Unfortunately, if you were expecting previous updates to the Album instance to be rolled back, you're out of luck. The changes have already been persisted when the Session was flushed! You can correct this in two ways; the first is to move the logic into a transactional service. Services are the subject of Chapter 11, so we'll be showing the latter option, which is to use programmatic transactions. Listing 10-32 shows the code updated to use the withTransaction method to demarcate the transactional boundaries.

Listing 10-32. *Using the withTransaction Method*

```
def save = {
    Album.withTransaction {
        def album = Album.get(params.id)
        album.title = "Changed Title"
        album.save(flush:true)
        ...
        // something goes wrong
        throw new Exception("Oh, sugar.")
    }
}
```

Grails uses Spring's PlatformTransactionManager abstraction layer under the covers. In this case, if an exception is thrown, all changes made within the scope of the transaction will be rolled back as expected. The first argument to the withTransaction method is a Spring TransactionStatus object, which also allows you to programmatically roll back the transaction by calling the setRollbackOnly() method, as shown in Listing 10-33.

Listing 10-33. *Programmatically Rolling Back a Transaction*

```
def save = {
    Album.withTransaction { status ->
        def album = Album.get(params.id)
        album.title = "Changed Title"
        album.save(flush:true)
        ...
        // something goes wrong
        if(hasSomethingGoneWrong()) {
            status.setRollbackOnly()
        }
    }
}
```

Note that you need only one withTransaction declaration. If you were to nest withTransaction declarations within each other, then the same transaction would simply be propagated from one withTransaction block to the next. The same is true of transactional services. In addition, if you have a JDBC 3.0–compliant database, then you can leverage save-points, which allow you to roll back to a particular point rather than rolling back the entire transaction. Listing 10-34 shows an example that rolls back any changes made after the Album instance was saved.

Listing 10-34. *Using Savepoints in Grails*

```
def save = {
    Album.withTransaction { status ->
        def album = Album.get(params.id)
        album.title = "Changed Title"
        album.save(flush:true)

        def savepoint = status.createSavepoint()
        ...
        // something goes wrong
        if(hasSomethingGoneWrong()) {
            status.rollbackToSavepoint(savepoint)
            // do something else
            ...
        }
    }
}
```

With transactions out of the way, let's revisit a topic that has been touched on at various points throughout this chapter: detached objects.

Detached Objects

The Hibernate Session is critically important to understand the nature of detached objects. Remember, the Session keeps track of all persistent instances and acts like a cache, returning instances that already exist in the Session rather than hitting the database again. As you can imagine, each object goes through an implicit life cycle, a topic we'll be looking at first.

The Persistence Life Cycle

Before an object has been saved, it is said to be transient. Transient objects are just like regular Java objects and have no notion of persistence. Once you call the save() method, the object is in a persistent state. Persistent objects have an assigned identifier and may have enhanced capabilities such as the ability to lazily load associations. If the object is discarded by calling the discard() method or if the Session has been cleared, it is said to be in a *detached* state. In other words, each persistent object is associated with a single Session, and if the object is no longer managed by the Session, it has been detached from the Session.

Figure 10-2 shows a state diagram describing the persistence life cycle and the various states an object can go through. As the diagram notes, another way an object can become detached is if the Session itself is closed. If you recall, we mentioned that a new Session is bound for each Grails request. When the request completes, the Session is closed. Any objects that are still around, for example, held within the HttpSession, are now in a detached state.

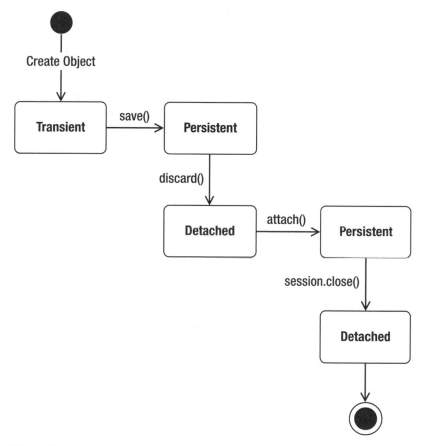

Figure 10-2. *The persistence life cycle*

So, what is the implication of being in a detached state? For one, if a detached object that is stored in the HttpSession has any noninitialized associations, then you will get a LazyInitializationException.

Reattaching Detached Objects

Given that it is probably undesirable to experience a LazyInitializationException, you can eliminate this problem by reassociating a detached object with the Session bound to the current thread by calling the attach() method, for example:

```
album.attach()
```

Note that if an object already exists in the Session with the same identifier, then you'll get an org.hibernate.NonUniqueObjectException. To get around this, you may want to check whether the object is already attached by using the isAttached() method:

```
if(!album.isAttached()) {
    album.attach()
}
```

Since we're on the subject of equality and detached objects, it's important to bring up the notion of object equality here. If you decide you want to use detached objects extensively, then it is almost certain that you will need to consider implementing equals and hashCode for all of your domain classes that are detached. Why? Well, if you consider the code in Listing 10-35, you'll soon see why.

Listing 10-35. *Object Equality and Hibernate*

```
def album1 = Album.get(1)
album.discard()

def album2 = Album.get(1)

assert album1 == album2 // This assertion will fail
```

The default implementation of equals and hashCode in Java uses object equality to compare instances. The problem is that when an instance becomes detached, Hibernate loses all knowledge of it. As the code in Listing 10-35 demonstrates, loading two instances with the same identifier once one has become detached results in you having two different instances. This can cause problems when placing these objects into collections. Remember, a Set uses hashCode to work out whether an object is a duplicate, but the two Album instances will return two different hash codes even though they share the same database identifier!

To get around this problem, you could use the database identifier, but this is not recommended, because a transient object that then becomes persistent will return different hash codes over time. This breaks the contract defined by the hashCode method, which states that the hashCode implementation must return the same integer for the lifetime of the object. The recommended approach is to use the *business key*, which is typically some logical property or set of properties that is unique to and required by each instance. For example, with the Album class, it may be the Artist name and title. Listing 10-36 shows an example implementation.

Listing 10-36. *Implementing equals and hashCode*

```
class Album {
    ...
    boolean equals(o) {
        if(this.is(o)) return true
        if( !(o instanceof Album) ) return false
        return this.title = o.title && this.artist?.name = o.artist?.name
    }
    int hashCode() {
        this.title.hashCode() + this.artist?.name?.hashCode() ?: 0
    }
}
```

An important thing to remember is that you need to implement equals and hashCode only if you are:

- Using detached instances extensively

- Placing the detached instances into data structures, like the Set and Map collection types, that use hashing algorithms to establish equality

The subject of equality brings us nicely onto another potential stumbling block. Say you have a detached Album instance held somewhere like in the HttpSession and you also have another Album instance that is logically equal (they share the same identifier) to the instance in the HttpSession. What do you do? Well, you could just discard the instance in the HttpSession:

```
def index = {
    def album = session.album
    if(album.isAttached()) {
        album = Album.get(album.id)
        session.album = album
    }
}
```

However, what if the detached album in the HttpSession has changes? What if it represents the most up-to-date copy and not the one already loaded by Hibernate? In this case, you need to consider merging.

Merging Changes

To merge the state of one, potentially detached, object into another, you need to use the static merge method. The merge method accepts an instance, loads a persistent instance of the same logical object if it doesn't already exist in the Session, and then merges the state of the passed instance into the loaded persistent one. Once this is done, the merge method then returns a new instance containing the merged state. Listing 10-37 presents an example of using the merge method.

Listing 10-37. *Using the merge Method*

```
def index = {
    def album = session.album
    album = Album.merge(album)
    render album.title
}
```

Performance Tuning GORM

The previous section on the semantics of GORM showed how the underlying Hibernate engine optimizes database access using a cache (the Session). There are, however, various ways to optimize the performance of your queries. In the next few sections, we'll be covering the different ways to tune GORM, allowing you to get the best out of the technology. You may want to enable SQL logging by setting logSql to true in DataSource.groovy, as explained in the previous section on configuring GORM.

Eager vs. Lazy Associations

Associations in GORM are lazy by default. What does this mean? Well, say you looked up a load of Album instances using the static list() method:

```
def albums = Album.list()
```

To obtain all the Album instances, underneath the surface Hibernate will execute a single SQL SELECT statement to obtain the underlying rows. As you already know, each Album has an Artist that is accessible via the artist association. Now say you need to iterate over each song and print the Artist name, as shown in Listing 10-38.

Listing 10-38. *Iterating Over Lazy Associations*

```
def albums = Album.list()
for(album in albums) {
    println album.artist.name
}
```

The example in Listing 10-38 demonstrates what is commonly known as the *N+1* problem. Since the artist association is lazy, Hibernate will execute another SQL SELECT statement (N statements) for each associated artist to add to the single statement to retrieve the original list of albums. Clearly, if the result set returned from the Album association is large, you have a big problem. Each SQL statement executed results in interprocess communication, which drags down the performance of your application. Listing 10-39 shows the typical output you would get from the Hibernate SQL logging, shortened for brevity.

Listing 10-39. *Hibernate SQL Logging Output Using Lazy Associations*

```
Hibernate:
    select
        this_.id as id0_0_,
        this_.version as version0_0_,
        this_.artist_id as artist3_0_0_,
        ...
    from
        album this_
Hibernate:
    select
        artist0_.id as id8_0_,
        ...
    from
        artist artist0_
    where
        artist0_.id=?
Hibernate:
    select
        artist0_.id as id8_0_,
            ...
    from
        artist artist0_
    where
        artist0_.id=?
...
```

A knee-jerk reaction to this problem would be to make every association eager. An eager association uses a SQL JOIN so that all Artist associations are populated whenever you query for Album instances. Listing 10-40 shows you can use the mapping property to configure an association as eager by default.

Listing 10-40. *Configuring an Eager Association*

```
class Album {
    ...
    static mapping = {
        artist fetch:'join'
    }
}
```

However, this may not be optimal either, because you may well run into a situation where you pull your entire database into memory! Lazy associations are definitely the most sensible default here. If you're merely after the identifier of each associated artist, then it is possible to retrieve the identifier without needing to do an additional SELECT. All you need to do is refer to the association name plus the suffix Id:

```
def albums = Album.list()
for(album in albums) {
    println album.artistId // get the artist id
}
```

However, as the example in Listing 10-38 demonstrates, there are certain examples where a join query is desirable. You could modify the code as shown in Listing 10-41 to use the fetch argument.

Listing 10-41. *Using the fetch Argument to Obtain Results Eagerly*

```
def albums =  Album.list(fetch:[artist:'join'])
for(album in albums) {
    println album.artist.name
}
```

If you run the code in Listing 10-41, instead of N+1 SELECT statements, you get a single SELECT that uses a SQL INNER JOIN to obtain the data for all artists too. Listing 10-42 shows the output from the Hibernate SQL logging for this query.

Listing 10-42. *Hibernate SQL Logging Output Using Eager Association*

```
select
    this_.id as id0_1_,
    this_.version as version0_1_,
    this_.artist_id as artist3_0_1_,
    this_.date_created as date4_0_1_,
    this_.genre as genre0_1_,
    this_.last_updated as last6_0_1_,
    this_.price as price0_1_,
    this_.title as title0_1_,
    this_.year as year0_1_,
    artist2_.id as id8_0_,
    artist2_.version as version8_0_,
    artist2_.date_created as date3_8_0_,
    artist2_.last_updated as last4_8_0_,
    artist2_.name as name8_0_
from
    album this_
inner join
    artist artist2_
        on this_.artist_id=artist2_.id
```

Of course, the static list() method is not the only case where you require a join query to optimize performance. Luckily, dynamic finders, criteria, and HQL can all be used to perform a join. Using a dynamic finder, you can use the fetch parameter by passing a map as the last argument:

```
def albums = Album.findAllByGenre("Alternative", [fetch:[artist:'join']])
```

Using criteria queries you can use the join method:

```
def albums = Album.withCriteria {
    ...
    join 'artist'
}
```

And, finally, with HQL you can use a similar syntax to SQL by specifying the inner join in the query:

```
def albums = Album.findAll("from Album as a inner join a.artist as artist")
```

Batch Fetching

As you discovered in the previous section, using join queries can solve the N+1 problem by reducing multiple SQL SELECT statements to a single SELECT statement that uses a SQL JOIN. However, join queries too can be expensive, depending on the number of joins and the amount of data being pulled from the database.

As an alternative, you could use batch fetching, which serves as an optimization of the lazy fetching strategy. With batch fetching, instead of pulling in a single result, Hibernate will use a SELECT statement that pulls in a configured number of results. To take advantage of batch fetching, you need to set the batchSize at the class or association level.

As an example, say you had a long Album with 23 songs. Hibernate would execute a single SELECT to get the Album and then 23 extra SELECT statements for each Song. However, if you configured a batchSize of 10 for the Song class, Hibernate would perform only 3 queries in batches of 10, 10, and 3. Listing 10-43 shows how to configure the batchSize using the mapping block of the Song class.

Listing 10-43. *Configuring the batchSize at the Class Level*

```
class Song {
    ...
    static mapping = {
        batchSize 10
    }
}
```

Alternatively, you can also configure the batchSize on the association. For example, say you loaded 15 Album instances. Hibernate will execute a SELECT every time the songs association of each Album is accessed, resulting in 15 SELECT statements. If you configured a batchSize of 5 on the songs association, you would only get 3 queries. Listing 10-44 shows how to configure the batchSize of the songs association.

Listing 10-44. *Configuring the batchSize of an Association*

```
class Album {
    ...
    static mapping = {
        songs batchSize:10
    }
}
```

As you can see from this discussion on eager vs. lazy fetching, a large part of optimizing an application's performance lies in reducing the number of calls to the database. Eager fetching is one way to achieve that, but you're still making a trip to the database even if it's only one.

An even better solution is to eliminate the majority of calls to the database by caching the results. In the next section, we'll be looking at different caching techniques you can take advantage of in GORM.

Caching

In the previous "The Semantics of GORM" section, you discovered that the underlying Hibernate engine models the concept of a Session. The Session is also known as the *first-level* cache, because it stores the loaded persistent entities and prevents repeated access to the database for the same object. However, Hibernate also has a number of other caches including the second-level cache and the query cache. In the next section, we'll explain what the second-level cache is and show how it can be used to reduce the chattiness between your application and the database.

The Second-Level Cache

As discussed, as soon as a Hibernate Session is obtained by GORM, you already have an active cache: the first-level cache. Although the first-level cache stores actual persistent instances for the scope of the Session, the second-level cache exists for the whole time that the SessionFactory exists. Remember, the SessionFactory is the object that constructs each Session.

In other words, although a Session is typically scoped for each request, the second-level cache is application scoped. Additionally, the second-level cache stores only the property values and/or foreign keys rather than the persistent instances themselves. As an example, Listing 10-45 shows the conceptual representations of the Album class in the second-level cache.

Listing 10-45. *How the Second-Level Cache Stores Data*

```
9 -> ["Odelay",1994, "Alternative", 9.99, [34,35,36], 4]
5 -> ["Aha Shake Heartbreak",2004, "Rock", 7.99, [22,23,24], 8]
```

As you can see, the second-level cache stores the data using a map containing multidimensional arrays that represent the data. The reason for doing this is that Hibernate doesn't have to require your classes to implement Serializable or some persistence interface. By storing only the identifiers of associations, it eliminates the chance of the associations becoming stale. The previous explanation is a bit of an oversimplification; however, you don't need to concern yourself too much with the detail. Your main job is to specify a cache provider.

By default, Grails comes preconfigured with OSCache as the cache provider. However, Grails also ships with Ehcache, which is recommended for production environments. You can change the cache configuration in `DataSource.groovy` by modifying the settings shown in Listing 10-46.

Listing 10-46. *Specifying a Cache Provider*

```
hibernate {
    cache.use_second_level_cache=true
    cache.use_query_cache=true
    cache.provider_class='com.opensymphony.oscache.hibernate.OSCacheProvider'
}
```

You can even configure a distributed cache such as Oracle Coherence or Terracotta, but be careful if your application is dependent on data not being stale. Remember, cached results don't necessarily reflect the current state of the data in the database.

Once you have a cache provider configured, you're ready to go. However, by default all persistent classes have no caching enabled. You have to be very explicit about specifying what data you want cached and what the cache policy is for that data.

There are essentially four cache policies available depending on your needs:

- `read-only`: If your application never needs to modify data after it is created, then use this policy. It is also an effective way to enforce read-only semantics for your objects because Hibernate will throw an exception if you try to modify an instance in a read-only cache. Additionally, this policy is safe even when used in a distributed cache because there is no chance of stale data.

- `nonstrict-read-write`: If your application rarely modifies data and transactional updates aren't an issue, then a `nonstrict-read-write` cache may be appropriate. This strategy doesn't guarantee that two transactions won't simultaneously modify a persistent instance. It is mainly recommended for usage in scenarios with frequent reads and only occasional updates.

- `read-write`: If your application requires users to frequently modify data, then you may want to use a `read-write` cache. Whenever an object is updated, Hibernate will automatically evict the cached data from the second-level cache. However, there is still a chance of phantom reads (stale data) with this policy, and if transactional behavior is a requirement, you should not use a `transactional` cache.

- `transactional`: A transactional cache provides fully transactional behavior with no chance of dirty reads. However, you need to make sure you supply a cache provider that supports this feature such as JBoss TreeCache.

So, how do you use these different cache levels in a Grails application? Essentially, you need to mark each class and/or association you want to cache using the cache method of the mapping block. For example, Listing 10-47 shows how to configure the default `read-write` cache for the `Album` class and a `read-only` cache for the songs association.

Listing 10-47. *Specifying a Cache Policy*

```
class Album {
    ...
    static mapping {
        cache true
        songs cache:'read-only'
    }
}
```

Now, whenever you query for results, before loading them from the database Hibernate will check whether the record is already present in the second-level cache and, if it is, load it from there. Now let's look at another one of Hibernate's caches: the query cache.

Query Caching

Hibernate, and hence GORM, supports the ability to cache the results of a query. As you can imagine, this is useful only if you have a frequently executed query that uses the same parameters each time. The query cache can be enabled and disabled using the `hibernate.cache.use_query_cache` setting in `DataSource.groovy`, as shown in Listing 10-46.

■**Note** The query cache works together with the second-level cache, so unless you specify a caching policy as shown in the previous section, the results of a cached query will not be cached.

By default, not all queries are cached. Like caching of instances, you have to specify explicitly that a query needs caching. To do so, in the `list()` method you could use the `cache` argument:

```
def albums = Album.list(cache:true)
```

The same technique can be used with dynamic finders using a map passed as the last argument:

```
def albums = Album.findAllByGenre("Alternative", [cache:true])
```

You can also cache criteria queries using the `cache` method:

```
def albums = Album.withCriteria {
    ...
    cache true
}
```

That's it for caching; in the next section, we'll cover the impacts of inheritance in ORM mapping.

Inheritance Strategies

As demonstrated in Chapter 3, you can implement inheritance using two different strategies called *table-per-hierarchy* or *table-per-subclass*. With a table-per-hierarchy mapping, one table is shared between the parent and all child classes, while table-per-subclass uses a different table for each subsequent subclass.

If you were going to identify one area of ORM technology that really demonstrates the object vs. relational mismatch, it would be inheritance mapping. If you go for table-per-hierarchy, then you're forced to have not-null constraints on all child columns because they share the same table. The alternative solution, table-per-subclass, could be seen as better since you avoid the need to specify nullable columns as each subclass resides in its own table.

The main disadvantage of table-per-subclass is that in a deep inheritance hierarchy you may end up with an excessive number of JOIN queries to obtain the results from all the parents of a given child. As you can imagine, this can lead to a performance problem if not used with caution; that's why we're covering the topic here.

Our advice is to keep things simple and try to avoid modeling domains with more than three levels of inheritance when using table-per-subclass. Alternatively, if you're happy sticking with table-per-hierarchy, then you're even better off because no JOIN queries at all are required. And with that, we end our coverage of performance tuning GORM. In the next section, we'll be covering locking strategies and concurrency.

Locking Strategies

Given that Grails executes within the context of a multithreaded servlet container, concurrency is an issue that you need to consider whenever persisting domain instances. By default, GORM uses optimistic locking with versioning. What this means is that the Hibernate engine does not hold any locks on database rows by performing a SELECT FOR...UPDATE. Instead, Hibernate versions every domain instance.

You may already have noticed that every table generated by GORM contains a version column. Whenever a domain instance is saved, the version number contained within the version column is incremented. Just before any update to a persistent instance, Hibernate will issue a SQL SELECT to check the current version. If the version number in the table doesn't match the version number of the instance being saved, then an org.hibernate. StaleObjectStateException is thrown, which is wrapped in a Spring org.springframework. dao.OptimisticLockingFailureException and rethrown.

The implication is that if your application is processing updates with a high level of concurrency, you may need to deal with the case when you get a conflicting version. The upside is that since table rows are never locked, performance is much better. So, how do you go about gracefully handling an OptimisticLockingFailureException? Well, this is a domain-specific question. You could, for example, use the merge method to merge the changes back into the database. Alternatively, you could return the error to the user and ask him to perform a manual merge of the changes. It really does depend on the application. Nevertheless, Listing 10-48 shows how to handle an OptimisticLockingFailureException using the merge technique.

Listing 10-48. *Dealing with Optimistic Locking Exceptions*

```
def update = {
    def album = Album.get(params.id)
    album.properties = params
    try {
        if(album.save(flush:true)) {
            // success
            ...
        }
        else {
            // validation error
            ...
        }
    }
    catch(OptimisticLockingFailureException e) {
        album = Album.merge(album)
        ...
    }
}
```

If you prefer not to use optimistic locking, either because you're mapping to a legacy database or because you just don't like it, then you can disable optimistic locking using the version method inside the mapping closure of a domain class:

```
static mapping = {
        version false
}
```

If you're not expecting a heavy load on your site, then an alternative may be to use pessimistic locking. Unlike optimistic locking, pessimistic locking will perform SELECT FOR...UPDATE on the underlying table row, which will block any other threads' access to the same row until the update is committed. As you can imagine, this will have an impact on the performance of your application. To use pessimistic locking, you need to call the static lock() method, passing the identifier of the instance to obtain a lock. Listing 10-49 shows an example of using pessimistic locking with the lock method.

Listing 10-49. *Using the lock Method to Obtain a Pessimistic Lock*

```
def update = {
    def album = Album.lock(params.id)
    ...
}
```

If you have a reference to an existing persistent instance, then you can call the `lock()` instance method, which upgrades to a pessimistic lock. Listing 10-50 shows how to use the lock instance method.

Listing 10-50. *Using the lock Instance Method to Upgrade to a Pessimistic Lock*

```
def update = {
    def album = Album.get(params.id)
    album.lock() // lock the instance
    ...
}
```

Note that you need to be careful when using the `lock` instance method because you still get an `OptimisticLockingFailureException` if another thread has updated the row in the time it takes to get the instance and call `lock()` on it! With locks out of the way, let's move on to looking at GORM's support for events.

Events Auto Time Stamping

GORM has a number of built-in hooks you can take advantage of to hook into persistence events. Each event is defined as a closure property in the domain class itself. The events available are as follows:

- `onLoad/beforeLoad`: Fired when an object is loaded from the database

- `beforeInsert`: Fired before an object is initially persisted to the database

- `beforeUpdate`: Fired before an object is updated in the database

- `beforeDelete`: Fired before an object is deleted from the database

- `afterInsert`: Fired after an object has been persisted to the database

- `afterUpdate`: Fired after an object has been updated in the database

- `afterDelete`: Fired after an object has been deleted from the database

These events are useful for performing tasks such as audit logging and tracking.

■**Tip** If you're interested in a more complete solution for audit logging, you may want to check out the Audit Logging plugin for Grails at `http://www.grails.org/Grails+Audit+Logging+Plugin`.

For example, you could have another domain class that models an `AuditLogEvent` that gets persisted every time an instance gets accessed or saved. Listing 10-51 shows this concept in action.

Listing 10-51. *Using GORM Events*

```
class Album {
    ...
    transient onLoad = {
        new AuditLogEvent(type:"read", data:title).save()
    }
    transient beforeSave = {
        new AuditLogEvent(type:"save", data:title).save()
    }
}
```

GORM also supports automatic time stamps. Essentially, if you provide a property called `dateCreated` and/or one called `lastUpdate`, GORM will automatically populate the values for these every time an instance is saved or updated. In fact, you've already been using this feature since the `Album` class has `lastUpdated` and `dateCreated` properties. However, if you prefer to manage these properties manually, you can disable automatic time stamping using the `autoTimestamp` method of the `mapping` block, as shown in Listing 10-52.

Listing 10-52. *Disable Auto Time Stamping*

```
class Album {
    ...
    static mapping = {
        autoTimestamp false
    }
}
```

Summary

And with that, you've reached the end of this tour of GORM. As you've discovered, thanks in large part to Hibernate, GORM is a fully featured dynamic ORM tool that blurs the lines between objects and the database. From dynamic finders to criteria, there is a plethora of options for your querying needs. However, it's not all clever tricks; GORM provides solutions to the harder problems such as eager fetching and optimistic locking.

Possibly the most important aspect of this chapter is the knowledge you have gained on the semantics of GORM. By understanding the ORM tool you are using, you'll find there are fewer surprises along the way, and you'll become a more effective developer. Although GORM pretty much eliminates the need for a data access layer like those you typically find in pure Java applications, it doesn't remove the need for a structured way to group units of logic. In the next chapter, we'll be looking at Grails services that provide exactly this. Don't go away!

CHAPTER 11

■■■

Services

A common pattern in the development of enterprise software is the so-called service layer that encapsulates a set of business operations. With Java web development, it is generally considered good practice to provide layers of abstraction and reduce coupling between the layers within an MVC application.

The service layer provides a way to centralize application behavior into an API that can be utilized by controllers or other services. Many good reasons exist for encapsulating logic into a service layer, but the following are the main drivers:

- You need to centralize business logic into a service API.

- The use cases within your application operate on multiple domain objects and model complex business operations that are best not mixed in with controller logic.

- Certain use cases and business processes are best encapsulated outside a domain object and within an API.

If your requirements fall into one of these categories, creating a service is probably what you want to do. Services themselves often have multiple dependencies; for example, a common activity for a service is to interact with the persistence layer whether that is straight JDBC or an ORM system like Hibernate.

Clearly, whichever system you use, you are potentially dependent on a data source or a session factory or maybe just another service. Configuring these dependencies in a loosely coupled way has been one of the main challenges facing early adopters of the J2EE technology.

Like many other software development challenges, this problem is solved by a software design pattern called Inversion of Control (IoC), or dependency injection, and projects such as Spring implement this pattern by providing an IoC container.

Grails uses Spring to configure itself internally, and it is this foundation that Grails builds on to provide services by convention. Nevertheless, let's jump straight into looking at what Grails services are and how to create a basic service.

Service Basics

Services, like other Grails artefacts, follow a convention and don't extend any base class. For example, say you decide to move much of the gTunes application's business logic into a service; you would need to create a class called StoreService located in the grails-app/services/ directory.

Unsurprisingly, there is a Grails target that allows you to conveniently create services. Building on what was just mentioned, to create the StoreService you can execute the create-service target, which will prompt you to enter the name of the service, as demonstrated in Listing 11-1.

Listing 11-1. *Running the create-service Target*

```
$ grails create-service

Welcome to Grails 1.1 - http://grails.org/
Licensed under Apache Standard License 2.0
Grails home is set to: /Development/Tools/grails

Base Directory: /Development/Projects/gTunes
Running script /Development/Tools/grails/scripts/CreateService.groovy
Environment set to development
Service name not specified. Please enter:
com.g2one.gtunes.Store
    [copy] Copying 1 file to /.../gTunes/grails-app/services/com/g2one/gtunes
Created Service for Store
    [copy] Copying 1 file to /.../gTunes/test/integration/com/g2one/gtunes
Created Tests for Store
```

Here you can enter com.g2one.gtunes.Store as the name of the service, and the target will create the StoreService class automatically and put it in the right place. The result will resemble something like Listing 11-2.

Listing 11-2. *grails-app/services/com/g2one/gtunes/StoreService.groovy*

```
package com.g2one.gtunes

class StoreService {

    boolean transactional = true

    def serviceMethod() {

    }
}
```

The service contains one method, which is just a placeholder for a real method. The more interesting aspect is the transactional property, which is discussed in detail later in this chapter.

Services and Dependency Injection

It is important to note that services are singletons by default, which means there is only ever one instance of a service. So, how do you go about getting a reference to a service within a controller, for example? Well, as part of Spring's dependency injection support, Spring has a concept called *autowiring* that allows dependencies to automatically be injected by name or type.

Grails services can be injected by name into a controller. For example, simply by creating a property with the name storeService within the StoreController, the StoreService instance will automatically be available to the controller. Listing 11-3 demonstrates how this is done.

Listing 11-3. *Injecting a Service Instance into a Controller*

```
class StoreController {
    def storeService
    ...
}
```

■Note The storeService property is dynamically typed in Listing 11-3. The property can be statically typed, and injection will work in the same way. It should be noted that using a dynamically typed reference allows for dummy versions of the service to easily be injected for the purpose of testing the controller.

The convention used for the name of the property is basically the property name representation of the class name. In other words, it is the class name with the first letter in lowercase following the JavaBean convention for property names. You can then invoke methods on the singleton StoreService instance, even though you have done nothing to explicitly look it up or initialize it. The underlying Spring IoC container handles all of this automatically.

You can use the same convention to inject services into other services, hence allowing your services to interact within one another.

It is important that you let Grails inject service instances for you. You should never be instantiating instances of service classes directly. Later in this chapter, we will discuss transactions, and you will see that there is some special magic going on when Grails is allowed to inject service instances for you. You will get none of those benefits if you are creating service instances yourself.

Now that you understand the basics of services, we'll show an example of implementing a service.

Services in Action

The StoreController in the gTunes application contains quite a bit of business logic and complexity at the moment. Pulling that logic out of the controller and into a service is a good idea.

In general, you should strive to keep your Grails controllers tight and concise. You should not let a lot of business complexity evolve in a controller. When much complexity starts to evolve in a controller, that should be a red flag to you, and you should consider refactoring the controller to pull out a lot of that complexity. Much of that complexity will fit perfectly into a service or multiple services.

Let's take a look at one specific area of the controller that is a good candidate for some refactoring. That area is the showConfirmation step in the buyFlow flow. Listing 11-4 shows a relevant piece of the StoreControllcr.

Listing 11-4. *Web Flow Logic in StoreController*

```
package com.g2one.gtunes

class StoreController {

    def buyFlow = {
        ...
        showConfirmation {
            on('confirm') {
                // NOTE: Dummy implementation of transaction processing
                // a real system would integrate an e-commerce solution
                def user = flow.user
                def albumPayments = flow.albumPayments
                def p = new Payment(user:user)
                flow.payment = p
                p.invoiceNumber = "INV-${user.id}-${System.currentTimeMillis()}"
                def creditCard = flow.creditCard
                assert creditCard.validate()
                // TODO: Use credit card to take payment
                // ...

                // Once payment taken update user profile
                for(ap in albumPayments) {
                    ap.user = user
                    // validation should never fail at this point
                    assert ap.validate()

                    p.addToAlbumPayments(ap)
                    assert p.save(flush:true)

                    ap.album.songs.each { user.addToPurchasedSongs(it) }
                    user.addToPurchasedAlbums(ap.album)
                    assert user.save(flush:true)
                }
            }.to 'displayInvoice'
```

```
        }
        ...
    }
    ...
}
```

There is a lot going on here, and this is just one step in a series of steps in a Web Flow. You should pull most of this code out of the controller and put it into a service.

Defining a Service

The code that is being refactored out of the `StoreController` should be put into a service called `StoreService`. The `StoreService` class should be defined in the `grails-app/services/com/g2one/gtunes/` directory. That refactoring would yield a `StoreService` like the one shown in Listing 11-5.

Listing 11-5. *The purchaseAlbums Method in the StoreService*

```
package com.g2one.gtunes

class StoreService {

    static transactional = true

    Payment purchaseAlbums(User user, creditCard, List albumPayments) {

        def p = new Payment(user:user)
        p.invoiceNumber = "INV-${user.id}-${System.currentTimeMillis()}"
        if(!creditCard.validate()) {
            throw new IllegalStateException("Credit card must be valid")
        }
        // TODO: Use credit card to take payment
        // ...

        // Once payment taken update user profile
        for(ap in albumPayments) {
            ap.user = user
            // validation should never fail at this point
            if(!ap.validate()) {
                throw new IllegalStateException("Album payment must be valid")
            }

            p.addToAlbumPayments(ap)
            if(!p.save(flush:true)) {
                throw new IllegalStateException("Payment must be valid")
            }
        }
```

```
                ap.album.songs.each { user.addToPurchasedSongs(it) }
                user.addToPurchasedAlbums(ap.album)
            }
            if(!user.save(flush:true)) {
                throw new IllegalStateException("User must be valid")
            }
            return p
        }
    }
}
```

Using a Service

The StoreController can now take advantage of the purchaseAlbums method in the StoreService. To do this, the StoreController needs to define the storeService property and then invoke the purchaseAlbums method on that property, as shown in Listing 11-6.

Listing 11-6. *Calling the purchaseAlbums Method in the StoreController*

```
package com.g2one.gtunes

class StoreController {

    def storeService

    def buyFlow = {
        ...
        showConfirmation {
            on('confirm') {
                // NOTE: Dummy implementation of transaction processing,
                // a real system would integrate an e-commerce solution
                def user = flow.user
                def albumPayments = flow.albumPayments
                flow.payment =
                  storeService.purchaseAlbums(user,
                                                flow.creditCard,
                                                flow.albumPayments)
            }
        }.to 'displayInvoice'
    }
    ...
}
```

Transactions

As mentioned previously, services often encapsulate business operations that deal with several domain objects. If an exception occurs while executing changes, you may not want any earlier changes to be committed to the database.

Essentially, you want an all-or-nothing approach, also known as a *transaction*. Transactions are essential for maintaining database integrity via their ACID properties, which have probably been covered in every book that has used a relational database. Nevertheless, we'll give you a quick look at them here. ACID stands for atomicity, consistency, isolation, and durability:

- *Atomicity*: This refers to how operations on data within a transaction must be atomic. In other words, all tasks within a transaction will be completed or none at all will be, thus allowing the changes to be rolled back.

- *Consistency*: This requires that the database be in a consistent state before and after any operations occur. There is no point attempting to complete a transaction if the database is not in a legal state to begin with, and it would be rather silly if an operation left the database's integrity compromised.

- *Isolation*: This refers to how transactions are isolated from all other operations. Essentially, this means other queries or operations should never be exposed to data that is in an intermediate state.

- *Durability*: Once a transaction is completed, durability guarantees that the transaction cannot possibly be undone. This is true even if system failure occurs, thus ensuring the committed transaction cannot at this point be aborted.

Grails services may declare a static property named transactional. When the transactional property is set to true, the methods of the service are configured for transaction demarcation by Spring. What this does is create a Spring proxy that wraps each method call and provides transaction management.

Grails handles the entire automatic runtime configuration for you, leaving you to concentrate on writing the logic within your methods. If the service does not require any transaction management, set the transactional property to false to disable transactions.

If a service needs to impose its own fine-grained control over transaction management, that is an option as well. The way to do this is to assign the transactional property a value of false and take over the responsibility of managing transactions yourself. The static withTransaction method may be called on any domain class, and it expects a closure to be passed as an argument. The closure represents the transaction boundary. See Listing 11-7 for an example.

Listing 11-7. *Using withTransaction in a Service*

```
package com.g2one.gtunes

class GtunesService {

    // turn off automatic transaction management
    static transactional = false

    void someServiceMethod() {

        Album.withTransaction {
            // everything in this closure is happening within a transaction
            // which will be committed when the closure completes
        }

    }

}
```

If the closure that is passed to the withTransaction method throws an exception, then the transaction will be rolled back. Otherwise, the transaction is committed.

If you want to take explicit control over rolling back the transaction, that is simple to do as well. It turns out that an instance of the org.springframework.transaction.TransactionStatus interface is being passed as an argument to the closure. One of the methods defined by the TransactionStatus interface is setRollbackOnly().[1] Calling the setRollbackOnly() method will ensure that the transaction gets rolled back. Listing 11-8 demonstrates how to take advantage of this.

Listing 11-8. *Using the TransactionStatus Argument*

```
package com.g2one.gtunes

class GtunesService {

    // turn off automatic transaction management
    static transactional = false

    void someServiceMethod() {

        Album.withTransaction { tx ->
            // do some work with the database
```

---

1. You can find the full documentation for the TransactionStatus interface at http://static. springframework.org/spring/docs/2.5.x/api/.

```
            // if the transaction needs to be rolled back for
            // any reason, call setRollbackOnly() on the
            // TransactionStatus argument...
            tx.setRollbackOnly()
        }

    }

}
```

Controllers and other Grails artefacts will, of course, need to get hold of a reference to the singleton StoreService. As described earlier in this chapter, the best way to get hold of a reference to a service is to take advantage of the automatic dependency injection provided by Grails.

Scoping Services

You must be careful about storing state in a service. By default all services are scoped as singletons and can be used concurrently by multiple requests. Further, access to service methods is not synchronized. For stateless services, none of that is a problem. If a service must maintain state, then it should be scoped to something other than singleton.

Grails supports several scopes for services. Which scope you use will depend on how your application uses the service and what kind of state is maintained in the service. The support scopes are as follows:

- prototype: A new service is created every time it is injected into another class.

- request: A new service will be created per request.

- flash: A new service will be created for the current and next requests only.

- flow: In Web Flows, the service will exist for the scope of the flow.

- conversation: In Web Flows, the service will exist for the scope of the conversation, in other words, a root flow and its subflows.

- session: A service is created for the scope of a user session.

- singleton (default): Only one instance of the service ever exists.

Note If a service uses flash, conversation, or flow scope, then the service class must implement the java.io.Serializable interface. Services using these scopes can be used only within the context of a Web Flow. See Chapter 9 for more details about Web Flow.

If a service is to be scoped using anything other than singleton, the service must declare a static property called scope and assign it a value that is one of the support scopes listed earlier. See Listing 11-9.

Listing 11-9. *A request-Scoped Service*

```
class LoanCalculationService {

    boolean transactional = true

    // this is a request scoped service
    static scope = 'request'

    ...

}
```

Choose the service scope carefully, and make sure your scope is consistent with the application's expectations of the service. Prefer stateless services; for these, the default scope of singleton is almost always optimum. When a service must maintain state, choose the scope that satisfies the application's requirements.

Testing Services

Since much of your business logic and complexity is encapsulated in services, it is important that these components are tested. As far as your tests are concerned, a service is just another class and can be tested as such. Note that integration tests participate in automatic dependency injection, so service instances can be injected into an integration test. Unit tests do not participate in automatic dependency injection. A unit test should create its own instances of a service class as necessary.

When unit testing a controller (or any other component) that uses a service, if the service is dynamically typed in the component that is being tested, then that component should be easy to test independent of the service dependency. For example, a Map or Expando object could be passed to a controller constructor to act as a dummy version of the service. An approach like this allows individual components to be unit tested in isolation. Isolation testing is all about testing individual components independently from their dependencies. Dynamic typing is one aspect of Groovy that makes isolation testing much easier to achieve compared to statically typed languages such as Java.

Exposing Services

The services you write as part of a Grails application contain a large share of the business logic involved in the application. Those services are easily accessed from just about anywhere in the application using Grails' automatic dependency injection. It makes sense that a lot of that business logic may be useful to other Grails applications. In fact, it may be useful to other applications that may not be Grails applications. The automatic dependency injection works only within the application. There really isn't any way to inject those services into other applications. However, it is possible to access those services from other applications, and Grails makes that really easy to do.

Making a service available to other process is known as *exposing* the service. A number of Grails plugins are available that support exposing services using various remoting technologies. For example, there is a plugin that greatly simplifies exposing services using the Java Management Extensions (JMX) technology.[2] JMX has been part of the Java Platform since the J2SE 5.0 release and provides a really simple mechanism for monitoring and managing resources within an application.

You can install the JMX plugin into a project using the `install-plugin` target, as shown in Listing 11-10.

Listing 11-10. *Installing the JMX Plugin*

```
$ grails install-plugin jmx

Welcome to Grails 1.1 - http://grails.org/
Licensed under Apache Standard License 2.0
Grails home is set to: /Development/Tools/grails

Base Directory: /Development/Projects/gTunes
Running script /Development/Tools/grails/scripts/InstallPlugin.groovy
Environment set to development
Reading remote plug-in list ...
Installing plug-in jmx-0.4
[mkdir] Created dir: /Users/jeff/.grails/1.1/projects/gTunes/plugins/jmx-0.4
    [unzip] Expanding: /.../plugins/grails-jmx-0.4.zip into /.../plugins/jmx-0.4
Executing remoting-1.0 plugin post-install script ...
Plugin jmx-0.4 installed
```

Like other remoting plugins that are available for Grails, the JMX plugin will look in all service classes for a property named expose. The expose property should be a list of `Strings`, and if the list contains the string jmx, then the plugin will expose that service using JMX.

Listing 11-11 shows a service in the gTunes application that has been exposed using JMX.

Listing 11-11. *The GtunesService Is Exposed Using JMX*

```
package com.g2one.gtunes

class GtunesService {

    static transactional = true

    static expose = ['jmx']
```

---

2. You can find more information about JMX at http://java.sun.com/javase/technologies/core/mntr-mgmt/javamanagement/.

```
    int getNumberOfAlbums() {
        Album.count()
    }

    int getNumberOfAlbumsForGenre(String genre) {
        Album.countByGenre(genre)
    }
}
```

The GtunesService contains a single method called getNumberOfAlbums, which returns the number of Album objects that are currently in the database. The service may contain any number of methods. All of the methods in the service will be exposed as JMX operations.

In terms of code, the only thing you need to do to expose your services using JMX is include jmx in the value of the expose property. It could not be simpler! There is another step that does not involve code. The way to enable remote access to services that have been exposed using JMX is to set the com.sun.management.jmxremote system property when the Grails application starts. A simple way to do this is to assign a value to the JAVA_OPTS environment variable. The value should include -Dcom.sun.management.jmxremote. Note that the property does not need to be assigned a value; the property just needs to be set. For example, in a Bash shell you could interactively set the environment variable using the code shown in Listing 11-12.

Listing 11-12. *Setting JAVA_OPTS in a Bash Shell*

```
export JAVA_OPTS=-Dcom.sun.management.jmxremote
```

In a Windows shell you could use the code shown in Listing 11-13.

Listing 11-13. *Setting JAVA_OPTS in a Windows Shell*

```
set JAVA_OPTS=-Dcom.sun.management.jmxremote
```

The com.sun.management.jmxremote system property must be set when the Grails application starts. Setting it after the Grails application has started will not affect the application.

Versions 5.0 and later of the J2SE include the Java Monitoring and Management Console known as JConsole. The JConsole application is a GUI tool for interacting with beans that have been exposed using JMX.

With your Grails application up and running, start JConsole by running the jconsole command at a command prompt. The application should open with the dialog box shown in Figure 11-1.

This dialog box allows you select which agent you want to connect to. Typically you will see just one agent in the list. Find your Grails application in the list, select it, and click the Connect button.

Once you have connected to an agent, the main JConsole window should appear, as shown in Figure 11-2.

Figure 11-1. *The Connect to Agent dialog box in JConsole*

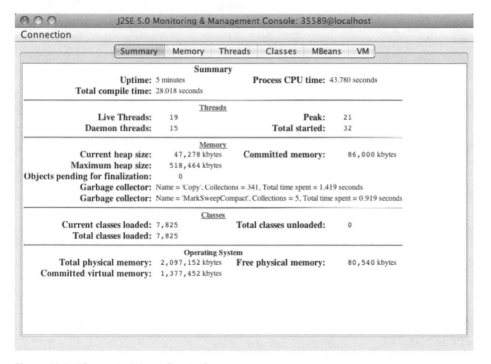

Figure 11-2. *The main JConsole window*

This main screen displays a lot of information about the Grails process. Click the "MBeans" tab at the top of the screen to view all the accessible beans. On that screen, you should see a list of all of your JMX exposed services under the "GrailsApp" folder on the left, as shown in Figure 11-3.

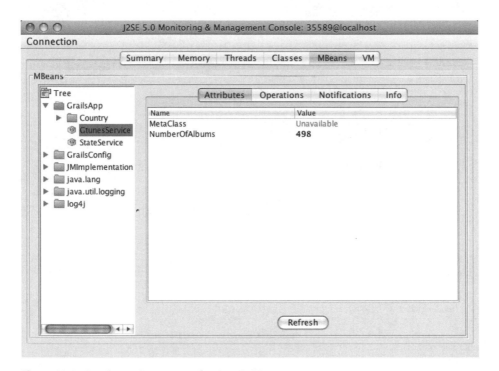

Figure 11-3. *Grails services exposed using JMX*

Notice the NumberOfAlbums property represented there. In Figure 11-3, that property has a value of 498. That value was just retrieved from the Grails application by invoking the getNumberOfAlbums method on the GtunesService. Just like that you have an entirely separate process communicating with your Grails service! In this case, the process is the JConsole application, but that process can be any JMX-aware client.

Select the "Operations" tab near the top of the screen. This tab will list all the operations that have been exposed by this bean, including all the methods defined in your service, as shown in Figure 11-4.

Notice that for operations that require parameters, JConsole provides a text box for you to define the value of the parameter. With that value filled in, you can click the button that contains the operation name. The operation will be invoked remotely, and the return value will be displayed.

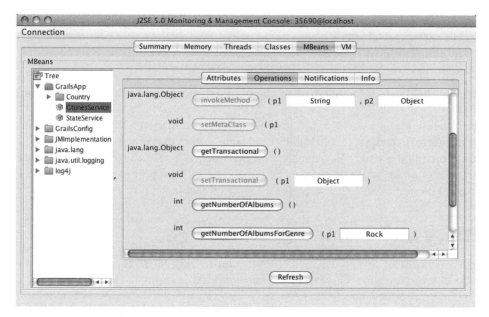

Figure 11-4. *JMX operations*

The JMX plugin is one of several Grails plugins that support exposing services using various remoting technologies. There is an XML-RPC plugin, and there is a Remoting plugin that allows services to be exposed via RMI, Hessian, Burlap, and Spring's HttpInvoker. The XFire plugin and the Axis2 plugin each support exposing services via SOAP. The XFire plugin is covered in detail in Chapter 15.

All of the remoting plugins use the same expose property in a service class as the trigger for exposing a service using any particular technology. Listing 11-14 shows how you would expose the GtunesService using JMX and XFire.

Listing 11-14. *Exposing a Service Using JMX and XFire*

```
package com.g2one.gtunes

class GtunesService {

    static transactional = true

    static expose = ['jmx', 'xfire']

    int getNumberOfAlbums() {
        Album.count()
    }
```

```
    int getNumberOfAlbumsForGenre(String genre) {
        Album.countByGenre(genre)
    }
}
```

Remember that in order for that to work, you need to have the JMX plugin and the XFire plugin installed.

Exposing Grails services is a great way to allow applications to access business logic inside a Grails application. In fact, you could build a Grails application that is just a service layer. That application might consist of nothing more than domain classes and services that provide access to the data, similar to the GtunesService shown earlier. The application would not necessarily need to have any controllers, any views, or anything else.

Summary

Services are an important component in almost any nontrivial Grails application. Services are where much of the application's business logic and complexity belong.

In this chapter, you saw how Grails helps simplify an application by encouraging the isolation of that complexity into services. You learned how you can easily take advantage of the power of Spring's dependency injection capabilities without the burden of having to write configuration files to instrument Spring.

You also saw how transaction management works with respect to Grails services. For most scenarios, the default method-level transaction demarcation is a perfect fit. For scenarios where the application needs more fine-grained control over transactions, Grails provides a really simple mechanism for dealing with those scenarios.

You have a lot of options for exposing Grails services using any number of remoting technologies.

You should make a habit of taking advantage of the power and flexibility provided by Grails services. If you do that, your applications will be easier to write, easier to understand, easier to maintain, and easier to test.

CHAPTER 12

■ ■ ■

Integrating Grails

So far, you've explored a number of the core concepts that underpin Grails. From controllers to GORM and services, you should now have a pretty good understanding of what makes Grails tick. In this chapter, you'll learn how you can fit Grails into your existing ecosystem. We hope what you'll get from this chapter is a good understanding of how to go about including Grails into your build system, development tools, reporting setup, and server environment.

There is a lot of ground to cover, so let's get started by taking a closer look at configuration in Grails.

Grails and Configuration

Using Convention over Configuration (CoC), Grails significantly reduces the amount of configuration you need to do. Crucially, however, it is convention *over* configuration, not instead of it. There are still a number of different ways you can configure Grails.

Most configuration can be done using Grails' central configuration mechanism. The file grails-app/conf/Config.groovy contains any global configuration for the application. You've already seen this file being used at various points throughout the book. In the following sections, we'll be taking a closer look at how configuration is done with Config.groovy and what configuration options are available to you.

Configuration Basics

The Config.groovy file is a Groovy script that is similar to a regular Java properties file. You can set properties using the dot dereference operator:

```
grails.mime.file.extensions = true
```

Since it's a Groovy script, all the type information is retained. So, in the previous example, a boolean property called grails.mime.file.extensions is set to true. To access this setting, you can use the config property of the grailsApplication object available in controllers and views:

```
assert grailsApplication.config.grails.mime.file.extensions == true
```

As well as supporting settings specified on a single line, like the grails.mime.file.extensions setting, you can also group settings using blocks, as shown in Listing 12-1.

Listing 12-1. *Grouping Settings in Config.groovy*

```
grails.mime {
    file.extensions = true
    types = [html: 'text/html']
}
```

The example in Listing 12-1 will produce two entries in `config`: `grails.mime.file.` `extensions` and `grails.mime.types`. You can also configure settings on a per-environment basis, which we'll cover in the next section.

Environment-Specific Configuration

As you discovered in Chapter 2, the `grails-app/conf/DataSource.groovy` file can be configured in an environment-specific way. This is because Grails uses the same mechanism to configure the `DataSource` as `Config.groovy` uses for the rest of the application.

Like with `DataSource.groovy`, by using `Config.groovy` you can specify environment-specific settings using the `environments` block, as shown in Listing 12-2.

Listing 12-2. *Environment-Specific Configuration*

```
// set per-environment serverURL stem for creating absolute links
environments {
    development {
        grails.serverURL = "http://localhost:8080"
    }
    production {
        grails.serverURL = "http://www.gtunes.com"
    }
}
```

As Listing 12-2 demonstrates, you can use the `environments` block to specify a different `grails.serverURL` setting for production and development environments. The `grails.` `serverURL` setting is one of a number of built-in settings that you'll be discovering through the course of this book.

Configuring Logging

Grails uses the popular Log4j (`http://logging.apache.org/log4j/`) library to configure logging. Traditionally, Log4j has been configured with either a properties file format or XML. Grails, however, provides a specific DSL for configuring logging. Within the `Config.groovy` script, you can set a property called `log4j` using a Groovy closure.

Within this closure, you can use the Log4j DSL to configure logging. Listing 12-3 shows the default Log4j configuration in Grails that sets up logging for a bunch of packages internal to Grails.

Listing 12-3. *The Default Log4j Configuration*

```
// log4j configuration
log4j = {
    error 'codehaus.groovy.grails.web.servlet', // controllers
            'codehaus.groovy.grails.web.pages', // GSP
            'codehaus.groovy.grails.web.sitemesh', // layouts
            'codehaus.groovy.grails.web.mapping.filter', // URL mapping
            'codehaus.groovy.grails.web.mapping', // URL Mapping
            'codehaus.groovy.grails.commons',// core / classloading
            'codehaus.groovy.grails.plugins',// plugins
            'codehaus.groovy.grails.orm.hibernate' // hibernate integration
}
```

As you can see from Listing 12-3, inside the body of the log4j closure there is an error method invoked that is passed a number of packages as arguments. The error method sets up the specified packages at the error debug level. The following debug levels are available going from least to most verbose:

- off: No logging at all.

- fatal: Log only fatal errors, which are typically errors that would cause an application to abort.

- error: Log all errors that occur but still allow the application to continue running.

- warn: Log scenarios that could be potentially harmful.

- info: Log informational messages that describe the progress of the application.

- debug: Log information that is used to debug an application.

- trace: The trace level is for even finer-grained events than the debug level.

- all: Log all messages that occur.

Sources within your own application can also be configured for logging. In Chapter 4 you learned about the log property available in every controller, tag library, or service. The output of this log property by default will use the root logging level of error. However, you can use the name of the class, starting with grails.app, to configure different logging behavior. For example, if you want to see output from all log statements in the UserController and AlbumArtService classes at the debug level, you could use the configuration in Listing 12-4.

Listing 12-4. *Setting the Debug Level*

```
log4j {
    debug 'grails.app.controller.UserController',
            'grails.app.service.AlbumArtService'
}
```

Using sensible defaults, Grails will automatically configure a console appender that logs to standard out, while the root logger is set to the error level. You can also create your own custom Log4j appenders. For example, the code in Listing 12-5 sets up an additional file appender that writes the log to a file.

Listing 12-5. *Configuring a File Appender*

```
log4j {
    appenders {
        rollingFile name:"myLog",
                        file:"/var/log/gtunes.log",
                        maxFileSize:"1MB",
                        layout: pattern(conversionPattern: '%c{2} %m%n')
    }
    ...
}
```

The example in Listing 12-5 uses a `rollingFile` appender, which is an `org.apache.log4j.RollingFileAppender` instance internally. Each named argument is a property of the `org.apache.log4j.RollingFileAppender` class, so to understand the configuration options, you just have to look at the Log4j APIs. The following is a list of the available Log4j appenders:

- `jdbc`: The `org.apache.log4j.jdbc.JDBCAppender` logs to a database connection.

- `null`: The `org.apache.log4j.varia.NullAppender` does nothing!

- `console`: The `org.apache.log4j.ConsoleAppender` logs to standard out.

- `file`: This is an `org.apache.log4j.FileAppender` that logs to a single file.

- `rollingFile`: This is an `org.apache.log4j.RollingFileAppender` that logs to a file that gets automatically backed up and re-created when a maximum size is hit.

You can also use the Log4j API yourself to create an appender programmatically and then simply call the appender method, passing your appender, to add your own appender. Notice also that Listing 12-5 uses the `pattern` method to define the `layout` property of the appender. This translates into an `org.apache.log4j.PatternLayout` instance. You can use a number of other layout styles, including the following:

- `xml`: An `org.apache.log4j.xml.XMLLayout` instance that outputs the log file in XML format.

- `html`: An `org.apache.log4j.HTMLLayout` instance that outputs the logs in HTML.

- `simple`: An `org.apache.log4j.SimpleLayout` instance that outputs to a preconfigured text format.

- `pattern`: An `org.apache.log4j.PatternLayout` instance that allows you to configure the output from Log4j. See the javadoc API for details.

Once you have an appender, you have to tell Log4j which packages need to be logged to that appender. Listing 12-6 shows an example of logging Hibernate output to the `rollingFile` appender defined earlier at the `trace` level.

Listing 12-6. *Using an Appender*

```
log4j {
    ...
    trace myLog:"org.hibernate"
    debug myLog:["org.codehaus.groovy.grails.web.mapping.filter",
                 "org.codehaus.groovy.grails.web.mapping"]
}
```

Notice that you reference the appender by the name given to it using the `name` argument. Finally, there is one special logger for stack traces, which we'll discuss in the next section.

Stack Trace Filtering

Whenever an exception is thrown in Grails, the exception's stack trace will be filtered of all Groovy and Grails internals before it is logged. This is very useful because it allows you to narrow the problem down to how it relates to your code. Otherwise, you could be sifting through a rather large stack trace because all the internal layers of Grails are exposed.

Normally, when an exception is thrown in development, you can work out from the filtered trace what the problem is. On a rare occasion, you may want to inspect the full nonfiltered stack trace. Grails, by default, sets up a special logger to which it will log the full stack trace. This logger writes to a file called `stacktrace.log` in the root of your project.

However, you can quite easily override this default behavior to provide your own custom logger for unfiltered stack traces. Listing 12-7 shows an example configuration that logs all unfiltered stack traces to a rolling file appender.

Listing 12-7. *Logging Unfiltered Traces*

```
log4j {
    appenders {
        rollingFile name:"stacktraceLog",
                        file:"/var/log/unfiltered-stacktraces.log",
                        maxFileSize:"1MB",
                        layout: pattern(conversionPattern: '%c{2} %m%n')
    }

    error stacktraceLog:"StackTrace"
}
```

You can also disable this functionality completely by passing the `grails.full.stacktrace` argument at the command line of your container or as an argument to the `run-app` command:

```
grails -Dgrails.full.stacktrace=true run-app
```

Externalized Configuration

During deployment, the `Config.groovy` file is compiled into a class and packaged into the WAR. Although this has its advantages, you may want to keep all configuration outside the main WAR file. For example, say you wanted to allow logging to be configured outside the application; to achieve this, you can use Grails' externalized configuration mechanism.

Essentially, within `Config.groovy` you can specify the `grails.config.locations` setting to contain a list of locations that need to be merged into the main configuration. Taking the logging example, Listing 12-8 shows how you could externalize the logging configuration to a file in the `USER_HOME` directory.

Listing 12-8. *Using Externalized Configuration*

```
grails.config.locations = ["file:${userHome}/gtunes-logging.groovy"]
```

You can even allow the `DataSource` to be configured externally using this mechanism. Although `DataSource.groovy` and `Config.groovy` are separate files on the file system, Grails merges them into a single logical configuration object. Hence, you can externalize not just logging, or any configuration, but also the `DataSource`, as shown in Listing 12-9.

Listing 12-9. *Externalizing DataSource Configuration*

```
grails.config.locations = ["file:${userHome}/.settings/gtunes-logging.groovy",
                           "file:${userHome}/.settings/gtunes-datasource.groovy"]
```

If you prefer to use static properties files in externalized configuration, you can do this too. Just use the extension `.properties` when referring to the files, and use regular `java.util.Properties` file semantics for configuration.

Understanding Grails' Build System

Grails' build system is powered by the Gant (`http://gant.codehaus.org`) build tool. Gant is a thin wrapper around Apache Ant (`http://ant.apache.org`), the ever-popular Java build system. Unlike Ant, which uses an XML format to describe a build, Gant uses a Groovy DSL. The benefit here is that you can easily mix build logic with scripting in Groovy code. Listing 12-10 shows a typical example of a Gant build script.

Listing 12-10. *An Example Gant Build Script*

```
targetDir = "build"
target(clean:"Cleans any compiled sources") {
    delete(dir:targetDir)
}
```

```
target(compile:"The compilation task") {
    depends(clean)
    mkdir(dir:"$targetDir/classes")
    javac(srcdir:"src/java",
             destdir:"$targetDir/classes" )
}
target(jar:"Creates a JAR file") {
    jar(destfile:"$targetDir/app.jar",basedir:"$targetDir/classes")
}
target(dist:"The default task") {
    depends(compile, jar)
}
setDefaultTarget ( dist )
```

Notice how the example in Listing 12-10 defines a number of targets by calling the `target` method. These are equivalent to Ant's `<target>` tag. Also, as you can see, you can specify dependencies between targets using the `depends` method:

```
depends(compile, jar)
```

If you install Gant outside of Grails, Gant includes its own command-line interface via the `gant` command. The `gant` command will search for a file called `build.gant`, the same way Ant looks for `build.xml`, and attempt to call it if found. Using the `gant` command, you can call an individual target or chain them, as shown here:

```
$ gant clean jar
```

It's at this point that you'll begin to realize the differences between vanilla Gant and Grails. Although Gant behaves much like Ant, Grails wraps Gant in its own `grails` command—the same one you've been using throughout the book. The `grails` command uses conventions within a Grails project to try to automatically figure out which script to execute. For example, when you run the following command:

```
$ grails create-app
```

Grails will search the following directories for a Gant script called `CreateApp.groovy` to execute:

- `PROJECT_HOME/scripts`: The `scripts` directory of the current project.

- `GRAILS_HOME/scripts`: The `scripts` directory of the location where you installed Grails.

- `PLUGINS_HOME/*/scripts`: Each installed plugin's `scripts` directory.

- `USER_HOME/.grails/scripts`: The `scripts` directory within the `.grails` directory of the current user's home directory. The location of this is operating system dependent.

If a matching Gant script is found, the `grails` command will execute the *default* target of the Gant script. In contrast to the `gant` command, the `grails` command is optimized for Grails' project layout, for the plugin system, and for the easy use of passing arguments.

Creating Gant Scripts

To help you understand this better, let's take a look at a simple "Hello World"–style example. Using the grails create-script command, create a new script called HelloWorld.groovy:

```
$ grails create-script hello-world
```

As expected, you'll end up with a new Gant script in the called HelloWorld.groovy in the scripts directory of your project. Figure 12-1 shows the script sitting snugly in place.

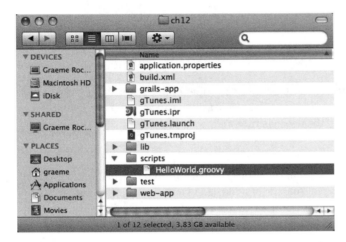

Figure 12-1. *The HelloWorld.groovy Gant script*

Grails uses lowercase names separated by hyphens—for example, hello-world—when referencing scripts but transforms the name into camel case for the script name. Listing 12-11 shows the contents of the generated HelloWorld.groovy script from Figure 12-1.

Listing 12-11. *The Script Template*

```
grailsHome = ant.project.properties."environment.GRAILS_HOME"

includeTargets << new File ( "${grailsHome}/scripts/Init.groovy" )

target(main: "The description of the script goes here!") {
    // TODO
}
setDefaultTarget(main)
```

As you can see, the template pulls in some existing functionality from a script called Init.groovy in the scripts directory of the location where you installed Grails. It then defines a single target, the default target, called main. To complete the "Hello World" example, you could use just a println statement or the echo target provided by Ant:

```
target(main: "The description of the script goes here!") {
    echo "Hello World!"
}
```

Now to run the `hello-world` script, all you need to do is run the following command using the grails executable:

```
$ grails hello-world
Welcome to Grails 1.1-SNAPSHOT - http://grails.org/
Licensed under Apache Standard License 2.0
...
Running script /Developer/grails-dev/book/dgg/code/ch12/scripts/HelloWorld.groovy
...
    [echo] Hello World!
```

Grails will perform a search of all the directories mentioned previously and find the `HelloWorld.groovy` script. Since the `main` target is the default target, Grails will execute it, which results in the "Hello World!" message being printed.

Of course, you have the entire Ant API at your disposal, which allows you to do a lot more than just print messages. Ant, and its plugins, provides access to targets that allow you to manipulate the file system, compile Java or Groovy code, perform XSLT transformations, and do just about anything you could dream of from the command line.

■Tip It may be useful, if you aren't already familiar with it as most Java developers are, to take a look at the Apache Ant manual (`http://ant.apache.org/manual/`). It provides comprehensive information about what you can do with Ant.

Command-Line Variables

The `Init.groovy` script that was imported by `HelloWorld.groovy` in Listing 12-11 provides a bunch of useful variables and targets. These are some of the variables you may find useful:

- `grailsVersion`: The version of Grails you're using

- `grailsEnv`: The environment Grails is executing in

- `basedir`: A String representing the base directory that the script is executing from

- `baseFile`: Similar to `basedir`, but a `java.io.File` representation

- `userHome`: The current user's home directory as a String

- `pluginsHome`: The location where plugins are installed

- `classesDir`: The location where classes are compiled to

The `grailsEnv` variable deserves special mention. If you recall from Chapter 2, you can tell Grails to run within the context of development, test, or production environments. As a recap, the following command will execute the `run-app` command using the production settings:

```
$ grails prod run-app
```

Your scripts can be equally environment-aware using the grailsEnv variable. For example, if you want a Gant script to run only in the development environment, you can write code like this:

```
if(grailsEnv == 'development') {
    // do something
}
```

Some of the other variables, such as the pluginsHome and classesDir variables, are automatically constructed by Grails. By default, Grails stores plugins and compiled resources in your USER_HOME directory under a special path. For example, you can find the gTunes application's compiled classes in the directory USER_HOME/.grails/1.1/projects/gTunes/classes. Figure 12-2 describes some of the tokens that make up this path.

Figure 12-2. *Grails compilation paths*

As you can see from Figure 12-2, Grails takes the Grails version number and the project name to formulate a path within the USER_HOME directory. If you are not happy with this location, then you can tell Graîls to use a different path by passing the grails.work.dir argument at the command line:

```
$ grails -Dgrails.work.dir=/tmp run-app
```

In fact, you can pass a whole load of different command-line arguments to customize the different locations that Grails uses:

- grails.work.dir: The base location where all Grails work occurs, including the test and source compilation directories

- grails.project.classes.dir: The location where project sources are compiled to

- grails.project.resource.dir: The location where project static resources (such as web.xml) are generated to

- grails.project.test.class.dir: The location where test sources are compiled to

- grails.plugins.dir: The location where plugins are installed

- grails.global.plugins.dir: The location where global plugins are installed

Parsing Command-Line Arguments

Unlike raw Gant, the grails command doesn't support chaining of targets, instead favoring the easy passing of command-line arguments. One useful target to depend on that is provided by the `Init.groovy` script is called the `parseArguments` target. The `parseArguments` target will read any command-line arguments and produce a variable called `argsMap` containing the values of the arguments in a more accessible form.

For example, say you wanted to enable the `HelloWorld.groovy` script to be able to print the name of the person to say hello to in either uppercase or lowercase. You could allow the name to be passed as a command-line argument and whether to print in uppercase or not as a command-line flag, as follows:

```
$ grails hello-world John -uppercase
```

Implementing the handling of these arguments manually would be somewhat tricky. Luckily, if you depend on the `parseArguments` target, all the heavily lifting is done for you. Listing 12-12 shows an updated `HelloWorld.groovy` Gant script that gracefully handles these arguments.

Listing 12-12. *Handling Command-Line Arguments*

```
depends(parseArguments)
def message = "Hello ${argsMap.params ? argsMap.params[0] : 'World'}"
if(argsMap.uppercase) {
    echo message.toUpperCase()
}
else {
    echo message
}
```

Notice that command-line flags (the arguments that start with - or --) are placed as boolean values into the `argsMap`. The example in Listing 12-12 shows how the -uppercase flag ends up as a boolean value with the key uppercase inside the `argsMap`. You can also have flags with values: for example, if you passed -uppercase=yes, then the value would be a `String` with the value yes in the `argsMap`.

All other arguments that are not flags are placed in the params key as a `List` that retains the order in which they were passed.

Documenting Your Scripts

You may have noticed from the script template in Listing 12-11 that the main target has a placeholder for the description of the target:

```
target(main: "The description of the script goes here!") {
```

You can provide additional information about a target so that others understand better how to go about using your script. For example, to give information about the hello-world script, you could modify this as follows:

```
target(main: "Prints 'hello world' to System.out") {
```

Then whenever another user of your script needs to get help on how to use the script, they can use the help command provided by Grails, as shown in Listing 12-13.

Listing 12-13. *Getting Help from Gant Scripts*

```
$ grails help hello-world
...
grails hello-world -- Prints 'hello world' to System.out
```

If one line of help is insufficient, you can take advantage of Groovy multiline strings to provide more detailed help, an example of which is shown in Listing 12-14.

Listing 12-14. *Using Multiline Strings to Provide Detailed Help*

```
target(main: """Prints 'hello world' to System.out
Type 'grails hello-world <name>' to say hello to someone specific

Available Flags:

-uppercase: Prints the message in uppercase
""") {
```

Reusing More of Grails

The inclusion of the `Init.groovy` script shown in Listing 12-11 is just one example of including an existing Grails script. You can in fact include a whole array of different scripts that provide different features. For example, say you want to make sure the tests run before your script is executed. You can include the `TestApp.groovy` script and depend on the `testApp` target, as shown in Listing 12-15.

Listing 12-15. *Executing Grails' Tests*

```
includeTargets << grailsScript("TestApp")
...
target(main: "The description of the script goes here!") {
    depends(parseArguments, testApp)

    ...
}
```

Alternatively, if you want to make sure that the container is up and running, maybe in order to perform some kind of automated functional tests, you can use the `RunApp.groovy` script. This script is the same one used when you type `grails run-app` at the command line, and it provides a target called `runApp` that you can use to load Grails' embedded Jetty container. As an extension to this, in the next section you'll look at how you can load Grails without even needing a container.

Bootstrapping Grails from the Command Line

If you need access to the Grails environment from the command line, you can load Grails using the GRAILS_HOME/scripts/Bootstrap.groovy script. This will enable you to, for example, use GORM from the command line for batch processing.

To get started, you need to include the Bootstrap.groovy script as follows:

```
includeTargets << grailsScript("Bootstrap")
```

and then call the bootstrap target:

```
bootstrap()
```

Once this is done, a number of new variables will be created including the following:

- grailsApp: A reference to the org.codehaus.groovy.grails.commons.GrailsApplication class that allows you to inspect the conventions in a running Grails application.

- appCtx: The Spring ApplicationContext instance that contains the bean definitions for the Grails application, as found at runtime.

- servletContext: A mock implementation of the ServletContext, usable from the command line.

- pluginManager: A reference to the org.codehaus.groovy.grails.plugins.GrailsPluginManager instance that allows you to inspect the currently installed plugins.

The most commonly used of these is the appCtx variable that allows access to all the beans contained within the Spring ApplicationContext. For example, if you need to obtain the Hibernate SessionFactory and/or SQL DataSource, you can easily do so using the appCtx:

```
DataSource dataSource = appCtx.getBean("dataSource")
SessionFactory sessionFactory = appCtx.getBean("sessionFactory")
```

With the basics out of the way, let's see a couple of examples of using Gant to boost your command-line productivity.

Gant in Action

Printing "Hello World!" to the command window is fun and all, but ultimately it not very useful. In the following sections, you'll be looking at a couple of real-world Gant scripts. The first is a script that will allow you to quickly deploy to Tomcat.

Automated Deployment to Tomcat

Writing a Tomcat deployment script in Ant is pretty trivial thanks to the targets that ship with Tomcat (see http://tomcat.apache.org/tomcat-6.0-doc/manager-howto.html). However, before you can start this example, you need to make sure you have Tomcat installed and TOMCAT_HOME set to the location where you installed it. Then run the grails create-script command as follows:

```
$ grails create-script tomcat-deploy
```

With that done, you should have a TomcatDeploy.groovy file in the scripts directory of your project, as shown in Figure 12-3.

Figure 12-3. *The TomcatDeploy.groovy script*

The TomcatDeploy.groovy script template will look identical to the HelloWorld.groovy template you saw earlier. To begin with, you're going to need to figure out the path to the Tomcat installation directory. Inspecting the TOMCAT_HOME environment variable can help you achieve this:

```
grailsHome = ant.project.properties."environment.GRAILS_HOME"
tomcatHome = ant.project.properties."environment.TOMCAT_HOME"
```

With knowledge of the Tomcat directory in hand, the next thing to do is include the War.groovy script available in GRAILS_HOME/scripts. The War.groovy template contains targets that allow you to construct a valid WAR file:

```
includeTargets << grailsScript("War")
```

To take advantage of the Tomcat Ant tasks, you have to define them by calling the taskdef method. This method relates to the <taskdef> target of Ant, so defining Ant tasks in Gant is pretty much identical to doing so in pure Ant—minus the angle brackets:

```
ant.path(id:"tomcat.lib.path") {
    fileset(dir:"${tomcatHome}/server/lib",includes:"*.jar")
}
ant.taskdef(name:"deploy",
            classname:"org.apache.catalina.ant.DeployTask",
            classpathref:"tomcat.lib.path")
```

As you can see, the only tricky part is ensuring that all the JAR files for the DeployTask class are placed onto the classpath appropriately using the JAR files available in your Tomcat installation directory. This is done using the classpathref named argument and a predefined Ant path called tomcat.lib.path.

Moving onto the `main` target of the `TomcatDeploy.groovy` script, you can change it to depend on the `war` target, which will ensure a valid WAR file is constructed before the rest of the code runs:

```
target(main: "Deploys the Grails application to Tomcat") {
    depends(parseArguments, war)
    ...
}
```

Once that is done, you need to establish the destination to publish the WAR to. You could, for example, accept the destination as the first argument to the command and otherwise default to `localhost`:

```
def dest = argsMap.params ? argsMap.params[0] : "http://localhost:8080/manager"
```

Once that is done, the rest is left to the `deploy` target supplied by the `org.apache.catalina.ant.DeployTask` class:

```
deploy(war:warName,
       url:dest,
       path:serverContextPath,
       username:"deployer",
       password:"secret")
```

The `warName` and `serverContextPath` variables are set up by the `War.groovy` script, which you can reuse here. The `deploy` target also requires that you pass `username` and `password` arguments whenever deploying to Tomcat. Given that you have a running instance of Tomcat locally, if you run the `tomcat-deploy` target now, you'll probably get a 401 error such as the following:

```
java.io.IOException: Server returned HTTP response code: 401 for URL:
http://localhost:8080/manager/deploy?path=%2FgTunes
```

The reason is that currently Tomcat doesn't have a user called `deployer` with a password of `secret` registered with it. To do so, you need to edit the `TOMCAT_HOME/conf/tomcat-users.xml` file and add a user who has access to the Tomcat `manager` application, as shown in Listing 12-16.

Listing 12-16. *Adding a Tomcat Deployer*

```
<?xml version='1.0' encoding='utf-8'?>
<tomcat-users>
  ...
  <user username="deployer" password="secret" roles="standard,manager"/>
</tomcat-users>
```

Once you have added the necessary Tomcat user, when you run the `tomcat-deploy` script, Grails will successfully deploy your application to Tomcat, as demonstrated in Listing 12-17.

Listing 12-17. *Deploying to Tomcat*

```
$ grails tomcat-deploy
...
Done creating WAR /Developer/grails-dev/book/dgg/code/ch12/gTunes-0.1.war
    [deploy] OK - Deployed application at context path /gTunes
```

You can of course take this further and write another tomcat-undeploy script or even combine them into two scripts. Nevertheless, Listing 12-18 shows the full code for the TomcatDeploy. groovy scripts.

Listing 12-18. *The TomcatDeploy.groovy Script*

```
grailsHome = ant.project.properties."environment.GRAILS_HOME"
tomcatHome = ant.project.properties."environment.TOMCAT_HOME"

includeTargets << grailsScript("War")

ant.path(id:"tomcat.lib.path") {
    fileset(dir:"${tomcatHome}/server/lib",includes:"*.jar")
}
ant.taskdef(name:"deploy",
                classname:"org.apache.catalina.ant.DeployTask",
                classpathref:"tomcat.lib.path")
target(main: "Deploys the Grails application to Tomcat") {
    depends(parseArguments, war)
    def dest = argsMap.params ? argsMap.params[0] : "http://localhost:8080/manager"

    deploy(war:warName,
           url:dest,
           path:serverContextPath,
           username:"deployer",
           password:"secret")
}
setDefaultTarget(main)
```

Exporting Data to XML

Another fairly common use of command-line scripts is to allow the migration of data. You could do this by performing a SQL dump of the database, but maybe you want to offer the ability to export all the content held in the database as XML as some web applications such as Atlassian Confluence and JIRA do.

■Note Although Grails, as of this writing, doesn't ship with a general-purpose migration solution for performing database migrations, you may want to take a look at the LiquiBase plugin (`http://www.liquibase.org/manual/grails`) and/or the DBMigrate plugin (`http://code.google.com/p/dbmigrate/wiki/Grails`), which both offer solutions to this problem.

Let's start by considering how you would write an export script that dumped all the relevant data from the gTunes application into a single parseable XML document. First you'll need to create a new Gant script called `export-library-to-xml`:

```
grails create-script export-library-to-xml
```

With that done, you're going to need to take advantage of the `GRAILS_HOME/scripts/Bootstrap.groovy` script we discussed earlier. To do so, simply change the import of the `Init.groovy` script to `Bootstrap.groovy`:

```
includeTargets << grailsScript("Bootstrap")
```

Inside the `main` target, you then need to depend on the `parseArguments` and `bootstrap` targets:

```
depends(parseArguments, bootstrap)
```

First, using the mechanics of the `parseArguments` target, you can work out the file to export to by either taking the first argument or creating a name programmatically:

```
def file = argsMap.params ?
              new File(argsMap.params[0]) :
              new File("./gtunes-data-${System.currentTimeMillis()}.xml")
```

As mentioned previously, the `bootstrap` target will set up a `grailsApp` variable that holds a reference to the `GrailsApplication` instance. The `GrailsApplication` instance can be used to dynamically load classes using the `classLoader` property. You need to do this because Gant scripts cannot directly reference the classes in your application, because they can't know whether those classes have been compiled yet. Luckily, it is pretty trivial to obtain a reference to any class using the `classLoader`:

```
def Artist = grailsApp.classLoader.loadClass("com.g2one.gtunes.Artist")
```

Unlike Java, with Groovy you can invoke any static method using a reference to `java.lang.Class`; hence, you can use regular GORM methods easily even with a dynamically loaded class reference. The first example of this is using the static `count()` method to figure out how many artists there are:

```
def artistCount = Artist.count()
```

Now it's time to create the XML. To do so, you're going to use Groovy's `StreamingMarkupBuilder` class. Listing 12-19 shows how to construct and use `StreamingMarkupBuilder`.

Listing 12-19. *Using StreamingMarkupBuilder to Write to a File*

```
new FileWriter(file) << new groovy.xml.StreamingMarkupBuilder().bind {
    music {
        ...
    }
}
```

Builders in Groovy allow you to construct hierarchies of nodes, a concept that fits nicely into the construction of XML. In this case, the `music` method will become the root element `<music>` of the XML document. In the next step, you initiate a transaction using the `withTransaction` method first discussed in Chapter 10.

The reason for using a transaction here is so that a common Hibernate `Session` is shared for the remainder of the code, hence avoiding a `LazyInitializationException` occurring when accessing uninitialized associations. Unlike in the server environment, Grails does not do any management of the Hibernate `Session` for you in scripts, but using `withTransaction` you can circumvent that:

```
Artist.withTransaction {
    ...
}
```

As well as `withTransaction`, you're going to take advantage of the `withSession` method to obtain a reference to the Hibernate `Session` object used. As discussed in Chapter 10, when reading a large amount of data into the Hibernate `Session`, you may run out of memory if you don't periodically clear the `Session`, and since you don't exactly know how much data is in the database, you're going to be doing that here:

```
Artist.withSession { session ->
    ...
}
```

The next step, if you'll excuse the pun, is to use the `step` method using the previously obtained `artistCount` variable to perform pagination of records. With this technique, you can obtain, say, ten `Artist` instances, including associations; manipulate them in some way; and then clear the `Session` before loading the next ten. Listing 12-20 shows the code in action.

Listing 12-20. *Using the step Method to Paginate Records*

```
0.step(artistCount, 10) { offset ->
    def artistList = Artist.list(offset:offset, max:10, fetch:[albums:'join'])
    ...
    session.clear()
}
```

With a list of Artist instances in hand, now it's just a matter of iterating over each one to create a bunch of <artist> XML elements:

```
for(currentArtist in artistList) {
    artist(name:currentArtist.name) {
        ...
    }
}
```

Finally, you also need to include all the Album instances associated with each Artist and all the Song instances associated with each Album. You can achieve this with a couple more nested loops:

```
for(currentAlbum in currentArtist.albums) {
    album(currentAlbum.properties['title', 'year', 'genre', 'price']) {
        for(currentSong in currentAlbum.songs) {
            song(currentSong.properties['title', 'duration'])
        }
    }
}
```

Notice how you can reference a subset of each Album instance's property values using the subscript operator and a List of property names:

```
currentAlbum.properties['title', 'year', 'genre', 'price']
```

And with that, the export-library-to-xml script is complete. Listing 12-21 shows the full code listing for the export-library-to-xml Gant script.

Listing 12-21. *The Full export-library-to-xml Code*

```
grailsHome = ant.project.properties."environment.GRAILS_HOME"

includeTargets << new File ( "${grailsHome}/scripts/Bootstrap.groovy" )

target(main: "Exports the gTunes library contained within the database to XML") {
    depends(parseArguments, bootstrap)

    def file = argsMap.params ?
                    new File(argsMap.params[0]) :
                    new File("./gtunes-data-${System.currentTimeMillis()}.xml")

    def Artist = grailsApp.classLoader.loadClass("com.g2one.gtunes.Artist")
    def artistCount = Artist.count()
```

```
      println "Creating XML for $artistCount artists"
      new FileWriter(file) << new groovy.xml.StreamingMarkupBuilder().bind {
          music {
              Artist.withTransaction {
                  Artist.withSession { session ->
                      0.step(artistCount, 10) { offset ->
                          def artistList = Artist.list(offset:offset,
                                                       max:10,
                                                       fetch:[albums:'join'])
                          for(currentArtist in artistList) {
                              artist(name:currentArtist.name) {
                                  for(currentAlbum in currentArtist.albums) {
                                      album(currentAlbum.properties['title', 'year',
                                                          'genre', 'price']) {
                                          for(currentSong in currentAlbum.songs) {
                                              song(currentSong.properties['title',
                                                                  'duration'])
                                          }
                                      }
                                  }
                              }
                          }
                          session.clear()
                      }
                  }
              }
          }
      }

      println "Done. Created XML export ${file.absolutePath}"
}
setDefaultTarget(main)
```

As you can see from the full code in Listing 12-21, you can also add a couple of `println` statements just to inform the user what is going on. You can now run the `export-library-to-xml` script using the grails command, and out will pop an XML document, as shown in Listing 12-22.

Listing 12-22. *Running the export-library-to-xml Script*

```
$ grails export-library-to-xml
...
Creating XML for 4 artists
Done. Created XML /Developer/grails-dev/gTunes/gtunes-data-122224970.xml
```

As you can see in this example, the script produces a file called gtunes-data-122224970.xml. The contents of this file contain the XML built by StreamingMarkBuilder; Listing 12-23 shows an example.

Listing 12-23. *Example Output XML*

```
<?xml version="1.0"?>
<music>
    <artist name="The Killers">
        <album year-"2006" title="Sam's Town" price="4.99" genre="Rock">
            <song title="Sam's Town" duration="246099"/>
            <song title="Enterlude" duration="49972"/>
            <song title="When You Were Young" duration="220499"/>
            ...
        </album>
    </artist>
    ...
</music>
```

Integration with Apache Ant

As discussed already, Grails' build system Gant builds on Ant. However, it may be a requirement for your organization to support a pure Ant build. If so, you have a number of options at your disposal. The first, and simplest, option is to use the build.xml file that is present in the root of every Grails project. This build.xml file simply delegates to Grails commands and hence relies on a copy of Grails being installed. Listing 12-24 shows an example of running the test target and the tests failing!

Listing 12-24. *Running a Target in the build.xml File*

```
$ ant test
Buildfile: build.xml

test:
    ...
    [exec] Running script /Developer/grails/scripts/TestApp.groovy

    ...
    [exec] Tests failed: 6 errors, 0 failures, 0 compilation errors.
      View reports in /Developer/grails-dev/gTunes/test/reports

BUILD FAILED
/Developer/grails-dev/gTunes/build.xml:30: exec returned: 1

Total time: 1 minute 9 seconds
```

As you can see from Listing 12-24, the build.xml file uses the Ant <exec> target to simply delegate responsibility to the grails command. Another approach to integrating Ant and Grails is to use the GRAILS_HOME/src/grails/grails-macros.xml file, which defines a <grails> macro target for calling Grails commands.

You can include the grails-macros.xml file in any normal Ant build using an Ant <import>:

```
<property environment="env" />
<import file="${env.GRAILS_HOME}/src/grails/grails-macros.xml"/>
```

In this example, you're using the location within GRAILS_HOME, but you could copy it to a more convenient location in your build if necessary. With that done, you can now use the new <grails> macro target to call Grails commands:

```
<grails command="test-app" />
```

The <grails> command works by looking up the appropriate classes from GRAILS_HOME. If the build environment you're working with doesn't have a GRAILS_HOME, then you'll need to use the <extend-classpath> element to tell the <grails> target where to look for the Grails JARs, as shown in Listing 12-25.

Listing 12-25. *Using the <extend-classpath> Element*

```
<grails command="run-app">
    <extend-classpath>
      <fileset dir="${lib.dir}"/>
    </extend-classpath>
</grails>
```

If you need to pass arguments to the `<grails>` command, you can use the args attribute. For example, the following usage will use Grails' `test-app` command to run the `UserControllerTests` unit test:

```
<grails command="test-app" args="UserController" />
```

Finally, if you need to pass system properties to the Grails command, such as to change the server port, you can do so with the `<sysprops>` element, as shown in Listing 12-26.

Listing 12-26. *Using the Element to Pass System Properties*

```
<grails command="run-app">
    <sysprops>
        <sysproperty key="server.port" value="7070"/>
    </sysprops>
</grails>
```

Dependency Resolution with Ivy

Apache Ivy is a dependency manager for Ant. With Ivy you can specify the JAR dependencies of your project in XML format. Your build then automatically downloads these dependencies. You can integrate Ivy into Grails in a couple of ways. One way is to just use the Ant `build.xml` file and integrate Ivy using the standard way described on the Ivy web site at `http://ant.apache.org/ivy/history/latest-milestone/tutorial/start.html`.

However, there is also a plugin for Grails that quickly integrates Ivy with Grails. To get started, you need to run the `install-plugin` command as follows:

```
grails install-plugin ivy
```

This installs Ivy for you locally without you having to download the Ivy distribution yourself. It will also automatically create the `ivy.xml` and `ivyconf.xml` files, both of which are necessary for transitive dependency resolution with Ivy. Figure 12-4 shows the two files nestled within the root directory of the target project.

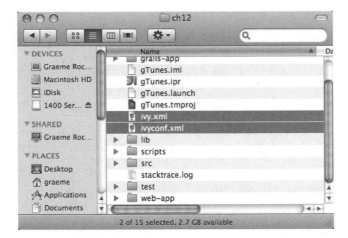

Figure 12-4. *The Ivy configuration files*

The `ivyconf.xml` file allows you to specify one or more resolvers to resolve dependencies. Typically you can leave this file alone, because you'll need to modify it only if you plan to configure additional repositories or even host your own repositories. The `ivy.xml` file is used to define the actual dependencies. Currently, the gTunes application defines a few dependencies that are contained in the `lib` directory, as shown in Figure 12-5.

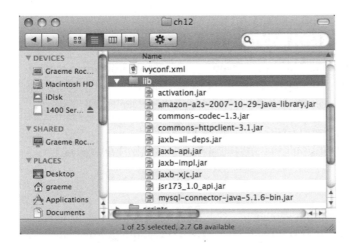

Figure 12-5. *Current JAR dependencies*

Some of these, like the Amazon JAR, won't necessarily be available in the repositories that Ivy scans. As mentioned, to make these available somewhere, you could host your own repositories and configure `ivyconf.xml` appropriately. Nevertheless, Listing 12-27 shows an example of configuring `ivy.xml` to resolve dependencies in the gTunes application.

Listing 12-27. *Configuring ivy.xml*

```
<ivy-module version="1.0">
    <info organization="codehaus" module="grails"/>
    <dependencies>
        <dependency org="commons-codec" name="commons-codec" rev="1.3"/>
        <dependency org="commons-httpclient" name="commons-httpclient" rev="3.1"/>
        <dependency org="mysql" name="mysql-connector-java" rev="5.1.6"/>
        ...
    </dependencies>
</ivy-module>
```

Ivy has the ability to use Maven repositories to resolve dependencies, and as you can see, you can use a similar format to the Maven pom.xml file to specify dependencies on the ivy.xml file. With the ivy.xml file configured, you can then download dependencies using the get-dependencies command:

```
grails get-dependencies
```

Listing 12-28 shows the output from Ivy as it automatically resolves and downloads the necessary dependencies.

Listing 12-28. *Example Output from Ivy*

```
[ivy-retrieve] :: resolving dependencies :: codehaus#grails;working@graeme...
[ivy-retrieve]     confs: [default]
[ivy-retrieve]         found commons-codec#commons-codec;1.3 in public
[ivy-retrieve]         found commons-httpclient#commons-httpclient;3.1 in public
[ivy-retrieve]         found commons-logging#commons-logging;1.0.4 in public
[ivy-retrieve]         found mysql#mysql-connector-java;5.1.6 in public
[ivy-retrieve] :: resolution report :: resolve 277ms :: artifacts dl 8ms
[ivy-retrieve]         :: evicted modules:
[ivy-retrieve]         commons-codec#commons-codec;1.2 by [commons-codec# ➥
                                     commons-codec;1.3] in [default]
        ---------------------------------------------------------------------
        |                   |          modules         ||   artifacts    |
        |        conf       | number|  search|dwnlded|evicted|| number|dwnlded|
        ---------------------------------------------------------------------
        |      default      |    5  |    0   |   0   |   1   ||   6   |   0   |
        ---------------------------------------------------------------------
[ivy-retrieve] :: retrieving :: codehaus#grails
[ivy-retrieve]     confs: [default]
[ivy-retrieve]         conflict on /Developer/grails-dev/book/dgg/code/ch12/lib/ ➥
                                     commons-codec-1.3.jar in [default]: 1.3
won
[ivy-retrieve]     0 artifacts copied, 4 already retrieved (0kB/12ms)
```

Now we'll cover how to integrate code coverage reporting into a Grails application.

Code Coverage with Cobertura

Even if you are an avid Test-Driven Development (TDD) practitioner, writing unit tests without knowing what code is covered by tests and what is not is a bit like shooting in the dark. Code coverage reports are incredibly useful because they will tell you what lines of code are covered by your unit tests and help you make an informed decision on what test you should be writing next. You'll often hear agile teams talking about improving their coverage. This decision is based on the analysis of coverage reports.

Out of the box, Grails does not produce code coverage reports, but thanks to the code-coverage plugin, it is easy to integrate the generation of code coverage reports into your application. To get started, as usual run the `install-plugin` command to install the code-coverage plugin:

```
$ grails install-plugin code-coverage
```

With that done, you can then run the `test-app-cobertura` command, which uses Cobertura (http://cobertura.sourceforge.net/), a code coverage tool for Java, to produce coverage reports. Cobertura uses byte code instrumentations and hence will slow down the running of your tests, but it will produce a nice set of reports in the `test/reports/cobertura` directory for you. Figure 12-6 shows an example.

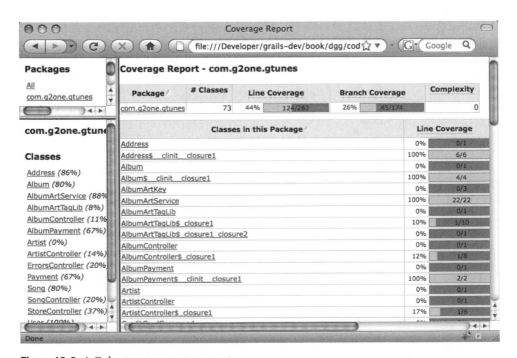

Figure 12-6. *A Cobertura coverage report*

You can click any of the class names in the report in Figure 12-6 to get line-by-line coverage information. As you can see, you still have some work to do to improve the coverage of the gTunes application. However, it is important to note that you may have 100 percent coverage and still have holes in your unit tests. Code coverage should be used to show the areas of code that need testing, not as a sign of test completeness.

Since coverage reports may take a while to produce, you don't want to have to create them every time you run your test suite. It may be better to delegate this responsibility to a build server. In the next section, we'll cover how to set up continuous integration to achieve this.

Continuous Integration with Hudson

Agile and test-driven philosophies have been debated endlessly and are a subject beyond the scope of this book. Nevertheless, if there is one agile practice that would bring immediate benefits to any project, whether "traditional" or agile, it is continuous integration.

Continuous integration involves setting up a server that continuously (either on a schedule or through monitoring for changes) builds the latest code, runs any tests, and produces a snapshot of the code for distribution. The continuous integration server can perform all manner of additional tasks from producing coverage reports to creating the latest documentation and even sending e-mails or SMS messages to notify of build failures.

In this section, we'll demonstrate how to use Hudson, an open source continuous integration server available at `https://hudson.dev.java.net/`. To get started, you need to download the `hudson.war` distribution of Hudson and deploy it to a container such as Apache Tomcat. Deployment with Tomcat is a simple matter of dropping the WAR into the `TOMCAT_HOME/webapps` directory and firing up Tomcat.

Then you can go to `http://localhost:8080/hudson`, assuming Tomcat is up and running on port 8080, and you'll be presented with the Hudson Dashboard shown in Figure 12-7.

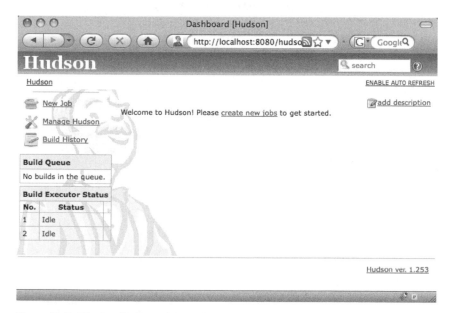

Figure 12-7. *The Hudson Dashboard*

The next step is to install the Grails plugin for Hudson. From the main Dashboard screen, click the "Manage Hudson" link, and then click the "Manage Plugins" link. On the Available tab, select the check box next to the Grails plugin, and click the "Install" button at the bottom of the page. Once you have installed the plugin, you'll need to restart Hudson.

Once the Grails plugin is installed, the next step is to configure your Grails installations in Hudson. The plugin does not come with its own version of Grails. The plugin uses a version of Grails that must be installed on the system separately from Hudson. The plugin allows you to configure as many different versions of Grails as you like. This is useful if you are building multiple Grails projects in the same Hudson instance and not all of those Grails projects are built with the same version of Grails.

To configure your Grails installations in Hudson, click the "Manage Hudson" link on the main Dashboard screen, and then click the "Configure System" link. Figure 12-8 shows the part of this screen that is used to configure your Grails installations.

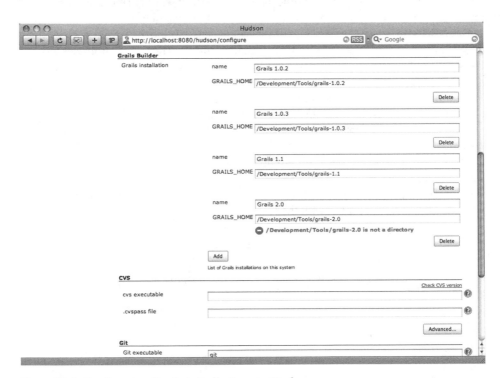

Figure 12-8. *Configuring Grails installations in Hudson*

You can see that each Grails installation has a name and a `GRAILS_HOME`. The name is simply an identifier that will help you select a particular version of Grails later when configuring jobs. The value of `GRAILS_HOME` must point to a specific Grails installation directory. Notice that there is validation built in to let you know whether the directory you have entered does not exist. The validation is not activated until you tab out of the text field.

Once you have configured all your Grails installations, make sure you scroll all the way to the bottom of the page and click the "Save" button.

With at least one Grails installation configured in Hudson, you are ready to create a job for a Grails project. You create a job for a Grails project in the same way you would for any other project in Hudson. From the main Dashboard screen, click the "New Job" link. Most often you will be creating a job for a so-called free-style software project, so you will select that radio button on the form to create a new job. See Figure 12-9.

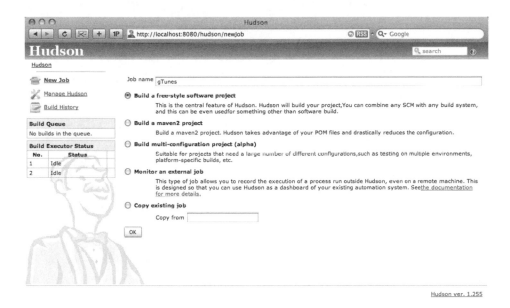

Figure 12-9. *Creating a new free-style job*

Once you click the "OK" button, you will be taken to the page where you configure all the details for how this build will be carried out. This page allows you to define which version control system you are using, paths to the project, a schedule for building the project, and so on. Near the bottom of the page is where you will configure the actual build steps. Once the Grails plugin is installed, a new build step should show up labeled "Build With Grails," as shown in Figure 12-10.

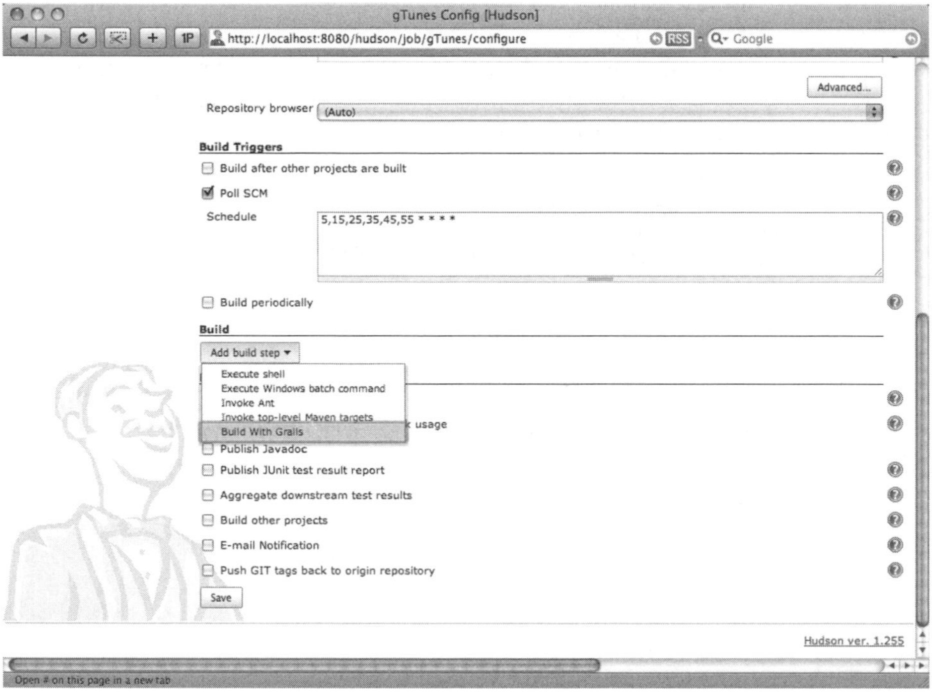

Figure 12-10. *The "Build With Grails" build step*

When you select the "Build With Grails" build step, the page will be updated with a form, which lets you configure the Grails build. This will include at a minimum specifying a version of Grails to use and which Grails targets to execute. A typical target to execute is the test-app target, but you can configure your job to execute whichever targets make sense. Figure 12-11 shows the details of a Grails build.

The "Grails Installation" drop-down will include all the Grails installations you configured earlier. Select the version of Grails that this job should be built with.

The "Targets" field lets you specify as many targets as you would like to be executed as part of this build. The targets will be executed in the order that they are specified in this text box. If any arguments are to be passed to any particular target, then the target name and the arguments should be surrounded by double quotes so the plugin knows to group them as one command.

There are fields for specifying the grails.work.dir and project.work.dir system properties.

The "Project Base Directory" field will typically be left blank but is important if the Grails project is not at the root of the job's working directory. For example, if your Grails project is in your SCM system at a path like /projects/development/code/grails/gTunes/ and for some reason you need to configure this job to check out everything under /projects/development/code/grails/gTunes/, then you will need to specify a value for the "Project Base Directory" field. The problem here is that the job root is /projects/development/code/grails/gTunes/, so the plugin will execute all Grails commands from that directory. Since that isn't the root of the Grails project itself, all the Grails commands will fail. To support this scenario, the "Project Base Directory" field should be given a value of /projects/development/code/grails/gTunes/, which is a relative path from the job root directory down to the root of the Grails project. With that in place, all of the Grails commands will be executed from the /projects/development/code/grails/gTunes/ directory.

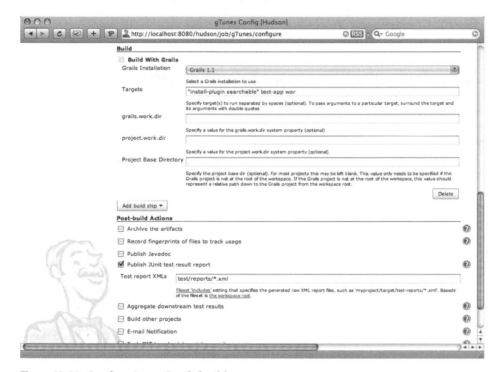

Figure 12-11. *Configuring a Grails build*

All other aspects of configuring a Grails job in Hudson are no different than they are for any other type of project.

Adding Support to Your Favorite IDE

Java developers in general have become particularly reliant on the comfort of modern integrated development environments (IDEs). This is largely because of the strictness of the Java language. From its static typing rules to quirks like its insistence on semicolons at the end of each line of code, it is hard to write anything in Java without a little nagging from the compiler. Fortunately, modern IDEs such as Eclipse and IntelliJ have made life a lot easier. In fact, they've done more than that. With the advent of refactoring tools, Java has become one of the most maintainable languages out there.

The tools in the dynamic language space are in general nowhere near as advanced as those available for Java. On the other hand, many developers create entire applications in simple text editors such as TextMate and jEdit, preferring their speed and efficiency to the relative clunkiness and slowness of a robust, richly featured IDE. This is possible because of the simplicity of frameworks such as Grails and the relatively forgiving Groovy grammar. It is our view that you can certainly get away with using the simpler tools during the early days of an application's life cycle.

However, as the application grows and enters the maintenance phase, the need for an IDE will also grow—particularly for refactoring and maintenance. Fortunately, although the tooling is much younger, you do have options available to you, which we will be covering in the following sections.

IntelliJ

By far the most complete IDE for Grails available at the moment is JetBrains' IntelliJ IDEA with the JetGroovy plugin installed. JetBrains worked closely with the Groovy team to make it the best possible environment to develop Groovy and Grails applications. In addition, although IntelliJ is a commercial IDE, JetBrains embraced the open source nature of Groovy by contributing back to the community. The joint compiler built into Groovy that allows Java and Groovy classes to be compiled together was contributed to Groovy during the development of JetGroovy.

JetGroovy contains the most complete support for code completion available for Groovy, performing completion on all statically typed references. Using type inference, JetGroovy can even sense completions on many dynamically typed references. JetGroovy also includes full circular refactoring, so if you rename a method in a Java source, it's picked up on the Groovy side. Likewise, if you rename a method in a Groovy source, all the Java code referencing that method changes accordingly.

JetGroovy will also complete all the dynamic methods added by Groovy at runtime, and you get many of the inspectors and quick fixes Java developers have come to expect. We recommend you take a look at the excellent marketing material JetBrains has put together on JetGroovy, which describes the features available in detail, at `http://www.jetbrains.com/idea/features/groovy_grails.html`. You can find even more documentation on JetGroovy on the Grails web site at `http://www.grails.org/IDEA+Integration`. Figure 12-12 shows the IntelliJ IDEA with JetGroovy in action.

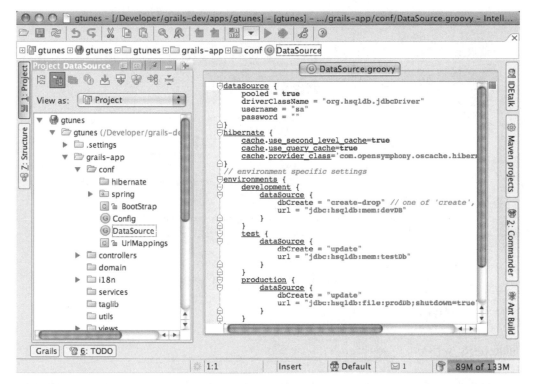

Figure 12-12. *IntelliJ IDEA with the JetGroovy plugin*

NetBeans

Of the open source IDEs available, NetBeans (http://www.netbeans.org/) provides the most advanced support for Groovy and Grails development. After making NetBeans one of the best Ruby IDEs on the market, Sun began investing in Groovy and Grails support, and with the release of NetBeans 6.5, the results of that investment have really begun to show. Featuring built-in Groovy support, the NetBeans plugin provides syntax highlighting, code completion, outline views, and menu options to easily access Grails commands. Figure 12-13 shows what NetBeans' Groovy editor looks like.

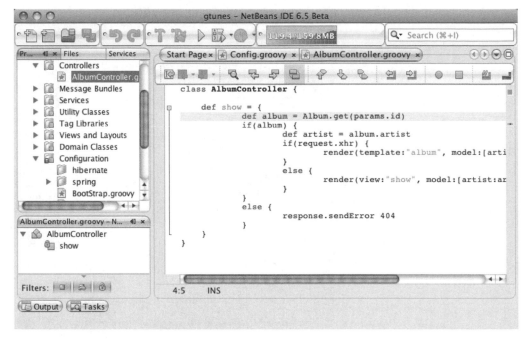

Figure 12-13. *NetBeans Groovy/Grails integration*

There is a good write-up on what is currently available in NetBeans on the Grails web site at http://www.grails.org/NetBeans+Integration.

Eclipse

The Eclipse plugin is available from the Groovy web site at http://groovy.codehaus.org/ Eclipse+Plugin where there are instructions on how to install it. It is still under active development, so we recommend retrieving it from Groovy's Subversion repository, building it, and installing it according to the instructions on the site. This will allow you to get the most benefit out of the currently implemented features. Alternatively, Groovy's update page is kept reasonably up-to-date.

The installation process with Eclipse is merely to drop the plugin ZIP file into the plugins directory located within your Eclipse installation. Once this is complete, just restart the IDE, and the plugin will be activated. There is one little bit of configuration to perform. The Groovy Eclipse plugin performs its own compilation process by default. This can get in the way of the

Grails-configured compiler, so you should disable this feature by selecting Project ➤ Properties ➤ Groovy Project Properties and checking the "Disable Groovy Compiler Generating Class Files" box.

Importing a Grails Project

Once you have the plugin installed, the next step is to import your Grails project. Luckily, Grails automatically creates Eclipse project and classpath files for you when you create the project. So, to import the project, right-click within the Package Explorer, and select the Import option, at which point the dialog box shown in Figure 12-14 will appear.

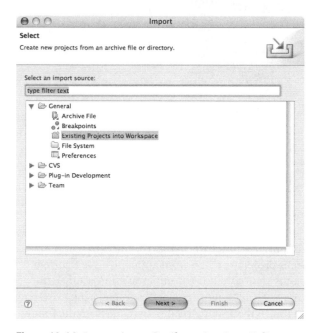

Figure 12-14. *Importing a Grails project into Eclipse*

Select the "Existing Projects into Workspace" option, and click the "Next" button. Now browse to the root of a Grails project using the "Browse" button, and click "Choose" or "OK." Once you have chosen the directory where the project is located, Eclipse will automatically detect that there are Eclipse project files within the specified root directory and even in subdirectories within the root. The result is that Eclipse displays a list of projects that you can import, as shown in Figure 12-15.

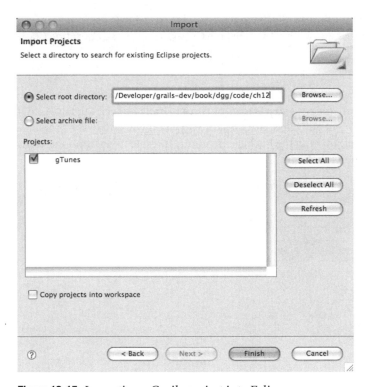

Figure 12-15. *Importing a Grails project into Eclipse*

Select the Grails project you want to import, and click the "Finish" button to complete the import. Don't be surprised that the Grails project you imported appears in the Package Explorer as "not compiling" and the Problems view contains a number of entries. Once the import is complete, there is one final step. Every Grails Eclipse project anticipates the existence of a GRAILS_HOME Eclipse variable; to create this (if it doesn't already exist), perform the following steps:

1. Right-click the project, and select Properties.

2. Select Java Build Path on the left menu.

3. Click the Libraries tab.

4. Click the "Add Variable" button.

5. Click the "Configure Variables" button.

6. Within the dialog box that appears, click "New."

7. Enter **GRAILS_HOME** into the "Name" field.

8. Click the "Folder" button, and browse to the location where Grails is installed.

9. Keep clicking OK until the changes are applied through all dialog boxes.

At this point, your project will be configured with the correct source directories and class-path. In the next section, we'll show how you can configure Grails as an external tool so that you can run a Grails application embedded within the IDE.

Running a Grails Application from Eclipse

You can run a Grails application from Eclipse using the Eclipse "External Tools" support. In the "External Tools" drop-down list, click "External Tools," as shown in Figure 12-16.

Figure 12-16. *Configuring an external tool for Grails in Eclipse*

Then under the Main tab, point the "Location" field to the `grails` executable, which is `GRAILS_HOME/bin/grails` on Unix or `GRAILS_HOME/bin/grails.bat` on Windows. Then set the "Working Directory" field to the location of your project within the Eclipse workspace. Finally, you can specify which Grails command to run using the "Arguments" field. Figure 12-17 shows an example configuration.

You'll also need to set the `GRAILS_HOME` environment variable to the location where you installed Grails on the Environments tab. Once this is done, you can click the "Run" button in the bottom right of the dialog box shown in Figure 12-17. Eclipse will run your Grails application, and you'll see the output in the Eclipse console.

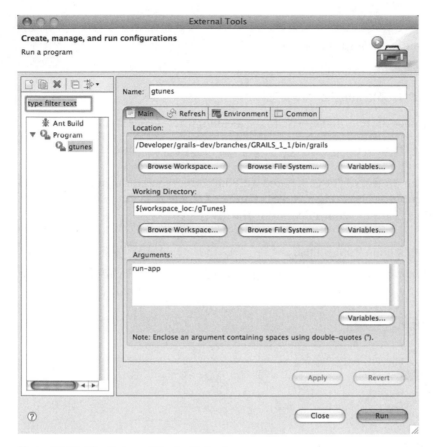

Figure 12-17. *The External Tools dialog box*

TextMate

If you happen to be lucky enough to work on a Mac (cue flame wars!), then you can take advantage of the excellent support for Groovy and Grails in the TextMate (`http://macromates.com/`) text editor. TextMate is a commercial text editor that is ultrafast, is extensible, and features nice features such as macros for pseudocode completion.

It also has really good integration with command-line processes and can be used as a complete replacement for Vi (`http://en.wikipedia.org/wiki/Vi`). On the downside, as mentioned, it is commercial and runs only on the Mac, but there are other great editors available that work with Grails, such as jEdit (`http://www.jedit.org/`), that are cross platform.

To get going, install TextMate, and then grab the TextMate bundles for Groovy and Grails from the TextMate repository at `http://macromates.com/svn/Bundles/trunk/Bundles/`. Typically you can just check these out using Subversion as follows:

```
svn co http://macromates.com/svn/Bundles/trunk/Bundles/Groovy.tmbundle/
svn co http://macromates.com/svn/Bundles/trunk/Bundles/Groovy%20Grails.tmbundle/
```

And then from Finder, simple double-click each one to install the bundle. Depending on your version of TextMate, there may be further steps; it is worth checking the http:// manual.macromates.com/en/bundles#getting_more_bundles page for the latest instructions if anything happens to go wrong. Once you have TextMate up and running, it's advisable to install the Terminal integration by selecting Help ➤ Terminal Usage and then clicking the "Create Link" button.

Once this is done, you can easily create a TextMate project from any directory via Terminal using the mate command. For example, from the root of the gTunes application, you can type this:

```
$ mate .
```

And like magic, you'll have a TextMate project ready to go. You can then open any unit test case, such as UserControllerTests, for example, and use the key combination Ctrl+Shift+Cmd+G to invoke the Grails menu. From this menu, you can choose to run the current test, all tests, or even the application. Figure 12-18 shows TextMate in action with the Grails context menu.

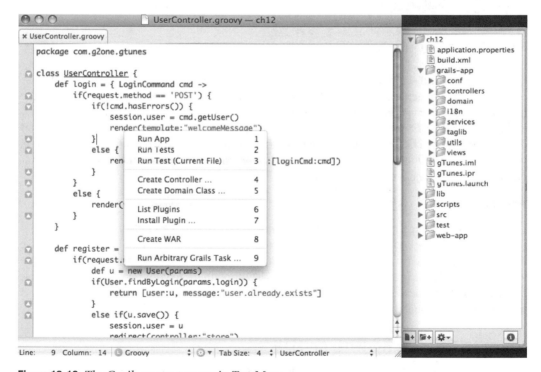

Figure 12-18. *The Grails context menu in TextMate*

If you choose to run all the tests, a new window will pop up and give you nicely formatted output of the test run, highlighting failed tests in red and good tests in green! Figure 12-19 shows the GrailsMate window that facilitates execution of tests in this manner.

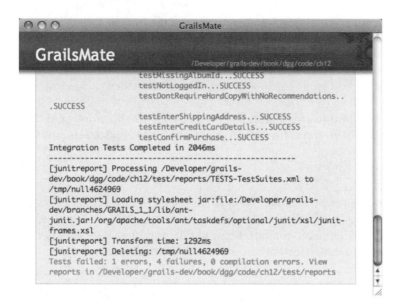

Figure 12-19. *Running tests in TextMate*

Another useful shortcut is Alt+Cmd+down arrow, which brings up the "Go to" option to quickly jump between resources that follow the same convention. For example, if you are editing the UserController class and you use the "Go to domain class" option, TextMate will open the User domain class by convention. Beyond these useful commands, there is a whole bunch of snippets that can be accessed by typing a shortcut and then hitting the Tab key. For example, you can type **rv** and then hit Tab, and you get the | character, indicating the location of your cursor, placed in a convenient location:

```
render(view:"|")
```

It is worth taking a look at the Bundles➤Groovy and Bundles➤Groovy Grails menus to see what is available because there are many useful shortcuts and commands that you can take advantage of. In our experience, if you're looking to get the best out of Grails' agile nature, it is worth using a simple text editor like TextMate as a complement to your regular IDE, whether it be IntelliJ, Eclipse, or NetBeans. It is very much the agile way to use the simplest possible tools to complete a job, and this applies to IDEs as well. You might even find Vi is good enough!

Remote Debugging with an IDE

You can remote debug Grails by running the grails-debug executable as a substitute for the grails executable.

■**Tip** The grails-debug executable simply sets up the necessary Java options to start Grails with a remote debugger. You could configure these yourself by setting the JAVA_OPTS environment variable.

The grails-debug executable will start Grails with a debug JVM. The debugger is listening on port 5005, which is the default debugger port for Java. You can then create a remote debug configuration in your IDE. For example, to do this with IntelliJ IDEA, you would go to the Debug menu and click Edit Configurations. Then click the plus icon in the top left and choose "Remote," which will give you a remote debug configuration, as shown in Figure 12-20.

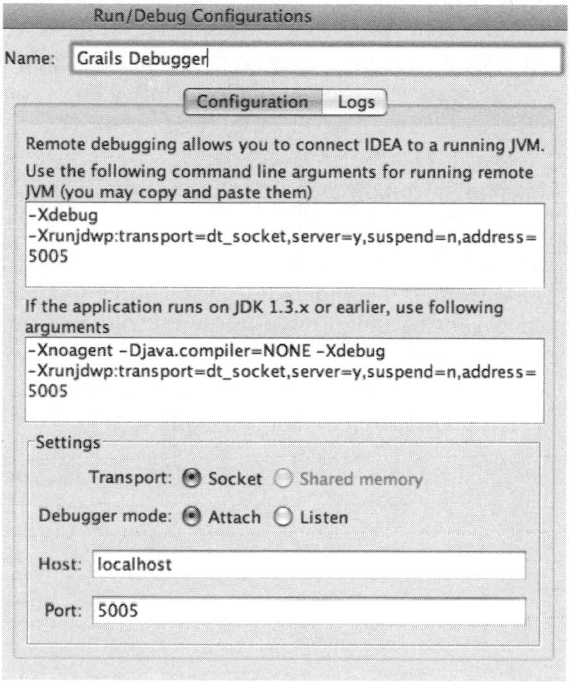

Figure 12-20. *An IntelliJ remote debug configuration*

You can leave the remaining settings as they are and just click the "OK" button in the bottom-right corner. With that done, just select the remote debug configuration and hit the "Debug" button, and IntelliJ will connect to the Grails remote server. You can then set breakpoints in your applications sources, and IntelliJ will stop at those points.

If you're willing to be adventurous, you can add Grails' source code to your path and step into the internals of Grails, but we'll leave that decision up to you! With IDEs out of the way, we're now going to talk about how you integrate Grails into the server environment. From mail servers to containers, there is still much to cover, so don't go away.

Integration with E-mail Servers

It has become a frequent use case for web applications to send e-mails. The Simple Mail Transfer Protocol (SMTP) is the enabler for mail delivery and has become pretty much the de facto standard for outgoing e-mail. A number of different server products support SMTP, from Microsoft Exchange Server to the open source Sendmail agent that is available on most Unix systems.

■**Note** The configuration of an SMTP server is beyond the scope of this book; we will show you how to set up Grails to talk to a successfully configured mail server.

You can integrate mail with Grails in several ways. Since Grails is built on Spring, you could use the `org.springframework.mail` abstraction, which provides a nicer API than JavaMail (http://java.sun.com/products/javamail/). However, that involves a lot of manual configuration, so what we'll be demonstrating is how to integrate the Grails Mail plugin into your application to enable the sending of confirmation e-mails whenever a user registers on gTunes or makes a purchase.

To get started, you need to install the Mail plugin with the `install-plugin` command:

```
$ grails install-plugin mail
```

The Mail plugin already comes with JavaMail and its dependencies, so you don't need to install any more libraries or dependencies. It uses sensible defaults and automatically assumes your mail server is running locally on port 25. However, if this is not the case, you can configure it using some settings in `grails-app/conf/Config.groovy`. For example, Listing 12-29 shows how you could configure the mail server to send e-mails using a Gmail account instead.

Listing 12-29. *Configuring the Mail Plugin*

```
grails {
   mail {
     host = "smtp.gmail.com"
     port = 465
     username = "youracount@gmail.com"
     password = "yourpassword"
     props = ["mail.smtp.auth":"true",
              "mail.smtp.socketFactory.port":"465",
              "mail.smtp.socketFactory.class":"javax.net.ssl.SSLSocketFactory",
              "mail.smtp.socketFactory.fallback":"false"]

   }
}
```

Notice in Listing 12-29 the usage of the props setting, which allows you to configure the properties of the JavaMail framework. However, for our purposes, we'll assume that a mail server running locally is good enough. Returning to the Mail plugin itself, the main addition is a new method called `sendMail` added to all controllers. Listing 12-30 shows an example of its usage at its simplest.

Listing 12-30. *Sending a Simple Mail Message*

```
sendMail {
    to "john@g2one.com"
    subject "Hello John"
    body "How are you?"
}
```

If you need to access the sendMail method from other places in your application, such as tag libraries and services, the Mail plugin provides a mailService that is available via dependency injection. Simply define a property called mailService in your tag library or service as follows:

```
def mailService
```

The sendMail method can then be called using the mailService instance, for example:

```
mailService.sendMail {
    ...
}
```

In the example in Listing 12-30, a simple String is used for the body of the e-mail. However, it is equally possible to use a GSP view to define the body, which is something you'll be doing to send registration confirmation e-mails to users of the gTunes application. Before you can do so, however, you need to modify the User domain class in order to add a new email property. Listing 12-31 shows the change to the User class.

Listing 12-31. *Adding an email Property to the User Class*

```
class User {
    String email
    ...
    static constraints = {
        ...
        email email:true, blank:false, unique:true
    }
}
```

As you can see in Listing 12-31, you've also applied a set of constraints to the email property. The email constraint ensures that it is a valid e-mail address, the blank constraint makes sure blank values are not allowed, and the unique constraint ensures that two users can't register with the same e-mail address. With this done, you need to modify the grails-app/views/user/register.gsp view to add a field for the email property to the registration form. Listing 12-32 shows the necessary change to the register.gsp file.

Listing 12-32. *Adding a Text Field for the email Property*

```
<g:form action="register" name="registerForm">
    ...
    <div class="formField">
        <label for="login">Email:</label>
        <g:textField name="email" value="${user?.email}"></g:textField>
    </div>
    ...
</g:form>
```

With that done, you now have an e-mail address to send confirmation e-mails to! To send an e-mail, you'll need to modify the `register` action of the `UserController` class to use the `sendMail` method to deliver an e-mail. Listing 12-33 shows the changes to the `register` action.

Listing 12-33. *Sending an E-mail Confirmation*

```
def register = {
    ...
        else if(u.save()) {
            session.user = u
            try {
                sendMail {
                    to u.email
                    subject "Registration Confirmation"
                    body view:"/emails/confirmRegistration",
                        model:[user:u]
                }
            }
            catch(Exception e) {
                log.error "Problem sending email $e.message", e
            }
            redirect(controller:"store")
        }
    ...
}
```

Notice how in Listing 12-33 you can use the `view` argument of the body method to define the name of the GSP view used to render the e-mail. As you can see, you can also pass a model with the `model` argument. The code is wrapped in a `try`/`catch` block just in case there is a problem sending the confirmation mail. At the moment, the code simply logs the error, but you could place the message into a queue to be re-sent later using a scheduled job—something you'll be looking at in the next section.

As for the GSP itself, you need to create a new view at the location grails-app/views/ emails/confirmRegistration.gsp. The example in Listing 12-33 uses an absolute path to this location. If you don't specify an absolute path then, as with regular views, the path is assumed to be relative to the current controller. Listing 12-34 shows the confirmRegistration view that renders the e-mail contents.

Listing 12-34. *The confirmRegistration View*

```
<%@ page contentType="text/plain"%>
Dear ${user.firstName} ${user.lastName},

Congratulations! You have registered with gTunes, giving you access to a huge
collection of music.

Your login id is: ${user.login}

You can use the following link to login: <g:createLink controller="store"
                                                        absolute="true" />

Kind Regards,

The gTunes Team
```

Note that the code in Listing 12-34 uses a GSP page directive to set the contentType to text/plain. The default contentType is text/html, so if you want to send HTML mail instead, you can omit this line. And with that, you've implemented e-mail confirmation of registration. However, that's not the end of our e-mail adventures; in the next section, you'll be learning how to send e-mails on a scheduled basis.

Scheduling Jobs

Another frequent use case in web applications is to perform some kind of scheduled execution. Whether it be to produce a monthly report that is too intensive to do via a web interface or to run some periodic system maintenance, scheduling jobs is a problem encountered time and again. In the Java world, the Quartz job scheduling library is one of the most popular open source solutions to this problem. Quartz allows you to schedule jobs that are to be executed on a scheduled basis, such as every 10 minutes or something more specific such as the last Thursday of every month at 1 a.m.

Grails features a plugin for Quartz (http://grails.org/Quartz+Plugin), which integrates Quartz seamlessly into Grails.

Installing the Quartz Plugin

To install the Quartz plugin, you need to run the install-plugin command, as shown in Listing 12-35.

Listing 12-35. *Installing the Quartz Plugin*

```
$ grails install-plugin quartz
...
Plugin provides the following new scripts:
-----------------------------------------
grails create-job
grails install-quartz-config
```

As you can see from the output, the Quartz plugin provides a couple of new commands. The most significant of these is the `create-job` command, which automates the process of creating a job. As an example, you'll create a job that sends out an automatically generated weekly newsletter detailing the latest new albums in the gTunes store. To get started, run the `create-job` command as follows:

```
$ grails create-job com.g2one.gtunes.NewsLetter
```

You'll end up with a new job class at the location `grails-app/jobs/com/g2one/gtunes/NewsLetterJob.groovy`. As you can see, the Quartz plugin has introduced an entirely new convention to Grails. All classes that are contained with the `grails-app/jobs` directory that end with the convention `Job` and contain an `execute` method are treated as scheduled jobs!

Simple Jobs

If you open the `NewsLetterJob.groovy` class, you'll notice it contains a single execute method as well as a `timeout` property, as shown in Listing 12-36.

Listing 12-36. *The Job Template*

```
class NewsLetterJob {
    def timeout = 1000l // execute job once in 5 seconds

    def execute() {
        // execute task
    }
}
```

By default, the job is configured to start immediately upon loading and execute every second. The `timeout` property is specified in milliseconds, so in the preceding example, there will be a 1-second interval between executions. Every second, the job's execute method will be called by the job scheduler. What you do within the execute method is entirely up to you. It could be some system maintenance task or maybe the execution of scheduled reports.

Occasionally, it's useful for a job to start after a set period of time; this is where the `startInterval` property comes in. Like the `timeout` property, `startInterval` accepts a time interval in milliseconds:

```
def startInterval = 10000
```

Here the job will execute 10 seconds after the scheduler first loads. The scheduler is, of course, started when a Grails application first loads. Jobs can also be placed in groups and given names using the name and group properties. Listing 12-37 shows how this is done.

Listing 12-37. *Job Naming and Grouping*

```
def name = "newsletter"
def group = "subscriptions"
...
```

The relevance of this will become more apparent in the section "Interacting with the Scheduler" later in this chapter. For the moment, however, it is time to look at an alternative way to schedule jobs that users of Unix's crontab command will be familiar with.

Cron Jobs

Using the timeout property is useful for simple cases, but what if you want the job to be executed on a set day in the month or week? For use cases such as this, the Quartz plugin allows you to specify a cron expression. If you have a Unix background, you are probably familiar with cron, the time-based scheduling service that got its name from the word *chronograph*.

A cron expression represents a firing schedule, such as "at 10:30 p.m. every last Sunday of the month," and is represented by six or seven fields representing seconds, minutes, hours, day of the month, month, day of the week, and year (optional), respectively. For example, the cron expression from the English language version would be as follows:

```
0 30 22 ? * 1L
```

This may seem a little baffling at first, but there is method to the madness. Table 12-1 should help make things a little clearer.

Table 12-1. *Cron Expression Fields*

Field Name	Allowed Values	Allowed Special Characters
Seconds	0–59	, - * /
Minutes	0–59	, - * /
Hours	0–23	, - * /
Day-of-month	1–31	, - * ? / L W C
Month	1–12 or JAN–DEC	, - * /
Day-of-week	1–7 or SUN–SAT	, - * ? / L C #
Year (optional)	Empty, 1970–2099	, - * /

Each field in the cron expression relates to one of the rows in the left column in the order in which it is defined. The second column of allowed values is simple enough, but the special characters (some of which are used in the example expression) might not be so clear:

- The asterisk (*) character is like a wildcard and means any value is allowed. It appears in the example expression to specify every month.

- The question mark (?) character is applicable only to the day-of-week and day-of-month fields and cannot be specified by both at the same time. It is used to allow no specific value in either field, equivalent to saying "any day of the week," for example. The example expression indicates there is no specific value for the day-of-month field.

- You can use commas (,) to specify a group of values. For example, the value SUN,THU,FRI in the day-of-week field translates to "on the days Sunday, Thursday, and Friday."

- A range of values can be specified using the hyphen (-) character between two values. For example, if you want the job to execute on workdays only, you could put MON-FRI in the day-of-week field.

- The forward slash (/) character allows increments to be specified in any of the fields. For example, if you have a frequently executed job, you may want to have a value of */15 in the seconds field, which means to execute the job on the seconds 0, 15, 30, and 45.

- The L character is an interesting one because it generally is shorthand for "last," and if placed in either the day-of-week or day-of-month field on its own, it means the last day of the week or month, respectively. However, this behavior changes if it is included after another character. The example specifies 1L in the day-of-week field, which means "the last Sunday of the month."

- Next, you have the W character that, when appended to the end of another character, means "the nearest weekday to the given day." For example, using 3W will result in the nearest weekday to the third of the month. If the third is a Sunday, this will be Monday; otherwise, if it's a Saturday, the job will execute on a Friday. In addition, W can be used in combination with L in the form LW to indicate the last weekday of the month.

- Finally, the # character is used between two numbers as in 5#2, which means "the second Thursday of the month." With this character, it is important to remember that if the second number is out of range, the job will never be executed.

So now that you have learned something about cron expressions, let's see how you go about specifying them in a Grails job, as shown in Listing 12-38.

Listing 12-38. *The Simple Job Is No Longer So Simple*

```
class NewsLetterJob {
    def cronExpression = "0 0 6 * * ?"
    ...
}
```

Here you have removed the timeout property and provided a cronExpression property that tells the job to execute at 6 a.m. in the morning every day. Again, the remaining configuration is handled for you at runtime. There is plenty more information on Quartz and cron expressions on the Quartz web site that is worth familiarizing yourself with. Table 12-2 presents some examples taken from the Quartz Javadoc of various possible cron expressions and their meanings.

Table 12-2. *Example Cron Expressions*

Expression	Meaning
0 0 12 * * ?	Fire at 12 p.m. (noon) every day.
0 15 10 ? * *	Fire at 10:15 a.m. every day.
0 15 10 * * ?	Fire at 10:15 a.m. every day.
0 15 10 * * ? *	Fire at 10:15 a.m. every day.
0 15 10 * * ? 2005	Fire at 10:15 a.m. every day during the year 2005.
0 * 14 * * ?	Fire every minute starting at 2 p.m. and ending at 2:59 p.m. every day.
0 0/5 14 * * ?	Fire every 5 minutes starting at 2 p.m. and ending at 2:55 p.m. every day.
0 0/5 14,18 * * ?	Fire every 5 minutes starting at 2 p.m. and ending at 2:55 p.m., *and* fire every 5 minutes starting at 6 p.m. and ending at 6:55 p.m. every day.
0 0-5 14 * * ?	Fire every minute starting at 2 p.m. and ending at 2:05 p.m. every day.
0 10,44 14 ? 3 WED	Fire at 2:10 p.m. and at 2:44 p.m. every Wednesday in the month of March.
0 15 10 ? * MON-FRI	Fire at 10:15 a.m. every Monday, Tuesday, Wednesday, Thursday, and Friday.
0 15 10 15 * ?	Fire at 10:15 a.m. on the 15th day of every month.
0 15 10 L * ?	Fire at 10:15 a.m. on the last day of every month.
0 15 10 ? * 6L	Fire at 10:15 a.m. on the last Friday of every month.
0 15 10 ? * 6L 2002-2005	Fire at 10:15 a.m. on every last Friday of every month during the years 2002, 2003, 2004, and 2005.
0 15 10 ? * 6#3	Fire at 10:15 a.m. on the third Friday of every month.

If you recall, we mentioned you could give a job a name or place it in a group. This comes in handy when interacting with the scheduler. More specifically, the scheduler has methods to retrieve existing jobs by name and group.

Interacting with the Scheduler

Quartz and its scheduler control all jobs in Grails. The scheduler itself is an instance of `org.quartz.Scheduler`, a rich interface for managing jobs that are currently executing and adding new jobs at runtime. The interface is a little too rich to list here, but you can browse through the methods via the Quartz web site: `http://www.opensymphony.com/quartz/api/org/quartz/Scheduler.html`.

First, though, you need to understand how to obtain a reference to the scheduler. The Spring container once again manages this for you, so obtaining a reference is a simple matter of defining the appropriate property in a controller or service class:

```
org.quartz.Scheduler quartzScheduler
```

The property will then be set for you automatically, after which you can start interacting with the scheduler. To start off with, let's take a look at how to obtain existing jobs from the scheduler. The scheduler provides a number of useful methods to achieve this, including those in Listing 12-39.

Listing 12-39. *Methods for Getting Jobs from the Scheduler*

```
class Scheduler {
    ...
    String[] getJobNames();
    String[] getJobGroupNames();
    JobDetail getJobDetail(String jobName, String jobGroupName);
    ...
}
```

The `getJobDetail(jobName,jobGroupName)` method will retrieve the `org.quartz.JobDetail` instance for a specified name and group. The `JobDetail` describes the job to be executed including information about the class that executes it. Remember that the name and group relate to the name and group properties defined when you create a job. For example, retrieving the `NewsLetterJob` could be done with the following:

```
def jobDetail = quartzScheduler.getJobDetail("newsletter","subscriptions")
```

Scheduling Jobs

Every `JobDetail` in Quartz when registered with the scheduler is associated with a trigger. A trigger is an instance of the `org.quartz.Trigger` interface and is responsible for activating the job. For example, once you obtain a reference to a `JobDetail`, you can register new triggers that fire at certain times, as in Listing 12-40.

Listing 12-40. *Registering New Triggers*

```
def trigger = TriggerUtils.makeDailyTrigger(11, 45)
  trigger.startTime = new Date()
  trigger.name = "myTrigger"
  quartzScheduler.scheduleJob(jobDetail, trigger)
```

The example in Listing 12-40 introduces another useful class, `org.quartz.TriggerUtils`, that contains various methods for constructing `Trigger` instances, one of which is shown in the example. Here you make a new `Trigger` that will execute the job daily at 11:45 a.m. The `Trigger` is then registered with the scheduler using the `JobDetail` instance. Of course, registering a new job is not all that is possible, and in the next few sections you'll see what else can be accomplished with the scheduler.

Pausing and Resuming Jobs

As well as allowing new jobs to be registered, the scheduler also gives you control over existing jobs, including pausing jobs that are currently scheduled. To pause all jobs currently scheduled, you could use the `pauseAll` method:

```
quartzScheduler.pauseAll()
```

Unsurprisingly, there is also a corresponding `resumeAll` method that will resume all scheduled jobs:

```
quartzScheduler.resumeAll()
```

Sometimes, however, it is useful to pause only a single job or group of jobs. This can be achieved with the `pauseJob` and `pauseJobGroup` methods:

```
quartzScheduler.pauseJob("newsletter","subscriptions")
quartzScheduler.pauseJobGroup("subscriptions")
```

The first statement will pause the `newsletter` within the `subscriptions` group, while the second will pause all jobs within the `subscriptions` group. Note that pausing a job or group of jobs will not stop currently executing jobs from running.

Triggering a Job

If for some reason you need to execute a job immediately and cannot wait for any predefined trigger, the scheduler provides methods to do just this. The aptly named `triggerJob` method should do the trick nicely:

```
quartzScheduler.triggerJob("newsletter","subscriptions")
```

Clearly, cron jobs put a lot of power at your fingertips, and it would be silly not to take advantage of at least some of this power for the gTunes application. In the next section, we'll cover how you can apply what you know so far about jobs to allow users of the gTunes application to receive an e-mail newsletter.

Adding and Removing Jobs

You've already seen one way of scheduling jobs with the `scheduleJob` method; the `addJob` method provides a way to add new jobs or replace existing ones. It takes two arguments: a `JobDetail` instance and a `Boolean` value that dictates whether it should replace an existing job of the same name and group.

To understand it, you need to explore how to create a JobDetail instance in the first place. At its simplest, the JobDetail class accepts three arguments: the name of the job, the group of the job, and a class that implements the org.quartz.Job interface.

The org.quartz.Job interface has a single method called execute. Therefore, to add a job, you first have to define a class that implements this interface and then register it with the scheduler using a JobDetail bean. However, a much easier alternative is to use Groovy's ability to coerce closures into an instance that implements a single method interface at runtime:

```
def job = {
    // implement the job here
} as org.quartz.Job
```

Notice the use of the as keyword to coerce the closure into an instance of the org.quartz.Job interface. Once you have a job, you can then construct a JobDetail instance, and using the addJob method, you can add it to the scheduler:

```
def jobDetail = new JobDetail("newsletter", "subscriptions", job)
quartzSchedular.addJob(jobDetails,true)
```

Note that just because you have added a job to the quartzScheduler does not mean it will execute. You have to schedule the job for execution as shown in the "Scheduling Jobs" section. To remove this job later, you can use the deleteJob method:

```
quartzScheduler.deleteJob("newsletter", "subscriptions")
```

Jobs in Action

To begin with, to avoid gTunes becoming a spamming machine, you're going to add an option to the registration page so that users can opt into the weekly newsletter. However, before you can do this, you're going to need to create a domain class that models a subscription. You can achieve this using the create-domain-class command:

```
$ grails create-domain-class com.g2one.gtunes.Subscription
```

Since there might be different subscription types, the Subscription domain class needs to have a property that defines what type of subscription you're dealing with. A nice way to achieve this if you're running on a Java 1.5 VM is to use a type-safe enum. Listing 12-41 shows the code for the new Subscription class.

Listing 12-41. *Modeling a Subscription*

```
package com.g2one.gtunes

class Subscription {
    SubscriptionType type
    User user
```

```
    static mapping = {
        user fetch:"join"
    }
}
enum SubscriptionType {
    NEWSLETTER
}
```

As you can see from Listing 12-41, you can use the SubscriptionType enum type to specify the type of Subscription a user is a member of. At the moment, there is only a single SubscriptionType, the NEWSLETTER type, but later you'll be adding other types of subscriptions to the gTunes application. Once this is done, you can update the grails-app/views/user/register.gsp view to ask the user whether they want to opt in to receiving the newsletter. Listing 12-42 shows the code added to the register.gsp view.

Listing 12-42. *Adding a Check Box to the register.gsp View*

```
<g:form action="register" name="registerForm">
    ...
    <div class="formField">
        Please tick the following box if you wish to subscribe to
        the weekly gTunes newsletter:
        <g:checkBox name="newsletter"></g:checkBox>
    </div>
    ...
</g:form>
```

Using the <g:checkBox> tag, you can add a new HTML check box component that will let users choose whether they want to receive the newsletter. Finally, to complete the picture, you can update the register action of the UserController class to create a new Subscription instance when a User registers. Listing 12-43 shows the changes to the register action.

Listing 12-43. *Updating the register Action*

```
def register = {
    ...
    else if(u.save()) {
        session.user = u
        if(params.newsletter) {
            new Subscription(type:SubscriptionType.NEWSLETTER, user:u).save()
        }
        ...
    }
    ...
}
```

It's time to return to the NewsLetterJob. First, since the job needs to run on the last Thursday of every month, you can use a cron expression to specify an appropriate schedule:

```
// fire at 7:15am on the last Thursday of every month
def cronExpression = "0 15 7 ? * 5L"
```

The cronExpression is pretty simple, but remember the L after the 5 for the day of the week! This signifies that it should be the *last* Thursday of every month instead of every Thursday. With the cronExpression in place, the next thing to consider is how the NewsLetterJob is going to deliver mails. Luckily, you learned about the Mail plugin in the previous section on integrating e-mail. The Mail plugin provides a service that can be injected into the job using dependency injection. Simply add the following property to the NewsLetterJob class definition:

```
def mailService
```

Now it's time to put the Subscription class to action within the execute method of the NewsLetterJob. First you need to look up all the subscribed e-mail addresses. You can do this with a single criteria query, as shown in Listing 12-44.

Listing 12-44. *Obtaining Subscribed E-mails*

```
def emails = Subscription.withCriteria {
    projections {
        user {
            property 'email'
        }
    }
    eq('type', SubscriptionType.NEWSLETTER)
}
```

Listing 12-44 is using GORM's withCriteria method to obtain a list of e-mail addresses that the mail needs to be sent out to. By using the projections method within the withCriteria method to specify that you want the email property of all the user properties within the Subscription class, you can load only the data you need. With a bunch of e-mail addresses in hand, the next thing to do is grab a list of the newest 10 albums from the last week. This can be achieved with a simple dynamic finder, as shown in Listing 12-45.

Listing 12-45. *Obtains the Newest 10 Albums from the Last Week*

```
def now = new Date()
def albumList =
        Album.findAllByDateCreatedBetween(now-7,
                                           now,
                                           [sort:'dateCreated',
                                           max:10,
                                           order:'desc'] )
```

Groovy overrides the minus operator on `java.util.Date` so that when you subtract a number from a date, Groovy will go back in time the equivalent number of days. The result is that the expression now-7 gives you a date from a week ago. The expression `findAllByDateCreatedBetween` will let you find all the `Album` instances for a given date range. With that done, it's now a simple matter of sending an e-mail to each user. Listing 12-46 shows the code that uses the `mailService` instance to fire off an e-mail to each e-mail address.

Listing 12-46. *Sending E-mails with the mailService*

```
def month = new GregorianCalendar().get(Calendar.MONTH)
for(email in emails) {
    mailService.sendMail {
        from "info@gtunes.com"
        to email
        title "The gTunes Monthly News Letter - $month"
        body view:"/emails/newsletter",
            model:[latestAlbums:albumList,
                   month:month]
    }
}
```

As you can see from the example in Listing 12-46, you can use regular Java APIs to get the current month and then simply get the `mailService` to deliver the mails. Once again, the code uses the `view` arguments of the body method to specify a view to render for the mail at the location grails-app/views/emails/newsletter.gsp. Listing 12-47 shows the full code listing for the NewsLetterJob.

Listing 12-47. *The NewsLetterJob Code*

```
package com.g2one.gtunes

class NewsLetterJob {
    // fire at 7:15am on the last Thursday of every month
    def cronExpression = "0 15 7 ? * 5L"

    def mailService
    def execute() {
        def emails = Subscription.withCriteria {
            projections {
                user {
                    property 'email'
                }
            }
            eq('type', SubscriptionType.NEWSLETTER)
        }
```

```
        def now = new Date()
        def albumList =
            Album.findAllByDateCreatedBetween(now-7,
                                              now,
                                              [sort:'dateCreated',
                                              max:10,
                                              order:'desc'])
    if(albumList) {
        def month = new GregorianCalendar().get(Calendar.MONTH)
        for(email in emails) {
            mailService.sendMail {
                from "info@gtunes.com"
                to email
                title "The gTunes Monthly News Letter - $month"
                body view:"/emails/newsletter",
                    model:[latestAlbums:albumList,
                           month:month]
            }
        }
    }
  }
}
```

To wrap things up, you can add a view that renders the newsletter. Listing 12-48 shows an example newsletter.gsp view that uses HTML mail to deliver the e-mail.

Listing 12-48. *The newsletter.gsp View*

```
<html>
    <head>
    </head>
    <body id="newsletter">
        <h1>The gTunes Month Newsletter for ${month}</h1>
        <p>Welcome to the gTunes monthly newsletter!
            Below are the latest releases
            available at <g:createLink controller="store"
                                       absolute="true" />
        </p>
        <h2>Latest Album Releases</h2>
        <g:each var="album" in="${latestAlbums}">
            <div class="albumArt">
                <b>Title</b>: <g:link controller="album"
                                      action="show"
                                      id="${album.id}">${album.title}</g:link>
                    <br>
```

```
            <b>Artist</b>: ${album.artist.name} <br>
            <div class="albumArt">
                <music:albumArt album="${album.title}"
                            artist="${album.artist.name}">
            </div>
        </div>
      </g:each>
    </body>
</html>
```

Well, that is it for jobs—for the time being, at least. Another thing to remember is that although Grails gives you the convenience of defining jobs by convention, the full power of Quartz and all its features are there for you to take advantage of. All in all, this makes for a pretty powerful and easy-to-use combination! Before you get too excited, however, let's take a look at a less glamorous task when integrating Grails: deployment.

Deployment

Moving your application from a development environment onto a production or test server often presents you with a number of choices. The options when deploying Grails are many and varied, and they run the gamut from simple to complex. In the following sections, you'll be looking at different ways of deploying Grails and how to customize the deployment process.

Deploying with Grails

If you're looking for a simple way to manage deployment and aren't too concerned about fine-tuning the details of your container, then deploying with Grails itself is certainly a simple way to go about it. To deploy with Grails, all you need to do is install Grails on the target server and then use the run-war command from the root of the project:

```
$ grails run-war
```

This will start a Jetty server on port 8080. On this point, you can configure the ubiquitous Apache HTTPD server (http://httpd.apache.org/) to use mod_proxy to relay requests to the Jetty server. The details of this are covered on the Jetty web site at http://docs.codehaus.org/display/JETTY/Configuring+mod_proxy. Alternatively, you could even run Jetty on port 80 so that it acts as the primary web server:

```
$ grails -Dserver.port=80 run-war
```

However, as simple as this approach is, many organizations favor a more structured approach to deployment using that standard Java stalwart, the WAR file.

Deploying to a Container

You learned about creating a WAR file as early as Chapter 2. When thinking about deployment in the Java world, the first thing that usually comes to mind is how to create a WAR. It is one of the strengths of the Java platform that you can take a WAR file and deploy it onto such a wide range of containers.

From the commercial 800-pound gorillas like IBM WebSphere and BEA WebLogic to the popular open source containers like Tomcat and JBoss, there are options aplenty. Against the background of all this helpful standardization, it is unfortunate that the way in which you deploy a WAR file is still not standardized.

On something like Tomcat, it's typically just a matter of dropping your WAR file into the `TOMCAT_HOME/webapps` directory, while on WebSphere there is a fancy GUI wizard that allows you to upload a WAR file via a browser. Nevertheless, there are some important things to consider when deploying to a container. The following is a list of key points to remember when deploying with Grails:

- Make sure that the `-server` flag is passed to the JVM that runs your container to enable the server VM. Running Grails on the client VM has a negative impact on performance.

- Depending on the number of GSP views you have, you may need to allocate more *permgen* space (the area of memory the JVM uses for dynamically compiled classes). GSP views are compiled at runtime on first load into byte code, so they require permgen space. You can allocate more permgen with the `-XX:MaxPermSize=256m` flag.

- It is advisable to allocate extra memory to the JVM when running a Grails application. Simple Grails applications have been known to perform well on shared virtual hosting with low memory, but the more you can allocate, the better. For example, to allocate 512MB of heap space, you can use the `-Xmx512M` flag.

Application Versioning and Metadata

You may have already noticed by now that when you run the `grails war` command, the generated WAR file has a version number on the end of the file name. You may be wondering where this mysterious version number comes from. Basically, when you create a Grails application, the version number of the application is set to 0.1 in the application's metadata.

You can change the version number by calling the `set-version` command, as shown in Listing 12-49.

Listing 12-49. *Setting the Application Version Number*

```
grails set-version 0.2
```

Then when you build a new WAR, the version number from Listing 12-49 will be used instead. At runtime you can inspect the application metadata using the `grailsApplication` object:

```
println grailsApplication.metadata."app.version"
```

or using the `<g:meta>` tag from a GSP, as shown in Listing 12-50.

Listing 12-50. *Using Application Metadata*

```
Version <g:meta name="app.version"/>
Built with Grails <g:meta name="app.grails.version"/>
```

Customizing the WAR

If you want to customize the way in which the WAR file is produced, you can consider taking advantage of a number of hooks. For example, say you wanted to provide a different base web.xml template in order to include your own custom servlets; you can do so with the grails.config. base.webXml setting in grails-app/conf/Config.groovy:

```
grails.config.base.webXml="file:${userHome}/.settings/my-web.xml"
```

Also, if you need to change the location where the WAR file is generated, you can do so using the grails.war.destFile property:

```
grails.war.destFile = "${tomcatHome}/webapps"
```

In terms of modifying the contents of the WAR, by default Grails will take everything from the web-app directory and include it in the WAR. If you prefer this not to happen, you can override this process with your own custom step using the grails.war.copyToWebApp setting:

```
grails.war.copyToWebApp = {
    fileset(dir:"/usr/var/mywar")
}
```

Alternatively, if you simply want to include additional resources in the WAR, you can do so with the grails.war.resources setting, as shown in Listing 12-51.

Listing 12-51. *Using the grails.war.resources Setting to Include Custom Resources*

```
grails.war.resources = { stagingDir ->
    // include static resources
    copy(dir:stagingDir) {
        fileset(dir:"/usr/var/www/htdocs")
    }
}
```

Notice how the closure assigned to grails.war.resources gets passed an argument that is the location of the directory where the WAR is being built. You can then use custom copy steps to include whatever extra resources you need. Once you actually have a WAR, you may want to perform some initial population of the database state when the application loads. We'll be covering how to do this in the next section.

Populating the Database with BootStrap Classes

Whenever an application loads for the first time, there may be some initial state that needs to be in place for the application to operate in a correct manner. One way to do this is with BootStrap classes. If you look at the grails-app/conf directory, you may have noticed a class called BootStrap.groovy. Listing 12-52 shows the template for this class.

Listing 12-52. *A BootStrap Class*

```
class BootStrap {

    def init = { servletContext ->
    }
    def destroy = {
    }
}
```

As you can see, there is an init method that is called when the container first loads and a destroy method. The destroy method is called on container shutdown, although it should be noted that it is not guaranteed to be invoked and hence shouldn't be relied upon for anything critical.

Within the Bootstrap class, you can use GORM to populate the database. Thanks to GORM's usage of fluent APIs,[1] it is pretty easy to create an object graph, as shown in Listing 12-53.

Listing 12-53. *Populating Data on Application Load*

```
def init = {
    def album = new Album(title:"Because of the Times")
                    .addToSongs(title:"Knocked Up")
                    .addToSongs(title:"Charmer")

    ...
    new Artist(name:"Kings of Leon")
                .addToAlbums(album)
                .save(flush:true)
}
```

If you need to populate per-environment data, then you can use the GrailsUtil class to obtain the environment and perform a switch. Listing 12-54 shows an example of this.

Listing 12-54. *Per-Environment Bootstrapping*

```
def init = {
    switch(grails.util.GrailsUtil.environment) {
        case "development":
            // initialize in development here
```

---

1. A fluent API is often referred to as *method chaining* because it involves writing methods that return objects in a manner so multiple methods can be chained in a sequence. See http://www.martinfowler.com/bliki/FluentInterface.html for a more complete definition.

```
        break
        case "production":
         // initialize in production here
        break
    }
}
```

Summary

Integrating Grails is a broad topic, as you have seen by the number of topics covered in this chapter. These range from integration with command-line tools to your development environment to the servers you finally deploy onto. Many options are available to you—so many in fact that an entire book on the subject wouldn't be inappropriate. The good news is that many of the deployment options and techniques that you use in the Java space are equally applicable to Grails.

Whether it be Java EE–compliant containers like Tomcat or your favorite build tool, there is typically a way to get Groovy and Grails to work seamlessly in your environment. In the next chapter, you'll learn about a whole new subject that is critical to the workings of Grails—the plugin system. Throughout the book you've been a user of many of Grails' more prominent plugins. In this chapter alone, you explored using the Mail and Quartz plugins.

Now it's time for you to turn into a plugin creator and learn how you can modularize your application through the use of plugins.

CHAPTER 13

■ ■ ■

Plugins

Up until now, you have been a consumer of the Grails plugin system at various points throughout the book. In Chapter 8, you used the Searchable plugin to add full-text search to your Grails application and explored how to use the Yahoo UI plugin as an alternative Ajax provider. And in the previous chapter, you had the chance to use both the Mail and Quartz plugins. Now it's time to turn the tables and become a plugin author. Plugins are, quite simply, the cornerstone of Grails. Grails itself is basically a plugin runtime with little knowledge beyond how to load and configure an installed set of plugins.

The Grails plugin system is very flexible—so much so that it would be quite reasonable to write an entire book on the subject. In this chapter, we aim to summarize the core concepts and demonstrate some common use cases for the plugin system. However, the full extent of what is achievable with the plugin system is left to your imagination.

Even if you don't plan to write a plugin to distribute to the world, we recommend you take the time to read this chapter. Grails plugins are not just a way to enhance the functionality of an existing Grails application; they are also an effective way to modularize your code. Later in this chapter, we will demonstrate how you can use plugins to split your Grails application into separate maintainable plugins that are composed together at runtime.

Plugin Basics

The core of Grails is a plugin runtime environment. However, to make it immediately useful, it ships with a default set of plugins that you have already been learning about, including GORM and Grails' MVC framework. Along with the default set of plugins, Grails ships with a set of commands to automatically discover and install new plugins. Let's take a look at these first.

Plugin Discovery

The Grails plugin community is a hive of activity and one of the most exciting areas of Grails. As of this writing, more than 80 plugins are available from the central repository. Providing a range of functionality from job scheduling to search to reporting engines, all the plugins are discoverable through the `grails list-plugins` command. To run the `list-plugins` command, simply type `grails list-plugins` in a command window, as shown in Listing 13-1.

Listing 13-1. *Running the list-plugins Command*

```
$ grails list-plugins
```

What this will do is go off to the Grails central repository and download the latest published plugin list. The list is then formatted and printed to the console. You can see some typical output from the list-plugins command in Listing 13-2, shortened for brevity.

Listing 13-2. *Output from the list-plugins Command*

```
Plug-in list out-of-date, retrieving..
     [get] Getting: http://plugins.grails.org/.plugin-meta/plugins-list.xml
....................................................................

Plug-ins available in the Grails repository are listed below:
-------------------------------------------------------------

acegi            <0.3>           -- Grails Spring Security 2.0 Plugin
aop              <no releases>   -- No description available
audit-logging    <0.4>           -- adds hibernate audit logging and onChange
                                    event handlers to GORM domain classes
authentication   <1.0>           -- Simple, extensible authentication services
                                    with signup support
...
```

In the left column, you can see the name of the plugin, while in the middle is the latest released version of the plugin. Finally, on the right of the output, you can see the short description for any given plugin. If you want to obtain more information about a particular plugin, you can use the plugin-info command. Listing 13-3 shows how to obtain more information about the audit-logging plugin from Listing 13-2 using the plugin-info command.

Listing 13-3. *Using the plugin-info Command to Get Detailed Plugin Information*

```
$ grails plugin-info audit-logging
...
--------------------------------------------------------------------------
Information about Grails plugin
--------------------------------------------------------------------------
Name: audit-logging    | Latest release: 0.4
--------------------------------------------------------------------------
adds hibernate audit logging and onChange event handlers to GORM domain classes
--------------------------------------------------------------------------
Author: Shawn Hartsock
--------------------------------------------------------------------------
Find more info here: http://www.grails.org/Grails+Audit+Logging+Plugin
--------------------------------------------------------------------------
```

The Audit Logging plugin adds an instance hook to domain
objects that allows you to hang Audit events off of them.
The events include onSave, onUpdate, onChange, onDelete and
when called the event handlers have access to oldObj and newObj definitions that
will allow you to take action on what has changed.

```
--------------------------------------------------------------------------
Available full releases:  0.3 0.4 0.4-SNAPSHOT
```

As you can see with the `plugin-info` command, you get more information about the plugin including a long description, a link to the documentation (in this case http://www.grails.org/ Grails+Audit+Logging+Plugin), who the author is, and all the past release version numbers.

Plugin Installation

This brings us nicely to the topic of plugin installation. To install the `audit-logging` plugin, you can use the `install-plugin` command as follows:

```
$ grails install-plugin audit-logging
```

However, if you require a specific version of the plugin, you can use one of the version numbers displayed in the `Available full releases:` field of Listing 13-3. Listing 13-4 demonstrates how to install version 0.3 of the `audit-logging` plugin.

Listing 13-4. *Installing a Specific Version of a Plugin with the install-plugin Command*

```
$ grails install-plugin audit-logging 0.3
```

After you install a Grails plugin, you can find out what plugins you already have installed by running the `list-plugins` command discussed in the previous section. You'll notice that, after the list of plugins available in the repository, the `list-plugins` command shows the plugins you currently have installed, as shown in Listing 13-5.

Listing 13-5. *Finding Out Which Plugins You Have Installed with list-plugins*

```
Plugins you currently have installed are listed below:
--------------------------------------------------------------

audit-logging       0.4                 -- adds hibernate audit logging and onChange
                                            event handlers to GORM domain classes
```

If you have multiple Grails applications in development that share a common set of plugins, it may well be useful to install a plugin globally for all applications. To do this, you can pass the -global flag to the `install-plugin` command. For example, Listing 13-6 shows how to install the `code-coverage` plugin, which provides test coverage reports powered by Cobertura, for all applications.

Listing 13-6. *Installing a Plugin Globally Using the -global Flag*

```
$ grails install-plugin -global code-coverage
```

If you no longer need a particular plugin, then you can use the counterpart to the `install-plugin` command, which is called, unsurprisingly, `uninstall-plugin`. The `uninstall-plugin` command works exactly like the `install-plugin` command; it simply takes the name of the plugin to uninstall, as shown in Listing 13-7.

Listing 13-7. *Uninstalling Plugins with the uninstall-plugin Command*

```
$ grails uninstall-plugin audit-logging
```

Local Plugins

Of course, the plugins you create may not necessarily live in the central Grails repository. Grails plugins are packaged as simple zip files, and if you downloaded a plugin from elsewhere, you can install it by simply running the `install-plugin` command and passing in the location on disk of the plugin. Listing 13-8 shows how to install a plugin located in your home directory on a Unix system.

Listing 13-8. *Installing a Local Plugin*

```
$ grails install-plugin ~/grails-audit-logging-0.3.zip
```

To ease distribution within your team, instead of keeping your plugins locally on disk, you may decide to host your plugins on a local web server. In that case, the `install-plugin` command also supports plugin installation over HTTP. Listing 13-9 shows how to install the `audit-logging` plugin over HTTP, bypassing Grails' plugin autodiscovery mechanism.

Listing 13-9. *Installing Plugins Over HTTP*

```
$ grails install-plugin http://plugins.grails.org/grails-audit-logging/tags/➥
LATEST_RELEASE/grails-audit-logging-0.4.zip
```

Now that you've learned the basics of plugin discovery and installation, let's move onto how you actually go about creating a plugin. We'll be demonstrating the basics of plugin creation and distribution. After that, we'll show you how to create some useful plugins to enhance and modularize the gTunes sample application.

Creating Plugins

Creating plugins in Grails is as simple as creating regular applications. All you need to do is run the `grails create-plugin` command and specify a name for your plugin. In fact, what you will soon discover is that a Grails plugin *is* a Grails application. To understand this, create a simple Grails plugin called `simple-cache` that can provide caching services to a Grails application. You do this using the `create-plugin` command, as shown in Listing 13-10.

Listing 13-10. *Creating a Plugin with the create-plugin Command*

```
$ grails create-plugin simple-cache
```

The result is what looks like a regular Grails application. You have all the typical resources that make up an application, including a `grails-app` directory. However, on closer inspection, you'll notice there is a file called `SimpleCacheGrailsPlugin.groovy` in the root of the project. This file contains a class that represents the *plugin descriptor*. Figure 13-1 shows the plugin descriptor residing snugly in the root of the project.

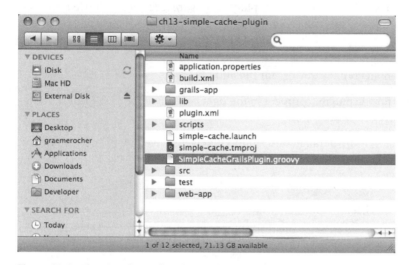

Figure 13-1. *The simple-cache plugin descriptor*

Providing Plugin Metadata

The plugin descriptor serves a number of purposes. The first and primary purpose is for the plugin author to provide metadata about the plugin such as the author name, version number, description, and so on. Listing 13-11 shows the `SimpleCacheGrailsPlugin` class and the placeholder fields used to supply this information.

Listing 13-11. *The SimpleCacheGrailsPlugin Plugin Descriptor*

```
class SimpleCacheGrailsPlugin {
    def version = 0.1
    def dependsOn = [:]
```

```
    // TODO Fill in these fields
    def author = "Your name"
    def authorEmail = ""
    def title = "Plugin summary/headline"
    def description = 'Brief description of the plugin.'
    ...
}
```

Properties such as author, title and so on, appear in the list-plugins and plugin-info commands when a plugin is published to a Grails plugin repository. The following list summarizes the available properties and what they represent:

- author: The name of the plugin author

- authorEmail: An e-mail contact address for the author

- title: A short title for the plugin to appear in the right column of the list-plugins command (see Listing 13-2)

- description: A longer, more detailed description that is displayed by the plugin-info command

- documentation: A link to the location of the documentation for the plugin

All the properties in this list are optional; however, providing this information will help others understand the purpose of your plugin. Listing 13-12 shows the simple-cache plugin's metadata information.

Listing 13-12. *The simple-cache Plugin Descriptor with Metadata Provided*

```
class SimpleCacheGrailsPlugin {
    def version = 0.1
    def dependsOn = [:]

    def author = "Graeme Rocher"
    def authorEmail = "graeme@g2one.com"
    def title = "A simple caching plugin"
    def description = 'A plugin that provides simple caching services'
    ...
}
```

You may have noticed the dependsOn property, which is currently assigned an empty Map literal. This property allows you to specify which plugin or plugins this plugin depends on. As an example, say your plugin depends on the presence of GORM in a Grails application; you can specify this by using the plugin name and version number:

```
def dependsOn = [hibernate:"1.1"]
```

As well as specifying a simple version number, the dependsOn version syntax also allows version ranges, including wildcards. As an example, the following two dependsOn expressions are equally valid:

```
def dependsOn = [hibernate:"1.0 > 1.1"]
def dependsOn = [hibernate:"* > 1.1"]
```

The first example specifies that the plugin depends on any version of the hibernate plugin between versions 1.0 and 1.1, while the second expression says that the plugin supports any version of the hibernate plugin up to version 1.1, inclusive.

Once the dependsOn property is specified, when a user installs a plugin via the install-plugin command, Grails will automatically attempt to install any dependent plugins if they aren't already installed. This technique is often referred to as *transitive dependencies resolution*, and it is implemented by many build systems (such as Ivy, which is discussed in Chapter 12) for JAR dependencies.

Supplying Application Artefacts

One of the more obvious ways a plugin can enhance an existing application is by providing a new artefact, such as a controller, tag library, or service.

■Note Throughout the source code and documentation of Grails, the word *artefact* is used to refer to a Groovy file that fulfills a certain concept (such as a controller, tag library, or domain class). It is spelled using the British English spelling of *artefact* as opposed to *artifact*, so we will be using that spelling throughout the book to maintain consistency with the APIs.

Because a Grails plugin is simply a Grails application, supplying an artefact is a simple matter of creating it just as you would in a regular application. For the simple-cache plugin, you're going to implement a service that provides application layer caching. To do so, simply use the create-service command from the root of the plugin:

```
$ grails create-service com.g2one.cache.Cache
```

Once completed, you'll end up with a new service at the location grails-app/services/com/g2one/cache/CacheService.groovy. Because it's pretty simple to do, you'll also be implementing a little tag library to perform content-level caching. To create the tag library, run the create-tag-lib command:

```
$ grails create-tag-lib com.g2one.cache.Cache
```

Note that since a Grails plugin is simply a Grails application, you can run it just like a Grails application! Just use the grails run-app command, and you're on your way. This has significant benefits for the plugin developer in that plugin development is not very different from regular application development. You can run your plugin like a regular application, and you can also test your plugin like a regular application using the `test-app` command. You can even install other plugins into a plugin, something that is critical when developing a plugin that has dependencies on other plugins.

As for the `CacheService` and the `CacheTagLib`, we'll get to the implementation details of these later. For the moment, all you need to know is that, when you package up your plugin for distribution, it will provide two new artefacts: a tag library and a service.

Plugin Hooks

Let's return to the plugin descriptor. As well as providing metadata about the plugin, the descriptor also enables you to supply hooks into the plugin runtime. Each hook is defined as a closure property and allows the plugin to participate in the various phases of the plugin life cycle. The hooks are listed here in the order of their execution:

- `doWithWebDescriptor`: This gets passed the XML for the `web.xml` file that has been parsed by Groovy's `XmlSlurper` into a `GPathResult`. See the "Modifying the Generated WAR Descriptor" section later in the chapter for more information on this one.

- `doWithSpring`: This allows participation in the runtime configuration of Grails' underlying Spring `ApplicationContext`. See the "Providing Spring Beans" section for more information.

- `doWithDynamicMethods`: Executed after the construction of the `ApplicationContext`, this is the hook that plugins should use to provide new behavior to Grails classes. See the "Using Metaprogramming to Enhance Behavior" section later in the chapter for more information.

- `doWithApplicationContext`: This is executed after Grails' `ApplicationContext` has been constructed. The `ApplicationContext` instance is passed to this hook as the first argument.

By default, the `simple-cache` plugin you created earlier comes with empty implementations of all of these. If you don't plan to implement any of these hooks, you can simply delete them from the plugin descriptor. Listing 13-13 shows the various plugin hooks, just waiting to be implemented.

■**Note** If you merely want to use plugins to provide application modularity, then you may want to skip to the "Packaging and Distributing a Grails Plugin" section because the following sections go into significant detail on how to hook into all aspects of the Grails plugin system.

Listing 13-13. *Plugin Hooks in the simple-cache Plugin*

```
class SimpleCacheGrailsPlugin {
    def version = 0.1
    ...
    def doWithWebDescriptor = { xml -> }
```

```
    def doWithSpring = {}

    def doWithDynamicMethods = { applicationContext -> }

    def doWithApplicationContext = { applicationContext -> }

}
```

Plugin Variables

A number of implicit variables are available within the context of these hooks that allow you to inspect the conventions within a running Grails application. The following are the available variables and associated descriptions:

- `application`: An instance of the `org.codehaus.groovy.grails.commons.GrailsApplication` class that provides information about the loaded classes and the conventions within them

- `manager`: An instance of the `org.codehaus.groovy.grails.plugins.GrailsPluginManager` class that allows you to find out what other Grails plugins are installed

- `plugin`: A reference to the `org.codehaus.groovy.grails.plugins.GrailsPlugin` class, which allows you to find out various information about the plugin including its name, version, and dependencies

The `GrailsApplication` class is typically the most critical to understand if you plan to implement any hooks that work with the Grails conventions. Essentially, it defines a number of dynamic properties that map to each concept in a Grails application. For example, to obtain a list of the controller classes in a `GrailsApplication`, you can do this:

```
def controllerClasses = application.controllerClasses
```

Note that when we refer to *classes*, we're not talking about instances of the `java.lang.Class` interface but of the `org.codehaus.groovy.grails.commons.GrailsClass` interface that defines a number of methods to inspect the conventions within a `GrailsApplication` for a particular artefact type.

For example, given the `CacheService` you created earlier, Listing 13-14 demonstrates some of the methods of the `GrailsClass` interface and how they behave.

Listing 13-14. *Using the Grails Convention APIs*

```
GrailsClass serviceClass =
                application.getServiceClass("com.g2one.cache.CacheService")

assert "CacheService" == serviceClass.shortName
assert "Cache" == serviceClass.name
assert "com.g2one.cache.CacheService" == serviceClass.fullName
assert "cacheService" == serviceClass.propertyName
assert "cache" == serviceClass.logicalPropertyName
assert "com.g2one.cache" == serviceClass.packageName
assert true == serviceClass.getPropertyValue("transactional")
```

You'll notice from Listing 13-14 the usage of the `getServiceClass` method to obtain the `CacheService` by name. The `getServiceClass` method is another dynamic method available on the `GrailsApplication` class. Essentially, for each artefact type, the `GrailsApplication` class provides dynamic methods to access the artefacts of that type, which are summarized here:

- `get*Classes`: Obtain a list of all the `GrailsClass` instances for a particular artefact type, such as with `getControllerClasses()` or via property access such as `controllerClasses`.

- `get*Class(String name)`: Obtain a specific `GrailsClass` instance by name, as in `getControllerClass("HelloController")`.

- `is*Class(Class theClass)`: Inquire if a given `java.lang.Class` is a particular artefact type, as in `isControllerClass(myClass)`.

The asterisk in the previous method names can be substituted for the relevant artefact type you are interested in. Table 13-1 summarizes the different artefact types, as well as shows an example of the typical usage for each.

Table 13-1. *Summary of Existing Artefact Types*

Artefact Type	Example
Bootstrap	`def bootstrapClasses = application.getBootstrapClasses()`
Codec	`def codecClasses = application.getCodecClasses()`
Controller	`def controllerClasses = application.getControllerClasses()`
Domain	`def domainClasses = application.getDomainClasses()`
Filters	`def filterClasses = application.getFiltersClasses()`
Service	`def serviceClasses = application.getServiceClasses()`
TagLib	`def tagLibClasses = application.getTagLibClasses()`
UrlMappings	`def urlMappingClasses = application.getUrlMappingsClasses()`

All of the artefact types in Table 13-1 cover existing artefacts, but Grails also allows you to add your own artefact types, which we'll look at in the next section.

Custom Artefact Types

Out of the box, Grails ships with a set of features, including controllers, domain classes, and so on. As you saw in the previous section, you can access all aspects of these via the `GrailsApplication` interface. However, what if you want to add a new artefact type? Take, for example, the existing Quartz plugin. As you discovered in Chapter 12, Quartz is a job-scheduling API that runs specified tasks on a scheduled basis. For example, you may want to run some code at 12 p.m. on the last Friday of every month. Quartz aims to solve these kinds of problems.

Now if you look at the existing artefact types, none of them models the idea of a job. So, how can you extend Grails and provide new knowledge to it about what a job is? Fortunately, you can find the answer in Grails' org.codehaus.groovy.grails.commons.ArtefactHandler interface. Listing 13-15 shows the key methods of the ArtefactHandler interface.

Listing 13-15. *The ArtefactHandler Interface*

```
public interface ArtefactHandler {
    String getType();
    boolean isArtefact(Class aClass);
    GrailsClass newArtefactClass(Class artefactClass);
}
```

The getType() method returns the type of the GrailsClass, which will be one of the values shown in the first column of Table 13-1. The isArtefact(Class) method is responsible for identifying whether a given class is of the current artefact type based on some convention. For example, does the class end with the convention *Controller*? If so, then it's a controller class.

The newArtefactClass(Class) method will create a new GrailsClass instance for the given java.lang.Class. The ArtefactHandler interface has other methods, but most of them are abstracted away from you because when implementing a custom ArtefactHandler, you'll typically extend the org.codehaus.groovy.grails.commons.ArtefactHandlerAdapter class. For example, take a look at Listing 13-16, which shows a possible implementation for the Quartz plugin.

Listing 13-16. *An ArtefactHandler for the Quartz Plugin*

```
1 class JobArtefactHandler extends ArtefactHandlerAdapter {
2
3     static final TYPE = "Job"
4
5     JobArtefactHandler() {
6         super(TYPE, GrailsClass, DefaultGrailsClass, TYPE)
7     }
8
9     boolean isArtefactClass(Class clazz) {
10        // class shouldn't be null and shoudd ends with Job suffix
11        if(!super.isArtefactClass(clazz)) return false
12        // and should have an execute method
13        return clazz.methods.find { it.name == 'execute' } != null
14    }
15 }
```

There are a few key things to look at in the JobArtefactHandler in Listing 13-16. First take a look at the constructor on lines 5 to 7:

```
5     JobArtefactHandler() {
6         super(TYPE, GrailsClass, DefaultGrailsClass, TYPE)
7     }
```

The constructor calls the super implementation, passing four arguments:

- *The artefact type*: In this case, you're using a constant called TYPE that has the value Job.

- *The interface to use for the artefact type*: You could extend the GrailsClass interface to provide a more specific interface such as GrailsJobClass.

- *The implementation of the interface for the artefact type*: Grails provides a default implementation in the DefaultGrailsClass, but you could subclass this if you want to provide custom logic within the artefact type.

- *The suffix that the class name should end with for a* java.lang.Class *to be considered of the artefact type*: The default implementation of the isArtefactClass method in ArtefactHandlerAdapter will perform a check on the passed java.lang.Class to ensure that the class name ends with the specified suffix. As you can see on line 11 of Listing 13-16, the logic from the superclass isArtefact method is being reused.

The next thing to note about the code in Listing 13-16 is the implementation of the isArtefactClass(Class) method, which checks that the class ends with the appropriate suffix by calling the superclass implementation of isArtefactClass(Class) and whether the class possesses an execute method. You can assert your expectations of the behavior of the JobArtefactHandler by writing a simple unit test, as shown in Listing 13-17.

Listing 13-17. *Testing an ArtefactHandler*

```
class JobArtefactHandlerTests extends GroovyTestCase {
    void testIsArtefact() {
        def handler = new JobArtefactHandler()
        assertTrue handler.isArtefactClass(TestJob)
        assertFalse handler.isArtefactClass(JobArtefactHandlerTests)

        GrailsClass jobClass = handler.newArtefactClass(TestJob)
        assertEquals "TestJob", jobClass.shortName
        assertEquals "Test", jobClass.name
        assertEquals "TestJob", jobClass.fullName
        assertEquals "testJob",jobClass.propertyName
        assertEquals "test",jobClass.logicalPropertyName
        assertEquals "", jobClass.packageName
    }
}
class TestJob {
    def execute() {}
}
```

At this point, there is one thing left to do. You have to tell your plugin about the ArtefactHandler. Say you were creating the Quartz plugin and you have a QuartzGrailsPlugin descriptor. If you add an artefacts property that contains a list of provided artefacts, the plugin will make Grails aware of the JobArtefactHandler:

```
def artefacts = [new JobArtefactHandler()]
```

So once the Quartz plugin is installed, if there is a class within the `grails-app/jobs` directory that looks like the one in Listing 13-18, the `JobArtefactHandler` will approve the class as being a "job."

Listing 13-18. *An Example Job*

```
class SimpleJob {
    def execute() {
        // code to be executed
    }
}
```

An added bonus of going through these steps is that suddenly the `GrailsApplication` object has become aware of the new artefact type you just added. With this hypothetical Quartz plugin installed, you can use all the dynamic methods on the `GrailsApplication` object first shown in Listing 13-14. Listing 13-19 demonstrates a few examples using the `SimpleJob` from Listing 13-18.

Listing 13-19. *Using the GrailsApplication Object to Inspect Jobs*

```
def jobClasses = application.getJobClasses()
GrailsClass simpleJobClass = application.getJobClass("SimpleJob")

assert application.isJobClass(SimpleJob)
```

The key thing to learn from this section is that Grails provides you with an *extensible* convention-based API. You are in no way restricted by the existing conventions and can easily start adding your own ideas to the mix. In the next section, we'll be looking at how the idea of Convention over Configuration (CoC) extends to the runtime configuration of Spring.

Providing Spring Beans

The `doWithSpring` hook allows you to specify new Spring beans to configure at runtime using Grails' `BeanBuilder` domain-specific language (DSL) for Spring. The intricacies of `BeanBuilder` will be described in far more detail in Chapter 16; however, we'll cover some of the basics here. Essentially, Grails is built completely on the Spring Framework. Grails has what is known as an `ApplicationContext`, which is essentially a container provided by Spring that holds one or more beans. By default, each bean is a singleton, meaning there is only one of them in the `ApplicationContext`.

As you learned in Chapter 11, Grails allows services to be autowired into controllers and tag libraries. This autowire feature is powered by the Spring container and is often referred to as *dependency injection*. It is an extremely powerful pattern that allows you to effectively separate out dependencies and the construction of those dependencies. That's the theory...now let's take a look at an example.

Earlier, you created a new service in the `simple-cache` plugin called `CacheService`. The `CacheService` is going to work in conjunction with a cache provider to provide application-layer caching to any user of the `simple-cache` plugin. Since it is a little pointless to reinvent the wheel and implement your own homegrown caching implementation, you're going to take advantage of the Ehcache library.

You may remember from Chapter 8 that you defined a bean in the `grails-app/conf/spring/resources.groovy` file for the gTunes application that used the `EhCacheFactoryBean` class provided by Spring. You're going to use that again here, within the context of `doWithSpring`. Listing 13-20 shows how to define a `globalCache` bean.

Listing 13-20. *Defining Beans in doWithSpring*

```
class SimpleCacheGrailsPlugin {
    ...
    def doWithSpring = {
        globalCache(org.springframework.cache.ehcache.EhCacheFactoryBean) {
            timeToLive = 300
        }
    }
}
```

As a reminder, the name of the bean is the name of the method, which in this case is `globalCache`. The bean class is the first argument, while the closure passed as the last argument allows you to set property values on the bean. In this case, a `globalCache` bean is configured to expire entries every 5 minutes (300 seconds). We've really only touched the surface of what is possible with `BeanBuilder` here and in Chapter 8, so if you're keen to know more, you could skip forward to Chapter 16, which contains detailed coverage.

With that done, let's begin implementing the `CacheService`. First you need to get a reference to the `globalCache` bean defined by the plugin. To do this, simply add a property that matches the name of the bean to the `CacheService`, as shown in Listing 13-21.

Listing 13-21. *Obtaining Beans Supplied by doWithSpring*

```
import net.sf.ehcache.Ehcache
class CacheService {
    static transactional = false

    Ehcache globalCache
    ...
}
```

The `globalCache` property is in bold in Listing 13-15. Note that transactions have been disabled for the service by setting `static transactional = false`, since transactions won't be a requirement for this service.

Now let's implement the caching logic. When implementing caching, the pattern is typically that you look up an object from the cache, and if it doesn't exist, you execute some logic that obtains the data to be cached. Listing 13-22 shows some pseudocode for this pattern.

Listing 13-22. *The Caching Pattern*

```
def obj = cache.get("myentry")
if(!obj) {
    obj = ... // do some complex task to obtain obj
    cache.put("myentry", obj)
}
return obj
```

However, given that you have the power of closures at your disposal, it makes more sense to take advantage of them to come up with a more elegant solution. Listing 13-23 shows how to implement caching of entire logical blocks using closures.

Listing 13-23. *Caching the Return Value of Blocks of Code Using Closures*

```
1 import net.sf.ehcache.Ehcache
2 import net.sf.ehcache.Element
3
4 class CacheService {
5    ...
6    def cacheOrReturn(Serializable cacheKey, Closure callable) {
7        def entry = globalCache?.get(cacheKey)?.getValue()
8        if(!entry) {
9            entry = callable.call()
10           globalCache.put new Element(cacheKey, entry)
11       }
12       return entry
13   }
14 }
```

To understand what the code is doing in Listing 13-23, let's step through it line by line. First, on line 7 an entry is obtained from the globalCache bean, which is an instance of the net.sf.ehcache.Ehcache class:

```
7 def entry = globalCache?.get(cacheKey)?.getValue()
```

Notice how you can use Groovy's safe-dereference operator ?. to make sure that a NullPointerException is never thrown when accessing the value, even if the globalCache property is null! The get method of the globalCache instance returns a net.sf.ehcache. Element instance, which has a getValue() method you can call to obtain the cached value. Next on lines 8 and 9 the code checks that the returned value is null, and if it is, the passed closure is invoked, which returns the result that needs to be cached:

```
8        if(!entry) {
9            def entry = callable.call()
```

The return value of the call to the closure is used to place a new cache entry into the cache on line 10:

```
10 globalCache.put new Element(cacheKey, entry)
```

Finally, on line 12 the cache entry is returned regardless of whether it is the cached version:

```
12 return entry
```

With that done, let's see how to implement the CacheTagLib that can take advantage of the CacheService in Listing 13-24.

Listing 13-24. *Adding Content-Level Caching*

```
class CacheTagLib {
    static namespace = "cache"

    CacheService cacheService
    def text = { attrs, body ->
        def cacheKey = attrs.key
        out << cacheService.cacheOrReturn(cacheKey) {
            body()
        }
    }
}
```

Once again, Listing 13-24 shows how to use dependency injection to get hold of a reference to the CacheService in the CacheTagLib. The cacheOrReturn method is then used to cache the body of the tag using the key attribute passed into the text tag. Notice how the CacheTagLib has been placed inside a namespace, a concept you first learned about in Chapter 5.

Users of the simple-cache plugin can now take advantage of content-level caching simply by surrounding the body of markup code they want to cache with the <cache:text> tag that the CacheTagLib provides. Listing 13-25 shows an example of its usage.

Listing 13-25. *Using the Tag Provided by the simple-cache Plugin*

```
<cache:text key="myKey">
  This is an expensive body of text!
</cache:text>
```

Dynamic Spring Beans Using Conventions

In the previous section, you implemented the simple-cache plugin using an Ehcache bean registered in the Spring ApplicationContext. What this example didn't demonstrate, though, is the ability to dynamically create beans on the fly using the conventions in the project.

In the "Custom Artefact Types" section, you explored how to create a plugin that identified Quartz jobs. In a typical Spring application, you would need to use XML to configure each individual job using the org.springframework.scheduling.quartz.JobDetailBean class. With a Grails plugin that knows about conventions, you can do it dynamically at runtime! Listing 13-26 shows this in action in a QuartzGrailsPlugin plugin descriptor.

Listing 13-26. *Dynamically Creating Beans at Runtime*

```
1 import org.springframework.scheduling.quartz.*
2
3 class QuartzGrailsPlugin {
4    ...
5    def doWithSpring ={
6        application.jobClasses.each { GrailsClass job ->
7            "${job.propertyName}"(JobDetailBean) {
8                name = job.name
9                jobClass = job.getClazz()
10           }
11       }
12    ...
13    }
14 }
```

To better understand the code in Listing 13-26, let's step through it. First, on line 6 the each method is used to iterate over all the artefacts of type Job:

```
6 application.jobClasses.each { GrailsClass job ->
```

Then on line 7, a new bean is dynamically created using Groovy's ability to invoke methods using a String (or a GString) as the method name:

```
7 "${job.propertyName}"(JobDetailBean) {
```

In this case, given the SimpleJob from Listing 13-18, you would end up with a bean called simpleJob in the Spring ApplicationContext that is an instance of the Quartz JobDetail class. The JobDetailBean class is a Spring-provided helper class for creating Quartz JobDetail instances as Spring beans. Finally, on lines 8 and 9, the name of the job and the class of the job are set using properties of the GrailsClass interface:

```
8                name = job.name
9                jobClass = job.getClazz()
```

To finish up the Quartz plugin, you could set up beans within doWithSpring for the Scheduler, using Spring's SchedulerFactoryBean, the triggers, and so on. However, since this serves mainly as a demonstration of what is possible, we recommend you take a look at the excellent existing Quartz plugin for Grails, which is installable with the following command:

```
$ grails install-plugin quartz
```

Using Metaprogramming to Enhance Behavior

In the previous section, you saw how plugins can participate in the configuration of the Spring ApplicationContext. Now let's look at another area that plugins typically contribute to: the application behavior. Groovy is a fully dynamic language that allows you to completely modify the behavior of a class at runtime through its metaprogramming APIs.

■**Tip** If you're looking for a book with significant coverage of the metaprogramming capabilities offered by Groovy, take a look at *Programming Groovy* by Venkat Subramaniam (Pragmatic Programmers, 2008).

Like other dynamic languages such as Smalltalk, Ruby, and Lisp, Groovy features a Meta Object Protocol (MOP). The key thing to remember is that it is the MOP that decides the behavior of Groovy code at runtime, so code that looks as though it may do one thing at compile time could be made to do something completely different. For each java.lang.Class that Groovy knows about, there is an associated MetaClass. The MetaClass is what dictates how a particular method, constructor, or property behaves at runtime.

Groovy's MetaClass allows you to add methods, properties, constructors, and static methods to any class. For example, consider the code in Listing 13-27.

Listing 13-27. *Adding New Methods to a Class*

```
class Dog {}
Dog.metaClass.bark = { "woof!" }
assert "woof!" == new Dog().bark()
```

Here you have a simple class called Dog. Instances of the Dog class cannot, as it stands, bark. However, by using the metaClass, you can create a bark method with this expression:

```
Dog.metaClass.bark = { "woof!" }
```

Clearly, this example has only brushed the surface of what is possible. If you refer to Appendix A, you'll find more detailed coverage of the metaprogramming APIs.

Let's look at an example within the context of a Grails plugin by trying to add the cacheOrReturn method to all controllers to eliminate the need to inject the service via Spring first. Listing 13-28 demonstrates how, by simply delegating to the CacheService, you can add a cacheOrReturn method to all controllers too.

■**Tip** If you prefer not to create a plugin but would still like to do metaprogramming in your Grails application, we recommend you do so within a Bootstrap class, a topic covered in Chapter 12.

Listing 13-28. *Adding Methods to All Controllers*

```
class SimpleCacheGrailsPlugin {
    ...
    def doWithDynamicMethods = { applicationContext ->
        def cacheService = applicationContext.getBean("cacheService")
        application
                .controllerClasses
            *.metaClass
            *.cacheOrReturn = { Serializable cacheKey, Closure callable ->
```

```
        cacheService.cacheOrReturn(cacheKey, callable)
    }
  }
}
```

Another important aspect to notice about the code in Listing 13-28 is the use of Groovy's spread dot operator *. to obtain all the metaClass instances from all the controllerClasses and also the use of a spread assignment to create a cacheOrReturn method for each MetaClass. That's far easier than adding a for or each loop!

Plugin Events and Application Reloading

As well as the plugin hooks discussed in the "Plugin Hooks" section, plugins can also participate in a number of events, including application reload events. Grails aims to minimize the number of application restarts required during development time. However, since reloading is typically different for each artefact type, the responsibility to reload is delegated to plugins.

A plugin can essentially listen for three core events: onChange, onConfigChange, and onShutdown. Let's take a look at onChange first because it is the most common event dealt with by plugins. Each individual plugin can monitor a set of resources. These are defined by a property called watchedResources. For example, as part of Grails core, there is a plugin that provides support for internationalization (covered in Chapter 7) through the use of message bundles that are found in the grails-app/i18n directory. The i18n plugin defines its watchedResources property as follows:

```
def watchedResources = "file:./grails-app/i18n/*.properties"
```

What this says is that the i18n plugin will monitor all files within the grails-app/i18n directory ending with the file extension .properties.

Tip If you're wondering about the file-matching patterns the watchedResources property uses, take a look at Spring's org.springframework.core.io.support.PathMatchingResourcePatternResolver class as well as the Spring Core IO package in general, which Grails uses under the covers.

Whenever one of the properties files in the grails-app/i18n directory changes, Grails will automatically trigger the onChange event of the plugin or plugins, monitoring the file passing in a change event object. The event object is essentially just a map containing the following entries:

- source: The source of the event, which is either a Spring org.springframework.core. io.Resource instance representing the file on disk or the recompiled and changed java.lang.Class instance if the watchResources property refers to Groovy classes

- application: A reference to the GrailsApplication instance

- manager: A reference to the GrailsPluginManager instance

- ctx: A reference to the Spring ApplicationContext instance

Typically the most important entry in the event map is the `source`, which contains a reference to the source of the change. In the case of the i18n plugin, the `source` entry would reference a Spring `org.springframework.core.io.Resource` instance since the properties files monitored by the i18n plugin are not Groovy classes. However, if you develop a plugin where you choose to monitor Groovy classes instead, Grails will automatically recompile the changed class and place the altered class within the `source` entry in the event map.

As an example, consider the Quartz plugin discussed in previous sections. The `watchedResources` definition for the Quartz plugin would look something like this:

```
def watchedResources = "file:./grails-app/jobs/**/*Job.groovy"
```

Whenever one of the Groovy files changes, Grails will recompile the class and pass you a reference to the `java.lang.Class` instance representing the job. However, that is all Grails will do. It is then up to you to make whatever changes you deem necessary to the running application to ensure it is now in the correct state. For example, in the "Dynamic Spring Beans Using Conventions" section, we showed you how to dynamically register new `JobDetail` beans for each job class. To implement reloading correctly for the Quartz plugin, you would need to ensure that those beans are replaced with the new class. Listing 13-29 shows a hypothetical implementation that takes the newly recompiled class and registers new beans with the `ApplicationContext`.

Listing 13-29. *Implementing onChange for the Quartz Plugin*

```
1 class QuartzGrailsPlugin {
2     def watchedResources = "file:./grails-app/jobs/**/*Job.groovy"
3     ...
4
5     def onChange = { event ->
6         Class changedJob = event.source
7         GrailsClass newJobClass = application.addArtefact(changedJob)
8         def newBeans = beans {
9             "${newJobClass.propertyName}"(JobDetailBean) {
10                name = newJobClass.name
11                jobClass = newJobClass.getClazz()
12            }
13        }
14        newBeans.registerBeans(applicationContext)
15    }
16 }
```

Although the code is pretty short, there are quite a few new concepts to understand, so let's walk through those starting on line 6 where a reference to the event's source is obtained:

```
6 Class changedJob = event.source
```

With the source in hand, the next thing the onChange event does is register the new Class with the GrailsApplication instance by calling the addArtefact method:

```
7 GrailsClass newJobClass = application.addArtefact(changedJob)
```

The code on line 8 is pretty interesting, because here the implicit beans method is used, which takes a block of code that uses the BeanBuilder syntax we discussed in the "Providing Spring Beans" section. The beans method returns a BeanBuilder instance containing the bean definitions (but not the instantiated beans themselves):

```
8 def newBeans = beans {
```

The code on lines 8 to 13 are essentially the same as you saw in Listing 13-26; all the code is doing is creating a new JobDetailBean bean definition from the new class. Line 14 is far more interesting because it shows how you can use the registerBeans method of the BeanBuilder class to register all the bean definitions defined within the BeanBuilder instance with the provided ApplicationContext:

```
14 newBeans.registerBeans(applicationContext)
```

Of course, not all plugins will need to register new beans based on an onChange event. This is a requirement only if you registered beans in the doWithSpring closure that require reloading behavior. It may be possible to work with the existing beans to implement effective reloading for a plugin. For example, the i18n plugin we discussed earlier simply clears the MessageSource cache, forcing it to be rebuilt:

```
def messageSource = applicationContext.getBean("messageSource")
if (messageSource instanceof ReloadableResourceBundleMessageSource) {
    messageSource.clearCache()
}
```

Other than the onChange event, the two other events available are onConfigChange and onShutdown. The onConfigChange event is fired if Grails' global configuration file found at grails-app/conf/Config.groovy is changed by the user. In the case of the onConfigChange event handler, the source of the change event is the altered ConfigObject. Often, plugins rely on settings found within Config.groovy for configuration. Remember, Grails uses Convention *over* Configuration, which means that conventions are used to ease development, but configuration is still possible if required. Later in this chapter we'll show an example that uses the Grails ConfigObject, which is obtainable using the getConfig() method of the GrailsApplication class.

Finally, the onShutdown event is fired when the shutdown() method of the GrailsPluginManager is called. This happens, for example, when a Grails application is undeployed from a container and the Grails servlet's destroy() method is invoked.

Modifying the Generated WAR Descriptor

As discussed in Chapter 12, the web.xml file Grails uses to integrate with servlet containers is generated programmatically. You saw in Chapter 12 that it is possible to modify the template used to generate web.xml by using the install-templates command. However, it is also possible for plugins to modify web.xml programmatically using the doWithWebDescriptor hook.

Essentially, when the web.xml file is generated, it gets parsed into memory by Groovy's XmlSlurper parser. This parser creates an in-memory representation of the XML that you can modify. The doWithWebDescriptor hook is passed a reference to the XML as the first argument to the doWithWebDescriptor closure. XmlSlurper allows you to use a builder-like syntax to make modifications to the XML.

As an example, one of the core Grails plugins is the URL mappings plugin, which provides the functionality covered in Chapter 6. The way the plugin works is to provide a Servlet filter that rewrites requests onto the main Grails servlet. To add this Servlet filter into the mix, the doWithWebDescriptor implementation of the URL mappings plugin looks something like the code in Listing 13-30.

Listing 13-30. *Example doWithWebDescriptor That Adds a New Servlet Filter*

```
1 def doWithWebDescriptor = { webXml ->
2    def filters = webXml.filter
3    def lastFilter = filters[filters.size()-1]
4    lastFilter + {
5        filter {
6            'filter-name'('urlMapping')
7            'filter-class'(UrlMappingsFilter.getName())
8        }
9    }
10   ...
11 }
```

To understand what the code in Listing 13-30 is doing, let's take a look at it line by line. First, on line 2, a GPath expression is used to get a list of all the existing <filter> elements contained within the web.xml file:

```
2 def filters = webXml.filter
```

Then, on line 3, a reference to the last <filter> element in the list is obtained:

```
3 def lastFilter = filters[filters.size()-1]
```

As you can see from the previous two examples, using Groovy's XML APIs is nothing like using a Java XML parser. The XML object parsed by XmlSlurper almost feels like a first-class object, with very little evidence that the underlying data structure is in fact XML. Finally, on lines 4 through 9, the overridden + operator is used to add a new `<filter>` element directly after the last `<filter>` element:

```
4    lastFilter + {
5        filter {
6            'filter-name'('urlMapping')
7            'filter-class'(UrlMappingsFilter.getName())
8        }
9    }
```

Notice how in Groovy you can use strings for method names; for instance, you can choose an idiomatic XML element name like `<filter-name>` as the name of a method. The previous code will append the following equivalent XML snippet to the `web.xml` document:

```
<filter>
    <filter-name>urlMapping</filter-name>
    <filter-class>org.codehaus.groovy.grails.web.mapping.filter. ➡
        UrlMappingsFilter</filter-class>
</filter>
```

As you can see, Grails makes it pretty easy to participate in the generation of the `web.xml` file. Although not a common thing to do in a plugin, it is sometimes useful when you want to integrate legacy servlets, filters, and so on. As mentioned previously, you could have used the `grails install-templates` command and modified the `web.xml` template directly, but this technique allows you to create plugins that automatically do this configuration for you. Reducing configuration, as well as embracing simplicity, is very much the Grails way, and `doWithWebDescriptor` is just another example of that.

Packaging and Distributing a Grails Plugin

Once you are confident that your plugin is ready for distribution, you can package it using the `grails package-plugin` command. In the command window, simply type `grails package-plugin` from the root of your plugin project, as shown in Listing 13-31.

Listing 13-31. *Packaging a Plugin*

```
$ grails package-plugin
...
[zip] Building zip: /Developer/grails/simple-cache/grails-simple-cache-0.1.zip
```

As you can see from the output in Listing 13-31, the `package-plugin` command generates a zip file using the name and version number of your plugin. In this case, you're packaging up the `simple-cache` plugin you developed earlier. Figure 13-2 shows an example of the resulting zip file.

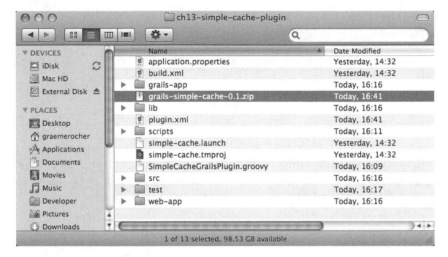

Figure 13-2. *The simple-cache plugin's packaged zip file*

Using the steps explained earlier in this chapter in the "Plugin Installation" section, you can now install the `simple-cache` plugin into other applications and make use of the tag library and services it provides.

If you want to distribute your plugin within the Grails central repository, you first need to obtain a plugin developer account for the Grails central Subversion (SVN) repository. You can find the steps to do so on the Grails web site at `http://grails.org/Creating+Plugins`.

Once you have obtained an account, releasing your plugin is as simple as typing the following command:

```
$ grails release-plugin
```

The `release-plugin` command will prompt you for the SVN username and password that you obtained when you set up a developer account. Grails does all the heavy lifting for you in making sure that the appropriate resources have been published in the repository and been tagged appropriately. The `release-plugin` command will also generate an updated plugin list so that your plugin appears whenever a Grails user types the `list-plugins` command.

Local Plugin Repositories

If you want to take advantage of Grails' plugin distribution and discovery mechanism on your own local network, then you can set up a local plugin repository. Grails' plugin repositories are currently backed by the SVN version control system, so all you need to do is set up an SVN repository on your local network, which you can do using the `svnadmin` command provided by SVN:

```
$ svnadmin create /path/to/repo
```

Once your SVN repository is created, you can configure additional repositories inside the `grails-app/conf/BuildConfig.groovy` file for each application or globally by creating a file in your USER_HOME directory at the location `USER_HOME/.grails/settings.groovy`. Either way, you can then provide additional named URLs of SVN repositories used for discovery and distribution. Listing 13-32 presents an example of configuring an additional plugin repository.

Listing 13-32. *Configuring Additional Plugin Repositories*

```
grails.plugin.repos.discovery.myRepository="http://foo.bar.com"
grails.plugin.repos.distrubtion.myRepository="https://foo.bar.com"
```

Notice in Listing 13-28 how Grails groups repositories under `discovery` and `distribution`. The URLs under `discovery` are used by the `list-plugins`, `install-plugin`, and `plug-info` commands discussed in the section on "Plugin Installation" to produce the plugin list that is presented to the user. The URLs under `distribution` are used by the `release-plugin` command, as discussed in the previous section.

By default, the `release-plugin` command will always try to publish to the Grails central repository. To tell the `release-plugin` command to publish to one of the repositories configured as in Listing 13-32, you need to add the name of the repository as an argument to the `release-plugin` command. For example:

```
$ grails release-plugin -repository=myRepository
```

And with that, we've reached the end of this tour of the plugin system. As you can imagine, you can take advantage of the plugin system in many different ways. In this section, we've touched on some ideas for plugins such as the `simple-cache` plugin and the Quartz plugin, but we think the plugin system is such a critical part of the Grails ecosystem that the lessons learned in this chapter should be put to further use. In the next section, you'll be applying what you've learned so far to create two new plugins for the gTunes application. Along the way, you'll discover how Grails' plugins can be used as both a way to extend the functionality of an existing application and as a way to effectively modularize your codebase.

Plugins in Action

So, you've learned what plugins are and the basics of creating plugins. It is now time to put that knowledge to work by developing a couple of plugins for the gTunes application. The first one you're going to create is a plugin that makes the album art service and tag library you developed in Chapter 8 into a reusable plugin. This is a perfect example of developing a plugin to add functionality and enhance behavior.

Plugins to Add Behavior

To start with, run the `create-plugin` command to create the basis of an `album-art` plugin:

```
$ grails create-plugin album-art
```

The next step is to move the `AlbumArtService.groovy` file and the `AlbumArtTagLib.groovy` file into the newly created plugin project. Once this is done, your plugin should be structured like Figure 13-3.

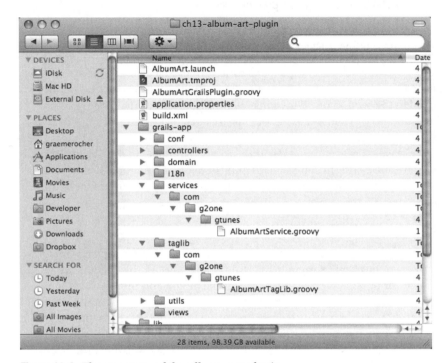

Figure 13-3. *The structure of the album-art plugin*

Of course, the `AlbumArtService` relies heavily on the Amazon web services library, so you should move those from the application into the plugin too. Figure 13-4 shows the `lib` directory with the necessary JAR files in place.

Also, don't forget to move the two tests that provide coverage for the `AlbumArtService` and `AlbumArtTagLib` from the application into the plugin. As mentioned previously, the great thing about plugins is that they can be developed and tested separately, which makes them useful for larger projects with multiple developers. With the `AlbumArtServiceTests` and `AlbumArtTagLibTests` test cases included in the `album-art` plugin, you can now immediately test whether your plugin is working by running the `test-app` command:

```
$ grails test-app
```

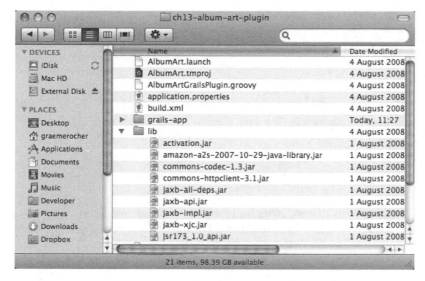

Figure 13-4. *The album-art plugin's dependencies*

With the tests passing, you can add the plugin metadata to the plugin descriptor that describes what this plugin is all about. Listing 13-33 shows the updated plugin descriptor with the metadata provided.

Listing 13-33. *Providing Metadata to the album-art Plugin*

```
class AlbumArtGrailsPlugin {

    def version = 0.1

    def author = "Graeme Rocher"
    def authorEmail = "graeme@g2one.com"
    def title = "Album art look-up plugin"
    def description = 'A plug-in that provides facilities to look-up album art'
    ...
}
```

One thing to consider is that when you developed the AlbumArtService in Chapter 8, it was designed to work in conjunction with an albumArtCache that used Ehcache provided by the application's grails-app/conf/spring/resources.groovy file. One solution to this would be to update the doWithSpring of the AlbumArtGrailsPlugin descriptor, as shown in Listing 13-34.

Listing 13-34. *Providing the albumArtCache with doWithSpring*

```
class AlbumArtGrailsPlugin {

    def version = 0.1
    ...
    def doWithSpring = {
        albumArtCache(org.springframework.cache.ehcache.EhCacheFactoryBean) {
            timeToLive = 300
        }
    }
}
```

However, since you previously developed a `simple-cache` plugin earlier in the chapter, it makes a lot more sense to take advantage of it. To do so, let's modify the `dependsOn` property on the `album-art` plugin descriptor, as shown in Listing 13-35.

Listing 13-35. *Using dependsOn to Depend on the simple-cache Plugin*

```
class AlbumArtGrailsPlugin {

    def dependsOn = [simpleCache:'0.1 > *']
    ...
}
```

■**Tip** When specifying dependencies, you need to use bean conventions instead of the hyphen-separated, lowercase name `simple-cache`. The reason for this Grails design decision is that a hyphen isn't valid in a variable name or map key in Groovy unless you put quotes around it.

To enable the ability to continue to test the `album-art` plugin in isolation, you can install the `simple-cache` plugin into the `album-art` plugin using the `install-plugin` command from the root of the `album-art` plugin directory:

```
$ grails install-plugin /path/to/simple-cache/grails-simple-cache-0.1.zip
```

When you package the `album-art` plugin, Grails will not include the `simple-cache` plugin within the `album-art` zip. It is your responsibility to ensure that when you install the `album-art` plugin into the target application, you install the `simple-cache` plugin first. If you don't, you will get an error because Grails will be unable to resolve the `album-art` plugins' dependency on the `simple-cache` plugin, unless the `simple-cache` plugin is available in one of the configured repositories.

Moving on, you now need to update the `album-art` plugin to use the `CacheService` provided by the `simple-cache` plugin. Listing 13-36 shows the changes made to the `AlbumArtService` highlighted in bold.

Listing 13-36. *Updating the AlbumArtService to Use the simple-cache Plugin*

```
class AlbumArtService {
    ...
    def cacheService

    String getAlbumArt(String artist, String album) {
        ...
                def key = new AlbumArtKey(album:album, artist:artist)
                return cacheService.cacheOrReturn(key) {
                    try {
                        def request = new ItemSearchRequest()
                        ...

                        def response = client.itemSearch(request)

                        // get the URL to the amazon image (if one was returned).
                        return response.items[0].item[0].largeImage.URL
                    }
                    catch(Exception e) {
                        log.error "Problem calling Amazon: ${e.message}", e
                        return DEFAULT_ALBUM_ART_IMAGE
                    }
                }
        ...
    }
}
```

The changes in Listing 13-36 will cause the tests for the `AlbumArtService` to fail with a `NullPointerException` because the `cacheService` is `null` within the context of the test. Instead of using a real implementation in the unit test, you can use duck typing to specify a mock implementation using Groovy's `Map` literal syntax, as shown in Listing 13-37.

Listing 13-37. *Mocking the cacheService*

```
albumArtService.cacheService = [cacheOrReturn:{key, callable-> callable() }]
```

Groovy allows maps, where the value of a given key is a closure, to act as if they are callable methods. In the example in Listing 13-37, by providing a `cacheOrReturn` key, you are able to mock the methods of the `CacheService`.

To spice things up even further, you're going to do a bit of metaprogramming, first by adding a `getAlbumArt` method to all controllers and second by allowing instances of the `Album` class from the gTunes application to retrieve their art simply by calling a `getArt()` method. The first case, in Listing 13-38, shows the necessary code, which just gets the `AlbumArtService` instance and adds a method to all controllers that delegates to the `AlbumArtService`.

Listing 13-38. *Adding a getAlbumArt Method to All Controllers*

```
class AlbumArtGrailsPlugin {
    ...
    def doWithDynamicMethods = { ctx ->
        def albumArtService = ctx.getBean("albumArtService")

        application.controllerClasses
                    *.metaClass
                    *.getAlbumArt = { String artist, String album ->
            return albumArtService.getAlbumArt(artist, album)
        }
    }
}
```

Adding a getArt() method to the Album class is a little trickier, because the plugin doesn't know anything about the Album class. So to implement this enhancement, you'll search the GrailsApplication instance for a domain class called Album and, if it exists, add the getArt() method to it. Listing 13-39 shows the modifications to the doWithDynamicMethods plugin hook.

Listing 13-39. *Adding a getAlbumArt Method to All Controllers*

```
class AlbumArtGrailsPlugin {
    ...
    def doWithDynamicMethods = { ctx ->
        ...
        def albumClass = application.domainClasses.find { it.shortName == 'Album' }
        if(albumClass) {
            albumClass.metaClass.getArt ={->
                    albumArtService.getAlbumArt(  delegate.artist?.name,
                                                  delegate.title)
            }
        }
    }
}
```

Notice how within the body of the new getArt method you can use the closure delegate to obtain the artist and title. The delegate property of a closure, when used in this context, is equivalent to referring to this in a regular method. With the code in Listing 13-39 in place, you can now obtain the URL to an Album instance's album art with the code shown in Listing 13-40.

Listing 13-40. *Using the getArt() Method to Obtain Album Art*

```
def album = Album.get(10)
println "The art for this album is at ${album.art}"
```

Note that, in Groovy, methods that follow bean conventions are accessible via the property access notation, so the expression album.art is equivalent to album.getArt(). And with that, you have completed the album-art plugin that can now be installed into any application that has a requirement to look up album art. The gTunes application is one such application. However, before you can install the `album-art` plugin, you need to install the `simple-cache` plugin that the `album-art` plugin is dependent on into the gTunes application:

```
$ grails install-plugin ../simple-cache/grails-simple-cache-0.1.zip
```

With that done, install the `album-art` plugin next:

```
$ grails install-plugin ../simple-cache/grails-album-art-0.1.zip
```

Now you can start up the gTunes application, and it will behave exactly as before, except it is utilizing the `album-art` plugin's functionality instead! One thing to note about the `album-art` plugin is that although it provides new functionality in the form of services, tag libraries, and new methods, it does not comprise an entire self-contained application. We'll be looking at how you can achieve this in the next section.

Plugins for Application Modularity

As well as making it possible to extend the available APIs within a Grails application, plugins can also provide entire modules of application functionality. Many newcomers dismiss plugins as purely for plugin developers who are willing to jump into the core Grails APIs, but in fact, plugins are an extremely effective way to modularize your application. In this section, we'll explain how you can create an entire application as a plugin that can be installed into the gTunes application.

To keep things simple, you'll tackle a very commonly demonstrated application in screencasts and presentations around Grails: the blog. Yes, as with any self-respecting modern Web 2.0 application, the gTunes application needs a blog where the proprietors of the gTunes store can make big announcements about new music, events, and so on. Luckily, a simple blog takes about five minutes to implement in Grails, so it shouldn't be too complicated.

The first step is to run the `create-plugin` command to create the blog plugin:

```
$ grails create-plugin blog
```

This will create the blog plugin and associated `BlogGrailsPlugin` descriptor. You can populate the descriptor with some plugin metadata; Listing 13-41 shows a sample blog plugin descriptor.

Listing 13-41. *Adding Metadata to the blog Plugin*

```
class BlogGrailsPlugin {
    def version = 0.1
    def author = "Graeme Rocher"
    def authorEmail = "graeme@g2one.com"
    def title = "A blogging plugin"
    def description = 'A plugin that provides a blog facility'
}
```

Now it's time to create a domain class that models a blog post:

```
$ grails create-domain-class com.g2one.blog.Post
```

After these two commands are complete, you should have a directory structure similar to that pictured in Figure 13-5.

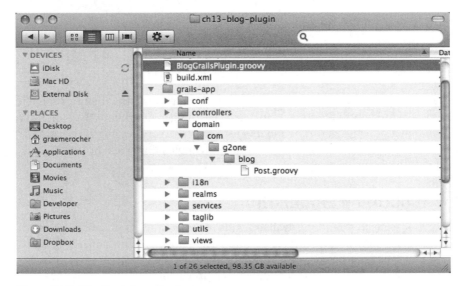

Figure 13-5. *The Post domain class*

Thinking about the Post domain class for a moment, it's going to have the obvious things like a title and a body, as well as a date posted. Putting this into practice, Listing 13-42 shows the Post domain class containing the necessary properties.

Listing 13-42. *The Post Domain Class*

```
package com.g2one.blog

class Post {
    String title
    String body
    Date dateCreated
    Date lastUpdated

    static constraints = {
        title blank:false
        body type:"text", blank:false
    }
}
```

Note that the Post domain class is using the property names dateCreated and lastUpdated to take advantage of Grails' auto time stamping capabilities that were first discussed in Chapter 10. With an appropriate domain class in place, to help you get started, you can use scaffolding to quickly generate a controller and views for the Post domain class:

```
$ grails generate-all com.g2one.blog.Post
```

For this first revision of the blog plugin, you're going to support the creation of new entries only; hence, you can remove the generated edit, update, and delete actions. In addition, you need to show only the first five posts; therefore, you can use the max parameter to the static list method of the Post class to specify that. Listing 13-43 shows the full code for the PostController.

Listing 13-43. *The PostController for the blog Plugin*

```
package com.g2one.blog

class PostController {
    def index = { redirect(action:list,params:params) }
    def allowedMethods = [save:'POST']

    def list = {
        [ postList: Post.list( max:5) ]
    }

    def create = {
        [post: new Post(params) ]
    }

    dcf save - {
        def post = new Post(params)
        if(!post.hasErrors() && post.save()) {
            flash.message = "Post ${post.id} created"
            redirect(action:list)
        }
        else {
            render(view:'create',model:[post:post])
        }
    }
}
```

Now let's move onto the views. In the case of the blog plugin, the list.gsp view is the most important because it will be responsible for showing each blog entry. However, Grails' default scaffolding displays the list view as a table, which is not very useful in this case. You can correct that by modifying the list.gsp view to render a _post.gsp template instead. Listing 13-44 shows the updated list.gsp code.

Listing 13-44. *The blog Plugin's list.gsp View*

```
<html>
    <head>
        <meta http-equiv="Content-Type" content="text/html; charset=UTF-8"/>
        <meta name="layout" content="${params.layout ?: 'main'}" />
        <title>Post List</title>
    </head>
    <body>

        <div class="nav">
            <span class="menuButton">
                <g:link class="create" action="create">New Post</g:link>
            </span>
        </div>
        <div class="blog">
            <h1>${grailsApplication.config.blog.title ?: 'No Title'}</h1>

            <g:render plugin="blog"
                        template="post"
                        var="post"
                        collection="${postList?.reverse()}" />
        </div>
    </body>
</html>
```

There are a few key things to mention about the list.gsp view in Listing 13-44. First, note that when using the <g:render> tag to render a template in a plugin view, you *must* specify the plugin that this template belongs to; otherwise, Grails will attempt to resolve the template within the application it is installed into. Second, take note of the usage of the grailsApplication variable to specify the blog title:

```
<h1>${grailsApplication.config.blog.title ?: 'No Title'}</h1>
```

Here the implicit grailsApplication object is used to read a configuration setting from the grails-app/conf/Config.groovy file. If the setting called blog.title is specified in Config.groovy, then the view will use that. Hence, users of this plugin are able to configure the blog to their needs. An alternative approach to doing this would be to use the <g:message> tag, in which case the plugin user has to specify the message in the grails-app/i18n/ messages.properties file. The choice is up to you.

Finally, take note of the HTML <meta> tag that dictates what layout the list.gsp uses:

```
<meta name="layout" content="${params.layout ?: 'main'}" />
```

What this does is if there is a layout parameter within the params object, it will use that for the layout; otherwise, use the main layout. The main layout will, of course, resolve to grails-app/views/layouts/main.gsp, but why the decision to allow customization via a parameter? The idea here is that the user of the plugin can very easily customize the layout of the blog through URL mappings. For example, consider the URL mapping in Listing 13-45.

Listing 13-45. *Using a URL Mapping to Customize the blog Plugin's Layout*

```
"/blog"(controller:"post", action:"list") {
    layout = "funky"
}
```

If you add the URL mapping in Listing 13-45 to your grails-app/conf/UrlMappings.groovy file, users can go to the /blog URL and have the list action of the PostController execute, which in turn renders the list.gsp view. However, notice how a property called layout is set inside the body of the closure passed to the URL mapping definition. As you learned in Chapter 6, it is possible to pass parameters in this way. The result is that for the /blog mapping, a layout called grails-app/views/layouts/funky.gsp will be used instead! This is a pretty powerful pattern because it allows you to apply a different layout simply by applying a new URL mapping to the same controller and action.

As for the _post.gsp template used in the <g:render> method of Listing 13-44, it is pretty simple and just formats each Post instance appropriately. You can see the code for the _post.gsp template in Listing 13-46.

Listing 13-46. *The _post.gsp Template*

```
<div id="post${post.id}" class="blogPost">
    <h2>${post.title}</h2>
    <div class="body">
        ${post.body}
    </div>

    <div class="desc">
        Posted on <g:formatDate date="${post.dateCreated}"
                                format="dd MMMMMM yy" />
    </div>

</div>
```

And with that, you have pretty much completed the list.gsp view. Figure 13-6 shows what the list.gsp view looks like when you run the blog plugin and head off to the list action of the PostController.

New Post

No Title

Figure 13-6. *The list view of the blog plugin*

Since the view renders each Post directly in the list.gsp view, the show.gsp view has been made redundant and can be deleted. Also, for the first revision, you're interesting in creating new posts only, so edit.gsp can be deleted too—you can always add editing later!

Moving on to the create.gsp view, it too could use a little cleaning up. Also, it would be nice to provide a rich text–editing capability for authoring the post. One of the plugins available for Grails is the fckeditor plugin, which adds support for FCKeditor (http://www.fckeditor. net/), a rich text–editing component. To install the fckeditor plugin into the blog plugin, run the following command:

```
$ grails install-plugin fckeditor
```

In addition to this, you need to update the BlogGrailsPlugin descriptor and add a dependsOn setting to ensure that when others install the blog plugin, FCKeditor is resolved too. Listing 13-47 shows the dependsOn set appropriately.

Listing 13-47. *Making the blog Plugin Depend on the fckeditor Plugin*

```
class BlogGrailsPlugin {
    def dependsOn = [fckeditor:'0.8 > *']
    ...
}
```

With that done, let's enable FCKeditor in create-gsp by using the <fck:editor> tag pro-vided by the fckeditor plugin. Listing 13-48 shows the updated create.gsp file with the usage of the <fck:editor> tag highlighted in bold. You will notice the logical name printed when you ran the blog plugin with grails run-app. Grails prints out a message such as this:

```
Loading with installed plug-ins: ["fckeditor", "blog"]
```

Listing 13-48. *Using the fckeditor to Enable Rich Text Editing*

```
<html>
    ...
    <body>
        <h1>Create Post</h1>
        <g:if test="${flash.message}">
        <div class="message">${flash.message}</div>
        </g:if>
        <g:hasErrors bean="${post}">
        <div class="errors">
            <g:renderErrors bean="${post}" as="list" />
        </div>
        </g:hasErrors>
        <g:form action="save" method="post" >
            <div class="dialog">
            <div id="titleField">
                    <label for="title">Title:</label>
                    <g:textField name="title"
                            value="${fieldValue(bean:post,field:'title')}"/>
            </div>
              <div id="bodyField">
                <fck:editor name="body"
                            width="500"
                            height="300"
                            toolbar="Basic">
                        ${fieldValue(bean:post,field:'body')}
                </fck:editor>
              </div>
            </div>
            <div class="buttons">
                <span class="button">
                    <input class="save" type="submit" value="Post" />
                </span>
            </div>
        </g:form>
    </body>
</html>
```

Using the `toolbar` attribute of the `<fck:editor>` tag, you can specify that you want only a simple toolbar with basic formatting options; otherwise, you'll get a toolbar with almost as many options as a word processor like Microsoft Word. Figure 13-7 shows the `create.gsp` view with the `<fck:editor>` tag doing the job of rendering a rich text–editing component.

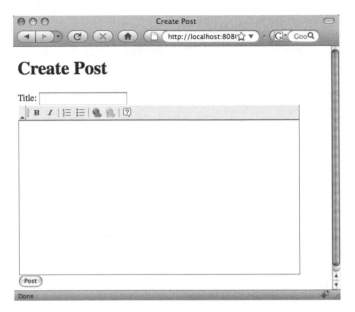

Figure 13-7. *Creating a post with FCKeditor*

Of course, both the `list.gsp` and `create.gsp` pages currently look rather uninspiring, but it is up to the application you install the `blog` plugin into to provide useful style information via CSS. Speaking of installing the `blog` plugin into an application, it is time to do exactly that! First package up the `blog` plugin by running the `package-plugin` command:

```
$ grails package-plugin
```

Then navigate to the gTunes application, and use `install-plugin` to install the `blog` plugin:

```
$ grails install-plugin ../blog/grails-blog-0.1.zip
```

Note how, in this case, since the FCKeditor plugin exists in the Grails central repository, the `install-plugin` command will automatically resolve the dependency. Now it would be useful to configure the blog's title using the `grails-app/conf/Config.groovy` file. Remember, the `blog.title` setting allows you to customize the blog title; simply adding the following setting to `Config.groovy` will do the trick:

```
// configuration for the blog
blog.title="The gTunes Weblog"
```

Run the gTunes application using the `run-app` command, and then navigate to the URL `http://localhost:8080/gTunes/post/list`. Like magic, you have the blog plugin running inside the gTunes application exactly as it was before—except that it is now taking advantage of the gTunes application's main layout. Clicking the "New Post" button will take you to the `create.gsp` view you developed earlier. Figure 13-8 shows the FCKeditor component running within the gTunes application.

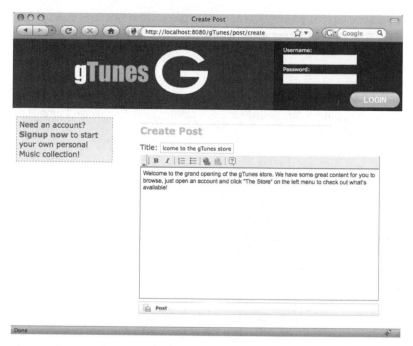

Figure 13-8. *Creating blog posts in the gTunes application*

If you type some content, including a title and body, and then hit the "Post" button, you're able to create new posts on the gTunes application blog, as shown in Figure 13-9.

Figure 13-9. *A blog post in the gTunes application*

Clearly, this is a very basic blog plugin at the moment with no support for RSS, comments, calendars, archives, and all that jazz. However, as a demonstration of the concept of using plugins to separate your application in reusable modules, it's a perfect example. A separate team of developers could happily work on the `blog` plugin and gradually integrate its functionality into the primary application over time. You could even create an automated build, as you learned in Chapter 12, to build and test all your plugins and install them into your main application for integrating testing. So, plugins are definitely worth a look, even if you don't intend to become an expert on Grails internals.

Summary

In this chapter, we hope you have learned the power of the Grails plugin system not just for plugins that provide API enhancements but equally for use cases that provide fully functional application modules like you saw in the previous section. Plugin development is a very broad topic, and this chapter only brushed the surface of what is possible; however, this chapter has given you enough knowledge to investigate developing your own plugins.

From the basics of creating and populating plugin metadata to the intricacies of developing the plugin itself and finally to the packaging and distribution of your plugins, this chapter has covered a lot of ground. As you have seen, Grails provides a broad set of functionality out of the box that can be extended without limits through its plugin system.

One thing you will have noticed during the development of the `blog` plugin in the previous section is that at the moment it allows pretty much anyone to post. Clearly, this is not desirable in the long term, so in the next chapter, we'll cover how you can refactor the simple security implementation in the gTunes application into one of the more fully featured security plugins that are available. Role-based security, here we come!

CHAPTER 14

■■■

Security

Security is a broad topic that is applicable across multiple layers of your application. From the view layer to the database, making your application immune to the various forms of attack is a nontrivial task. Scary things like cross-site scripting (XSS) and SQL injection attacks require careful attention when building your application. As well as covering techniques that help avoid such attacks, in this chapter we'll cover how you can secure your application through authentication and authorization.

Authentication refers to the act of establishing a client's identity. The ubiquitous login form is typically used to establish identity in web applications. *Authorization*, on the other hand, is about granting a client specific rights (often referred to as *privileges* or *permissions*).

Of course, there is no point in reinventing the wheel, so we'll cover how you can use one of the security frameworks already available to implement a more generic solution for authentication and authorization.

Securing Against Attacks

Hacking Internet sites has become a challenge for not just malicious individuals but also for security firms that research potential holes in an application's makeup. The more media coverage an application has, the more likely it is subject to such attacks. Banks and large Internet sites are at particular risk.

When developing an application, you should pay careful attention to the security requirements. Is it exposed to the outside world, or is it an intranet application? What are the implications of a breach? An application with heightened security requirements will take longer to develop and require more user acceptance testing and probing.

As for Grails, some vulnerabilities are completely beyond its control. No matter how cautious you are, Grails won't save you if there is a vulnerability at the operating system or web server level. Having said that, Grails does provide you with the tools to implement *application*-layer security, but ultimately it is up to you to keep security at the forefront of your mind. Unit and functional testing can help you spot problems in this area. Your application can be breached in many ways. In the next few sections, we'll cover some of those ways and how you can help avoid any issues occurring in the first place.

SQL or HQL Injection

One way to launch a Denial of Service (DoS) attack is to use SQL or HQL injection. Essentially, if you use HQL that is built up from values obtained from request parameters, it is possible for an attacker to modify the incoming parameters to give the HQL a different meaning. This may cause invalid data to be returned from the HQL query or, worse still, data held in the database to be removed or changed! To illustrate the problem, consider the code in Listing 14-1.

Listing 14-1. *An Action Vulnerable to HQL Injection*

```
def search = {
    Album.findAll("from Album as a where a.title='"+ params.title +"'")
}
```

With the code in Listing 14-1, an attacker could pass a value as the title parameter that could compromise the query and lead to a DoS attack. For example, say the attacker decided to send a request parameter with the following value:

```
' or a.title not null
```

This would result in the following HQL query:

```
from Album as a where a.title='' or a.title not null
```

The result is that instead of returning only a few records, the query could return thousands or millions of records, causing a potential OutOfMemoryError. Worse still, if the attacker initiates 10,000 requests using the same parameters, you could get threads blocking while these long-running queries execute. With no threads left in the pool, your server will become unresponsive, and the hacker will have successfully completed a DoS attack.

Of course, this phenomenon is not specific to Grails; any application that builds HQL or SQL up dynamically comes up against it. So, how do you prevent such an attack? The secret is never, ever to build up queries from String values, as you saw in Listing 14-1. Instead, use either named or ordinal parameters for the query or, even better, criteria queries. Listing 14-2 shows four possible alternatives to the query from Listing 14-1.

Listing 14-2. *Alternatives That Avoid HQL Injection*

```
// using ordinal parameters
Album.findAll("from Album as a where a.title = ?", [params.title])

// using named parameters
Album.findAll("from Album as a where a.title = :title", [title:params.title])

// using criteria
Album.withCriteria {
    eq('title', params.title)
}

// using a dynamic finder
Album.findAllByTitle(params.title)
```

In all the examples from Listing 14-2, Hibernate will automatically deal with escaping the values passed into the query, making it impossible to execute an HQL injection attack. In the next section, we'll show another potential avenue for attack that is specific to Groovy and Grails—Groovy injection.

Groovy Injection

HQL injection vulnerabilities are dangerous for sure, but the unguarded parsing of Groovy scripts from user input could be even more harmful. Called *Groovy injection*, this involves accepting input from a user that is then executed as a Groovy script. Listing 14-3 shows an example of this technique.

Listing 14-3. *Groovy Injection*

```
def execute = {
    new GroovyShell().evaluate(params.script)
}
```

Writing code like that shown in Listing 14-3 is, to be blunt, not the smartest thing to do. Bringing the whole container down is a simple matter of sending a parameter with the following value:

```
System.exit(1)
```

Or worse, the user could send code that modifies key system files, corrupting the operating system. The GroovyShell class places no restrictions on what code the user is able to run. Generally, as is the case with other dynamic languages such as Ruby and JavaScript, it is not advisable to dynamically evaluate user input in this manner. If you *really* must have this functionality, then you need to make sure the GroovyShell instance is set up with the appropriate Java security permissions. The Groovy website has good documentation on how to achieve this at http://groovy.codehaus.org/Security.

Cross-Site Scripting (XSS)

XSS attacks are probably the most well known but least understood security exploit. The technique involves injecting JavaScript written by the attacker into the page. An attacker able to control the JavaScript on your site is an incredibly dangerous scenario. She could do all manner of things, from stealing a user's cookie to changing a login form so that it sends requests to another server that captures usernames and passwords.

XSS attacks are amazingly common; the site xssed.com even keeps an up-to-date list of the latest known vulnerabilities in major public sites. You'll notice many prominent industry names there; as you can see, even some of the most well-known companies in the software industry make mistakes. The main reason XSS attacks are so common is that they are very hard to test for. Automated testing in most cases is insufficient to trace every potential XSS problem.

In fact, the current implementation of the gTunes application already has an XSS vulnerability that we left in there on purpose (honest!). To reproduce it, try the following:

1. Click the "Signup now" link to load the register form.

2. Enter a valid login, password, email, and last name.

3. For the "First Name" field, enter the text `<script type="text/javascript">alert ('hello')</script>`.

4. Click the "Register" button.

Figure 14-1 shows the form populated with the data from these steps.

Registration

Complete for the form below to create an account!

Login:	baduser1
Password:	●●●●●●●
Confirm Password:	●●●●●●●
Email:	bad1@bad.com
First Name:	>t">alert('hello')</script>
Last Name:	Fake name

Please tick the following box if you wish to subscribe to the weekly gTunes newsletter: ☐

Register

Figure 14-1. *Entering malicious data into the registration form*

When you click the "Register" button, you'll see an alert box pop up with the message "hello." The JavaScript you entered into the "First Name" field has been executed! The gTunes application is currently vulnerable to an XSS attack. Figure 14-2 shows an example of the message box appearing in Firefox.

Figure 14-2. *An XSS vulnerability in action*

But why? The reason for the vulnerability lies in the `grails-app/views/user/` `_welcomeMessage.gsp` template. If you look at the code for the template, it has the following snippet of HTML:

```
Welcome back <span id="userFirstName">${session?.user?.firstName}!</span><br><br>
```

Using the GSP expression syntax `${..}` on the first name simply dumps out the value; there is no HTML escaping happening here. So, what is the solution? A robust and future-proof solution would be to make all `${..}` expressions HTML escaped by default using the `grails.views.default.codec` setting in `grails-app/conf/Config.groovy`:

```
grails.views.default.codec="html"
```

By setting the default codec Grails uses to encode data in GSP views to HTML, you can ensure all GSP expressions are HTML escaped by default. The downside of this approach is that if you're using GSPs to produce any format other than HTML, such as JSON or raw text, then this may be problematic since the setting is global. An alternative is to use the `defaultCodec` page directive to enable HTML escaping on a page-by-page basis:

```
<%@ defaultCodec="html" %>
```

By inserting the previous line of code at the top of a GSP, you can enable escaping all expressions for only the current page. Finally, you can also use the `encodeAsHTML()` method provided by Grails to explicitly encode the data, as shown in Listing 14-4.

Listing 14-4. *Using encodeAsHTML to HTML Escape a Value*

```
Welcome back
<span id="userFirstName">${session?.user?.firstName?.encodeAsHTML()}!</span><br><br>
```

Another important thing to note is that Grails' built-in form tags, such as `<g:textField>`, automatically use the `encodeAsHTML()` method for you. So, you need to be concerned only when the data is being used outside of Grails' built-in tags.

XSS and URL Escaping

In the previous section, you saw how a user can launch an XSS exploit if you don't correctly encode data as HTML by calling the `encodeAsHTML()` method. However, when creating URLs programmatically from user input, it is equally important to URL encode the data used to make up a link. If you're using Grails' built-in `<g:link>` tag and all the other built-in tags that use URLs, then you don't have to worry. Grails will ensure all the data is appropriately URL encoded.

However, if you decide to bypass the built-in tags and do your own link creation, maybe through a tag library, then it is critical you URL escape the programmatically created links. Listing 14-5 shows an example of a potentially vulnerable link.

Listing 14-5. *A Vulnerable Link*

```
<a href="/gTunes/albums?title=${params.title}">Show Album</a>
```

Simply by fiddling with the `title` parameter in a `GET` request an attacker could perform an XSS attack. To avoid this problem, you can call the `encodeAsURL()` method on any data to be included in the URL. Listing 14-6 shows an example of this.

Listing 14-6. *Escaping URLs*

```
<a href="/gTunes/albums?title=${params.title?.encodeAsURL()}">Show Album</a>
```

You'll be learning more about the `encodeAsHTML()` and `encodeAsURL()` methods in the section "Using Dynamic Codecs." For now, let's stay on the topic of vulnerabilities with a further look into DoS attacks.

Denial of Service (DoS)

You've already seen how HQL injection can be used to cause a DoS attack and bring your system down. However, there are other ways you can be vulnerable to a DoS attack even if you avoid using `String` concatenation to build queries. One of the most common ways is through pagination. As you'll recall, GORM methods like `list` and the dynamic finders accept parameters such as `offset` and `max` that allow you to paginate through the records available in the database. Listing 14-7 presents an example of a simple `list` action that does this.

Listing 14-7. *Listing All Albums*

```
def list = {
    if(!params.max) params.max = 10
    [albumList: Album.list(params)]
}
```

As innocent as it may seem, the code in Listing 14-7 is vulnerable to a DoS attack. The reason is that the code doesn't set the maximum value of the `max` argument. An attacker could pass a `max` value of 1000000, and you could end up with a million records loading and the same `OutOfMemoryError` and thread blocking issues we mentioned earlier. Ouch!

A better solution is to ensure that you constrain the value of the `max` parameter passed to a query to not exceed a specific value. Listing 14-8 shows an example implementation that ensures the `max` parameter can only ever reach 100.

Listing 14-8. *Constraining the Maximum Value for Pagination*

```
def list = {
    params.max = Math.min( params.max?.toInteger() ?: 0, 100)
    [albumList: Album.list(params)]
}
```

As you can see from the code in Listing 14-8, you can use the `Math.min` method to get a safe maximum value to use when paginating data. We're not done with potential vulnerabilities just yet, though. In the next section, you'll look at one that affects data binding.

Batch Data Binding Vulnerability

Many web frameworks, including Grails, allow you to bind the data of incoming request parameters to objects. In the case of Grails, these are typically domain instances. Data binding was covered in depth in Chapter 4, but just as a reminder, with Grails it can be done with the following constructor:

```
def album = new Album(params)
```

or alternatively using the `properties` property of an existing domain instance:

```
def album = Album.get(params.id)
album.properties = params
```

In many scenarios, this is not a problem, because a trusted source may be performing the update. However, in some cases, using this technique can be undesirable. Consider, for example, a scenario where you used a simple flag on a `User` domain class to signify whether the `User` is an administrator:

```
class User {
    ...
    boolean administrator
}
```

Administrators have far-reaching powers over the system that only a select few are allowed to have. To set the scene further, say you had a profile page where a user can change her password, phone number, and various personal details. Listing 14-9 shows the server-side code to update the `User` instance.

Listing 14-9. *Vulnerable Controller Action*

```
def update = {
    def user = User.get(params.id)
    user.properties = params
    if(user.save()) {
        redirect(action:"profile", id:user.id)
    }
    ...
}
```

The form that sends the request to the `update` action in Listing 14-9 has fields that only the `User` is allowed to edit. However, a particularly malicious individual could spoof a request so that it sent a parameter called `administrator` with a value of true. The result would be the `User` gaining newfound powers and, potentially, compromising your system.

In this scenario, you should make sure you are explicit about what properties can be updated. Listing 14-10 shows a corrected version of the code in Listing 14-9 that uses the subscript operator on the `properties` property to specify which properties are subject to data binding.

Listing 14-10. *Correcting the Data Binding Vulnerability*

```
def update = {
    def user = User.get(params.id)
    user.properties['firstName', 'lastName', 'phoneNumber','password'] = params
    if(user.save()) {
        redirect(action:"profile", id:user.id)
    }
    ...
}
```

The key message with all these attacks is to make sure that when you accept input from the user, you are aware of the risks of doing so. Grails provides you with all the tools necessary to avoid attacks but will not magically save you from writing vulnerable code. So far in this chapter, you've seen the use of encodeAsURL() and encodeAsHTML(); in the next section, we'll cover how these methods came about and how you can add your own custom versions.

Using Dynamic Codecs

Throughout the course of the chapter so far, you've seen examples of the encodeAsHTML() and encodeAsURL() methods. These methods didn't magically appear out of nowhere; codec classes that ship with Grails provide them. For example, the encodeAsHTML() method is implemented in Grails as shown in Listing 14-11.

Listing 14-11. *An Example Codec Class*

```
import org.springframework.web.util.HtmlUtils

class HTMLCodec {
    static encode( theTarget ) {
        HtmlUtils.htmlEscape(theTarget?.toString())
    }

    static decode( theTarget ) {
        HtmlUtils.htmlUnescape(theTarget?.toString())
    }
}
```

Essentially, a codec class is one that ends with the convention Codec and includes encode and/or decode methods. Grails will automatically create encodeAsHTML() and decodeHTML() methods that delegate to the HTMLCodec class in Listing 14-11 at runtime. The interesting thing is that you can provide your own custom codecs. For example, say you wanted to provide the ability to encrypt data using the Blowfish encryption algorithm that is part of the Java Cryptography Extension (JCE) provided by Sun at http://java.sun.com/javase/technologies/security/. Thanks to custom codecs, this is pretty easy: all you need to do is create a new codec class in the grails-app/utils directory called BlowfishCodec.groovy and populate it with the code in Listing 14-12.

Listing 14-12. *A Blowfish Encryption Codec Class*

```
import org.codehaus.groovy.grails.commons.ConfigurationHolder as CH

import java.security.*;
import javax.crypto.*;
import javax.crypto.spec.*;

class BlowfishCodec {
    static encode(target) {
        def cipher = getCipher(Cipher.ENCRYPT_MODE)
        return cipher.doFinal(target.bytes).encodeBase64()
    }

    static decode(target) {
        def cipher = getCipher(Cipher.DECRYPT_MODE)
        return new String(cipher.doFinal(target.decodeBase64()))
    }

    private static getCipher(mode) {
        def keySpec = new PBEKeySpec(getPassword())
        def cipher = Cipher.getInstance("Blowfish")
        def keyFactory = SecretKeyFactory.getInstance("Blowfish")
        cipher.init(mode, keyFactory.generateSecret(keySpec))
    }
    private static getPassword() { CH.config.secret.key.toCharArray() }
}
```

The BlowfishCodec implementation shown in Listing 14-12 uses the Java cryptography APIs to construct a Cipher using a password set in grails-app/conf/Config.groovy. The method getPassword() inspects the config object provided by importing the org.codehaus.groovy.grails.commons.ConfigurationHolder class:

```
private static getPassword() { CH.config.secret.key.toCharArray() }
```

The getCipher(mode) then uses the getPassword() method to construct an instance of the javax.crypto.spec.PBEKeySpec class that is used for password-based encryption. A javax.crypto.Cipher instance is then obtained using the Blowfish algorithm and initialized using the appropriate mode:

```
private static getCipher(mode) {
        def keySpec = new PBEKeySpec(getPassword())
        def cipher = Cipher.getInstance("Blowfish")
        def keyFactory = SecretKeyFactory.getInstance("Blowfish")
        cipher.init(mode, keyFactory.generateSecret(keySpec))
}
```

Finally, the encode and decode closures then use the cipher to encrypt and decrypt the necessary bytes. Notice how this codec is actually using the Base64Codec built into Grails to return the byte[] as a Base-64 encoded String. Now to encrypt data, you can simply call the encodeAsBlowfish() method:

```
def encrypted = "This is some secret info".encodeAsBlowfish()
```

And to perform the associated decryption, you can call the decodeBlowfish() method:

```
def unencrypted = encrypted.decodeBlowfish()
```

We'll leave to your imagination what else might be possible with codec classes. They're certainly a pretty powerful way to provide common encoding and decoding methods across your application and yet another example of the use of conventions in Grails to enhance behavior. In the next section, we'll take a diversion into the topic of authentication and authorization, including coverage of the available security plugins for Grails.

Authentication and Authorization

Application-layer security, which consists of *authenticating* users at login and *authorizing* authenticated users to perform certain functions, is used in most nontrivial applications. In Chapter 4, you saw how to roll your own authentication mechanism with the UserController class, a trivial implementation that simply checks that a user exists in the database. Until now, however, we have not explained how authorization works through roles and permissions.

As simple as it is to implement your own login mechanism, as your application grows you'll feel the need for more complex security rules. You could use roles to distinguish access to parts of the system—for example, is the user an administrator or a regular user? You may also want fine-grained permission access to individual resources. Typically, but not always, a role consists of multiple permissions.

Rolling your own solution for all of these, potentially complex, security scenarios is rather wasteful given the abundance of security frameworks available for Grails. Currently, three widely used plugins offer security features to Grails:

- Acegi (Spring Security) plugin (http://www.grails.org/AcegiSecurity+Plugin): This integrates Grails with Spring Security (http://static.springframework.org/spring-security/site/, formerly Acegi), a security framework that is part of the Spring portfolio of products.

- Authentication plugin (http://www.grails.org/Authentication+Plugin): The Authentication plugin is a simple security plugin that provides login and registration out of the box. Designed to use sensible defaults to configure most aspects authentication automatically, it lets you customize the behavior of the plugin via events.

- JSecurity plugin (http://www.grails.org/JSecurity+Plugin): The JSecurity plugin integrates the JSecurity framework for Java (http://www.jsecurity.org/) with Grails. It provides helpers to automatically generate login and registration functionality.

In the next section, we'll cover filters, a feature of Grails that underpins all of these frameworks. After that, we'll dive headfirst into integrating the JSecurity plugin into the gTunes application.

Grails Filters

Security is one of those problems that Aspect-Oriented Programming (AOP) advocates often point to as a prime example of a crosscutting concern. In other words, security rules often apply to multiple URIs, classes, and even methods across an application. Getting your security logic mixed in with your business logic is definitely undesirable. Typically, you need to authorize a user to execute certain methods, which can result in security logic being mixed with application logic.

In Grails, you can use filters to execute code before and after a controller action. To add a set of filters in Grails, you need to create a class that ends with the convention *Filters* in your application. A typical place to do this is in the `grails-app/conf` directory. For example, Listing 14-13 shows a `LoggingFilters` implementation that logs request information before and after each request.

Listing 14-13. *An Example Filters Class*

```
class LoggingFilters {
    static filters = {
        all(controller:"*", action:"*") {
            before = {
                log.debug "Parameters: ${params.inspect()}"
            }
            after = { model ->
                log.debug "Model: ${model?.inspect()}"
            }
        }
    }
}
```

As you can see from Listing 14-13, within the `LoggingFilters` definition you define a single static property called `filters` that is assigned a block of code. Then, within the body of this block of code, you can define one or more filters. The example in Listing 14-13 defines a single filter called `all` that applies to all actions within all controllers:

```
all(controller:"*", action:"*") {
```

Notice the usage of the wildcard (*) character to signify that this filter applies to all actions and controllers. Instead of a wildcard, you can also define a specific controller and/or action:

```
secure(controller:"admin", action:"*") {
```

Alternatively, if you prefer URI-based filters, then you can use the `uri` argument:

```
secure(uri:"/admin/**") {
```

In addition, the values you pass to any of the arguments, such as `controller` and `action`, are actually just regular expressions. Hence, if you need to apply a filter to multiple controllers, you can use regex:

```
secure(controller:"(admin|secure)", action:"*") {
```

The last argument of each filter definition is a block of code that you can use to define a before filter:

```
before = {
        log.debug "Parameters: ${params.inspect()}"
}
```

A before filter can also return false, which signifies that the intercepted action should not be executed, something that is critical for security plugins. As well as the before filter, there is also an after filter:

```
after = { model ->
        log.debug "Model: ${model?.inspect()}"
}
```

As you can see, the after filter is a little special because it gets passed the model that the view will use to render. Note also that the after filter gets executed before view rendering. If you want to execute a filter after the view has rendered, you can use the afterView filter, as shown in Listing 14-14.

Listing 14-14. *Using the afterView Filter*

```
after = {
    request.currentTime = System.currentTimeMillis()
}
afterView = {
    log.debug "View took ${System.currentTimeMillis()-request.currentTime}ms"
}
```

Listing 14-14 shows an example that profiles how long it takes for view rendering to complete. As you can see, filters provide an excellent mechanism for implementing crosscutting concerns, because they can be applied across multiple controllers and/or actions. For example, Listing 14-15 shows a very trivial security filter that checks whether a user is logged in.

Listing 14-15. *A Security Filter*

```
class SecurityFilters {
   def filters = {
       loginCheck(controller:'*', action:'*') {
           before = {
               if(!session.user && actionName != 'login') {
                   redirect(action:'login')
                   return false
               }
           }
       }
} } }
```

The security plugins available for Grails make extensive usage of its filters mechanism. In the next section, we'll talk about the JSecurity plugin as an example.

The JSecurity Plugin

The JSecurity plugin builds on the excellent JSecurity library (`http://www.jsecurity.org/`) to provide authentication and authorization to a Grails application. The JSecurity plugin works by combining a set of one or more security filters with a security *realm*. The realm is the bridge between JSecurity and Grails, and it provides methods that you can implement to facilitate authentication and authorization. To get started with JSecurity, you have to install the plugin by running the `install-plugin` command, as shown in Listing 14-16.

Listing 14-16. *Running the install-plugin command*

```
$ grails install-plugin jsecurity
...
Plugin jsecurity-0.2.1 installed
Plug-in provides the following new scripts:
-----------------------------------------
grails create-auth-controller
grails create-db-realm
grails create-ldap-realm
grails quick-start
```

As you can see from the output in Listing 14-16, the JSecurity plugin provides various additional commands that help you integrate it with Grails, the details of which are listed here:

- `create-auth-controller`: This creates a controller that implements logging in and logging out using JSecurity APIs.

- `create-db-realm`: If you don't already have a domain model that represents users and roles, this command will create one that uses GORM to store user information to the database.

- `create-ldap-realm`: This creates a realm that authenticates users against a configured LDAP server.

- `quick-start`: This combines the `create-db-realm` and `create-auth-controller` commands to set up JSecurity in a single command.

Authentication Realms

Both the `create-db-realm` and `create-ldap-realm` classes set up a realm class that deals with rights management. In other words, the realms dictate who can access your system, as well as what roles and permissions they have once the user has authenticated. A *realm class* is a class that lives in the `grails-app/realms` directory and that ends with the convention *Realm*. Although there are no further requirements, for realm classes to be useful they should implement some or all of the methods shown in Listing 14-17.

Listing 14-17. *Methods of a Realm*

```
def authenticate(authToken)
def hasRole(principal, roleName)
def isPermitted(principal, permission)
```

The authenticate method is called when a user tries to sign in to your application. The argument passed to the authenticate method is an instance of the org.jsecurity.authc. AuthenticationToken interface. The default implementation assumed by JSecurity is org. jsecurity.authc.UsernamePasswordToken, which uses username/password-based authentication. However, you can change the authentication token mechanism used by setting the authTokenClass static property of the realm class:

```
static authTokenClass = org.jsecurity.authc.UsernamePasswordToken
```

The hasRole and isPermitted methods both accept a principal, which is the unique value used to identify the user returned by the authenticate method. We'll be returning to roles and permissions in a moment; first we'll address the notion of subjects and principals.

Subjects and Principals

A subject, in JSecurity terms, is a person or entity who is currently accessing your application. Modeled by the class org.jsecurity.subject.Subject, a subject does not have to be logged in and can be in one of three states:

- Unknown: The application doesn't know who the user is.

- Remembered: The application remembers the user from a previous session.

- Authenticated: The user has successfully logged in, by entering their credentials, and the application knows who they are.

You can obtain the current Subject instance at any time using the org.jsecurity. SecurityUtils class, which has a static getSubject() method, as shown in Listing 14-18.

Listing 14-18. *Using SecurityUtils to Obtain the Subject*

```
def subject = org.jsecurity.SecurityUtils.getSubject()
println "User ${subject.principal} is authenticated? ${subject.authenticated}"
```

As shown in Listing 14-18, the Subject has a getPrincipal() method that returns the principal. As mentioned, the principal is the unique identity of a user such as a login name, email address, or Social Security number.

Roles and Permissions

In a role-based system, a role represents a function or set of responsibilities a user may have. If you were developing a content management system (CMS), you might have roles such as Administrators, Editors, and Users. Although an Administrator would have overall access to all parts of the system, lesser beings such as simple Users would be able to access only a limited set of functions. Permissions, on the other hand, represent a much finer-grained level of control. In fact, a role typically consists of a collection of permissions. For example, considering the gTunes application permissions might include asking the following questions:

- Can the user create blog entries?

- Can the user play music from Album X?

- Can the user upload new music to the system?

In JSecurity, a permission is modeled by the `org.jsecurity.authz.Permission` interface shown in Listing 14-19.

Listing 14-19. *The org.jsecurity.authz.Permission Interface*

```
package org.jsecurity.authz

interface Permission {
    boolean implies(Permission p)
}
```

As you can see from Listing 14-19, the `Permission` interface defines a single method called `implies(Permission)`. The idea here is that typically a user gets assigned a collection of permissions. If one of the permissions assigned to that user allows access to the `Permission` passed as an argument to the `implies(Permission)` method, then `true` will be returned. As an example, to create an Administrator user, you could use the `org.jsecurity.authz.permission.AllPermission` permission, which *implies* access to all other permissions by always returning `true` from the `implies(Permission)` method.

The validation of roles and permissions can and should occur at multiple levels, from the view to the controller layer. In the next section, we'll show how to apply these ideas to the gTunes application by using JSecurity to secure access to various parts of the application.

JSecurity in Action

As mentioned previously, JSecurity comes with built-in commands that allow you to generate a domain model and authentication realm. However, since you already have a domain model and because it will help you understand the intricacies of JSecurity, you're going to build a custom JSecurity realm class.

Implementing Authentication with JSecurity

To get started, you need to create new realm class in the grails-app/realms directory. In Figure 14-3 you can see we've created a new realm class called AuthRealm in the com.g2one. gtunes package.

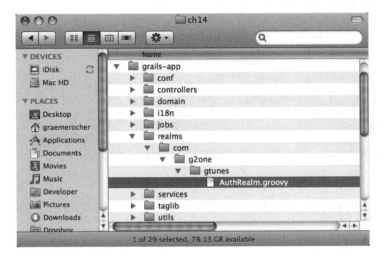

Figure 14-3. *The AuthRealm class*

The next step is to implement the authenticate method for the AuthRealm class, as shown in Listing 14-20.

Listing 14-20. *The authenticate Method of the AuthRealm*

```
class AuthRealm {
    static authTokenClass = org.jsecurity.authc.UsernamePasswordToken

    CredentialsMatcher credentialMatcher

    def authenticate(authToken) {
        ...
    }
}
```

As you can see, the code uses the org.jsecurity.authc.UsernamePasswordToken class for the authToken instance that will be passed to the authenticate method. Since there is already an existing com.g2one.gtunes.User domain class that contains login and password properties, the UsernamePasswordToken class is a logical choice here.

Another thing you'll note from the code in Listing 14-20 is the credentialMatcher property. This property is injected by Spring at runtime. The default implementation used is the org.jsecurity.authc.credential.Sha1CredentialsMatcher, which expects that credentials that are stored are SHA hashed, a pretty common practice.

You can, however, replace the CredentialsMatcher implementation simply by defining a new Spring bean in the grails-app/conf/spring/resources.groovy file called credentialMatcher. For example, the following code defines a CredentialsMatcher that uses MD5 hashing instead:

```
credentialMatcher(org.jsecurity.authc.credential.Md5CredentialsMatcher)
```

Returning to the authenticate method, the UsernamePasswordToken instance defines a username property that you can use to obtain the username of the user, as shown in Listing 14-21.

Listing 14-21. *Obtaining the Username of a User*

```
def username = authToken.username

// Null username is invalid
if (username == null) {
    throw new AccountException('Null usernames are not allowed by this realm.')
}
```

As you can see from Listing 14-21, if the username is null, an org.jsecurity.authc. AccountException is thrown. JSecurity provides a number of built-in exception types within the org.jsecurity.authc package, the examples of which are listed here:

- AccountException: Thrown because of a problem with the account under which an authentication attempt is being executed

- ConcurrentAccessException: Thrown when an authentication attempt has been received for an account that has already been authenticated

- DisabledAccountException: Thrown when attempting to authenticate and the corresponding account has been disabled for some reason

- ExcessiveAttemptsException: Thrown when a system is configured to allow only a certain number of authentication attempts over a period of time and the current session has failed to authenticate successfully within that number

- ExpiredCredentialsException: Thrown during the authentication process when the system determines the submitted credentials has expired and will not allow a login

- IncorrectCredentialsException: Thrown when attempting to authenticate with credential(s) that do not match the actual credentials associated with the account principal

- UnknownAccountException: Thrown when attempting to authenticate with a principal that doesn't exist in the system (for example, by specifying a username that doesn't relate to a user account)

It is up to your implementation of the authenticate method to throw the appropriate exceptions for each reason, but as you can see, JSecurity provides exception types for most common cases. For example, Listing 14-22 shows the next step needed to implement authenticate appropriately by throwing an UnknownAccountException if the User instance is not found for the specified username.

Listing 14-22. *Throwing an UnknownAccountException If a User Is Not Found*

```
def user = User.findByLogin(username)

if (!user) {
    throw new UnknownAccountException("No account found for user $username")
}
```

As you can see from Listing 14-22, it is at this point that you are able to connect JSecurity with your existing domain model. However, if a User instance is found, you want to make sure that said user's password is correct. Listing 14-23 shows an example of how to achieve this.

Listing 14-23. *Validating User Credentials*

```
def account = new SimpleAccount(username, user.password, "gTunesRealm")
if (!credentialMatcher.doCredentialsMatch(authToken, account)) {
    throw new IncorrectCredentialsException("Invalid password for $username")
}
```

Notice how in Listing 14-23 you need to construct an instance of the org.jsecurity. authc.SimpleAccount class, which takes the principal (in this case the username), the credentials, and the name of the realm. Once constructed, you can then use the credentialMatcher instance's doCredentialsMatch method to validate the user's authentication token. If the token is not valid, an IncorrectCredentialsException is thrown. If all is well, the final thing to do is to return the user's principal:

```
return username
```

And with that, you've completed the implementation of the authenticate method. Listing 14-24 shows the full code listing from the authenticate method.

Listing 14-24. *The authenticate Method*

```
def authenticate(authToken) {
    def username = authToken.username

    // Null username is invalid
    if (username == null) {
        throw new AccountException('Null usernames are not allowed by this realm.')
    }

    // Get the user with the given username. If the user is not
    // found, then they don't have an account and we throw an
    // exception.
    def user = User.findByLogin(username)
    if (!user) {
        throw new UnknownAccountException("No account found for $username")
    }
```

```
    // Now check the user's password against the hashed value stored
    // in the database.
    def account = new SimpleAccount(username, user.password, "gTunesRealm")
    if (!credentialMatcher.doCredentialsMatch(authToken, account)) {
        throw new IncorrectCredentialsException("Invalid password for  $username")
    }
    return username
}
```

Now all that is left to do is implement a controller that can take advantage of the realm. A simple way to do this is to run the create-auth-controller command, which will generate a controller that uses JSecurity to authenticate. However, since the gTunes application already has a UserController, you're going to modify that instead and at the same time get a chance to explore JSecurity's APIs.

To authenticate with JSecurity, you need a reference to the org.jsecurity.mgt. SecurityManager instance, the interface for which is shown in Listing 14-25.

Listing 14-25. *The org.jsecurity.mgt.SecurityManager Interface*

```
interface SecurityManager {
    Subject getSubject()
    Subject login(AuthenticationToken authenticationToken)
    void logout(PrincipalCollection subjectIdentifier)
}
```

To obtain a reference to the SecurityManager, you need to use dependency injection via Spring using a bean called jsecSecurityManager. If you recall, the current UserController uses a command object, called LoginCommand, to handle login processing. Command objects can participate in dependency injection using Spring by simply declaring a property within the command class that matches the bean name:

```
def jsecSecurityManager
```

Using the SecurityManager instance's login(AuthenticationToken) method, you can then authenticate users based on the parameters bound to the LoginCommand. Listing 14-26 shows the updated LoginCommand class that uses the jsecSecurityManager for authentication.

Listing 14-26. *A LoginCommand Definition That Uses JSecurity for Authentication*

```
class LoginCommand {
    String login
    String password

    def jsecSecurityManager

    boolean authenticate() {
        def authToken = new UsernamePasswordToken(login, password)
        try{
            this.jsecSecurityManager.login(authToken)
```

```
                return true
            }
            catch (AuthenticationException ex){
                return false
            }
        }
    }
    static constraints = {
        login blank:false, validator:{ val, cmd ->
            if(!cmd.authenticate())
                return "user.invalid.login"
        }
        password blank:false
    }
}
```

You can see the guts of the logic in the authenticate() method of the LoginCommand in Listing 14-26. Initially, a new UsernamePasswordToken instance is constructed and passed to the jsecSecurityManager bean's login(AuthenticationToken) method. If the login (AuthenticationToken) method completes without an exception being thrown, the authenticate() method returns true, signaling a successful login. Otherwise, if an exception is thrown, false is returned. The other major change to the LoginCommand is that the login constraint now calls the command's authenticate() method and returns a code called user.invalid.login if authentication failed.

You could write code to handle specific AuthenticationException instances, such as UnknownAccountException, and return different error codes based on each exception. Nevertheless, the code serves to demonstrate how to use a command object to authenticate via JSecurity. As for the login action of the UserController, it doesn't need any changes since the command object itself encapsulates the logic of logging in.

However, what does need a change is the register action. This currently stores passwords in plain-text form, but JSecurity is expecting an SHA1 hash of the password by default. Listing 14-27 shows the changes made to the register action to provide an SHA1 hash of the password.

Listing 14-27. *Hashing a Password with SHA1*

```
import org.jsecurity.crypto.hash.Sha1Hash

class UserController {
    ...
    def register = {
        if(request.method == 'POST') {
            ...
                if(u.validate()) {
                    u.password = new Sha1Hash(u.password).toHex()
                    u.save()
                    ...
```

```
                }
            ...
        }
    }
    ...
}
```

Securing Your Site with JSecurity Filters

Adding the ability to authenticate users wouldn't be of much use if you didn't have the ability to secure areas of a Grails application that require authentication. The JSecurity plugin for Grails uses the filters mechanism discussed earlier in the chapter in order to authenticate users. To begin with, you need to define a filters class. For example, you could create an AuthFilters class, as shown in Figure 14-4.

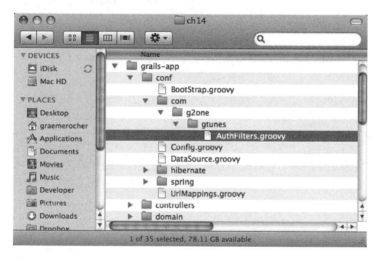

Figure 14-4. *The grails-app/conf/com/g2one/tunes/AuthFilters.groovy file*

With the filters class in place, you need to define a static filters property that is assigned a block of code, the body of which will contain the filter definitions. Listing 14-28 shows the AuthFilters class with the filters static property in place.

Listing 14-28. *The AuthFilters Class*

```
package com.g2one.gtunes

class AuthFilters {
    static filters = {
        ...
    }
}
```

By default JSecurity allows all requests through without authentication, so you need to define which controllers, actions, and/or URIs require authentication. You can do so by calling the accessControl method within the definition of a before filter. For example, users are required to log in to purchase music, so you need to secure the buy action of the StoreController, as shown in Listing 14-29.

Listing 14-29. *Securing an Action*

```
static filters = {
    purchasing(controller:"store", action:"buy") {
        before = {
            accessControl()
        }
    }
    ...
}
```

To deal with authentication failures that arise from a filters class, you need to implement the onNotAuthenticated(Subject, controller) method. Listing 14-30 shows the implementation used by the gTunes application.

Listing 14-30. *Implementing the onNotAuthenticated Method*

```
def onNotAuthenticated(subject, d) {
    if (d.request.xhr) {
        d.render(template:"/user/loginForm", model:[message:"user.not.logged.in"])
    }
    else {
        // Redirect to login page.
        d.flash.message = "user.not.logged.in"
        if(d.actionName == 'buy') {
            d.redirect(controller:"album", action:"display", id:d.params.id)
        }
        else {
            d.redirect(controller:"store", action:"shop")
        }
    }
}
```

The logic here is a bit more convoluted because it deals both with Ajax requests, by checking the request.xhr property, and with regular requests. Additionally, if the actionName is the buy action, then there is some logic in there to take the user back to the Album they were trying to buy. You could, of course, redirect to the original URI using the forwardURI property, but since there isn't a use case yet for this in the gTunes application, the implementation in Listing 14-30 will do fine.

If you need to secure access for a specific role, you can pass a block to the accessControl method that contains a call to the method role(name) that defines the role. For example, the blogging feature you added via a plugin in Chapter 13 can be secured so that only administrators can access the feature using the following syntax:

```
blogEditing(controller:"blog", action:"(create|save)") {
    before = {
        accessControl {
            role('ADMINISTRATOR')
        }
    }
}
```

Notice how the previous filter applies to both the create and save actions of the BlogController. Currently the role(name) method is being called to allow access to a role named ADMINISTRATOR, but if you wanted to allow access to more than one role, you can use the | operator:

```
accessControl {
    role('ADMINISTRATOR') | role('EDITOR')
}
```

Here users who are in either the ADMINISTRATOR role or the EDITOR role can create blog posts. Of course, you have not yet implemented the hasRole method in the AuthRealm class, so no one at this point has access to these areas of the gTunes site. In the next section, you'll rectify that by implementing role-based security.

Implementing Role-Based Security

Currently, the gTunes domain model does not define the concept of a role. To correct this, you need to create a new domain class called Role using the create-domain-class command:

```
$ grails create-domain-class com.g2one.gtunes.Role
```

Once complete, you'll end up with a new domain class in the grails-app/domain/com/g2one/gtunes directory called Role.groovy. A good way to implement a role is using a type-safe enum. Listing 14-31 shows the code for the Role class that uses an enum called RoleName containing the different role names.

Listing 14-31. *The Role Domain Class*

```
package com.g2one.gtunes

class Role implements Serializable {
    RoleName name
}
enum RoleName {
    USER, EDITOR, ADMINISTRATOR
}
```

The next step is to update the `com.g2one.gtunes.User` domain class to associate a user with a set of roles. Listing 14-32 shows the changes to the `User` domain class with the addition of a roles association.

Listing 14-32. *Adding a roles Association to the User Domain Class*

```
class User implements Serializable{
    ...
    static hasMany = [ purchasedAlbums:Album,
                       purchasedSongs:Song,
                       roles:Role ]
}
```

In addition, users who register with the gTunes site should be assigned the default role of `USER`. To achieve this, you can update the `register` action, as shown in Listing 14-33, to call the `addToRoles` method, passing the `RoleName` as an argument.

Listing 14-33. *Updating the register Action to Include Roles*

```
def register = {
    ...
    if(u.validate()) {
        u.password = new Sha1Hash(u.password).toHex()
        u.addToRoles(name:RoleName.USER)
        u.save()
        ...
    }
    ...
}
```

Now it is time to consider the `AuthRealm`, which currently does not implement the `hasRole` method. Listing 14-34 shows a simple implementation that inspects the `roles` association of the `User` domain class.

Listing 14-34. *Using Criteria to Query User Roles*

```
def hasRole(principal, roleName) {
    def user = User.findByLogin(principal, [fetch:[roles:'join']])
    return user.roles.any { it.name == RoleName.valueOf(roleName) }
}
```

Notice how in Listing 14-34 you use the `principal` argument passed to the `hasRole` method to look up the `User` based on their unique `login` name. If the `User` doesn't have a `Role` within its roles association that matches the specified `RoleName`, then the `hasRole` method will return `false`. With this in place, the controller actions secured with the `accessControl` method in the `AuthFilters` class will not allow users to access those controller actions unless the `User` has the specified role.

Securing the View

In addition to securing via the AuthFilters class, you can also secure the view layer using a variety of tags provided by the JSecurity plugin. You may recall that previously the gTunes application checked whether a User existed within the session object to control the state of the view. As a refresher, the code in question can be found within the grails-app/views/layouts/main.gsp layout, as shown in Listing 14-35.

Listing 14-35. *The Old Way of Securing the View*

```
<div id="loginBox" class="loginBox">
    <g:if test="${session?.user}">
        <g:render template="/user/welcomeMessage"></g:render>
    </g:if>
    <g:else>
        <g:render template="/user/loginForm"></g:render>
    </g:else>
</div>
```

In the example in Listing 14-35, the loginBox <div> displays different content depending on whether the user is logged in. Using JSecurity, there are two equivalents tags to achieve this: <jsec:isLoggedIn> and <jsec:isNotLoggedIn>. Listing 14-36 shows the code updated to use the JSecurity model.

Listing 14-36. *Checking Whether a User Is Authenticated with JSecurity*

```
<div id="loginBox" class="loginBox">
    <jsec:isLoggedIn>
        <g:render template="/user/welcomeMessage"></g:render>
    </jsec:isLoggedIn>
    <jsec:isNotLoggedIn>
        <g:render template="/user/loginForm"></g:render>
    </jsec:isNotLoggedIn>
</div>
```

■**Tip** If you're not keen on the naming of the <jsec:isLoggedIn> and <jsec:isNotLoggedIn> tags, you may want to use <jsec:authenticated> and <jsec:notAuthenticated>, which mean the same thing.

Additionally, the grails-app/views/user/_welcomeMessage.gsp template was particularly reliant on the existence of a user object within the session with the following snippet of code:

```
Welcome back <span id="userFirstName">${session?.user?.firstName}!</span><br><br>
```

If you merely want to output the currently logged in user's login name, then you could use the `<jsec:principal />` tag instead:

```
Welcome back <span id="userFirstName"><jsec:principal />!</span><br><br>
```

However, in this case, you really want to print the user's first name. To facilitate this, you may want to add another filter that makes the actual User instance available to the request, as shown in Listing 14-37.

Listing 14-37. *Making the User Object Available in the Request*

```
userInRequest(controller:"*", action:"*") {
    before = {
        def subject = SecurityUtils.getSubject()
        if(subject && subject?.principal) {
            request.user = User.findByLogin(subject.principal)
        }
    }
}
```

As you can see from Listing 14-37, you can use the SecurityUtils class to get a reference to the Subject and then, using the principal, look up the User instance and place it within the request. As you saw in Chapter 10, with a good caching policy in place, you can avoid hitting the database in most cases. Now within the _welcomeMessage.gsp template you can use the user object held in the request to output the User instance's firstName property:

```
Welcome back <span id="userFirstName">${request?.user?.firstName}!</span><br><br>
```

Returning to roles, as well as the `<jsec:isLoggedIn>` tag, you can also check whether a User has a particular Role within the view using the `<jsec:hasRole>` or `<jsec:hasAllRoles>` tag. Listing 14-38 shows an example of using the `<jsec:hasRole>` tag.

Listing 14-38. *Restricting Access Based on Role*

```
<jsec:hasRole name="ADMINISTRATOR">
    <g:link controller="blog" action="create">Create Blog Entry</g:link>
</jsec:hasRole>
<jsec:hasRole in="['ADMINISTRATOR', 'USER']">
    <g:link controller="blog" action="list">Show Blog Entries</g:link>
</jsec:hasRole>
```

Now it is time to try something a little more fun. In the next section, you're going to implement the "My Music" section of the gTunes application that will allow you to play the music you have purchased. Of course, this has to be dealt with in a secure manner, because users should be able to play only the music they have actually purchased. Luckily, JSecurity has great support for implementing permission-based security, which will help solve this problem.

Implementing the "My Music" Section with Permissions

As it stands at the moment, the gTunes application is capable of allowing users to purchase albums. However, there is currently no way to play the music the User has purchased, which is not particularly useful. To fix this problem, you're going to implement the "My Music" section, which will show the currently logged in user's collection of music and allow them to play individual songs.

To do so, first create a link to the "My Music" section by editing the grails-app/views/ layouts/main.gsp layout and modifying the navButtons <div>, as shown in Listing 14-39.

Listing 14-39. *Adding the "My Music" Link*

```
<div id="navPane">
    <div id="navButtons" style="display:${request.user? 'block' :'none'}">
        <ul>
            <li><g:link controller="user" action="music">My Music</g:link></li>
            <li><g:link controller="store" action="shop">The Store</g:link></a></li>
        </ul>
    </div>
    ...
</div>
```

The added <g:link> tag links to a new music action of the UserController. The music action is responsible for building up a model representing the user's library of music. Listing 14-40 shows an example implementation.

Listing 14-40. *Obtaining Information About the User's Music Collection*

```
def music = {
    def albumList = AlbumPayment.withCriteria {
        projections {
            property "album"
        }
        eq("user", request.user)
    }

    def artistList = albumList.collect { it.artist }.unique()
    return [artists:artistList, albums:albumList ]
}
```

As you can see, you can obtain information about the user's purchases using the AlbumPayment class. In Listing 14-40, a projection is used to select the album property of each AlbumPayment instance in the criteria query. Projections were discussed in more detail in Chapter 10. With a list of albums and artists in hand, you can then use a view to render this information appropriately. Listing 14-41 shows the grails-app/views/user/music.gsp view that goes through each Artist instance and displays an album art link to each album.

Listing 14-41. *The music.gsp View*

```
<g:applyLayout name="libraryLayout">
    <div id="musicLibrary" class="musicLibrary">
        <g:if test="${!artists}">
            You haven't purchased any music just yet.
            Why don't you take a <g:link controller="store"
             action="shop">look at the store</g:link>
             to see what's available.
        </g:if>
        <g:each var="artist" in="${artists}">
            <div id="artist${artist.id}" class="artist">
                <h2>${artist.name}</h2>
                <g:each var="album"
                        in="${albums.findAll { it.artist.name == artist.name}}">
                    <span class="purchasedAlbum">
                        <g:remoteLink update="musicLibrary"
                                              controller="album"
                                              action="display"
                                              id="${album.id}">
                            <music:albumArt artist="${artist.name}"
                                                    album="${album.title}"
                                                    alt="${album.title}"/>

                        </g:remoteLink>
                    </span>

                </g:each>
            </div>
        </g:each>
    </div>
</g:applyLayout>
```

Notice that in Listing 14-41 the music.gsp view is using a new layout called libraryLayout.
This makes sense, since typically you don't want the same information about the store within
your music library. You can see the grails-app/views/layouts/libraryLayout.gsp file in
Listing 14-42.

Listing 14-42. *The libraryLayout.gsp View*

```
<html>
    <head>
        <meta http-equiv="Content-type" content="text/html; charset=utf-8">
        <meta name="layout" content="main">
        <title>gTunes Store</title>
    </head>
```

```
<body id="body">
    <h1>Your Music</h1>
    <div id="musicPanel">
        <g:layoutBody />
    </div>
</body>
```

```
</html>
```

Currently, the libraryLayout.gsp view in Listing 14-42 is pretty simple, but you could easily augment it with additional functionality such as recommendations based on the user's current collection of music, and so on. All in all, after applying a few CSS tweaks, the new "My Music" section looks like Figure 14-5.

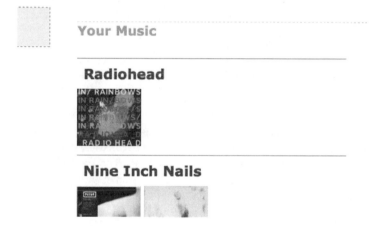

Figure 14-5. *The "My Music" section of the gTunes application*

Next, since this section of the gTunes application relates specifically to personal data of individual users, you need to ensure that said users are logged in before accessing the music action of the SongController. To do this, add a new filter definition in the AuthFilters class that secures the music action, as shown in Listing 14-43.

Listing 14-43. *Securing the music Action*

```
library(controller:"user", action:"music") {
    before = {
        accessControl()
    }
}
```

If you refer to the code in Listing 14-41, you'll notice that the <g:remoteLink> tag used links to the display action of the AlbumController. Currently, this will just render an Album exactly as shown in the store. Figure 14-6 shows an example of the current behavior.

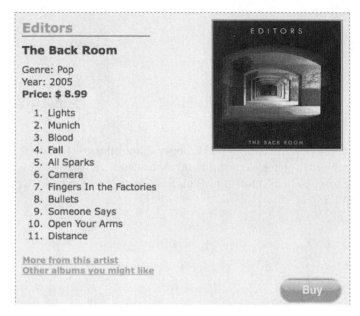

Figure 14-6. *The current presentation of Album information*

As you can see, even if you purchased the Album, the gTunes application is still showing the price, the "Buy" button, and so on. Somehow you need to give the user *permission* to access this Album. It is in use cases like this that JSecurity's permissions mechanism comes in handy. To model permissions, you're going to need to create a new com.g2one.gtunes.Permission class using the create-domain-class command:

```
$ grails create-domain-class com.g2one.gtunes.Permission
```

The Permission domain class is going to implement the org.jsecurity.authz.Permission interface, providing some default behavior. Listing 14-44 shows the code for the Permission domain class.

Listing 14-44. *The Permission Domain Class*

```
package com.g2one.gtunes

class Permission implements org.jsecurity.authz.Permission, Serializable{

    static belongsTo = [user:User]

    boolean implies(org.jsecurity.authz.Permission p) { false }
}
```

As you can see from Listing 14-44, the Permission domain class is also associated with an individual User using a belongsTo static property. To make this a bidirectional relationship, you can add a hasMany definition on the User side of the association, as shown in Listing 14-45.

Listing 14-45. *Updating the User Class with the Permissions Association*

```
class User implements Serializable{
    ...
    static hasMany = [ purchasedAlbums:Album,
                       purchasedSongs:Song,
                       roles:Role,
                       permissions:Permission]
}
```

Returning to Listing 14-44, the default behavior is to return `false` from the `implies` `(Permission)` method, granting the `User` no additional permissions. To provide additional behavior, you can subclass the `Permission` domain class. As an example, currently you need to restrict the access users have to `Album` instances they have purchased. To do this, you can implement an `AlbumPermission` by extending the `Permission` class. Simply run the create-domain-class command again to create the `AlbumPermission` class:

```
grails create-domain-class com.g2one.gtunes.AlbumPermission
```

With that done, you need to extend the `com.g2one.gtunes.Permission` class and add the necessary behavior to restrict access to individual `Album` instances. Listing 14-46 shows a sample implementation.

Listing 14-46. *The AlbumPermission Class*

```
package com.g2one.gtunes

class AlbumPermission extends Permission {
    Album album

    boolean implies(org.jsecurity.authz.Permission p) {
        if(p instanceof AlbumPermission) {
            if(album.id == p.album?.id) {
                return true
            }
        }
        return false
    }

    String toString() { "Album Permission: ${album}"}
}
```

As you can see from Listing 14-46, each `AlbumPermission` is associated with an `Album` instance. If the `Permission` supplied to the `implies(Permission)` method contains the same `Album` instance, then the `User` has permission to access the `Album` and `true` is returned; otherwise, `false` is returned.

To finalize permission handling, you need to add code to the `purchaseAlbum` method of the `StoreService` you created in Chapter 11 to associate an `AlbumPermission` with a `User` when they purchase an Album. Listing 14-47 shows how you can use the addToPermissions method to achieve this in the StoreService class.

Listing 14-47. *Assigning an AlbumPermission to a User*

```
class StoreService {

    static transactional = true

    Payment purchaseAlbums(User user, creditCard, List albumPayments) {
        // Once payment taken update user profile
        for(ap in albumPayments) {
            ...
            user.addToPurchasedAlbums(ap.album)
            user.addToPermissions(new AlbumPermission(album:ap.album))
        }
        ...
    }
}
```

At this point, you need to consider the AuthRealm, which currently implements the hasRole method, but not the isPermitted method that is necessary for permission handling. Listing 14-48 shows an example implementation that obtains a list of Permission instances for a User and verifies them against the supplied Permission instance.

Listing 14-48. *Implementing isPermitted in the AuthRealm Class*

```
def isPermitted(principal, requiredPermission) {
    if(requiredPermission instanceof com.g2one.gtunes.Permission) {
        def permissions = Permission.withCriteria {
            user {
                eq('login', principal)
            }
        }
        return permissions.any { permission ->
                permission.implies(requiredPermission)
        }
    }
    else {
        return true
    }
}
```

Notice, in Listing 14-48, the usage of the any method on the list of permissions. The any method will return true if any of the expressions within the passed closure evaluate to true. The result is that if any of the Permission instances return true from the implies(Permission) method, then the any method will return true.

Now it is time to return to the grails-app/views/album/_album.gsp template that is currently showing the price and insisting users purchase the Album again, even if they have already purchased it. To resolve this situation, you can create a new `permission` variable using the `AlbumPermission` class with the `<g:set>` tag:

```
<g:set var="permission"
            value="${new com.g2one.gtunes.AlbumPermission(album:album)}" />
```

Then you can use the `<jsec:lacksPermission>` tag to display information only if the user doesn't have permission to access the `Album`. For example, the price shouldn't be shown if the user has already purchased the `Album`, as shown in Listing 14-49.

Listing 14-49. *Using the <jsec:lacksPermission> Tag to Restrict Access*

```
<div class="albumInfo">
    Genre: ${album.genre ?: 'Other'}<br>
    Year: ${album.year}<br>
    <jsec:lacksPermission permission="${permission}">
        <strong>Price: $ ${album.price}</strong>
    </jsec:lacksPermission>
</div>
```

You can also at this point supply a link that allows the user to play an individual `Song` if they have purchased the `Album` using a combination of the `<jsec:lacksPermission>` and `<jsec:hasPermission>` tags, as shown in Listing 14-50.

Listing 14-50. *Using the <jsec:hasPermission> Tag to Allow Access*

```
<g:each in="${album.songs}" var="song">
    <li>
        <jsec:lacksPermission permission="${permission}">
            ${song.title}
        </jsec:lacksPermission>
        <jsec:hasPermission permission="${permission}">
            <g:link controller="song" action="play"
                id="${song.id}">${song.title}</g:link>
        </jsec:hasPermission>
    </li>
</g:each>
```

As you can see from Listing 14-50, the code links to the `play` action of the `SongController`. We'll talk about implementing this action in a moment; for now, the last step in updating the `_album.gsp` template is to disable the "Buy" button if the user has already purchased the `Album`, as shown in Listing 14-51.

Listing 14-51. *Disabling the "Buy" Button*

```
<div id="buttons" style="float:right;">
    <jsec:hasPermission permission="${permission}">
        <g:link controller="user" action="music">Back to My Music</g:link>
    </jsec:hasPermission>
```

```
    <jsec:lacksPermission permission="${permission}">
        <g:link controller="store" action="buy" id="${album.id}">
            <img src="${createLinkTo(dir:'images',file:'buy-button.gif')}"
                    border="0">
        </g:link>
    </jsec:lacksPermission>
</div>
```

You'll notice from the GSP code in Listing 14-51 that if the User does have access to the Album, then a "Back to My Music" link is displayed instead, allowing the user to navigate easily back to their music. Figure 14-7 shows the updated interface in place with the AlbumPermission class having the desired effect.

Figure 14-7. *The updated _album.gsp template with permissions working*

At this point, you need to consider how to enable users to play music they have purchased. You could leverage various technologies that allow the streaming of media. From Windows Media Player to Flash, each has its own advantages and disadvantages. For the gTunes application, the powers that be have decided on QuickTime (http://www.apple.com/quicktime/) as the preferred technology, since it works well on most mainstream platforms (even on Unix-flavors via WINE; see http://appdb.winehq.org/appview.php?appId=1029) and is simple to use.

To allow embedding of QuickTime audio easily, it would be good to wrap the functionality of QuickTime into a tag library. To do so, run the grails create-tag-lib command as follows:

```
$ grails create-tag-lib com.g2one.gtunes.Streaming
```

This will create a new tag library called StreamingTagLib.groovy at the location grails-app/com/g2one/gtunes, as shown in Figure 14-8.

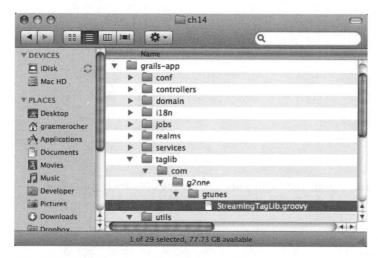

Figure 14-8. *The StreamingTagLib.groovy file*

We chose a generic name on purpose, just in case the requirement to add support for other media players, such as Flash, arises. Nevertheless, Listing 14-52 shows the code that embeds a QuickTime movie using the StreamingTagLib.

Listing 14-52. *The StreamingTagLib Implementation*

```
package com.g2one.gtunes

class StreamingTagLib {

    static namespace = "media"

    def player = { attrs, body ->
        def userAgent = request.getHeader('User-Agent')
        def src = attrs.src
        def width = attrs.width ?: 100
        def height = attrs.height ?: 100
        def autoplay = attrs.autoplay ?: false
        out.write """
<OBJECT CLASSID=\"clsid:02BF25D5-8C17-4B23-BC80-D3488ABDDC6B\"
                WIDTH=\"${width}\"
                HEIGHT=\"${height}\"
                CODEBASE=\"http://www.apple.com/qtactivex/qtplugin.cab\">
```

```
<PARAM name=\"SRC\" VALUE=\"${src}\">
<PARAM name=\"AUTOPLAY\" VALUE=\"${autoplay}\">
<EMBED SRC=\"${src}\"
                WIDTH=\"${width}\"
                HEIGHT=\"${height}\"
                AUTOPLAY=\"${autoplay}\"
                CONTROLLER=\"true\"
                LOOP=\"false\"
                PLUGINSPAGE=\"http://www.apple.com/quicktime/download/\">
</EMBED>
</OBJECT>"""
    }
}
```

There are a couple of interesting things to note about the code in Listing 14-52. First, as you can see, the media namespace is used for this tag library, making the name of the tag `<media:player>`.

Second, notice the usage of Groovy multiline Strings to easily write out a bunch of markup. If you wanted, you could refactor this out to a separate GSP template, but for now this simple solution will do. Now let's take advantage of the `<media:player>` tag by implementing the play action of the `SongController`.

Of course, you don't want users who don't have permission to be able to play a Song from an Album they have purchased. Luckily, using the ability to call tags as methods in Grails, you can use the same `<jsec:hasPermission>` and `<jsec:lacksPermission>` tags in a controller. Listing 14-53 shows this in action.

Listing 14-53. *The play Action of the SongController*

```
def play = {
    def song = Song.get(params.id)
    if(song) {
        def albumPermission = new AlbumPermission(album:song.album)
        jsec.hasPermission(permission:albumPermission) {
            render(view:"play", model:[song:song])
        }
        jsec.lacksPermission(permission:albumPermission) {
            response.sendError 401
        }
    }
    else {
        response.sendError 404
    }
}
```

As demonstrated by Listing 14-53, you can construct an instance of the AlbumPermission class and then use it as an argument to the jsec.hasPermission method. The closure, which is equivalent to the tag body in GSP, will be invoked only if the user has permission. In the case where the User lacks permission, an HTTP 401 error is sent back signaling that the User is forbidden from accessing this resource.

Otherwise, if all is well, a new view called grails-app/views/song/play.gsp is rendered. Listing 14-54 shows the GSP markup for the play.gsp view, which takes advantage of the <media:player> tag you developed earlier.

Listing 14-54. *The play.gsp View*

```
<g:applyLayout name="libraryLayout">
    <div id="musicLibrary" class="musicLibrary">
        <div class="songPlayer">
            <h2>${song.artist.name} - ${song.title}</h2>
            <div class="albumArt">
                <music:albumArt artist="${song.artist.name}"
                                album="${song.album.title}"  />
            </div>
            <div class="player">
                <media:player src="${createLink(controller:'song',
                                               action:'stream',
                                               id:song.id)}"
                              autoplay="true"
                              height="20"
                              width="200" />
            </div>
            <div class="links" style="float:right;">
                    <g:remoteLink controller="album"
                                          action="display"
                                          id="${song.album.id}"
                                          update="musicLibrary">
                                Back to Album
                    </g:remoteLink><br>
                    <g:link controller="user"
                            action="music">
                                Back to My Music
                    </g:link><br>
            </div>
        </div>
    </div>
</g:applyLayout>
```

You'll notice from the code in Listing 14-54 that the src attribute of the <media:player> tag is another action called stream. The stream action is responsible for sending back the music file. Of course, at the moment, there isn't any music! To rectify that, add a new file property to the Song domain class, as shown in Listing 14-55.

Listing 14-55. *Adding a file Property to the Song Class*

```
class Song implements Serializable {

    String file
    ...
    static constraints = {
        ...
        file validator:{ val ->
            if(!new File(val).exists())
                return "song.does.not.exist"
        }
    }
}
```

As you can see, the file property uses a custom validator that ensures you can't add a Song that doesn't exist on the file system. Now all you need to do is stream the data from the file back to the User. Listing 14-56 shows an example implementation that uses Java I/O techniques.

Listing 14-56. *Implementing the stream Action*

```
1 static final BUFFER_SIZE = 2048
2 def stream = {
3      def song = Song.get(params.id)
4     if(song) {
5          def albumPermission = new AlbumPermission(album:song.album)
6          jsec.hasPermission(permission:albumPermission) {
7              try {
8                  def file = new File(song.file)
9                  def type = file.name[-3..-1]
10                  response.contentType = "audio/x-${type}"
11                  def out = response.outputStream
12                  def bytes = new byte[BUFFER_SIZE]
13                  file.withInputStream { inp ->
14                      while( inp.read(bytes) != -1) {
15                          out.write(bytes)
16                          out.flush()
17                      }
18                  }
19              }
```

```
20              catch(Exception e) {
21                  log.error "Error streaming song $file: $e.message", e
22                  response.sendError 500
23              }
24
25          }
26          jsec.lacksPermission(permission:albumPermission) {
27              response.sendError 401
28          }
29      }
30      else {
31          response.sendError 404
32      }
33 }
```

Notice that in Listing 14-56, the code once again secures access to the Song using the AlbumPermission you created earlier and the <jsec:hasPermission> and <jsec:lacksPermission> tags. If the User does have permission, then a new java.io.File is created, and the response contentType is set based on the file extension on lines 8 to 10:

```
8               def file = new File(song.file)
9               def type = file.name[-3..-1]
10              response.contentType = "audio/x-${type}"
```

■**Note** The technique of using the file extension to produce the MIME type for the contentType works for MP3 and M4A formats but may be a little naive if the application later needs to support other formats like WMA and so on.

With that done, the next step is to obtain the java.io.OutputStream to write to and from the response and create a buffer to read bytes from the file with the following:

```
11              def out = response.outputStream
12              def bytes = new byte[BUFFER_SIZE]
```

A trivial way to read the bytes of the File would be to call the readBytes() method. However, this reads the entire contents of the File into memory and, since audio files are quite large, may not scale too well.

■**Note** Speaking of scaling, a better solution may be to use something like Amazon's Simple Storage Service (S3) to serve the files from the cloud instead. You can find an Amazon S3 plugin for Grails that can help simplify this task at http://grails.org/Amazon+S3+Plugin.

Instead, the code in Listing 14-56 uses a 2KB buffer to read and stream parts of the file back to the User on lines 13 to 18:

```
13                  file.withInputStream { inp ->
14                    while( inp.read(bytes) != -1) {
15                        out.write(bytes)
16                        out.flush()
17                    }
18                }
```

And with that, you've completed the "My Music" section of the gTunes application and allowed users to securely stream the music they have purchased! Figure 14-9 shows the interface that allows users to play their music.

Figure 14-9. *Streaming music with QuickTime*

In the next section, you'll learn how having a better understanding of your URL mappings will enable you to keep an eye on how users can access your application.

Limiting Access Through URL Mappings

A good technique to adopt when considering securing your application is to have greater control over the way URLs map onto controllers. The default URL mapping scheme that Grails uses is dynamic in that the parameters in the URI dictate what action is executed (see Listing 14-57).

Listing 14-57. *The Default URL Mapping Scheme*

```
"/$controller/$action?/$id?"()
```

It is easy with a URL mapping like the one in Listing 14-57 to accidentally expose an action that should be secured. If security is of a high priority, we recommend you take control of your URL mappings and create mapping rules for each URL that is exposed. Listing 14-58 shows an example `grails-app/conf/UrlMappings.groovy` file for the gTunes application that provides mappings for each exposed controller.

Listing 14-58. *Fine-Grained URL Mapping Configuration*

```
// User access
"/your/music"(controller:"user", action:"music")
"/login"(controller:"user", action:"login")
"/logout"(controller:"user", action:"logout")
"/register"(controller:"user", action:"register")
"/stream/$id"(controller:"song", action:"stream")
"/play/$id"(controller:"song", action:"play")
"/buy/$id"(controller:"store", action:"buy")

// Anonymous browsing
"/"(controller:"store")
"/album/$id"(controller:"album", action:"display")
"/song/$id"(controller:"song", action:"display")
"/artist/$id"(controller:"artist", action:"display")
"/store"(controller:"store", action:"shop")
"/search"(controller:"store", action:"search")
"/genre/$name"(controller:"store", action:"genre")
"/blog"(controller:"blog", action:"list")
```

Another advantage of this approach is that you can then configure a dynamic URL mapping purely for administrator access, as shown in Listing 14-59.

Listing 14-59. *Administrator URL Mappings*

```
// Administrator access
"/admin/$controller/$action?/$id?"()
```

As you can see from Listing 14-59, all URIs that start with /admin can now be used for administrator access. If you then secure this URI within the AuthFilters class, as shown in Listing 14-60, you have created an area of the site that is accessible only to administrators.

Listing 14-60. *Securing the /admin URI*

```
admin(uri:'/admin/*') {
    before = {
        accessControl {
            role("ADMINISTRATOR")
        }
    }
}
```

If you want to add some quick administrative features, then you could take advantage of dynamic scaffolding, a topic covered in Chapter 2. As an example, try adding the following line to the AlbumController class:

```
def scaffold = Album
```

Now if you go to the URL `http://localhost:8080/gTunes/admin/album/create`, you can create new `Album` instances using the CRUD interface provided. You can also go to the URL `http://localhost:8080/gTunes/admin/album/list` to get a list of existing `Album` instances in case you need to modify any of them. Thanks to Grails' scaffolding feature, you have managed to add a basic admin facility to the gTunes application that is secured with JSecurity in only a few lines of code!

Summary

In this chapter, you explored the importance of security when developing a Grails application. From preventing malicious users from penetrating your application to cross-site scripting and DoS attacks to implementing authentication and authorization using a framework such as JSecurity, we covered a lot of ground. Security is, however, a domain-specific topic, and a variety of options are available to you when developing a Grails application. If JSecurity doesn't fulfill your requirements, then you have the Acegi plugin or the Authentication plugin to try. Alternatively, you could continue the "home-grown" security model. It is really up to you.

In the next chapter, we'll cover how to implement web services in Grails. Using key technologies such as SOAP, REST, and RSS/Atom, there is a lot to cover in this particularly interesting area of web development. Don't go away!

CHAPTER 15

■ ■ ■

Web Services

The idea of web services has been a dream of the IT industry for what seems like forever. The ability to compose applications from multiple, disparate services available over the Web was initially put forward by the SOAP standard. SOAP defined a protocol for exchanging XML messages over a network in a language-neutral way. Although still widely used, SOAP has never really fulfilled its potential, and a simpler model has emerged called Representational State Transfer[1] (REST). REST is a simple architectural style that utilizes the nature of the Web and its HTTP protocol to enable web services communication.

Unlike SOAP, REST is not really a standard and in fact doesn't even specify a requirement for the type of the payloads sent between client and server. For example, some users of REST services choose to use JavaScript Object Notation (JSON) or a custom format instead of XML in their REST APIs. Nevertheless, the idea behind REST is to use simple messages for communication and to take advantage of HTTP methods like GET, PUT, POST, and DELETE to model the different verbs found in Create/Read/Update/Delete (CRUD) applications.

While REST embraces the very nature of the Web, SOAP, on the other hand, tries to stay protocol neutral and has no dependency on HTTP. SOAP is designed to be used in conjunction with a set of tools or libraries that generate the client stub and server skeleton code to facilitate communication either ahead of time or at runtime. Both have their respective advantages and disadvantages. SOAP is very comprehensive, defining web service standards for everything from security to metadata. However, it is also extremely complex in comparison to REST, which targets simplicity.

As you may recall, the main aim of Grails is to embrace simplicity, and in this sense, REST is a far better fit for Grails than SOAP—so much so that Grails provides REST support out of the box. However, several organizations are still committed to the SOAP standard, and in this chapter, you will see how to add both SOAP and the REST APIs to a Grails application.

In addition, we'll be looking at the related syndication technologies Really Simple Syndication (RSS) and Atom.[2] Although not strictly web services related, RSS and Atom are similar in that they provide a way to publish information over the Web using a standard XML format. In fact, Google's GData web service APIs have standardized on an Atom-based format for XML payloads.

---

1. REST is a broad subject, the full details of which are beyond the scope of this book, but we recommend you read Roy Fielding's original dissertation on the subject at http://www.ics.uci.edu/~fielding/pubs/dissertation/top.htm.
2. Atom refers to a pair of related standards, the Atom Syndication Format and Atom Publishing Protocol (APP); see http://en.wikipedia.org/wiki/Atom_(standard).

REST

As already mentioned, REST defines an architectural style for defining web services. Each HTTP method, such as POST and GET, signifies a verb or action that can be executed on a noun. Nouns are represented by URL patterns often referred to as *resources* in REST. Data is typically exchanged using Plain Old XML (POX), an acronym established to differentiate web services that use regular XML for data exchange from specialized versions of XML, such as the one found in SOAP. However, many public REST web services also use JSON as the data transfer format. Ajax clients in particular get massive benefit from JSON web services because client-side JavaScript found in the browser has fewer problems parsing JSON data.

So, how does REST fit into a Grails-based architecture? If you think about it, the HTTP "verbs" map nicely onto controller actions. Each controller is typically associated with a domain class that represents the noun. All you need is a good way to get Grails to execute different actions based on the HTTP verb. One way to do this is to define a default index action that uses a switch statement, as shown in Listing 15-1.

Listing 15-1. *Manually Implementing a RESTful Controller*

```
class AlbumController {
    def index = {
        switch(request.method) {
            case "GET":
                return show()
                break
            case "PUT":
                return save()
                break
            ...
        }
    }
}
```

The approach shown in Listing 15-1 is a bit repetitive and ugly. Luckily, there is a better way using URL mappings.

RESTful URL Mappings

For any given URL mapping, you can tell Grails to execute different actions based on the incoming request method. Listing 15-2 shows the syntax to achieve this.

Listing 15-2. *Mapping onto Different Actions Based on the HTTP Method*

```
static mappings = {
    "/album/$id?"(controller:"album") {
        action = [GET:'show', PUT:'save', POST:'update', DELETE:'delete']
    }
}
```

By assigning a map literal, where the keys are the HTTP method names, to the action parameter in the body of the closure passed to the URL mapping, you can tell Grails to map different HTTP methods to different actions. Now if you open up a browser and go the URI /album, Grails will detect the HTTP GET request and map to the show action of the AlbumController. If you then created an HTML form that used the HTTP POST method to submit, the update action would be used instead.

Of course, the example in Listing 15-2 is still using the database identifier to identify albums. One of the defining aspects of REST is to use the semantics of the Web when designing your URI schemes. If you consider for a moment that in the gTunes application you have artists, albums, and songs, it would be great if REST clients could navigate the gTunes store simply by using the URI. Take a look at the URL mapping in Listing 15-3, which presents an example of using URL mappings that better represents the nouns within the gTunes application.

Listing 15-3. *RESTful URL Example*

```
static mappings = {
    "/music/$artist/$album?/$song?"(controller:"store") {
        action = [GET:'show', PUT:'save', POST:'update', DELETE:'delete']
    }
}
```

The example in Listing 15-3 shows a URL mapping that allows semantic navigation of the gTunes store. For example, if you wanted to retrieve information about the Artist Beck, you could go to /music/Beck. Alternatively, if you're interested in a particular Album by Beck, you could go to /music/Beck/Odelay, and so on.

The disadvantage of the approach in Listing 15-3 is that you are essentially mapping the entire pattern onto a single controller—the StoreController. This places a load of burden on the StoreController because it needs to know about artists, albums, and songs. Really, it would be desirable to map differently depending on which URL tokens have been specified. To achieve this, you could use a closure to define the name of the controller to map to, as shown in Listing 15-4.

Listing 15-4. *Dynamically Mapping to a Controller*

```
"/music/$artistName/$albumTitle?/$songTitle?"{
    controller = {
        if(params.albumTitle && params.songTitle) return 'song'
        else if(params.albumTitle) return 'album'
        else return 'artist'
    }
    action = [GET:'show', PUT:'save', POST:'update', DELETE:'delete']
}
```

The code in Listing 15-4 shows a technique where you can use a closure to change the controller (or action or view) to map to using runtime characteristics such as request parameters. In this case, if you have enough information to retrieve a Song (such as the artist name, album title, and song title), then the SongController is mapped to; otherwise, if only the artist name and album title are specified, the AlbumController is mapped to, and so on.

One of the powerful characteristics of REST that you may have already noticed is that it behaves very much like a regular web application. The same `AlbumController` can be used to deal with both incoming REST requests and regular web requests. Of course, you need to be able to know whether to send back an XML response, in the case of a web service, or a plain HTML page. In the next section, you'll see how to achieve this with content negotiation.

Content Negotiation

Grails controllers have the ability to deal with different incoming request content types automatically through a mechanism known as *content negotiation*. Although not specific to web services (you could equally use this technique with Ajax or to support different browser types), content negotiation is often used in conjunction with RESTful web services. The idea behind content negotiation is to let a controller automatically detect and handle the content type requested by the client. A few mechanisms can be used to achieve this:

- Using the `ACCEPT` or `CONTENT_TYPE` HTTP headers, Grails can detect which is the preferred content type requested by the client. The mechanics of this will be explained in the next section.

- Using a `format` request parameter, clients can request a specific content type.

- And finally, content negotiation can also be triggered using the file extension in the URI, as in `/album/list.xml`.

We'll cover each of these mechanisms in the next few sections, starting with content negotiation via the HTTP `ACCEPT` header.

Content Negotiation with the ACCEPT Header

Every browser that conforms to the HTTP standards is required to send an `ACCEPT` header. The `ACCEPT` header contains information about the various MIME types[3] the client is able to accept. For example, a mobile client that supports only responses in the Wireless Application Protocol,[4] often found in mobile phones, would send an `ACCEPT` header something like this:

```
application/vnd.wap.wmlscriptc, text/vnd.wap.wml
```

■**Tip** For a detailed overview of the `ACCEPT` header, take a look at the specification provided by the W3C at `http://www.w3.org/Protocols/rfc2616/rfc2616-sec14.html`.

---

3. Multipurpose Internet Mail Extensions (MIME) is an Internet standard for describing content types; see `http://en.wikipedia.org/wiki/MIME`.
4. The Wireless Application Protocol (WAP) is a wireless communication standard to enable Internet access on mobile devices; see `http://en.wikipedia.org/wiki/Wireless_Application_Protocol`.

The list of supported MIME types is defined as a comma-separated list, where the most appropriate MIME type is first in the list. Modern browsers such as Firefox 3 typically send an ACCEPT header like the following:

```
text/html,application/xhtml+xml,application/xml;q=0.9,*/*;q=0.8
```

Notice the q parameter after application/xml? The ACCEPT header can specify a "quality" rating for each MIME type. The default quality is 1.0, and the higher the quality, the more appropriate the MIME type. As you can see from the Firefox 3 header, text/html has the highest priority. For Grails to know which MIME types it should handle, you may need to provide additional configuration in grails-app/conf/Config.groovy using the grails.mime.types setting. You'll notice that Grails provides a default set of configured types for each project, an example of which is shown in Listing 15-5.

Listing 15-5. *Configuring Additional MIME Types*

```
grails.mime.types = [ html: ['text/html','application/xhtml+xml'],
                             xml: ['text/xml', 'application/xml'],
                             js: 'text/javascript',
                             ...
                      ]
```

To tell Grails to handle other types beyond the preconfigured ones, you need to add a new entry into the grails.mime.types map where the key is the file extension of the format typically used and the value is the MIME type found in the ACCEPT header. For example, to add support for WAP, where Wireless Markup Language (WML) files are typically served, you can add the following configuration:

```
grails.mime.types = [ html: ['text/html','application/xhtml+xml'],
                             wml: ['text/vnd.wap.wml'],
                             ...
                      ]
```

Of course, if you don't need to support any niche formats such as WML, you can skip this configuration. For the purposes of REST web services, Grails is already preconfigured to be able to handle XML requests. So, how exactly do you deal with a request that needs to send back multiple formats? If you simply want to know the format of an incoming request in order to use branching logic, you can use the format property of the request object:

```
assert request.format == 'xml'
```

However, Grails provides a more elegant way to deal with different format types using the withFormat method of controllers. Using withFormat, you can tell a controller to handle XML, HTML, and even WML requests differently. For example, take a look at the code in Listing 15-6.

Listing 15-6. *Using the withFormat Method*

```
1 import grails.converters.*
2 class ArtistController {
3     def show = {
```

```
4          def artist = params.artistName ? Artist.findByName(params.artistName) :
5                                                       Artist.get(params.id)
6
7          if(artist) {
8              withFormat {
9                  html artist:artist, albums:artist?.albums
10                 xml { render artist as XML }
11             }
12         }
13         else {
14             response.sendError 404
15         }
16     }
17     ...
18 }
```

The code in Listing 15-6 shows how to handle a request when the URL mapping in Listing 15-4 ends up mapping to the ArtistController. Quite a few new concepts have been introduced in such a small snippet of code, so to understand it fully, let's step through it line by line starting with line 1:

```
1 import grails.converters.*
```

Here the grails.converters package is imported, which provides features to enable the marshaling of Java objects into XML or JSON. You'll see the significance of this later; for the moment, take a look at the first change to the code on line 7:

```
8      withFormat {
```

Using the withFormat method, which takes a block, you can send different responses for different request formats. Each nested method within the passed closure matches the name of a format; for example, the html method on line 9 handles regular browser requests:

```
9          html artist:artist, album:album
```

Notice that you can pass a model to the view to be rendered. In this case, the withFormat method will pass control to a view called grails-app/views/artist/show.gsp, which doesn't exist just yet. Finally, on line 10, you can see the code that deals with an XML response:

```
10         xml { render artist as XML }
```

In this example, you can see the first usage of the grails.converters package. The expression render artist as XML uses the imported grails.converters.XML converter to automatically marshal the Artist instance into the XML format. That's pretty simple, but how does a client go about communicating with this XML API? Well, think about how you interact with the application using your browser. For example, load the gTunes application, go to the store, and navigate to one of the existing artists using the REST URI conventions you established in Listing 15-4 such as /music/Kings of Leon.

Unsurprisingly, you get a 404 error since the `grails-app/views/artist/show.gsp` view does not exist. You can create it quickly, as shown in Listing 15-7.

Listing 15-7. *The Artist show.gsp View*

```
<g:applyLayout name="storeLayout">
    <g:render template="artist" model="[artist:artist]"></g:render>
</g:applyLayout>
```

As you can see, the `show.gsp` view is pretty trivial since you already created a template called `_artist.gsp` that does the hard work. Now if you refresh, you should get the view rendered appropriately, as shown in Figure 15-1.

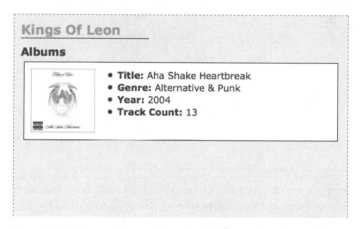

Figure 15-1. *The grails-app/views/artist/show.gsp view rendered*

Take note of the URL in the address bar. If you have set up the URL mappings as shown in Listing 15-2, you should have a URL something like `http://localhost:8080/gTunes/music/Kings of Leon`. Now load the Grails console by typing the command `grails console` into a separate command window from the root of the gTunes project. With that done, try the script in Listing 15-8.

Listing 15-8. *Communicating with a REST API*

```
url = new URL("http://localhost:8080/gTunes/music/Kings%20of%20Leon")

conn = url.openConnection()
conn.addRequestProperty("accept","application/xml")

artist = new XmlSlurper().parse(conn.content)

println "Artist Name = ${artist.name}"
```

Notice how in Listing 15-8 the addRequestProperty method of the URLConnection object is used to set the ACCEPT header to application/xml. The result is that instead of the HTML response you got from the browser, you get an XML one. If you want to see the XML sent back from the server, try replacing the XmlSlurper parsing code with the following line:

```
println conn.content.text
```

The response sent back by the withFormat method and its usage of the expression render artist as XML will result in XML that can be parsed with a parser like Groovy's XmlSlurper, an example of which is shown in Listing 15-9.

Listing 15-9. *Grails' Automatic XML Marshaling Capabilities*

```
<?xml version="1.0" encoding="UTF-8"?>
<artist id="4">
  <albums>
    <album id="4"/>
  </albums>
  <dateCreated>2008-08-04 21:05:08.0</dateCreated>
  <lastUpdated>2008-08-04 21:05:08.0</lastUpdated>
  <name>Kings of Leon</name>
</artist>
```

Grails has used the ACCEPT header in combination with the withFormat method to establish what kind of response the client is anticipating. Since the topic of marshaling to XML is a pretty important one when it comes to REST, we'll be looking at it in more detail later in the chapter. First, however, let's look at one gotcha related to ACCEPT header content negotiation.

The ACCEPT Header and Older Browsers

Depending on the clients you expect to serve, the ACCEPT header might not be so reliable. There is a nasty catch when using the ACCEPT header in that older browsers, including Internet Explorer 6 and older, simply specify */* within the ACCEPT header, meaning they accept any format.

So, how does Grails deal with an ACCEPT header of */*? Well, if you look at the withFormat definition in Listing 15-6, you'll notice that the html method is called first, followed by the xml method. If the ACCEPT header contains */*, then Grails will invoke the first method it finds within the withFormat method, which in this case is the html method. The result is that, even on older browsers, HTML will be served by default.

If this is not the desired behavior, you can also specify a method within the withFormat block to deal with an ACCEPT header containing */*. You may have noticed that the grails.mime.types setting of the grails-app/conf/Config.groovy file matches a MIME type of */* to a format called all:

```
grails.mime.types = [ ...,
                           all: '*/*']
```

What this means is that within the withFormat block, you can define a method to handle the all format type, as shown in the example in Listing 15-10.

Listing 15-10. *Dealing with the all Format*

```
withFormat {
    html artist:artist, albums:artist?.albums
    all artist:artist, albums:artist?.albums
    xml { render artist as XML }
}
```

In this case, Listing 15-10 is not doing anything differently, but you could have your own custom logic to deal with all if required. If this is too dreadful to contemplate and you prefer not to use the ACCEPT header, then consider the techniques in the following sections.

Content Negotiation with the CONTENT_TYPE Header

An alternative to using the ACCEPT header is to use the HTTP CONTENT_TYPE header, which is designed to specify the incoming content type of the request. To try a client that uses the CONTENT_TYPE header, open the Grails console again, and run the script in Listing 15-11.

Listing 15-11. *Communicating with a REST API Using the CONTENT_TYPE Header*

```
url = new URL("http://localhost:8080/gTunes/music/Kings%20Of%20Leon")

conn = url.openConnection()
conn.addRequestProperty("content-type","application/xml")

artist = new XmlSlurper().parse(conn.content)

println "Artist Name = ${artist.name}"
```

The code is identical to Listing 15-8 except that the CONTENT-TYPE header is passed to the addRequestProperty method. The CONTENT_TYPE header always takes precedence over the ACCEPT header if both are specified. Another advantage of using the CONTENT_TYPE header is that the API support for manipulating the content type is a little simpler for Ajax clients. For example, you could use some JavaScript and the Prototype library in Listing 15-12 to call the web service and manipulate the incoming XML.

Listing 15-12. *Calling REST Web Services from JavaScript*

```
new Ajax.Request("http://localhost:8080/gTunes/music/Kings%20Of%20Leon",
                 {    contentType:"text/xml",
                    onComplete:function(response) {
                        var xml = response.responseXML;
                        var root = xml.documentElement;
                        var elements = root.getElementsByTagName("name")
                        alert("Artist name = " + elements[0].firstChild.data);
                    }
                 })
```

■**Note** The JavaScript in Listing 15-12 works only because it is being run from the same host and port as the server application. One of the limitations of JavaScript is that cross-domain Ajax is forbidden for security reasons. However, there are ways around these limitations by using subdomain tricks and also by allowing users of the web service to include JavaScript served by your server. There is even an initiative to create a standard for cross-domain communication (see `http://ajaxian.com/archives/the-fight-for-cross-domain-xmlhttprequest`). However, the topic is broad and beyond the scope of this book.

As you can see in Listing 15-12, by specifying the `contentType` option passed to Prototype's `Ajax.Request` object, you can tell Prototype to send a different `CONTENT_TYPE` header in the request. The `onComplete` event handler can then take the resulting XML and manipulate it via the JavaScript Document Object Model (DOM). So, that's it for the HTTP headers involved in content negotiation. In the next couple of sections, we'll cover some alternative ways to handle different formats.

Content Negotiation Using File Extensions

One of the easiest ways to specify that the client needs a particular format is to use the file extension in the URI. As an example, open the Grails console again, and try the script in Listing 15-13.

Listing 15-13. *Using the File Extension for Content Negotiation*

```
url = new URL("http://localhost:8080/gTunes/music/Kings%20Of%20Leon.xml")

conn = url.openConnection()
artist = new XmlSlurper().parse(conn.content)

println "Artist Name = ${artist.name}"
```

Notice that, unlike the script in Listing 15-11, the definitions of the `CONTENT_TYPE` and `ACCEPT` headers have been removed from this example. Instead, the extension `.xml` is specified in the URI, from which Grails automatically recognizes that XML is being requested and sends back an XML response.

If you remove the XML MIME type definition from the `grails.mime.types` setting in `grails-app/conf/Config.groovy`, Grails will no longer deal with the `.xml` file extension. If you prefer to not use this feature at all, you can disable it completely by setting `grails.mime.file.extensions` in `Config.groovy` to `false`:

```
grails.mime.file.extensions=false
```

Content Negotiation with a Request Parameter

The final form of content negotiation is to use the `format` request parameter. For example, the code in Listing 15-13 can be adapted to use the `format` request parameter simply by changing the first line:

```
url = new URL("http://localhost:8080/gTunes/music/Kings%20Of%20Leon?format=xml")
```

Notice how instead of using the file extension `.xml`, the `format` parameter is passed with a value of `xml`. As an alternative to specifying the `format` parameter in the URL itself, you could provide it via a URL mapping. For example, consider the code added to the `grails-app/conf/UrlMappings.groovy` file in Listing 15-14.

Listing 15-14. *Proving the format Parameter in a URL Mapping*

```
"/music/$artist"(controller:"artist") {
    action = "show"
    format = "xml"
}
```

Highlighted in bold in Listing 15-14 is the `format` parameter. As you learned in Chapter 6, you can provide parameters directly in the URL mapping!

And with that, we have completed the tour of the different ways to trigger content negotiation. However, a typical scenario in content negotiation is to have multiple different views for different format types. In the next section, you'll find out how to achieve this.

Content Negotiation and the View

Consider for a moment the usage of the `withFormat` method in Listing 15-6. You'll note that currently the code is handling two different format types: `xml` and `html`. In the case of `xml`, the code renders some XML directly to the response, and in the case of `html`, it is utilizing a view. However, what if you changed the code to look like the snippet in Listing 15-15?

Listing 15-15. *Multiple View Delegates Within withFormat*

```
withFormat {
    html artist:artist, albums:artist?.albums
    wml artist:artist, albums:artist?.albums
    xml { render artist as XML }
}
```

Notice how in Listing 15-15 there is the addition of a new `withFormat` handler that deals with `wml`. It too delegates to a view, so now you have two different format types delegating to the same view! That's putting a lot of responsibility on the view to know exactly which format type it's dealing with. Imagine the hideous `if/else` branching you would have to do to serve both

HTML and WML in the same view! Luckily, there is another way. If you include the file extension at the end of the view name but before the `.gsp` extension, Grails will choose the view that is most specific.

For example, in the case of Listing 15-15, if you had a view called `grails-app/views/artist/show.wml.gsp`, then that view would be responsible for serving WML pages, and if you had a view called `grails-app/views/artist/show.html.gsp`, that view would deal with standard HTML. Of course, if a view can't be found to match a particular format, then Grails falls back on the usual conventions by using the regular `show.gsp` view. Nevertheless, as you can see, Grails makes it easy to serve different views for different format types using the power of Convention over Configuration.

So, in the earlier "Content Negotiation with the ACCEPT Header" section, we touched on XML marshaling with the `grails.converters` package. In the next few sections, you'll get a more detailed look at the marshaling *and* unmarshaling of XML, including the different ways it can be done.

Marshaling Objects to XML

In the previous sections, we touched on the `render artist as XML` expression used to marshal objects into XML in one line of code. If you take a look back at Listing 15-9, the XML is produced by Grails' built-in converters in the `grails.converters` package. Notice how the `albums` collection has been marshaled into a set of identifiers only. The client could use these identifiers to utilize a separate web service to obtain the XML for each `Album`. Alternatively, you could use the converters provided in the `grails.converters.deep` package that traverse the relationships of a domain class, converting each into XML. All you need to change is the import at the top of the `ArtistController` class to the following:

```
import grails.converters.deep.*
```

The downside is, of course, that you get a much larger XML response, an example of which is shown in Listing 15-16, shortened for brevity.

Listing 15-16. *Marshaling XML with the Deep Converter*

```
<?xml version="1.0" encoding="UTF-8"?>
<artist id="4">
  <albums>
    <album id="4">
      <artist reference="/artist"/>
      <dateCreated>2008-08-04 21:05:08.0</dateCreated>
      <genre>Rock</genre>
      <lastUpdated>2008-08-04 21:05:08.0</lastUpdated>
      <price>10.99</price>
```

```
    <songs>
      <song id="37">
        <album reference="/artist/albums/album"/>
        <artist reference="/artist"/>
        <dateCreated>2008-08-04 21:05:08.0</dateCreated>
        <duration>430346</duration>
        <genre>Rock</genre>

        <lastUpdated>2008-08-04 21:05:08.0</lastUpdated>
        <title>Knocked Up</title>
        <trackNumber>1</trackNumber>
        <year>2007</year>
      </song>
      ...
    </songs>
    <title>Because of the Times</title>
    <year>2007</year>
  </album>
</albums>
<dateCreated>2008-08-04 21:05:08.0</dateCreated>
<lastUpdated>2008-08-04 21:05:08.0</lastUpdated>
<name>Kings of Leon</name>
</artist>
```

The upside is that the client gets a lot more information, which can be parsed and dealt with. Returning to the Grails console, try the script in Listing 15-17.

Listing 15-17. *Using the Deep Converters Results*

```
url = new URL("http://localhost:8080/gTunes/music/Kings%20of%20Leon")

conn = url.openConnection()
conn.addRequestProperty("accept","application/xml")

artist = new XmlSlurper().parse(conn.content)

println "Artist Name = ${artist.name}"
println "Albums ---"
for(album in artist.albums.album) {
    println "Album Title = $album.title"
    println "Songs ---"
    album.songs.song.eachWithIndex { song, i ->
        println "${i+1}) $song.title"
    }
}
```

Notice how in Listing 15-17 you can find out not only about the Artist but also about all of their albums and the songs within those albums. The output from running this script is something like this:

```
Artist Name = Kings of Leon
Albums ---
Album Title = Because of the Times
Songs ---
1) Knocked Up
2) Charmer
...
```

Of course, the XML in Listing 15-16 may not be optimal because it contains a lot of data that the client may not need. Luckily, Grails also provides a simple way to marshal XML using a builder approach. Listing 15-18 shows the ArtistController class using the render method's capability to take a closure that represents the builder code needed to output XML.

Listing 15-18. *Using an XML Builder to Output XML*

```
class ArtistController {
    def show = {
        def a = params.artistName ? Artist.findByName(params.artist) :
                                    Artist.get(params.id)

        if(a) {
            withFormat {
                html artist:a, albums:a?.albums
                xml {
                    render(contentType:"text/xml") {
                        artist(name:a.name) {
                            for(alb in a.albums) {
                                album(title:alb.title,
                                        year:alb.year,
                                        genre:alb.genre,
                                        price:alb.price) {
                                    for(s in alb.songs) {
                                        song(title:s.title,
                                                number:s.trackNumber,
                                                duration:s.duration)
                                    }
                                }
                            }
                        }
```

```
                }
            }
          }
        }
      }
      else {
          response.sendError 404
      }
    }
}
```

To trigger the builder, you can use the render method, passing a contentType argument with a value of text/xml and a closure containing the builder code. The way the builder works is that each method name relates to an XML element. You'll notice from the code in Listing 15-18 that you have to be very careful not to define local variables using names you plan to use for XML elements; otherwise, Groovy will try to invoke them, thinking the variable is a closure. Nevertheless, you can see the result of the code in Listing 15-18 in Listing 15-19.

Listing 15-19. *Output Using the Builder Approach*

```xml
<?xml version="1.0"?>
<artist name="Kings of Leon">
    <album title="Because of the Times" year="2007" genre="Rock" price="10.99">
        <song title="Knocked Up" number="1" duration="430346"/>
        <song title="Charmer" number="2" duration="176893"/>
        ...
    </album>
</artist>
```

As you can see, the XML in Listing 15-19 is far more concise than that produced by the deep converter. Of course, it depends very much on your domain model. For most common cases, the grails.converter package is fine; however, if you do need fine-grained control over the XML produced, then the builder approach is a good alternative.

Marshaling Objects to JSON

As mentioned previously, REST is not limited to XML as a transport medium. JSON is a popular choice for REST web services that have many Ajax clients because of the ease with which it is possible to parse JSON using JavaScript—somewhat unsurprising given JSON is native JavaScript itself.

Fortunately, Grails makes it pretty easy to convert objects and other data structures to JSON using the grails.converters package. Listing 15-20 shows how you can use the render object as JSON expression to output JSON.

Listing 15-20. *Dealing with the all Format*

```
import grails.converters.*
...
withFormat {
    html artist:artist, albums:artist?.albums
    all artist:artist, albums:artist?.albums
    xml { render artist as XML }
    json { render artist as JSON }
}
```

Using file extension content negotiation, if you open a browser and hit the URL
`http://localhost:8080/gTunes/music/Kings Of Leon.json`, Grails will return a JSON
response. Depending on your browser, you may be asked to download the file, since the
rendering of JSON is not typically supported by browsers in the same way XML is. Nevertheless, Grails will do its best to marshal whatever you pass to the render method into
appropriate JSON, an example of which is shown in Listing 15-21.

Listing 15-21. *Example JSON Response*

```
{ "id":26,
  "class":"Artist",
  "albums":[{"class":"Album","id":4}],
  "dateCreated":"2008-08-04T21:05:08Z",
  "lastUpdated":"2008-08-04T21:05:08Z",
   "name":"Kings Of Leon"
}
```

So, now that you have some JSON, what conceivable benefit does it have over XML? Well,
compared to the angle-bracketed XML, it is a little terser. However, the main benefit is to Ajax
clients. Using a library like Prototype, it is trivial to parse the JSON in Listing 15-21, as shown in
Listing 15-22.

Listing 15-22. *Parsing JSON on the Client*

```
new Ajax.Request('http://localhost:8080/gTunes/music/Kings Of Leon.json', {
  method:'get',
  requestHeaders: {Accept: 'application/json'},
  evalJSON: true,
  onSuccess: function(response){
    var artist = response.responseJSON;

    alert("Artist Name = " + artist.name);
  }
});
```

Compare the simplicity of evaluating a block of JSON to the pain of JavaScript DOM programming, and you will realize that JSON is certainly the better choice if your primary audience is Ajax clients. Furthermore, many popular Ajax toolkits, such as Yahoo UI and Ext-JS, allow you to use JSON data sources to populate rich components such as dynamic data tables, which may influence your choice in deciding whether to use JSON.

As well as rendering simple responses, the JSON converter, like the XML converter, also supports deep nested graphs of objects by changing the import to the `grails.converters.deep` package:

```
import grails.converters.deep.JSON
```

Grails also features a builder for constructing custom JSON responses, similar to the XML builder demonstrated in Listing 15-23.

Listing 15-23. *Using the JSON Builder*

```
..
withFormat {
    ...
    json {
        render(contentType:"text/json") {
            name a.name
            albums {
                for(alb in a.albums) {
                    album name:alb.title
                }
            }
        }
    }
}
```

As you can see, to trigger the JSON builder, you can pass the `contentType` parameter with a value of `text/json` or `application/json`. Then, within the body of the closure passed as the last argument, you can construct the JSON. Each method call in the JSON builder creates a new entry in the JSON object. You can create JSON arrays by passing a closure to a method and invoking a method for each array entry. Listing 15-24 shows the result of the JSON builder notation in Listing 15-23.

Listing 15-24. *Result of Using the JSON Builder*

```
{
 "name":"Kings of Leon",
 "albums":[  {"name":"Because of the Times"},
             {"name":"Aha Shake Heartbreak"} ]
}
```

Unmarshaling XML or JSON

Everything you have seen so far is modeled around the use of the HTTP GET method to read data from a REST web service. GET requests in REST are undoubtedly the most common; however, many REST web services also allow users to perform write operations on the server. A key principle of REST is that a GET request should *never* cause the state of the server to change. Other HTTP methods such as POST, PUT, and DELETE should be used in a REST model to perform write operations.

Many public web services that claim to use a RESTful approach in fact ignore this philosophy and design everything around the GET method. A GET is a lot easier to interact with because you can simply type the URL of the web service into your browser to issue a GET request. Other kinds of requests such as POST, PUT, and DELETE, however, require you to use HTTP utilities such as the Firefox Poster plugin or Fiddler, an HTTP debugging proxy, for Windows machines.

Nevertheless, it is best practice to follow the REST philosophy. Modeling everything around GET could be very damaging if you have certain GET requests that fundamentally change the data on your system. Web spiders, such as Google's search engine crawler, could quite easily step on the toes of your application by inadvertently sending GET requests to your web services! In this book, we'll be following the REST philosophy as it was designed to be implemented, even if it's a bit fussier.

Another great thing about REST is that as soon as you read data from a REST web service, you implicitly know how to perform updates to REST resources. Remember, REST stands for Representational *State* Transfer. This implies that when a REST web service sends you some data in XML or JSON, in order to perform a write operation all you need to do is send the changed data back in the same form it was sent to you.

Let's start by looking at the POST request first. In the context of REST, the POST method is used when a web service user wants to update data. For example, assuming you're using the render album as XML approach, if you access one of the albums from the gTunes application using the RESTful paths you established earlier, you'll get some XML back like that shown in Listing 15-25.

Listing 15-25. *XML Returned from a GET Request*

```xml
<?xml version="1.0" encoding="UTF-8"?>
<album id="12">
  <artist id="26"/>
  <dateCreated>2008-08-21 14:26:40.0</dateCreated>
  <genre>Alternative &amp; Punk</genre>
  <lastUpdated>2008-08-21 14:26:40.0</lastUpdated>
  <price>8.99</price>
  <songs>
    <song id="134"/>
    ...
  </songs>
  <title>Aha Shake Heartbreak</title>
  <year>2004</year>
</album>
```

To get the XML in Listing 15-25, you can access the URI `/music/Kings%20of%20Leon/` `Aha%20Shack%20Heartbreak.xml` using file extension content negotiation. Now, immediately you know how to update the data because the format has been sent to you in the `GET` request. But here is the catch. How do you test sending `POST` data to the server? Unlike sending a `GET` request, you can't just type the URI into the browser. To send a `POST` request, you're going to need a little help from the Firefox Poster plugin available from `https://addons.mozilla.org/` `en-US/firefox/addon/2691`.

Once installed, the Poster plugin will add a little "P" icon into the Firefox system tray, as shown in Figure 15-2.

Figure 15-2. *The Poster plugin tray icon*

When you click the Poster icon, it will load a new window separate to the main Firefox window that contains the features of the Poster plugin. Fundamentally, it allows you to specify a URL to send a request to, plus a bunch of other stuff like the HTTP method, any content to send, and so on. Figure 15-3 shows the Poster window with the URL to the XML from Listing 15-25 specified.

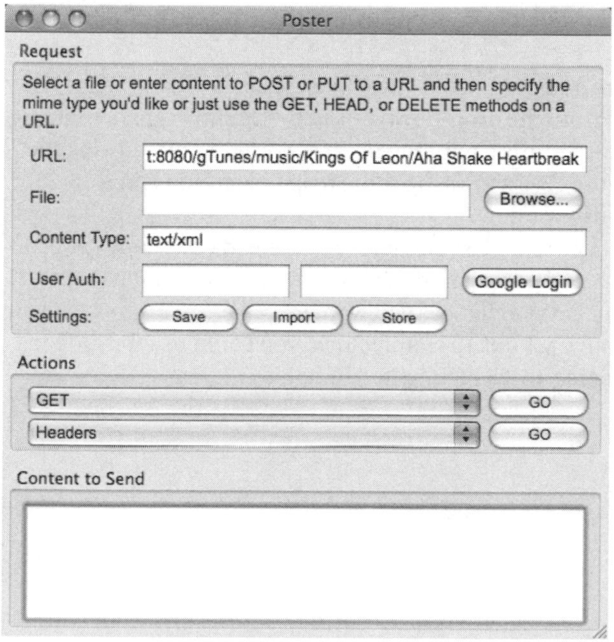

Figure 15-3. *The Poster plugins main window*

In the "Actions" pane, you can add headers like the ACCEPT header by selecting the "Headers" drop-down list and clicking the "Go" button. Figure 15-4 shows how to specify an ACCEPT header of text/xml.

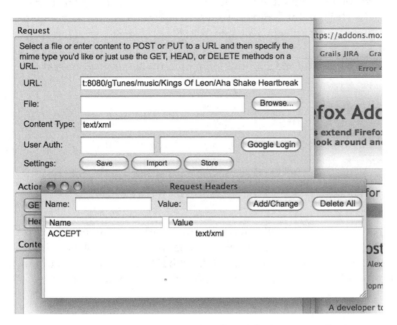

Figure 15-4. *Specifying an ACCEPT header with the Poster plugin*

Once the necessary ACCEPT headers and parameters have been specified, you can send a request by choosing the HTTP method from the drop-down box in the "Actions" panel and hitting the "Go" button. You'll then get the response popping up in a new window showing the XML coming back from the server. Figure 15-5 shows the same response from Listing 15-25 appearing in the Poster plugin's response window.

Now here's the trick to send data back to a REST service. All you need do is copy the text from the response shown in Figure 15-5 and paste it into the Poster plugin's "Content to Send" field. Then simply modify the data to reflect the changes you want to make. For example, if you want to change the genre from Alternative & Punk to simply Rock, you could use the XML in Listing 15-26 with the changes from Listing 15-25 highlighted in bold.

Figure 15-5. *The Poster plugins response window*

Listing 15-26. *Updating the XML to Send to a REST Service*

```
<?xml version="1.0" encoding="UTF-8"?>
<album id="12">
  <artist id="26"/>
  <dateCreated>2008-08-21 14:26:40.0</dateCreated>
  <genre>Rock</genre>
  <lastUpdated>2008-08-21 14:26:40.0</lastUpdated>
  <price>8.99</price>
  <songs>
    <song id="134"/>
    ...
  </songs>
  <title>Aha Shake Heartbreak</title>
  <year>2004</year>
</album>
```

Finally, to send the request use the first drop-down box in the "Actions" panel, change the method to the POST request, and hit the "Go" button. Unfortunately, in this case, the response from the server is a 404. Why? Well, currently the gTunes application can deal with GET requests but not POST requests. If you recall, the URL mapping from Listing 15-2 mapped POST requests onto an action called update, which doesn't exist yet.

Let's add the code necessary to implement the update action. Listing 15-27 shows the complete code, which we will step through in a moment.

Listing 15-27. *Handling POST Requests in a REST Web Service*

```
1 def update = {
2       def album = Album.get(params['album']?.id)
3         if(album) {
4             album.properties = params['album']
5             album.save()
6             withFormat {
7                 html {
8                     render(view:"show", [album:album, artist:album.artist])
9                 }
10                 xml {
11                     if(!album.hasErrors()) {
12                         render album as XML
13                     }
14                     else {
15                         render album.errors as XML
16                     }
17                 }
18             }
19
20         }
21         else {
22             response.sendError 404
23         }
24     }
25 }
```

Listing 15-27 is one of the longer listings you've seen so far in the book and there is a lot going on there, so we'll walk you through the code so you can understand what it is doing. First, on line 2, the Album instance is obtained using the id of the album contained within the params object:

```
2       def album = Album.get(params['album']?.id)
```

But hold on. Aren't you dealing with an XML request here? Where are the reams of XML parsing code? And where did this magical album within the params object come from? Quite simply, when Grails detects an incoming XML request, it will automatically parse it and config-ure the params object based on the contents of the XML. The power of this pattern is that as far as you are concerned, dealing with an XML (or JSON) request is no different from dealing with a regular form submission.

■**Note** Automatic unmarshaling works only with XML that matches the conventions used within the `render as XML` and `render as JSON` automatic marshaling capabilities. If you are using a custom format, then it is your responsibility to unmarshal appropriately.

You can submit the same request to the `update` action using form data that starts with the `album` prefix. Remember how we mentioned that REST models the natural behaviors of the Web? Here you have a prime example of how Grails embraces that by allowing you to eliminate the need to differentiate between regular form submissions and REST web service requests. Another example of this can be seen on line 5, where Grails' normal data-binding pattern, which you learned in Chapter 4, is used to update the `Album` instance:

```
4          album.properties = params['album']
```

Then on line 5, the `Album` instance is saved:

```
5          album.save()
```

With that done, it's time for the `withFormat` method to do its thing and deal with both HTML and XML formats on line 6:

```
6          withFormat {
```

In the case of HTML, for the moment it just renders the `show.gsp` view again:

```
7              html {
8                  render(view:"show", [album:album, artist:album.artist])
9              }
```

The `show.gsp` view could be updated to utilize the `<g:renderErrors>` tag to display any update errors to the user. In the case of XML, the logic is a little different. If there are no errors, then you can simply send the `Album` back to the caller of the REST API with the changes reflected on lines 10 to 13:

```
10             xml {
11                 if(!album.hasErrors()) {
12                     render album as XML
13                 }
                   ...
18             }
```

However, if there are validation errors, you can send an error response using the `errors` property of the `Album` instance. By using the `render` method, you can automatically marshal errors to XML:

```
15                     render album.errors as XML
```

Now you can try calling the `update` action via a REST web service. First, return to the Firefox Poster plugin, and try to resubmit the `POST` request. This time when you submit the `POST` request, you can see the `<genre>` element in the XML has been updated in the response! If you tried to send an invalid value such as a blank `Album` title to the web service, you would get an error response like the one shown in Listing 15-28.

Listing 15-28. *An Error Response from a REST Web Service*

```
<errors>
  <error object= "com.g2one.gtunes.Album"
         field= "title"
         message= "Property [title] of class..."
         rejected-value="" />
</errors>
```

And with that, you have added support, not only for reading information about albums and artists via a REST API but also for updating album details. Feel free to explore the capability further by implementing support for updating artists and songs via `POST` requests. This exercise is similar in each instance and will give you good practice in using Grails' REST support.

Note that adding support for `PUT` and `DELETE` is largely similar to what you've already seen. In the case of a `PUT` request, instead of looking up an existing instance, as you saw on line 3 of Listing 15-27, you would create a brand new instance by passing the `params` object into the constructor, as shown in Listing 15-29.

Listing 15-29. *Binding XML Data to New Instances*

```
def save = {
    def album = new Album(params["album"])
    ...
}
```

The remaining code to deal with `PUT` requests is much like the `update` action in Listing 15-27. As for the `DELETE` requests, you just have to obtain the instance and call the `delete()` method. It's pretty simple really. However, one thing we haven't yet discussed is security.

REST and Security

In Chapter 14, you used the JSecurity framework to secure the gTunes application. Having an open REST API that allows any user to update the data in the gTunes application is probably not desirable. There are a number of different ways to implement security with REST. In fact, the issue of security in REST is one of the hottest points in the SOAP vs. REST debate, because—unlike SOAP, which defines a standard for security called WS-Security—there is no standard for REST security.

If you plan to maintain a completely stateless client API, then you could use request headers such as the `Authorization` HTTP header with some form of token-based authentication. This is a model followed by Google and Amazon in their REST APIs. Alternatively, you could use Secure Sockets Layer (SSL) communication over HTTPS with basic authentication provided by the web server. The topic of security in REST is broad and has many ramifications.

Assuming it's OK to maintain stateful clients, then another, possibly simpler, alternative is to use the JSecurity framework and provide a REST API onto your application's login system. The downside is that clients would be required to support cookies in order for the server to be aware that the client is logged in. The Apache Commons HttpClient (http://hc.apache.org/httpclient-3.x/authentication.html) project is an example of a client-side library that supports cookies, which clients can take advantage of.

Atom and RSS

Atom and RSS are two competing standards to allow the publishing of web feeds. The two formats have proven very popular with many applications, including modern web browsers that support RSS and Atom feeds to provide news headlines, as well as with blog aggregators. Nearly every website you visit nowadays has either an RSS or Atom feed that you can subscribe to, to get the latest news or information. Although the provision of RSS or Atom feeds is not a web service in the traditional sense, it is very similar in that the mechanics involve the exchange of XML data over HTTP.

Moreover, Google is actually standardizing on Atom and the Atom Publishing Protocol (APP) as the format used in all of its web services APIs, so there is clearly a lot of crossover between REST and the syndication formats Atom and RSS. Currently, Grails doesn't provide support for RSS and Atom out of the box, but an excellent Feeds plugin is available in the plugin repository. In the following sections, we'll be covering how to install the Feeds plugin and provide RSS and Atom feeds that show the latest additions to the gTunes library.

To get started, you first need to install the Feeds plugin by running the following command:

```
$ grails install-plugin feeds
```

Creating RSS and Atom Feeds

What the Feeds plugin does is add functionality to the render method to facilitate the rendering of RSS and Atom feeds. Under the covers, the plugin is using the popular Rome library (http://rome.dev.java.net/) to produce the feeds; Rome is yet another example of how Grails promotes reuse of the existing Java ecosystem. Let's look at an example in code of how to use the Feeds plugin; see Listing 15-30.

Listing 15-30. *Rendering RSS and Atom Feeds with the Feeds Plugin*

```
1 def latest = {
2    def newestAlbums = Album.list(max:5, sort:"dateCreated", order:"desc")
3
4    def feed = {
5        title = "Newest Additions to gTunes"
6        link = g.createLink(controller:"store",
7                                          action:"latest",
8                                           params:[format:request.format])
```

```
9            description = "Track the newest additions to the gTunes music store"
10      for(a in newestAlbums) {
11            entry(a.title) {
12                link = g.createLink(controller:"album", action:"show", id:a.id)
13                g.render(template:"/album/album", model:[album:a, artist:a.artist])
14            }
15        }
16    }
17
18    withFormat {
19        rss { render(feedType:"rss", feed) }
20        atom { render(feedType:"atom", feed) }
21    }
22 }
```

The code in Listing 15-30 adds a new action to the StoreController that provides RSS and Atom feeds of the five most recent additions to the albums within gTunes' library of music. Once again, the code takes advantage of Grails' content negotiation feature described earlier in the chapter to deliver both RSS and Atoms feeds. First, on line 2, the five most recent albums are obtained using GORM's list method:

```
2    def newestAlbums = Album.list(max:5, sort:"dateCreated", order:"desc")
```

Then on line 4, the feed is constructed using the builder syntax defined by the Feeds plugin:

```
4    def feed = {
```

The Feeds plugin uses a domain-specific language (DSL) to wrap the inner workings of the Rome API. Your job is limited to specifying the feed title, description, and entries.

■**Tip** For a more comprehensive overview of the syntax supported by the Feeds plugin, refer to the documentation available at http://grails.org/Feeds+Plugin.

Lines 5 to 9 do the job of setting a title for the feed, as well as a more detailed description and a link back to the feed URL:

```
5        title = "Newest Additions to gTunes"
6        link = g.createLink(controller:"store",
7                                        action:"latest",
8                                        params:[format:request.format])
9        description = "Track the newest additions to the gTunes music store"
```

Notice how on line 6 you can take advantage of the `<g:createLink>` tag called as a method to create a link back to the feed with the appropriate format prepopulated. In this example, `title` and `description` have been hard-coded, but you could just as easily pull this information from an i18n message bundle using the `<g:message>` tag called as a method, as described in Chapter 7:

```
title = g.message(code:"gtunes.latest.feed.title")
```

With all the metadata provided to the feed, the next job is to create the entries for the feed. The syntax used by the Feeds plugin is to call a method called `entry`, passing in the entry title and a closure. Within the body of the closure, you are able to set metadata about the entry, including a link back to it. Finally, the return value of the closure is used to populate the markup contained within the body of the feed entry. You can see the mechanics of this in action on lines 11 to 14:

```
11          entry(a.title) {
12              link = g.createLink(controller:"album", action:"show", id:a.id)
13              g.render(template:"/album/album", model:[album:a,
artist:a.artist])
14          }
```

Notice how once again you can use the `<g:createLink>` tag to create a link to the album. Also, to populate the body content of the entry, you can take advantage of the `<g:render>` tag called as a method to render the grails-app/albums/_album.gsp template, which already knows how to format an album appropriately. With that done, it's time to use the feed, and once again you see the `withFormat` method in action on line 18:

```
18    withFormat {
      ...
21    }
```

However, unlike in previous examples, instead of handling HTML or XML, this example uses content negotiation to deliver RSS and Atom formats:

```
19          rss { render(feedType:"rss", feed) }
20          atom { render(feedType:"atom", feed) }
```

There are a few key things to notice about the previous code. First, as you can see within the `withFormat` method, you can enable the handling of RSS and Atom feeds by calling the `rss` and `atom` methods, respectively, passing in a closure that should be invoked in each case. Within the body of each closure, you can see the `render` method used in combination with the `feedType` argument to specify either `rss` or `atom`. To maintain the DRYness[5] of the code, notice how you can pass the same reference to the `feed` closure regardless of whether you are rendering an Atom or an RSS feed.

One final thing to do is to create a new URL mapping in the grails-app/conf/UrlMappings.groovy file so that the feeds are exposed:

---

5. Don't Repeat Yourself (DRY) is an acronym used in programming circles to describe the philosophy of avoiding repetition at all costs.

```
"/store/latest"(controller:"store",action:"latest")
```

Your efforts are complete. To access the RSS feed, you can use the URL http://
localhost:8080/gTunes/store/latest.rss, while the Atom feed can be accessed by
changing the .rss extension to .atom. If you access the RSS feed within Firefox, which
supports RSS, you'll get a page rendered like the one in Figure 15-6.

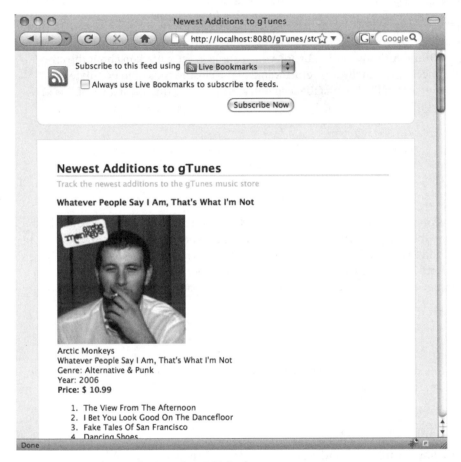

Figure 15-6. *Firefox rendering of an RSS feed*

RSS and Atom Link Discovery

Another feature of most RSS and Atom-enabled browsers is the ability to automatically discover
feed links for the currently viewed page. For example, if you go to http://news.bbc.co.uk in Firefox, you'll notice a little blue feed icon appear in the address bar, as shown in Figure 15-7.

Figure 15-7. *Firefox RSS feed detection in action*

It may seem like magic, but the way it works is that developers need to provide the necessary HTML <meta> headers that link to the RSS or Atom feed. Only then will a browser such as Firefox discover the feed. Luckily, the Feeds plugin provides support for doing just this using the <feed:meta> tag. Say, for example, you wanted the RSS or Atom icon to appear in the browser when users visited the gTunes store; you could quite easily enable this by modifying the grails-app/views/layouts/storeLayout.gsp layout as shown in Listing 15-31.

Listing 15-31. *Providing RSS and Atom Metadata*

```
<html>
    <head>
        <feed:meta kind="rss"
                              version="2.0"
                              controller="store"
                              action="latest"
                              params="[format:'rss']"/>
        <feed:meta kind="atom"
                              version="1.0"
                              controller="store"
                              action="latest"
                              params="[format:'atom']"/>
        ...
    </head>
    ...
</html>
```

Now if you go to http://localhost:8080/gTunes/store, you'll see the same browser address bar links in Firefox as you did on the BBC! And with that, it is now time to look at a different web services paradigm via the SOAP specifications.

SOAP

SOAP is a specification for web services that originated in a joint Microsoft and IBM effort. SOAP was originally an acronym for Simple Object Access Protocol; however, after discovering it wasn't simple or an access protocol and didn't have anything to do with objects, the creators decided to ditch the acronym, so now it's just called SOAP.

Although REST is designed to be used with simple tools like your browser, SOAP as a technology cannot be used effectively without good tooling and technological support. The premise of SOAP is that, through the use of tools, you generate a web service descriptor using the Web Services Description Language (WSDL). SOAP clients can then use the WSDL to generate (using tooling support) a client that is capable of invoking the SOAP service in their language of choice.

Although REST is all about resources and transferring XML representations of those resources, SOAP is fundamentally a Remote Procedure Call (RPC) technology. Instead of being an architectural pattern like REST, it encourages developers to continue to think in objects and function calls. It just so happens that those objects and function calls are remote web services.

To support this RPC model, the SOAP specification includes the facility to describe within the WSDL (in XML Schema) how objects should be marshaled to and from XML. Each data type is described in XML Schema, and Java tools digest the WSDL and attempt to automatically marshal objects to and from XML using the schema.

The primary goal of SOAP is to enable interoperability between different languages and tools using XML as the transport medium, something that REST achieves just as well. However, SOAP also includes a number of complementary standards, under the WS-* banner, that cover everything from security and transactions to management and discovery. Furthermore, unlike REST, which is primarily based on HTTP, SOAP doesn't mandate the protocol and could be used over a range of protocols including SMTP and FTP. All in all, it's a lofty goal; unfortunately, the various SOAP specifications have gone through a number of drafts, and the implementors of the specifications have continually had to play catch-up.

To make matters worse, it has taken a while for SOAP vendors and users to decide what the best practices are for implementing SOAP (see `http://www.ibm.com/developerworks/webservices/library/ws-whichwsdl/`). Some early adopters settled on a pattern for binding called RPC/encoded (rpc-enc) for the SOAP message bodies. Later, another pattern called *document/literal* (doc-lit) became popular. Currently, four styles are in existence:

- RPC/encoded (rpc-enc)

- RPC/literal (rpc-lit)

- Document/encoded (doc-enc)

- Document/literal (doc-lit)

The result is that not all SOAP implementations can communicate with one another. To mitigate this problem, a Web Services Interoperability (WS-I, `http://www.ws-i.org/`) group was formed that is designed to make sense of all the SOAP standards from the W3C and Oasis and provide recommendations as to what can be used and what cannot because of problems with interoperability. All in all, SOAP could be viewed as a bit of a mess, but the good news is things can only get better, and the SOAP stacks are improving. There are advantages to using SOAP over REST, including a defined specification for security called WS-Security. Additionally, there are many existing adopters of SOAP, so it isn't going away anytime soon. Competition is good, and REST has helped drive massive improvements in the SOAP stacks as they play catch-up to the simplicity provided by REST.

In the following sections, we'll cover the different ways you can implement SOAP web services in Grails and also how you can invoke SOAP web services from Grails.

SOAP Web Services via Plugins

If you are looking to expose a SOAP service with Grails, you are currently rather spoiled for choice. Three plugins add the capability to expose SOAP services, each using a different underlying framework. The plugins are as follows:

- XFire Plugin (`http://www.grails.org/XFire+plugin`): The XFire plugin builds on the original XFire project (`http://xfire.codehaus.org/`), allowing you to expose Grails services as SOAP services. The XFire plugin is, as of this writing, the most mature of the SOAP plugins.

- Axis 2 Plugin (`http://www.grails.org/Apache+Axis2+Plugin`): The Axis 2 plugin builds on the Apache Axis 2 framework (Axis 1 was the first open source SOAP stack available for Java). The plugin works by integrating the WSO2 Web Services for Spring project (`http://wso2.org/projects/wsf/spring`) that integrates Axis 2 with Spring. Since Grails is built on Spring, anything that can integrate with Spring can integrate with Grails.

- Metro Plugin (`http://jax-ws-commons.dev.java.net/grails/`): This is a plugin that integrates with Metro (`http://metro.dev.java.net/`), the web services stack that is part of the Glassfish umbrella project. The Metro plugin allows you to use standard JSR-224 Java API for XML-based Web Services (JAX-WS) annotations on Grails service classes to expose a SOAP web service.

So, you have several options. Each is pretty trivial to use, but we'll take a look at how to go about using the XFire plugin as an example. First you need to install the plugin by running the `grails install-plugin` command as follows:

```
$ grails install-plugin xfire
```

Once the plugin is installed, it works by integrating with the Grails service classes that were described in Chapter 11. The way it does this is by making each service available as a SOAP web service under the `/services` URI. To ensure this URI is not dealt with by Grails, you need to add a constraint to the default URL mapping in `grails-app/conf/UrlMappings.groovy`, as shown in Listing 15-32.

Listing 15-32. *Changing the Grails URL Mappings to Exclude the /services URI*

```
  "/$controller/$action?/$id?"{
    constraints {
        controller(matches:/.*[^(services)].*/)
    }
 }
```

As you can see in Listing 15-32, by using the matches constraint you can tell Grails not to match the /services URI. Now, let's try to create an example SOAP service by running the following command:

```
$ grails create-service com.g2one.gtunes.Album
```

You'll end up with a new service class called AlbumService located in the grails-app/services directory under the package com.g2one.gtunes. Now try to write a method in the AlbumService that finds all the album titles for a given artist. Listing 15-33 shows the code for the AlbumService class.

Listing 15-33. *The AlbumService Class*

```
package com.g2one.gtunes

class AlbumService {

    String[] findAlbumsForArtist(String artistName) {
        def artist = Artist.findByName(artistName)
        def albums = []
        if(artist) {
            albums = Album.findAllByArtist(artist)
        }
        return albums.title as String[]
    }
}
```

You can write a simple unit test that tests the behavior of this method using the generated test in the test/unit directory called AlbumServiceTests. Listing 15-34 shows an example test for the findAlbumsForArtist method.

Listing 15-34. *Testing the Service Code*

```
import grails.test.*

void testFindAlbumsForArtist() {
    def artist = new Artist(name:"Beck")
    MockUtils.mockDomain(Artist, [artist])
    MockUtils.mockDomain(Album, [new Album(title:"Odelay", artist:artist),
                                 new Album(title:"Guero", artist:artist)])

    def albumService = new AlbumService()

    def results =  albumService.findAlbumsForArtist("Beck")
    assertEquals 2,results.size()
    assertEquals "Odelay", results[0]

    results =  albumService.findAlbumsForArtist("Rubbish")

    assertEquals 0, results.size()
}
```

With that done, it's time to utilize the features of the XFire plugin. All you need to do to expose the AlbumService as a SOAP web service is to add a single line to the AlbumService class definition as follows:

```
static expose = ['xfire']
```

What this says is that you want to "expose" the AlbumService class to the world as a web service using the XFire plugin. You'll see this convention used elsewhere in Grails and its plugins. For example, using the Remoting plugin (http://grails.org/Remoting+Plugin), which allows you to expose Grails services over the Remote Method Invocation (RMI) standard, is configured as follows:

```
static expose = ['rmi']
```

To test the SOAP web service, run Grails with the grails run-app command. The XFire plugin uses the /services URI to map to SOAP web services. In the case of the AlbumService, the full URI to the exposed web service is /services/album where the /album part is taken from the name of the service. To get the WSDL for the AlbumService, you can access the URL http://localhost:8080/gTunes/services/album?wsdl. The XFire plugin generates the WSDL for each service automatically at runtime. The WSDL itself is a rather long and unwieldy XML format that is far too long to list here—heaven knows how authors of SOAP books manage! Nevertheless, Listing 15-35 shows a much shortened version of the XML you're likely to get back.

Listing 15-35. *Example Generated WSDL*

```
<?xml version="1.0" encoding="UTF-8"?>
<wsdl:definitions targetNamespace="http://gtunes.g2one.com"
                  xmlns:tns="http://gtunes.g2one.com"
                  xmlns:wsdlsoap="http://schemas.xmlsoap.org/wsdl/soap/"
                  xmlns:soap12="http://www.w3.org/2003/05/soap-envelope"
                  xmlns:xsd="http://www.w3.org/2001/XMLSchema"
                  xmlns:soapenc11="http://schemas.xmlsoap.org/soap/encoding/"
                  xmlns:soapenc12="http://www.w3.org/2003/05/soap-encoding"
                  xmlns:soap11="http://schemas.xmlsoap.org/soap/envelope/"
                  xmlns:wsdl="http://schemas.xmlsoap.org/wsdl/">
  <wsdl:types>
    <xsd:schema xmlns:xsd="http://www.w3.org/2001/XMLSchema"
            attributeFormDefault="qualified"
            elementFormDefault="qualified"
            targetNamespace="http://gtunes.g2one.com">
        <xsd:element name="findAlbumsForArtist">
          <xsd:complexType>
          ..
          </xsd:complexType>
          ..
        </xsd:element>
        ...
    </xsd:scema>
        ...
  </wsdl:types>
  ...
</wsdl:definitions>
```

As you can see, it's not something that mere mortals should have to digest given that even the namespace definitions take ten lines. Fortunately, SOAP is designed to be used in conjunction with good tools and frameworks—enter the Groovy-WS project.

Calling SOAP from the Client

Unlike REST, calling SOAP services requires jumping through several hoops. It is worth investigating what SOAP tools are available on your platform. On the Mac, there is the excellent Mac SOAP Client project (http://code.google.com/p/mac-soapclient/) that provides a useful graphical utility for testing SOAP web services. Figure 15-8 shows an example of its usage. Notice how you can specify the URL to the WSDL, which is then automatically digested by the Mac SOAP client.

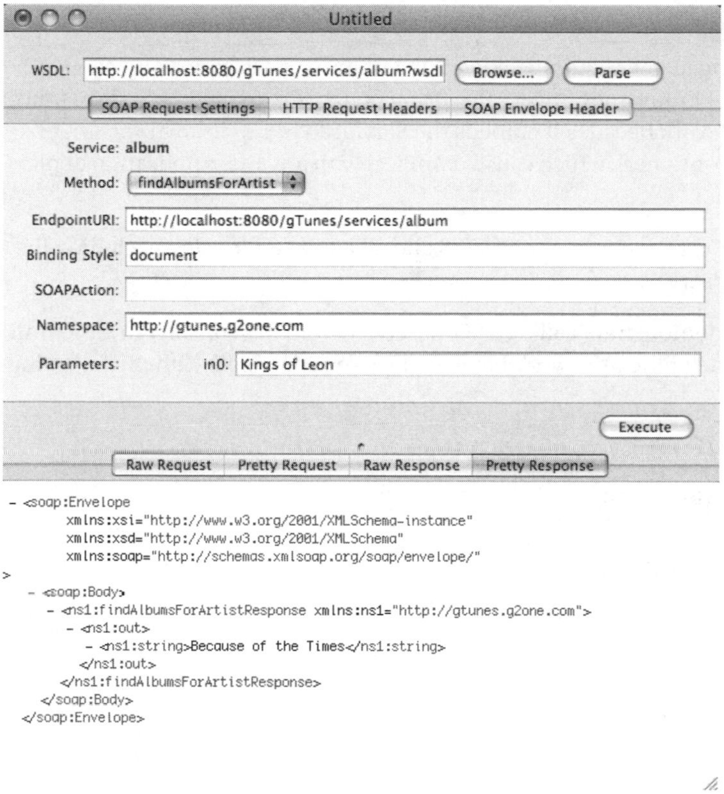

Figure 15-8. *The Mac SOAP client*

As you can see, you can specify in the drop-down the method of the SOAP service to execute and what parameters to pass. The tabs at the bottom allow you to see the outgoing request and the response from the SOAP service. That's all very useful for debugging your SOAP services, but let's look at how you can call a SOAP service from Groovy. To do so, you can use the Groovy-WS project available at `http://groovy.codehaus.org/GroovyWS`.

■**Note** The current XFire plugin for Grails is based on the original XFire project, while Groovy-WS is based on Apache CXF, which is the successor to XFire. As of this writing, there isn't a CXF plugin for Grails. However, it can be configured manually as described in the "Grails + CXF Example" tutorial at `http://docs.codehaus.org/pages/viewpage.action?pageId=85983334`.

Two downloads are available:

- The full JAR containing all the required dependencies for both the server and client portions of Groovy-WS including the Servlet APIs. If you plan to use Groovy-WS from Grails, then this JAR *will not* work because it embeds the Servlet APIs and its own version of Jetty (Grails' default container), which causes conflicts with any web application deployment (including Grails).

- A trimmed-down JAR that contains Groovy-WS and all its dependencies, excluding the Servlet APIs and Jetty server.

For this example, we'll demonstrate calling a SOAP service from the console, so either JAR will do. Simply download one of the JARs, and then run the Groovy console with the following command:

```
$ groovyConsole -cp /path/to/groovyws-all-0.3.1.jar
```

Now try the script in Listing 15-36.

Listing 15-36. *Calling a SOAP Web Service*

```
import groovyx.net.ws.WSClient

def proxy = new WSClient("http://localhost:8080/gTunes/services/album?wsdl",
                         this.class.classLoader)

albums = proxy.findAlbumsForArtist("Tracy Chapman")

println "Found (${albums.string.size()}) Albums"
println "-------------"
albums.string.each {
    println it
}
```

The example in Listing 15-31 uses the Groovy-WS project's dynamic SOAP client called groovyx.net.ws.WSClient that automatically digests the WSDL and creates an appropriate interface for interacting with it. Using the proxy created by WSClient, you can invoke the findAlbumsForArtist method as if it were a regular method.

Oddly, the JAXB specification requires that array types in Java be returned as ArrayOf<Type> definitions on the client. Hence, the findAlbumsForArtist method returns a type that is actually ArrayOfString and not a String[] as you might expect. The intricacies of how SOAP and SOAP frameworks marshal objects from one type to another from client to server is beyond the scope of this book. To obtain the actual String[], you can call the ArrayOfStrings.getString() method, as shown in the example in Listing 15-31. To wrap things up, Figure 15-9 shows what the result of this script looks like in the Groovy console.

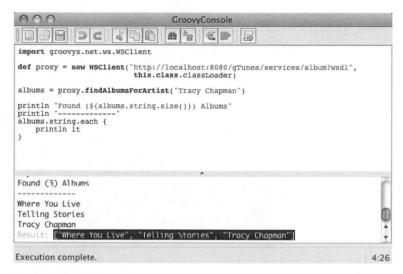

Figure 15-9. *Calling a SOAP service from the Groovy console*

Summary

Once again, a lot of ground has been covered in this chapter. Now you should have a good understanding of the options available to you when developing web services on the Grails platform. Whether you choose REST or SOAP depends on a number of factors, some possibly outside your control. Nevertheless, you are safe in the knowledge that there is good support for both paradigms in Grails.

In your exploration of REST, you learned how to leverage Grails content negotiation features to deal with REST requests. You explored how to marshal both XML and JSON and how to invoke REST web services from Groovy and JavaScript clients. On the SOAP side, you discovered how to expose a Grails service as a SOAP service and how to use the Groovy-WS project to invoke SOAP web services. You even got to explore a little bit outside the realms of strict web services by creating RSS and Atom feeds for the gTunes application.

There is still ground to be covered, however, and in the next chapter you'll be learning how to take advantage of Grails' close integration with the Spring framework. Stay tuned.

CHAPTER 16

■ ■ ■

Leveraging Spring

The ever-popular Spring Framework (http://www.springframework.org) was one of the first frameworks to pioneer simplified development in the Java space. Promoting the use of Plain Old Java Objects (POJOs), rather than objects tied to specific Java APIs such as EJB and JMS, Spring shot to prominence and is now integrated into pretty much every popular Java open source framework. However, it's not just the open source software advocates who have been quick to integrate Spring; major software vendors such as BEA (now part of Oracle) have chosen to base their software on the Spring Framework.

In this chapter, we'll cover what Spring is, how it relates to Grails, and how you can leverage it to do some pretty interesting things. Spring is a huge framework in itself that provides wrappers and utility classes for pretty much every common problem found using Java technology; hence, full coverage of Spring is beyond the scope of this book. Nevertheless, we'll go through a quick overview so you can garner a basic understanding of what Spring is.

Spring Basics

Spring is the engine that underpins Grails. At its core, it is a dependency injection container that allows you to configure and wire together dependencies. When using raw Spring, this is typically done in an XML format, as shown in Listing 16-1.

Listing 16-1. *Spring's XML Format*

```
<beans>
  <bean id="myDataSource" class="org.apache.commons.dbcp.BasicDataSource"
              destroy-method="close">
    <property name="driverClassName" value="org.hsqldb.jdbcDriver"/>
    <property name="url" value="jdbc:hsqldb:hsql://localhost:9001"/>
    <property name="username" value="sa"/>
    <property name="password" value=""/>
  </bean>
```

```
    <bean id="mySessionFactory"
                class="org.springframework.orm.hibernate3.LocalSessionFactoryBean">
      <property name="dataSource" ref="myDataSource"/>
      <property name="mappingResources">
        <list>
          <value>product.hbm.xml</value>
        </list>
      </property>
      <property name="hibernateProperties">
        <value>
          hibernate.dialect=org.hibernate.dialect.HSQLDialect
        </value>
      </property>
    </bean>
</beans>
```

■**Note** In recent times, Spring has been extended to allow this type of configuration to be done using Java 5 annotations instead of XML. See `http://static.springframework.org/spring/docs/2.5.x/reference/beans.html#beans-annotation-config` for further information.

The example in Listing 16-1 defines two Spring "beans" using the `<bean>` element:

- `myDataSource`: An instance of the `org.apache.commons.dbcp.BasicDataSource` class that uses an HSQLDB database running on port 9001

- `mySessionFactory`: A Hibernate `SessionFactory` using the `HSQLDialect` and a single Hibernate XML mapping file called `product.hbm.xml`

You set the properties of each bean using the `<property>` element. Notice how you can reference beans you have defined using the `ref` attribute:

```
<property name="dataSource" ref="myDataSource"/>
```

As an alternative to explicitly managing dependencies as in the previous example, you can configure beans for "autowiring," in which case Spring will try to wire your dependencies together automatically. Autowiring can be configured using the type or the name on the `<bean>` element:

```
<bean autowire="byType" ...>
   ...
</bean>
```

In this case, the type of class is used to calculate how beans are wired together; however, you can also specify autowiring to happen by bean name using a value of byName for the autowire attribute. See `http://static.springframework.org/spring/docs/2.5.x/reference/beans.html#beans-factory-autowire` for more information.

Once you have configured a bunch of beans, you can construct an `org.springframework.context.ApplicationContext` instance. You can do this in a number of different ways. With XML, you could use a `ClassPathXmlApplicationContext` instance that searches the classpath for the given XML file name:

```
ApplicationContext applicationContext =
                        new ClassPathXmlApplicationContext("beans.xml")
```

Once you have an `ApplicationContext`, you can query it for any configured beans, as shown in Listing 16-2.

Listing 16-2. *Using the ApplicationContext*

```
SessionFactory sessionFactory = applicationContext.getBean("mySessionFactory")
```

With that rather simplistic introduction out the way, let's look at the Spring and Grails combo.

Spring and Grails

You may well be wondering at this point how all this relates to Grails. Essentially, the way Grails works is that it does what Spring's XML does for you at runtime. Instead of you defining an XML file with all the dependencies configured, Grails makes some decisions based on the conventions in the project and automatically configures Spring using sensible defaults. However, all Grails objects are essentially Spring beans that have been configured for autowiring by name.

Dependency Injection and Grails

The way Grails allows you to inject services into other Grails classes is powered by Spring. Grails takes the class name and infers a bean name from it. For example, the `com.g2one.gtunes.StoreService` becomes the bean called `storeService`. Then you can simply define a property with the appropriate name and have it injected by Spring:

```
def storeService
```

If you prefer to look up beans explicitly, then you can always use the `ApplicationContext` directly. All you have to do is implement the interface `org.springframework.context.ApplicationContextAware`, and Grails will inject the `ApplicationContext` instance into your class. Listing 16-3 shows the updates to the `StoreController` class needed to achieve this.

Listing 16-3. *Implementing ApplicationContextAware*

```
import org.springframework.context.*

class StoreController implements ApplicationContextAware {
    ApplicationContext applicationContext

    StoreService getStoreService() {  applicationContext.getBean("storeService") }
    ...
}
```

A concern about Grails often raised by Spring users is that they will lose some control without the fine-grained ability to micromanage each bean definition. This concern is unfounded because although Grails does configure beans for you, you retain the ability to override any bean definition and add your own bean definitions.

You can achieve this in a couple of ways. If you are used to Spring's XML format and prefer it, then you can create a file called `grails-app/conf/spring/resources.xml` and add your XML bean definitions in the regular Spring way. However, the preferred way in Grails is to use the Spring DSL provided by Grails. In the next section, you'll learn about the Spring DSL and how you can use it to manipulate Grails' Spring configuration.

The BeanBuilder DSL

In early versions of Grails, a Grails application was configured by generating the necessary Spring XML at runtime. The generated XML would then be parsed into bean definitions. All in all, it was a rather clunky solution to the problem of creating Spring bean definitions at runtime. Later, the Grails developers came up with a new way of configuring Spring encapsulated by the `grails.spring.BeanBuilder` class.

Essentially, Grails searches the directory `grails-app/conf/spring` for any Groovy scripts. By default, Grails creates a single script called `resources.groovy` in the `grails-app/conf/spring` directory when you create a project. Figure 16-1 shows the `resources.groovy` script nested snugly within the gTunes project.

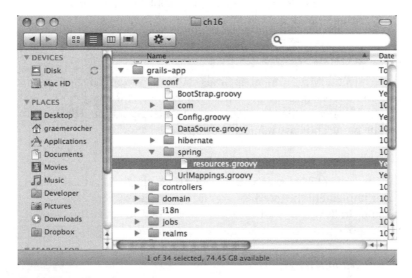

Figure 16-1. *The resources.groovy script*

The `resources.groovy` script itself contains a single property called beans that is assigned a block of code, as shown in Listing 16-4.

Listing 16-4. *The beans Property*

```
beans = {
    // Place your Spring DSL code here
}
```

The beans property is equivalent to the root <beans> element in Spring XML. Now let's find out how to define a Spring bean using the BeanBuilder DSL.

Defining Spring Beans

To define a bean with BeanBuilder, you need to invoke a method with the bean class as the first argument. For example, the myDataSource bean from Listing 16-1 can be defined using BeanBuilder, as shown in Listing 16-5.

Listing 16-5. *Defining a Bean*

```
myDataSource(org.apache.commons.dbcp.BasicDataSource) { bean ->
    bean.destroyMethod = "close"
    driverClassName"org.hsqldb.jdbcDriver"
    url="jdbc:hsqldb:hsql://localhost:9001"
    username="sa"
    password=""
}
```

The Spring bean identifier is taken from the method name you invoke, while the class of the bean is the first argument. The final argument to the method is a Groovy closure that lets you define the properties of the bean.

The example in Listing 16-5 sets the driverClassName, url, username, and password properties of the myDataSource bean within the closure. Notice also that the closure's first argument allows you to set any property on the Spring org.springframework.beans.factory.support. AbstractBeanDefinition class. The example in Listing 16-5 sets the destroyMethod of the bean to close using this technique:

```
bean.destroyMethod = "close"
```

This is equivalent to the destroy-method attribute used in the <bean> element of Spring XML. You may want to set a number of other useful properties in the bean argument, including the following:

- autowire: Allows you to control whether a bean is a candidate for autowiring. This can be set to true (defaults to autowiring by name), byName, byType, or byConstructor.

- abstract: Whether this bean is an abstract bean (see the section "Abstract Beans").

- dependsOn: Specify the names of the beans that the bean depends on as a List. Spring will ensure dependent beans are initialized first.

- destroyMethod: The method to call when the bean is destroyed, because of container shutdown.

- `factoryBean`: The bean that is used to construct instances of this bean (see the section "Factory Beans").

- `initMethod`: The method to call when the bean is initialized.

- `parent`: The parent of this bean definition (see the section "Abstract Beans").

- `scope`: The scope of the bean (see the section "Bean Scopes").

Each of these properties allows you to control the manner in which a bean is constructed and disposed of. One thing to note is that the code in Listing 16-5 works because the `BasicDataSource` class has a default constructor. If there is no default constructor, then you can pass arguments to the bean's constructor by simply appending them after the class name:

```
helloWorldString(String, "hello world!")
```

In this case, a new `java.lang.String` will be created as a bean called `helloWorldString` using the `String(String)` constructor. Also, `BeanBuilder` supports Groovy's additional default constructor that takes a `Map` that allows you to set properties on the instance after it is constructed. This is quite common in GORM; for example, to create a new `Album` instance, you can do the following:

```
new Album(title:"The Bends", genre:"Alternative")
```

To do the same thing with `BeanBuilder`, you can do the following:

```
theBendsAlbum(Album, title:"The Bends", genre:"Alternative")
```

As you can see from the previous example, by specifying a sequence of named arguments after the class, you can set properties on the bean.

Overriding Spring Beans

Any Spring bean that is automatically defined by Grails can be overridden by creating a bean of the same name in the `grails-app/conf/spring/resources.groovy` file or the equivalent XML version. You can find a complete list of names of the beans that Grails configures automatically in the "Plugins" section of the reference documentation for Grails at `http://grails.org/doc/1.1.x`.

As you learned in Chapter 13, Grails itself is configured by plugins, and each plugin typically defines a `doWithSpring` closure that uses `BeanBuilder` syntax to configure Spring in some way. The following are some of the more critical beans that Grails configures that you may want to consider overriding:

- `dataSource`: The `javax.sql.DataSource` instance that represents the connection to the database.

- `jspViewResolver`: The `org.springframework.web.servlet.ViewResolver` instance that Grails uses to resolve GSP or JSP views. You can override this bean to integrate custom view technologies, such as FreeMarker (`http://freemarker.org/`), into Grails.

- `localeResolver`: The `org.springframework.web.servlet.LocaleResolver` instance that Grails uses to resolve the `Locale` of an incoming request.

- messageSource: The org.springframework.context.MessageSource instance that Grails uses to resolve i18n messages (discussed in Chapter 7).

- multipartResolver: The org.springframework.web.multipart.MultipartResolver instance that Grails uses to handle file uploads (discussed in Chapter 4).

- sessionFactory: The org.hibernate.SessionFactory instance used to configure Hibernate.

- transactionManager: The org.springframework.transaction.PlatformTransactionManager instance Grails uses to manage transactions using Spring's transaction abstraction (discussed in Chapter 11).

As an example, say you wanted to override the dataSource bean to use a C3PO (http://sourceforge.net/projects/c3p0) connection pool. All you have to do is provide a bean in the grails-app/conf/spring/resources.groovy file with the corresponding name, as shown in Listing 16-6.

Listing 16-6. *Overriding the dataSource Bean*

```
dataSource(com.mchange.v2.c3p0.ComboPooledDataSource) { bean ->
    bean.destroyMethod = "close"
    driverClass"org.hsqldb.jdbcDriver"
    jdbcUrl="jdbc:hsqldb:hsql://localhost:9001"
    user="sa"
    password=""
}
```

Factory Beans

A common pattern in Spring is the factory bean, essentially a bean that constructs another bean. In Spring, factory beans are encapsulated by the org.springframework.beans.factory.FactoryBean interface, as shown in Listing 16-7.

Listing 16-7. *The FactoryBean Interface*

```
public interface FactoryBean {
    Object getObject() throws Exception;
    Class getObjectType();
    boolean isSingleton();
}
```

You've already seen a factory bean being used in the Spring XML in Listing 16-1. The org.springframework.orm.hibernate3.LocalSessionFactoryBean class is a FactoryBean instance that constructs a Hibernate org.hibernate.SessionFactory instance. The LocalSessionFactoryBean class implements the FactoryBean interface so that the getObject() method returns a fully constructed SessionFactory instance.

In other words, although the type of the factory bean is LocalSessionFactoryBean, the finally constructed bean is actually an instance of the SessionFactory class. Listing 16-8 shows an example of using the LocalSessionFactoryBean instance with BeanBuilder.

Listing 16-8. *Using LocalSessionFactoryBean with BeanBuilder*

```
mySessionFactory(org.springframework.orm.hibernate3.LocalSessionFactoryBean) {
    dataSource = myDataSource
    mappingResources = ['product.hbm.xml']
    hibernateProperties = ['hibernate.dialect':'org.hibernate.dialect.HSQLDialect']
}
```

There are a few interesting things to note about the example in Listing 16-8. First, as you can see, you can reference other beans simply by referencing the name of the bean:

```
dataSource = myDataSource
```

Here, the `myDataSource` bean that was defined in Listing 16-5 is referenced. You can even reference beans that haven't been defined yet or that are defined by Grails. For example, to reference the `dataSource` bean constructed by Grails instead, you can use the `ref` method:

```
dataSource = ref("dataSource")
```

Second, note the usage of Groovy `Map` and `List` literals in Listing 16-8 when defining bean properties:

```
mappingResources = ['product.hbm.xml']
hibernateProperties = ['hibernate.dialect':'org.hibernate.dialect.HSQLDialect']
```

Compared to the Spring XML, the Groovy syntax is far more concise and readable. Now, typically factory beans do implement the `FactoryBean` interface defined earlier, but it is important to note that you don't have to implement this interface to use factory beans. By using the `factoryMethod` property, you can implement similar logic. For example, Listing 16-9 constructs a `java.util.Calendar` instance that is prototyped. This means that a new bean is constructed every time you call the `getBean(String)` method of the `ApplicationContext` class or the bean is wired into another bean (you'll learn more in the "Bean Scopes" section).

Listing 16-9. *Using the factoryMethod Property*

```
calendarBean(java.util.Calendar) { bean ->
    bean.factoryMethod = "getInstance"
    bean.scope = "prototype"
}
```

Notice how in Listing 16-9 the `factoryMethod` property of the bean argument is used to specify that in order to construct a `Calendar` instance the static `getInstance()` method must be called. You can even use other beans as factories. For example, to create another bean from the `calendarBean` in Listing 16-9, you can simply pass the name of the bean as an argument to the bean-defining method:

```
USCalendar(calendarBean) {
    firstDayOfWeek = Calendar.SUNDAY
}
```

```
frenchCalendar(calendarBean) {
    firstDayOfWeek = Calendar.MONDAY
}
```

In this example, two new beans are defined, called USCalendar and frenchCalendar, that both use the calendarBean as their factory and set a different firstDayOfWeek property for each bean. The fun with factory beans doesn't end there. You can also define a method that needs to be called to construct the bean:

```
timeZoneBean(calendarBean:"getTimeZone")
```

In this example, a new bean called timeZoneBean will be constructed by invoking the get-TimeZone() method of the calendarBean instance.

Inner Beans

Occasionally you may need to define a bean that you don't want to expose to clients because it relates to the internal workings of another bean. To achieve this, you can use inner beans. To define an inner bean, you can assign a closure to a property where the first argument to the closure is the bean type. For example, if you wanted to define the myDataSource bean as an inner bean of the mySessionFactory bean, you could do so, as shown in Listing 16-10.

Listing 16-10. *Using Inner Beans*

```
mySessionFactory(org.springframework.orm.hibernate3.LocalSessionFactoryBean) {
    dataSource = { org.apache.commons.dbcp.BasicDataSource bd ->
        driverClassName"org.hsqldb.jdbcDriver"
        url="jdbc:hsqldb:hsql://localhost:9001"
        username="sa"
        password=""
    }
    mappingResources = ['product.hbm.xml']
    hibernateProperties = ['hibernate.dialect':'org.hibernate.dialect.HSQLDialect']
}
```

With the example in Listing 16-10, only the mySessionFactory bean will be exposed because the dataSource property has been defined using an inner bean.

Abstract Beans

An abstract bean in Spring is more akin to the template pattern than an abstract class in Java. Essentially, you can define an incomplete, or *abstract*, bean that provides a set of common properties but that is not itself instantiated. Other beans can then extend from the abstract bean and inherit any properties defined on said abstract bean.

For example, consider the case where you are defining multiple data sources. Each data source uses the same driver, so it would be painful and would waste time to have to repeat this information over and over. Instead, you could define an abstract bean that sets the driverClassName property, and any other common properties, and then create individual beans that use the abstract bean as a parent. Listing 16-11 shows an example.

Listing 16-11. *Using Abstract Beans*

```
dataSourceCommons {
    driverClassName"org.hsqldb.jdbcDriver"
    username="sa"
    password=""
}
firstDataSource(org.apache.commons.dbcp.BasicDataSource) { bean ->
    bean.parent = dataSourceCommons
    url="jdbc:hsqldb:hsql://localhost:9001"
}
secondDataSource(org.apache.commons.dbcp.BasicDataSource) { bean ->
    bean.parent = dataSourceCommons
    url="jdbc:hsqldb:hsql://localhost:9002"
}
```

In Listing 16-11, the code defines an abstract bean called dataSourceCommons. BeanBuilder assumes that if you don't pass a class name as the first argument, then the bean is abstract. Alternatively, if you have a bean definition that accepts a class name and you want it to be abstract, then you can set the abstract property of the bean argument to true:

```
dataSourceCommons(org.apache.commons.dbcp.BasicDataSource) { bean ->
    bean.abstract = true
    driverClassName"org.hsqldb.jdbcDriver"
    username="sa"
    password=""
}
```

Returning to Listing 16-11, the remaining code then constructs a further two beans called firstDataSource and secondDataSource, each of which sets the parent property of the bean argument to dataSourceCommons. This allows these beans to inherit the properties set on the abstract bean dataSourceCommons.

Bean Scopes

By default, all Spring beans are singleton scoped. This means that there is only ever one instance of the bean within the Spring container. As you saw in the "Factory Beans" section, beans can also be prototype scoped. In this case, a new instance of the bean is created every time the bean is requested. Several other scopes are available, listed here in order of their longevity:

- prototype: A new bean is created every time the getBean(name) method of the ApplicationContext is called or every time the bean is injected into another bean.

- request: A new bean is created for each request.

- flash: A new bean is created and stored in flash scope, making it available for the current and next requests only.

- flow: When using Web Flows (see Chapter 9), a new bean is created and placed into flow scope. The bean is disposed of when the flow terminates.

- conversation: When using Web Flows, a new bean is created and placed in conversation scope. The bean is disposed of when the conversation ends.

- session: A new bean is created and stored in the client session. The bean is disposed of when the session is invalidated.

- singleton: A single bean exists for the life of the Spring container.

Tip You can even create your own scopes; see the section on custom scopes in the Spring user guide at http://static.springframework.org/spring/docs/2.5.x/reference/beans.html#beans-factory-scopes-custom.

As you've already seen, to register a bean that utilizes one of the previously mentioned scopes, you need to set the scope property of the bean argument:

```
frenchCalendar(calendarBean) { bean ->
    bean.scope = "prototype"
    firstDayOfWeek = Calendar.MONDAY
}
```

Dynamically Creating Beans

The major benefit of BeanBuilder in comparison to Spring's static XML format is that because the BeanBuilder DSL is Groovy code, you can create beans dynamically, on the fly. For example, it is often useful to configure different beans for different environments. This is nontrivial to achieve in raw Spring. You often have to use a combination of FactoryBean instances and the org.springframework.beans.factory.config.PropertyPlaceholderConfigurer class to substitute different values for different environments in your build.

With BeanBuilder, this isn't really necessary. Take, for example, the mySessionFactory bean you saw earlier. You could configure the SessionFactory differently for development than for production. Listing 16-12 shows an example.

Listing 16-12. *Dynamically Configuring Beans*

```
def hibProps = ['hibernate.dialect':'org.hibernate.dialect.HSQLDialect']
if(grails.util.GrailsUtil.isDevelopmentEnv()) {
    hibProps."hibernate.show_sql" = "true"
    hibProps."hibernate.format_sql" = "true"
}
mySessionFactory(org.springframework.orm.hibernate3.LocalSessionFactoryBean) {
    dataSource = myDataSource
    mappingResources = ['product.hbm.xml']
    hibernateProperties = hibProps
}
```

As you can see from Listing 16-12, using regular Groovy code you can check whether you're in the development environment and, if so, set up some properties that are useful for development only. In the example in Listing 16-12, the code configures the `hibernate.show_sql` and `hibernate.format_sql` properties, which allow you to debug Hibernate SQL, to be enabled only in the development environment.

However, it is not just the properties of the beans you can configure dynamically. Thanks to Groovy's ability to invoke methods using strings, you can easily create the beans themselves dynamically (see Listing 16-13).

Listing 16-13. *Dynamic Bean Creation*

```
def dataSources = [firstDataSource: 9001, secondDataSource:9002]

dataSources.each { name, port ->
    "$name"(org.apache.commons.dbcp.BasicDataSource) { bean ->
        bean.destroyMethod = "close"
        driverClassName"org.hsqldb.jdbcDriver"
        url="jdbc:hsqldb:hsql://localhost:$port"
        username="sa"
        password=""
    }
}
```

As you can see from Listing 16-13, which uses a map of data source names and ports, you can create bean names dynamically by invoking the bean-defining method using a `String`:

```
"$name"(org.apache.commons.dbcp.BasicDataSource) { bean ->
```

This code will create two beans called `firstDataSource` and `secondDataSource` using the keys of the `dataSources` map.

Spring in Action

Now that you've learned what can be achieved with `BeanBuilder`, let's put some of that knowledge to work and have some fun with Spring. We'll take you through a couple of examples that will build on the gTunes application. The first involves taking advantage of Spring's excellent support for the JMS API.

Integrating JMS with Spring JMS

What many people fail to realize when evaluating Spring is that it is far more than just a dependency injection container. It is an entire abstraction layer over Java EE standards and popular open source software, which promotes POJO programming. The idea behind Spring is that you should rarely, if ever, have to refer to framework code in your own code. The Spring JMS support is one such an example, where Spring allows you to define Message-Driven POJOs (see `http://static.springframework.org/spring/docs/2.5.x/reference/jms.html#jms-asynchronousMessageReception`).

In the following sections, we'll show how you can use BeanBuilder to set up Spring's support for Message-Driven POJOs with JMS. The functionality you're going to implement will allow users to subscribe to a particular Artist. When the Artist releases a new Album, an e-mail notification needs to be sent to all subscribed users. The mechanics of this are going to be implemented using asynchronous, reliable messaging. But before you can do that, you're going need a JMS container. A popular open source solution is the Apache ActiveMQ project.

Setting up ActiveMQ

To get started using ActiveMQ, download the distribution from http://activemq.apache.org/, and extract it somewhere locally. Figure 16-2 shows an example of the ActiveMQ distribution once installed.

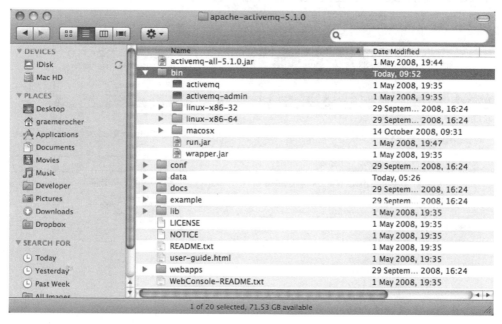

Figure 16-2. *The ActiveMQ installation directory*

■**Tip** You'll find detailed installation instructions covering multiple platforms on the ActiveMQ web site at http://activemq.apache.org/getting-started.html.

Now to get started using ActiveMQ, you need to start up the ActiveMQ container. You can do this by running the bin/activemq command or one of the OS-specific commands such as bin/macosx/activemq, as shown in Listing 16-14.

Listing 16-14. *Starting ActiveMQ*

```
$ activemq start
Starting ActiveMQ Broker...
```

You can verify that ActiveMQ has started up correctly by opening the ActiveMQ web console, which you can typically find on port 8161 at the URL http://localhost:8161/admin/. Figure 16-3 shows an example of the ActiveMQ web console.

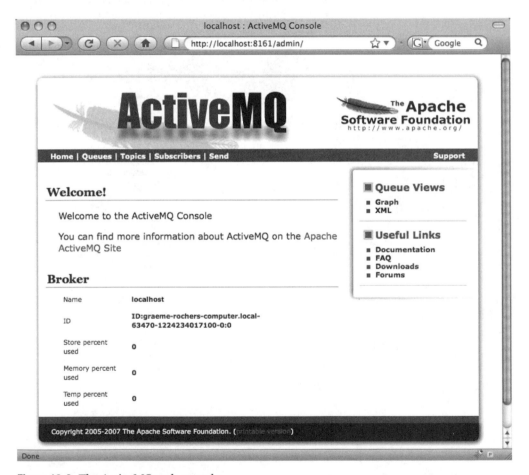

Figure 16-3. *The ActiveMQ web console*

Configuring ActiveMQ with BeanBuilder

With ActiveMQ running, it's now time to configure the gTunes application so that it can use the ActiveMQ instance. A prerequisite to using JMS is obtaining a reference to a javax.jms.ConnectionFactory instance. ActiveMQ provides an implementation of this interface through the org.apache.activemq.ActiveMQConnectionFactory class.

Before you can use it, you need to add the necessary JAR files to the `lib` directory of the gTunes application. Figure 16-4 shows the `activemq-core-5.0.0.jar` file and the necessary geronimo JARs, which you can obtain from the `ACTIVEMQ_HOME/lib` directory, in place.

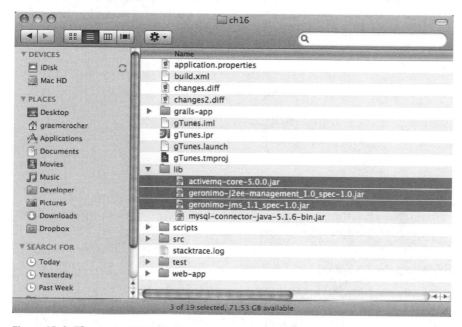

Figure 16-4. *The ActiveMQ JAR files*

■**Tip** There is actually an ActiveMQ plugin (`http://grails.org/ActiveMQ+Plugin`) for Grails that performs all the setup you can see in this section using a Grails plugin. But since you're learning about Spring, we'll continue to describe the manual way!

The next step is to open the `grails-app/conf/spring/resources.groovy` file and register a new Spring bean that points to the URL of the ActiveMQ container. Listing 16-15 shows the necessary BeanBuilder code.

Listing 16-15. *Configuring the JMS ConnectionFactory for ActiveMQ*

```
jmsFactory(org.apache.activemq.ActiveMQConnectionFactory) {
    brokerURL = "tcp://localhost:61616"
}
```

The example in Listing 16-15 sets up a single bean called `jmsFactory` that is an instance of the `ActiveMQConnectionFactory` class. It also sets the `brokerURL` property to the location of the ActiveMQ server, which by default runs on port 61616. One thing that is pretty common, though, is to use a pool of `ConnectionFactory` instances for sending messages, in the same way as you would pool a database `java.sql.Connection`. You can easily achieve this by using the `org.apache.activemq.pool.PooledConnectionFactory` class, as shown in Listing 16-16.

Listing 16-16. *Using a ConnectionFactory Pool*

```
jmsFactory(org.apache.activemq.pool.PooledConnectionFactory) { bean ->
    bean.destroyMethod = "stop"
    connectionFactory = { org.apache.activemq.ActiveMQConnectionFactory cf ->
        brokerURL = "tcp://localhost:61616"
    }
}
```

As you can see in Listing 16-16, the code defines the `connectionFactory` property of the `PooledConnectionFactory` class using an inner bean definition. You learned about inner beans in the section of that name earlier in the chapter.

Sending JMS Messages with Spring

To send JMS messages using the `jmsFactory` bean, you can take advantage of Spring's excellent `org.springframework.jms.core.JmsTemplate` class that provides helper methods for sending messages. You can define the `JmsTemplate` as another Spring bean, as shown in Listing 16-17.

Listing 16-17. *Defining the jmsTemplate Bean*

```
jmsTemplate(org.springframework.jms.core.JmsTemplate) {
    connectionFactory = jmsFactory
}
```

Notice how in Listing 16-17 the `connectionFactory` property is referencing the `jmsFactory` bean you defined earlier. Now you need to consider how to send a notification when a new `Album` is created. A good way to achieve this is to use a GORM event, as described in Chapter 10.

A useful thing about domain classes in Grails is that they too are Spring beans that can participate in autowiring. So, to get a reference to the `jmsTemplate` from the `Album` class, you simply need to define a property within the `Album` domain class that matches the bean name. Listing 16-18 shows the updates to the `Album` domain class.

Listing 16-18. *Injecting the jmsTemplate into the Album Domain Class*

```
class Album {
    ...
    transient jmsTemplate
}
```

You'll notice that in Listing 16-18 the `jmsTemplate` property is defined as `transient`. This is to avoid the `JmsTemplate` instance being serialized along with the `Album` class when it is sent in a JMS message or stored in a flow. Now you can define an afterInsert event, which is fired after an Album instance is inserted into the database that sends a JMS message containing the Album instance. Listing 16-19 shows the necessary code.

Listing 16-19. *Sending a JMS Message*

```
class Album {
    ...
    transient afterInsert = {
        try {
            jmsTemplate.convertAndSend("artistSubscriptions", this)
        }
        catch(e) {
            log.error "Error sending JMS message: ${e.message}",e
        }
    }
}
```

As you can see from Listing 16-19, the afterInsert event uses the JmsTemplate class' convertAndSend method to send the current Album instance to a JMS Queue called artistSubscriptions. Additionally, if an exception occurs, such as when the JMS container is down, the exception is logged at the error level.

If you now attempt to create a new Album using the administrative tools you created in Chapter 14, a JMS message will be sent when you do so. If you visit the ActiveMQ web console and click the Queues section, you'll notice that the artistSubscription queue has appeared in the list, as shown in Figure 16-5.

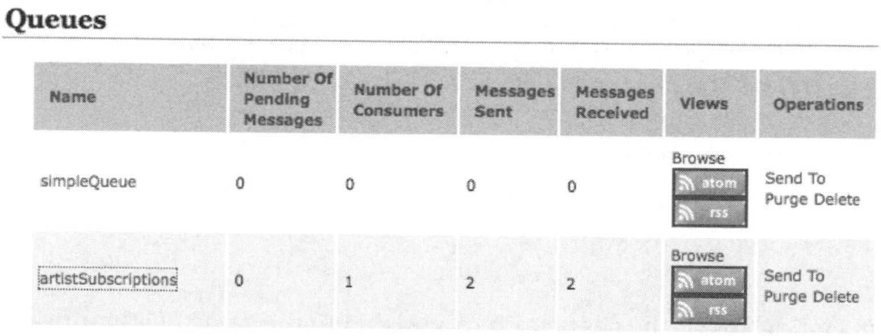

Queues

Name	Number Of Pending Messages	Number Of Consumers	Messages Sent	Messages Received	Views	Operations
simpleQueue	0	0	0	0	Browse atom rss	Send To Purge Delete
artistSubscriptions	0	1	2	2	Browse atom rss	Send To Purge Delete

Figure 16-5. *The available JMS queues*

Consuming JMS Messages with Spring

At this point, you need to consider how to consume the JMS messages that have been sent. Luckily, Spring provides some excellent ways to achieve this too. A central concept is the notion of Message-Driven POJOs.[1] A Message-Driven POJO is a normal Java class that has a method that is triggered by a JMS message. To implement a Message-Driven POJO, you can

---

1. There is an excellent introductory article on Message-Driven POJOs on the SpringSource Team blog at http://blog.springsource.com/2006/08/11/message-driven-pojos/.

use the `org.springframework.jms.listener.adapter.MessageListenerAdapter` class, which is capable of listening for JMS messages and delegating the message to another bean.

A nice thing about Grails' Spring integration is that you can reuse the beans Grails defines automatically within your own bean definitions. So, for example, if you wanted to create a `MessageListenerAdapter` that delegates to a new method called onNewAlbum in the `com.g2one.gtunes.StoreService`, you can do so using the code shown in Listing 16-20.

Listing 16-20. *Using MessageListenerAdapter to Delegate to a Grails Service*

```
import org.springframework.jms.listener.adapter.*
...
jmsMessageListener(MessageListenerAdapter, ref("storeService")) {
    defaultListenerMethod = "onNewAlbum"
}
```

Notice how in Listing 16-20 the code uses the `ref(beanName)` method to create a reference to the `storeService` bean, which is one of the beans Grails automatically creates, and passes it to the constructor of the `MessageListenerAdapter` bean. If you don't specify the `defaultListenerMethod` property, then Spring will try to delegate to a method called handleMessage. That may be fine, but to increase the clarity of your code, you can change this as the example in Listing 16-20 does.

For the `jmsMessageListener` to receive messages, you need to set up an instance of the `org.springframework.jms.listener.DefaultMessageListenerContainer` class as a Spring bean. The `DefaultMessageListenerContainer` class works with the JMS `ConnectionFactory` to monitor for JMS messages. Listing 16-21 shows how to configure an instance of `DefaultMessageListenerContainer` with `BeanBuilder`.

Listing 16-21. *Configuring a DefaultMessageListenerContainer Instance*

```
jmsContainer(org.springframework.jms.listener.DefaultMessageListenerContainer) {
    connectionFactory = jmsFactory
    destinationName = "artistSubscriptions"
    messageListener = jmsMessageListener
    transactionManager = ref("transactionManager")
    autoStartup = false
}
```

As you can see from Listing 16-21, the `destinationName` is set to the same destination used by the `jmsTemplate` in Listing 16-19. The `messageListener` property is set to the `jmsMessageListener` bean you created earlier, and, interestingly, the `transactionManager` property is set to refer to Grails' built-in `transactionManager` instance.

The importance of this will become clear later; for now the last thing to note is that `autoStartup` is set to `false`. This is done to make sure Grails has sufficient time to load before the consumer starts receiving messages from the JMS container. The downside is that you have to take responsibility for starting the `jmsContainer` bean yourself. To do this, you can use the `grails-app/conf/BootStrap.groovy` class' init method. Listing 16-22 shows the changes to `BootStrap.groovy` to achieve this.

Listing 16-22. *Starting the jmsContainer Instance*

```
class BootStrap {

    def jmsContainer
    def init = { servletContext ->
        ...
        log.info "Starting JMS Container"
        jmsContainer.start()
    }
}
```

As with other Grails classes, the BootStrap class can obtain references to any Spring bean simply by defining a property that matches the bean name. In Listing 16-22, a jmsContainer property is defined, resulting in the DefaultMessageListenerContainer instance being injected, at which point the start() method can be called. To complete the picture, you need to implement the onNewAlbum method within the com.g2one.gtunes.StoreService class. For now, simply provide an implementation that prints the album title, as shown in Listing 16-23.

Listing 16-23. *A Simple onNewAlbum Implementation*

```
class StoreService {
    ...
    void onNewAlbum(Album album) {
        println "-- Got album $album.title"
    }
}
```

Now if you create a new Album instance, a JMS message will be sent to the ActiveMQ server and placed on the queue. The Spring jmsContainer bean is already listening for messages, and as soon as it gets one from the queue, the onNewAlbum message will be triggered, and a message such as the following will be printed:

```
-- Got album The Bends
```

All of this happens asynchronously and so doesn't interfere with the actual workflow of creating an Album instance. Spring is also doing a lot of magic under the surface to automatically translate what is in fact a javax.jms.ObjectMessage instance into the correct arguments to pass to the onNewAlbum method. The StoreService itself, you'll notice, has no direct references to the JMS APIs. It is a simple POJO (or POGO, as the case may be).

Enabling Artist Subscriptions

At the moment, the onNewAlbum method is not doing anything of great value. To rectify this situation, you first need to implement the capability for users to subscribe to a particular Artist. There is already a com.g2one.gtunes.Subscription domain class that models subscriptions. Of course, the Subscription needs to know what Artist it relates to. To do this, you can create a subclass of Subscription called ArtistSubscription by running the grails create-domain-class command:

```
$ grails create-domain-class com.g2one.gtunes.ArtistSubscription
```

After adding a new enum value called ARTIST to the SubscriptionType enum in the parent class, the ArtistSubscription implementation looks like Listing 16-24.

Listing 16-24. *The ArtistSubscription Class*

```
package com.g2one.gtunes

class ArtistSubscription extends Subscription {

    ArtistSubscription() {
        type = SubscriptionType.ARTIST
    }

    static belongsTo = [artist:Artist]
}
```

With the ArtistSubscription class in place, you need to consider how to allow users to subscribe. To do so, you can develop a GSP template that renders a "Subscribe" link if the user is not subscribed or an "Unsubscribe" link if they are. Listing 16-25 shows the code for the grails-app/views/artist/_subscribe.gsp template.

Listing 16-25. *The subscribe Template*

```
<jsec:isLoggedIn>
    <div id="subscription">
        <gtunes:isSubscribed artist="${artist}">
                <g:remoteLink update="subscription"
                    controller="artist"
                    action="unsubscribe"
                    id="${artist.id}">Unsubscribe</g:remoteLink> -
                    Click here to no longer receive e-mail updates when
                    <strong>${artist.name}</strong> release a new album.
        </gtunes:isSubscribed>
        <gtunes:notSubscribed artist="${artist}">
            <g:remoteLink update="subscription"
                controller="artist"
                action="subscribe"
                id="${artist.id}">Subscribe</g:remoteLink>
                Click here to receive e-mail updates when
                <strong>${artist.name}</strong> release a new album.
        </gtunes:notSubscribed>
    </div>
</jsec:isLoggedIn>
```

The template in Listing 16-25 uses the `<jsec:isLoggedIn>` tag to ensure that the subscription controls are displayed only if the user is logged in. Then it uses two tags that haven't been created yet: `<gtunes:isSubscribed>` and `<gtunes:notSubscribed>`. The idea behind these two tags is to render different markup according to whether the user is subscribed. In Listing 16-25, the tags render either a "Subscribe" or "Unsubscribe" `<g:remoteLink>` tag that makes an Ajax call and updates the surrounding `<div>`.

To implement these tags, you need to create a new tag library. You can do so by running the `grails create-tag-lib` command:

```
$ grails create-tag-lib com.g2one.gtunes.Subscription
```

This command will create a new tag library at the location *grails-app/taglib/com/g2one/gtunes/SubscriptionTagLib.groovy*. Listing 16-26 shows the template for the `SubscriptionTagLib` class.

Listing 16-26. *The SubscriptionTagLib Implementation*

```
package com.g2one.gtunes

class SubscriptionTagLib {
    static namespace = "gtunes"

}
```

Notice that the `SubscriptionTagLib` in Listing 16-26 is using the gtunes namespace. To implement the `<gtunes:isSubscribed>` tag, you need a way to check whether a user is subscribed. You can do so by writing a utility method that uses GORM to query the database. Listing 16-27 shows a possible implementation.

Listing 16-27. *Checking Whether a User Is Subscribed*

```
boolean checkSubscribed(user, artist) {
    user && artist &&
        ArtistSubscription.findByUserAndArtist(user, artist, [cache:true])
}
```

Using the `ArtistSubscription` class you created earlier, the code in Listing 16-27 uses a dynamic finder called `findByUserAndArtist` to locate the `Subscription` instance. Note that the code uses the `cache:true` argument so that the query is cached, because it is likely to be used quite frequently. With the `checkSubscribed` method in place, writing a couple of tags to take advantage of it is pretty easy. Listing 16-28 shows the code for the `<gtunes:isSubscribed>` and `<gtunes:notSubscribed>` methods.

Listing 16-28. *Implementing the SubscriptionTagLib Tags*

```
def isSubscribed = { attrs, body ->
    if(checkSubscribed(request.user, attrs.artist)) {
        out << body()
    }
```

```
}
def notSubscribed = { attrs, body ->
    if(!checkSubscribed(request.user, attrs.artist)) {
        out << body()
    }
}
```

Of course, testing is crucial too. You could test the tag library using the GroovyPagesTestCase class you used to test the AlbumArtTagLib. However, since the SubscriptionTagLib is mainly about branching logic and not markup rendering, it is probably easier to take advantage of the grails.test.TagLibUnitTestCase class that lets you unit test tag libraries but not the markup they generate. Simply create a new a unit test in the test/unit/com/g2one/gtunes directory called SubscriptionTagLibTests that extends from the TagLibUnitTestCase class, as shown in Listing 16-29.

Listing 16-29. *Using the TagLibUnitTestCase Class*

```
package com.g2one.gtunes

class SubscriptionTagLibTests extends grails.test.TagLibUnitTestCase {
    ...
}
```

You can then write a couple of simple tests that check the behavior of the <gtunes: isSubscribed> and <gtunes:notSubscribed> tags. Listing 16-30 shows two tests called testIsSubscribed and testNotSubscribed.

Listing 16-30. *Testing the SubscriptionTagLib Class*

```
void testIsSubscribed() {
    mockDomain(ArtistSubscription)

    def artist = new Artist(name:"Kings of Leon")
    def user = new User(login:"testuser")
    new ArtistSubscription(artist:artist, user:user).save()

    tagLib.request.user = user
    tagLib.isSubscribed(artist:artist) {
        "subscribed"
    }
    tagLib.notSubscribed(artist:artist) {
        "notsubscribed"
    }

    assertEquals "subscribed", tagLib.out.toString()
}

void testNotSubscribed() {
```

```
    mockDomain(ArtistSubscription)

    def artist = new Artist(name:"Kings of Leon")
    def user = new User(login:"testuser")

    tagLib.request.user = user
    tagLib.isSubscribed(artist:artist) {
        "subscribed"
    }
    tagLib.notSubscribed(artist:artist) {
        "notsubscribed"
    }

    assertEquals "notsubscribed", tagLib.out.toString()
}
```

A closure can be passed as the body of the tag, as long as it returns a String representing the body contents. In Listing 16-30, either "subscribed" or "notsubscribed" will be written to the mock out variable. OK, with the tests out of the way, the next thing to do is to modify the grails-app/views/artist/_artist.gsp template to include the new _subscribe.gsp template. Listing 16-31 shows the necessary code changes highlighted in bold.

Listing 16-31. *Updates to the _artist.gsp Template*

```
<div id="artist${artist.id}" class="artistProfile" style="display:none;">
    <div class="artistDetails">
        ...
        <g:render template="subscribe" model="[artist:artist]"></g:render>
    </div>
</div>
```

Now when you visit one of the artist pages, you'll see a new "Subscribe" link, as shown in Figure 16-6.

Figure 16-6. *The "Subscribe" link*

Unfortunately, when you click the link, you'll receive a "Page not found" 404 error. To resolve this issue, you need to implement the server logic for the subscribe and unsubscribe actions that the <g:remoteLink> tags in Listing 16-25 refer to. Open the ArtistController class, and add a new action called subscribe that persists a new ArtistSubscription if one doesn't already exist. Listing 16-32 shows an example implementation.

Listing 16-32. *Implementing the subscribe Action*

```
def subscribe = {
    def artist = Artist.get(params.id)
    def user = request.user
    if(artist && user) {
        def subscription = ArtistSubscription.findByUserAndArtist(user, artist)
        if(!subscription) {
            new ArtistSubscription(artist:artist, user:user).save(flush:true)
        }
        render(template:"/artist/subscribe", model:[artist:artist])
    }
}
```

As you can see from the code in Listing 16-32, the subscribe action reuses the _subscribe.gsp template to render an Ajax response to the client. The logic in the SubscriptionTagLib deals with the rest. To add the unsubscribe logic, you simply need to delete the ArtistSubscription instance if it exists, as shown in Listing 16-33.

Listing 16-33. *Implementing the unsubscribe Action*

```
def unsubscribe = {
    def artist = Artist.get(params.id)
    def user = request.user
    if(artist && user) {
        def subscription = ArtistSubscription.findByUserAndArtist(user, artist)
        if(subscription) {
            subscription.delete(flush:true)
        }
        render(template:"/artist/subscribe", model:[artist:artist])
    }
}
```

Finally, you need to add a couple of URL mappings in order to expose the subscribe and unsubscribe actions, as shown in Listing 16-34.

Listing 16-34. *The Subscriptions URL Mappings*

```
"/artist/subscribe/$id"(controller:"artist", action:"subscribe")
"/artist/unsubscribe/$id"(controller:"artist", action:"unsubscribe")
```

Implementing Asynchronous E-mail Notifications

Now with users able to subscribe to their favorite artists, it is time to consider the onNewAlbum method of the StoreService class again. Whenever a JMS message is received, you're going to need to find all the subscribers for the Artist associated with the passed Album and send an e-mail to each one.

To do this, you first need a reference to the mailService bean, provided by the Mail plugin installed in Chapter 12, which can be obtained by defining a property of the same name:

```
def mailService
```

Next, you need to obtain a list of all the User instances subscribed to the Artist associated with the Album. To do this, you can get a reference to the Artist via the artist property:

```
def artist = album.artist
```

Then use a criteria query to obtain a list of users:

```
def users = ArtistSubscription.withCriteria {
    projections {
        property "user"
    }
    eq('artist', artist)
}
```

Notice the use of the projections block to specify that you want the result to contain the user property of each ArtistSubscription found. Once you have a list of users, you can now use the mailService to send an e-mail to each one:

```
for(user in users) {
    mailService.sendMail {
        from "notifications@gtunes.com"
        to user.email
        title "${artist.name} has released a new album: ${album.title}!"
        body view:"/emails/artistSubscription", model:[album:album,
                                     artist:artist,
                                     user:user]
    }
}
```

As you can see, the body method is used to specify that the e-mail is to be rendered by a view called /emails/artistSubscription. We'll return to this view in a moment. For completeness, Listing 16-35 contains the full code listing for the onNewAlbum(Album) method.

Listing 16-35. *The onNewAlbum(Album) Method*

```
void onNewAlbum(Album album) {
    try {
        def artist = album.artist
```

```
            def users = ArtistSubscription.withCriteria {
                projections {
                    property "user"
                }
                eq('artist', artist)
            }

            for(user in users) {
                mailService.sendMail {
                    from "notifications@gtunes.com"
                    to user.email
                    title "${artist.name} has released a new album: ${album.title}!"
                    body view:"/emails/artistSubscription", model:[album:album,
                                                                   artist:artist,
                                                                   user:user]
                }
            }


        }
        catch(Exception e) {
            log.error "Error sending album $album notification message: $e.message", e
            throw e
        }
}
```

One addition that we didn't cover previously is the surrounding try/catch block in Listing 16-35. An exception could occur if there was an error sending a mail or communicating with the database. Notice how the exception is logged and rethrown within the catch block. So, why rethrow the exception?

Essentially, the StockService is a *transactional* service class. It is using Grails' transactionManager underneath the surface. If you recall, the jmsContainer bean was given a reference to the Grails transactionManager in Listing 16-21. As a reminder, here is the relevant snippet from grails-app/conf/spring/resources.groovy:

```
jmsContainer(org.springframework.jms.listener.DefaultMessageListenerContainer) {
    ...
    transactionManager = ref("transactionManager")
    autoStartup = false
}
```

If an exception is thrown, Grails will automatically roll back the transaction. Since the jmsContainer has a reference to the transactionManager, it will be made aware that the transaction was rolled back. The result is that the JMS transaction will be rolled back, effectively marking the message as undelivered. ActiveMQ will then try to deliver the message again later. Thanks to Spring's transaction abstraction layer, you get a reliable messaging system, with guarantees of message redelivery.

The last thing to do is to finish up the subscription implementation by providing the view that renders the e-mail. Listing 16-36 shows the grails-app/views/emails/artistSubscription.gsp view.

Listing 16-36. *The artistSubscription View*

```
<%@ page contentType="text/plain"%>
Dear ${user.firstName} ${user.lastName},

One of your favorite artists ${artist.name} has released
a new album called ${album.title}!

It is available now on gTunes at
<g:createLink controller="album"
              action="display"
              id="${album.id}" absolute="true" />

Kind Regards,

The gTunes Team
```

Mixing Groovy and Java with Spring

Although Grails already takes advantage of Groovy's joint compiler, allowing you to integrate Java code seamlessly into a Grails application, it is often nice to provide this integration via Spring.

As an example, currently the gTunes application is using some Groovy code to stream music to the user. You can find the relevant code in the stream action of the SongController, which is shown in Listing 16-37.

Listing 16-37. *The Stream action of the SongController Class*

```
def file = new File(song.file)
try {
    def type = file.name[-3..-1]
    response.contentType = "audio/x-${type}"
    def out = response.outputStream
    def bytes = new byte[BUFFER_SIZE]
    file.withInputStream { inp ->
        while( inp.read(bytes) != -1) {
            out.write(bytes)
            out.flush()
        }
    }
}
```

```
catch(Exception e) {
    log.error "Error streaming song $file: $e.message", e
    response.sendError 500
}
```

Performance-wise, Java undoubtedly has the edge on Groovy when writing low-level IO code like that in Listing 16-37. You may want to optimize the stream action of the SongController to use a Java class instead. To do so, create a new Java class called StreamingService in the src/java/com/g2one/gtunes directory, as shown in Figure 16-7.

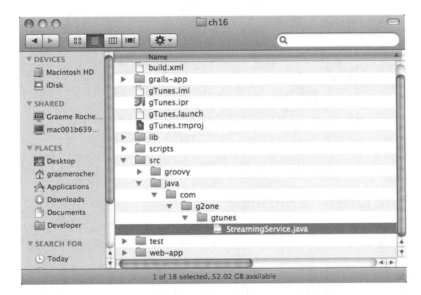

Figure 16-7. *The StreamService.java file*

Rather than reading each byte, you could take advantage of the java.nio.channels package that allows optimized file transfer. Of course, you could use the java.nio.channels package from Groovy, but we're currently shooting for maximum performance by writing the class in Java. Listing 16-38 shows the implementation of the StreamingService class, which provides a method called streamSong that can be used to transfer the bytes of a Song instance to the given OutputStream.

Listing 16-38. *The StreamingService Class*

```
package com.g2one.gtunes;

import java.io.*;
import java.nio.channels.*;
import org.apache.commons.logging.*;
```

```
public class StreamingService
{
    private static final int BUFFER_SIZE = 2048;
    private static final Log LOG = LogFactory.getLog(StreamingService.class);

    /**
     * Streams the given song to the given OutputStream
     */
    public void streamSong(Song song, OutputStream out) {
        if(song != null) {
            File file = new File(song.getFile());
            FileInputStream input = null;
            try {
                input = new FileInputStream(file);
                FileChannel in = input.getChannel();
                in.transferTo(0,in.size(), Channels.newChannel(out));
                out.flush();
            }
            catch(Exception e) {
                throw new RuntimeException(e.getMessage(), e);
            }
            finally {
                try {
                    input.close();
                }
                catch(IOException e) {
                    // ignore
                }
            }
        }
    }
}
```

One important thing to note is that this Java class references the domain class com.g2one.gtunes.Song, which is written in Groovy. Groovy's joint compiler allows Java classes to resolve Groovy classes, something that, as of this writing, is not possible in any other dynamic language on the JVM. The remainder of the code simply obtains a FileChannel instance and then calls the transferTo method to transfer the file to the response OutputStream.

Now you could just use the new operator to create a new instance of the StreamingService class within the SongController. But a nicer way to do this is to use Spring. Simply register a new bean in the grails-app/conf/spring/resources.groovy file for the StreamingService class, as shown in Listing 16-39.

Listing 16-39. *Creating a streamingService Bean*

```
streamingService(com.g2one.gtunes.StreamingService)
```

Now to obtain a reference to this bean in `SongController`, just create the equivalent property:

```
def streamingService
```

The `stream` action can then be modified to take advantage of the `streamingService` instance, as shown in Listing 16-40.

Listing 16-40. *Using the streamingService Bean*

```
def stream = {
    ...
    if(song) {
        def albumPermission = new AlbumPermission(album:song.album)
        jsec.hasPermission(permission:albumPermission) {
            ...
                response.contentType = "audio/x-${song.file[-3..-1]}"
                streamingService.streamSong(song, response.outputStream)
            ...
        }
        ...
    }
    ...
}
```

As you can see from Listing 16-40, the `streamSong` method is called, passing in the Song instance and the `response` object's `outputStream` property. You now have a much better-performing implementation that uses the `java.nio.channels` package instead. Since it is a Spring bean, if you one day decided to change the `StreamingService` implementation—for example, to stream the music from Amazon S3 instead—then all you would need to do is alter the `grails-app/conf/spring/resources.groovy` file and register a different implementation.

The `SongController` would need no changes at all since it is using duck typing to invoke the `streamSong` method. If you prefer static typing, then you could introduce an interface that the `StreamingService` class can implement, exactly as you would do in Java.

Summary

This chapter gave you some revealing insight into the inner workings of Grails and its Spring underpinnings. Moreover, you have learned that just because Grails embraces Convention over Configuration, it does not mean that configuration is not possible. Quite the contrary—every aspect of Grails is customizable thanks to Spring.

Grails provides such a clean abstraction over Spring that often users of Grails simply don't know Spring is there. In this chapter, you saw how you can reach out to great Spring APIs, such as the JMS support, to help you solve commons problems. Having said that, Spring is an enormous framework that provides far more features and benefits than we could possibly cover in this chapter. There are Spring abstractions for pretty much every major Java standard and many of the popular open source projects too.

If you really want to get to grips with Spring, we recommend you invest some time reading the excellent reference documentation at `http://static.springframework.org/spring/docs/ 2.5.x/reference/` or take a look at Apress' excellent array of Spring books.[2] Doing so will help improve your knowledge of Grails too, because fundamentally Grails is just Spring and Hibernate in disguise! In the next chapter, we'll look at one of the other major frameworks that Grails builds on for its persistence concerns: Hibernate.

---

2. Some recent Spring books published by Apress include *Pro Spring 2.5* by Jan Machacek et al. (Apress, 2008), *Spring Recipes: A Problem-Solution Approach* by Gary Mak (Apress, 2008), and *Pro Java EE Spring Patterns: Best Practices and Design Strategies Implementing Java EE Patterns with the Spring Framework* by Dhrubojyoti Kayal (Apress, 2008).

CHAPTER 17

■ ■ ■

Legacy Integration with Hibernate

Throughout the book, you have been constructing what is essentially a green field[1] application. There has been no legacy data to deal with, no database administrators (DBAs) are nagging you, and in general life has been good. Unfortunately, in the real world, many applications do have to be reengineered from existing sources and data.

Shockingly enough, these older projects may not follow the conventions that Grails uses to define its database schema. The database tables may use completely different column and table naming conventions. The strategy used to generate the database identifier may differ from the native one Grails uses by default.

Fortunately, the Hibernate team has been on a mission to solve the object-relational mismatch[2] for years. Hibernate is capable of mapping onto more than 90 percent of all database schemas and has broad support for different database vendors. In this chapter, we'll cover how you can reach out and call upon Hibernate's more advanced features in Grails. First, we'll cover Grails' mapping DSL that provides access to most of the common Hibernate features. Later, we'll delve into writing some Hibernate XML and even EJB 3 annotations with Grails.

Legacy Mapping with the ORM DSL

The most common mismatches experienced with Grails occur when the table and column names that Grails expects don't match the underlying database. You can control most aspects of how Grails maps onto the underlying database using the object-relational mapping (ORM) domain-specific language (DSL).

You've actually already had a chance to take advantage of the ORM DSL in Chapter 10 to control fetch strategies and cache configuration. If you recall, to use the ORM DSL, you need to define a mapping static variable that is assigned a Groovy closure, as shown in Listing 17-1.

---

1. In software engineering jargon, a *green field* project is one that is free of any constraints imposed by prior work. See http://en.wikipedia.org/wiki/Greenfield_project.
2. *Object-relational mismatch* is a term used to describe the technical difficulties in mapping an object-oriented-programming language onto a relational database system; see http://en.wikipedia.org/wiki/Object-Relational_impedance_mismatch.

Listing 17-1. *Defining the Mapping Closure*

```
static mapping = {
    ...
}
```

Within the body of the closure, you can control how Grails maps classes onto the underlying database. Let's start with looking at how to change table and column names.

Changing Table and Column Name Mappings

To change the table a class maps onto, you can call the table method and pass the name of the table. For example, by default the com.g2one.gtunes.Album class maps onto a table called album. If you wanted to map onto a table called RECORDS instead, you could do so as shown in Listing 17-2.

Listing 17-2. *Changing the Table Name*

```
class Album {
    ...
    static mapping = {
        table "RECORDS"
    }
}
```

You can change the column that individual properties map onto by invoking a method that matches the property name. Then using a named argument, called column, you can set the column name. Listing 17-3 shows an example that maps the title property onto a column called R_TITLE.

Listing 17-3. *Changing a Column Name Mapping*

```
class Album {
    String title
    ...
    static mapping = {
        table "RECORDS"
        title column: "R_TITLE"
    }
}
```

Occasionally, you may run into a scenario where the name of a domain class or a property on a domain class conflicts with a SQL keyword. For example, say you have a domain class called Order. The Order domain class by default maps onto a table called order. The name order conflicts with the SQL ORDER BY syntax. At this point, you have two options. You can rename your domain class, or you can use backticks to escape the name of the table:

```
table "`order`"
```

Mapping simple properties such as `title` is, well, simple. Associations tend to require a little more thought. In the next section, we'll cover how you can change the way different kinds of associations map onto the underlying database.

Changing Association Mappings

Grails has special logic that deals with mapping different kinds of associations onto a database. For a simple one-to-one or many-to-one association, Grails will map a foreign key column. For example, the `artist` property of the `Album` class will map to a column called `artist_id` that contains the foreign key reference for the artist. You can change this in the same way as any simple mapping, as shown in Listing 17-4.

Listing 17-4. *Changing a Column Name for a Many-to-One Association*

```
class Album {
        static belongsTo = [artist:Artist]
        ...
        static mapping = {
                artist column: "R_CREATOR_ID"
        }
}
```

The example in Listing 17-4 maps the `artist` property to a column called R_CREATOR_ID. A one-to-many association requires a little more thought. First you need to consider whether the one-to-many association is unidirectional or bidirectional. With a unidirectional one-to-many association, GORM will use a join table to associate the two tables, since there isn't a foreign key available on the many side of the association. Figure 17-1 illustrates this.

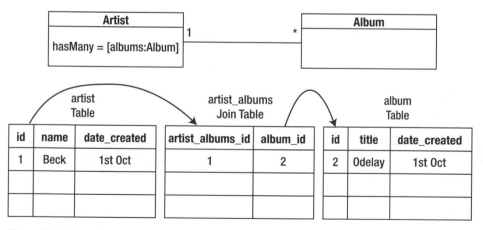

Figure 17-1. *How GORM maps a unidirectional one-to-many association*

As you can see from Figure 17-1, if the `albums` association were unidirectional, GORM would create an intermediate `artist_albums` join table in order to map the association correctly. The `album_id` column, containing the `Album` identifier, has a unique constraint applied that ensures the join table can't be used for a many-to-many association. For a unidirectional association to work, a join table *must* available. However, you can change the name of this join table and the columns it uses to create the join.

To do so, you need to use the `joinTable` argument on the one side of the association. Listing 17-5 shows an example of using the `joinTable` argument on the `albums` property of the `Artist` class.

Listing 17-5. *Using a joinTable Mapping*

```
class Artist {
        static hasMany = [albums:Album]
        ...
        static mapping = {
                albums joinTable:[name:'Artist_To_Records',
                                  key:'Artist_Id',
                                  column:'Record_Id']
        }
}
```

In the example in Listing 17-5, the `joinTable` argument is used to map the unidirectional `albums` association onto a join table called `Artist_To_Records`. The key argument is used to specify the column to store the identifier of the one side, which in this case is the `id` property of the `Artist`. Conversely, the `column` argument is used to specify the name of the column to store the identifier of the many side.

Crucially, the mapping in Listing 17-5 works only for a unidirectional one-to-many because with a bidirectional one-to-many mapping a join table is not used. Instead, a foreign key association is created. Figure 17-2 shows how GORM maps a bidirectional one-to-many association.

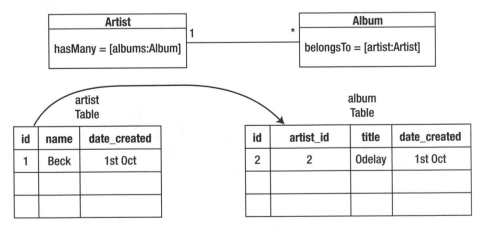

Figure 17-2. *A bidirectional one-to-many association*

As you can see from Figure 17-2, since there is a two-ended association, no join table is necessary. The foreign key column `artist_id` is used to map the `albums` association. If you simply need to change the column that is used to establish the foreign key association, then you can do so using the `column` argument on either end of the association. Listing 17-6 shows an example that uses the `column` argument with the `artist` property of the `Album` class.

Listing 17-6. *Changing the Foreign Key for a Bidirectional One-to-Many Association*

```
class Album {
    ...
    static mapping = {
        artist column: "R_Artist_Id"
    }
}
```

One final relationship type to consider is a many-to-many association. A many-to-many association is mapped using a join table in a similar way to a unidirectional one-to-many association. Figure 17-3 shows an example of how a many-to-many association works if you created a hypothetical `Composer` domain class. Each `Composer` has many albums, while each `Album` has many composers, making this a many-to-many relationship.

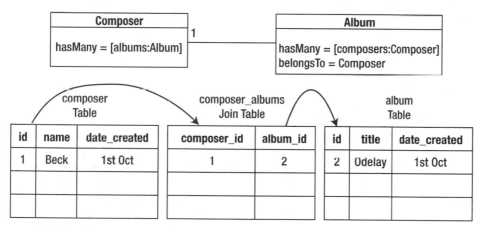

Figure 17-3. *How Grails maps a many-to-many association*

You can change the way a many-to-many association maps onto the underlying database using the same `joinTable` argument used to configure a unidirectional one-to-many association. Listing 17-7 shows an example of changing the table and column names for the relationship that Figure 17-3 models.

Listing 17-7. *Changing Table and Column Name Mappings for a Many-to-Many*

```
class Composer {
    static hasMany = [albums:Album]
    static mapping = {
        table "MUSICIAN"
        albums joinTable: "MUSICIAN_TO_RECORD", column: "RECORD_ID"
    }
}
```

```
class Album {
      static hasMany = [composers:Composer]
      static belongsTo = Composer
      static mapping = {
         ...
         composers joinTable: "MUSICIAN_TO_RECORD", column: "MUSICIAN_ID"
      }
}
```

The example in Listing 17-7 will map to a join table called MUSICIAN_TO_RECORD. Figure 17-4 shows an example of what the table looks like.

MUSICIAN_TO_RECORD
Join Table

MUSICIAN_ID	RECORD_ID
1	2

Figure 17-4. *The MUSICIAN_TO_RECORD join table*

Understanding Hibernate Types

Hibernate by default knows how to persist a range of different common Java types. For example, it will assume a java.lang.String maps to a java.sql.Types.VARCHAR SQL type.

The org.hibernate.Hibernate class contains a number of constants that represent the different types that Hibernate knows about by default. For example, the constant Hibernate.STRING represents the type used to persist String instances by default. The SQL VARCHAR type is typically limited to 255 characters, and in some cases this may not be practical.

Using the ORM DSL, you can change the default type used to map a specific column. Listing 17-8 shows an example of changing the title property of the Album class to a Hibernate.TEXT type.

Listing 17-8. *Changing the Hibernate Type*

```
class Album {
      ...
      String title
      static mapping = {
            title type: "text"
      }
}
```

As Listing 17-8 demonstrates, you can refer to the different Hibernate types by name when doing the mapping. The text type will map the text property to a java.sql.Types.CLOB column.

In addition to this, Hibernate allows you to specify custom implementations of the `org.hibernate.usertype.UserType` interface to allow Hibernate to persist other types. As an example, say you wanted to use the excellent JodaTime Java date and time API (`http://joda-time.sourceforge.net`). Hibernate by default doesn't know how to persist instances of the JodaTime API such as the `org.joda.time.DateTime` class.

Fortunately, JodaTime provides a number of custom `UserType` implementations that can be used to persist JodaTime objects. Listing 17-9 shows an example that uses the `org.joda.time.Duration` class to represent the duration of a song, instead of an integer.

Listing 17-9. *Using the JodaTime Hibernate UserType*

```
class Song {
    ...
    org.joda.time.Duration duration
    static mapping = {
        duration type: org.joda.time.contrib.hibernate.PersistentDuration
    }
}
```

■**Note** The example in Listing 17-9 assumes you have the necessary JodaTime JAR files within the `lib` directory, including the JodaTime Hibernate integration library found at `http://joda-time.sourceforge.net/contrib/hibernate/index.html`.

With Hibernate types, including custom `UserType` instances, the choice of underlying SQL type is made by the implementation. The `sqlTypes()` method of the `org.hibernate.usertype.UserType` interface is responsible for returning an array of SQL types that the `UserType` maps to. Why an array? Well, a `UserType` may use multiple columns for storage, so a type is needed for each column used to store data.

For example, the `PersistentDuration` class from Listing 17-9 returns an array containing a single entry—the `Types.VARCHAR` SQL type. If you need to override the SQL type used, then you can use the `sqlType` argument, as shown in Listing 17-10.

Listing 17-10. *Using the sqlType Argument*

```
class Song {
    ...
    org.joda.time.Duration duration
    static mapping = {
        duration type: org.joda.time.contrib.hibernate.PersistentDuration,
            sqlType: "VARCHAR(120)"
    }
}
```

■Note Be careful when using the `sqlType` argument because you may lose database independence since you are referring directly to underlying SQL types of the database that sometimes differ from vendor to vendor.

Now let's look at a more complex example. Currently, the gTunes application uses a simple `Float` to represent the `price` property of the `Album` class. Say you wanted to have an object that encapsulates not just the price but also the currency. Listing 17-11 shows the `MonetaryAmount` class that contains properties for both the value and the currency of a given amount.

Listing 17-11. *The MonetaryAmount Class*

```groovy
package com.g2one.gtunes

class MonetaryAmount implements Serializable {
    private final BigDecimal value
    private final Currency currency

    MonetaryAmount(value, Currency currency) {
        this.value = value.toBigDecimal()
        this.currency = currency
    }

    BigDecimal getValue() { this.value }
    Currency getCurrency() { this.currency }

    boolean equals(o) {
        if (!(o instanceof MonetaryAmount)) return false
        return o.value == this.value && o.currency == this.currency
    }

    int hashCode() {
        int result = 23468
        result += 37 * this.value.hashCode()
        result += 37 * this.currency.hashCode()
        return result
    }
}
```

This class lives in the `src/groovy` directory, so it is not a persistent domain class. Unfortunately, Hibernate has no way of knowing how to persist instances of the `MonetaryAmount` class. To get around this, you need to implement a custom `UserType`. Listing 17-12 shows the code for the `MonetaryAmountUserType`, which stores the properties of the `MonetaryAmount` class in two different columns.

Listing 17-12. *The MonetaryAmountUserType Hibernate User Type*

```
package com.g2one.gtunes

import java.sql.*
import org.hibernate.*
import org.hibernate.usertype.UserType

class MonetaryAmountUserType implements UserType {

    private static final SQL_TYPES = [ Types.NUMERIC, Types.VARCHAR ] as int[]

    public int[] sqlTypes() { SQL_TYPES }
    public Class returnedClass() { MonetaryAmount }
    public boolean equals(x, y) { x == y }
    public int hashCode(x) { x.hashCode() }
    public Object deepCopy(value) { value }
    public boolean isMutable() { false }

    Serializable disassemble(value)  { value }
    def assemble(Serializable cached, owner)  { cached  }
    def replace(original, target, owner) { original  }


    public Object nullSafeGet(ResultSet resultSet,
                              String[] names,
                              Object owner)
          throws HibernateException, SQLException {
        if (resultSet.wasNull()) return null

        def value = resultSet.getBigDecimal(names[0])
        def currency = Currency.getInstance(resultSet.getString(names[1]))
        return new MonetaryAmount(value, currency)
    }

    void nullSafeSet(PreparedStatement statement,
                     Object amount,
                     int index) {

        if (amount == null) {
            statement.setNull(index, SQL_TYPES[index])
            statement.setNull(index + 1, SQL_TYPES[index + 1])
        }
```

```
        else {
            def currencyCode = amount.currency.currencyCode
            statement.setBigDecimal(index, amount.value)
            statement.setString(index + 1, currencyCode)
        }
    }
}
```

The crucial parts of the code in Listing 17-12 are the implementations of the nullSafeGet and nullSafeSet methods. The nullSafeGet method is responsible for reading the java.sql.ResultSet and creating a new instance of the target type:

```
def value = resultSet.getBigDecimal(names[0])
def currency = Currency.getInstance(resultSet.getString(names[1]))
return new MonetaryAmount(value, currency)
```

The nullSafeSet method is used to populate the PreparedStatement used to store an instance of the target type. The last argument of the nullSafeSet method is the current index, which you can use to set ordinal-based arguments on the PreparedStatement instance:

```
def currencyCode = amount.currency.currencyCode
statement.setBigDecimal(index, amount.value)
statement.setString(index + 1, currencyCode)
```

One final thing to note is the definition of the SQL types used:

```
private static final SQL_TYPES = [ Types.NUMERIC, Types.VARCHAR ] as int[]
```

Since there are two entries in the array, the MonetaryAmountUserType will require two columns to function correctly. Now let's look at how to take advantage of the MonetaryAmount class in gTunes. Listing 17-13 shows the updates to the com.g2one.gtunes.Album class.

Listing 17-13. *Using Custom User Types*

```
class Album {
    MonetaryAmount price
    ...
    static mapping = {
        price type: MonetaryAmountUserType, {
                column name: "price"
                column name: "currency_code"
        }
    }
}
```

As you can see from Listing 17-13, you can use the type argument to specify the MonetaryAmountUserType implementation. Then you need to configure the mapping of the columns used by a MonetaryAmountUserType by passing a closure. Within the body of the closure, you can set the column names used. Notice that order of the column definitions must match the order of the values returned by the sqlType() method of the MonetaryAmountUserType class.

In addition, if you need to override the underlying SQL type used by each of the columns in the `MonetaryAmountUserType` class, then you can use the `sqlType` argument you saw earlier. Listing 17-14 shows an example.

Listing 17-14. *Using sqlType with Custom User Types*

```
class Album {
    MonetaryAmount price
    ...
    static mapping = {
        price type: MonetaryAmountUserType, {
                column name: "price"
                column name: "currency_code", sqlType: "text"
        }
    }
}
```

Changing the Database Identity Generator

The default strategy that GORM uses to obtain an identifier for a newly persisted domain class instance is to use the native database generator. The actual algorithm chosen depends on the capabilities of the underlying database. For example, in MySQL GORM will ask the database to generate an identifier from the `id` column in a given table.

Many databases don't use an identity column, instead relying on other techniques such as sequences or user-generated identifiers. Fortunately, with Hibernate there is a nice API for defining the identifier generation strategy that is accessible through GORM. Extracted from the Hibernate documentation, this is a list of available identity generators:

- `increment`: Generates identifiers of type `long`, `short`, or `int` that are unique only when no other process is inserting data into the same table. This strategy should not be used with Grails since multiple threads accessing the table could result in non-unique identifiers.

- `identity`: Supports identity columns in DB2, MySQL, MS SQL Server, Sybase, and HypersonicSQL. The returned identifier is of type `long`, `short`, or `int`.

- `sequence`: Uses a sequence in DB2, PostgreSQL, Oracle, SAP DB, and McKoi, or uses a generator in Interbase. The returned identifier is of type `long`, `short`, or `int`.

- `hilo`: Uses a high/low algorithm to efficiently generate identifiers of type `long`, `short`, or `int`, given a table and column (by default `hibernate_unique_key` and `next_hi`, respectively) as a source of high values. The high/low algorithm generates identifiers that are unique only for a particular database.

- `seqhilo`: Uses a high/low algorithm to efficiently generate identifiers of type `long`, `short`, or `int`, given a named database sequence.

- `uuid`: Uses a 128-bit UUID algorithm to generate identifiers of type `string`, unique within a network (the IP address is used). The UUID is encoded as a string of hexadecimal digits of length 32.

- `guid`: Uses a database-generated GUID string on MS SQL Server and MySQL.

- `native`: Picks `identity`, `sequence`, or `hilo` depending upon the capabilities of the underlying database.

- `assigned`: Leaves the application to assign an identifier to the object before `save()` is called.

- `select`: Retrieves a primary key assigned by a database trigger by selecting the row by some unique key and retrieving the primary key value.

- `foreign`: Uses the identifier of another associated object. This is usually used in conjunction with a one-to-one primary key association.

- `sequence-identity`: A specialized sequence generation strategy that utilizes a database sequence for the actual value generation but combines this with JDBC 3's `getGeneratedKeys` to actually return the generated identifier value as part of the insert statement execution. This strategy is known to be supported only on Oracle 10g drivers targeted for JDK 1.4.

As you can see, you can choose form many different options, the details of which are covered in far more detail in the Hibernate reference documentation at `http://www.hibernate.org/hib_docs/reference/en/html/mapping.html#mapping-declaration-id-generator`. Nevertheless, as an example of configuring a custom generator in Grails, Listing 17-15 shows how to configure a `hilo` generator.

Listing 17-15. *Configuring a hilo Generator*

```
class Album {
  ..
  static mapping = {
        id generator:'hilo', params:[table:'hi_value',
                                            column:'next_value',
                                            max_lo:100]
  }
}
```

The example in Listing 17-15 uses a `hilo` generator that uses a table called `hi_value` that contains a column called `next_value` to compute an identifier. If you are familiar with Hibernate, you will have noticed that the map passed to the `params` argument is equivalent to the `<param>` element in Hibernate XML mapping. For example, to achieve the equivalent mapping in Hibernate XML, you could use the XML in Listing 17-16.

Listing 17-16. *Configuring hilo Generator in XML*

```
<id name="id" type="long" column="cat_id">
        <generator class="hilo">
                <param name="table">hi_value</param>
                <param name="column">next_value</param>
                <param name="max_lo">100</param>
        </generator>
</id>
```

If the target database doesn't have a numeric identifier but instead uses assigned `String` values as identifiers, then you can use the `assigned` generator. For example, say you wanted to use the `title` property of the `Album` class as the identifier instead. You could do so with the code in Listing 17-17.

Listing 17-17. *Configuring an assigned Generator*

```
class Album {
        String title
        ...
        static mapping = {
                id name: "title", generator: "assigned"
        }
}
```

The `name` argument is used to signify the name of the property used for the identifier, while the generator argument is set to `assigned`.

Using Composite Identifiers

Staying on the topic of identifiers, with Grails you can also use composite identifiers. A composite identifier is an identifier consisting of two or more unique properties of a domain class. For example, the `Album` domain class could use the `title` and `artist` properties to form a composite identifier, as shown in Listing 17-18.

Listing 17-18. *Configuring a Composite Identifier*

```
class Album implements Serializable {
        String title
        Artist artist
          ...
        static mapping = {
            id composite:[ "title","artist"]
        }
}
```

In Listing 17-18, the `composite` argument is used to pass a list of property names that form the composite primary key. To retrieve domain instances that utilize a composite identifier, you need to pass an instance of the domain class to the get method. For example, given the composite identifier from Listing 17-18, you can use the following code to retrieve an `Album` instance:

```
def a = Artist.findByName("Tool")
def album = Album.get(new Album(artist:a, title: "Lateralus"))
```

Note that when using composite identifiers, your domain class must implement the `java.io.Serializable` interface; otherwise, you will receive an error. And that completes this tour of the mapping features available through GORM. In the next section, we'll cover how you can use raw Hibernate to achieve a lot of what you've seen so far, and you'll learn how to access the full range of Hibernate configuration options.

Mapping with Hibernate XML

So far in this chapter, you saw how Grails integrates with Hibernate by providing an alternative mapping mechanism that uses convention instead of configuration. What's not tackled in that chapter is that this integration doesn't preclude you from using one of Hibernate's other mapping strategies.

Essentially, Hibernate defines two built-in mapping strategies. The first, and more common, is to use XML mapping files that define how an object is mapped to its related database table. In the next section, you will see how this can be achieved with Grails to gain greater flexibility and control over the mapping options available to you.

Although Hibernate XML is not nearly as concise and simple to work with as GORM, what it does provide is *flexibility*. It allows fine-grained control over how a class is mapped onto the underlying database, giving you access to the mapping features not available in the ORM DSL.

An important point is that you don't have to map *all* classes with Hibernate; you can mix and match where you think it's appropriate. This allows GORM to handle the typical case and allows Hibernate to do the heavy lifting.

To get going, the first thing you need to do is create the `hibernate.cfg.xml` file within the `grails-app/conf/hibernate` directory of the gTunes application. Figure 17-5 shows an example of how do to this.

Figure 17-5. *The hibernate.cfg.xml file*

The `hibernate.cfg.xml` file serves to configure the Hibernate `SessionFactory`, the class that Hibernate uses to interact with the database via sessions. Grails, of course, manages all this for you via the dynamic persistent methods discussed in Chapters 3 and 10.

All we're concerned with at this point is mapping classes from the domain model onto tables in a database. As it stands, the content of the `hibernate.cfg.xml` file looks something like Listing 17-19.

Listing 17-19. *The hibernate.cfg.xml File*

```
<?xml version="1.0" encoding="UTF-8"?>
<!DOCTYPE hibernate-configuration PUBLIC
                  "-//Hibernate/Hibernate Configuration DTD 3.0//EN"
                  http://hibernate.sourceforge.net/hibernate-configuration-
3.0.dtd">
<hibernate-configuration>
    <session-factory>
            <!-- Mapping goes here -->
    </session-factory>
</hibernate-configuration>
```

At the moment, there is just an empty configuration file. To map individual classes, it is good practice to create individual mapping files for each class and then *refer to* them in the main `hibernate.cfg.xml` file.

Listing 17-20 shows how you can use the `<mapping>` tag within the `hibernate.cfg.xml` file to achieve this.

Listing 17-20. *Adding Mapping Resources to hibernate.cfg.xml*

```
<?xml version="1.0" encoding="UTF-8"?>
<!DOCTYPE hibernate-configuration PUBLIC
                  "-//Hibernate/Hibernate Configuration DTD 3.0//EN"
                  "http://hibernate.sourceforge.net/hibernate-configuration-
3.0.dtd">
<hibernate-configuration>
    <session-factory>
        <mapping resource="com/g2one/gtunes/User.hbm.xml"/>
    </session-factory>
</hibernate-configuration>
```

The additional mapping is defined in bold with a new mapping resource reference for the `com.g2one.gtunes.User` class. Of course, the `User.hbm.xml` file does not yet exist at this point, so you need to create it. Figure 17-6 demonstrates what the state of the directory structure should look like after you've created the mapping file.

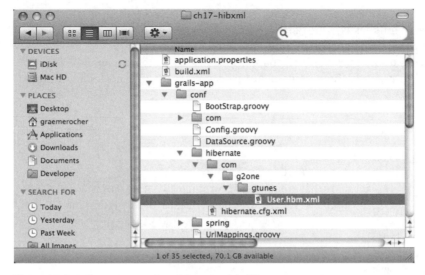

Figure 17-6. *Hibernate config with mapping files*

Mapping files contain the actual mappings between the object model and relational table. They're normally located in the same package as the mapped class and follow the naming convention of the class. For example, the mapping file that handles the User mapping is User.hbm. xml, the contents for which are shown in Listing 17-21.

Listing 17-21. *The User.hbm.xml Mapping File*

```
<?xml version="1.0"?>
<!DOCTYPE hibernate-mapping PUBLIC
        "-//Hibernate/Hibernate Mapping DTD 3.0//EN"
        "http://hibernate.sourceforge.net/hibernate-mapping-3.0.dtd">
<hibernate-mapping>
  <class name="com.g2one.gtunes.User" table="user_table" lazy="true">
     <comment>The User domain object</comment>

     <id name="id" column="user_id">
         <generator class="native"/>
     </id>
     <natural-id mutable="true">
         <property name="login"
                        length="10"/>
     </natural-id>
     <property name="password"
                   not-null="true"
                   column="u_pwd"/>
```

```
        <property name="email"/>
        <property name="firstName" column="u_first_name"/>
        <property name="lastName" column="u_last_name"/>
        ...
    </class>
</hibernate-mapping>
```

Listing 17-21 shows how you can map the User class onto a table called user_table that has a natively generated identifier and a natural identifier. A *natural identifier*, demonstrated by the use of the <natural-id> tag in Listing 17-21, is a property or a combination of properties that is unique to an instance of the User class. In this case, the login property is unique for each User instance and hence has been identified as the natural identifier.

Hibernate will create unique and not-null constraints when creating the database schema for the natural identifier.

Additionally, Hibernate recommends implementing equals and hashCode based on the natural id where possible. In fact, this is recommended even without Hibernate in place. Listing 17-22 shows the amends made to the User domain class to complete this example.

Listing 17-22. *User Domain Class Modifications*

```
class User {
    ...
    boolean equals(obj) {
        if(this--obj) return true
        if(!obj || obj.class != this.class) return false
        return login?.equals(obj.login) ? true : false
    }
    int hashCode() {
        return login ? login.hashCode() : super.hashCode()
    }
}
```

Although not strictly necessary, or even enforced by Hibernate, implementing equals and hashCode will help Hibernate behave correctly when dealing with collections of objects and querying.

With that strategy covered, let's move onto another alternative mapping strategy that uses annotations in the next section.

EJB 3–Compliant Mapping

In its latest incarnation, version 3.0, EJB has drawn inspiration from Hibernate. In many senses, EJB 3.0 responds to Hibernate's market dominance by offering an API that has the same feel as Hibernate but is vendor neutral.

One part of the specification is the Java Persistence API (JPA) that defines a set of annotations for persisting POJO objects using object-relational mapping. Although Grails doesn't support JPA directly (this support is still on the road map at the time of writing), what you can do is write EJB 3.0–compliant entity beans using JPA annotations. As well as annotations, JPA uses Java's Generics feature to establish the type of objects contained within collections and other generic interfaces. Generics were added to Java to increase type safety and avoid unnecessary casting when working with generic objects such as the collections API.

In the next example, you'll use JPA annotations to map a Java version of the com.g2one.gtunes.Address class within the gTunes.

To get started, make sure you have the gTunes application imported into Eclipse as described in Chapter 3.

Next, create new Address Java class in com.g2one.gtunes under the src/java tree using the New Java Class dialog box shown in Figure 17-7.

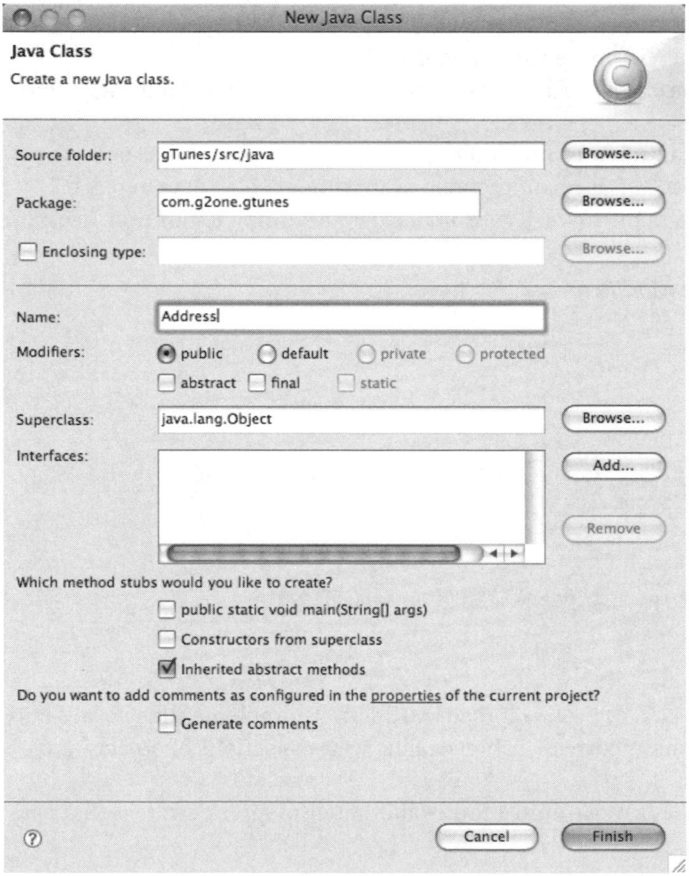

Figure 17-7. *The Eclipse New Java Class dialog box*

Figure 17-7 shows how to create the Address class within the aforementioned package. Once the Address class has been created, Eclipse's Package Explorer shows a source structure something like Figure 17-8.

Figure 17-8. *The Address class*

Now it's time to write some Java code. First open the `Address` class and add the `@Entity` annotation to the class name. To get the class to compile correctly, you will need to import the `javax.persistence.Entity` annotation as per Listing 17-23.

Listing 17-23. *The Class Address.java*

```
package com.g2one.gtunes;

import javax.persistence.Entity;
import javax.persistence.Table;

@Entity
@Table(name="address_table")
public class Address {
  // class body
}
```

As the previous code example shows, you will also need to use the `@Table` annotation to specify the table name previously used in the section "Mapping with Hibernate XML."

Now create private fields that match the names of the previous `Address` GORM domain class as per Listing 17-24.

Listing 17-24. *The Address Entities Fields*

```
package com.g2one.gtunes;
...
public class Address {
    private Long id;
    private Long version;
    private String number;
    private String street;
    private String city;
    private String state;
    private String postCode;
    private String country;
}
```

Once this has been done, you need to create public getters and setters for each field so that the Address class becomes a fully fledged JavaBean. Eclipse can help you here by accessing the Source/Generate Getters and Setters menu option. This will make each field into what is known as a *property*.

Once the properties have been generated, you need to annotate certain properties with additional information defining their purpose, starting with the id property in Listing 17-25.

Listing 17-25. *The id Property*

```
@Id
@Column(name="address_id")
@GeneratedValue
public Long getId() {
    return id;
}
```

In Listing 17-25 the id property is the primary key, it maps to a column called address_id, and its value is generated natively by the database. Next, the Address class's version property needs to be annotated with the @Version annotation. The @Version annotation is needed to specify the property used for optimistic locking (see Chapter 10 for more information about optimistic locking). Listing 17-26 shows how to annotate the getVersion() method with the @Version annotation.

Listing 17-26. *The login Property*

```
@Version
public Long getVersion() {
    return version;
}
```

The city, country, and postcode properties require different column names. Again, you can adjust this by using the @Column annotation, as shown in Listing 17-27.

Listing 17-27. *Mapping Individual Columns*

```
@Column(name="a_city")
public String getCity() {
    return city;
}
@Column(name="a_country")
public String getCountry() {
    return country;
}
@Column(name="a_post_code")
public String getPostCode() {
    return postCode;
}
```

You will, of course, have to add the imports for the @Column, @GeneratedValue, and @Id annotations used so far, but Eclipse or any good IDE will likely do this for you. Once complete, the new EJB 3–compliant Address class will look like the following:

```
package com.g2one.gtunes;

import javax.persistence.*;

@Entity
@Table(name="address_table")
public class Address {
    private Long id;
    private Long version;
    private String number;
    private String street;
    private String city;
    private String state;
    private String postCode;
    private String country;


    @Id
    @GeneratedValue
    public Long getId() {
        return id;
    }
    public void setId(Long id) {
        this.id = id;
    }

    @Version
    public Long getVersion() {
        return version;
    }
    public void setVersion(Long version) {
        this.version = version;
    }
    public String getCity() {
        return city;
    }
    public void setCity(String city) {
        this.city = city;
    }
    public String getCountry() {
        return country;
    }
```

```
    public void setCountry(String country) {
        this.country = country;
    }
    public String getNumber() {
        return number;
    }
    public void setNumber(String number) {
        this.number = number;
    }
    public String getPostCode() {
        return postCode;
    }
    public void setPostCode(String postCode) {
        this.postCode = postCode;
    }
    public String getState() {
        return state;
    }
    public void setState(String state) {
        this.state = state;
    }
    public String getStreet() {
        return street;
    }
    public void setStreet(String street) {
        this.street = street;
    }
```

```
}
```

With that rather long listing out of the way, there are a few things left to do to complete the migration to an EJB 3.0 entity. First, you need to update each DataSource in the grails-app/conf directory to tell Grails that you want to use an annotation configuration strategy. Listing 17-28 shows the necessary changes to the development DataSource.

Listing 17-28. *Specifying the Annotation Configuration Strategy*

```
import org.codehaus.groovy.grails.orm.hibernate.cfg.*
class DevelopmentDataSource { // Groovy
   def configClass = GrailsAnnotationConfiguration
   ...
}
```

With that done, the hibernate.cfg.xml file located in the grails-app/conf/hibernate directory needs updating to reflect the fact that you are no longer using Hibernate XML mapping. Listing 17-29 shows the update Hibernate configuration file with each class refer-enced using the `class` attribute of the `mapping` tag.

Listing 17-29. *Updated hibernate.cfg.xml File*

```xml
<?xml version="1.0" encoding="UTF-8"?>
<!DOCTYPE hibernate-configuration PUBLIC
                "-//Hibernate/Hibernate Configuration DTD 3.0//EN"
                "http://hibernate.sourceforge.net/hibernate-configuration-3.0.dtd">
<hibernate-configuration>
    <session-factory>
        <mapping package="com.g2one.gtunes"/>
        <mapping class="com.g2one.gtunes.Address" />
    </session-factory>
</hibernate-configuration>
```

The previous mapping simply tells Hibernate which classes are persistent, and the config-uration of the mapping is then delegated to the annotations contained within the classes themselves.

You now need to delete the Groovy version of the `Address` domain class in `grails/domain`, since its Java equivalent has superseded it.

You can now start Grails using `grails run-app`, and the gTunes application will operate as if nothing has changed. The remarkable thing here is that the `Address` class is written in Java, and yet all of the dynamic finder and persistence methods work as if by magic.

Grails is an *unobtrusive* framework, and by that we mean it doesn't require your domain objects to have any knowledge of the framework itself. Grails will magically inject the necessary behavior to support dynamic persistence and query methods into each EJB 3.0 entity using Groovy's Meta Object Protocol.

Grails' unobtrusive nature makes it an appealing proposition, because you can essentially reuse an existing Hibernate domain model and get all the benefits of the dynamic nature of Grails when you need to. On the other hand, if you want to reuse the domain model and map-ping from an older application, you can use the *same* domain model, because there are no framework specifics tying domain objects to Grails.

This is an incredibly powerful concept and one of the defining aspects of Grails that sets it apart from other frameworks and allows you to adopt a blended approach. By *blended* we mean having the *choice* to use static typing when you want to or, if you so choose, harnessing the power of dynamic typing when it suits your needs.

Before we continue, there is one thing you should do just to be sure that your application is working exactly as it was before you migrated the domain model: execute the tests. In fact, if you execute `grails test-app` at this point, you will get a number of failures. Why? During the migration you lose the power that GORM's constraints mechanism offers.

So, how do you create constraints for EJB 3 entities? In the next section we tackle this very issue.

Using Constraints with POJO Entities

Clearly, one of the powerful features of Grails is its constraints mechanism (discussed in Chapter 3). It allows a flexible way to specify metainformation about a class that can then be used in features such as validation and scaffolding. The reason there are failing test cases, as mentioned at the end of the previous section, is that your validation logic for the Address class is no longer working because of missing constraints.

Why is it not working? Quite simply, it's because it is not there! Java doesn't support closures or builders, so you can't just include the necessary code inside a Java class. Luckily, however, Grails has an elegant solution to this problem, again based on the convention approach.

What you need to do is create a new Groovy *script* in the same package and directory (yes, a Groovy file is now placed under src/java/...) as the class for which the constraints are being applied. The scripts name needs to start with the name of the class and end with Constraints. Figure 17-9 shows a new Groovy script called AddressConstraints.groovy.

The reason the previous file is a script is that it doesn't make sense to define an entirely new class just to define constraints on an existing class. All you are really interested in is applying a set of constraints in the same form as shown inside GORM classes. Listing 17-30 shows how to apply constraints within the AddressConstraints.groovy script.

That is all the file contains: no class definition, no configuration, just the constraints that apply to the Address class. At runtime, Grails will load and execute this script to retrieve the constraints that apply to the Address class, hence allowing Java domain classes to have constraints in the same format as GORM classes.

Figure 17-9. *Creating the AddressConstraints.groovy script*

Listing 17-30. *Applying Constraints to the Address Class*

```
package com.g2one.gtunes
constraints = {
    number blank:false, maxSize:200
    street blank:false, maxSize:250
    city blank:false, maxSize:200
    postCode blank:false, maxSize:50
    country blank:false, maxSize:200
}
```

Summary

In this chapter, you learned the fundamental message behind Grails, even if you didn't realize it until now. Grails strives to make the common, repetitive tasks that Java developers face every day ridiculously simple.

On the other hand, Grails provides all the underlying power and flexibility that you get in traditional Java web frameworks. Need to integrate with an LDAP directory? No problem. Want to expose a SOAP API onto a Grails service? That's possible too. In fact, whatever you can configure with Spring can be integrated with Grails.

In addition, you found out that you can write your domain model in Java and *still* take advantage of all the advanced Grails features such as dynamic finders, criteria, and scaffolding. Grails takes integration with Java extremely seriously, with the whole goal being to provide an environment for blended development. This also makes committing to Grails a safe choice, since you can always use Java where deemed necessary.

The reality is that there are many cases where static typing is the better choice, and conversely, there are many where dynamic typing is favorable. Groovy and Grails provide a platform to use a mix of approaches that allows you to switch between environments without requiring a large mental shift or making you deal with incompatibilities between programming platforms and paradigms.

■ ■ ■

The Groovy Language

Groovy is an all-purpose programming language for the JVM. It was born in 2003 when James Strachan and Bob McWhirter founded the Groovy project with the goal of creating a glue language to easily combine existing frameworks and components. Groovy is a language that aims to bring the expressiveness of languages such as Ruby, Lisp, and Python to the Java platform while still remaining Java friendly.

It attracted much excitement with these ambitious goals, because the majority of other scripting languages on the Java platform either used an entirely alien syntax and APIs or were simply Java without the need to specify types.

Despite its youth, Groovy is a stable, feature-rich language that forms the perfect base for Grails. This is a fantastic achievement, given the limited resources available to an open source project such as Groovy.

Groovy was an obvious choice as a platform for the Grails framework, because it provides the necessary underlying infrastructure to create the diverse range of miniature domain-specific languages utilized throughout Grails.

Note Martin Fowler has written an excellent article about domain-specific languages: `http://www.mar-tinfowler.com/bliki/DomainSpecificLanguage.html`.

What does this mean? Well, the syntax you see used throughout the book has often been magically enhanced and shortened by using a combination of Groovy's already concise syntax and its support for metaprogramming. Groovy performs a lot of magic under the covers, abstracted away from the developer. This removes the burden from the programmer who would otherwise be required to write reams of unnecessary, repetitive code.

Before we start our journey through the diverse syntax offered by Groovy, it is worth understanding how it compares to its cousin Java. In the next section, you will see how seamlessly Groovy integrates with Java at the syntax level.

Groovy and Java: A Comparison

Groovy's resemblance to Java is often quite striking. Some Groovy code is almost indistinguishable from Java. If your Groovy code looks too much like Java, you can improve its expressiveness by writing more idiomatic Groovy. Groovy code, when written by an experienced Groovy developer, typically occupies 40–60 percent fewer lines of code when compared to the equivalent Java. In the following sections, we'll cover the key similarities and differences between Groovy and the Java language.

What's the Same?

Java and Groovy actually have many similarities. This is what makes Groovy so appealing from a Java developer's perspective. There is no huge mental shift necessary to start working with Groovy. The Groovy syntax can almost be seen as a superset (although this is not the case) of the Java language, with the following taken directly from Java's syntax:

- Keywords and statements
- `try/catch/finally` exception handling
- Class, interface, field, and method definitions
- Instantiation of objects using the `new` operator
- Packaging and imports
- Operators, expressions, and assignment
- Control structures
- Comments
- Annotations, Generics, static imports, and `enum` types from Java 5

More importantly, though, Groovy shares the same object and runtime model as Java, so the infrastructure that you are operating in (the JVM) is the same. What does this mean? Well, although Groovy is a dynamic language like Ruby or Python, it is *not* interpreted. All Groovy code, be it executed as a script or a fully qualified class, is compiled down to byte code and then executed.

You shouldn't underestimate the significance of this, because it means that a Groovy class *is* a Java class and that Groovy and Java can interoperate with each other seamlessly. A Java class can call methods on a class implemented in Groovy without ever knowing any different.

So, that's what is the same; again, we've given a brief overview, but really the similarities become obvious quite quickly once you start working with Groovy. Of equal significance, however, is what is *different* about Groovy.

What's Different?

One of the things that makes Groovy different is that a number of things are optional, including parentheses, `return` statements, and semicolons at the end of statements.

■ Note The rules that govern optional parentheses are unambiguous, but it's generally good style to include parentheses in all but the simplest of cases (for example, in a `println` statement).

In addition, some `import` statements are optional, because Groovy automatically imports the following packages for you:

- `groovy.lang.*`
- `groovy.util.*`
- `java.lang.*`
- `java.util.*`
- `java.util.regex.*`
- `java.net.*`
- `java.io.*`
- `java.math.BigDecimal, java.math.BigInteger`

Besides these differences, Groovy's main goal is to add features that make the common tasks faced by Java developers trivial. To facilitate this, Groovy supports the following:

- Closures (similar to anonymous code blocks but with different scoping rules)
- Advanced `String` support with interpolation (described in the "Groovy Strings" section of this chapter), regular expressions, and template generation
- True object oriented programming with autoboxing/unboxing
- Operator overloading and syntactic structures to ease access to existing Java classes
- Improved syntax for existing data types augmented by new types
- An extended library of methods onto existing Java classes

At this point, we've tackled many of the similarities and differences with Java but have yet to show any actual code. In the next section, you'll start your journey into Groovy by getting the basics right first.

The Basics

The Groovy syntax is extremely closely aligned to that of Java; this does not mean you can copy and paste Java code into Groovy, and vice versa (although in some cases this does work), but it does mean that it all feels very familiar.

Fundamentally, Groovy can be written either in classes or as a script. Implementing the "Hello World!" example as a Groovy script would involve one line of code:

```
println 'Hello World!'
```

Assuming you've saved this code in a file called `Hello.groovy`, executing it is trivial too:

```
groovy Hello.groovy
```

Groovy automatically creates an executable *class* from the script. The reason this is high-lighted is that it is important to note that even though no class has been declared, the previous code will inevitably still become a class that extends `groovy.lang.Script`.

■**Note** The `groovy.lang.Script` class is the superclass used by Groovy to provide support for running arbitrary snippets of code as scripts.

Like Java, everything in Groovy must be a class.

Declaring Classes

Class declaration is simple and familiar enough. Listing A-1 shows an example of a simple `HelloController` class from a Grails application.

Listing A-1. *HelloController.groovy*

```
class HelloController {
    def world = {
        render "Hello World it's " + new java.util.Date()
    }
}
```

Here we have defined a class called `HelloController` that contains a single property called `world`. The property itself has been assigned a value, which is a closure. Java developers may be a little confused at the moment as how this simple declaration can be a property given the ver-bosity of the property syntax in Java.

Essentially, another difference from Java is that Groovy has no concept of the default visibility (also known as *package-level visibility*). Instead, properties declared at the default level, without any explicit modifiers such as `private`, `protected`, or `public`, are assumed to be JavaBean properties, and the appropriate getters and setters are generated for you.

The lack of default visibility also becomes clear when defining methods, because methods are assumed to be `public` if no modifier is specified.

In the next few sections, we'll cover some of these, as well as some of the other powerful features that Groovy offers, starting with built-in assertions.

Language-Level Assertions

Assertions are a concept introduced to the Java language in JDK 1.4 that allow you to verify application state at a certain point. Like Java, Groovy has an `assert` keyword.

Assertions are primarily useful to avoid the scenario where code is executed under an invalid state and, to this end, are a useful debugging tool. In terms of this book, assertions are also useful for revealing what the current state of an executing Groovy program is. Listing A-2 shows an example of an assertion in action.

Listing A-2. *Groovy Assertions*

```
def num = 1
...
assert num == 1
```

Here we simply verify that the variable called num still has a value of 1 at the point of execution in the code. Assertions will be utilized throughout many of the following examples, including in our coverage of Groovy strings, which we'll cover next.

Groovy Strings

Groovy supports a concept found in many other languages such as Perl and Ruby called *string interpolation*. Because this is rather a mouthful in Groovy-land, they're simply (or comically, depending on which way you look at it) known as GStrings.

A GString is just like a normal string, but it allows the embedding of variables within it, using the familiar ${..} syntax found in many popular Java frameworks including Spring, Ant, and an array of view technologies. The curly braces can be omitted if it is simply the variable name that is required. Listing A-3 also demonstrates another powerful feature of Groovy's string support: multiline strings. These are defined with the triple-quotation syntax.

Listing A-3. *GStrings in Action*

```
def person = "John"

println """
${new Date()}

Dear $person,

This is a Groovy letter!

Yours Sincerely,
The XYZ Company
"""
```

On the first line of the listing, a variable called `person` is defined that is then later referenced from the `String` itself. The multiline `String` can span several lines and includes all new line characters, tabs, and spaces in its output. The resulting output of the listing is as follows:

```
Wed Jan 14 06:20:58 BST 2009

Dear John,

This is a Groovy letter!

Yours Sincerely,
The XYZ Company
```

Coming from Java, where every new line has to be closed with a quote and contain the + concatenation character, this example comes as rather a relief. This also brings us nicely to another difference from Java in the way that Groovy interprets strings vs. characters. In Java, a character is defined using the single-quotation syntax, while in Groovy it could represent either a regular `String` (that is, one not of the `GString` variety) or a character. For example, the declarations in Listing A-4 are all valid in Groovy, while in Java the first and third would produce compilation errors.

Listing A-4. *String and Characters in Groovy*

```
String hello = 'Hello' // a regular String
String greeting = "$hello World!" // a GString
def c = '\n' as char // A java.lang.Character new line character
char c = '\n' // the same as above
```

Believe it or not, there is yet another alternative for declaring strings in Groovy. It is known as the *slashy* syntax and allows easy definition of regular expressions (regex) without the need to introduce escape characters as with Java.

■Note Regular expressions are a way of doing pattern matching against strings. Commonly referred to as *regex*, they define a set of matching operators that can be used to match almost any pattern in a string. A full discussion of regex is beyond the scope of this book, but many references are available online about the topic.[1]

This allows you to omit the backslash (\) escape character that cripples Java's regex support. Consider the example in Listing A-5.

---

1. *Java Regular Expressions: Taming the java.util.regex Engine* by Mehran Habibi (Apress, 2004) is an excellent book that covers the intricacies of regular expressions on the Java platform.

Listing A-5. *Groovy vs. Java Regex*

```
def file = /C:\this\will\need\escaping\afile.pdf/
// This is what you need in Java
assert file ==~ "\\w{1}:\\\\.+\\\\.+\\\\.+\\\\.+\\\\.+\\.pdf"
// And here is how you do it in Groovy
assert file ==~ /\w{1}:\\.+\\.+\\.+\\.+\\.+\.pdf/
```

This example attempts to match a file reference on a Windows system. Since Windows uses the backslash character in file references, it means you would need to escape every one of these in the Java regex expression on line 3 twice—once because Java requires you to escape the backslash character and again because so does regex!

But thanks to Groovy's slashy syntax, on line 5 you are able to avoid this particular nightmare by at least having to escape the backslash character only once.

In addition to the slashy syntax, Groovy's regex support goes even further, with support for specialized regex operators, some examples of which are shown in Listing A-6.

Listing A-6. *Groovy Regular Expressions*

```
1  import java.util.regex.*
2
3  // usage of the matching operator, which returns a Boolean
4  assert 'abababab' ==~ /(ab)+/
5
6
7     // Here the pattern operator is used
8     // to create a java.util.regex.Pattern instances
9      def pattern = ~/foo/
10    assert pattern instanceof Pattern
11
12   // The matcher operator allows you to create a
13   // java.util.regex.Matcher instance
14   def matcher = "cheesecheese" =~ /cheese/
15   assert matcher instanceof Matcher
```

The first example on line 4 uses the match ==~ operator, which will attempt to match the entire string against the provided regex. Next, line 9 demonstrates how to create an instance of java.util.regex.Pattern using the pattern operator.

Essentially, by starting a string with the ~ character, it creates the Pattern instance instead of a String. The pattern operator is commonly seen applied directly before slashy strings in the format ~/.../ but can in fact be applied to any string.

■Note It is important to notice the space between the equals sign and the ~ character that differentiates the pattern operator from the find =~ operator on line 14.

Lastly, the find =~ operator on line 14 will find the first match in the supplied String and, if used in an assignment as shown in the example, will return a java.util.regex.Matcher instance. A full discussion on regular expressions is rather beyond the scope of this book; nevertheless, what you have seen so far serves to introduce the capabilities Groovy has to offer in terms of regex support.

The next section should be pretty interesting as we explore Groovy's closure support. The closure, as a construct, is beginning to get much traction among the software development community as the benefits (and also the limitations of languages that don't have them) have started to become abundantly clearer.

Closures

Closures can essentially be seen as reusable code blocks (often called *anonymous code blocks*). At the syntax level, they are a sequence of statements surrounded by curly braces. They can be quite difficult to understand in the beginning at a conceptual level, but once you begin using them, it becomes hard to imagine how you ever lived without them.[2] Let's take a look at the basic example shown in Listing A-7.

Listing A-7. *Simple Closure*

```
def square = { it * it }
assert [1,4,9] == [1,2,3].collect(square)
```

The previous example is similar to creating a function pointer in C, although the behavior of closures differs significantly. First you define a closure and assign it to a variable called square that takes the default argument and multiplies it by itself. The default argument in Groovy is called it and becomes useful for simple definitions.

The square closure is then passed to another of Groovy's built-in methods called collect that will collect each element from the list and apply the passed closure to its value. In this case, the result is a list of numbers that represent the square root of each element in the original list.

Clearly, it's useful to be able to pass blocks of code around in this fashion, but another useful way to use closures is inline as an argument to a method. This is like using an anonymous inner class in Java, except the syntax is significantly more elegant, as Listing A-8 demonstrates.

Listing A-8. *Groovy step Method*

```
def lastRevision = 0.9

0.1.step(lastRevision, 0.1) { currentRevision ->
    println( currentRevision )
}
```

---

2. Many people feel now is the time for Java to introduce closure support, and this may happen in the future. See http://mindprod.com/jgloss/closure.html for information on why Java doesn't currently support closures.

The previous code steps through all the revisions of an imaginary version control reposi-tory and outputs each revision number. The last argument of the method is a closure, which is executed on each iteration (or *step*, if we're using the method's verb).

Note The step method itself takes three arguments. The last of these is a closure instance. Note how Groovy allows the closure to be specified at the end of the expression.

Clearly, closures take some getting used to when coming from Java, but if you think of them as a type of anonymous inner class, it will go a long way to aid your understanding. You'll see many more examples of their usage in the coming chapters as well as see them combined with another powerful Groovy concept: builders.

In the next section, we'll look at how Groovy greatly simplifies the Java collections API by providing language-level constructs for common Java types, as well as one of its own.

Lists, Maps, and Ranges

Groovy contains first-class constructs for two of the most commonly used collections in Java: List and Map.

This new syntax, combined with operator overloading and additional methods that use closures (provided by Groovy to extend the Java collection API), is a powerful combination best illustrated with some examples. See, for instance, Listing A-9.

Listing A-9. *Collections in Action*

```
1    // prints 1 2 3 separated by new lines to standard out
2    [1,2,3].each { num -> println num }
3    // create an empty list
4    def list = []
5    // use overloaded left shift operator to append items
6    list << 'one' << 'two' << 'three'
7    // check that we have 3 items
8    assert list.size() == 3
9    // Use Groovy's findAll method to find all words containing the letter "o"
10   assert list.findAll { item -> item.contains('o') }.size() == 2
11   // Merges a list into a string using the supplied string
12   assert list.join(',') == 'one,two,three'
13
14   // map of contact numbers
15   def contacts = [ Fred : '903-0200-1565',
16                    Wilma: '903-0207-7401' ]
17   contacts.each { key, value ->
18       println "calling $key on $value"
19   }
20   // add new contact
```

```
21  contacts.Dino = '903-0207-0349'
22  assert contacts.size() == 3
```

Here you can see various usages of Groovy lists and maps. First in line 2 there is an example of using Groovy's each method to iterate over a list of integer values:

```
2   [1,2,3].each { num -> println num }
```

The example calls each directly on the list definition and prints each element of the list using println, resulting in this output:

```
1
2
3
```

Next, there is an interesting use of the left shift << operator to append elements to the list. In Groovy, the left shift operator is generally available on all objects that have the concept of *appending* such as lists, buffers, and streams:

```
6   list << 'one' << 'two' << 'three'
```

Groovy then checks the size of the list using the size method. The size method is interesting in that even though it does exist for collections, it can be used on pretty much any object that has the concept of size or length. Java is extremely inconsistent in its handling of size and length, and there are different ways to obtain this information, depending on whether you are working with strings, arrays, or collections. Groovy attempts to unify this into a single method:

```
8   assert list.size() == 3
```

Here, on line 10 Groovy's findAll method is used on the list to locate all strings within the list that contain the letter *O*. The closure passed to findAll is evaluated as the criteria on each element of the list:

```
10  assert list.findAll { item -> item.contains('o') }.size() == 2
```

Another useful method in the toolbox is join, which allows you to merge any list or array into a string using the passed arguments as the separator. Here you create a comma-separated string of all elements in the collection:

```
12  assert list.join(',') == 'one,two,three'
```

The next example demonstrates Groovy's built-in syntax for defining maps:

```
15  def contacts = [ Fred : '903-0200-1565',
16                   Wilma: '903-0207-7401' ]
```

Here you create a java.util.Map that has two elements representing contact information for Fred and Wilma. Groovy allows you to omit the quotes around keys within the map syntax, so the keys Fred and Wilma in the example translate into strings.

█Note The map concept in Java is equivalent to what is known as a *hash* in many other languages. In fact, the default implementation used is `java.util.LinkedHashMap`.

Sometimes you want to use something other than a string as the key and want to resolve an object from the surrounding scope as the key. If this is the case, you need to surround the key with brackets (…).

Lines 17–19 in the example demonstrate how you can use the each method to iterate over a map in the same way as other collection objects, with the key and value as arguments to the method. More interestingly, however, is the use of the dereference operator on line 21:

```
21 contacts.Dino = '903-0207-0349'
```

This will actually create a new key called Dino, with the value being the telephone number. Why is this interesting? Well, it allows you to treat maps almost like dynamic objects. Speaking of dynamic objects, there is a particular type of Groovy object called Expando.

Expando Objects

It is often useful to be able to create an object dynamically at runtime, particularly if it is not a frequently used one that warrants a class definition. This is where Expando comes in handy. Consider the example in Listing A-10.

Listing A-10. *Expandos in Action*

```
fred = new Expando()

fred.firstName = "Fred"
fred.lastName = "Flintstone"

fred.age = 45
fred.happyBirthday = {
    fred.age++
}

fred.happyBirthday()
assert fred.age == 46
```

As you can see, Expando allows you to programmatically define an object, its properties, and its methods at runtime. This example creates an Expando object called fred and then simply goes about assigning some properties with some initial values. A method is defined by setting a closure to a property that can be later called like a regular method.

So far, you've seen quite a range of Groovy features, and with that particular pun out of the way, we're going to move onto another type introduced by Groovy: ranges.

Ranges

Groovy supports the concept of inclusive and exclusive ranges at the language level. A range consists of a left value and a right value, with a strategy for moving from left to right. Ranges can be used on numbers, strings, dates, and any other object that implements the `Comparable` interface and defines next and previous methods.

■**Note** The `java.lang.Comparable` interface is Java's way of comparing two objects. It defines a single method called `compareTo(Object)` that returns an integer. The method should return 1 if the passed object is greater than this object, −1 if it is less than this object, and 0 if they are equal.

Listing A-11 shows some examples of using ranges in combination with Groovy's advanced switch statement.

Listing A-11. *Ranges in Action*

```
def person = Expando()
person.name = "Fred"
person.age = 45

def child = 0..16 // inclusive range
def adult = 17..<66 // exclusive range
def senior = 66..120 //

switch(person.age) {
      case child:
            println "You're too young ${person.name}!"
      break
      case adult:
            println "Welcome ${person.name}!"
      break
      case senior:
            println "Welcome ${person.name}! Take a look at our senior citizen
rates!"
      break
}
```

This example has three ranges plus Groovy's advanced switch capabilities to print different messages depending on the age of the user. Ranges are commonly used in Groovy as a replacement for the traditional Java for loop using Groovy's for..in syntax and in combination with the subscript operator.

Listing A-12 shows how to use the for loop with a range applied to a String using the subscript operator.

Listing A-12. *The Groovy for Loop and Ranges*

```
def text = 'print me'
for(i in 0..<4) {
    println text[i]
}
assert 'print' == text[0..4]
```

Here, you're looping through the first four characters of the supplied text (remember, the previous example is an exclusive range) and printing out each character. The output of the for loop equates to the following:

```
p
r
i
n
```

And that concludes this whirlwind tour of Groovy basics. You've explored a lot, and although this section is by no means comprehensive, it should give you an idea of what Groovy is capable of as a general-purpose language.

In the next section, you'll start to explore the features that make Grails a possibility. What you've seen so far is great, but there is much more to Groovy, making it one of the most powerful dynamic languages available on the JVM today.

Groovy Power Features

The next sections are by no means a prerequisite for using Groovy, but they will help you understand what makes Groovy so powerful when compared to some of its sister dynamic languages that run on the JVM.

You'll explore three features in particular detail:

- True object oriented programming

- Metaprogramming

- Builders

Everything Is an Object

Unlike Java, which mixes primitive and reference types, in Groovy everything is an object. How does Groovy manage this while maintaining integration with Java? Well, before Java 5.0 was even introduced with Generics and autoboxing, Groovy was doing this for you in Java 1.4.

When a primitive type gets passed into the Groovy world, it is automatically "boxed" into its object equivalent, and vice versa. This allows Groovy to support some interesting concepts, which we will cover in the following sections:

- Methods on primitives

- Operator overloading

- The Groovy truth

In this respect, Groovy is far closer to object-oriented languages such as Smalltalk than Java, since even operators such as ==, !=, +, and – are translated into method calls at runtime.

Note Groovy's == operator differs from Java's in that it does not evaluate object identity, but it delegates to the object's equals method. For object identity, Groovy introduces a special is method: left.is(right).

To get you on your way to understanding the implications and possibilities that true object oriented programming offers, the first thing we're going to look at is Groovy's ability to support methods on primitives.

Methods on Primitives

Since Groovy performs autoboxing at runtime, you automatically have all the methods available in the concrete class equivalent (the Java primitive type int becomes java.lang.Integer, for example) as well as some additional ones provided by Groovy.

Combine this feature with Groovy's closure support, and having methods on primitives provides some interesting use cases. Listing A-13 provides various examples of calling methods on integers.

Listing A-13. *Methods on Numbers*

```
3.times {
    println it
}
// iterates from 3 to 9
3.upto(9) {
    println it
}
// iteratives from 3 to 9 in increments of 3
3.step(9,3) {
    println it
}
```

The previous examples provide a little taster of what allowing methods on primitive types means to Java developers. For others, this may not seem so revolutionary, but it's another string to Groovy's bow.

Operator Overloading

Operator overloading, which has a love-hate relationship in the world of C++, has been incorporated into the Groovy language in an extremely elegant fashion. As mentioned previously, Groovy is a true object-oriented language, and this extends to the operators themselves. Operators in Groovy are just method calls that follow a naming convention.

Table A-1 lists the Groovy operators and their equivalent methods; to utilize operators, simply add the necessary method to your object.

Table A-1. *Groovy Operator Method Names*

Operator	Method
a + b	a.plus(b)
a - b	a.minus(b)
a * b	a.multiply(b)
a / b	a.divide(b)
a++ or ++a	a.next()
a-- or --a	a.previous()
a[b]	a.getAt(b)
a[b] = c	a.putAt(b, c)
a << b	a.leftShift(b)

It doesn't end here, however; Groovy also uses operator overloading to overload the comparison operators. Table A-2 shows these operators and the methods or expressions they evaluate to.

Table A-2. *Groovy Comparison Operator Method Names*

Operator	Method
a == b	a.equals(b)
a != b	! a.equals(b)
a <=> b	a.compareTo(b)
a > b	a.compareTo(b) > 0
a >= b	a.compareTo(b) >= 0
a < b	a.compareTo(b) < 0
a <= b	a.compareTo(b) <= 0

In addition, Groovy provides a number of built-in operators on common Java types that let you work with them in intuitive ways. As an illustration, you can use the left shift << operator to do the following:

- Append an item to a `java.util.List`

- Output data to a `java.io.Writer` or a `java.io.OutputStream`

- Append characters onto a `java.lang.StringBuffer`

Groovy provides many more such operators across the JDK classes—too many to list here—so it is worthwhile to explore what is available in terms of operators within the Groovy documentation and source code. As your knowledge of Groovy grows, you will find yourself using them more and more and even providing your own.

The Groovy Truth

What is true and what isn't is very different in Groovy in comparison to Java, but not in a bad way. The phrase "the Groovy Truth" was coined by Dierk Koenig, Groovy committer and author of *Groovy in Action*[3] to differentiate Groovy's concept of what is true and what is not. As an example, the following, by no means comprehensive, list can be passed to `if` statements in Groovy and will evaluate to `false`:

- A `null` reference

- An empty or `null` string

- The number zero

- A regex `Matcher` that doesn't match

This makes for infinitely cleaner code and decreases the burden on the programmer to make sure that `null` checks are valid, that they're checking that a string is not `null` and is not zero length (boy, that's a mouthful), and that they're checking a whole hoard of other possibilities that cause error-prone code.

In the context of web applications, this is extremely useful given the amount of string evaluation necessary (remember, request parameters come in as strings).

Using the Groovy Truth, the `if`, `while`, and `assert` statements become rather more intelligent than their equivalents in Java. However, it simply wouldn't be Groovy if it wasn't taken even further. In Java, the `switch` statement is rarely used. Why? Well, it's fairly limiting in that it operates only in conjunction with the `int` or `char` primitive types (as well as `Enum` since Java 5).

In Groovy, however, the `switch` statement is your best friend and one of the more frequently used constructs. Groovy's `switch` accepts *any* object that implements the method `isCase`. Default implementations of `isCase` are provided for many of the commonly used types; if none is provided, then `isCase` simply delegates to the `equals` method. Listing A-14 shows the `switch` statement in action and how it can be used in conjunction with a variety of types.

---

3. *Groovy in Action* by Dierk Koenig et al. (Greenwich, CT: Manning Publications, 2007)

Listing A-14. *Usage of Groovy Switch*

```
switch (x) {
  case 'Graeme':
    println "you're Graeme!"
    break
  case 18..65:
    println "ok you're old enough"
    break
  case ~/Gw?+e/:
    println 'your name starts with G and ends in e!'
    break
  case Date:
    println 'got a Date instance'
    break
  case ['John', 'Ringo', 'Paul', 'George']:
    println "You're one of the Beatles! "
    break
  default:
    println "That is something entirely different"
}
```

The previous example is just a taster of what is possible with the Groovy switch. Try doing some experiments of your own to get used to the behavior of switch and how isCase behaves for each type.

Given what you've seen so far of Groovy's ability to dynamically dispatch operators and methods and box primitive types in objects, you would think that we've covered the parts that make Groovy truly dynamic. Not quite. In the next section, we'll cover Groovy's metaprogramming support, which makes Groovy extremely compelling and powerful and helps put it on an even keel with languages such as Ruby and Python.

Metaprogramming

Any concept that has a colorful name such as *metaprogramming* sounds scary, but fundamentally metaprogramming in Groovy is the ability to add behavior to classes at runtime. You've seen this in action many times already with Groovy's seemingly magical ability to add new methods to existing Java classes.

Given that Java's class-loading mechanism dictates that classes, once loaded, cannot be changed, you may be wondering how this is possible at all.

What Groovy does is that for every class loaded by the Groovy runtime there is an associated MetaClass that is used when dispatching methods to the class itself. Think of it in terms of a proxy that delegates to the actual implementation. The remarkable thing with Groovy, however, is that it doesn't just cover method dispatching. Constructors, fields, operators (because of operator overloading), properties, static, and instance methods can all be added, intercepted, or modified at runtime thanks to Groovy's Meta Object Protocol (MOP).

Outside of Groovy, the way this has been done is through software tools such as AspectJ, an implementation of Aspect-Oriented Programming (AOP) for Java, which does byte code weaving. In Groovy, byte code manipulation is unnecessary, and through Groovy's meta facility, Grails is able to perform a lot of magic in one line of code that would otherwise have taken reams of complicated Java code.

None of Grails' classes extends any special framework-specific classes, and the necessary behavior is instead injected into your classes at runtime via the MetaClass. Let's step through a few examples of how Groovy makes all this possible through its metaprogramming APIs.

Inspecting the MetaClass

As mentioned, every java.lang.Class has an associated groovy.lang.MetaClass instance. The MetaClass for a given Class can be obtained using the metaClass property on any instance. For example, if you wanted to find out all the methods available on a given instance, you could use the metaClass property, as shown in Listing A-15.

Listing A-15. *Inspecting Methods at Runtime Using the MetaClass*

```
def text = "hello world"
text.metaClass.methods.each { method ->
        println method.name
}
```

The code in Listing A-15 uses the methods property of the MetaClass, which returns a list of groovy.lang.MetaMethod instances, to output each method name, resulting in output such as the following:

```
replaceAll
replaceFirst
split
split
startsWith
startsWith
subSequence
substring
substring
toCharArray
toLowerCase
...
```

As well as the methods property, a properties property will obtain a list of groovy.lang. MetaProperty instances representing each property available on an instance. Occasionally, you'll just want to find whether an individual instance has a particular method or property and act accordingly. Listing A-16 shows how you can use the respondsTo and hasProperty methods to achieve this.

Listing A-16. *Using respondsTo and hasProperty*

```
def text = "hello world"
if(text.respondsTo("toUpperCase")) {
     println text.toUpperCase()
}
if(text.hasProperty("bytes")) {
     println text.bytes.encodeBase64()
}
```

The technique in Listing A-16 is often referred to as *duck typing*, a term that originates from the saying, "If it walks like a duck and quacks like a duck, I would call it a duck." In other words, in dynamic languages, objects can fulfill an implicit contract through duck typing, without needing to implement any special interface, as you would be required to do in a statically typed language like Java.

Adding Behavior at Runtime

Much of the Grails magic involves adding behaviors, in the form of methods, properties, and constructors, at runtime. In early versions of Grails, this was done through custom MetaClass implementations. However, this soon grew tedious, and the developers of Grails ended up creating a special kind of MetaClass called the ExpandoMetaClass.

ExpandoMetaClass provided a DSL for modifying MetaClass instances, and after stabilizing from its roots in the Grails project, ExpandoMetaClass soon became part of the Groovy language itself. Adding methods using ExpandoMetaClass is incredibly easy. Listing A-17 shows an example that adds a method called swapCase to the String class.

Listing A-17. *Adding Methods to Classes at Runtime Using ExpandoMetaClass*

```
String.metaClass.swapCase = {->
     def sb = new StringBuffer()
     delegate.each {
         sb << (Character.isUpperCase(it as char) ?
                   Character.toLowerCase(it as char) :
                   Character.toUpperCase(it as char))
     }
     sb.toString()
}
assert "Hello".swapCase() == "hELLO"
```

As you can see from Listing A-17, you can add or override methods at runtime by assigning a closure to a property of the MetaClass. Within the scope of the closure, the delegate variable is equivalent to this in a standard method.

This is exactly how the APIs such as GORM, discussed in Chapter 10, work. Grails inspects all the domain classes within a project and automagically adds new behavior to each one. Since the Grails runtime constructs a Spring `ApplicationContext`, closures can be used to inject methods that interact with Spring and Hibernate.

Listing A-18 shows an example of how the save method looks in Grails internally.

Listing A-18. *Adding the save Method at Runtime*

```
def t = new HibernateTemplate(applicationContext.getBean("sessionFactory"))
for(domainClass in application.domainClasses) {
        domainClass.metaClass.save = { t.saveOrUpdate(delegate) }
}
```

The real implementation is a bit more involved than that, but at a simple level Listing A-18 serves to demonstrate the concept. Of course, Groovy doesn't allow the addition of just instance methods but static methods, constructors, and properties too. Listing A-19 shows a few examples of adding different kinds of behaviors.

Listing A-19. *Enhancing the Behavior of a Class*

```
def dateFormat = new java.text.SimpleDateFormat("MM/dd/yyyy")
// Add a static method
Date.metaClass.static.format = { fmt -> dateFormat.format(new Date()) }
// Add a property
String.metaClass.getDate = {-> dateFormat.parse(delegate) }
// Add a constructor
String.metaClass.constructor { Date d -> dateFormat.format(d) }

String today = Date.format()
println "Today is $today"
Date todaysDate = today.date
today = new String(todaysDate)
println "Today is still $today"
```

As you can see from Listing A-19, with Groovy's metaprogramming capabilities you can modify and extend pretty much any aspect of a class behavior. However, it is not just classes that can be altered. Groovy also supports per-instance modifications of behavior. In Listing A-19, the changes to the `MetaClass` apply globally because the code is using the `metaClass` property of the `java.lang.Class` instance that is being modified.

To apply behavior to only one instance, you can use the `metaClass` property of the instance, in which case only that instance will be altered. This has several advantages; the major one is that changes to behavior can be isolated to the thread that the instance is created in. Global modifications apply to all threads, so should only ever be made once at start-up time to avoid inconsistent behavior.

Listing A-20 shows an example of adding the `swapCase` method from Listing A-17 to an instance of `java.lang.String`.

Listing A-20. *Using Per-Instance Metaprogramming*

```
def text = "Hello".

text.metaClass.swapCase = {->
      def sb = new StringBuffer()
      delegate.each {
          sb << (Character.isUpperCase(it as char) ?
                     Character.toLowerCase(it as char) :
                     Character.toUpperCase(it as char))
      }
      sb.toString()
}
assert text.swapCase() == "hELLO"
```

The examples of metaprogramming you have seen so far are neat, but many languages (including JavaScript and Python) allow you to add methods at runtime. However, Groovy belongs to a select group of languages that takes this concept even further by allowing you to modify the semantics of a program by intercepting method dispatch itself. In the next section, we'll cover how to achieve this.

Intercepting Method Dispatch

You can intercept method dispatch in Groovy in a number of ways. If you're the author of the class, then a trivial way is just to override the invokeMethod method. When you implement invokeMethod, Groovy will route all calls to methods that don't exist to your invokeMethod implementation.

Listing A-21 shows a trivial implementation that simply prints out the current method name, instead of throwing an exception, if a method doesn't exist.

Listing A-21. *Overriding invokeMethod*

```
class InterceptAndPrint {
   def out
   InterceptAndPrint (out) { this.out = out }
   def invokeMethod(String name, args) {
       out << name
   }
}
def i = new InterceptAndPrint (System.out)
i.hello()
i.world()
```

As you can see, by implementing invokeMethod, you can change the way Groovy's method dispatch is represented at runtime. You can achieve the same thing with properties by overriding the getProperty(name) and setProperty(name,value) methods.

Intercept, Cache, Invoke

As you saw in the previous section, you can intercept method dispatch by overriding the invokeMethod method. This is a pretty powerful pattern because you're injecting new behavior into your application. However, it has its overheads because Groovy has to go through various layers of dispatch logic before eventually reaching the invokeMethod method.

Another approach is to take advantage of *code synthesis* using the Intercept, Cache, Invoke pattern. The basics steps are as follows:

- *Intercept*: Intercept failed method dispatch using the methodMissing method.

- *Cache*: Create a new method on the fly, caching the behavior in the MetaClass.

- *Invoke*: Invoke the new behavior and return the result.

The advantage of this approach is that many new methods can be created at runtime. These new methods will incur a cost on first creation, but subsequent calls to the same method will be quicker. This is the technique that GORM uses to implement dynamic finders, a subject discussed in Chapter 10.

Listing A-22 shows an example of how you could implement your own version of dynamic finders using raw SQL instead of Hibernate using the methodMissing hook.

Listing A-22. *Implementing Intercept, Cache, Invoke*

```
url = "jdbc:hsqldb:mem:testDB"
driver = "org.hsqldb.jdbcDriver"
user = "sa"
pass = ""
Album.metaClass.static.methodMissing = { String name, args ->
    if(name.startsWith("findBy") && args) { // intercept
        def propertyName = name[6..-1]
        propertyName = propertyName[0].toLowerCase() + propertyName[1..-1]

        def newMethod = { Object[] varArgs ->
            def results = []
            def sql = groovy.sql.Sql.newInstance(url,user,pass, driver)
            sql.eachRow("select * from ${ Album.name} where $propertyName=?",
                        [varArgs[0]] ) {
                results << new Album (title:it.title, genre:it.genre)
            }
            return results
        }
        Album.metaClass."$name" = newMethod // cache
        return newMethod.call(args) // invoke
    }
}
```

```
    else {
        throw new MissingMethodException(name, Album,args)
    }
}

albums = Album.findByTitle("The Backroom")
albums.each {
    println it.title
    println it.genre
}
```

The steps of the Intercept, Cache, Invoke pattern are highlighted in bold in Listing A-22. Essentially, using `methodMissing`, you can intercept method dispatch, and if the method name starts with *findBy*, then a new method is automatically created that uses Groovy's SQL APIs to execute a query and return the results. The new behavior is then cached by creating a new method using the `MetaClass` at runtime:

```
Album.metaClass."$name" = newMethod // cache
```

This will ensure that the next time the method is invoked, Groovy doesn't have to go through the various phases of dispatch logic before giving up and calling `methodMissing`. Finally, the cached method is then invoked, resulting in the new behavior being executed:

```
return newMethod.call(args) // invoke
```

And that is how you implement GORM-style dynamic finders using raw SQL. Of course, the implementation in Listing A-22 is pretty limited compared to GORM, but you get the general idea.

The `MetaClass` concept in combination with Groovy's advanced syntax is also what enables a concept called *builders*. In the next section, we'll explain what builders are, what's the driving force behind their conception, and why they're so important to the overall picture.

Understanding Builders

A builder is an object that implements the builder pattern. The Gang of Four's book[4] introduces one particular pattern known as the *builder* pattern. The idea behind it is to construct complex objects from another object or builder. For example, you may need to build a complex markup hierarchy with the root object being the document itself. A builder would encapsulate the logic to construct, or *build*, this object for you.

The builder pattern is extremely difficult to implement in Java because of the limitations of the syntax. (Some would say it is impossible and that current implementations are merely mimicking a true builder, although efforts have been made in projects such as Commons CLI and IntelliJ IDEA PSI.) Groovy, however, has no such problem, thanks to its support for named arguments, closures, and optional parentheses.

---

4. *Design Patterns: Elements of Reusable Object-Oriented Software* by Erich Gamma, Richard Helm, Ralph Johnson, and John Vlissides (Addison-Wesley, 1995)

Note Groovy doesn't support true named arguments but allows the method to specify a map as the only argument, hence mimicking this capability. This limitation is mainly down to Java byte code itself, which does not associate names (only types) with method parameters.

Groovy ships with a number of builders (excuse the pun) built-in, including but not limited to the following:

- The `MarkupBuilder` for constructing, typically XML, markup

- The `DOMBuilder` for constructing W3C DOM trees

- The `AntBuilder` to provide scripting for Apache Ant

- The `SwingBuilder` for constructing Swing GUI interfaces

As an example, take a look at the usage of the `MarkupBuilder`, shown in Listing A-23, which allows construction of markup documents such as XML or HTML.

Listing A-23. *MarkupBuilder in Action*

```
// construct builder that outputs to standard out
def mkp = new groovy.xml.MarkupBuilder()

// write markup
mkp.authors {
    author(name:'Stephen King') {
        book( title:'The Shining')
        book( title:'The Stand')
    }
    author(name: 'James Patterson') {
        book( title:'Along Came a Spider' )
    }
}
```

This example demonstrates the construction of a `groovy.xml.MarkupBuilder` instance using standard out and the usage of closures and named arguments to represent the markup. Listing A-24 shows the result.

Listing A-24. *Result of MarkupBuilder*

```
<authors>
    <author name="Stephen King">
        <book title="The Shining" />
        <book title="The Stand" />
    </author>
    <author name="James Patterson">
        <book title="Along Came a Spider" />
    </author>
</authors>
```

It is interesting at this point to take a closer look at Listing A-23. In this example, we passed an "anonymous" closure to the authors() method of the MarkupBuilder instance, but consider the possibility of assigning this closure to a variable and then passing as an argument the same closure to different builders, one that renders XML and another that outputs the same data as a PDF document or renders it in a GUI.

Unlike the XML produced in Listing A-24, the builder code in Listing A-23 is pure Groovy code and can therefore leverage the full power of the language: conditionals, looping, referencing, inheritance, and so on.

Builders are an extremely powerful concept, and if you're willing to delve into some Groovy development by extending the BuilderSupport class to create your own builders, you can create some pretty amazing constructs that could end up as domain-specific languages within your application.

Grails utilizes builders all over the place, from constructing Hibernate criteria to rendering markup to the HTTP response. Builders are a key element in the conciseness and power that Grails brings to web application development.

Summary

That completes this dash through the Groovy language. As we have already admitted, it was by no means comprehensive. Groovy has many more fantastic features; it is really worth investing the time to learn more about it. But this quick overview should give you an idea of why some of Groovy's features are so important to Grails and how they make life easier developing today's web applications.

You saw that Groovy looks pretty much like Java at first glance, allowing a smooth transition into the new world of dynamic programming. Since Groovy is fully integrated with the Java platform and works directly on JDK objects, your investment in learning Java and your experience with the platform are fully protected.

What's new is that Groovy gives you more immediate control over types such as lists and maps. New concepts such as closures and ranges complete the picture. The combination of syntax enhancements, new types, improvements to JDK classes, and metaprogramming leads to an idiomatic Groovy style that is both simple and powerful.

Index